MW00344490

Program Composition
(Page in Text)

Subprogram section (177)
  Procedure definition (175–176,
               183–185)

```
PROCEDURE ReadCodes
            ( VAR Department, Employee : char );
{-- Read department & employee codes --}
BEGIN
  write( 'Enter dept. & employee codes: ' );
  readln( Department, Employee )
END {ReadCodes};
```

  Function definition (217–219)

```
FUNCTION RoundCents( Amount : real ) : real;
{-- Round Amount to nearest cent --}
BEGIN
  RoundCents := round(100 * Amount) / 100
END {RoundCents};
```

Statement part (67, 105)

```
BEGIN {**** main program ****}
  statement-1;
        .
        .
        .
  statement-n
END {main program}.
```

Unit format
  Unit heading
  Interface part
  Implementation part

Unit heading (266)

```
UNIT DaysIO;
```

Interface part (267)
  USES clause (optional)
  Declaration part (modified)

```
INTERFACE
  USES Printer;
  TYPE
    DayType = (Sun, Mon, Tues, Wed,
               Thur, Fri, Sat);
    PROCEDURE PrintDay( Day : DayType);
```

Implementation part (267–268)
  USES clause (optional)

```
IMPLEMENTATION
  VAR
   i : integer;
```

  Declaration part

```
  PROCEDURE PrintDay( Day : DayType);
    BEGIN
      writeln( ord(DAY) )
    END {PrintDay};
```

Initialization part

```
  BEGIN
    FOR i := 1 TO 5 DO
      writeln
    END {DaysIO}.
```

TURBO PASCAL®
Programming and
Problem Solving

**Second
Edition**

SANFORD LEESTMA
LARRY NYHOFF

Department of Mathematics and Computer Science
Calvin College

MACMILLAN PUBLISHING COMPANY
New York

MAXWELL MACMILLAN CANADA
Toronto

MAXWELL MACMILLAN INTERNATIONAL PUBLISHING GROUP
New York   Oxford   Singapore   Sydney

Editor(s): David Johnstone, John Griffin
Production Supervisor: Ron Harris
Production Manager: Roger Vergnes
Text Designer: Susan Frankenberry
Cover Designer: Natasha Sylvester
Cover Painting: Chris Overvoorde
Illustrations: Precision Graphics

This book was set in 10½ × 12 Times Roman by York Graphics, printed and bound by Arcata/Hawkins. The cover was printed by Phoenix Color Corp.

Trademark acknowledgments: MS DOS and Windows are registered trademarks of Microsoft Corporation; Turbo Pascal is a registered trademark of Borland International, Inc.; IBM is a registered trademark of International Business Machines Corporation; Mathematica is a registered trademark of Wolfram Research, Inc.

Macmillan Publishing Company
866 Third Avenue, New York, New York 10022

Macmillan Publishing Company is part
of the Maxwell Communication Group of Companies.

Maxwell Macmillan Canada, Inc.
1200 Eglinton Avenue East
Suite 200
Don Mills, Ontario M3C 3N1

Library of Congress Cataloging in Publication Data
Leestma, Sanford.
    Turbo Pascal : programming and problem solving / Sanford Leestma,
Larry Nyhoff. — 2nd ed.
        p.   cm.
    Includes indexes.
    ISBN 0-02-388701-X
    1. Pascal (Computer program language)   2. Turbo Pascal (Computer
file)   I. Nyhoff, Larry R.   II. Title.
QA76.73.P2L443   1993
005.26'2—dc20   92-45178
                                                                   CIP

Printing: 2 3 4 5 6 7 8   Year: 3 4 5 6 7 8 9 0 1 2

Dedicated to the memory of

DAVID JOHNSTONE

who will be sorely missed by all of us who knew and admired this sincere, kind, and gentle man.

We thank God for him and for the privilege of working with him and of having him for a friend.

PREFACE

Recently, a new set of curriculum recommendations was published in *Computing Curricula 1991: Report of the ACM/IEEE-CS Joint Curriculum Task Force*. A major theme of this report is that the introductory computer science courses should include an introduction to the various areas of computer science:

- Architecture
- Artificial Intelligence and Robotics
- Database and Information Retrieval
- Human–Computer Communication
- Numerical and Symbolic Computation
- Operating Systems
- Programming Languages
- Software Methodology and Engineering
- Social, Ethical, and Professional Context

Feeling that this was an important objective in the early computer science courses, we included several examples and exercises from several of these areas in the previous edition of this text.

In this new edition we have expanded and improved these examples, trying to capture the spirit of these curriculum guidelines in a natural, unobtrusive way. We were guided by the recommendations of the Curriculum '91 report and by suggestions made by reviewers and users of the previous edition. These examples have been carefully selected to provide an overview of the discipline of computer science and to provide a foundation for further study in theoretical and/or applied computer science. They have been highlighted in seventeen special PART OF THE PICTURE sections, which we marked with an icon in the shape of a puzzle piece. These sections include:

- History of Computing
- Computer Organization
- Social, Professional, and Ethical Issues
- Syntax and Semantics
- Numeric Computation (Curve Fitting: Least Squares Line; Solving Equations; Numerical Integration; Matrix Multiplication; Solving Linear Systems)

- Databases
- Data Structures and Data Types
- Sorting and Searching
- Analysis of Algorithms
- Data Encryption
- Computer Graphics (Plotting Graphs and Density Plots)
- Programming Languages (Compilers; Finite State Automata and Lexical Analysis)
- Introduction to OOP

A solid base is thus established on which later courses in theoretical and/or applied computer science can build.

In this new edition we have retained those features from the previous edition that users and reviewers urged us to keep:

- Complete but concise treatment, yet with sufficient detail to aid students.
- Programming Pointers at chapter ends to highlight important points, especially common programming pitfalls and proper techniques of design and style.
- More than sixty complete programs and sample runs throughout the text that illustrate basic programming concepts and demonstrate good structure and style. In the spirit of Curriculum '91, they are chosen from a wide range of applications. Copies of all those marked in the text with a disk icon are on the data disk that accompanies this text.
- Use of color to emphasize and highlight important features and not simply for decoration.
- Exercise sets that include short written exercises as well as a large number of programming exercises and projects drawn from a wide range of application areas.

The major new features of this edition include the following:

- An expanded chapter on software development that includes a discussion of problem analysis and specification; design; coding; verification and validation; and software engineering.
- Inclusion of PART OF THE PICTURE sections that illustrate the breadth of computer science and its applications as suggested in Curriculum '91.
- New placement of and expanded treatment of procedures and functions.
- More formal specification of algorithms and subprograms, spelling our their input, output, purpose, and items accepted and/or returned.
- Specification boxes to highlight language features, making them stand out so they are easy to locate.
- New layout and design.
- New chapter on abstract data types and object-oriented programming.
- Integrated treatment of input, output, and data files.
- Increased emphasis on modular design. (A new chapter is devoted entirely to this topic.)
- Later introduction to recursion when students are better able to understand and apply it.

Another recommendation in the Curriculum '91 report is that the introductory courses in computer science include a laboratory component to supplement and apply the class lectures. To meet this need, Professors Linda Elliott and Jane Turk from LaSalle University have prepared a lab manual to accompany this text. It contains 16 lab modules and includes a disk containing all the programs, drivers, and data files referenced in the manual.

Supplementary Materials

A number of supplementary materials are available from the publisher. These include the following:

- The lab manual and disk prepared by Professors Elliott and Turk.
- An instructor's manual containing lecture notes, sample test questions, and transparency masters.
- A solutions manual that contains solutions to the exercises in the text, including most of the programming exercises.
- Data disks containing solutions to most of the programming exercises.
- Data disks containing all the sample programs and data files used in the text. Each listing of a program, unit, or file in the text that is accompanied by a disk icon is on these disks. A program in Figure X.Y will be named `FIGX-Y.PAS`; a data file in Figure X.Y will be named `FILX-Y.DAT`.
- A test bank, both in printed form and on disk.
- Data disks containing all the exercises of the text.

Acknowledgments

We express our sincere appreciation to all who helped in any way in the preparation of this text. We will miss our erudite editor David Johnstone, whose professional competence kept us on course, whose words of encouragement kept us going, and whose friendship over the years made textbook writing for Macmillan an enjoyable experience. We must also thank our punctilious production supervisor Ronald Harris, whose attention to details and deadlines has compensated for our lack thereof and whose encouraging words and kind admonitions (when needed) have prodded us to action; working without him is almost unthinkable. The comments and suggestions made by the following reviewers were also valuable and their work is also much appreciated: Prof. Michael Pitt, Eastfield College; Prof. Mark LeBlanc, University of New Hampshire; Prof. J. Richard Rinewalt, Texas Christian University; Mr. Harry Shea, University of Maine; Prof. James McKenna, SUNY Fredonia; Prof. William Leslie, SUNY Fredonia; Prof. Susan Simons, Memphis State University; Prof. David Valentine, SUNY Potsdam; Prof. Gregory Carmichael, University of Iowa; Prof. Vicki Varner, University of Texas-Arlington; Prof. Kay Chen, Bucks County Community College; Prof. Ernst Rilke, Harper College; Prof. John Lowther, Michigan Technical University; Prof. Kathy Edgeworth, Louisiana State University; Prof. Donald Marois, United States Military Academy; Prof. Thomas Taylor, SUNY Fredonia; Prof. Cathy Bareiss, Olivet Nazarene College; Prof. James Williams, University of Maryland; Prof. Thomas Mertz, Millersville University; and Prof. Dale Parsons, Millersville University. And, of course, we must once again thank our wives, Shar and Marge, whose love and understanding have kept us going through another year of textbook writing, and to Jeff, Dawn and Rebecca, Jim, Julie, Joan, Michelle and Paul, Sandy, and Michael, for not complaining about the times that their needs and wants were slighted by our busyness. Above all, we give thanks to God for giving us the opportunity, ability, and stamina to prepare another new edition of this text.

L. R. N.
S. C. L.

CONTENTS

APPENDIXES

GLOSSARY

INDEX OF EXAMPLES AND EXERCISES

INDEX

THE COMPUTER SCIENCE PICTURE

1

Is computer science a science? An engineering discipline? Or merely a technology, an inventor and purveyor of computing commodities? What is the intellectual substance of the discipline? Is it lasting, or will it fade within a generation?
FROM THE 1989 REPORT OF THE TASK FORCE ON THE CORE OF COMPUTER SCIENCE

I wish these calculations had been executed by steam.
CHARLES BABBAGE

For, contrary to the unreasoned opinion of the ignorant, the choice of a system of numeration is a mere matter of convention.
BLAISE PASCAL

CHAPTER CONTENTS

As the title indicates, the primary focus of this text is on problem solving and programming. Although these are fundamental skills, computer science as a discipline consists of much more. The breadth of the discipline is evidenced by the following list of the main areas of computer science from *Computing Curricula 1991: Report of the ACM/IEEE–CS Joint Curriculum Task Force:*[1]

- **Algorithms and Data Structures.** This area deals with specific classes of problems and their efficient solutions. The performance characteristic of algorithms and the organization of data relative to different access requirements are major components.
- **Architecture.** Methods of organizing efficient, reliable computing systems provide a central focus of this area. It includes the implementation of processors, memory, communications, and software interfaces, as well as the design and control of large, reliable computational systems.
- **Artificial Intelligence and Robotics.** The basic models of behavior and the building of (virtual or actual) machines to simulate animal and human behavior are included here. Inference, deduction, pattern recognition, and knowledge representation are major components.
- **Database and Information Retrieval.** This area is concerned with organizing information and algorithms for the efficient access and update of stored information. The modeling of data relationships, security and protection of information in a shared environment, and characteristics of external storage devices are included in this area.
- **Human–Computer Communication.** The efficient transfer of information between humans and machines is the central focus of this area. Graphics, human factors that affect efficient interaction, and the organization and display of information for effective utilization by humans are included.
- **Numerical and Symbolic Computation.** General methods for using computers efficiently and accurately to solve equations from mathematical models are central to this area. The effectiveness and efficiency of various approaches to solve equations and the development of high-quality mathematical software packages are important components.
- **Operating Systems.** This area deals with control mechanisms that allow multiple resources to be efficiently coordinated during the execution of programs. Included are appropriate services of user requests, effective strategies for resource control, and effective organization to support distributed computation.
- **Programming Languages.** The fundamental questions addressed by this area involve notations for defining virtual machines that execute algorithms, the efficient translation from high-level languages to machine codes, and the various extension mechanisms that can be provided in programming languages.
- **Software Methodology and Engineering.** The major focus of this area is the specification, design, and production of large software systems. Principles of programming and software development, verification, and validation

---

[1] Allen B. Tucker, ed., *Computing Curricula 1991: Report of the ACM/IEEE–CS Joint Curriculum Task Force* (ACM Press and IEEE Computer Society Press, 1991).

of software, and the specification and production of software systems that are safe, secure, reliable, and dependable are of special interest.

■ **Social and Professional Context.** This area is concerned with the cultural, social, legal, and ethical issues related to the discipline of computing.

To help students develop an accurate and balanced picture of computer science as a discipline, a first course in computing should touch on many of these areas. This is especially important to students majoring in computer science, for whom this introduction to the discipline will be fleshed out in later courses, as well as to those majoring in other disciplines, for whom the portrayal of computer science should be a realistic one. Thus, although most of this text is devoted to developing problem-solving and programming skills, we attempt to paint a more complete picture of computer science by including special "PART OF THE PICTURE" sections throughout the text that introduce topics from several of these areas.

1.1 PART OF THE PICTURE: **The History of Computing**

The modern electronic computer is one of the most important inventions of the twentieth century. It is an essential tool in many areas, including business, industry, government, science, and education; indeed, it has touched nearly every aspect of our lives. The impact of this twentieth-century information revolution brought about by the development of high-speed computing systems has been nearly as widespread as the impact of the nineteenth-century Industrial Revolution. As part of the picture of computer science, it is necessary to be aware of some of the events that led up to modern-day computing.

Two important concepts in the history of computation are the **mechanization of arithmetic** and the concept of a **stored program** for the automatic control of computations. We shall focus on some of the devices that have implemented these concepts.

The Mechanization of Arithmetic

A variety of mechanical devices were used in ancient civilizations to assist in computation. One of the earliest is the **abacus** (Figure 1.1), which has movable beads strung on rods to count and to do calculations. Although its exact origin is unknown, the abacus was used by the Chinese perhaps three thousand to four thousand years ago and is still used today throughout Asia. The ancient British stone monument **Stonehenge** (Figure 1.2), located in southern England, was built between 1900 and 1600 B.C. and evidently was an astronomical calculator used to predict the changes of the seasons. Five hundred years ago, the Inca Indians of South America used a system of knotted cords called **quipus** (Figure 1.3) to count and record divisions of land among the various tribal groups. In Western Europe, **Napier's bones** (Figure 1.4) and tables of **logarithms** were designed by the Scottish mathematician John Napier (1550–1617) to simplify calculations. These led to the subsequent invention of the **slide rule** (Figure 1.5).

In 1642, the young French mathematician **Blaise Pascal** (1623–1662) invented one of the first mechanical adding machines (Figure 1.6), a device that used

FIGURE 1.1   Abacus.

FIGURE 1.2   Stonehenge.

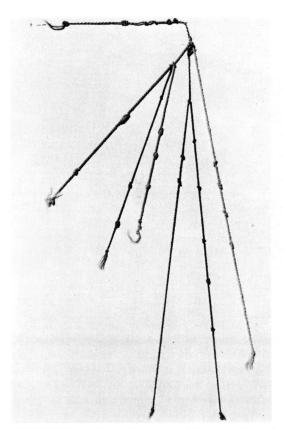

FIGURE 1.3 Quipus. (Courtesy of the American Museum of Natural History)

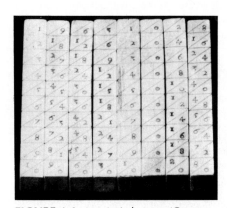

FIGURE 1.4 Napier's bones. (Courtesy of the Smithsonian Institution)

FIGURE 1.5 Slide rule.

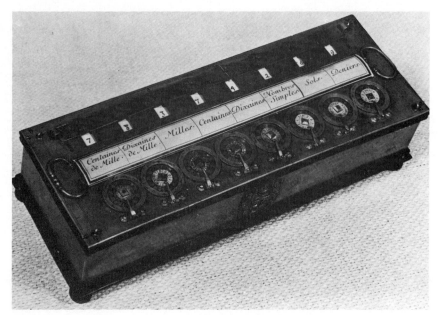

FIGURE 1.6   Pascal's adder. (Courtesy of IBM)

a system of gears and wheels similar to that found in odometers and other counting devices. **Pascal's adder** could both add and subtract and was invented to calculate taxes. Pascal's announcement of his invention reveals the motivation for its development:

> Dear reader, this notice will serve to inform you that I submit to the public a small machine of my invention, by means of which you alone may, without any effort, perform all the operations of arithmetic, and may be relieved of the work which has often times fatigued your spirit, when you have worked with the counters or with the pen. As for simplicity of movement of the operations, I have so devised it that, although the operations of arithmetic are in a way opposed the one to the other—as addition to subtraction, and multiplication to division—nevertheless they are all performed on this machine by a single movement. The facility of this movement of operation is very evident since it is just as easy to move one thousand or ten thousand dials, all at one time, if one desires to make a single dial move, although all accomplish the movement perfectly. The most ignorant find as many advantages as the most experienced. The instrument makes up for ignorance and for lack of practice, and even without any effort of the operator, it makes possible shortcuts by itself, whenever the numbers are set down.

Although Pascal built more than fifty of his adding machines, his commercial venture failed because the devices could not be built with sufficient precision for practical use.

In the 1670s, the German mathematician **Gottfried Wilhelm von Leibniz** (1646–1716) produced a machine that was similar in design to Pascal's but somewhat more reliable and accurate (Figure 1.7). Leibniz's calculator could perform all four of the basic arithmetic operations of addition, subtraction, multiplication, and division.

A number of other mechanical calculators followed that further refined Pascal's and Leibniz's designs. By the end of the nineteenth century, these calculators had become important tools in science, business, and commerce.

FIGURE 1.7 Leibniz's calculator. (Courtesy of IBM)

The Stored Program Concept

As noted earlier, the second fundamental idea to emerge in the history of computing was the concept of a stored program to control the calculations. One early example of an automatically controlled device is the weaving loom (Figure 1.8) invented by the Frenchman **Joseph Marie Jacquard** (1752–1834). This automatic

FIGURE 1.8 Jacquard loom. (Courtesy of IBM)

loom, introduced at a Paris exhibition in 1801, used metal cards punched with holes to position threads for the weaving process. A collection of these cards made up a program that directed the loom. Within a decade, eleven thousand of these machines were being used in French textile plants, resulting in what may have been the first incidence of unemployment caused by automation. Indeed, unemployed workers rioted and destroyed several of the new looms and cards. According to Jacquard, ''The iron was sold for iron, the wood for wood, and I its inventor delivered up to public ignominy.'' The **Jacquard loom** is still used today, although modern versions are controlled by programs stored on magnetic tape rather than punched cards.

Mechanical Computers

The two fundamental concepts, mechanized calculation and stored program control, were combined by the English mathematician **Charles Babbage** (1792–1871), who began work in 1822 on a machine that he called the **Difference Engine** (Figure 1.9). This machine was designed to compute polynomials for the preparation of mathematical tables. Babbage continued his work until 1833 with support

FIGURE 1.9   Babbage's Difference Engine.

from the British government, which was interested in possible military applications of the Difference Engine. But Babbage later abandoned this project, because according to the curator of the London Science Museum, Doran Swade, the contankerous Babbage argued with his engineer, ran out of money, and was beset by personal rivalry. Babbage nonetheless went on to design a more sophisticated machine that he called his **Analytical Engine** (Figure 1.10). This machine had several special-purpose components that were intended to work together. The "mill" was supposed to carry out the arithmetic computations; the "store" was the machine's memory for storing data and intermediate results; and other components were designed for the input and output of information and for the transfer of information between components. The operation of this machine was to be fully automatic, controlled by punched cards, an idea based on Jacquard's earlier work. In fact, as Babbage himself observed: "The analogy of the Analytical Engine with this well-known process is nearly perfect." **Ada Augusta,** Lord George Byron's daughter, the countess of Lovelace, and lifelong friend of Babbage, understood how the device was to operate and supported Babbage in his work. Considered by some to be the first programmer, Lady Lovelace described the similarity of Jacquard's and Babbage's inventions: "The Analytical Engine weaves algebraic patterns just as the Jacquard loom weaves flowers and leaves." Although Babbage's machine was not built during his lifetime, it is nevertheless an important part of the history of computing because many of the concepts of its design are used in modern computers.

A related development in the United States was the census bureau's use of punched-card systems to help compile the 1890 census (Figure 1.11). These systems, designed by **Herman Hollerith,** a young mathematician employed by the bureau, used electrical sensors to interpret the information stored on the punched

FIGURE 1.10 Babbage's Analytical Engine. (Courtesy of IBM)

FIGURE 1.11   Hollerith equipment. (Courtesy of IBM)

cards. In 1896, Hollerith left the census bureau and formed his own tabulating company, which in 1924 became the International Business Machines Corporation (IBM).

The development of computing devices continued at a rapid pace in the United States. Some of the pioneers in this effort were Howard Aiken, John Atanasoff, J. P. Eckert, J. W. Mauchly, and John von Neumann. Repeating much of the work of Babbage, Aiken designed a system consisting of several mechanical calculators working together. This work, which was supported by IBM, led to the invention in 1944 of the electromechanical **Mark I** computer (Figure 1.12). This machine is the best-known computer built before 1945 and may be regarded as the first realization of Babbage's Analytical Engine.

Early Electronic Computers

The first fully electronic computer was developed by **John Atanasoff** at Iowa State University. With the help of his assistant, **Clifford Berry,** he built a prototype in 1939 and completed the first working model in 1942 (Figure 1.13). The best known of the early electronic computers was the **ENIAC** (Electronic Numerical Integrator and Computer), constructed in 1946 by J. P. Eckert and J. W. Mauchly at

FIGURE 1.12   Mark I. (Courtesy of IBM)

the Moore School of Electrical Engineering of the University of Pennsylvania (Figure 1.14). This extremely large machine contained over 18,000 vacuum tubes and 1500 relays and nearly filled a room 20 feet by 40 feet in size. It could multiply numbers approximately one thousand times faster than the Mark I could, though it was quite limited in its applications and was used primarily by the Army Ordnance

FIGURE 1.13   Atanasoff–Berry computer. (Courtesy of Iowa State University)

FIGURE 1.14   ENIAC. (Courtesy of Sperry Corporation)

Department to calculate firing tables and trajectories for various types of shells. Eckert and Mauchly later left the University of Pennsylvania to form the Eckert–Mauchly Computer Corporation, which built the **UNIVAC** (Universal Automatic Computer), the first commercially available computer designed for both scientific and business applications. The first UNIVAC was sold to the census bureau in 1951.

The instructions, or program, that controlled the ENIAC's operation were entered into the machine by rewiring some parts of the computer's circuits. This complicated process was very time-consuming, sometimes taking several people several days, and during this time, the computer was idle. In other early computers, the instructions were stored outside the machine on punched cards or some other medium and were transferred into the machine one at a time for interpretation and execution. A new scheme, developed by Princeton mathematician John von Neumann and others, used internally stored commands. The advantages of this stored program concept are that internally stored instructions can be processed more rapidly and, more important, that they can be modified by the computer itself while computations are taking place. The stored program concept made possible the general-purpose computers so commonplace today.

Modern Computers

The actual physical components used in constructing a computer system are its **hardware.** Several generations of computers can be identified by the type of hardware used. The ENIAC and UNIVAC are examples of **first-generation** computers, which are characterized by their extensive use of vacuum tubes. Advances in electronics brought changes in computing systems, and in 1958, IBM introduced the first of the **second-generation** computers, the IBM 7090. These computers were built between 1959 and 1965 and used transistors in place of vacuum tubes. Consequently, these computers were smaller, required less power, generated far less heat, and were more reliable than their predecessors. They were also less expensive, as illustrated by the introduction of the first **minicomputer** in 1963, the PDP-8, which sold for $18,000, in contrast with earlier computers whose six-digit price tags limited their sales to large companies. The **third-generation** computers that followed used integrated circuits and introduced new techniques for better system utilization, such as multiprogramming and time-sharing. The IBM System/360 introduced in 1964 is commonly accepted as the first of this generation of computers. Computers of the 1980s and 1990s, commonly called **fourth-generation** computers, use very large-scale integrated circuits (VLSI) on silicon chips and other microelectronic advances to shrink their size and cost still more while enlarging their capability. A typical chip is equivalent to many thousands of transistors, is smaller than a baby's fingernail, weighs a small fraction of an ounce, requires only a trickle of power, and costs but a few dollars. One of the pioneers in the development of transistors was Robert Noyce, one of the cofounders of the Intel Corporation, which introduced the 4004 microprocessor in 1971. Noyce contrasted microcomputers with the ENIAC as follows:

> An individual integrated circuit on a chip perhaps a quarter of an inch square now can embrace more electronic elements than the most complex piece of electronic equipment that could be built in 1950. Today's microcomputer, at a cost of perhaps $300, has more computing capacity than the first electronic computer, ENIAC. It is twenty times faster, has a larger memory, consumes the power of a light bulb rather than that of a locomotive, occupies 1/30,000 the volume and costs 1/10,000 as much. It is available by mail order or at your local hobby shop.

Microprocessors like the Intel 4004 made possible the development of the personal computers so common today. One of the most popular personal computers was the **Apple II,** constructed in a makeshift production facility in a garage and introduced in 1977 by **Steven Jobs** and **Steve Wozniak,** then 21 and 26 years old, respectively. They founded the Apple Computer Company, one of the major manufacturers of microcomputers today. This was followed by the introduction in 1981 of the first of **IBM's PCs,** which have become the standard for the microcomputer in business and industry (Figure 1.15).

Continued advances in technology have produced a wide array of computer systems, ranging from portable **laptop** and **notebook** computers to powerful desktop machines known as **workstations** and to **supercomputers** capable of performing billions of operations each second and to **massively parallel computers** which use a large number of microprocessors working together in parallel to solve large problems. Someone once noted that if progress in the automotive industry had been as rapid as in computer technology since 1960, today's automobile would have an engine that is less than 0.1 inch in length, would get 120,000 miles to a gallon of gas, have a top speed of 240,000 miles per hour, and would cost $4.00.

Computer Software

The stored program concept, introduced by John Von Neumann, was a significant improvement over manual programming methods, but early computers still were

FIGURE 1.15   A modern personal computer. (Courtesy of IBM)

difficult to use because of the complex coding schemes required for the representation of programs and data. Consequently, in addition to improved hardware, computer manufacturers began to develop collections of programs known as **system software,** which make computers easier to use. One of the more important advances in this area was the development of **operating systems,** which allocate storage for programs and data and carry out many other supervisory functions. In particular, an operating system acts as an interface between the user and the machine. It interprets commands given by the user and then directs the appropriate system software and hardware to carry them out. One of the most commonly used operating systems is UNIX, begun in 1971 but still undergoing development today. It is the only operating system that has been implemented on computers ranging from microcomputers to supercomputers. The most popular operating system for personal computers has for many years been MS-DOS, the first version of which was developed by the Microsoft Corporation in 1981. In more recent years, **graphical user interfaces (GUI),** such as that of the Apple MacIntosh and Microsoft's Windows, have been devised to provide a simpler and more intuitive interface between humans and computers.

Another important advance in system software was the development of **high-level languages,** which allow users to write programs in a language similar to natural language. A program written in a high-level language is known as a **source program.** For most high-level languages, the instructions that make up a source program must be translated into **machine language,** that is, the language used directly by a particular computer for all its calculations and processing. This machine language program is called an **object program.** The programs that translate source programs into object programs are called **compilers.**

One of the first high-level languages to gain widespread acceptance was **FORTRAN** (**FOR**mula **TRAN**slation), which was developed for the IBM 704 computer by **John Backus** and a team of thirteen other programmers at IBM over a three-year period (1954–1957). Since that time many other high-level languages have become popular, including ALGOL, BASIC, COBOL, Pascal, C, Ada, and Modula-2. In this text we use the Pascal programming language.

Pascal, named in honor of the French mathematician Blaise Pascal, was designed by Niklaus Wirth at the Eidgenössiche Technishe Hochschule (ETH) in Zurich, Switzerland. The first Pascal compiler appeared in 1970, and the first report on the language was published in 1971.[2] A revised user manual and report was published in 1974.[3] The first two paragraphs of the introduction to this report describe Wirth's reasons for developing Pascal:

> The development of the language Pascal is based on two principal aims. The first is to make available a language suitable to teach programming as a systematic discipline based on certain fundamental concepts clearly and naturally reflected by the language. The second is to develop implementations of this language which are both reliable and efficient on presently available computers.
>
> The desire for a new language for the purpose of teaching programming is due to my dissatisfaction with the presently used major languages whose features and constructs too often cannot be explained logically and convincingly and which too often defy systematic reasoning. Along with this dissatisfaction goes my conviction that the language in which the student is taught to express his ideas profoundly influences his habits of thought and invention, and that the disorder governing these languages directly imposes itself onto the programming style of the students.

For Pascal, Wirth used much of the framework of ALGOL. Pascal itself has served as the basis for more recent programming languages such as Ada (named after Ada Augusta) and Modula-2 (also developed by Wirth).

Summary

The history of computation and computational aids began several thousands of years ago, and in some cases, the theory underlying such devices progressed much more rapidly than did the technical skills required to produce working models. Although the modern electronic computer, with its mechanized calculation and automatic program control, has its roots in the mid-nineteenth-century work of Charles Babbage, the electronic computer is a fairly recent development. The rapid changes that have marked its progression since its inception in 1945 can be expected to continue into the future.

---

[2] N. Wirth, ''The Programming Language Pascal,'' *Acta-Informatica* 1 (1971): 35–63.

[3] K. Jensen and N. Wirth, *Pascal User Manual and Report* (Heidelberg: Springer-Verlag, 1974).

1.2   PART OF THE PICTURE: Computer Organization

In our discussion of the history of computing, we noted that Babbage designed his Analytical Engine as a system of several separate components, each with its own particular function. This general scheme was incorporated in many later computers and is, in fact, a common feature of most modern computers. In this section we briefly describe the major components of a modern computing system and how program instructions and data are stored and processed.

Computing Systems

The heart of any computing system is its **central processing unit,** or **CPU.** The CPU controls the operation of the entire system, performs the arithmetic and logic operations, and stores and retrieves instructions and data. The instructions and data are stored in a high-speed **memory unit,** and the **control unit** fetches these instructions from memory, decodes them, and directs the system to execute the operations indicated by the instructions. Those operations that are arithmetical or logical in nature are carried out using special registers and circuits of the **arithmetic–logic unit (ALU)** of the CPU.

The memory unit is called the **internal** or **main** or **primary memory** of the computer system. It is used to store the instructions and data of the programs being executed. Most computing systems also contain components that serve as **external** or **auxiliary** or **secondary memory.** Common forms of this type of memory are magnetic disks and magnetic tapes. These **peripheral devices** provide long-term storage for large collections of information. The rate of transfer of information to and from them is considerably slower than that for internal memory.

Other peripherals are used to transmit instructions, data, and computed results between the user and the CPU. These are the **input/output devices,** which have a variety of forms, such as terminals, scanners, voice input devices, printers, and plotters. Their function is to convert information from an external form understandable to the user to a form that can be processed by the computer system, and vice versa.

Figure 1.16 shows the relationship between these components in a computer system. The arrows indicate how information flows through the system.

Memory Organization

The devices that comprise the memory unit of a computer are two-state devices. If one of the states is interpreted as 0 and the other as 1, then it is natural to use a **binary scheme,** using only the two binary digits (**bits**) 0 and 1 to represent information in a computer. These two-state devices are organized into groups called **bytes,** each of which contains a fixed number of these devices, usually eight, and thus can store a fixed number of bits. Memory is commonly measured in bytes, and a block of $2^{10} = 1024$ bytes is called **1K** of memory. Thus, a 512K memory usually refers to a memory that consists of $512 \times 2^{10} = 2^9 \times 2^{10} = 2^{19} = 524,288$ bytes, or, equivalently, $2^{19} \times 2^3 = 2^{22} = 4,194,304$ bits (1 byte = 8 bits).

A larger grouping of bits and bytes is into **words.** Word sizes vary with computers, but common sizes are 16 bits (=2 bytes) and 32 bits (=4 bytes). Each word

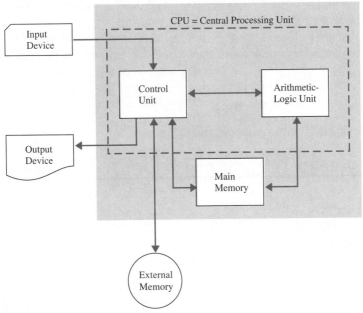

FIGURE 1.16 Major components of a computing system.

or byte is identified by an **address** and can be directly accessed using this address. This makes it possible to store information in a specific memory location and then to retrieve it later. To understand how this is done, we must first examine the binary number system.

Number Systems

The number system that we are accustomed to using is a **decimal** or **base-10** number system, which uses the digits 0, 1, 2, 3, 4, 5, 6, 7, 8, and 9. The significance of these digits in a numeral depends on the positions that they occupy in that numeral. For example, in the numeral

$$485$$

the digit 4 is interpreted as

$$4 \text{ hundreds}$$

and the digit 8 as

$$8 \text{ tens}$$

and the digit 5 as

$$5 \text{ ones}$$

Thus, the numeral 485 represents the number four-hundred eighty-five and can be written in **expanded form** as

$$(4 \times 100) + (8 \times 10) + (5 \times 1)$$

or

$$(4 \times 10^2) + (8 \times 10^1) + (5 \times 10^0)$$

The digits that appear in the various positions of a decimal (base-10) numeral thus are coefficients of powers of 10.

Similar positional number systems can be devised using numbers other than 10 as a base. The **binary** number system uses 2 as the base and has only two digits, 0 and 1. As in a decimal system, the significance of the bits in a binary numeral is determined by their positions in that numeral. For example, the binary numeral

$$101$$

can be written in expanded form (using decimal notation) as

$$(1 \times 2^2) + (0 \times 2^1) + (1 \times 2^0)$$

that is, the binary numeral 101 has the decimal value

$$4 + 0 + 1 = 5$$

Similarly, the binary numeral 111010 has the decimal value

$$(1 \times 2^5) + (1 \times 2^4) + (1 \times 2^3) + (0 \times 2^2) + (1 \times 2^1) + (0 \times 2^0)$$
$$= 32 + 16 + 8 + 2$$
$$= 58$$

When necessary, to avoid confusion about which base is being used, it is customary to write the base as a subscript for nondecimal numerals. Using this convention, we could indicate that 5 and 58 have the binary representations just given by writing

$$5 = 101_2$$

and

$$58 = 111010_2$$

Two other nondecimal numeration systems are important in the study of computer systems: **octal** and **hexadecimal.** The octal system is a base-8 system and uses the eight digits 0, 1, 2, 3, 4, 5, 6, and 7. In an octal numeral such as

$$1703_8$$

the digits are coefficients of powers of 8; this numeral is therefore an abbreviation for the expanded form

$$(1 \times 8^3) + (7 \times 8^2) + (0 \times 8^1) + (3 \times 8^0)$$

and thus has the decimal value

$$512 + 448 + 0 + 3 = 963$$

A hexadecimal system uses a base of 16 and the digits 0, 1, 2, 3, 4, 5, 6, 7, 8, 9, A (10), B (11), C (12), D (13), E (14), and F (15). The hexadecimal numeral

$$5E4_{16}$$

has the expanded form

$$(5 \times 16^2) + (14 \times 16^1) + (4 \times 16^0)$$

which has the decimal value

$$1280 + 224 + 4 = 1508$$

Table 1.1 shows the decimal, binary, octal, and hexadecimal representations for the first 31 nonnegative integers.

TABLE 1.1   Numeric Representations

Decimal	Binary	Octal	Hexadecimal
0	0	0	0
1	1	1	1
2	10	2	2
3	11	3	3
4	100	4	4
5	101	5	5
6	110	6	6
7	111	7	7
8	1000	10	8
9	1001	11	9
10	1010	12	A
11	1011	13	B
12	1100	14	C
13	1101	15	D
14	1110	16	E
15	1111	17	F
16	10000	20	10
17	10001	21	11
18	10010	22	12
19	10011	23	13
20	10100	24	14
21	10101	25	15
22	10110	26	16
23	10111	27	17
24	11000	30	18
25	11001	31	19
26	11010	32	1A
27	11011	33	1B
28	11100	34	1C
29	11101	35	1D
30	11110	36	1E
31	11111	37	1F

Data Storage

Integers.   When an integer value must be stored in the computer's memory, the binary representation of that value is typically stored in one memory word. To illustrate, consider a computer whose word size is sixteen bits, and suppose that the integer value 58 is to be stored. A memory word is selected, and a sequence of sixteen bits formed from the binary representation 111010 of 58 is stored there:

Memory

| 0 | 0 | 0 | 0 | 0 | 0 | 0 | 0 | 0 | 0 | 1 | 1 | 1 | 0 | 1 | 0 |

Negative integers must be stored in a binary form in which the sign of the integer is part of the representation. There are several ways that this can be done, but one of the most common is the **two's complement** representation. In this scheme, positive integers are represented in binary form as just described, with the leftmost bit set to 0 to indicate that the value is positive. The representation of a negative integer $-n$ is obtained by first finding the binary representation of n, complementing it—that is, changing each 0 to 1 and each 1 to 0—and then adding 1 to the result. For example, the two's complement representation of -58 using sixteen bits is obtained as follows:

1. Represent 58 by a 16-bit binary numeral:

$$0000000000111010$$

2. Complement this bit string:

$$1111111111000101$$

3. Add 1:

$$1111111111000110$$

Note that the leftmost bit in this two's complement representation of a negative integer is always 1, indicating that the number is negative.

The fixed word size limits the range of the integers that can be stored. For example, the largest positive integer that can be stored in a 16-bit word is

$$0111111111111111_2 = 2^{15} - 1 = 32767$$

and the smallest negative integer is

$$1000000000000000_2 = -2^{15} = -32768$$

The range of integers that can be represented using a 32-bit word is

$$10000000000000000000000000000000_2 = -2^{31} = -2147483648$$

through

$$01111111111111111111111111111111_2 = 2^{31} - 1 = 2147483647$$

Representation of an integer outside the allowed range would require more bits than can be stored in a single word, a phenomenon known as **overflow.** This limitation may be partially overcome by using more than one word to store an integer. Although this enlarges the range of integers that can be stored exactly, it does not solve the problem of overflow; the range of representable integers is still finite.

Real Numbers. Numbers that contain decimal points are called **real numbers** or **floating point numbers.** In the decimal representation of such numbers, each digit is the coefficient of some power of 10. Digits to the left of the decimal point are coefficients of nonnegative powers of 10, and those to the right are coefficients of negative powers of 10. For example, the decimal numeral 56.317 can be written in expanded form as

$$(5 \times 10^1) + (6 \times 10^0) + (3 \times 10^{-1}) + (1 \times 10^{-2}) + (7 \times 10^{-3})$$

or, equivalently, as

$$(5 \times 10) + (6 \times 1) + \left(3 \times \frac{1}{10}\right) + \left(1 \times \frac{1}{100}\right) + \left(7 \times \frac{1}{1000}\right)$$

Digits in the binary representation of a real number are coefficients of powers of two. Those to the left of the **binary point** are coefficients of nonnegative powers of two, and those to the right are coefficients of negative powers of two. For example, the expanded form of 110.101 is

$$(1 \times 2^2) + (1 \times 2^1) + (0 \times 2^0) + (1 \times 2^{-1}) + (0 \times 2^{-2}) + (1 \times 2^{-3})$$

and thus has the decimal value

$$4 + 2 + 0 + \frac{1}{2} + 0 + \frac{1}{8} = 6.625$$

There is some variation in the schemes used for storing real numbers in computer memory, but one common method is illustrated by the following. The binary representation

$$110.101_2$$

of the real number 6.625 can also be written as

$$0.110101_2 \times 2^3$$

Typically, one part of a memory word (or words) is used to store a fixed number of bits of the **mantissa** or **fractional part,** 0.110101_2, and another part to store the **exponent,** $3 = 11_2$. For example, if the leftmost eleven bits in a 16-bit word are used for the mantissa and the remaining five bits for the exponent, 6.625 can be stored as

$$\boxed{0|1|1|0|1|0|1|0|0|0|0|0|0|0|1|1}$$

$$\underbrace{\hspace{4cm}}_{\text{mantissa}} \quad \underbrace{\hspace{2cm}}_{\text{exponent}}$$

where the first bit in each part is reserved for the sign.

Because the binary representation of the exponent may require more than the available number of bits, the overflow problem discussed in connection with the integer representation may also occur when storing a real number. Also, there obviously are some real numbers whose mantissas have more than the allotted number of bits; consequently, some of these bits will be lost when storing such numbers. In fact, most real numbers do not have finite binary representations and thus cannot be stored exactly in any computer. For example, the binary representation of the real number 0.7 is

$$(0.10110011001100110 \ldots)_2$$

where the block 0110 is repeated indefinitely. If only the first eleven bits are stored and all remaining bits are truncated, the stored representation of 0.7 will be

$$0.10110011002$$

which has the decimal value 0.69921875. If the binary representation is rounded to eleven bits, the stored representation for 0.7 will be

$$0.10110011012$$

which has the decimal value 0.700195312. In either case, the stored value is not exactly 0.7. This error, called **roundoff error,** can be reduced, but not eliminated, by using a larger number of bits to store the binary representation of real numbers.

Boolean and Character Values.   Computers store and process not only numeric data but also boolean or logical data (false or true), character data, and other types of nonnumeric information. Storing logical values is easy: False can be encoded as 0, true as 1, and these bits stored.

The schemes used for the internal representation of character data are based on the assignment of a numeric code to each of the characters in the character set. Several standard coding schemes have been developed, such as **ASCII** (American Standard Code for Information Interchange) and **EBCDIC** (Extended Binary Coded Decimal Interchange Code). Table 1.2 shows these codes for capital letters. A complete table of ASCII and EBCDIC codes for all characters is given in Appendix A.

Characters are represented internally using these binary codes. A byte consisting of eight bits can thus store the binary representation of one character, and a 16-bit word consisting of two bytes can store two characters. For example, the character string HI can be stored in a single 16-bit word with the code for H in the left byte and the code for I in the right byte; with ASCII code, the result is as follows:

```
0 1 0 0 1 0 0 0 0 1 0 0 1 0 0 1
```
          H   I

TABLE 1.2   Character Codes

Character	ASCII		EBCDIC	
	Decimal	Binary	Decimal	Binary
A	65	01000001	193	11000001
B	66	01000010	194	11000010
C	67	01000011	195	11000011
D	68	01000100	196	11000100
E	69	01000101	197	11000101
F	70	01000110	198	11000110
G	71	01000111	199	11000111
H	72	01001000	200	11001000
I	73	01001001	201	11001001
J	74	01001010	209	11010001
K	75	01001011	210	11010010
L	76	01001100	211	11010011
M	77	01001101	212	11010100
N	78	01001110	213	11010101
O	79	01001111	214	11010110
P	80	01010000	215	11010111
Q	81	01010001	216	11011000
R	82	01010010	217	11011001
S	83	01010011	226	11100010
T	84	01010100	227	11100011
U	85	01010101	228	11100100
V	86	01010110	229	11100101
W	87	01010111	230	11100110
X	88	01011000	231	11100111
Y	89	01011001	232	11101000
Z	90	01011010	233	11101001

Memory words of size 32 (bits) are usually divided into four bytes and thus can store four characters. Character strings of a length greater than the number of bytes in a word are usually stored in two or more consecutive memory words.

Instruction Processing

We have now seen how various types of data can be stored in a computer's memory. Program instructions for processing data must also be stored in memory. As an example, suppose that three values, $8 = 1000_2$, $24 = 11000_2$, and $58 = 111010_2$, have been stored in memory locations with addresses 4, 5, and 6 and that we want to multiply the first two values, add the third, and store the result in memory word 7.

Address	Memory	
0		
1		
2		
3		
4	0000000000001000	← 8
5	0000000000011000	← 24
6	0000000000111010	← 58
7		← Result

$\vdots$

To perform this computation, the following instructions must be executed:

1. Fetch the contents of memory word 4 and load it into the accumulator register of the ALU.
2. Fetch the contents of memory word 5 and compute the product of this value and the value in the accumulator.
3. Fetch the contents of memory word 6 and add this value to the value in the accumulator register.
4. Store the contents of the accumulator register in memory word 7.

In order to store these instructions in computer memory, they must be represented in binary form. The addresses of the data values present no problem, as they can easily be converted to binary addresses:

$$4 = 100_2$$
$$5 = 101_2$$
$$6 = 110_2$$
$$7 = 111_2$$

The operations load, multiply, add, store, and other basic machine instructions are represented by numeric codes, called **opcodes;** for example,

$$LOAD = 16 = 10000_2$$
$$STORE = 17 = 10001_2$$
$$ADD = 35 = 100011_2$$
$$MULTIPLY = 36 = 100100_2$$

Using part of a word to store the opcode and another part for the address of the **operand,** we can represent our sequence of instructions in **machine language** as

1. 0001000000000100
2. 0010010000000101
3. 0010001100000110
4. 0001000100000111

$$\underbrace{\qquad}_{\text{opcode}} \underbrace{\qquad}_{\text{operand}}$$

These instructions can then be stored in four (consecutive) memory words. When the program is executed, the control unit will fetch each of these instructions, decode it to determine the operation and the address of the operand, fetch the operand, and then perform the required operation, using the ALU if necessary.

Programs for early computers had to be written in such machine language. Later it became possible to write programs in **assembly language,** which uses mnemonics (names) in place of numeric opcodes and variable names in place of numeric addresses. For example, the preceding sequence of instructions might be written in assembly language as

1. LOAD A
2. MULT B
3. ADD C
4. STORE X

An **assembler,** which is part of the system software, translates such assembly language instructions into machine language.

Today, most programs are written in a high-level language such as Pascal, and a **compiler** translates each statement in this program into a sequence of basic machine (or assembly) language instructions.

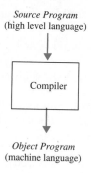

Source Program
(high level language)

Compiler

Object Program
(machine language)

For example, for the preceding problem, the programmer could write the Pascal statement

$$X := A * B + C$$

which instructs the computer to multiply the values of **A** and **B**, add the value of **C**, and assign the value to **X**. The compiler then translates this statement into a sequence of four machine (or assembly) language instructions like those given earlier.

As the preceding diagram indicates, a compiler translates the entire source program into an equivalent object program consisting of machine language instructions. After this translation is complete, this object program is executed by the computer. Some languages are processed using an **interpreter** rather than a compiler. An interpreter also examines a source program statement by statement. However, after each statement is translated, the resulting machine language instructions are immediately executed before the next statement is examined; no object program is actually produced. Still another approach is to compile the source program into simple machine-independent language called **intermediate code.** The resulting program may be either interpreted or compiled. In any case, the original source program in a high-level language must be translated into strings of 0s and 1s that represent machine instructions.

Exercises

1. Describe the importance of each of the following persons to the history of computing:

   (a) Charles Babbage   (b) Blaise Pascal
   (c) John von Neumann   (d) Herman Hollerith
   (e) Joseph Jacquard   (f) Gottfried Wilhelm von Leibniz
   (g) John Atanasoff   (h) Steven Jobs
   (i) Robert Noyce   (j) J. P. Eckert
   (k) Niklaus Wirth   (l) Steve Wozniak

2. Describe the importance of each of the following devices to the history of computing:

   (a) ENIAC   (b) Analytical Engine
   (c) Jacquard loom   (d) UNIVAC
   (e) Mark I

3. Distinguish the four different generations of computers.

4. Briefly define each of the following terms:

   (a) stored program concept   (b) FORTRAN
   (c) Pascal   (d) CPU
   (e) ALU   (f) peripheral devices
   (g) bit   (h) byte
   (i) word   (j) UNIX
   (k) MS-DOS   (l) source program
   (m) object program   (n) assembly language
   (o) machine language   (p) K

5. What are the main functions of

   (a) an operating system
   (b) a compiler
   (c) an assembler

6. Convert each of the following unsigned binary numerals to base 10:

   (a) 1001   **(b)** 110010
   (c) 1000000   **(d)** 111111111111111 (fifteen 1s)
   (e) 1.1   **(f)** 1010.10101

7. Convert each of the following octal numerals to base 10:

   (a) 123   **(b)** 2705   **(c)** 10000
   (d) 77777   **(e)** 7.2   **(f)** 123.45

8. Convert each of the following hexadecimal numerals to base 10:

   (a) 12   **(b)** 1AB   **(c)** ABC
   (d) FFF   **(e)** 8.C   **(f)** AB.CD

9. Conversion from octal representation to binary representation is easy, as we need only replace each octal digit with its three-bit binary equivalent. For example, to convert 617_8 to binary, replace 6 with 110, 1 with 001, and 7 with 111, to obtain 110001111_2. Convert each of the octal numerals in Exercise 7 to binary numerals.

10. Imitating the conversion scheme in Exercise 9, convert each of the hexadecimal numerals in Exercise 8 to binary numerals.

11. To convert a binary numeral to octal, place the digits in groups of three, starting from the binary point, or from the right end if there is no binary point, and replace each group with the corresponding octal digit. For example, $10101111_2 = 010\ 101\ 111_2 = 257_8$. Convert each of the binary numerals in Exercise 6 to octal numerals.

12. Imitating the conversion scheme in Exercise 11, convert each of the binary numerals in Exercise 6 to hexadecimal numerals.

13. One method for finding the **base-b** representation of a whole number given in base-10 notation is to divide the number repeatedly by b until a quotient of zero results. The successive remainders are the digits from right to left of the base-b representation. For example, the binary representation of 26 is 11010_2, as the following computation shows:

$$
\begin{array}{rl}
0 & \text{R } 1 \\
2\overline{)1} & \text{R } 1 \\
2\overline{)3} & \text{R } 0 \\
2\overline{)6} & \text{R } 1 \\
2\overline{)13} & \text{R } 0 \\
2\overline{)26} &
\end{array}
$$

Convert each of the following base-10 numerals to (i) binary, (ii) octal, and (iii) hexadecimal:

   (a) 27   **(b)** 99   **(c)** 314   **(d)** 5280

14. To convert a decimal fraction to its base-b equivalent, repeatedly multiply the fractional part of the number by b. The integer parts are the digits from left to right of the base-b representation. For example, the decimal numeral 0.6875 corresponds to the binary numeral 0.1011_2, as the following computation shows:

$$
\begin{array}{r|l}
 & .6875 \\
 & \times 2 \\
\hline
1 & .375 \\
 & \times 2 \\
\hline
0 & .75 \\
 & \times 2 \\
\hline
1 & .5 \\
 & \times 2 \\
\hline
1 & .0 \\
\end{array}
$$

Convert the following base-10 numerals to (i) binary, (ii) octal, (iii) hexadecimal:

(a) 0.5 **(b)** 0.25 **(c)** 0.625
(d) 16.0625 **(e)** 8.828125

15. Even though the base-10 representation of a fraction may terminate, its representation in some other base need not terminate. For example, the following computation shows that the binary representation of 0.7 is $(0.10110011001100110011001100110\ldots)_2$, where the block of bits 0110 is repeated indefinitely. This representation is commonly written as $0.1\overline{0110}_2$.

$$
\begin{array}{r|l}
 & .7 \\
 & \times 2 \\
\hline
1 & .4 \\
 & \times 2 \\
\hline
0 & .8 \\
 & \times 2 \\
\hline
1 & .6 \\
 & \times 2 \\
\hline
1 & .2 \\
 & \times 2 \\
\hline
0 & .4 \\
\end{array}
$$

Convert the following base-10 numerals to (i) binary, (ii) octal, (iii) hexadecimal:

(a) 0.3 **(b)** 0.6 **(c)** 0.05 **(d)** $0.\overline{3} = 0.33333\cdots = 1/3$

16. Find the decimal value of each of the following 16-bit integers, assuming a two's complement representation:

(a) 0000000001000000 **(b)** 1111111111111110
(c) 1111111110111111 **(d)** 0000000011111111
(e) 1111111100000000 **(f)** 1000000000000001

17. Find the 16-bit two's complement representation for each of the following integers:

(a) 255   (b) 1K
(c) −255   (d) −256
(e) −34567$_8$ (f) −3ABC$_{16}$

18. Assuming two's complement representation, what range of integers can be represented in 8-bit words?

19. Assuming an 11-bit mantissa and a 5-bit exponent, as described in the text, and assuming that two's complement representation is used for each, indicate how each of the following real numbers would be stored in a 16-bit word if extra bits in the mantissa are (i) truncated or (ii) rounded:

(a) 0.375   (b) 37.375
(c) 0.03125   (d) 63.84375
(e) 0.1   (f) 0.01

20. Using the tables for ASCII and EBCDIC in Appendix A, indicate how each of the following character strings would be stored in 2-byte words using (i) ASCII or (ii) EBCDIC:

(a) TO   (b) FOUR   (c) AMOUNT
(d) ETC.   (e) J. DOE   (f) A#∗4−C

21. Using the instruction mnemonics and opcodes given in the text, write a sequence of (a) assembly language and (b) machine language instructions equivalent to the Pascal statement

```
X := (A + B) * C
```

For the machine language instructions, assume that the values of A, B, and C are stored in memory words 15, 16, and 17, respectively, and the value of X is to be stored in memory word 23.

22. Repeat Exercise 21 for the Pascal statement

```
X := (A + B) * (C + D)
```

assuming that the value of D is stored in memory word 18.

PROGRAM DEVELOPMENT

People always get what they ask for; the only trouble is that they never know, until they get it, what it actually is that they have asked for.
ALDOUS HUXLEY

CHAPTER CONTENTS

We noted in Chapter 1 that the computer has become an indispensable tool in many areas. Its applications are far too many to enumerate, and the following list is intended only to show some of the diverse uses of computers:

- Business and Finance
    Mailing lists and billings
    Payroll, accounts receivable, accounts payable
    Inventory control
    Reservations systems (airlines, car rentals, etc.)
    Word processing
    Data management
    Spreadsheets
    EFT (electronic funds transfer)
    ATMs (automatic teller machines)
    Electronic mail
    Home banking
    Financial planning
    Processing of insurance claims
- Industry
    Robots in assembly lines
    CAD (computer-aided design)
    CAM (computer-aided manufacturing)
    CIM (computer-integrated manufacturing)
    Market analysis
    Project management and control
    Production scheduling
- Government
    Defense systems
    Space programs
    Compilation of census data
    Weather forecasting by NOAA (National Oceanic and Atmospheric Administration)
    Automated traffic-control systems
    State and local lotteries
    The FBI's NCIS (national crime information system)
- Medicine
    CAT (computerized axial tomography) and MR (magnetic resonance) scans
    On-line access to patients' medical records
    Monitoring life-support systems
    Expert diagnosis systems
- Entertainment
    Animation, colorization, and creation of special effects in the film industry
    Video games
- Science
    Analysis of molecules
    Study of crystal structures
    Testing food quality
    Simulation of large dynamical systems

These and many other applications all require the development of software, and although the problems themselves and specific techniques used in their solutions vary, there are several phases or steps that are common in the software development process:

1. Problem analysis and specification.
2. Design.
3. Coding.
4. Verification and validation.
5. Maintenance.

In this chapter we begin by describing and illustrating the first four steps of this **software life cycle,** using three problems, each of which can be solved with a simple program. In the last section, we discuss the fifth step, software maintenance, and also some of the questions and complications that software developers face in real-world applications.

2.1 Problem Analysis and Specification

Because the initial description of a problem may be somewhat vague and imprecise, the first step in the development of a program to solve the problem is to analyze the problem and formulate a precise **specification** of it. This specification must include a description of the problem's **input**—what information is given and which items are important in solving the problem—and its **output**—what information must be produced to solve the problem. Input and output are the two major parts of the problem's specification, and for a problem that appears in a programming text, they are usually not too difficult to identify. In a real-world problem encountered by a professional programmer, the specification of the problem often includes other items, like those described in Section 2.5, and considerable effort may be required to formulate it completely. In this section we illustrate this first step of program development with three simple examples.

PROBLEM 1: Calculating Revenue

Sam Shyster installs coaxial cable for the Cawker City Cable Company. For each installation, there is a basic service charge of $25.00 and an additional charge of $2.00 for each foot of cable. During the month of January, Sam installed a total of 263 yards of cable at 27 different locations. What was the total revenue that Sam generated for the month?

Identifying the input and output in this textbook problem is easy:

Input	Output
Basic service charge: $25.00	Revenue generated
Unit cable cost: $2.00	
Number of installations: 27	
Yards of cable: 263	

The other given items of information—the employee's name, his job, the name of the company, and the month—are not relevant (at least not for this problem) and can be ignored.

The revenue that Sam Shyster generated can be easily calculated by hand, or still more easily by using a calculator, and does not warrant developing a computer program for its solution. A program written to solve this particular problem would probably be used just once. If Sam installs cable at 42 locations in February using 455 yards of cable or if the basic service charge or the unit cost of cable changes, we would have a new problem requiring a new program. This is obviously a waste of effort, since it is clear that each such problem is a special case of the more general problem of finding the revenue generated for any number of installations, any amount of cable, any basic service charge, and any unit cost of cable. A program that solves the general problem can be used in many situations and is consequently more useful than one designed to solve only the original special problem.

One important aspect of problem analysis, therefore, is **generalization.** The effort involved in later phases of the problem-solving process demands that the program eventually developed be sufficiently flexible, that it solve not only the given specific problem but also any related problem of the same kind with little, if any, modification required. In this example, the specification of the problem could thus be better formulated in general terms:

Input	Output
Basic service charge	Revenue generated
Unit cable cost	
Number of installations	
Yards of cable	

Obviously, we could generalize still more—allow several employees, other kinds of charges, different kinds of cable, and so on—but we must stop somewhere. In this elementary introduction to the problem-solving process, we wish to keep our examples quite simple.

PROBLEM 2: Pollution Index

The level of air pollution in the city of Dogpatch is measured by a pollution index. Readings are made at 12:00 P.M. at three locations: the Abner coal plant, downtown at the corner of Daisy Avenue and 5th Street, and at a randomly selected location in a residential area. The average of these three readings is the pollution index, and a value of 50 or greater for this index indicates a hazardous condition, whereas values lower than 50 indicate a safe condition. Because this index must be calculated daily, the Dogpatch environmental statistician would like a program that calculates the pollution index and then determines the appropriate condition, safe or hazardous.

The relevant given information consists of three pollution readings and the cutoff value used to distinguish between safe and hazardous conditions. A solution to the problem consists of the pollution index and a message indicating the condition. Generalizing so that any cutoff value, not just 50, can be used, we could specify the problem as follows:

Input	Output
Three pollution readings	Pollution index = the average of the pollution readings
Cutoff value to distinguish between safe and hazardous condition	Condition: safe or hazardous

PROBLEM 3: Mean Time to Failure

One important statistic that is used in measuring the reliability of a component in a circuit is the *mean time to failure,* which can be used to predict the circuit's lifetime. This is especially important in situations in which repair is difficult or even impossible, such as a computer circuit in a space satellite. Suppose that an engineering laboratory has been awarded a contract by NASA to evaluate the reliability of a particular component for a future space probe to Jupiter. As part of this evaluation, an engineer at this laboratory tested several of these circuits and recorded the time at which each failed. She now wishes to develop a program to process this data and determine the mean time to failure.

The input for this problem is obviously a collection of failure times for the component being tested, and the output is clearly the average or mean of these times. To calculate this mean, we must know how many tests were conducted, but this information is not given in the statement of the problem. We cannot assume, therefore, that it is part of the input, and so the program will have to be flexible enough to process any number of measurements. A specification of the input and output for this problem thus might be

Input	Output
A collection of numeric values (number unknown)	The number of values The mean of the values

2.2 Design

Once the specification of a problem has been given, a **design plan** for developing a program or a system of programs that meets the specification must be formulated. Two important aspects of design are selecting appropriate structures to organize and store the data to be processed and designing procedures to process the data. For the problems considered in the first several chapters of this text, the data items will be processed and stored using variables much like those used in mathematics to name quantities in algebraic formulas and equations; more complex structures will be discussed in later chapters.

Because the computer is a machine possessing no inherent problem-solving capabilities, the procedures developed to solve a problem must be formulated as a detailed sequence of simple steps. Such procedures are called **algorithms.**

The steps that comprise an algorithm must be organized in a logical and clear manner so that the program that implements this algorithm will be similarly well structured. **Structured algorithms** and **programs** are designed using three basic methods of control:

1. *Sequential:* Steps are performed in a strictly sequential manner, each step being executed exactly once.
2. *Selection:* One of a number of alternative actions is selected and executed.
3. *Repetition:* One or more steps are performed repeatedly.

These three structures are individually quite simple, but in fact they are sufficiently powerful that any algorithm can be constructed using them.

Programs to implement algorithms must be written in a language that the computer can understand. It is natural, therefore, to describe algorithms in a language that resembles that used to write computer programs, that is, in a "pseudoprogramming language" or, as it is more commonly called, **pseudocode.**

Unlike the definitions of high-level programming languages such as Pascal, there is no set of rules that precisely define pseudocode. It varies from one programmer to another. Pseudocode is a mixture of natural language and symbols, terms, and other features commonly used in high-level languages. Typically one finds the following features in various pseudocodes:

1. The usual computer symbols are used for arithmetic operations: + for addition, − for subtraction, * for multiplication, and / for division.
2. Symbolic names (identifiers) are used to represent the quantities being processed by the algorithm.
3. Some provision is made for including comments, often by enclosing each comment between special symbols such as (* and *).
4. Certain key words that are common in high-level languages may be used: for example, Read or Enter to indicate input operations and Display, Print, or Write for output operations.
5. Indentation is used to indicate certain blocks of instructions.

The structure of an algorithm may be displayed in a **structure diagram** that shows the various tasks that must be performed and their relation to one another. These diagrams are especially useful in describing algorithms for more complex problems and will be described in more detail in Section 2.5. In this section we restrict our attention to the three simple examples introduced in the preceding section. Using these examples, we illustrate the three basic control structures—sequence, selection, and repetition—and how to present algorithms using pseudocode.

PROBLEM 1: Calculating Revenue—Sequential Structure

As we noted in the preceding section, the input for this problem consists of the basic service charge, unit cable cost, number of installations, and yards of cable used; the output to be produced is the amount of revenue generated. We will use the variables *ServiceCharge, UnitCost, Installations, YardsOfCable,* and *Revenue* to represent these quantities.

The first step in an algorithm for solving this problem is to obtain the values for the input items—*ServiceCharge, UnitCost, Installations,* and *YardsOfCable.* The next step is to determine the number of feet of cable used, by multiplying the number of yards of cable by 3. The revenue generated can then be obtained by multiplying the unit cable cost by the number of feet of cable and the number of installations by the basic service charge, and adding these two products. Finally, the output value—revenue generated—must be displayed.

This algorithm can be expressed in pseudocode as follows. Note that we have included the problem's specification and a brief description of the algorithm's purpose as a comment at the beginning of the algorithm. Such **documentation** is important and should always be included in the statement of an algorithm.

ALGORITHM FOR REVENUE CALCULATION

(* Input: A basic *ServiceCharge,* a *UnitCost* for cable, number of
             Installations, and *YardsOfCable* used.
   Purpose: This algorithm calculates the revenue generated by the
             installation of a certain number of yards of cable at a number of
             locations. For each installation there is a fixed basic service
             charge and an additional charge for each foot of cable.
   Output: *Revenue* generated. *)

1. Enter *ServiceCharge, UnitCost, Installations,* and *YardsOfCable.*
2. Calculate *FeetOfCable* = 3 * *YardsOfCable.*
3. Calculate

$$Revenue = Installations * ServiceCharge + UnitCost * FeetOfCable$$

4. Display *Revenue.*

This algorithm uses only sequential control; the steps are executed in order, from beginning to end, with each step being performed exactly once. For other problems, however, the solution may require that some of the steps be performed in some situations and bypassed in others. This is illustrated by our second example.

PROBLEM 2: Pollution Index—Selection Structure

Recall that for Problem 2, the input consists of three pollution readings and a cutoff value that distinguishes between safe and hazardous conditions. These will be represented by the variables *Level1, Level2, Level3,* and *Cutoff,* respectively. The output to be produced consists of the pollution index, which is the average of the three readings and will be stored in the variable *Index,* and a message indicating the appropriate condition.

Once again, the first step in an algorithm to solve this problem is to obtain values for the input items—*Level1, Level2, Level3,* and *Cutoff.* The next step is to calculate the pollution index by averaging the three readings. Now, one of two possible actions must be selected. Either a message indicating a safe condition or a message indicating a hazardous condition must be displayed. The appropriate action is selected by comparing the pollution index with the cutoff value. In the pseudocode description of this algorithm, this selection is indicated by

If *Index* < *Cutoff* then
    Display 'Safe condition'
Else
    Display 'Hazardous condition'

ALGORITHM FOR POLLUTION INDEX PROBLEM

(* Input: Three pollution levels and a cutoff value.
    Purpose: This algorithm reads three pollution levels, *Level1, Level2,* and *Level3,* and a *Cutoff* value. It then calculates the pollution *Index.* If the value of *Index* is less than *Cutoff,* a message indicating a safe condition is displayed; otherwise, a message indicating a hazardous condition is displayed.
    Output: The pollution *Index* and a message indicating the air quality. *)

1. Enter *Level1, Level2, Level3,* and *Cutoff.*
2. Calculate

$$Index = \frac{Level1 + Level2 + Level3}{3}$$

3. Display *Index.*
4. If *Index* < *Cutoff* then
    Display 'Safe condition'
Else
    Display 'Hazardous condition'.

In addition to the sequential processing and selection illustrated in the first two examples, the solution of other problems may require that a step or a collection of steps be repeated. This is illustrated in our third example.

PROBLEM 3: Mean Time to Failure—Repetition Structure

In Problem 3, the input is a set of numbers, each representing the failure time of a component in a circuit. The output is the number of data values and their average, which is then the mean time to failure for this component.

In developing algorithms to solve problems like this, one useful method is to begin by considering how the problem could be solved without using a computer, perhaps instead using pencil and paper and/or a calculator. To solve the problem in this manner, we enter the values one at a time, counting each value as it is entered and adding it to the sum of the preceding values. We see that the procedure thus involves two quantities:

1. A counter that is incremented by 1 each time a value is entered.
2. A running sum of the data values.

Data Value	Count	Sum
	0	0.0
3.4	1	3.4
4.2	2	7.6
6.0	3	13.6
5.5	4	19.1
. . .	. . .	. . .

The procedure begins with 0 as the value of the counter and 0.0 as the initial value of the sum. At each stage, a data value is entered, the value of the counter is incremented by 1, and the data value is added to the sum, producing a new sum. These steps are repeated until all the data values have been processed, and the sum is then divided by the count to obtain the mean value.

When solving this problem by hand, it is clear when the last data value has been entered, but if this procedure is to be performed by a program, some method is needed to indicate that all of the data values have been processed. A common technique is to signal this by entering an artificial value called a **data flag** or **data sentinel,** which is distinct from any possible valid data item. This value is not processed as a regular data value but serves only to terminate the repetition.

A pseudocode description of this algorithm follows.

ALGORITHM TO CALCULATE MEAN TIME TO FAILURE

(* Input: A collection of failure times.
  Purpose: Algorithm to read failure times, count them, and find the mean time to failure (*MeanFailTime*). *FailTime* represents the current failure time entered, *NumTimes* is the number of failure times, and *Sum* is their sum. Values are read until an end-of-data flag is encountered.
  Output: *MeanFailTime* and *NumTimes*. *)

1. Initialize *NumTimes* to 0 and *Sum* to 0.0.
2. Enter the first value for *FailTime*.
3. While *FailTime* is not the end-of-data flag, do the following:
    a. Increment *NumTimes* by 1.
    b. Add *FailTime* to *Sum*.
    c. Enter next value for *FailTime*.
4. If *NumTimes* $\neq$ 0 then
    a. Calculate *MeanFailTime* = *Sum* / *NumTimes*.
    b. Display *MeanFailTime* and *NumTimes*.
  Else
    Display a 'No Data' message.

In this algorithm, the repetition is indicated by

While *FailTime* is not the end-of-data flag, do the following:
  a. Increment *Count* by 1.
  b. Add *FailTime* to *Sum*.
  c. Enter next value for *FailTime*.

This specifies that Statements 3a, 3b, and 3c are to be repeated as long as the value of *FailTime* is not the end-of-data flag. Thus, when the flag signaling the end of data is entered, this repetition is terminated, and the remaining statements of the algorithm are performed.

The three control structures in these examples, **sequential, selection,** and **repetition,** are used throughout this text in designing algorithms to solve problems. The implementation of each of them in the Pascal language is considered in detail in later chapters.

2.3   Coding

The first two steps of the program development process are extremely important, because the remaining phases will be much more difficult if the first two steps are skipped or are not done carefully. On the other hand, if the problem has been carefully analyzed and specified and if an effective design plan has been developed, the third step of program coding is usually straightforward.

Coding is the process of implementing in some programming language the variables (and structures) used to store the data and the algorithms for solving the problem. In the design plan, the variables and algorithms may be described in a natural language or pseudocode, but the program that implements that algorithm must be written in the vocabulary of a programming language and must conform to the **syntax,** or grammatical rules, of that language. The major portion of this text is concerned with the vocabulary and syntax of the programming language Pascal. In this section, we introduce some elementary features of this language and give an example of a simple Pascal program. These features will be discussed in detail in subsequent chapters.

Variables

In the three examples in the preceding section, we used variables to store various quantites. In the first example, the variables *ServiceCharge, UnitCost, Installations,* and *YardsOfCable* represented the basic service charge, the cost per foot of cable, the number of installations, and the yards of cable used, respectively. The output in this example was the revenue generated and was represented by the variable *Revenue.* In the second example, the variables *Level1, Level2, Level3, Cutoff,* and *Index* were used, and in the third example, the variables were *FailTime, NumTimes, Sum,* and *MeanFailTime.*

In Pascal, variable names must begin with a letter, which may be followed by any number of letters and digits. Turbo Pascal, however, allows an underscore (_) in addition to letters and digits. This allows us to choose names that suggest what the variable represents, for example, `ServiceCharge`, `UnitCost`, `Installations`, `YardsOfCable`, `Revenue`, `Level1`, `FailTime`, and `Sum`. *Meaningful variable names should always be used because they make a program easier to read and understand.*

Types

In the examples we have been considering, two types of numbers are used. The values of `YardsOfCable`, `FeetOfCable`, and `Installations` in the first example, `Level1`, `Level2`, `Level3`, `Cutoff`, and `Index` in the second example, and `NumTimes` in the third example are integers, whereas the values of `ServiceCharge`, `UnitCost`, and `Revenue` in the first example and `FailTime`, `Sum`, and `MeanFailTime` in the third example are real, that is, they have fractional parts. Pascal distinguishes between these two types of numeric data, and the types of the values that each variable may have must be specified. This is done by placing variable declarations of the form

```
VAR
    list1 : integer;
    list2 : real;
```

at the beginning of the program, where *list1* is a list of the variable names of integer type and *list2* is a list of variable names of real type. Thus, the types of the Pascal variables in the first example can be specified by

```
VAR
    YardsOfCable, FeetOfCable, Installations : integer;
    ServiceCharge, UnitCost, Revenue : real;
```

and those in the third example by

```
VAR
    NumTimes : integer;
    MeanFailTime, FailTime, Sum : real;
```

In these examples, **VAR** is one of the **reserved words** in Pascal. Reserved words may not be used for any purpose other than those designated by the rules of the language. For example, reserved words may not be used as variable names. In this text reserved words will always be written in uppercase to emphasize their special status.

Operations

Addition and subtraction are denoted in Pascal by the usual + and - symbols. Multiplication is denoted by *, real division by /, and integer division by **DIV**. The assignment operation is denoted by := in Pascal programs. For example, the statement

```
FeetOfCable := 3 * YardsOfCable;
```

calculates the value of the product

```
3 * YardsOfCable
```

and assigns this value to the variable `FeetOfCable`.

Input/Output

In the pseudocode description of an algorithm in the preceding section we used the words "enter" and "read" for input operations and "display," "print," and "write" for output operations. One Pascal statement that may be used for input is the **readln** statement. A simple form of this statement is

```
readln( list )
```

where *list* is a list of variables for which values are to be read. For example, the statement

```
readln( ServiceCharge, UnitCost, Installations, YardsOfCable );
```

reads values for the variables **ServiceCharge**, **UnitCost**, **Installations**, and **YardsOfCable** entered by the user from some input device.

A simple output statement in Pascal is the **writeln** statement of the form

```
writeln( list )
```

where *list* is a list of items to be displayed. For example, the statement

```
writeln( 'Revenue generated = $', Revenue )
```

displays the label

```
Revenue generated = $
```

followed by the value of the variable **Revenue**.

Comments

Comments can also be incorporated into Pascal programs. They are indicated by enclosing them within braces

```
{ comment }
```

or within (* and *)

```
(* comment *)
```

Program Composition

Figure 2.1 shows a Pascal program for the algorithm to solve the revenue calculation problem considered earlier in this chapter. The program begins with the **program heading**

```
PROGRAM CalculateRevenue( input, output );
```

where **CalculateRevenue** is the name assigned to the program by the programmer, **input** indicates that information will be input to the program from an external source, and **output** indicates that the program will also produce some output. In Turbo Pascal, the program heading is optional, but it is considered good programming practice to include it in all programs.

FIGURE 2.1 Calculating revenue.

```
PROGRAM CalculateRevenue( input, output );
{*****************************************************************

     Input (keyboard): A basic service charge, cost per foot of cable,
                       number of installations, and yards of cable are
                       input to the program.
     Purpose:          Program to calculate the revenue generated by an
                       employee installing coaxial cable.
     Output:           Revenue generated.


     *****************************************************************}

VAR
     Installations,          {number of installations}
     YardsOfCable,           {yards of cable used}
     FeetOfCable : integer;  {equivalent feet of cable}
     ServiceCharge,          {basic service charge}
     UnitCost,               {cost per foot of cable}
     Revenue : real;         {revenue generated}

BEGIN
     writeln( 'Enter service charge, cost of one foot of cable,' );
     writeln( 'number of installations, and yards of cable used:' );
     readln( ServiceCharge, UnitCost, Installations, YardsOfCable );
     FeetOfCable := 3 * YardsOfCable;
     Revenue := ServiceCharge * Installations + UnitCost * FeetOfCable;
     writeln;
     writeln( 'Revenue generated = $', Revenue:7:2 )
END.
```

Sample run:

```
Enter service charge, cost of one foot of cable,
number of installations, and yards of cable used:
25.00 2.00 27 263

Revenue generated = $2253.00
```

This is followed by documentation in the form of a comment that describes the program. It specifies what is input to the program, what the purpose of the program is, and what output it produces. The next part of the program consists of the variable declarations that specify the types of all the variables used in the program and comments to explain them.

The first step in the algorithm is an input instruction to enter values for the variables *ServiceCharge, UnitCost, Installations,* and *YardsOfCable:*

1. Enter *ServiceCharge, UnitCost, Installations,* and *YardsOfCable.*

This is translated into the following statements in the program:

```
writeln( 'Enter service charge, cost of one foot of cable,' );
writeln( 'number of installations, and yards of cable used:' );
readln( ServiceCharge, UnitCost, Installations, YardsOfCable );
```

The two **writeln** statements are used to prompt the user that values are to be entered. The **readln** statement actually assigns the four values entered by the user to the four variables **ServiceCharge**, **UnitCost**, **Installations**, and **YardsOfCable**. Thus, in the sample run shown, when the user enters

> 25.00 2.00 27 263

the value **25.00** is assigned to **ServiceCharge**, **2.00** to **UnitCost**, **27** to **Installations**, and **263** to **YardsOfCable**.

The next two steps in the algorithm

2. Calculate *FeetOfCable* = 3 ∗ *YardsOfCable*.
3. Calculate
   Revenue = *ServiceCharge* ∗ *Installations* + *UnitCost* ∗ *FeetOfCable*.

translate into the Pascal assignment statements

```
FeetOfCable := 3 * YardsOfCable;
Revenue := ServiceCharge * Installations + UnitCost * FeetOfCable;
```

The output instruction

4. Display *Revenue*.

is translated into the Pascal statement

```
writeln( 'Revenue generated = $', Revenue:7:2 );
```

The *format descriptor* **:7:2** appended to the variable name **Revenue** indicates that this is a real value to be displayed in an output zone of size seven and is to be rounded to two decimal places.

The end of the program is indicated by the Pascal reserved word **END** followed by a period. Note that the statements in the program are separated by semicolons.

2.4 Verification and Validation

Errors may occur in any of the phases of the program development process. For example, the specifications may not accurately reflect information given in the problem; the algorithms may contain logical errors; and the program may not be coded correctly. The detection and correction of errors is an important part of software development and is known as validation and verification. **Validation** is concerned with checking that the algorithms and the program meet the problem's specifications. **Verification** refers to checking that they are correct and complete. Validation is sometimes described as answering the question "Are we solving the correct problem?'' and verification as answering the question ''Are we solving the problem correctly?''

One important part of verification and validation is executing the program with various sets of test data. The procedure for entering a program into the computer varies from one machine to another. Here and in Appendix G we describe the system known as the Turbo Pascal *integrated environment,* in which it is especially easy to enter and execute programs. Additional details about it can be obtained from your instructor, computer center personnel, or user manuals.

The Turbo Pascal environment is entered by giving the command **TURBO**. This activates the main menu screen similar to that shown in Figure 2.2.[1] The *main menu bar* at the top of the screen shows the various operations available to the user, and the *status line* at the bottom of the screen shows function-key equivalents for some of the commonly used commands. The area between these is the *desktop* or *editing window* in which programs are entered and modified; **NONAME00.PAS** is the name that will be given to such a program, but the user can assign a more meaningful name later when saving the program on disk.

In Turbo Pascal 7.0, once this main menu screen appears, we can simply begin typing the program in the editing window (see Appendix G for additional details). After it has been entered, the operations shown in the main menu bar are used to save, compile, execute, and modify this program. Using a mouse, we can select one of the menu titles simply by clicking on its name, which causes a *pull-down menu* to appear. Clicking on one of the commands on this menu (or dragging down to the

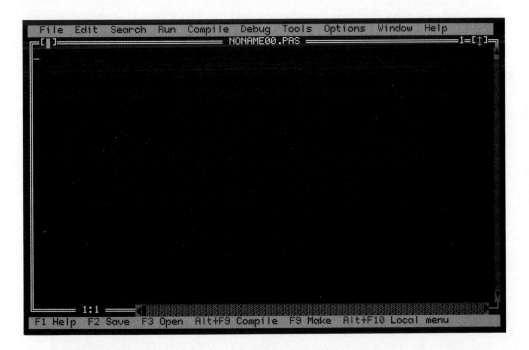

FIGURE 2.2 The main menu screen in Turbo 7.0.

---

[1] The screen shown here is that for Version 7.0 of Turbo Pascal. See Appendix G for a description of the Turbo integrated environment for Versions 5.5 and 6.0.

command and then releasing) will cause that command to be executed. Using only the keyboard, we can activate one of the pull-down menus in either of the following ways:

1. Press **F10** to activate the main menu bar; move the highlight bar to the desired menu title by using the left and right arrow keys (← and →) or by typing the first letter of the title; then press the **Enter** key.
2. Type the first letter of the title while holding down the **Alt** key; for example, **Alt+F** will activate the **File** menu.

Any of the commands on the pull-down menu can then be selected by using the up and down arrow keys (↑ and ↓) to move the highlight bar to it or by typing the highlighted letter of the command. Pressing the **Enter** key causes execution of the selected command to begin.

To illustrate, suppose that we have entered the program in Figure 2.1 and now wish to save it on disk. For this we use the **Save as** command on the **File** menu. Figure 2.3 shows the screen after this command has been selected (for example, by typing **Alt+F** and then **a**). When the **Enter** key is pressed, a *dialog box* appears that requests us to enter a name for the program. This name must be a legal MS-DOS name consisting of eight or fewer letters, digits, and certain other special characters, followed by the extension **.PAS**, for example **SAMPLE.PAS**. (If we enter only **SAMPLE**, the system will automatically attach the extension **.PAS**.)

To compile the program, we use the **Compile** operation. When the **Compile** menu is activated (see Figure 2.4), the **Compile** command is highlighted, and we need only press the **Enter** key (or the letter **C**) to begin compilation of the program. (As indicated on this pull-down menu, a shortcut way to compile a program is to

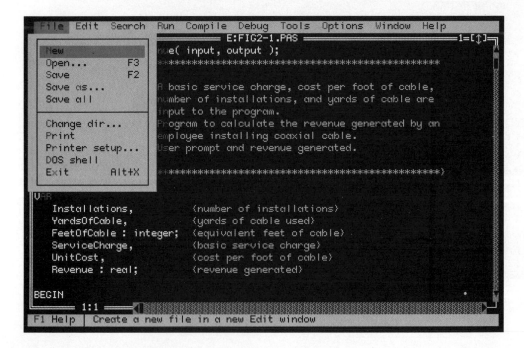

FIGURE 2.3 The **File** menu.

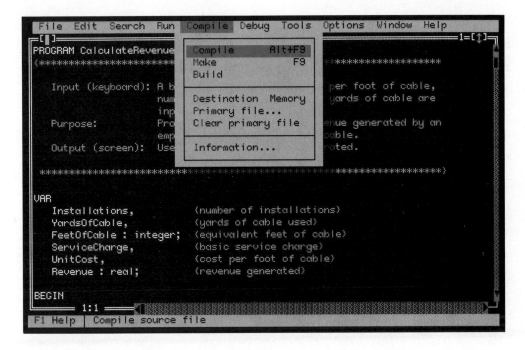

FIGURE 2.4   The **Compile** menu.

use **Alt+F9**.) If no errors are detected, a message indicating successful compilation will be displayed:

    Compile successful: Press any key

Pressing any key reactivates the edit window.

We use the **Run** operation to execute the resulting object program. When the **Run** menu is activated (see Figure 2.5), the **Run** option is highlighted, so that pressing the **Enter** key (or the letter **R**) will cause the program to be executed. (As the menu indicates, **Ctrl+F9** provides a shortcut method to accomplish this same thing.) The program will first display a message prompting the user to enter four values:

    Enter service charge, cost of one foot of cable,
    number of installations, and yards of cable used.

After these values are entered (as shown in color in the following), the desired output value is calculated and displayed:

    Enter service charge, cost of one foot of cable,
    number of installations, and yards of cable used.
    25.00 2.00 27 263

    Revenue generated = $2253.00

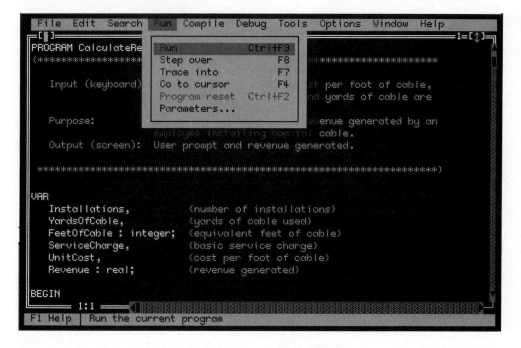

FIGURE 2.5   The **Run** menu.

This output will be displayed only briefly, however, and the main menu becomes active once again. To review the output, we can use the **User screen** command on the **Debug** menu or, more simply, press **Alt+F5**. The output will reappear and remain on the screen until the edit window is reactivated by pressing any key.

In this example, we illustrated the **interactive mode** of processing, in which the user enters data values **25.00**, **2.00**, **27**, and **263** during program execution (from the keyboard), and the output produced by the program is displayed directly to the user (on the screen). Another mode of operation is **batch processing,** in which a file containing the data is prepared in advance, and execution then proceeds without any user interaction, with data values being read from this file as needed.

In this example, the program was entered, compiled, and executed without error. Usually, however, a programmer makes some errors when designing the program or when attempting to enter and execute it. Errors may be detected at various stages of program processing and may cause the processing to be terminated (''aborted''). Errors in the program's syntax, such as incorrect punctuation or misspelled key words, are detected during compilation. Such errors are called **syntax errors** or **compile-time errors** and usually make it impossible to complete the compilation and execution of the program. For example, if the first **writeln** statement that prompts the user to enter values is mistakenly entered as

```
writeln( 'Enter service charge, cost of one foot of cable,' ;
```

with the right parenthesis missing, an attempt to compile the program results in the following message, signaling a "fatal" error:

    Error 89: ")" expected.

In the Turbo environment, the cursor will be positioned in the edit window at the point in the program where the error was detected so that it can be corrected and the program recompiled.

Other errors, called **run-time errors,** are not detected until execution of the program has begun. For example, an attempt to divide by zero in an arithmetic expression produces the error message

    Error 200: Division by zero

Once again, the cursor will be positioned in the edit window at the location of the error in the program.

Errors that are detected by the computer system are relatively easy to identify and correct. There are, however, other errors that are more subtle and difficult to identify. These are **logical errors** that arise in the design of the algorithm or in the coding of the program that implements the algorithm. For example, if the statement

    FeetOfCable := 3 * YardsOfCable;

in the program of Figure 2.1 were mistakenly entered as

    FeetOfCable := 3 + YardsOfCable;

with the multiplication symbol (*) replaced by the symbol for addition (+), the program would still be syntactically correct. No error would occur during its compilation or execution. But the output produced by the program would not be correct because an incorrect formula was used to calculate **FeetOfCable**. Thus, if the values **25.00**, **2.00**, **27**, and **263** were entered for the variables **ServiceCharge**, **UnitCost**, **Installations**, and **YardsOfCable**, respectively, the output produced by the program would be

    Revenue generated = $1207.00

instead of the correct output

    Revenue generated = $2253.00

as shown in the sample run in Figure 2.1.

Since it may not be obvious whether the results produced by a program are correct, *it is important that the user run a program several times with input data for which the correct results are known in advance.* For the preceding example, it is easy to calculate by hand the correct answer for values such as **1.00**, **2.00**, **3**, and **4**, for **ServiceCharge**, **UnitCost**, **Installations**, and **YardsOfCable**, respectively, to check the output produced by the program. This process of **program testing** is extremely important, as a *program cannot be considered to be correct* *until it has been checked with several sets of test data.* The test data should be carefully selected so that each part of the program is tested.

2.5   Software Engineering

Programming and problem solving is an art in that it requires a good deal of imagination, ingenuity, and creativity. But it is also a science in that certain techniques and methodologies are commonly used. The term **software engineering** has come to be applied to the study and use of these techniques.

As we noted in the introduction to this chapter, the **life cycle** of software consists of five basic phases:

1. Problem analysis and specification.
2. Design.
3. Coding.
4. Verification and Validation.
5. Maintenance.

In the preceding sections we described the first four phases and illustrated them with some examples. We deliberately kept these examples simple, however, so that we could emphasize the main ideas without getting lost in a maze of details, but in real-world applications and in problems later in this text, these phases may be considerably more complex. In this section we reexamine each of these phases and describe some of the additional questions and complications that professional programmers face, together with some of the software engineering techniques used in dealing with them.

Problem Analysis and Specification

Like the exercises and problems in most programming texts, the examples we have considered thus far were quite simple and, we hope, clearly stated. Analyzing these problems to identify the input and output is, therefore, quite easy. This is not the case, however, with most real-world problems, which are often stated vaguely and imprecisely because the person posing the problem does not fully understand it. For example, the president of a land development company might ask a programmer to "computerize the payroll system for the Cawker City Construction Company."

In these situations, many questions must be answered in order to complete the problem's specifications. Some of these answers are required to describe more completely the problem's input and output. What information is available for each employee? How is the program to access this data? Has this information been validated, or must the program provide error checking? In what format should the output be displayed? Are paychecks being printed? Must additional reports be generated for company executives and/or government agencies?

Other questions deal more directly with the required processing. Are employees paid on an hourly or a salary basis, or are there some of each? What premium, if any, is paid for overtime? What items must be withheld—for federal, state, and city income taxes, retirement plans, insurance, and the like—and how are they to be computed?

Many other questions must be answered before the specification of the problem is complete and the design of the algorithms and programs can begin. Will the users be technically sophisticated, or will they be novices so that the software must be made extra user friendly and robust? How often will the software be used? What are the response time requirements? How critical is the application in which the software is being used? If fault-free performance is required, must a proof of correctness accompany the software? As the specification of the problem is being formulated, decisions must be made regarding the feasibility of a computer solution. Is it possible to design programs to carry out the required processing? If so, is it economically feasible? What hardware and software are available? Could the problem be solved better manually? How soon must the software be ready? What is its expected lifetime; that is, how long will it be used, and what changes can be expected in the future?

Although this list is by no means exhaustive, it does indicate the wide range of information that must be obtained in analyzing and specifying the problem. In some situations this is done by a **systems analyst,** but in others it is part of the programmer's responsibility.

The statement of the specifications developed in this phase becomes the formal statement of the problem's requirements. This **problem specification** document serves as the major reference document that guides the development of the software, and it is the *standard* or *benchmark* used in validating the final system to determine whether it does in fact solve the problem. For this reason, a number of **formal methods** have been developed for formulating specifications. These methods are usually studied in more advanced software engineering courses, and in this text we will state the problem specifications somewhat less formally.

Design

Once the specification of a problem has been given, we can begin designing a solution for the problem. As we noted in Section 2.2, two important parts of the design plan are the selection of structures to organize and store the data and the design of algorithms to process the data. For example, in the payroll problem we are considering, a file of employee records containing names, social security numbers, number of dependents, and so on contains permanent information that must be stored in some structure so that this information can be accessed and processed. Other information such as hours worked will be entered during program execution and can perhaps be stored in simple variables, as in the examples we considered in previous sections.

A real-world problem may be so complex that it is difficult to visualize or anticipate at the outset all the details of a complete solution to the problem. To solve such problems, a **divide-and-conquer** strategy is used, in which the original problem is partitioned into simpler subproblems, each of which can be considered independently. We begin by identifying the major tasks to be performed to solve the problem and arranging them in the order in which they are to be carried out. These tasks and their relation to one another can be displayed in a **structure diagram.** For example, a first structure diagram for the problem might be

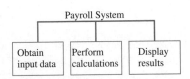

Usually one or more of these first-level tasks is still quite complex and must be divided into subtasks. For example, we noted that for the payroll system, some of the input information is permanent, whereas other information will be entered during program execution. Consequently, the task "Obtain input data" can be subdivided into two subtasks:

1. Obtain permanent employee information.
2. Obtain current information.

Similarly, the task "Perform calculations" may be split into three subtasks:

1. Calculate gross pay.
2. Calculate withholding.
3. Calculate net pay.

Finally, the third task, "Display results," may be subdivided into

1. Print paychecks.
2. Print summary reports.

In a structure diagram, these subtasks are placed on a second level below the corresponding main task, as pictured in Figure 2.6. These subtasks may require further division into still smaller subtasks, resulting in additional levels, as illustrated in Figure 2.7. This **successive refinement** continues until each subtask is sufficiently simple that the design of an algorithm for that subtask is straightforward.

This **top–down** approach to software development allows the programmer to design and test an algorithm and the corresponding program **module** for each subproblem independently of the others. For very large projects a team approach might be used in which the low-level subtasks are assigned to different programmers. The individual program modules they develop are eventually combined into one complete program that solves the original problem.

Program Coding

Coding is the process of implementing data structures and algorithms in some programming language. If the design plan has been developed carefully and completely, this translation process is nearly automatic. As we noted, large software systems are developed in a top–down manner in which a problem is partitioned into a number of subproblems and individual modules are developed to solve the

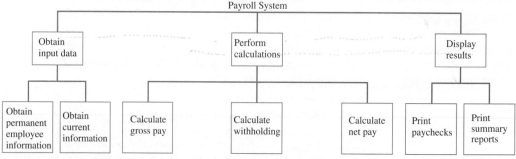

FIGURE 2.6 Second structure diagram.

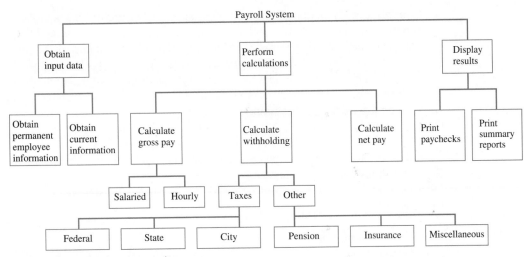

FIGURE 2.7 Third structure diagram.

subproblems. **Integration** is the process of combining these program units into a complete program or system of programs. Such integration is usually done incrementally by adding the units one at a time. If an error occurs when a new module is added to the system, the developer can be reasonably confident that it was caused by this module and not by one added earlier.

The first decision that must be made when translating an algorithm into a program is what programming language to use. This obviously depends on the languages available to the programmer and those that he or she is able to use, but other factors also influence the decision. The problem may have characteristics that make one language more appropriate than another. For example, if the problem requires scientific computing with extended precision and/or complex numbers, FORTRAN may be the most suitable language. Problems that involve a large amount of file input/output and report generation can perhaps best be handled in COBOL. Applications in artificial intelligence that require making logical inferences might best be solved using PROLOG. Structured algorithms, especially those developed as a collection of subalgorithms in a top–down manner, can best be implemented in a structured language such as Pascal, Modula-2, Ada, C, or C++.

Regardless of which language is used, certain programming practices contribute to the development of *correct, readable, and understandable programs.* One principle is that *programs should be well structured.* Two helpful guidelines in this regard are to

- *Use a top–down approach when developing a program for a complex problem.* Divide the problem into simpler and simpler subproblems, and write individual subprograms to solve these subproblems.
- *Strive for simplicity and clarity.* Avoid clever programming tricks intended only to demonstrate the programmer's ingenuity or to produce code that executes only slightly more efficiently.

A second principle is that *each program unit should be documented.* In particular:

- *Each program unit should include opening documentation.* Comments should be included at the beginning of each program (procedure, function) to explain what it does, how it works, any special algorithms it uses, a summary of the problem's specification, assumptions, and so on, and they may also include other items of information such as the name of the programmer, the date the program was written and when it was last modified, and references to books and manuals that give additional information about the program. In addition, it is a good practice to explain the variables that are being used in the program.

■ *Comments should also be used to explain key program segments and/or segments whose purpose or design is not obvious.* However, too many detailed or unnecessary comments clutter the program and only make it more difficult to read and understand.

■ *Meaningful identifiers should be used.* For example, the statement

```
Wages := HoursWorked * HourlyRate
```

is more meaningful than

```
W := H * R
```

or

```
X7 := R * ZEKE
```

Don't use "skimpy" abbreviations just to save a few keystrokes when entering the program. Also, follow what has been called the "Shirley Temple principle" and avoid "cute" identifiers, as in

```
BaconBroughtHome := SlaveLabor * LessThanImWorth
```

A third principle has to do with a program's appearance. *A program should be aesthetically pleasing; it should be formatted in a style that enhances its readability.* The following are some guidelines for good program style:

■ *Use spaces between the items in a statement to make it more readable,* for example, before and after each operator (+, -, <, :=, etc.).

■ *Insert a blank line between sections of a program and wherever appropriate in a sequence of statements to set off blocks of statements.*

■ *Adhere rigorously to alignment and indentation guidelines to emphasize the relationship between various parts of the program.* For example, indent those statements that make up the body of a loop.

It is often difficult for beginning programmers to appreciate the importance of learning good programming habits that lead to the design of readable and understandable programs. The reason for this is that programs written in an academic environment are often quite different from those developed in real-world situations, in which program style and form are critical. Student programs are usually quite short (usually less than a few hundred lines of code); are executed and modified only a few times (almost never, once they have been handed in); are rarely examined in detail by anyone other than the student and the instructor; and are not developed within the context of budget constraints. Real-world programs, on the other hand, may be very long (several thousand lines of code); are developed by teams of programmers; are commonly used for long periods of time and thus require maintenance if they are to be kept current and correct; and are often maintained by someone other than the original programmer. As hardware costs continue to decrease and programmer costs increase, the importance of reducing programming and maintenance costs and the corresponding importance of writing programs that can be easily read and understood by others continue to grow.

As we discuss features of the Pascal language in the following chapters, additional principles for program design will be given. It is important for beginning programmers to follow these guidelines, even in early simple programs, so that good habits are established and carried on into the design of more complex programs.

Program Execution and Testing

Obviously the most important characteristic of any program is that it be *correct*. No matter how well structured, how well documented, or how nice the program looks, if it does not produce correct results, it is worthless. But as we have seen, the fact that a program executes without producing any error messages is no guarantee that it is correct. The results produced may be wrong because of logical errors that the computer system cannot detect. It is the responsibility of the programmer to test each program in order to ensure that it is correct.

Since errors may occur at each phase of the development process, different kinds of tests are required to detect them: **unit tests** in which each program unit is tested individually; **integration tests** that check that these units have been combined correctly, and **system tests** that test to see whether the overall system functions correctly. These correspond to the various phases of the software life cycle, as indicated by the following diagram of the ''V'' Life Cycle Model:[2]

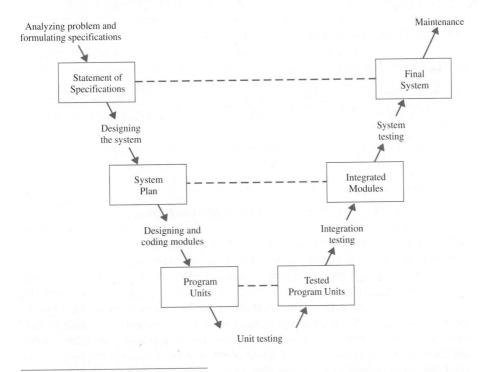

Analyzing problem and
formulating specifications

Statement of
Specifications

Designing
the system

System
Plan

Designing and
coding modules

Program
Units

Tested
Program Units

Unit testing

Integration
testing

Integrated
Modules

System
testing

Final
System

Maintenance

---

[2] Additional information about the ''V'' Life Cycle Model and about software testing can be found in Dorothy Graham, *Software Test and Debug: Techniques and Tools* (Manchester, England: A National Computing Centre Limited Technical Report, 1989).

System testing measures the correctness and performance of the final system against the problem's specification. Integration tests are considered in Section 5.7, where we illustrate top–down design. Unit testing is probably the most time-consuming and is surely the most fundamental kind of testing, since incorrectness of any part of the system implies incorrectness of the system as a whole.

The specification document for the original problem serves as a standard for validating the entire system. Similarly, specifications of the subproblems obtained in a top–down design process are needed as standards against which the individual modules are tested. Each of these specifications should include at least a description of

1. The purpose of the module.
2. Items input to the module (from input devices).
3. Items *accepted* from other modules.
4. Items output by the module (to output devices).
5. Items *returned* to other modules.

When a correctness proof of the module is required, the specifications must also include **preconditions** and **postconditions** that describe the state of processing before and after the module is executed. When it is appropriate in the examples of this text, we will include informal descriptions of pre- and postconditions in the descriptions of the module's input/accepted items and output/returned items, respectively. (See Section 4.6 for more about program testing.)

Maintenance

The life cycle of a program written by a student programmer normally ends with the fourth phase; that is, once the program has been written, executed, and tested, the assignment is complete. Programs in real-world applications, however, are often used for several years and are likely to require some modification. Software systems, especially large ones developed for complex projects, often have obscure bugs that were not detected during testing and that surface after the software has been placed in use. One important aspect of software maintenance is fixing such flaws in the software.

It may also be necessary to modify software to improve its performance, to add new features, and so on. Other modifications may be required owing to changes in the computer hardware and/or the system software such as the operating system. External factors may also force program modification; for example, changes in the tax laws may mean revising part of a payroll program. These changes are easier to make in systems that are developed in a modular manner with well-structured modules than in poorly designed ones, because the changes can often be made by modifying only a few of the modules or by adding new modules.

Software maintenance is a major component of the life cycle of software. Studies have shown that in recent years more than 50 percent of computer center budgets and more than 50 percent of programmer time have been devoted to software maintenance and that worldwide, billions and perhaps trillions of dollars have been spent on software maintenance. A major factor that has contributed to this high cost in money and time is that many of the original programs and systems had poor structure, documentation, and style. This problem is complicated by the fact that maintenance must often be done by someone not involved in the original design. Thus it is mandatory that programmers do their utmost to design programs and systems of programs that are readable, well documented, and well structured so that they are easy to understand and modify and are thus easier to maintain than is much of the software developed in the past.

2.6 PART OF THE PICTURE: Social, Professional, and Ethical Issues

We noted in Chapter 1 that the impact of the computer revolution on modern society is as great as was the impact of the nineteenth-century Industrial Revolution, and in the introduction to this chapter, we gave a number of examples to illustrate the wide range of computer applications. As the diversity of applications continues to grow, computing will affect more and more individuals, groups, and institutions. As a result, the influence exerted by computer professionals, either wittingly or unwittingly, will continue to increase, as will the importance of responsible and ethical conduct. Like all technology, computer technology is inherently neither good nor evil. It is the responsibility of computer professionals to ensure that it is used for the benefit, and not to the detriment, of society.

Some of the ethical concerns that are raised by the growth of computer technology are

- *Privacy.* Computing technology has made possible the construction of large databases of information about individuals and institutions. Although the purpose for which this information was collected may be legitimate (credit ratings, crime networks, medical records, and government records), there is always the potential for the misuse of sensitive information by unauthorized individuals.[3] Indeed, such misuse has become so prevalent in recent years that state and federal governments have enacted statues such as the Electronic Communication Privacy Act of 1986 to combat such invasions of privacy. Computer professionals and computer scientists perhaps more than others have the knowledge and ability to access private information. Therefore, they have a special responsibility to respect the rights of others by not accessing these databases without authorization and, in applications that require access to these databases, using this information only for the purpose for which it was intended. Those who design these databases and/or software to process them also have a responsibility to maintain the integrity and security of that information. In particular, this most assuredly means that they have no right to develop programs like computer viruses that damage, destroy, or interfere in any way with other people's computer systems or the data stored in these systems. The worm program injected into the Internet in November 1988 by Robert T. Morris, a computer science graduate student at Cornell University, and the more recent Michelangelo virus are but two of many examples of malicious programs that attacked computers around the world, shutting down thousands of them and/or de-

---

[3] See the quotation in Section 6.3, PART OF THE PICTURE: Databases.

stroying data files. Such irresponsible behavior obviously is not appropriate to those who call themselves, or who aspire to be, computer professionals.

■ *Intellectual Property.* Computer hardware and software are the property of the individuals or companies that developed them. Those who wish to use these products should obtain them through legal channels and abide by the conditions that govern their use. It has been estimated, however, that 60 to 80 percent of all software used today has been pirated and that the resulting loss to the software industry exceeds several billion dollars per year. It is important that all computer professionals have respect for their fellow professionals and do not create, use, or disseminate illegal copies of software. This applies not only to copyrighted software but also to shareware that is distributed with the understanding that those who use it will register their copy with the developer and pay the nominal fee for its use.

■ *Truth in Software.* Computer professionals are responsible for ensuring that the software or hardware they are developing functions in the manner claimed. This means that these products should be thoroughly tested and made as error free as possible before they are delivered to the customer. It also means that potential users be made fully aware of the hardware and software needed to use the product and that errors found and difficulties encountered after the product is released are remedied promptly.

The major societies for computer professionals such as ACM (Association for Computing Machinery), BCS (British Computer Society), DPMA (Data Processing Management Association), and IEEE (Institute of Electrical and Electronics Engineers) recognize the importance of the ethical issues that arise in computing and have published codes of conduct for computer professionals. These codes describe the computer professional's obligations to (1) society, (2) employers, (3) clients, and (4) coprofessionals and professional societies. In a recent article, C. Dianne Martin and David H. Martin identify seven common themes in these codes:[4]

1. Dignity and worth of other people.
2. Personal integrity and honesty.
3. Responsibility for work.
4. Confidentiality of information.
5. Public safety, health, and welfare.
6. Participation in professional societies to improve standards of the profession.
7. The notion that knowledge and access to technology is equivalent to social power.

Summaries of the codes of ACM, IEEE, and DPMA follow:

ACM CANONS OF CONDUCT

Preamble: Recognition of professional status by the public depends not only on skill and dedication but also on adherence to a recognized Code of Professional Conduct. The following Code sets forth the general principles (Canons) followed by professional ideals (Ethical Considerations) . . . applicable to each member . . . An ACM member shall:

---

[4] C. Dianne Martin and David H. Martin, "Professional Codes of Conduct and Computer Ethics Education," *Computers and Society* 20 (1990): 18–29. (Reprinted from *Social Science Computer Review,* vol. 9, Duke University Press, 1990)

Canon 1. *Act at all times with integrity:*

EC1.1. . . . properly qualify expressed opinions outside the member's areas of competence.

EC1.2. . . . preface any partisan statement about information processing by indicating clearly on whose behalf they are made.

EC1.3. . . . act faithfully on behalf of employers or clients.

Canon 2. *Strive to increase competence and prestige of the profession:*

EC2.1. . . . encouraged to extend public knowledge, understanding, and appreciation of information processing, and to oppose any false or deceptive statements relating to information processing of which the member is aware.

EC2.2. . . . not use professional credentials to misrepresent the member's competence.

EC2.3. . . . shall undertake only those professional assignments and commitments for which the member is qualified.

EC2.4. . . . strive to design and develop systems that adequately perform the intended functions and that satisfy employer's or client's operational needs.

EC2.5. . . . maintain and increase competence through a program of continuing education encompassing the techniques, technical standards, and practices in the member's field of professional activity.

EC2.6. . . . provide opportunity and encouragement for professional development and advancement of both professionals and those aspiring to become professionals.

Canon 3. *Accept responsibility for own work:*

EC3.1. . . . accept only those assignments for which there is a reasonable expectancy of meeting requirements or specifications, and shall perform assignments in a professional manner.

Canon 4. *Act with professional responsibility:*

EC4.1. . . . not use ACM membership for professional advantage or to misrepresent the authority of the member's statements.

EC4.2. . . . conduct professional activities on a high plane.

EC4.3. . . . be encouraged to uphold and improve professional standards of the Association through participation in their formulation, establishment, and enforcement.

Canon 5. *Use special knowledge and skills for advancement of human welfare:*

EC5.1. . . . consider health, privacy, and general welfare of public in performance of work.

EC5.2. . . . whenever dealing with data concerning individuals, always consider the principle of the individual's privacy and seek the following:

–to minimize the data collected.
–to limit authorized access to the data.
–to provide proper security for the data.
–to determine the required retention period of the data.
–to ensure proper disposal of the data.

IEEE CODE OF ETHICS

Preamble: Engineers, scientists and technologists affect the quality of life for all people in our complex technological society. In the pursuit of their profession, therefore, it is vital that IEEE members conduct their work in an ethical manner so that they merit the confidence of colleagues, employers, clients and the public. This IEEE Code of Ethics represents such a standard of professional conduct for IEEE members in the discharge of their responsibilities to employees, to clients, to the community, and to their colleagues in this Institute and other professional societies.

Article I. *Members shall maintain high standards of diligence, creativity, and productivity and shall:*

a. Accept responsibility for their actions;
b. Be honest and realistic in stating claims or estimates from available data;
c. Undertake technological tasks and accept responsibility only if qualified by training or experience, or after full disclosure to their employers or clients of pertinent qualifications;
d. Maintain their professional skills at the level of the state of the art, and recognize the importance of current events in their work;
e. Advance the integrity and prestige of the profession by practicing in a dignified manner and for adequate compensation.

Article II. *Members shall, in their work:*

a. Treat fairly all colleagues and co-workers, regardless of race, religion, sex, age or national origin;
b. Report, publish and disseminate freely information to others, subject to legal and proprietary restraints;
c. Encourage colleagues and co-workers to act in accord with this Code and support them when they do so;
d. Seek, accept, and offer honest criticism of work, and properly credit the contributions of others;
e. Support and participate in the activities of their professional societies;
f. Assist colleagues and co-workers in their professional development.

Article III. *Members shall, in their relations with employers and clients:*

a. Act as faithful agents or trustees for their employers or clients in professional and business matters, provided such actions conform with other parts of this Code;
b. Keep information on business affairs or technical processes of an employer or client in confidence while employed, and later, until such information is properly released, provided that such actions conform with other parts of this Code;
c. Inform their employers, clients, professional societies or public agencies or private agencies of which they are members or to which they make presentations, of any circumstance that could lead to a conflict of interest;
d. Neither give nor accept, directly or indirectly, any gift payment or service of more than nominal value to or from those having business relationships with their employers or clients.
e. Assist and advise their employers or clients in anticipating the possible consequences, direct or indirect, immediate or remote, of the projects, work or plans of which they have knowledge.

Article IV. *Members shall, in fulfilling responsibility to community:*

a. Protect safety, health, and welfare of the public and speak out against abuses in these areas affecting the public interest;
b. Contribute professional advice, as appropriate, to civic, charitable, or other nonprofit organizations;
c. Seek to extend public knowledge and appreciation of the profession and its achievements.

DPMA CODE OF ETHICS

I acknowledge:

1. *That I have an obligation to management,* therefore, I shall promote the understanding of information processing methods and procedures to management using every resource at my command.

2. *That I have an obligation to my fellow members,* therefore I shall uphold the high ideals of DPMA as outlined in its Association Bylaws. Further, I shall cooperate with my fellow members and shall treat them with honesty and respect at all times.
3. *That I have an obligation to society* and will participate to the best of my ability in the dissemination of knowledge pertaining to the general development and understanding of information processing. Further, I shall not use knowledge of a confidential nature to further my personal interest, nor shall I violate the privacy and confidentiality of information entrusted to me or to which I may gain access.
4. *That I have an obligation to my employer* whose trust I hold, therefore I shall endeavor to discharge this obligation to the best of my ability, to guard my employer's interests, and to advise him or her wisely and honestly.
5. *That I have an obligation to my country,* therefore, in my personal business and social contacts, I shall uphold my nation and shall honor the chosen way of life of my fellow citizens.

I accept these obligations as a personal responsibility, and as a member of this Association. I shall actively discharge these obligations and I dedicate myself to that end.

In reading these codes you may note that they are not computer-specific codes but, rather, consist of general principles and guidelines that might apply to almost any profession. This is perhaps because computer science is a relatively young discipline, which, unlike well-established professions such as medicine and law, has not benefited from hundreds and perhaps thousands of years of forming, analyzing, and interpreting ethical principles and practices. The development of specific ethical principles for computing has also been complicated by rapid advances in computer technology and the explosive growth of computer applications, several of which have raised new ethical problems and dilemmas. Since this trend will undoubtedly continue, the need to formulate and continually revise ethical guidelines is critical. Even more important is the necessity for future computer professionals to gain not only technical expertise but also an awareness of ethical and moral issues and a commitment to responsible use of the computer.

Exercises

1. Consider the following algorithm:

    1. Initialize X to 0, Y to 5, Z to 25.
    2. While $X \leq 4$ do the following:
        a. Set $Y = Z - Y$, $A = X + 1$, and then increment X by 1.
        b. If $A > 1$ then
            Set $Z = Z - 5$, $A = A^2$, and then set $B = Z - Y$.
    3. Display A, B, X, Y, and Z.

Complete the following **trace table** for this algorithm, which displays the labels of the statements in the order in which they are executed and the values of the variables at each stage:

Statement	A	B	X	Y	Z	
1	?	?	0	5	25	
2	"	"	"	"	"	
2a	1	"	1	20	"	(?=undefined)
2b	"	"	"	"	"	
2a	2	"	2	5	"	
.	.	.	.	.	.	
.	.	.	.	.	.	
.	.	.	.	.	.	
3	"	"	"	"	"	

2. Construct a trace table similar to that in Exercise 1 for the following algorithm, assuming that the value entered for A is (a) 0.1, (b) 0.3, (c) 1.0:

   1. Enter A.
   2. While $A \leq 0.3$ do the following:
      a. Increment A by 0.1.
      b. If $A \neq 0.3$ then do the following:
         i. Set S and X to 0, T to 1.
         ii. While $T \leq 6$ do the following:
            (a) Add T to X and then increment T by 2.
      c. Else do the following:
         i. Set T to 0, X to 1, and $S = 3 * S$.
         ii. While $T \leq 5$ do the following:
            (a) Increment T by 1 and then set $X = X * T$.
      d. Display A, S, and X.

3. Construct a trace table similar to that in Exercise 1 for the following algorithm, for each of the sets of values for b, h, and k given in the following table:

b	h	k
3	6	1
4	3	2
5	2	0
2	6	2

   1. Initialize I, A, and X to 0.
   2. While $I < 4$ do the following:
      a. Increment I by 1.
      b. Enter b, h, k.
      c. If $k \geq 1$ then do the following:
         i. Set $A = \dfrac{bh}{2}$.
         ii. If $k \geq 2$ then do the following:
            (a) Set $X = \dfrac{bh^3}{36}$.
      d. Display I, b, h, A, and X.

For each of the problems described in Exercises 4 through 13, identify both the information that must be produced to solve the problem and the given information that will be useful in obtaining the solution. Then design an algorithm to solve the problem.

4. Calculate and display the perimeter and area of a square with a given side.

5. Two common temperature scales are the Fahrenheit and Celsius scales. The boiling point of water is 212° on the Fahrenheit scale and 100° on the Celsius scale. The freezing point of water is 32° on the Fahrenheit scale and 0° on the Celsius scale. Assuming a linear relationship ($F = a \cdot C + b$) between these two temperature scales, convert a temperature on the Celsius scale to the corresponding Fahrenheit temperature.

$$\frac{180}{100}$$

$$\frac{9}{5}$$

6. Calculate and display the largest and the smallest of three given test scores.

7. Calculate and display the largest number, the smallest number, and the range (largest number minus smallest number) for any given set of test scores.

8. The business manager of a certain company wants a program to calculate the wages for the company's employees. This program should accept an employee number, base pay rate per hour, and the number of hours worked. All hours above 40 are to be paid at the overtime rate of 1.5 times the base rate. For each employee, the program should print the employee number, total number of hours worked, base pay rate, and total wages, and it should also print the total of all wages paid by the company.

9. A certain city classifies a pollution index of less than 35 as pleasant, 35 through 60 as unpleasant, and above 60 as hazardous. The city's pollution control officer desires a program that will accept several values of the pollution index and produce the appropriate classification for each.

10. Suppose that a professor gave a quiz to her class and compiled a list of scores ranging from 50 through 100. She intends to use only three grades: A if the score is 90 or above, B if it is below 90 but above or equal to 75, and C if it is below 75. She would like a program to assign the appropriate letter grades to the numeric scores.

11. The "divide and average" algorithm for approximating the square root of any positive number A is as follows: Take any initial approximation X that is positive, and then find a new approximation by calculating the average of X and A/X; that is, $(X + A/X)/2$. Repeat this procedure with X replaced by this new approximation, stopping when X and A/X differ in absolute value by some specified error allowance, such as 0.00001.

12. Several quadratic equations of the form $Ax^2 + Bx + C = 0$ are to be solved or it is to be determined that no real solutions exist. If the discriminant $B^2 - 4AC$ is positive, the equation has two real solutions given by the quadratic formula

$$\frac{-B \pm \sqrt{B^2 - 4AC}}{2A}$$

if the discriminant is zero, the equation has one real solution, $-B/2A$; and if the discriminant is negative, there are no real solutions.

13. The Rinky Dooflingy Company currently sells 200 dooflingies per month, at a profit of $300 per dooflingy. The company now spends $2000 per month on advertising and has a fixed operating cost of $10,000 per month that does not depend on the volume of sales. If the company doubles the amount spent on advertising, its sales will increase by 20 percent. The company president would like to know, beginning with the company's current status and successively doubling the amount spend on advertising, at what point the net profit will "go over the hump," that is, begin to decline.

14. Enter and execute the following short Pascal program on your computer system:

```
PROGRAM Exercise14( output );
{******************************* *********************

    Purpose:          Perform various arithmetic
                      operations on two numbers X and Y.
    Output (screen): Results of the operations.


******************************* ********************}

VAR
    X, Y,                   {two given numbers}
    Sum : integer;          {sum of the numbers}

BEGIN
    X := 214;
    Y := 2057;
    Sum := X + Y;
    writeln( 'Sum of', X, Y, ' is', Sum )
END.
```

15. Make the following changes in the program in Exercise 14 and execute the modified program:

(a) Change 214 to 1723 in the statement assigning a value to X.
(b) Change the variable names X and Y to Alpha and Beta throughout.
(c) Insert the comment

   {Calculate the sum}

   before the statement

   Sum := Alpha + Beta;

(d) Insert the following comment and statement before the `writeln` statement:

```
{Now calculate the difference}
Difference := Alpha - Beta;
```

change the variable declaration to

```
VAR
    Alpha, Beta,          {two given numbers}
    Sum,                  {sum of the numbers}
    Difference : integer; {difference of the numbers}
```

and add the following statement after the `writeln` statement:

```
writeln( 'Difference of', Alpha, Beta, ' is', Difference )
```

Note: For the modified program to work correctly, you must also insert a semicolon at an appropriate location.

16. Using the program in Figure 2.1 as a guide, write a Pascal program for the algorithm in Exercise 4.

17. Using the program in Figure 2.1 as a guide, write a Pascal program for the algorithm in Exercise 5.

18. Search recent issues of the *New York Times, Time, Newsweek,* or other newspapers or news magazines to find articles that describe

(a) A new or novel application of computing.
(b) A problem caused by a computer error, either in hardware or software.
(c) Difficulties caused by a computer virus, worm, or other scheme that causes a computer system to shut down or to function abnormally, that destroys or damages data stored in the computer, or that generally is intended to interfere with the normal operation of or use of one or many computer systems.
(d) A break-in by a hacker or a group of hackers to databases containing sensitive information.

Write a report that summarizes the article and your reaction to it, especially to any ethical and moral issues that are involved.

19. Many of the publications of the professional computing societies contain articles that are of interest to and can be understood by students. Select one or several of the publications in the following list, locate an article dealing with some current ethical issue, and prepare a written summary of the article, the ethical or moral problem or difficulty involved, suggestions for dealing with the problem, and your reaction.

Communications of the ACM
Computers and Society, a publication of the ACM Special Interest Group on Computers & Society

COMPUTERWORLD

IEEE *Computer*

IEEE *Software*

IEEE *Spectrum*

New Scientist

SIGCAPH Newsletter, a publication of the ACM Special Interest Group on Computers and the Physically Handicapped

SIGCHI bulletin, a publication of the ACM Special Interest Group on Computer & Human Interaction

Software Engineering Notes, an informal newsletter of the ACM Special Interest Group on Software Engineering

BASIC PASCAL

*Kindly enter them in your notebook.
And, in order to refer to them
conveniently, let's call them A, B, and Z.*
THE TORTOISE IN LEWIS CARROLL'S
What the Tortoise Said to Achilles

In language, clarity is everything.
CONFUCIUS

CHAPTER CONTENTS

One important part of using the computer to solve a problem is implementing the algorithm for solving that problem as a program. Whereas algorithms can be described somewhat informally in a pseudoprogramming language, the corresponding program must be written in strict compliance with the rules of some programming language. In this chapter we begin a detailed study of the language Pascal.

As we noted in Chapter 1, Pascal was developed in the late 1960s and early 1970s by the Swiss computer scientist Niklaus Wirth. For several years the *Pascal User Manual and Report* written by Wirth and Kathleen Jensen and published in 1974 served as the de facto standard for the language. In 1983, however, an official standard was prepared by committees of the American National Standards Institute (ANSI) and the Institute of Electrical and Electronic Engineers (IEEE) and was published as the *American National Standard Pascal Computer Programming Language.* A number of other versions of Pascal that provide useful variations of and extensions to the standard have appeared. One of the most popular versions for microcomputers is Turbo Pascal, developed by Borland International, Inc., and it is this version of Pascal that is used in this text.

3.1   Data Types + Algorithms = Programs

Two important concepts emerge from our examination of the first two steps of the problem-solving process: **data types** and **algorithms.** Every problem processes data of various types. It may be numeric data representing times or temperatures, or character data representing names, or logical data used in designing a circuit, and so on. Consequently, a program for solving a problem must be written in a language that can store and process various types of data.

Pascal is designed to handle four basic types of data:

```
integer
real
char
boolean
```

The first two are numeric types and are used to process different kinds of numbers. In addition to these standard types, Turbo Pascal provides the types **shortint**, **longint**, **byte**, **word**, **single**, **double**, **extended**, and **comp** for processing various types of numeric values. The type **char** is used to process character data, and Turbo Pascal also provides the type **string** for processing strings of characters. The type **boolean** is used to process boolean or logical data; such data may have either the value **true** or the value **false**. Pascal also provides other data types, including some that are used to structure collections of data; these additional types are described in later chapters.

The second important aspect of a design plan for solving a problem is developing algorithms to process the input data and produce the required output. A program for solving a problem must be written in a language that provides operations for processing data and instructions that carry out the steps of the algorithm. For example, Pascal provides basic arithmetic operations for numeric computations, input and output instructions for entering and displaying data, instructions for implementing the basic control structures, and so on.

Since these two basic aspects of problem solving, data types and algorithms, cannot be separated, a program for solving a problem must incorporate both aspects; that is, some part of the program must specify the data being processed, and another part must contain the instructions to do the processing. A Pascal program contains a **declaration part,** in which the names and types of constants and variables used to store input and output values as well as intermediate results are declared. This is followed by a **statement part,** which contains the statements that carry out the steps of the algorithm.

The general form of a program in Turbo Pascal is

Pascal Program

> program heading
> **USES** clause
> declaration part
> statement part.

(Note the required period that follows the statement part.) The first statement of a Pascal program is the **program heading.** This statement is optional in Turbo Pascal, but it may be used to give the program a name and to indicate the kinds of input/output operations that will be performed. The heading should be followed by some **opening documentation** in the form of comments about the program's input, output, and purpose and may include other relevant information such as special algorithms that it implements, the date the program was written, when it was last modified, the name of the programmer, and so on. This may be followed by a **USES** clause that specifies units containing special items such as graphics procedures that are used by the program but are defined elsewhere. Each of the parts of a program is described in detail in the following sections.

3.2   Constants and Variables

As we noted in Section 3.1, organizing the data is an important aspect of programming, and a problem may involve several different types of data. In this section we describe integer, real, character, string, and boolean constants in Pascal and how the types of variables used to store constants are declared.

Constants

Constants are quantities whose values do not change during program execution. They may be of numeric, character, string, or boolean type (or one of the other types considered later). An **integer** constant of type **integer** is a string of digits that does not include commas or a decimal point; negative integer constants must be preceded by a negative sign, but a plus sign is optional for nonnegative integers. Thus

```
     0
   137
 -2516
+17745
```

are valid integer constants, whereas the following are invalid for the reasons indicated:

5,280	(Commas are not allowed in integer constants.)
16.0	(Integer constants may not contain decimal points.)
--5	(Only one algebraic sign is allowed.)
7-	(The algebraic sign must precede the string of digits.)

In Turbo Pascal, constants of type **integer** are limited to the range −32768 through 32767. Constants of the other integer types have the same forms as integer constants but are limited to the ranges specified in the following table:

Type	Range
byte	0 through 255
shortint	−128 through 127
integer	−32768 through 32767
word	0 through 65535
longint	−2147483648 through 2147483647

Turbo Pascal also allows integer constants to be written in hexadecimal notation (see Section 1.2). A hexadecimal integer constant is indicated by placing a dollar sign ($) in front of its hexadecimal representation. For example, **$12A** represents the integer constant 298.

Another type of numeric data is the **real** type. Constants of this type may be represented as ordinary decimal numbers or in scientific notation. The **decimal** representation of real constants must include exactly one decimal point, and it must be embedded; that is, there must be at least one digit before the decimal point and at least one digit after it. As in the case of integer constants, no commas are allowed. Negative real constants must be preceded by a minus sign, but a plus sign is optional for nonnegative reals. Thus

$$1.234$$
$$-0.1536$$
$$+56473.0$$

are valid real constants, whereas the following are invalid for the reasons indicated:

1,752.63	(Commas are not allowed in real constants.)
82	(Real constants in decimal form must contain a decimal point.)
.01	(Real constants may not begin with a decimal point.)
24.	(Real constants may not end with a decimal point.)

The **exponential** or **floating point** representation of a real constant consists of an integer or real constant in decimal form followed by the letter **E** (or **e**) followed by an integer constant that is interpreted as an exponent on the base 10. For example, the real constant 337.456 may also be written as

$$3.37456E2$$

which means

$$3.37456 \times 10^2$$

or it may be written in a variety of other forms, such as

```
0.337456E3
337.456E0
33745.6E-2
337456E-3
```

In addition to type **real**, Turbo Pascal also provides the types **single**, **double**, and **extended** for processing real values and **comp** for processing integer values that are stored in a real format.[1] The range of values and the number of significant digits for each of these real types are given in the following table:

Type	Range	Significant Digits
real	2.9E−39 through 1.7E+38	11–12
single	1.5E−45 through 3.4E+38	7–8
double	5.0E−324 through 1.7E+308	15–16
extended	1.9E−4951 through 1.1E+4932	19–20
comp	1−2E+63 through 2E+63−1	8

A **character** is one of the symbols in the Pascal character set. Although this character set may vary from one Pascal implementation to another, it usually includes digits 0 through 9; uppercase letters A through Z; lowercase letters a through z; usual punctuation symbols such as the semicolon (;), comma (,), and period (.); and special symbols such as +, =, >, and ↑. Turbo Pascal allows a character to be any symbol from the ASCII character set (see Appendix A).

A **character constant** (of type **char**) consists of a single character enclosed within single quotes (apostrophes); for example,

```
'A', '+', '3', ':'
```

If a character constant is to consist of an apostrophe, it must appear as a pair of apostrophes enclosed within single quotes (apostrophes):

```
''''
```

A sequence of characters is commonly called a **string,** and a **string constant** (of type **string**) consists of a string enclosed within single quotes. Turbo Pascal limits the length of a string to 255 characters. Thus

```
'John Q. Doe'
```

and

---

[1] The special compiler directive for numeric processing (`{$N}`) must be turned on when using these data types. This is all that is required if your machine has an 8087 coprocessor. If it does not, a special emulation directive (`{$E}`) can be turned on to provide 8087 emulation in software.

```
'PDQ123-A'
```

are valid string constants. Again, if an apostrophe is one of the characters in a string constant, it must appear as a pair of apostrophes; for example,

```
'Don''t'
```

The type **boolean** is named for the nineteenth-century mathematician George Boole, who originated the logical calculus. There are only two **boolean constants,**

```
true
```

and

```
false
```

These constants are called **logical** constants in some programming languages.

Identifiers

Identifiers are names given to programs, constants, variables, and other entities in a program. Identifiers must begin with a letter, which may be followed by any number of letters, digits, or underscores, but only the first 63 characters are used. *This allows the user to choose meaningful identifiers that suggest what they represent.*

Pascal **reserved words** such as **VAR**, **BEGIN**, and **END** may not be used as identifiers, since they have a special meaning in Pascal. A complete list of reserved words is given in Appendix B. Pascal also uses certain **standard identifiers,** such as **integer**, **real**, **true**, **false**, **read**, **readln**, **write**, and **writeln**. *These identifiers have predefined meanings, but they are not reserved words. Consequently, they may be redefined by the programmer, but it is not good practice to do so.* A list of frequently used standard identifiers is given in Appendix B.

Pascal makes no distinction between uppercase and lowercase (except in character and string constants). For example, **HourlyRate** is a valid identifier and will not be distinguished from **HOURLYRATE**, **hourlyrate**, or **HoURlyRaTE**, even if one form is used in one place in the program and another is used somewhere else. It is usually considered good programming style to use uppercase and lowercase letters to improve a program's readability. A common practice—and one that we use in the sample programs in this text—is to write all reserved words in uppercase and all identifiers in lowercase, usually capitalizing the first letter if they are user defined. If an identifier is made up of several words, we usually capitalize the first letter of each.

Named Constants

Certain constants occur so frequently that they are given names. For example, the name "pi" is commonly given to the constant 3.14159 . . . and "e" to the base 2.71828 . . . of natural logarithms. Pascal allows the programmer to assign identifiers to certain constants in the **constant section** of the program's declaration part:

Constant Section

Form:

```
CONST
    identifier-1 = constant-expression-1;
    identifier-2 = constant-expression-2;
              .
              .
              .
    identifier-n = constant-expression-n;
```

where:

CONST is a reserved word;

each *identifier-i* is a valid Pascal identifier;

each *constant-expression-i* is a valid Pascal constant or an expression (as described in the next section) that contains only constants and previously defined constant identifiers.

Purpose:

Assigns names to constants; each *identifier-i* can be used in the program wherever the associated *constant-expression-i* can be used.

For example, the constant section

```
CONST
    Pi = 3.14159;
    NegPi = -Pi;
    TwoPi = 2 * Pi;
    MyName = 'John Doe';
    Year = 1992;
```

associates the names **Pi**, **NegPi**, and **TwoPi** with the real constants **3.14159**, **-3.14159**, and **6.28318**, respectively; **MyName** with the string constant **'John Doe'**; and **Year** with the integer **1992**. These names can then be used anywhere in the program that the corresponding constant value can be used.

One reason for using named constants is to make the program easier to read and to modify. Programmers should not use "magic numbers" that suddenly appear without explanation, as in

```
PopChange := (0.1758 - 0.1257) * Population;
```

because if these numbers must be changed, someone must search through the program to determine what they represent and which are the appropriate ones to change, and to locate all the places where they appear. It is thus better to use named constants, as in

```
CONST
    BirthRate = 0.1758;
    DeathRate = 0.1257;
```

and to rewrite the preceding statement as

```
PopChange := (BirthRate - DeathRate) * Population;
```

Readability is improved and the flexibility of the program is increased, because if these constants must be changed, one need only change the definitions of **BirthRate** and **DeathRate** in the constant section at the beginning of the program.

Pascal also includes three predefined constant identifiers: the boolean constant identifiers **true** and **false** and the integer constant identifier **maxint**. The value of **maxint** is the largest integer that can be represented in the particular computer being used. In Turbo Pascal this value is 32767 ($2^{15} - 1$). Turbo Pascal also provides the predefined constant identifier **MaxLongInt** whose value is 2147483647 ($2^{31} - 1$).

Variables

In mathematics, a symbolic name is often used to refer to a quantity. For example, the formula

$$A = l \cdot w$$

is used to calculate the area (denoted by A) of a rectangle with a given length (denoted by l) and a given width (denoted by w). These symbolic names, A, l, and w, are called **variables.** If specific values are assigned to l and w, this formula can be used to calculate the value of A, which then is the area of a particular rectangle.

Variables were also used in Chapter 2 in the discussion of algorithms and programs. When a variable is used in a Pascal program, the compiler associates it with a particular memory location. The value of a variable at any time is the value stored in the associated memory location at that time. One might think of a variable and its memory location as a mailbox with the name of the variable on the outside and the values of the variable placed inside:

Variable names are identifiers and thus must follow the rules for forming valid identifiers.

The type of a Pascal variable must be one of the four data types described earlier (or one of the other data types discussed later), and the type of each variable determines the type of value that may be stored in that variable. It is therefore necessary to specify the type of each variable in a Pascal program. This is done in the **variable section** of the program's declaration part (or in a constant section, as described later).

Variable Section

Form:

```
VAR
    variable-list-1 : type-1;
    variable-list-2 : type-2;
                  .
                  .
                  .
    variable-list-m : type-m;
```

where:
VAR is a reserved word;
each *variable-list-i* is a single variable or a
list of variables separated by commas;
each *type-i* is one of the Pascal data types
integer, **real**, **char**, **string**, or **boolean** (or
some other Turbo Pascal type discussed later).

Purpose:
Declares the types of variables that are used in the
program. Each variable in *variable-list-i* is
declared to be of type *type-i*.

For example, the variable declaration section

```
VAR
    EmpNumber : integer;
    EmpName : string;
    DeptCode : char;
    CityResident : boolean;
    Hours : real;
    Rate : real;
    Wages : real;
```

or equivalently,

```
VAR
    EmpNumber : integer;
    EmpName : string;
    DeptCode : char;
    CityResident : boolean;
    Hours, Rate, Wages : real;
```

declares that only the seven variables `EmpNumber`, `EmpName`, `DeptCode`,
`CityResident`, `Hours`, `Rate`, and `Wages` are used in the program and that
`EmpNumber` is of type `integer`; `EmpName` is of type `string`; `DeptCode` is of type
`char`; `CityResident` is of type `boolean`; and `Hours`, `Rate`, and `Wages` are of type
`real`.

It is good programming practice to use meaningful variable names that suggest what they represent, since this makes the program more readable and easier to understand. It is also good practice to include a **data dictionary** *consisting of brief comments that indicate what the variables represent, how they are to be used, and so on.* These comments may be included in the variable declaration section. The following illustrates:

Data dictionary
↓

```
VAR
  EmpNumber : integer;          {employee's number,}
  EmpName : string;             {name,}
  DeptCode : char;              {and department code}
  CityResident : boolean;       {indicates if employee is a city resident}
  Hours : real;                 {hours worked by employee}
  Rate : real;                  {employee's hourly pay rate}
  Wages : real;                 {total wages earned by employee}
```

Variable Initialization

In Turbo Pascal, it is possible to assign an initial value to a variable when it is declared. Such initial values are assigned during compilation, not during execution. Unfortunately, Turbo Pascal uses a nonstandard form of a constant section (rather than a variable section) to do this initialization. For example, the constant section.

```
CONST
    Year : integer = 1992
    CompanyName : string = 'Cawker City Cookie Company';
    TaxRate : real = 0.33;
```

declares the variable **CurrentYear** to be of type **integer** with an initial value of **1992**, the variable **CompanyName** to be of type **string** with an initial value of **Cawker City Cookie Company**, and the variable **TaxRate** to be of type **real** with an initial value of **0.33**. Although the term is a misnomer, these initialized constants are called **typed constants** in Turbo Pascal. It must be noted that *this initialization is only done once, during compilation, before execution of the program begins.* In particular, this means that the variables cannot be reinitialized while the program is being executed.

Exercises

1. Which of the following are legal Pascal identifiers?

(a) XRay	(b) X-Ray	(c) Jeremiah	(d) R2D2
(e) 3M	(f) PDQ123	(g) PS.175	(h) x
(i) 4	(j) N/4	(k) $M	(l) ZZZZZZ
(m) night	(n) ngiht	(o) nite	(p) to day

2. Classify each of the following as an integer constant, real constant, or neither:

(a) 12	(b) 12.	(c) 12.0	(d) '12'
(e) 8 + 4	(f) -3.7	(g) 3.7-	(h) 1,024

(i) +1   (j) $3.98   (k) 0.357E4   (l) 24E0
(m) E3   (n) five   (o) 3E.5   (p) .000001
(q) 1.2 x 10   (r) -(-1)   (s) 0E0   (t) 1/2

3. Which of the following are legal string constants?

    (a) 'X'   (b) '123'   (c) IS'   (d) 'too yet'
    (e) 'DO''ESNT'   (f) 'isn''t'   (g) 'constant'   (h) '$1.98'
    (i) 'DON'T'   (j) '12 + 34'   (k) '''twas'   (l) 'A''B''C'

4. For each of the following, write constant sections to name each given constant with the specified name:

    (a) 1.25 with the name **Rate**.
    (b) 40.0 with the name **RegHours** and 1.5 with the name **OvertimeFactor**.
    (c) 1776 with the name **Year**, 'F' with **Female**, and a blank character with **Blank**.
    (d) **true** with the name **Exist**, 0 with **Zero**, * with **Asterisk**, an apostrophe with **Apostrophe**, and the string CPSC151A with **Course**.

5. Write variable sections to declare:

    (a) **Item**, **Number**, and **Job** to be of type **real**.
    (b) **ShoeSize** to be of type **integer**.
    (c) **Mileage** to be of type **real** and **Cost** and **Distance** to be of type **integer**.
    (d) **Alpha** and **Beta** to be of type **integer**, **Code** to be of type **char**, **Root** to be of type **real**, and **RootExists** to be of type **boolean**.

6. For each of the following, write constant sections to declare each variable to have the specified type and initial value:

    (a) **FirstMonth** to be of type **string** and having the string **January** as its initial value.
    (b) **NumberOfDeposits** and **NumberOfChecks** to be of type **integer**, each with an initial value of 0; **TotalDeposits** and **TotalChecks** to be of type **real**, each with an initial value of 0; and **ServiceCharge** to be of type **real** with an initial value of 0.25.
    (c) **Symbol1** and **Symbol2** to be of type **char** and with a blank character and a semicolon for the initial value, respectively; **Debug** to be of type **boolean** with an initial value of **false**; and **CourseName** to be of type **string** and having the string CPSC 151A as its initial value.

3.3 Arithmetic Operations and Functions

In the preceding section we considered variables and constants of various types. These variables and constants can be processed by using operations and functions appropriate to their types. In this section we discuss the arithmetic operations and functions that are used with numeric data.

Operations

In Pascal, addition and subtraction are denoted by the usual plus (+) and minus (-) signs. Multiplication is denoted by an asterisk (*). This symbol must be used to denote every multiplication. Thus to multiply **n** by **2**, we must use **2*n** or **n*2**, not **2n**. There are three other arithmetic operations in Pascal: a real division operation denoted by a slash (/); an integer division operation denoted by the reserved word **DIV**; and an integer operation denoted by the reserved word **MOD**, which reduces one integer modulo another. The following table summarizes these arithmetic operations:

Operator	Operation
+	addition
-	subtraction, unary minus
*	multiplication
/	real division
DIV	integer division
MOD	remainder in integer division

For the operators +, -, and *, the operands may be of either integer or real type. If both are integer, the result is integer, but if either is of real type, the result is real. For example,

```
2 + 3 = 5
2 + 3.0 = 5.0
2.0 + 3 = 5.0
2.0 + 3.0 = 5.0
```

The division operator / produces a real result regardless of the type of the operands; for example,

```
 7 / 2 = 3.5
7.0 / 2 = 3.5
 7 / 2.0 = 3.5
7.0 / 2.0 = 3.5
 12 / 3 = 4.0
```

For the operators **DIV** and **MOD**, both the operands must be of integer type, and the result is also of integer type. If **i** and **j** are of integer type, then **i DIV j** produces the integer quotient that results when **i** is divided by **j**. In Turbo Pascal, the value of **i MOD j** is the remainder that results when **i** is divided by **j**.[2] For example,

---

[2] In standard Pascal, the value of **i MOD j** is the value obtained when **i** is reduced modulo **j**. When both **i** and **j** are positive, this value is the remainder that results when **i** is divided by **j**. This is not the case when **i** is negative, however; for example, **(-8) MOD 3 = 1**. Also, **i MOD j** is not defined when **j** is negative.

```
      7 DIV 2 = 3        7 MOD 2 = 1
     12 DIV 3 = 4       12 MOD 3 = 0
      0 DIV 5 = 0        0 MOD 5 = 0
      4 DIV 5 = 0        4 MOD 5 = 4
   (-8) DIV 3 = -2    (-8) MOD 3 = -2
```

The expressions i DIV j and i MOD j are defined for all nonzero integers i and j.

There are two **priority levels** for these arithmetic operators: high and low. The high-priority operators are *, /, DIV, and MOD, and the low-priority operators are + and -. When an expression containing several of these operators is evaluated, first all high-priority operations are performed in the order in which they occur, from left to right, and then all low-priority operations are carried out in the order in which they occur, from left to right.

To illustrate, consider the expression

$$7 * 10 - 5 \text{ MOD } 3 * 4 + 9$$

The leftmost multiplication is performed first, giving the intermediate result

$$70 - 5 \text{ MOD } 3 * 4 + 9$$

The next high-priority operator encountered is MOD, which gives

$$70 - 2 * 4 + 9$$

The second multiplication is the final operation of high priority; when it is performed, it yields

$$70 - 8 + 9$$

Next, the low-priority operations are performed in the order in which they occur, from left to right. The subtraction is thus performed first, giving

$$62 + 9$$

and then the addition is carried out, giving the final result

$$71$$

The standard order of evaluation can be modified by using parentheses to enclose subexpressions within an expression. These subexpressions are first evaluated in the standard manner, and the results are then combined to evaluate the complete expression. If the parentheses are "nested," that is, if one set of parentheses is contained within another, the computations in the innermost parentheses are performed first.

For example, consider the expression

$$(7 * (10 - 5) \text{ MOD } 3) * 4 + 9$$

The subexpression 10 - 5 is evaluated first, producing

$$(7 * 5 \text{ MOD } 3) * 4 + 9$$

Next the subexpression 7 * 5 MOD 3 is evaluated in the standard order, giving

$$2 * 4 + 9$$

Now the multiplication is performed, giving

$$8 + 9$$

and the addition produces the final result

$$17$$

Care must be taken in writing expressions containing two or more operations to ensure that they are evaluated in the order intended. Even though parentheses may not be required, they should be used freely to clarify the intended order of evaluation and to write complicated expressions in terms of simpler expressions. One must make sure, however, that the parentheses balance, that is, that they occur in pairs, since an unpaired parenthesis results in an error.

The symbols + and - can also be used as **unary operators;** for example, -x and +(a + b) are allowed. But unary operators must be used carefully, since Pascal does not allow two operators to follow in succession. For example, the expression n * -2 is not allowed; rather, it must be written n * (-2). These unary operations have low priority, the same as that of the corresponding binary operations.

In summary, the following rules govern the evaluation of arithmetic expressions:

Priority Rules

High-Priority Operators: *, /, DIV, and MOD

Low-Priority Operators: +, -, unary +, unary -

1. The high-priority operations are performed before the low-priority operations.
2. Operators having the same priority are performed in order, from left to right.
3. If an expression contains subexpressions enclosed within parentheses, these are evaluated first, using the standard order specified in Rules 1 and 2. If there are nested parentheses, the innermost subexpressions are evaluated first.

TABLE 3.1 Predefined Arithmetic Functions

Function	Description	Type of Parameter	Type of Value[3]
abs(x)	Absolute value of **x**	integer or real	Same as argument
arctan(x)	Inverse tangent of **x** (value in radians)	integer or real	real
cos(x)	Cosine of **x** (in radians)	integer or real	real
exp(x)	Exponential function e^x	integer or real	real
*frac(x)	Fractional part of **x**	real	real
*int(x)	Integer part of **x**	real	integer
ln(x)	Natural logarithm of **x**	integer or real	real
*pi	Returns value of π	None	real
round(x)	**x** rounded to nearest integer	real	integer
sin(x)	Sine of **x** (in radians)	integer or real	real
sqr(x)	x^2	integer or real	Same as argument
sqrt(x)	Square root of **x**	integer or real	real
trunc(x)	**x** truncated to its integer part	real	integer

In addition to the basic arithmetic operations +, -, *, /, DIV, and MOD, Turbo Pascal also provides bitwise operations that can be applied to integer data: NOT, AND, OR, XOR (exclusive or), SHL (shift left), and SHR (shift right). These are described in Appendix G.

Functions

Pascal also contains a number of predefined arithmetic functions, as shown in Table 3.1. (These marked with an asterisk are not provided in standard Pascal.) To use any of these functions, we simply give the function name followed by its parameter—the constant, variable, or expression to which the function is to be applied—enclosed in parentheses. Thus, to calculate the square root of 5, we write

```
sqrt(5)
```

and to calculate $\sqrt{b^2 - 4ac}$, we could use

```
sqrt(sqr(b) - 4 * a * c)
```

If the value of the expression `sqr(b) - 4 * a * c` is negative, an error results, because the square root of a negative number is not defined.

Exercises

1. Find the value of each of the following expressions, or explain why it is not a valid expression:

    (a) 9 - 5 - 3

    (b) 2 DIV 3 + 3 / 5   *not valid because 3/3 isn't an integer*

---

[3] If the special compiler directive for numeric processing ({$N+}) is on, real values are of type extended.

(c) 9 DIV 2 / 5
(d) 9 / 2 DIV 5
(e) 2.0 / 4
(f) (2 + 3) MOD 2
(g) 7 MOD 5 MOD 3
(h) (7 MOD 5) MOD 3
(i) 7 MOD (5 MOD 3)
(j) (7 MOD 5 MOD 3)
(k) 25 * 1 / 2
(l) 25 * 1 DIV 2
(m) 25 * (1 DIV 2)
(n) -3.0 * 5.0
(o) 5.0 * -3.0
(p) 12 / 2 * 3
(q) ((12 + 3) DIV 2) / (8 - (5 + 1))
(r) ((12 + 3) DIV 2) / (8 - 5 + 1)
(s) (12 + 3 DIV 2) / (8 - 5 + 1)
(t) sqrt(sqr(4))
(u) sqrt(sqr(-4))
(v) sqr(sqrt(4))
(w) sqr(sqrt(-4))
(x) trunc(8 / 5) + round(8 / 5)

2. If **R1** and **R2** are of type **real**, **I1**, **I2**, **I3** are of type **integer**, and **R1** = 2.0, **R2** = 3.0, **I1** = 4, **I2** = 5, and **I3** = 8, find the value of each of the following:

(a) R1 + R2 + R2
(b) I3 DIV 3
(c) I3 / 3
(d) (R2 + R1) * I1
(e) I3 DIV I2 * 5.1
(f) sqr(I1) / sqr(R1)
(g) sqr(I2) / sqr(R1)
(h) sqrt(R1 + R2 + I1)

3. Write Pascal expressions to compute the following:

(a) $10 + 5B - 4AC$.
(b) Three times the difference $4 - n$ divided by twice the quantity $m^2 + n^2$.
(c) The square root of $a + 3b^2$.
(d) The square root of the average of m and n.
(e) $|A/(m + n)|$ ($|x|$ denotes the absolute value of x).
(f) a^x, computed as $e^{x \ln a}$ (where ln is the natural logarithm function).
(g) The real quantity *Amount* rounded to the nearest hundredth.

3.4 The Assignment Statement

The **assignment statement** is used to assign values to variables:

Assignment Statement

Form:

> variable := expression

where:
    variable is a valid Pascal identifier.
    expression may be a constant, another variable
       to which a value has previously been assigned,
       or a formula to be evaluated.

Purpose:
Assigns the value of *expression* to *variable*.

For example, suppose that **xCoord** and **yCoord** are real variables, **Number** and **Position** are integer variables, **Code** is a character variable, **Name** is a string variable, and **Found** is a boolean variable as declared by the following variable section:

```
VAR
    xCoord, yCoord : real;
    Number, Position : integer;
    Code : char;
    Name : string;
    Found : boolean;
```

These declarations associate memory locations with the seven variables. This might be pictured as follows, with the question marks indicating that these variables are initially undefined:

xCoord	?
yCoord	?
Number	?
Position	?
Code	?
Name	?
Found	?

Now consider the following assignment statements:

```
xCoord := 5.23;
yCoord := sqrt(25.0);
Number := 17;
Code := 'M';
Name := 'Smith';
Found := false;
```

Note that the boolean constant **false** is not enclosed in quotes; **'false'** is a string constant, not a boolean constant. Also note that the value of a variable of type **char** is a single character and not a string of characters.

The first assignment statement assigns the real constant **5.23** to the real variable **xCoord**, and the second assigns the real constant **5.0** to the real variable **yCoord**. The next four assignment statements assign the integer constant **17** to the integer variable **Number**, the character **M** to the character variable **Code**, the string **Smith** to the string variable **Name**, and the boolean value **false** to the boolean variable **Found**. Thinking of variables as mailboxes, as described in Section 3.2, we might picture the results as follows:

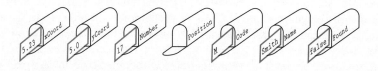

More precisely, when these assignment statements are executed, the values **5.23**, **5.0**, **17**, **M**, **Smith**, and **false** are stored in the memory locations associated with the variables **xCoord**, **yCoord**, **Number**, **Code**, **Name**, and **Found**, respectively. The variable **Position** is still undefined, and the content of the memory location associated with it is uncertain.

xCoord	5.23
yCoord	5.0
Number	17
Position	?
Code	M
Name	Smith
Found	false

These values are substituted for the variables in any subsequent expression containing these variables. Thus, in the assignment statement

```
Position := Number DIV 3 + 2;
```

the value **17** is substituted for the variable **Number**; the expression **Number DIV 3 + 2** is evaluated yielding **7**, and this value is then assigned to the integer variable **Position**; and the value of **Number** is unchanged.

xCoord	5.23
yCoord	5.0
Number	17
Position	7
Code	M
Name	Smith
Found	false

In the assignment statement

```
xCoord := 2.0 * xCoord;
```

the variable **xCoord** appears on both sides of the assignment operator (**:=**). In this case, the current value **5.23** for **xCoord** is used in evaluating the expression **2.0 * xCoord**, yielding the value **10.46**; this value is then assigned to **xCoord**. The old value **5.23** is lost because it has been replaced with the new value **10.46**.

xCoord	10.46
yCoord	5.0
Number	17
Position	7
Code	M
Name	Smith
Found	false

In every assignment statement, the variable to be assigned a value must appear on the left of the assignment operator (**:=**), and a legal expression must appear on the right. Furthermore, both the variable and the expression must be of the same type. However, *it is legal to assign an integer value to a real variable;* the integer value will be converted to the corresponding real value. *It is not legal to assign a real value to an integer variable.*

The following are examples of invalid Pascal assignment statements. A reason is given for each to explain why it is not valid. The variables in these statements are assumed to have the types specified earlier.

Statement	Error
`5 := Number`	Variable must appear on the left of the assignment operator.
`xCoord + 3.5 := 2.7`	Arithmetic expressions may not appear on the left of the assignment operator.
`Code := 5`	Numeric value may not be assigned to a character variable.
`Code := 'ABC'`	Value of a **char** variable is a single character.
`Number := '5'`	Character constant may not be assigned to a numeric variable.
`Number := 3.4`	Real value may not be assigned to an integer variable.
`Number := '2' + '3'`	`'2' + '3'` is not a legal expression.
`Position := Number := 1`	`Number := 1` is not a legal expression.
`Found := 'false'`	`'false'` is not a boolean expression.

It is important to remember that *the assignment statement is a replacement statement.* Some beginning programmers forget this and write an assignment statement like

    A := B

when the statement

    B := A

is intended. These two statements produce very different results: The first assigns the value of **B** to **A**, leaving **B** unchanged, and the second assigns the value of **A** to **B**, leaving **A** unchanged.

$$
\begin{array}{ccc}
A \;\boxed{8.5} & A := B & A \;\boxed{9.37} \\
B \;\boxed{9.37} & \longrightarrow & B \;\boxed{9.37}
\end{array}
$$

$$
\begin{array}{ccc}
A \;\boxed{8.5} & B := A & A \;\boxed{8.5} \\
B \;\boxed{9.37} & \longrightarrow & B \;\boxed{8.5}
\end{array}
$$

To demonstrate further the replacement property of an assignment, suppose that the integer variables **Alpha** and **Beta** have values **357** and **59**, respectively, and that we wish to interchange these values. For this, we use an auxiliary integer variable **Temp** to store the value of **Alpha** while we assign **Beta**'s value to **Alpha**; then we can assign this stored value to **Beta**.

    Temp := Alpha;
    Alpha := Beta;
    Beta := Temp;

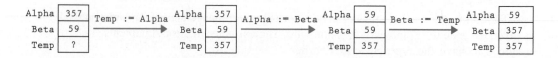

As another example, consider the statement

```
Sum := Sum + Counter
```

Such a statement, in which the same variable appears on both sides of the assignment operator, often confuses beginning programmers. Execution of this statement causes the values of **Sum** and **Counter** to be substituted for these variables to evaluate the expression **Sum + Counter**, and the resulting value is then assigned to **Sum**. The following diagram illustrates this for the case in which the integer variables **Sum** and **Counter** have the values **120** and **16**, respectively:

```
Sum    | 120 |     Sum := Sum + Counter      Sum    | 136 |
Counter | 16 |    ──────────────────────▶    Counter | 16 |
```

Note that the old value of the variable **Sum** is lost because it was replaced with a new value.

Another statement in which the same variable appears on both sides of the assignment operator is

```
Counter := Counter + 1
```

This statement implements the operation "increment **Counter** by 1." When it is executed, the current value of **Counter** is substituted for this variable to evaluate the expression **Counter + 1**, and this new value is then assigned to **Counter**. For example, if **Counter** has the value **16**, the value of **Counter + 1** is **16 + 1 = 17**, which is then assigned as the new value for **Counter:**

```
                    Counter := Counter + 1
Counter | 16 |     ──────────────────────▶    Counter | 17 |
```

Note once again that the old value of the variable has been lost because it was replaced with a new value.

Turbo Pascal also provides two special statements that can be used to increment or decrement integer variables. The general form of the **increment statement** is

```
Inc( variable, step )
```

where *variable* is an integer variable whose value is to be incremented by *step*, where *step* is an integer-valued expression. For example, the assignment statement

```
Sum := Sum + Counter
```

can also be written

```
Inc( Sum, Counter )
```

If the step size is omitted so the statement has the form

```
Inc( variable )
```

then it is taken to be 1. For example, an alternative way of writing the statement

```
Counter := Counter + 1
```

is

```
Inc( Counter )
```

The **decrement statement** has the form

```
Dec( variable, step )
```

or simply

```
Dec( variable )
```

if the step size is 1. For example, the statement

```
Dec( Counter )
```

or

```
Dec( Counter, 1 )
```

is an alternative to the assignment statement

```
Counter := Counter - 1
```

In a Pascal program, *variables are undefined until their values have been explicitly specified* by an assignment statement or by one of the other statements discussed later. The results of attempting to use undefined variables are unpredictable.

Exercises

1. Assuming that **Number** is of integer type, **xValue** and **yValue** are of real type, **Grade** is of character type, and **Found** is of boolean type, determine which of the following are valid Pascal assignment statements. If they are not valid, explain why they are not.

   (a) `XValue := 2.17828`   (b) `3 := Number`
   (c) `Grade := 'B+'`   (d) `Number := Number + 1`
   (e) `xValue := 1`   (f) `Grade := A`
   (g) `Number + 1 := Number`   (h) `xValue := '1'`
   (i) `Found := Grade`   (j) `yValue := yValue`
   (k) `xValue := A`   (l) `Grade := Grade + 10`
   (m) `Found := 'true'`   (n) `xValue := Number`
   (o) `Number := yValue`

2. Given that **R1**, **R2**, **R3**, and **xCoord** are real variables with **R1** = **2.0**, **R2** = **3.0**, and **R3** = **4.0**; **I1**, **I2**, and **I3** are integer variables with **I1** = 8, and **I2** = 5; and **Numeral** and **Symbol** are character variables with **Numeral** = '2', find the value assigned to the given variable by each of the following, or indicate why the statement is not valid:

(a) `xCoord := (R1 + R2) * R2`
(b) `xCoord := (R2 + R1 / R3) * 2`
(c) `xCoord := I1 / I2 + 5`
(d) `I3 := I1 DIV I2 + 5`
(e) `xCoord := sqr(I2) / sqr(I1)`
(f) `I3 := sqr(I2) / sqr(I1)`
(g) `Symbol := 4`
(h) `Symbol := Numeral`
(i) `Symbol := '4'`
(j) `Symbol := R3`
(k) `R1 := 2`
(l) `R1 := '2'`
(m) `R1 := Numeral`
(n) `I1 := I1 + 2`
(o) `I3 := 1 + Numeral`
(p) `I3 := round(sqr(I1 MOD I2) / R3)`

3. For each of the following, write (i) an assignment statement and (ii) a statement using **Inc** or **Dec** that changes the value of the integer variable **Number** by the specified amount:

(a) Increment **Number** by 77.
(b) Decrement **Number** by 3.
(c) Increment **Number** by twice its value.
(d) Add the rightmost digit of **Number** to **Number**.
(e) Decrement **Number** by the integer part of the real value **X**.

4. Write a Pascal assignment statement for each of the following that calculates the given expression and assigns the result to the specified variable. Assume that all variables are of type **real**, except where otherwise noted.

(a) **Rate** times **Time** to **Distance**.
(b) **X** incremented by an amount **DeltaX** to **X**.
(c) $\dfrac{1}{\dfrac{1}{R1} + \dfrac{1}{R2} + \dfrac{1}{R3}}$ to **Resistance**.
(d) Area of a triangle of base **b** and height **h** (one-half base times height) to **Area**.
(e) The last three digits of the integer **StockNumber** with a decimal point before the last two digits to **Price** (e.g., if **StockNumber** is 1758316, **Price** is assigned the value **3.16**).
(f) **Tax** rounded to the nearest dollar to **Tax**.

5. For each of the following, give values for the integer variables **a**, **b**, and **c** for which the two given expressions have different values:

(a) a * (b DIV c) and a * b DIV c
(b) a DIV b and a * (1 / b)
(c) (a + b) DIV c and a DIV c + b DIV c

3.5   Input/Output

In the preceding section we considered the assignment statement, which enables us to calculate the values of expressions and store the results of these computations by assigning them to variables. An assignment statement does not, however, display these results on some output device, nor does it allow the user to enter new values during execution. For example, a program to calculate the wages earned by John Doe, employee #31564, for 38.5 hours of work at an hourly rate of $8.75 could contain the variable section

```
VAR
    EmpName : string;       {employee name}
    EmpNumber : integer;    {and number}
    Hours,                  {hours worked}
    Rate,                   {hourly pay rate}
    Wages : real;           {total wages}
```

and the statement part

```
BEGIN
    EmpName := 'John Doe';
    EmpNumber := 31564;
    Hours := 38.5;
    Rate := 8.75;
    Wages := Hours * Rate
END.
```

The value of **Wages** is calculated as desired but is stored only internally in the memory location associated with **Wages** and is not displayed to the user. Moreover, if the same wage calculation is to be done for Mary Smith, employee #31565, who worked 37.5 hours at an hourly rate of $9.25, the statement part of the program must be almost completely rewritten, as follows:

```
BEGIN
    EmpName := 'Mary Smith';
    EmpNumber := 31565;
    Hours := 37.5;
    Rate := 9.25;
    Wages := Hours * Rate
END.
```

The output statement that we consider in this section provides a method for easily displaying information. We also consider an input statement that provides a convenient method of assigning values from an external source to variables during execution of the program.

Program Heading

Any collection of data to be input to a program or output from a program is called a **file.** Some programs do not require any input from a file, since all values to be processed are assigned within the program. This is true, for example, in the preceding program segments. All useful programs, however, do produce some output, because the results obtained would not otherwise be displayed to the user.

The program heading in a Pascal program has the following form:

Program Heading

Form:

    PROGRAM *name*(*file-list*);

where:
  PROGRAM is a reserved word;
  name is a valid Pascal identifier;
  file-list is a list of identifiers representing
      names of files.

Purpose:
Names the program with the specified *name* and declares that the files named in *file-list* are used in the program.

Two standard files provided by the Pascal language are **input** and **output**. The file **input** refers to a system input device, and the file **output** refers to a system output device. In Turbo Pascal these are the keyboard and the monitor's screen, respectively. An appropriate program heading for a Pascal program that does not require input could have the form

    PROGRAM *name*(output);

A program that requires input and produces output could have a program heading of the form

    PROGRAM *name*(input, output);

These forms of the program heading may also be used in Turbo Pascal, but a simpler form in which the file list is omitted is also allowed:

    PROGRAM *name*;

In fact, the entire program heading is optional, but we shall include it in the sample programs in this text to identify the program and the type of input/output operations that it performs.

Output

There are two output statements in Pascal, the **write** and the **writeln** (read "write-line") statements:

write and writeln Statements

Forms:

```
write( output-list )
writeln( output-list )
writeln
```

where:
   write and **writeln** are predefined output procedures;
   output-list is a single expression or a list of expressions separated by commas. Each of these expressions may be a constant, a variable, or a formula.

Purpose:
Execution of these output statements displays the values of the items in the **output-list** on the current line; **writeln** then advances to the next line so that subsequent output will appear on a new line, whereas **write** produces no such advance. The last form of **writeln** with no output list terminates output to the current line, so that subsequent output begins on a new line.

For example, the statements

```
writeln( Alpha, Beta );
writeln( Gamma, Delta );
```

display the values of **Alpha** and **Beta** on one line and the values of **Gamma** and **Delta** on the next line. Subsequent output would begin on yet another line.

The values of the expressions in the output list are displayed in **fields,** which are zones of consecutive positions in the output line. To illustrate, suppose that **Counter, RealNum, Code, Name,** and **BooleVar** are variables declared by

```
VAR
    Counter : integer;
    RealNum : real;
    Code : char;
    Name : string;
    BooleVar : boolean;
```

and consider the following statements:

```
Counter := 16;
RealNum := 123.456;
Code := 'A';
Name := 'Blaise Pascal';
BooleVar := true;
writeln( 'Counter' );
writeln( Counter );
writeln( Counter, ' is even', Counter + 1, ' is odd' );
writeln( RealNum, RealNum / 70000 );
writeln( Code, 'B', 'C', '***' );
writeln( Name, '***' );
writeln( BooleVar, false );
```

These statements produce output similar to the following:

```
Counter
      16
      16 is even       17 is odd
 1.234560000E+02 1.763657143E-03
ABC***
Blaise Pascal***
TRUE FALSE
```

For an integer, the field width is the number of digits (and sign) in the integer. For character, string, and boolean values, it is the number of characters to be displayed. Real values are displayed in floating point notation in 17-space fields.

When a **write** statement is executed, the values are displayed on the current line, but *there is no advance to a new line.* Consequently, any subsequent output will be displayed on this same line. For example, the statements

```
write( 'A' );
write( 'B' );
write( 'C' );
writeln( 'DEF' );
writeln( 'GHI' );
```

produce as output

```
ABCDEF
GHI
```

The **writeln** statement, but not **write**, may also be used with no output list to advance to a new line. In this case, the parentheses used to enclose the output list are also omitted, and so the statement has the form

```
writeln
```

Execution of this statement produces a blank line unless the last preceding output statement was a **write** statement, in which case output to the current line is terminated and subsequent output begins on a new line. For example, consider the statements

```
Counter := 16;
write( Counter, ' is even ' );
write( Counter + 1, ' is odd' );
writeln;
writeln( '**********' );
writeln( '*          *' );
writeln( '**********' );
writeln;
writeln( 2 * Counter, ' is even' );
```

These statements produce as output:

```
16 is even 17 is odd
**********
*          *
**********

32 is even
```

In an earlier example in this section we considered the problem of calculating wages for an employee. To display some of the relevant information from this example, we might add several **writeln** statements, as shown in the program in Figure 3.1.

FIGURE 3.1   Calculating wages—version 1.

```
PROGRAM WageCalculation( output );
{*****************************************************************************

    Input:          None.
    Purpose:        This program calculates wages as hours * rate for
                    a given number of hours worked and a given hourly
                    rate for some employee identified by his/her
                    employee name and number.
    Output (screen): The employee's name, number, hours worked,
                    hourly rate, and total wages.


*****************************************************************************}

VAR
    EmpName : string;       {employee name}
    EmpNumber : integer;    {employee number}
    Hours,                  {hours worked by employee}
    Rate,                   {employee's hourly rate}
    Wages : real;           {gross wages earned by employee}
```

FIGURE 3.1   Calculating wages—version 1. (cont.)

```
BEGIN
   EmpName := 'John Doe';
   EmpNumber := 31564;
   Hours := 38.5;
   Rate := 8.75;
   Wages := Hours * Rate;
   writeln( 'Employee name: ', EmpName );
   writeln( 'Employee #', EmpNumber );
   writeln( 'Hours worked:  ', Hours );
   writeln( 'Hourly rate:  $', Rate );
   writeln( 'Total Wages:  $', Wages )
END.
```

Sample run:

```
Employee name: John Doe
Employee #31564
Hours worked:   3.8500000000e+01
Hourly rate:  $ 8.7500000000e+00
Total Wages:  $ 3.3687500000e+02
```

Format Descriptors

The output produced by the preceding program is not really satisfactory because the real values are displayed in an exponential form that is not suitable for monetary values. This deficiency can be remedied by specifying the format of the output, by appending **format descriptors** to the items in the output list.

Format Descriptors

Forms:

> :w
> :w:d

where:
   w and d are integer-valued expressions.

Purpose:
When appended to an item in an output list, these format descriptors specify the output format for the value of that item:

:w specifies that the value is to be displayed in a field consisting of w spaces. The value will be right justified in this field. Real values will be displayed in exponential form. If the

> size of the field is too small, the field will be enlarged for numeric values, but for character, string, or boolean values, only the leftmost *w* characters will be displayed.
>
> :*w*:*d*   is used to display real values in decimal form; *w* is the field width; and *d* is the number of digits to be displayed to the right of the decimal point. The value will be rounded to *d* places or zero padded as necessary.

To illustrate the first kind of format descriptor, consider the statement

```
writeln( Counter:2, ' is even', Counter + 1:5, ' is odd' );
```

The format descriptor :2 specifies that the value of Counter is to be displayed in a field of width 2, and the format descriptor :5 specifies that the value of Counter + 1 is to be displayed in a field of width 5. If Counter has the value 16, the output produced by this statement will be

```
16 is even   17 is odd
```

If Zone is an integer variable with value 2, the statement

```
writeln( Counter:Zone, ' is even', Counter + 1:Zone + 3, ' is odd' );
```

will produce this same output. The statement

```
writeln( Counter : 1, ' is even', Counter + 1:1, ' is odd' );
```

produces

```
16 is even17 is odd
```

As this last example demonstrates, if a value is too large for the specified field, then the field is automatically enlarged to accommodate it. Thus because the value 16 of Counter has two digits, the field of size 1 specified for it by Counter:1 is enlarged so that both digits are displayed. Similarly, the output produced by the statement

```
writeln( Counter:1, ' is even':7, Counter + 1:1, ' is odd':5 );
```

is

```
16 is even17 is odd
```

If the field width is larger than necessary, the value is *right justified* in the field. Thus, the output produced by the statement

```
writeln( Counter:5 , 'is even':8 , Counter + 1:10 , 'is odd':8 );
```

is

```
___16_is_even_____17__is_odd
```

If a real value is output using the format descriptor :*w*, it is displayed in exponential form. If the usual decimal form for a real value is desired, a format descriptor of the form :*w*:*d* must be used. In this descriptor, *d* is an integer expression specifying the number of digits to be displayed to the right of the decimal point. To illustrate, suppose that **Alpha** and **Beta** are real variables, with values 3.51 and −123.47168, respectively. The statements

```
write( Alpha:4:2 );
write( Beta:12:5 );
writeln;
```

produce the output

```
3.51___-123.47168
```

Note that the values are right justified in the specified fields.

If *d* is larger than the number of digits to the right of the decimal point in the value being displayed, zeros are added as necessary. For example, the statement

```
writeln( Alpha:8:4 , Beta:12:6 );
```

produces the output

```
__3.5100_-123.471680
```

If the value of *d* is too small, the value to be displayed is *rounded* to *d* decimal places. Thus the output produced by the statements

```
writeln( Alpha:8:2 , Beta:12:3 );
writeln( Alpha:8:1 , Beta:12:1 );
```

is

```
____3.51_____-123.472
_____3.5_____-123.5
```

If *w* is too small, the field is enlarged as necessary. For example, the statement

```
writeln( Alpha:3:1 , Beta:3:1 );
```

produces the output

```
3.5-123.5
```

Either *w* or *d* in a descriptor of the form :*w*:*d* may be an expression. To illustrate, suppose that `Zone` and `NumDigits` are integer variables with the values 8 and 2, respectively. The statements

```
writeln( Alpha + 3:Zone:NumDigits );
writeln( Beta + 1:Zone + 1:NumDigits + 1 );
```

produce the output

```
      6.51
   -122.472
```

We remarked earlier that the output produced by the program in Figure 3.1 is not really satisfactory. The program in Figure 3.2 is a modification that uses format descriptors to display the results in a more acceptable format.

FIGURE 3.2 Calculating wages—version 2.

```
PROGRAM WageCalculation( output );
{******************************************************************

    Input:          None.
    Purpose:        This program calculates wages as hours * rate for
                    a given number of hours worked and a given hourly
                    rate for some employee identified by his/her
                    employee number.
    Output (screen): The employee's name, number, hours worked,
                    hourly rate, and total wages.


******************************************************************}

VAR
    EmpName : string;        {employee name}
    EmpNumber : integer;     {employee number}
    Hours,                   {hours worked by employee}
    Rate,                    {employee's hourly rate}
    Wages : real;            {gross wages earned by employee}

BEGIN
    EmpName := 'John Doe';
    EmpNumber := 31564;
    Hours := 38.5;
    Rate := 8.75;
    Wages := Hours * Rate;
    writeln( 'Employee Name: ', EmpName );
    writeln( 'Employee # ', EmpNumber:1 );
    writeln( 'Hours worked:  ', Hours:7:2 );
    writeln( 'Hourly rate:  $', Rate:7:2 );
    writeln( 'Total wages:  $', Wages:7:2 )
END.
```

FIGURE 3.2 Calculating wages—version 2. (cont.)

Sample run:

```
Employee Name:   John Doe
Employee # 31564
Hours worked:     38.50
Hourly rate:  $    8.75
Total wages:  $ 336.88
```

Input

There are two input statements in Pascal, the `read` and `readln` (read ''read line'') statements:

read and readln Statements

Forms:

```
readln( input-list )
read( input-list )
readln
```

where:

read and **readln** are predefined input procedures;

input-list is a single variable or a list of variables separated by commas.

Purpose:

Execution of these input statements reads values from the standard file **input** and assigns them to the variables in the **input-list**. After values have been read for all the variables, **readln** causes an advance to a new input line from which subsequent values will be read, whereas **read** causes no such advance. The last form of **readln** with no input list terminates input from the current line, so that subsequent input begins on a new line.

Recall that in Turbo Pascal the standard file **input** refers to the keyboard, so that data values are entered by the user during program execution. To illustrate, consider the statement

```
readln( EmpNumber, Hours, Rate );
```

where **EmpNumber** is an integer variable and **Hours** and **Rate** are real variables. If the data values

```
31564  38.5  8.75
```

are entered, the value `31564` is assigned to the variable `EmpNumber`, `38.5` to `Hours`, and `8.75` to `Rate`. Thus this single `readln` statement can replace the three assignment statements

```
EmpNumber := 31654;
Hours  := 38.5;
Rate  := 8.75;
```

used in the programs of Figures 3.1 and 3.2.

Data values entered for the variables in the input list of a `readln` statement must be constants, and consecutive numbers should be separated by one or more blanks, and the type of each value must agree with the type of the variable to which it is to be assigned. Assignment of a real value to an integer variable is not allowed, although an integer value may be read and assigned to a real variable.

After values have been read for all of the variables in the input list, a `readln` statement causes an advance to a new input line from which subsequent values will be read. Consequently, if there are more values in the current input line than there are variables in the input list, the first data values are read, but all remaining values are ignored.

If there are fewer entries in a line of input data than variables in the input list, successive lines of input data are processed until values for all variables in the input list have been obtained. Thus for the statement

```
readln( EmpNumber, Hours, Rate );
```

the values for `EmpNumber`, `Hours`, and `Rate` can all be entered on the same line:

```
31564 38.5 8.75
```

or on three separate lines:

```
31564
38.5
8.75
```

or with the value for `EmpNumber` on the first line and the values for `Hours` and `Rate` on the next line:

```
31564
38.5 8.75
```

The `readln` statement can also be used to read values for string variables and character variables. The simplest way to read a value for a string variable is to use a `readln` statement in which the variable is the only item in the input list,

```
readln( string-variable )
```

and then enter the string value on a line by itself. For example, to read a value for the string variable `EmpName`, we could use the statement

```
readln( EmpName );
```

and enter the employee's name on a single line:

   John Doe

When a **readln** statement is encountered, program execution is suspended until the user enters values for all variables in the input list. Program execution then automatically resumes. Because execution is interrupted and because the correct number and types of values must be entered before execution can resume, *it is good practice to provide some message to prompt the user when it is necessary to enter data values.* This is accomplished by preceding input statements with output statements that display appropriate prompts. The program in Figure 3.3 illustrates this by prompting the user when values for **EmpNumber**, **Hours**, and **Rate** are to be entered; it is a modification of the program in Figure 3.2. Values entered by the user are underlined.

   FIGURE 3.3 Calculating wages—version 3.

```
PROGRAM WageCalculation( input, output );
{******************************************************************

    Input (keyboard): An employee name, number, hours worked, and
                      hourly rate.
    Purpose:          This program calculates wages as hours * rate
                      for an employee identified by his/her name and
                      employee number.
    Output (screen):  Prompts to the user, employee's name, number,
                      hours worked, hourly rate, and total wages.


    ******************************************************************}

VAR
    EmpName : string;        {employee name}
    EmpNumber : integer;     {employee number}
    Hours,                   {hours worked by employee}
    Rate,                    {employee's hourly rate}
    Wages : real;            {gross wages earned by employee}

BEGIN
    write( 'Enter employee name: ' );
    readln( EmpName );
    write( 'Enter employee number: ' );
    readln( EmpNumber  );
    write( 'Enter hours worked and hourly rate: ' );
    readln( Hours, Rate );
    Wages := Hours * Rate;
    writeln( 'Employee # ', EmpNumber:1 );
    writeln( 'Hours worked:  ', Hours:7:2 );
    writeln( 'Hourly rate:   $', Rate:7:2 );
    writeln( 'Total wages:   $', Wages:7:2 )
END.
```

FIGURE 3.3   Calculating wages—version 3. (cont.)

Sample run:

```
Enter employee name: John Doe
Enter employee number: 31564
Enter hours worked and hourly rate: 38.5 8.75
Employee name: John Doe
Employee # 31564
Hours worked:    38.50
Hourly rate:  $   8.75
Total wages:  $ 336.88
```

As we noted in our description of the Turbo environment in Section 2.4, when program execution is complete, the output produced by the program is displayed only briefly before the edit window is reactivated. We described there how it can be reviewed by using the **User Screen** option of the **Window** menu (**Run** menu in Version 5.5) or equivalently, by using **Alt-F5**. An alternative is to place a **readln** statement of the form

```
readln
```

with an empty input list at the end of the program to suspend execution so that the output can be examined. For example, we might append a semicolon to the last **writeln** statement in the program in Figure 3.3 and add the statements

```
write( 'Press the Enter key to terminate execution.' );
readln
```

for this purpose. When the **readln** statement is encountered, program execution is suspended, providing an opportunity for the user to examine the output. When the **Enter** key is pressed, program execution is completed, the output disappears, and the edit window is reactivated.

The **read** statement is similar to the **readln** statement except that it does *not* advance to a new input line after values have been read for the variables in the input list. To illustrate, consider the statement

```
read( EmpNumber, Hours, Rate )
```

and suppose that the data values are entered as follows:

```
31564 38.5 8.75 31523
40.0 8.25
```

As in the case of the earlier **readln** statement, the values read for **EmpNumber**, **Hours**, and **Rate** are 31564, 38.5, and 8.75, respectively. If this statement is executed again, the value 31523 will be read for **EmpNumber**, 40.0 for **Hours** (end of lines are ignored for numeric input), and 8.25 for **Rate**.

1. Assuming that **Alpha** and **Beta** are real variables with values -567.392 and 0.0004, respectively, and that **Rho** is an integer variable with a value 436, show precisely the output that each of the following sets of statements produces, or explain why an error occurs:

(a) ```
writeln(Rho);
writeln(Rho + 1);
writeln(Rho + 2);
```

(b) ```
write( Rho );
write( Rho + 1 );
writeln( Rho + 2 );
```

(c) ```
write('Alpha =');
write(Alpha:9:3);
write('Beta =':7);
writeln(Beta:7:4);
```

(d) ```
write( Rho:5, 2 * Rho:5 );
writeln;
writeln( Beta:10:5 );
```

(e) ```
writeln(Alpha:8:1, Rho:5);
writeln('Tolerance:', Beta:8:5);
```

(f) ```
writeln( 'Alpha =', Alpha:12:5 );
writeln( 'Beta =', Beta:6:2, ' ':4, 'Rho =', Rho:6 );
writeln( Alpha + 4.0 + Rho:15:3 );
```

(g) ```
write('Tolerance =':8);
writeln(Beta:5:3);
writeln;
writeln;
writeln(Rho:2, Alpha:4:2);
```

(h) ```
writeln( 10 * Alpha:8:1, trunc(10 * Alpha):8,
          round(10 * Alpha):8 );
writeln( sqr(Rho DIV 100):5, sqrt(Rho DIV 100):5 );
```

(i) ```
writeln('Rho =':7, Rho:8:2);
writeln('*****');
```

(j) ```
write( Alpha:10 );
write;
writeln( Beta:10 );
```

2. Assuming that **I** and **J** are integer variables with **I = 15** and **J = 8**, that **C** and **D** are character variables with **C = 'C'** and **D = '-'**, and that **X** and **Y** are real variables with **X = 2559.50** and **Y = 8.015**, show precisely the output that each of the following sets of statements produce:

(a) ```
writeln('New balance =':I, X:J:2);
writeln(C:I MOD 10, Y:J:J - 6);
```

(b) ```
write( 'I =':I );
write( I:I );
writeln( 'J =':J, J:J );
writeln;
writeln( I:J, J:I );
writeln( trunc(X / J):J, J - Y:I:J, D:J DIV 7 );
```

3. Assume that **N1** and **N2** are integer variables with values 39 and −5117, respectively; that **R1** and **R2** are real variables with values 56.7173 and −0.00247, respectively; and that **C** is a character variable with value **F**. For each of the following, write a set of output statements that use these variables to produce the given output:

(a) `__56.7173___F___39`
`-5117PDQ-0.00247__`

(b) `__56.717____-0.0025***39__F`
`____56.72__39-5117_____`

(c) `ROOTS_ARE__56.717_AND_-0.00247`

(d) `APPROXIMATE_ANGLES:__56.7_AND_-0.0`
`MAGNITUDES_ARE_____39_AND__5117___`

4. Assuming that **A**, **B**, and **C** are integer variables and **X**, **Y**, and **Z** are real variables, and **S** and **T** are string variables, tell what value, if any, will be assigned to each of these variables, or explain why an error occurs, when each of the following sets of statements is executed with the given input data:

(a) `readln( A, B, C, X, Y, Z );`   Input: 1 2 3
                                              4 5.5 6.6

(b) `readln( A, B, C );`   Input: 1
    `readln( X, Y, Z );`   2
                                              3
                                              4
                                              5
                                              6

(c) `read( A, X );`   Input: 1 2.2
    `read( B, Y );`   3 4.4
    `read( C, Z );`   5 6.6

(d) `read( A, B, C );`   Input: 1 2.2
    `readln( X, Y, Z );`   3 4.4
                                             5 6.6

(e) `read( A );`   Input: 1 2 3
    `readln( B, C );`   4 5.5 6.6
    `read( X, Y );`
    `readln( Z );`

(f) `readln( A );`   Input: 1 2 3
    `read( B, C );`   4 5.5 6.6
    `readln( X, Y );`
    `read( Z );`

```
(g) read( A, B );                    Input:  1    2    3
    readln;                                  4 5.5 6.6
    read( C );                               7 8.8 9.9
    read( X );                              10 11.11 12.12
    readln;                                 13 14.14 15.15
    readln( Y );                            Pascal
    readln;                                 Leibniz
    readln( Z );                            Babbage
    readln( S );
    readln;
    readln( T );
```

3.6 Program Composition

Pascal Program

As noted in Section 3.1, a Pascal program consists of four parts:

> program heading
> **USES** clause
> declaration part
> statement part

These four parts *must* appear in the order shown.

Program Heading

The **program heading** is a single statement of the form

```
PROGRAM name( file-list );
```

as described in the preceding section. The name assigned to the program must be a legal Pascal identifier. In Turbo Pascal, the file list may be omitted, giving the simpler form

```
PROGRAM name;
```

and in fact, the entire program heading is optional. The program heading should normally be followed by **opening documentation** in the form of comments that describe what the program does, how it works, any special algorithms it uses, a summary of the problem's specification, assumptions, and so on, and they may also include other items of information such as the name of the programmer, the date the program was written and when it was last modified, and references to books and manuals that give additional information about the program. In addition, it is a good practice to explain the variables that are being used in the program.

USES Clause

The **USES clause** has the form

```
USES list;
```

where **list** is a list of names of units containing special items to be imported into the program. Most of the sample programs use no such items, and so the **USES** clause will not be needed. (The **USES** clause is described in more detail in Chapter 5.)

Declaration Part

The **declaration part** of a Pascal program may contain up to five sections that define various entities used in the program:

label section
constant section
type section
variable section
subprogram section

Turbo Pascal allows any number of different sections of each kind, and they may appear in any order. It is common practice to follow standard Pascal, however, and to use only one section of each kind and arrange them in the order given here.

Constant Section

A **constant section** has the form

```
CONST
    identifier-1 = constant-expression-1;
    identifier-2 = constant-expression-2;
                     .
                     .
                     .
    identifier-k = constant-expression-k;
```

and is used to assign names to constants, as described in Section 3.2.

Variable Section

A **variable section** has the form

```
VAR
    variable-list-1 : type-1;
    variable-list-2 : type-2;
                     .
                     .
                     .
    variable-list-m : type-m;
```

and is used to declare the variables used in the program, that is, to specify their names and types. This also was discussed in Section 3.2. We also noted there that special constant sections of the form

```
CONST
   variable-1 : type-1 = value-1;
   variable-2 : type-2 = value-2;
                 .
                 .
                 .
   variable-n : type-n = value-n;
```

can be used to declare variables and to assign them initial values at compile time. The other sections of the declaration part will be discussed later.

Statement Part

The **statement part** of the program has the form

```
BEGIN
   statement-1;
   statement-2;
        .
        .
        .
   statement-n
END
```

This part of the program contains the statements that implement the steps of an algorithm. It may include such statements as assignment statements, input/output statements, and other statements considered in subsequent chapters of this book.

Correct punctuation is critical in a Pascal program, and each of the sections must be punctuated exactly as indicated. In particular, the program heading, each constant definition, and each variable declaration must end with a semicolon. In the statement part, the statements are *separated* by semicolons, but there need be no semicolon following the last statement. Finally, note that a period must follow the reserved word **END** that closes the statement part of the program.

Comments

We have seen that comments are indicated in a Pascal program by enclosing them in braces:

```
{ comment }
```

or between (∗ and ∗):

```
(∗ comment ∗)
```

These comments are not program statements and may be placed anywhere in the program except, of course, in the middle of a reserved word, an identifier, a constant, and so on. As discussed in Section 2.5, comments should be used to explain the use of variables, to explain the purpose of the program or a program segment, and to provide other pertinent information about the program. Such documentation is intended to clarify the purpose and structure of the program. It is invaluable if revisions and modifications are made to the program in the future, especially if such maintenance is done by persons other than the original programmer.

3.7   Example: Truck Fleet Accounting

Problem

Suppose that a manufacturing company maintains a fleet of trucks to deliver its products. On each trip, the driver records the distance traveled in miles, the number of gallons of fuel used, the cost of the fuel, and the other costs of operating the truck. As part of the accounting process, the controller needs to calculate and record for each truck and for each trip the miles per gallon, the total cost of that trip, and the cost per mile. A simple program is to be designed to carry out these calculations.

Specification

From the preceding description of the problem, it is easy to determine the problem's input and output:

Input:	Miles traveled
	Gallons of fuel used
	Fuel cost
	Other operating costs
Output:	Miles per gallon
	Total cost of the trip
	Cost per mile

Design

The calculations required to solve this program are quite simple. The miles per gallon is obtained by dividing the number of miles traveled by the number of gallons of fuel used. The total cost is obtained by adding the cost of fuel to the other operating costs. This sum is divided by the number of miles traveled to yield the cost per mile.

Expressing this algorithm in pseudocode is straightforward once we select the appropriate variable names to represent the quantities involved. Selecting names that are self-documenting, we use the following:

VARIABLES FOR TRUCK COST PROBLEM

`Miles`	Total miles traveled
`Fuel`	Total gallons of fuel used
`FuelCost`	Total cost of fuel
`OperCost`	Total of other operating costs
`Mpg`	Miles per gallon
`TotalCost`	Total cost of the trip
`CostPerMile`	Cost per mile

A pseudocode description of the algorithm is the following:

ALGORITHM FOR TRUCK COST PROBLEM

(* Input: *Miles, Fuel, FuelCost, OperCost.*
   Purpose: This algorithm calculates miles per gallon, total cost of the trip,
             and cost per mile, given the number of miles traveled, gallons of
             fuel used, cost of the fuel, and other operating costs.
   Output: *Mpg, TotalCost, CostPerMile.* *)

1. Enter *Miles, Fuel, FuelCost,* and *OperCost.*
2. Calculate *Mpg = Miles / Fuel.*
3. Calculate *TotalCost = FuelCost + OperCost.*
4. Calculate *CostPerMile = TotalCost / Miles.*
5. Display *Mpg, TotalCost,* and *CostPerMile.*

Coding and Testing

A Pascal program implementing this algorithm and two sample runs using test data
are shown in Figure 3.4.

FIGURE 3.4 Trucking costs.

```
PROGRAM TruckCosts( input, output );
{*****************************************************************

   Input (keyboard): Miles traveled, fuel consumed, cost of fuel, and
                     other operating costs.
   Purpose:          This program calculates the total cost and miles
                     per gallon for the operation of a vehicle based
                     on the miles traveled, fuel consumed, cost per
                     gallon of fuel, and operating cost per mile.
   Output (screen):  Miles per gallon, total cost, and cost per mile.

   *****************************************************************}


VAR
    Miles : integer;       {total miles traveled}
    Fuel,                  {total gallons of fuel used}
    FuelCost,              {total cost of fuel}
    OperCost,              {total of other operating costs}
    Mpg,                   {miles per gallon}
    TotalCost,             {total cost of the trip}
    CostPerMile : real;    {cost per mile}
```

FIGURE 3.4   Trucking costs. (cont.)

```
BEGIN
    writeln( 'Enter miles traveled, gallons of fuel used,' );
    writeln( 'total cost of fuel, and total of other costs:' );
    readln( Miles, Fuel, FuelCost, OperCost );
    Mpg := Miles / Fuel;
    TotalCost := FuelCost + OperCost;
    CostPerMile := TotalCost / Miles;
    writeln( 'Miles per gallon:', Mpg:7:2 );
    writeln( 'Total cost:      $', TotalCost:7:2 );
    writeln( 'Cost per mile:  $', CostPerMile:7:2 )
END.
```

Sample runs:

```
Enter miles traveled, gallons of fuel used,
total cost of fuel, and total of other costs:
10 1 1.50 3.50
Miles per gallon:   10.00
Total cost:      $    5.00
Cost per mile:   $    0.50


Enter miles traveled, gallons of fuel used,
total cost of fuel, and total of other costs:
100 10 15 10
Miles per gallon:   10.00
Total cost:      $   25.00
Cost per mile:   $    0.25
```

3.8   PART OF THE PICTURE: Syntax and Semantics

In this chapter we introduced enough of the basic features of the Pascal language that we can write simple Pascal programs like that in the preceding section. We have described the general structure of a program as well as some of the declarations, operations, statements, and other items that make up a program. In each case we described the general form of these items and what they are intended to accomplish.

Recall from Section 1.2 that Pascal programs must be compiled before they can be executed. A **compiler** is a system program that accepts as input the stream of characters that make up the Pascal program and separates these characters into meaningful groups such as reserved words, constants, and identifiers. These groups are called *tokens,* and the compiler groups these tokens into larger structures such as arithmetic expressions and statements. If these tokens and structures are formed according to the rules of the Pascal language, the compiler will be able to recognize them and translate them into machine instructions, which can then be executed.

The rules that specify the form of a Pascal program and of each of its components are called the **syntax rules** of the language. These rules must be stated very clearly and precisely, and various methods have been used to accomplish this. Two of the most common methods are **Backus–Naur Form** (**BNF**), which uses an algebraic notation, and **syntax diagrams,** which present the rules graphically.

To illustrate, the syntax rule discussed in Section 3.2 for forming identifiers stated that an identifier consists of a letter followed by any number of letters, digits, or underscores. In BNF, this syntax rule would be stated as:

$<$identifier $> :: = \ <$ letter $> \ [<$letter $> \ | < $ digit $> | \ \_ \ ]$

The symbol $::=$ is read as "is defined as," the vertical bar ($|$) as "or," and the square brackets [and] are used to enclose items that can be repeated zero or more times. Angular brackets, $<$ and $>$, are used to enclose items like "letter" and "digit" that also must be defined:

$<$letter $> :: = \ $ a $|$ b $|$ c $|$ d $|$ e $|$ f $|$ g $|$ h $|$ i $|$ j $|$ k $|$ l $|$ m $|$ n $|$ o $|$ p $|$ q $|$ r $|$
s $|$ t $|$ u $|$ v $|$ w $|$ x $|$ y $|$ z $|$
A $|$ B $|$ C $|$ D $|$ E $|$ F $|$ G $|$ H $|$ I $|$ J $|$ K $|$ L $|$ M $|$ N $|$ O $|$ P $|$ Q $|$ R $|$ S $|$ T $|$
U $|$ V $|$ W $|$ X $|$ Y $|$ Z $|$

$<$digit $> :: = $ 0 $|$ 1 $|$ 2 $|$ 3 $|$ 4 $|$ 5 $|$ 6 $|$ 7 $|$ 8 $|$ 9

The syntax rule for identifiers can also be given by the following syntax diagram:

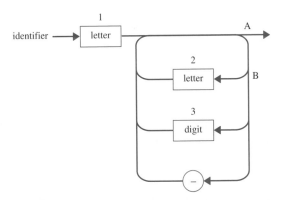

To use this diagram as a syntax rule for forming identifiers, we begin on the left and proceed to the right. Each time we pass through one of the boxes, we record a character of the specified type. At a junction in the diagram, any one of the paths may be followed. When we exit from the right, we will have formed a legal identifier. For example, the identifier **x14a** can be formed as follows: Beginning on the left and passing through the first box, we record the letter **x**. Moving to the right, at Junction A we loop back, passing through Box 3, and record the digit **1**. When we return to Junction A, we loop back again and record the digit **4** when we pass through Box 3. At Junction A we loop back one final time, but this time at Junction B we take the path through Box 2 and record the letter **a**. Finally, at Junction A we proceed to the right and exit, having formed the identifier **x14a**. (We labeled the boxes and junctions of the syntax diagram to facilitate our discussion, though normally such labels are not used.)

In a syntax diagram such as this one, the rectangular boxes indicate a language construct for which syntax rules must be specified. A syntax diagram for digits is

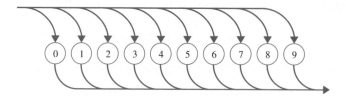

and a syntax diagram for letters would be similar. Circles and ovals indicate symbols or reserved words in Pascal that must appear exactly as shown.

The graphical representation of syntax rules afforded by syntax diagrams is easier to read than is the algebraic notation of BNF. Thus we use syntax diagrams rather than BNF to present syntax rules in this text.

A syntax diagram may also be used to specify the form of a Pascal program:

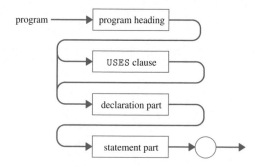

Each of the three parts can also be described by a syntax diagram. For example,

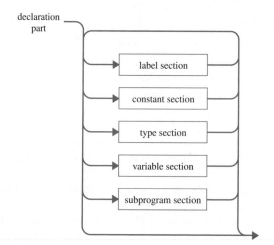

specifies the structure of the declaration part and

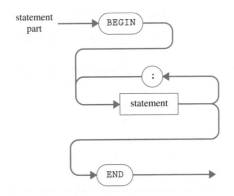

specifies the syntax of the statement part.

Each Pascal statement can also be specified by a syntax diagram. For example, a syntax diagram specifying the correct form of an assignment statement is the following:

Syntax diagrams provide a convenient mechanism for precisely defining the syntax rules for Pascal, and in subsequent chapters, we will use them to summarize the syntax of each new Pascal feature. A complete set of syntax diagrams for the various components of a Turbo Pascal program is given in Appendix C.

Note that a syntax rule specifies only the form of an item and not its meaning. For example, the preceding syntax diagram specifies only the form of an assignment statement, but additional information must be given to describe the meaning of this statement, namely, that the expression is evaluated and this value is then assigned to a variable of appropriate type; that is, it is stored in the memory location associated with the variable. The interpretation or meaning of an item is called its **semantics** and must be specified in some other way. Although formal methods and notations analogous to BNF and syntax diagrams are available for specifying semantics, they are beyond the scope of this introductory text. Instead, we will describe semantics of new items informally and illustrate them by means of examples.

Exercises

1. A "thing" is defined by the following syntax diagrams:

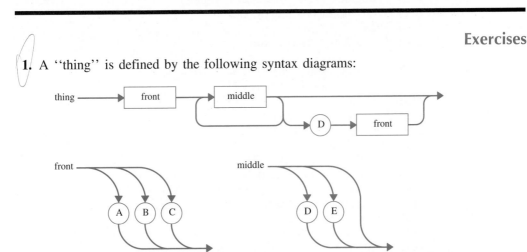

Determine which of the following are valid things:

(a) ADDDDDDA   (b) ADDA   (c) ADA   (d) ABC   (e) ADC   (f) A

2. Use BNF to state the syntax rules defined by the syntax diagrams in Exercise 1.

3. A widget is defined by:

(a) A widget is a jabber followed by a wocky followed by a slash (/).
(b) A jabber is a thunk or a thunk followed by * or a thunk followed by a wocky.
(c) A thunk is the letter T followed by one of the digits 1, 2, or 3.
(d) A wocky is a thunk or a list of thunks separated by commas.

Give a complete set of syntax rules for widgets using (i) BNF (ii) syntax diagrams.

4. Write a program heading for a program named **Sample**, which will involve both input and output, a constant section to name **1900** with the name **Year** and the string **Nat'l Science** with **FieldOfStudy**, and a variable section that declares **Number** and **Prime** to be of integer type and **Initial** to be of character type.

5. (a) Verify that the expression **round(100.0 * Cost)/100** converts the real value **Cost** to dollars, rounding to the nearest cent, using the following values of **Cost**:

(i) 12.342   (ii) 12.348   (iii) 12.345   (iv) 12.340   (v) 13.0

(b) Write an expression similar to that in part (a) that rounds a real amount **X** to the nearest tenth.
(c) Write an expression similar to that in part (a) that rounds a real amount **X** to the nearest thousandth.

6. Describe the syntax errors in the following program:

```
{ 1}    PROGRAM Error (output; input)
{ 2}        {'Example BEGIN END'}
{ 3}    VAR
{ 4}        Alpha, Beta, Rho
{ 5}        : real;
{ 6}        Add, Sub, Mult, Div : integer
{ 7}    CONST Year := 1776;
{ 8}    BEGIN
{ 9}        Mult := 3.14;
{10}        readln( Div );
{11}        ALPha := 3;
{12}        Beta = Alpha + 1;
{13}        Rho := Beta MOD 3;
{14}        writeln( 'Value is, Alpha:3:1 );
{15}        writeln( 'Gamma isn''t negative' );
{16}        writeln( Mult:3:1 );
{17}        Year := Year + 1
{18}    END
```

7. Write a program that reads two three-digit integers and then calculates and prints their product and the quotient and the remainder that result when the first is divided by the second. The output should be formatted to appear as follows:

```
   739
x   12
-----
  8868
```

```
        61 R    7
      -----
   12 ) 739
```

8. Write a program to read the lengths of the two legs of a right triangle, and to calculate and print the area of the triangle (one-half the product of the legs) and the length of the hypotenuse (square root of the sum of the squares of the legs).

9. Write a program to read values for the coefficients A, B, and C of the quadratic equation $Ax^2 + Bx + C = 0$, and then find the two roots of this equation by using the quadratic formula

$$\frac{-B \pm \sqrt{B^2 - 4AC}}{2A}$$

Execute the program with several values of A, B, and C for which the quantity $B^2 - 4AC$ is nonnegative, including $A = 4$, $B = 0$, $C = -36$; $A = 1$, $B = 5$, $C = -36$; $A = 2$, $B = 7.5$, $C = 6.25$.

10. Write a program to convert a measurement given in feet to the equivalent number of (a) yards, (b) inches, (c) centimeters, and (d) meters (1 ft = 12 in., 1 yd = 3 ft, 1 in. = 2.54 cm, 1 m = 100 cm). Read the number of feet, and print, with appropriate labels, the number of inches, number of centimeters, and number of meters.

11. Write a program to read a student's number, his or her old GPA (grade point average), and the old number of course credits (e.g., 31479, 3.25, 66) and to then print these with appropriate labels. Next, read the course credit and grade for each of four courses; for example, `Course1 = 5.0`, `Grade1 = 3.7`, `Course2 = 3.0`, `Grade2 = 4.0`, and so on. Calculate:

old # of honor points = (old # of course credits) * (old GPA)
new # of honor points = `Course1` * `Grade1` +
`Course2` * `Grade2` + · · ·
total # of new course credits = `Course1` + `Course2` + · · ·

$$\text{current GPA} = \frac{\text{\# of new honor points}}{\text{\# of new course credits}}$$

Print the current GPA with appropriate label. Finally, calculate

$$\text{cumulative GPA} = \frac{(\text{\# of old honor points}) + (\text{\# of new honor points})}{(\text{\# of old course credits}) + (\text{\# of new course credits})}$$

and print this with a label.

12. The shipping clerk at the Rinky Dooflingy Company (Exercise 13 of Section

2.6) is faced with the following problem: Dooflingies are very delicate and must be shipped in special containers. These containers are available in four sizes, huge, large, medium, and small, which can hold 50, 20, 5, and 1 dooflingy, respectively. Write a program that reads the number of dooflingies to be shipped and prints the number of huge, large, medium, and small containers needed to send the shipment in the minimum number of containers and with the minimum amount of wasted space. Use constant definitions for the number of dooflingies each type of container can hold. The output should be similar to the following:

```
Container  Number
=========  ======
  Huge       21
  Large       2
  Medium      1
  Small       3
```

Execute the program for 3, 18, 48, 78, and 10,598 dooflingies.

13. Write a program that reads the amount of a purchase and the amount received in payment (both amounts in cents) and then computes the change in dollars, half-dollars, quarters, dimes, nickels, and pennies.

14. Angles are often measured in degrees (°), minutes ('), and seconds ("). There are 360 degrees in a circle, 60 minutes in one degree, and 60 seconds in one minute. Write a program that reads two angular measurements given in degrees, minutes, and seconds and then calculates and prints their sum. Use the program to verify each of the following:

$$74°29'13'' + 105°8'16'' = 179°37'29''$$
$$7°14'55'' + 5°24'55'' = 12°39'50''$$
$$20°31'19'' + 0°31'30'' = 21°2'49''$$
$$122°17'48'' + 237°42'12'' = 0°0'0''$$

15. Write a program that reads two three-digit integers and then prints their product in the following format:

```
  749
x 381
-------
  749
 5992
2247
-------
285369
```

Execute the program with the following values: 749 and 381; −749 and 381; 749 and −381; −749 and −381; 999 and 999.

Programming Pointers

In this section we consider some aspects of program design and suggest guidelines for good programming style. We also point out some errors that may occur in writing Pascal programs.

Program Design

1. *Programs cannot be considered correct if they have not been tested.* Test all programs with data for which the results are known or can be checked by hand calculations.

2. *Programs should be readable and understandable.*

   ■ *Use meaningful identifiers.*
   For example,

   ```
   Wages := Hours * Rate
   ```

   is more meaningful than

   ```
   W := H * R
   ```

   or

   ```
   Z7 := Alpha * X
   ```

   Also, avoid "cute" identifiers, as in

   ```
   BaconBroughtHome := HoursWasted * Pittance
   ```

   ■ *Use comments to describe the purpose of a program or other key program segments.*

   However, don't clutter the program with needless comments; for example, the comment in the statement

   ```
   Counter := Counter + 1   {add 1 to counter}
   ```

   is not helpful and should not be used.

   ■ *Label all output produced by a program.* For example,

   ```
   writeln( 'Employee #', EmpNumber:5, ' Wages = $', Wages:8:2 )
   ```

   produces more informative output than does

   ```
   writeln( EmpNumber:5, Wages:8:2 )
   ```

3. *Programs should be general and flexible.* They should solve a class of problems rather than one specific problem. It should be relatively easy to modify a program to solve a related problem without changing much of the program. Using named constants instead of "magic numbers," as described in Section 3.2, is helpful in this regard.

Potential Problems

1. *Real constants must have at least one digit before and at least one digit after the decimal point.* Thus 2. and .1 are not valid real constants.

2. *String constants must be enclosed within single quotes.* If either the beginning or the ending quote is missing, an error will result. An apostrophe is represented in a character constant or a string constant as a pair of apostrophes, for example, `'isn''t'`.

3. *Single characters, not strings of several characters, are assigned to variables of type* char.

4. *The boolean constants* true *and* false *are not the same as the string constants* 'true' *and* 'false'.

5. *Parentheses within expressions must be paired.* That is, for each left parenthesis there must be exactly one matching right parenthesis that appears later in the expression.

6. *Real division is denoted by* /, *integer division by* DIV. Thus 8 / 5 = 1.6, 8 DIV 5 = 1, 8.0 / 4.0 = 2.0, but 8.0 DIV 4.0 is not a valid expression.

7. *All multiplications must be indicated by* *. For example 2 * n is valid, but 2n is not.

8. *A semicolon must appear*

- *at the end of the program heading.*
- *at the end of each constant declaration.*
- *at the end of each variable declaration.*
- *between statements.*

No semicolon is necessary after the last statement of a program. However, it is not an error if one is used; for example,

```
BEGIN
   .
   .
   .
   writeln( 'Hourly rate: $', Rate );
   writeln( 'Total Wages: $', Wages );
END.
```

The semicolon at the end of the last **writeln** statement produces an **empty statement** between this statement and the reserved word **END**.

9. *Comments are enclosed within* { *and* } *or* (* *and* *). Each beginning delimiter { or (* must have a matching end delimiter } or *), respectively. Failure to use these in pairs can produce strange results. For example, in the statement part

```
BEGIN
   {Read employee data
   readln( EmpNumber, Hours, Rate );
   {Calculate wages}
   Wages := Hours * Rate
END.
```

everything from "**Read employee data . . .** " through "**Calculate wages**," including the **readln** statement, is a single comment. No values are read for **EmpNumber**, **Hours**, and **Rate**, and so **Hours** and **Rate** are undefined when the statement **Wages := Hours * Rate** is executed.

10. *There must be a period after the reserved word* END *at the end of the program.* Failure to include it is an error.

11. *All identifiers must be declared.* Failure to declare an identifier used in a program is an error.

12. *Turbo Pascal does not distinguish between uppercase and lowercase letters except in string constants.* For example, Sum, sum, and SUM all represent the same identifier. Thus, variable declarations such as

    ```
    VAR
        Sum : integer;
        sum : real;
    ```

    produce an error, since the same identifier is declared more than once.

13. *All variables are initially undefined.* This means that it is not possible to predict the contents of the memory location associated with a variable until a value has been explicitly assigned to that variable. For example, the statement y := x + 1 will produce a "garbage" value for y if x has not previously been assigned a value, as in

    ```
    x := 0;
        .
        .
        .
    y := x + 1;
    ```

14. *All variables should be initialized in the statement part of the program.* Using typed constants to initialize variables is usually unwise, since this practice can lead to logical errors because this initialization is done at compile time, not during execution.

15. *The type of a variable and the type of its value must be the same.* Thus, entering the value 2.7 for the integer variable Counter in the statement

    ```
    readln( Counter )
    ```

    may generate an error message such as

    ```
    ERROR 106: Invalid numeric format
    ```

    Similarly, the assignment statement

    ```
    Counter := 2.7
    ```

    is also incorrect. An integer value may, however, be assigned to a real variable and is automatically converted to real type.

16. *Reserved words, identifiers, and constants, as well as the assignment operator, may not be broken at the end of a line, nor may they contain blanks (except, of course, a string constant may contain blanks).* Thus, the statements

```
Emp Number := 12 345;
writeln( 'The number of the current employee
           is ', EmpNumber:5 );
```

are not valid. If it is necessary to split a string, as in the second statement, over two lines, you can split the string into two separate strings:

```
writeln( 'The number of the current employee ',
           'is ', EmpNumber:5 );
```

or split the statement into two separate statements:

```
write( 'The number of the current employee ' );
writeln( 'is ', EmpNumber:5 );
```

17. *An equal sign* (=) *is used in constant declarations to associate an identifier with a constant. The assignment operator* (:=) *is used in assignment statements to assign a value to a variable.* These two operators are not interchangeable; do not confuse them. Also, note that := is a single operator; : and = may not be separated by a blank.

Program Style

In the examples in this text, we adopt certain stylistic guidelines for Pascal programs, and you should write your program in a similar style. In this text the following standards are used; others are described in the Programming Pointers of subsequent chapters.

1. *Put each statement of the program on a separate line.*

2. *Use uppercase and lowercase letters in a way that contributes to program readability;* for example, put reserved words in uppercase and identifiers in lowercase, capitalizing the first letter if it is user defined.

3. *Put the program heading and the reserved words* BEGIN, END, CONST, *and* VAR *on separate lines.*

4. *When a statement is continued from one line to another, indent the continuation line(s).*

5. *Each* BEGIN *and its corresponding* END *should be aligned. The statements enclosed by* BEGIN *and* END *are indented.*

6. *Indent each constant declaration and each variable declaration;* for example,

```
CONST
    TaxRate = 0.1963;
    InterestRate = 0.185

VAR
    EmpNumber : integer;
    Hours, Rate, Wages : real;
```

7.   *Insert a blank line before a* **CONST** *section, a* **VAR** *section, the beginning of the statement part of the program, and wherever appropriate in a sequence of statements to set off blocks of statements.*

8.   *Use spaces between the items in a statement to make it more readable.*

Standard Pascal

Several of the features of Turbo Pascal described in this chapter are not supported in standard Pascal. Some of these are the following:

- The only predefined numeric data types are **integer** and **real**.
- There is no predefined string type.
- Integers may not be represented in hexadecimal notation.
- The only predefined numeric constant is **maxint**.
- **ABSOLUTE, EXTERNAL, IMPLEMENTATION, INLINE, INTERFACE, INTERRUPT, SHL, SHR, STRING, UNIT, USES,** and **XOR** are not reserved words.
- Identifiers may contain only letter and digits.
- The value of **i MOD j** is the value obtained by reducing **i** modulo **j** (rather than the remainder obtained when **i** is divided by **j**). Also, **j** may not be negative in an expression of the form **i MOD j**.
- The operators **SHL, SHR,** and **XOR** are not provided, and the operators **NOT, AND,** and **OR** may not be used to perform bitwise operations on integer values.
- The arithmetic functions **FRAC, INT,** and **PI** are not provided.
- A complete program heading is required.
- Each of the sections in the declaration part may appear at most once and must appear in the following order: label section, constant section, type section, variable section, subprogram section.
- Typed constants are not supported.

STRUCTURED PROGRAMMING

A journey of a thousand miles begins with a single step.
ANCIENT PROVERB

Then Logic would take you by the throat, and force you to do it!
ACHILLES IN LEWIS CARROLL'S
What the Tortoise Said to Achilles

But what has been said once can always be repeated.
ZENO OF ELEA

CHAPTER CONTENTS

In Chapter 2 we described several software engineering techniques that assist in the design of programs that are easy to understand and whose logical flow is easy to follow. Such programs are more likely to be correct when first written than are poorly structured programs; and if they are not correct, the errors are easier to find and correct. Such programs are also easier to modify, which is especially important, since such modifications may be required long after the program was originally written and are often made by someone other than the original programmer.

In this chapter we continue our study of basic software engineering principles and describe some of the features of Pascal that facilitate the development of well-structured programs. In a **structured program,** the logical flow is governed by three basic control structures, **sequence, selection,** and **repetition.** Pascal provides several constructs that implement these control structures, and we now consider four of them: compound statements, the **IF** statement, and the **WHILE** statement. Others are described in the Chapter 7.[1]

4.1   Sequential Structure: Compound Statements; BEGIN and END

Sequential structure, as illustrated in the following diagram, refers to the execution of a sequence of statements in the order in which they appear so that each statement is executed exactly once. The arrows in this diagram, called **flow lines,** indicate the order in which the statements are executed. In the case of a sequential structure, they clearly show the "straight line" pattern of execution. All the sample programs in Chapter 3 are "straight-line" programs in which the only control used is sequential.

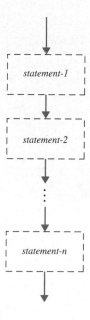

---

[1] Pascal provides one additional selection structure, the **CASE** statement, and two other repetition structures, the **FOR** statement and the **REPEAT—UNTIL** statement. Those who prefer to study all of Pascal's control structures at this point should look at Section 7.1 after considering the **IF** statement and Sections 7.2 and 7.3 after considering the **WHILE** statement.

Compound Statements

In a Pascal program, a sequential structure is implemented by a **compound statement** whose syntax diagram is

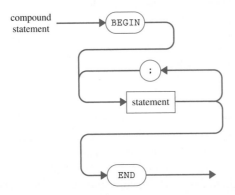

A compound statement thus consists of the reserved word **BEGIN**, followed by a sequence of statements, followed by the reserved word **END**:

Compound Statement

Form:

```
BEGIN
   statement-1;
   statement-2;
         .
         .
         .
   statement-n
END
```

where:
   BEGIN and **END** are reserved words;
   each *statement-i* is a Pascal statement.

Purpose:
Combines a sequence of statements into a single statement; *statement-1*, *statement-2*, . . . , *statement-n* are executed in order so that each statement is executed exactly once.

Note that semicolons are used to separate the statements that make up a compound statement.

Execution of the statements in a compound statement proceeds sequentially. For example, the compound statement

```
BEGIN
   write( 'Enter two numbers: ' );
   readln( Number1, Number2 );
   Sum := Number1 + Number2;
   writeln( 'Sum = ', Sum )
END
```

first displays a prompt to the user and then reads two numbers; next, it calculates their sum; and finally, it displays the result.

4.2   The Boolean Data Type

Several of the most useful Pascal statements for implementing selection and repetition structures involve boolean expressions. Consequently, before we can describe these statements, we must examine in more detail the **boolean** data type.

Recall that there are two boolean constants, **true** and **false**, and that boolean variables may have only these values. The type identifier **boolean** is used to specify the type of a boolean variable; for example,

```
VAR
     Female, Graduate, OnDeansList, OddValue : boolean;
```

declares that **Female, Graduate, OnDeansList**, and **OddValue** are boolean variables.

Three predefined boolean-valued functions are provided in Pascal. One is the function **odd,** which returns the value **true** or **false** according to whether its integer parameter is an odd or even number. For example, if the integer variable **Number** has the value 17, then the value of the boolean expression

```
odd(Number)
```

is **true**. The other two predefined boolean-valued functions, **eoln** and **eof**, are used in connection with file processing and are described in Chapter 6.

Boolean values may be displayed with **write** or **writeln** statements, as described in Section 3.5, but values for boolean variables cannot be read (except from certain types of files, as described in Chapter 15). A boolean variable may, however, be assigned a value with an assignment statement of the form

boolean-variable := boolean-expression

For example,

```
Female := true;
```

assigns the boolean constant **true** to the boolean variable **Female**, and if the value of **Number** is 17,

```
OddValue := odd(5 * Number + 1);
```

assigns **false** to **OddValue**.

Simple Boolean Expressions

Boolean expressions may be either **simple** or **compound.** Boolean constants and variables, as well as references to boolean-valued functions, are simple boolean expressions, as are expressions of the form

```
expression-1  relational-operator  expression-2
```

where *expression-1* and *expression-2* are of the same type and the **relational operator** may be any of the following:

Relational Operator	Definition
<	Is less than
>	Is greater than
=	Is equal to
<=	Is less than or equal to
>=	Is greater than or equal to
<>	Is not equal to

These relational operators may be used with any of the standard data types: `integer`, `real`, `boolean`, `char`, and `string` (as well as other ordinal types considered in Chapter 8). The following are examples of boolean expressions formed using these relational operators:

```
x < 5.2
sqr(b) >= 4*a*c
Number = 500
Initial <> 'Q'
```

For character data, the ASCII numeric codes (see Section 1.2) are used to establish an ordering for the character set. Thus

```
'A' < 'F'
```

is a true boolean expression, since the ASCII code of **A** (65) is less than the ASCII code of **F** (70). Comparison of characters and strings is discussed in more detail in Chapters 8 and 10.

For boolean values, the constant `false` is less than the constant `true`. Thus

```
false < true
true > false
```

are valid boolean expressions, and each has the value `true`.

For numeric data, the relational operators are the standard ones used to compare numbers. Thus, if **x** has the value 4.5, the expression **x < 5.2** is true. If **Number** has the value 17, the expression **Number = 20** is false.

The Effect of Roundoff Errors

When using the relational operators = and <> to compare numeric quantities, it is important to remember that *many real values cannot be stored exactly. Consequently, boolean expressions formed by comparing real quantities with = are often evaluated as false, even though these quantities are algebraically equal.* The program in Figure 4.1 demonstrates this by showing that for most real values **X**, the value of **Y** computed by

```
Y := X * (1.0 / X);
```

is not 1. In this program, the assignment statement

```
EqualsOne := (Y = 1.0);
```

calculates the value of the boolean expression **Y = 1.0** and assigns this value to the boolean variable **EqualsOne**. The value of this expression is the boolean constant **true** if the value of **Y** is equal to 1.0 and is **false** otherwise.

FIGURE 4.1   The effect of roundoff error.

```
PROGRAM RoundoffError( input, output );
{*****************************************************************

    Input (keyboard):  A real number.
    Purpose:           Show inexact representation of reals by showing
                       that for some real values X, X * (1 / X) is
                       not equal to 1.
    Output (screen):   Prompts to the user, the value of X, the value
                       of Y = X * (1.0 / X), and the value of the
                       boolean expression  Y = 1.0.

*****************************************************************}
VAR
   X,                      {real number entered}
   Y : real;               {Y = X * (1 / X)}
   EqualsOne : boolean; {indicates if value of Y is 1}

BEGIN
   write( 'Enter real # :   ' );
   readln( X );
   Y := X * (1.0 / X);
   writeln( 'X = ', X:7:5, '   Y = X*(1/X) = ', Y:7:5,
            '   1.0 - Y = ', 1.0 - Y:12 );
   EqualsOne := (Y = 1.0);    {Assigns true to EqualsOne if Y
                               is equal to one; false otherwise}
   writeln( 'Y equals 1?   ', EqualsOne )
END.
```

FIGURE 4.1   The effect of roundoff error. (cont.)

Sample runs:

```
Enter real # :  0.5
X = 0.50000   Y = X*(1/X) = 1.00000    1.0 - Y = 0.00000E+00
Y equals 1?   TRUE


Enter real # :  0.25
X = 0.25000   Y = X*(1/X) = 1.00000    1.0 - Y = 0.00000E+00
Y equals 1?   TRUE


Enter real # :  0.77117
X = 0.77117   Y = X*(1/X) = 1.00000    1.0 - Y = 9.09495E-13
Y equals 1?   FALSE


Enter real # :  6.39631
X = 6.39631   Y = X*(1/X) = 1.00000    1.0 - Y = 9.09495E-13
Y equals 1?   FALSE
```

The algebraic expression $X * (1 / X)$ is identically 1 for all nonzero values of X. However, as the preceding program demonstrates, the value of the boolean expression **X * (1.0 / X)** may not be equal to 1. The reason for this is that most real numbers cannot be stored exactly (see Section 1.2). Thus when the value **0.77117** was entered for **X**, the value was not stored exactly, with the result that the value calculated for **X * (1.0 / X)** was not exactly equal to **1.0**, even though the displayed value might suggest that it was because it was rounded to **1.00000**. Inexact representation of real values is a "fact of life" for computer programmers. Instead of using a boolean expression of the form

```
RealValue1 = RealValue2
```

to compare two real values that are subject to roundoff error, one should use

```
ABS(RealValue1 - RealValue2) < Epsilon
```

where **Epsilon** is a small real value such as **1E-7**.

Compound Boolean Expressions

Compound boolean expressions are formed by combining boolean expressions using the **boolean operators**

```
NOT
AND
OR
XOR
```

(Standard Pascal does not provide **XOR**.) These operators are defined as follows:

Boolean Operator	Boolean Expression	Definition
NOT	NOT p	*negation* of p: **NOT** p is false if p is true; **NOT** p is true if p is false.
AND	p AND q	*conjunction* of p and q: p **AND** q is true if both p and q are true; it is false otherwise.
OR	p OR q	*disjunction* of p and q: p **OR** q is true if either p or q or both are true; it is false otherwise.
XOR	p XOR q	*exclusive or* of p and q: p **XOR** q is true if either p or q is true, but not both; it is false otherwise.

These definitions are summarized by the following **truth tables,** which display all possible values for p and q and the corresponding values of the boolean expression:

p	NOT p
true	false
false	true

p	q	p AND q
true	true	true
true	false	false
false	true	false
false	false	false

p	q	p OR q
true	true	true
true	false	true
false	true	true
false	false	false

p	q	p XOR q
true	true	false
true	false	true
false	true	true
false	false	false

In a boolean expression containing several of these operators, the operations are performed in the order **NOT, AND, OR** and **XOR.** Parentheses may be used to indicate subexpressions that should be evaluated first. For example, given the boolean variables **Female, OnDeansList,** and **Graduate,** we can form boolean expressions such as

```
Female AND OnDeansList
NOT Female AND Graduate
Female AND (OnDeansList OR Graduate)
```

The first expression **Female AND OnDeansList** is true only in the case that both **Female** and **OnDeansList** are true. In the second example, the subexpression **NOT Female** is evaluated first, and this result is then combined with the value of **Graduate,** using the operator **AND.** The entire expression is therefore true only in the case that **Female** is false and **Graduate** is true. In the last example, the subexpression **OnDeansList OR Graduate** is evaluated first; the possible values it may have are displayed in the following truth table:

Female	OnDeansList	Graduate	Female AND (OnDeansList OR Graduate)
true	true	true	true
true	true	false	true
true	false	true	true
true	false	false	false
false	true	true	true
false	true	false	true
false	false	true	true
false	false	false	false

This value is then combined with the value of **Female** using the operator **AND**:

Female	OnDeansList	Graduate	Female AND (OnDeansList OR Graduate)	
true	true	true	true	true
true	true	false	true	true
true	false	true	true	true
true	false	false	false	false
false	true	true	false	true
false	true	false	false	true
false	false	true	false	true
false	false	false	false	false

As this truth table indicates, the entire expression is true only in the case that **Female** is true and either **OnDeansList** or **Graduate** (or both) is true.

The evaluation of a boolean expression that contains an assortment of arithmetic operators, boolean operators, and relational operators is carried out using the following **priority levels:**

Operator	Priority
NOT	1 highest (performed first)
/, *, DIV, MOD, AND	2
+, -, OR, XOR	3
<, >, =, <=, >=, <>	4 lowest (performed last)

As an example, consider the expression

    (N <> 0) AND (X < 1/N)

Had the parentheses not been used to enclose the two simple boolean expressions, the resulting expression

    N <> 0 AND X < 1/N

would be equivalent to the expression

    N <> (0 AND X) < 1/N

since the highest priority operator **AND** is evaluated first. This is clearly not a valid expression because the boolean operator **AND** cannot be applied to numeric operands.

In Turbo Pascal, boolean expressions of the form *p* **AND** *q* and *p* **OR** *q* are evaluated from left to right, and this allows so-called **short-circuit evaluation** in certain cases. For example, if *p* is false, the expression *p* **AND** *q* is false regardless of the value of *q*, and thus *q* need not be evaluated in this case. This means that no division-by-zero error can occur in evaluating the expression.

```
(N <> 0) AND (X < 1 / N)
```

for if **N** is 0, the first expression **N <> 0** is false, and so the second expression **X < 1 / N** is not evaluated. Similarly, if *p* is true, the expression *p* **OR** *q* is true regardless of the value of *q*, so that *q* need not be evaluated in this case. Thus no division-by-zero error will occur when evaluating the boolean expression

```
(N = 0) OR (X >= 1 / N)
```

for if **N** is 0, the first expression **N = 0** is true, and so the second expression is not evaluated.

4.3   Example: Logical Circuits

As an application of boolean expressions, consider the following logical circuit, called a **binary half-adder,** which can be used to add two binary digits.

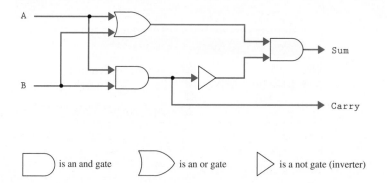

This circuit is designed to accept two inputs, **A** and **B**, and produce two outputs, **Sum** and **Carry**. It contains four basic electronic components called **gates, two AND** gates, one **OR** gate, and one **NOT** gate (also called an *inverter*). The inputs to these gates are pulses of current applied to the lines leading into the gates, and the outputs are pulses of current on the lines emanating from the gates. In the case of an **AND** gate, an output pulse is produced only when there are pulses on both input lines. An **OR** gate produces an output pulse only when there is an input pulse on at least one of the input lines. A **NOT** gate produces an output pulse only when there is no incoming pulse. If we associate the logical expression ''a pulse is present'' with each line, that is, if we interpret **true** as the presence of a pulse and **false** as the absence of a pulse, then the boolean operators **AND**, **OR**, and **NOT** can be used to model **AND**, **OR**, and **NOT** gates, respectively.

Boolean expressions can thus be used to model logical circuits. For example, the output **Sum** in the circuit for a binary half-adder can be represented by the boolean expression

(A OR B) AND NOT (A AND B)

(or equivalently, **A XOR B**) and the output **Carry** by

A AND B

The values of these boolean expressions are displayed in the following truth table:

A	B	Carry	Sum
true	true	true	false
true	false	false	true
false	true	false	true
false	false	false	false

If we now take the value **false** to represent the binary digit 0 and **true** to represent the binary digit 1, the preceding truth table can be written as

A	B	Carry	Sum
1	1	1	0
1	0	0	1
0	1	0	1
0	0	0	0

If we interpret **Sum** and **Carry** as the sum and carry bits produced when two binary digits are added as specified by the addition table

+	0	1
0	0	1
1	1	10

then we see that the circuit does in fact carry out this addition correctly.

The program in Figure 4.2 reads binary values (0 or 1) for **ANum** and **BNum** and converts them to boolean values for **A** and **B** with

0 ↔ false
1 ↔ true

by means of the assignment statements

```
A := (ANum = 1);
B := (BNum = 1);
```

The values of the two boolean expressions representing the sum and carry outputs are then assigned to boolean variables **Sum** and **Carry**, respectively, and are displayed.

FIGURE 4.2   A binary half-adder.

```
PROGRAM HalfAdder( input, output );
{*********************************************************************

   Input (keyboard): Two binary digits.
   Purpose:          Calculate the outputs from a logical circuit
                     that represents a binary half-adder.
   Output (screen):  Two boolean values representing the sum and
                     carry that result when the input values are
                     added.

*********************************************************************}

VAR
   ANum, BNum : integer;    {the two binary inputs to the circuit}
   A, B,                    {their boolean equivalents}
   Sum, Carry : boolean;    {the outputs of the circuit}

BEGIN
   write( 'Enter two binary inputs: ' );
   readln( ANum, BNum );

   {Find boolean equivalents of ANum and BNum,
        0 <-> FALSE, 1 <-> TRUE
      and calculate Sum and Carry outputs}

   A := (ANum = 1);
   B := (BNum = 1);
   Sum := (A OR B) AND NOT (A AND B);
   Carry := A AND B;

   {Display boolean equivalents of binary outputs}

   write( 'Carry = ', Carry, '  Sum = ',Sum );
   writeln( '  (FALSE = 0, TRUE = 1)' );
END.
```

FIGURE 4.2   A binary half-adder. (cont.)

Sample runs:

```
Enter two binary inputs: 0 0
Carry = FALSE   Sum = FALSE   (FALSE = 0, TRUE = 1)

Enter two binary inputs: 0 1
Carry = FALSE   Sum = TRUE    (FALSE = 0, TRUE = 1)

Enter two binary inputs: 1 0
Carry = FALSE   Sum = TRUE    (FALSE = 0, TRUE = 1)

Enter two binary inputs: 1 1
Carry = TRUE    Sum = FALSE   (FALSE = 0, TRUE = 1)
```

Exercises

1. Assuming that **a**, **b**, and **c** are boolean variables, use truth tables to display the values of the following boolean expressions for all possible values of **a**, **b**, and **c**:

   (a) a OR NOT b   **(b)** NOT (a AND b)
   (c) NOT a OR NOT B   **(d)** a AND true OR (1 + 2 = 4)
   (e) a AND (b OR c)   **(f)** (a AND b) OR (a AND c)

2. Write boolean expressions to express the following conditions:

   (a) **x** is greater than 3.
   (b) **y** is strictly between 2 and 5.
   (c) **r** is negative and **z** is positive.
   (d) Both **Alpha** and **Beta** are positive.
   (e) **Alpha** and **Beta** have the same sign (both are negative or both are positive).
   (f) $-5 < x < 5$.
   (g) **a** is less than 6 or is greater than 10.
   (h) p = q = r.
   (i) **x** is less than 3, or **y** is less than 3, but not both.

3. Given the boolean variables **a**, **b**, and **c**, write a boolean expression that is

   (a) true if and only if **a** and **b** are true and **c** is false.
   (b) true if and only if **a** is true and at least one of **b** or **c** is true.
   (c) true if and only if exactly one of **a** and **b** is true.

4. In a certain region, pesticide can be sprayed from an airplane only if the temperature is at least 70 degrees, the relative humidity is between 15 and 35 percent, and the wind speed is at most 10 miles per hour. Write a program that accepts three numbers representing temperature, relative humidity, and wind speed; assigns the value true or false to the boolean variable **OkToSpray** according to these criteria; and displays this value.

5. The Cawker City Credit Company will approve a loan application if the applicant's income is at least $25,000 or the value of his assets is at least $100,000; in addition, his total liabilities must be less than $50,000. Write a program that accepts three numbers representing income, assets, and liabilities, assigns the value **true** or **false** to the boolean variable **CreditOK** according to these criteria, and displays this value.

6. A *binary full-adder* has three inputs: the two bits **A** and **B** being added and a "carry-in" bit **CIn** (representing the carry bit that results from adding the bits to the right of **A** and **B** in two binary numbers). It can be constructed from two binary half-adders and an **OR** gate:

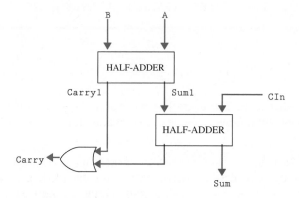

(a) Write boolean expressions for
   (i) **Sum1** and **Carry1** in terms of **A** and **B**.
   (ii) **Sum** and **Carry** in terms of **CIn**, **Sum1**, and **Carry1**.
(b) Write a program to implement this binary full-adder, and use it to verify the results shown in the following table:

A	B	CIn	Sum	Carry
0	0	0	0	0
0	0	1	1	0
0	1	0	1	0
0	1	1	0	1
1	0	0	1	0
1	0	1	0	1
1	1	0	0	1
1	1	1	1	1

7. An *adder* to calculate binary sums of two-bit numbers

$$\begin{array}{r} \text{A2 A1} \\ + \text{ B2 B1} \\ \hline \text{COut S2 S1} \end{array}$$

where **S1** and **S2** are the sum bits and **COut** is the carry-out bit, can be constructed from a binary half-adder and a binary full-adder:

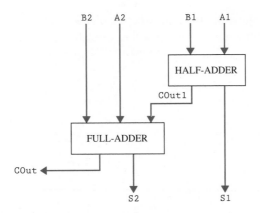

(a) Write logical expressions for
   (i) S1 and COut1 in terms of A1 and B1.
   (ii) S2 and COut in terms of A2, B2, and COut1.
(b) Write a program to implement this adder and use it to demonstrate that $00 + 00 = 000$, $01 + 00 = 001$, $01 + 01 = 010$, $10 + 01 = 011$, $10 + 10 = 100$, $11 + 10 = 101$, and $11 + 11 = 110$.

8. Write a program that reads three real numbers and assigns the appropriate value **true** or **false** to the following boolean variables:

Triangle:	**true** if the real numbers can represent lengths of the sides of a triangle, and **false** otherwise (the sum of any two of the numbers must be greater than the third).
Equilateral:	**true** if **Triangle** is **true** and the triangle is equilateral (the three sides are equal).
Isosceles:	**true** if **Triangle** is **true** and the triangle is isosceles (at least two sides are equal).
Scalene:	**true** if **Triangle** is **true** and the triangle is scalene (no two sides are equal).

The output from your program should have a format like the following:

```
Enter 3 lengths: 2, 3, 3
Triangle is:     TRUE
Equilateral is:  FALSE
Isosceles is:    TRUE
Scalene is:      FALSE
```

4.4   Selection Structure: The IF Statement

A **selection structure** makes possible the selection of one of a number of alternative actions, depending on the value of a boolean expression.

Simple IF Statement

In the simplest selection structure, a sequence of statements is executed or bypassed depending on whether a given boolean expression is true or false. This is pictured in the following diagram, where a diamond indicates the evaluation of a boolean expression, and the two possible execution paths are indicated using arrows.

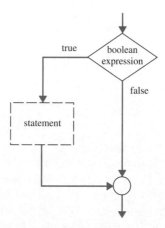

This selection structure can be implemented in Pascal using a simple form of the **IF statement:**

IF Statement (Simple Form)

Form:

> IF *boolean-expression* THEN
>   *statement*

where:
   IF and **THEN** are reserved words;
   statement is a Pascal statement.

Purpose:
If the boolean expression is true, the specified statement is executed; otherwise it is bypassed. In either case, execution continues with the next statement in the program.

For example, in the statement

```
IF Score <= 60 THEN
    writeln( 'F' );
```

the boolean expression **Score <= 60** is evaluated, and if it is true, the letter **F** is displayed. Otherwise, the **writeln** statement is bypassed. In either case, execution continues with the statement following this **IF** statement. The statement that appears in an **IF** statement may be a compound statement; for example,

```
IF Hours > 40 THEN
   BEGIN
      Overtime := Hours - 40;
      OvertimePay := 1.5 * Overtime * Rate
   END {IF};
```

Here the values of **Overtime** and **OvertimePay** are calculated only in the case that the boolean expression **Hours > 40** is true. Similarly, for the **IF** statement

```
IF (1 < X) AND (X < 3) THEN
   BEGIN
      Y := X * X;
      W := sqrt(x)
   END {IF};
```

Y is set equal to the square of **X** and **W** is set equal to the square root of **X** only in the case that **X** is strictly between 1 and 3; otherwise, these assignment statements are not executed and the values of **Y** and **W** are unchanged.

In these examples of an **IF** statement, we have attached a comment **{IF}** to the reserved word **END** that marks the end of the compound statement. As we shall see, compound statements may be used in several other Pascal constructs, and attaching such comments to each clearly indicates the structure in which it is contained.

General IF Statement

In the preceding selection structure, the selection is between (1) executing a given statement and (2) bypassing this statement. In the two-way selection pictured in the following diagram, the selection is between (1) executing one statement and (2) executing another statement:

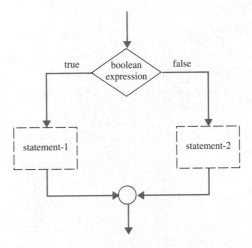

This selection structure is implemented in Pascal by an **IF** statement that allows the programmer not only to specify the statement selected for execution when the boolean expression is true but also to indicate an alternative statement for

execution when it is false. This **IF** statement (together with the earlier form) is specified by the following syntax diagram:

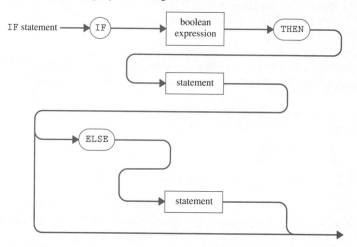

As the diagram indicates, an **IF** statement may contain an optional else part and thus may have two forms:

IF Statement (General Form)

Form:

```
IF boolean-expression THEN
    statement
```

or

```
IF boolean-expression THEN
    statement-1
ELSE
    statement-2
```

where:
  IF, **THEN**, and **ELSE** are reserved words;
  statement, *statement-1*, and *statement-2* are
    Pascal statements.

Purpose:
In the first form, if the boolean expression is true, the specified statement is executed; otherwise it is bypassed, and execution continues with the next statement in the program.

In the second form, if the boolean expression is true, *statement-1* is executed and *statement-2* is bypassed; otherwise *statement-1* is bypassed and *statement-2* is executed. In either case, execution continues with the next statement in the program.

Example: Pollution Index Problem

A problem that requires this two-alternative selection structure is the pollution index problem considered in Chapter 2. In this problem, a pollution index is to be calculated, and if this index is less than some cutoff value, a message indicating a safe condition must be displayed; if not, a message indicating a hazardous condition must be displayed. This selection was indicated in the algorithm for solving this problem (Section 2.2) by

> If *Index* < *Cutoff* then
>   Display 'Safe condition'
> Else
>   Display 'Hazardous condition'

and is implemented in the Pascal program in Figure 4.3 by the following Pascal statement:

```
IF Index < Cutoff THEN
   writeln( 'Safe condition' )
ELSE
   writeln( 'Hazardous condition' );
```

FIGURE 4.3 Pollution index.

```
PROGRAM PollutionIndex( input, output );
{*****************************************************************

   Input (keyboard): Three pollution levels and a cutoff value.
   Purpose:          Read 3 pollution levels, calculate a
                     pollution index as their average, and then
                     display an appropriate air-quality message.
   Output (screen):  The pollution index and a "safe condition"
                     message if this index is less than the cutoff
                     value, otherwise a "hazardous condition"
                     message.

*****************************************************************}

CONST
   Cutoff = 50;              {bottom line for a safe condition}

VAR
   Level1, Level2, Level3,   {three pollution readings}
   Index : integer;          {pollution index}
```

FIGURE 4.3   Pollution index. (cont.)

```
BEGIN
   write( 'Enter 3 pollution readings: ' );
   readln( Level1, Level2, Level3 );
   Index := (Level1 + Level2 + Level3) DIV 3;
   writeln( 'Pollution index = ', Index );
   IF Index < Cutoff THEN
      writeln( 'Safe condition' )
   ELSE
      writeln( 'Hazardous condition' )
END.
```

Sample runs:

```
Enter 3 pollution readings: 55 39 48
Pollution index = 47
Safe condition
```

```
Enter 3 pollution readings: 68 49 57
Pollution index = 58
Hazardous condition
```

Example: Grade Calculation—Version 1

As another illustration of using an **IF** statement to implement a two-alternative selection structure, suppose that students in a computer programming class will receive a passing grade if their final course average is 60 or above and will fail otherwise. The final average is computed as a weighted average of the homework average, the average on tests, and the exam score:

$$Average = 0.2 * Homework + 0.5 * Tests + 0.3 * Exam$$

A program is to be written to determine the pass/fail grade for a given student in this class. An algorithm for calculating grades is as follows:

GRADE ASSIGNMENT ALGORITHM—VERSION 1

(* Input: A student's homework average, test average, and final exam score.

Purpose: Determine the pass/fail *Grade* for a student using a weighted *Average* of the student's *Homework* average, average on *Tests*, and *Exam* score.

Output: The weighted average and pass/fail grade. *)

1. Read *Homework, Tests,* and *Exam.*
2. Calculate

$$Average = 0.2 * Homework + 0.5 * Tests + 0.3 * Exam.$$

3. If *Average* ≥ 60 then
    Set *Grade* = 'P'
   Else
    Set *Grade* = 'F'.
4. Display *Average* and *Grade*.

A Pascal program to implement this algorithm is given in Figure 4.4. An **IF** statement is used to implement the selection structure that makes the appropriate grade assignment, depending on the boolean expression *Average* ≥ 60. Note the use of the four constant identifiers *HWWeight, TestWeight, ExamWeight,* and *PassFailLine* in place of the constants 0.2, 0.5, 0.3, and 60. These identifiers are defined in the constant section and then used throughout the program. If the program has to be modified to assign grades when weighting factors are different or the pass/fail line changes, we need only change the definitions of these constant identifiers; the statement part of the program need not be modified.

 FIGURE 4.4 Grade assignment—version 1.

```pascal
PROGRAM GradeAssignment1( input, output );
{*************************************************************

    Input (keyboard): Three real numbers representing a student's
                      homework average, average on tests, and a final
                      exam score.
    Purpose:          Compute a final course average using the
                      homework average, average on tests, and final
                      exam score;  a pass or fail grade is then assigned.
    Output (screen):  User prompt, the weighted average, and the
                      pass/failgrade.

    *************************************************************}

CONST
    HWWeight = 0.2;         {weight factors for homework,}
    TestWeight = 0.5;       {    tests,}
    ExamWeight = 0.3;       {    and the exam}
    PassFailLine = 60.0;    {pass/fail line}

VAR
    Homework, Tests, Exam,  {homework, test, and exam averages}
    Average : real;         {final course average}
    Grade : char;           {grade assigned (P or F)}
```

FIGURE 4.4 Grade assignment—version 1. (cont.)

```
BEGIN
   write( 'Enter homework, test and exam scores: ' );
   readln( Homework, Tests, Exam );
   Average := HWWeight * Homework + TestWeight * Tests
           + ExamWeight * Exam;
   IF Average >= PassFailLine THEN
      Grade := 'P'
   ELSE
      Grade := 'F';
   writeln( 'Average = ', Average:5:1, ' Grade = ', Grade )
END.
```

Sample runs:

```
Enter homework, test and exam scores: 60 60 60
Average =   60.0 Grade = P


Enter homework, test and exam scores: 60 70 80
Average =   71.0 Grade = P


Enter homework, test and exam scores: 55.2 50.7 45.5
Average =   50.0 Grade = F


Enter homework, test and exam scores: 99.5 58.3 75
Average =   71.6 Grade = P
```

Example: Grade Calculation—Version 2

The statements in an **IF** statement may themselves contain other **IF** statements. In this case, one **IF** statement is said to be **nested** within the other **IF** statement. To illustrate, suppose that in the preceding example, students who pass are awarded special honors if their average is 80 or above. The following algorithm solves this problem:

GRADE ASSIGNMENT ALGORITHM—VERSION 2

(* Input: A student's homework average, test average, and final exam score.

   Purpose: Determine the pass/fail *Grade* for a student using a weighted *Average* of the student's *Homework* average, average on *Tests,* and *Exam* score. Passing students are awarded *Honors* if their average is sufficiently high.

   Output: The weighted average, honors indicator, and pass/fail grade. *)

1. Read *Homework, Tests,* and *Exam.*
2. Calculate

   Average = 0.2 * *Homework* + 0.5 * *Tests* + 0.3 * *Exam.*

3. Set *Honors* equal to a blank.
4. If *Average* ≥ 60 then
   a. Set *Grade* = 'P'
   b. If *Average* ≥ 80 then
        Set *Honors* equal to 'H'.
   Else
      Set *Grade* = 'F'.
5. Display *Average* and *Grade.*

The pseudocode description of the algorithm clearly shows the selection structure for determining honors designation based on the condition *Average* ≥ 80 nested within the larger selection structure based on the condition *Average* ≥ 60. This nested selection structure is implemented in the Pascal program in Figure 4.5 by nested **IF** statements.

FIGURE 4.5 Grade assignment—version 2.

```
PROGRAM GradeAssignment2( input, output );
{*********************************************************************

    Input (keyboard): Three real numbers representing a student's
                      homework average, average on tests, and a final
                      exam score.
    Purpose:          Compute a final course average using the
                      homework average, average on tests, and final
                      exam score;  a pass or fail grade is then
                      assigned.  Passing students receive an honors
                      grade if their averages are sufficiently high.
    Output (screen):  User prompt, the weighted average, an honors
                      indicator, and the pass/fail grade.


    *********************************************************************}

CONST
    HWWeight = 0.2;          {weight factors for homework,}
    TestWeight = 0.5;        {    tests,}
    ExamWeight = 0.3;        {    and the exam}
    PassFailLine = 60.0;     {pass/fail line}
    HonorsLine = 80.0;       {honors/no honors line}

VAR
    Homework, Tests, Exam,   {homework, test, and exam averages}
    Average : real;          {final course average}
    Grade,                   {grade assigned (P or F)}
    Honors : char;           {honors designation (H or blank)}
```

FIGURE 4.5   Grade assignment—version 2. (cont.)

```
BEGIN
    write( 'Enter homework, test and exam scores: ' );
    readln( Homework, Tests, Exam );
    Average := HWWeight * Homework + TestWeight * Tests
            + ExamWeight * Exam;
    Honors := ' ';
    IF Average >= PassFailLine THEN
        BEGIN
            Grade := 'P';
            IF Average >= HonorsLine THEN
                Honors := 'H'
        END {IF}
    ELSE
        Grade := 'F';
    writeln( 'Average = ', Average:5:1, '   Grade = ', Honors, Grade )
END.
```

Sample runs:

```
Enter homework, test and exam scores: 60 60 60
Average =   60.0   Grade =   P


Enter homework, test and exam scores: 60 70 80
Average =   71.0   Grade =   P


Enter homework, test and exam scores: 55.2 50.7 45.5
Average =   50.0   Grade =   F


Enter homework, test and exam scores: 99 98 97
Average =   97.9   Grade = HP
```

In a nested **IF** *statement, each* **ELSE** *clause is matched with the nearest preceding unmatched* **IF**. For example, in the statement

```
IF x > 0 THEN
    IF y > 0 THEN
        z := sqrt(x) + sqrt(y)
    ELSE
        readln( z );
```

the **ELSE** clause is associated with the **IF** statement containing the boolean expression **y > 0**. Consequently, the **readln** statement is executed only in the case that **x** is positive and **y** is nonpositive. If we wish to associate this **ELSE** clause with the outer **IF** statement, we can write

```
IF x > 0 THEN
    BEGIN
        IF y > 0 THEN
            z := sqrt(x) + sqrt(y)
    END {IF x}
ELSE
    readln( z );
```

Here the **readln** statement is executed whenever **x** is nonpositive.

Note that in these examples, each **ELSE** clause is aligned with the corresponding **IF**. This alignment emphasizes the relationship between each **IF** and its associated **ELSE**.

IF—ELSE IF Construct

The selection structures considered thus far involve selecting one of two alternatives. It is also possible to use the **IF** statement to design selection structures that contain more than two alternatives. These **multialternative selection structures** can be constructed using nested **IF** statements, but such compound **IF** statements may become quite complex, and the correspondence between **IF**s and **ELSE**s may not be clear if the statements are not indented properly. A better format that clarifies the correspondence between **IF**s and **ELSE**s and also emphasizes that the statement implements a multialternative selection structure is an **IF—ELSE IF** construct:

IF—ELSE IF Construct

Form:

```
IF boolean-expression-1 THEN
    statement-1
ELSE IF boolean-expression-2 THEN
    statement-2
            .
            .
            .
    ELSE
        statement-n
```

where:
  IF, THEN, and **ELSE** are reserved words;
  statement-1, statement-2, . . . ,
    statement-n are Pascal statements;
  and the **ELSE** clause is optional.

Purpose:
When an **IF—ELSE IF** construct is executed, the boolean expressions are evaluated to determine the first expression that is true. The associated state-

ment is executed, and execution then continues with the statement following the construct. If none of the boolean expressions is true, the statement associated with the **ELSE** clause is executed, and execution then continues with the statement following the construct; if the **ELSE** part is omitted, execution "falls through" to the next statement of the program. This **IF–ELSE IF** construct therefore implements an *n*-way selection structure in which exactly one of *statement-1*, *statement-2*, . . . , *statement-n* is executed.

Example: Grade Calculation—Version 3

As an illustration of multialternative selection, suppose that the grade assignment program in Figure 4.4 is to be modified so that letter grades are assigned as indicated in the following table:

Average	Letter Grade
Average ≥ 90	A
$80 \leq$ average < 90	B
$70 \leq$ average < 80	C
$60 \leq$ average < 70	D
Average < 60	F

The algorithm for solving this problem is an easy modification of that given earlier:

GRADE ASSIGNMENT ALGORITHM—VERSION 3

(* Input: A student's homework average, test average, and final exam score.

Purpose: Determine a letter *Grade* for a student using a weighted *Average* of the student's *Homework* average, average on *Tests,* and *Exam* score.

Output: The weighted average and the letter grade. *)

1. Read *Homework, Tests,* and *Exam.*
2. Calculate

$$Average = 0.2 * Homework + 0.5 * Tests + 0.3 * Exam.$$

3. If *Average* ≥90 then
    Set *Grade* = 'A'
  Else if *Average* ≥80 then
    Set *Grade* = 'B'
  Else if *Average* ≥70 then
    Set *Grade* = 'C'
  Else if *Average* ≥60 then
    Set *Grade* = 'D'
  Else
    Set *Grade* = 'F'.
4. Display *Average* and *Grade*.

The program in Figure 4.6 implements this algorithm, using the following **IF** statement to implement the five-way selection structure in Step 3:

```
IF Average >= ABLine THEN
    Grade := 'A'
ELSE IF Average >= BCLine THEN
    Grade := 'B'
ELSE IF Average >= CDLine THEN
    Grade := 'C'
ELSE IF Average >= DFLine THEN
    Grade := 'D'
ELSE
    Grade := 'F';
```

 FIGURE 4.6 Grade assignment—version 3.

```
PROGRAM GradeAssignment3( input, output );
{*****************************************************************
```

Input (keyboard):	Three real numbers representing a student's homework average, average on tests, and a final exam score.
Purpose:	Compute a final course average using the homework average, average on tests, and final exam score; a letter grade is then assigned.
Output (screen):	User prompt, the weighted average, and the letter grade.

```
*****************************************************************}
CONST
    HWWeight = 0.2;        {weight factors for homework,}
    TestWeight = 0.5;      {    tests,}
    ExamWeight = 0.3;      {    and the exam}
    ABLine = 90.0;         {A/B line}
    BCLine = 80.0;         {B/C line}
    CDLine = 70.0;         {C/D line}
    DFLine = 60.0;         {D/F line}
```

FIGURE 4.6   Grade assignment—version 3. (cont.)

```
VAR
    Homework, Tests, Exam,    {homework, test, and exam averages}
    Average : real;           {final course average}
    Grade : char;             {grade assigned (A, B, C, D or F)}

BEGIN
    write( 'Enter homework, test and exam scores: ' );
    readln( Homework, Tests, Exam );
    Average := HWWeight * Homework + TestWeight * Tests
             + ExamWeight * Exam;
    IF Average >= ABLine THEN
        Grade := 'A'
    ELSE IF Average >= BCLine THEN
        Grade := 'B'
    ELSE IF Average >= CDLine THEN
        Grade := 'C'
    ELSE IF Average >= DFLine THEN
        Grade := 'D'
    ELSE
        Grade := 'F';
    writeln( 'Average = ', Average:5:1, ' Grade = ', Grade )
END.
```

Sample runs:

```
Enter homework, test and exam scores: 100 100 100
Average = 100.0 Grade = A


Enter homework, test and exam scores: 30 40 50
Average =  41.0 Grade = F


Enter homework, test and exam scores: 56.2 62.7 66.5
Average =  62.5 Grade = D


Enter homework, test and exam scores: 87.5 91.3 80
Average =  87.2 Grade = B
```

Exercises

1. Write a Pascal statement for each of the following:

   (a) If `TaxCode` is `'T'`, increase `Price` by adding `TaxRate` percentage of `Price` to it.

   (b) If `Code` has the value 1, read values for x and y, and calculate and print the sum of x and y.

   (c) If A is strictly between 0 and 5, set B equal to $1/A^2$; otherwise set B equal to A^2.

(d) Assign **true** to the boolean variable **LeapYear** if the integer variable **Year** is the number of a leap year. (A leap year is a multiple of 4, and if it is a multiple of 100, it must also be a multiple of 400.)

(e) Assign the value **Cost** corresponding to the value of **Distance** given in the following table:

Distance	Cost
0 through 100	5.00
More than 100 but not more than 500	8.00
More than 500 but less than 1000	10.00
1000 or more	12.00

(f) Display the number of days in the month corresponding to the value of **Month** (1, 2, . . . , 12). Use part (d) to determine the number of days if the value of **Month** is 2, assuming that a value has been assigned to **Year**.

2. Describe the output produced by the following poorly indented program segment:

```
Number := 4;
Alpha := -1.0;
IF Number > 0 THEN
   IF Alpha > 0 THEN
      writeln( 'First writeln' )
ELSE
   writeln( 'Second writeln' );
writeln( 'Third writeln' ) ;
```

3. A student used the following **IF** statement in a program:

```
IF Honors = true THEN
   IF Awards = true THEN
      GoodStudent := true
   ELSE
      GoodStudent := false
ELSE IF Honors = false THEN
   GoodStudent := false;
```

(a) Write a simpler **IF** statement that is equivalent to this one.

(b) Write a single assignment statement that is equivalent to this **IF** statement.

4. Write a program to check a quadratic equation of the form $Ax^2 + Bx + C = 0$ to see if it has real roots, and if so, find these roots. If there are no real roots, display an appropriate message (see Exercise 12 of Section 2.6). Execute the program with the following values for A, B, and C: 1, −5, 6; 1 −2, 1; 1, 0, 4; 1, 1, 1; 2, 1, −3.

5. A certain city classifies a pollution index less than 35 as "pleasant," 35 through 60 as "unpleasant," and above 60 as "hazardous." Write a program that reads a number representing a pollution index and displays the appropriate classification of it. Execute the program with the following data: 20, 45, 75, 35, 60.

6. Write a program that reads an employee's number, hours worked, and hourly rate and calculates his or her wages. All hours over 40 are paid at 1.5 times the regular hourly rate. Execute the program with the following values for employee number, hours worked, and hourly rate: 123, 38, 7.50; 175, 39.5, 7.85; 223, 40, 9.25; 375, 44.5, 8.35.

7. Write a wage calculation program like that in Exercise 6, but with the following modification: If an employee's number is greater than or equal to 1000, the program should read an annual salary and calculate the employee's weekly pay as this salary divided by 52. If the employee's number is less than 1000, wages are calculated on an hourly basis, as described in Exercise 6. Execute the program with the data in Exercise 6 and the following data: 1217, 25500; 1343, 31775.

8. Suppose that charges by a gas company are based on consumption according to the following table:

Gas Used	Rate
First 70 cubic meters	$5.00 minimum cost
Next 100 cubic meters	5.0¢ per cubic meter
Next 230 cubic meters	2.5¢ per cubic meter
Above 400 cubic meters	1.5¢ per cubic meter

Write a program in which the meter reading for the previous month and the current meter reading are entered, each a four-digit number and each representing cubic meters, and that then calculates the amount of the bill. *Note:* The current reading may be less than the previous one; for example, the previous reading may have been 9897, and the current one is 0103. Execute the program with the following meter readings: 3450, 3495; 8810, 8900; 9950, 0190; 1275, 1982; 9872, 0444.

4.5 Repetition Structure: The WHILE Statement

The third basic control structure is a **repetition structure** or **loop** that makes possible repeated execution of one or more statements. Pascal provides three statements that implement repetition structures: the **WHILE** statement, the **FOR** statement, and the **REPEAT—UNTIL** statement. In this chapter we consider the first of these statements, the **WHILE** statement. (The **FOR** and **REPEAT—UNTIL** statements are described in Chapter 7.) This statement can be used to implement a repetition structure called a **while loop** in which repetition is controlled by a boolean expression and continues while this expression remains true, terminating when it becomes false.[2]

---

[2] Turbo Pascal 7.0 provides a **Break** procedure that can be used to terminate repetition of loops and a **Continue** procedure to continue with the next iteration of a loop. See Section H.1 of Appendix H.

The syntax diagram for a **WHILE statement** is

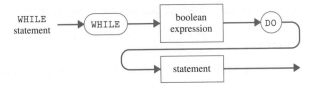

The form of a **WHILE** statement and its semantics can be specified as follows:

WHILE Statement

Form:

    WHILE *boolean-expression* DO
        statement

where:
   WHILE and **DO** are reserved words;
   statement is a Pascal statement.

Purpose:
The boolean expression is evaluated, and if it is true, the specified statement, called the **body** of the loop, is executed. The boolean expression is then reevaluated, and if it is still true, this statement is executed again. This process of evaluating the boolean expression and executing the specified statement is repeated as long as the boolean expression is true. When it becomes false, repetition is terminated.

The preceding description of how a **WHILE** statement functions can be summarized graphically as

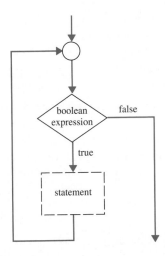

Note that repeated execution of the body of the loop must eventually cause the value of the boolean expression to become false, since otherwise repetition would continue *ad infinitum* (except as noted in footnote 2 on page 150).

Example: Summation

To illustrate the use of a while loop, consider the following problem:

> For a given value of *Limit,* what is the smallest positive *Number* for which the sum
>
> $$1 + 2 + \cdots + Number$$
>
> is greater than *Limit,* and what is the value of this sum?

To solve this problem we use three variables:

Number: A positive integer added to the sum.
Sum: $1 + 2 + \cdots + Number.$
Limit: The specified limit for the sum.

We begin with *Number* and *Sum* initialized to 0. If this value of *Sum* exceeds the value of *Limit,* the problem is solved. Otherwise we increment *Number* by 1, add it to *Sum,* and then check to see if this value of *Sum* exceeds *Limit.* Once again, if it does, the problem is solved; and if not, *Number* must again be incremented and added to *Sum.* This process is continued as long as the value of *Sum* is less than or equal to *Limit.* Eventually the value of *Sum* will exceed *Limit* and the problem is solved. This leads to the following algorithm:

ALGORITHM FOR SUMMATION PROBLEM

(* Input: An integer *Limit.*
   Purpose: Find the smallest positive integer *Number* for which the sum
             $1 + 2 + \cdots + Number$ is greater than *Limit.*
   Output: *Number* and *Sum.* *)

1. Enter *Limit.*
2. Set *Number* equal to 0.
3. Set *Sum* equal to 0.
4. While *Sum* $\leq$ *Limit* do the following:
       a. Increment *Number* by 1.
       b. Add *Number* to *Sum.*
5. Display *Number* and *Sum.*

In this algorithm, the body of the while loop in Step 4 consists of two statements, but in Pascal, a **WHILE** statement may contain only one statement. Consequently, we must combine the two statements into one compound statement:

```
WHILE Sum <= Limit DO
   BEGIN
      Number := Number + 1;
      Sum := Sum + Number
   END {WHILE};
```

The program in Figure 4.7 uses this **WHILE** statement in implementing this algorithm.

 FIGURE 4.7 Calculating sums.

```
PROGRAM Summation( input, output );
{*****************************************************************************

    Input (keyboard):   An integer Limit.
    Purpose:            Find the smallest positive integer Number for
                        which the sum
                                    1 + 2 + ... + Number
                        is greater than the value of Limit.
    Output (screen):    User prompt, number, and the value of this Sum.


*****************************************************************************}

VAR
    Number,             {positive integer added to the sum}
    Sum,                {1 + 2 + ... + Number}
    Limit : integer;    {limit for sum}

BEGIN
    write( 'Enter value that 1 + 2 + ... + ? is to exceed: ' );
    readln( Limit );
    Number := 0;
    Sum := 0;
    WHILE Sum <= Limit DO
        BEGIN
            Number := Number + 1;
            Sum := Sum + Number
        END {WHILE};
    writeln( '1 + ... + ', Number:1, ' = ', Sum:1, ' > ', Limit:1 )
END.
```

Sample runs:

```
Enter value that 1 + 2 + ... + ? is to exceed: 10
1 + ... + 5 = 15 > 10


Enter value that 1 + 2 + ... + ? is to exceed: 10000
1 + ... + 141 = 10011 > 10000


Enter value that 1 + 2 + ... + ? is to exceed: -1
1 + ... + 0 = 0 > -1
```

In the first sample run of Figure 4.7 in which the value 10 is entered for `Limit`, the body of the while loop is executed five times, as indicated in the following table, which traces its execution:

Number	Sum	Sum <= Limit	Action
0	0	true	Execute body of while loop
1	1	true	Execute body of while loop
2	3	true	Execute body of while loop
3	6	true	Execute body of while loop
4	10	true	Execute body of while loop
5	15	false	Terminate repetition

A similar trace table for the second sample run would show that the loop body is executed 141 times. The third sample run demonstrates that the boolean expression in a **WHILE** statement is evaluated before repetition begins. When the value **-1** is entered for `Limit`, the **WHILE** statement causes an immediate transfer of control to the `writeln` statement that displays the value **0** for both **Number** and **Sum**.

Sentinel-Controlled While Loops

One important use of while loops is in reading and processing a set of data values. Usually the number of data values is not known in advance, and so some method must be devised to determine when all of the data values have been read. One commonly used method is to use a **sentinel-controlled while loop** in which we append to the data an artificial data value called an **end-of-data flag** or **sentinel,** which is distinct from any possible data item. As each data item is read, it is checked to determine whether it is this end-of-data flag. If it is not, the value is processed. When the end-of-data flag is read, it must not be processed as a regular data value, but, rather, should serve only to terminate repetition.

This scheme can be implemented by using a sentinel-controlled while loop of the following form[3]:

1. Read the first data value.
2. While the data value is not the data sentinel, do the following:
    a. Process the data value.
    b. Read the next data value.

Note the two input instructions, one before the while loop and one at the bottom of the while loop. The first data value must be read before the while loop is entered for the first time, since otherwise the condition that controls repetition cannot be checked. Within the while loop, after the current data value has been processed, a new value must be read before the next pass through the loop. This standard technique for reading and processing data values is used in the following example.

Example: Calculating the Mean Time to Failure

Consider again Problem 3 of Chapter 2 in which failure times of some device are to be read and counted and the mean time to failure is to be calculated. Since the

---

[3] An alternative sentinel-controlled loop that uses the **Break** procedure of Turbo Pascal 7.0 to terminate repetition is described in Section H.1 of Appendix H.

number of failure times is not known in advance, a sentinel-controlled while loop is an appropriate repetition structure to use. This technique for reading and processing data values was used in the algorithm given in Section 2.2 for solving this problem:

ALGORITHM TO CALCULATE MEAN TIME TO FAILURE

(* Input: A collection of failure times.
Purpose: Algorithm to read failure times, count them, and find the mean time to failure (*MeanFailTime*). *FailTime* represents the current failure time entered, *NumTimes* is the number of failure times, and *Sum* is their sum. Values are read until an end-of-data flag is encountered.
Output: *MeanFailTime* and *NumTimes*. *)

1. Initialize *NumTimes* to 0 and *Sum* to 0.0.
2. Enter the first value for *FailTime*.
3. While *FailTime* is not the end-of-data flag, do the following:
   a. Increment *NumTimes* by 1.
   b. Add *FailTime* to *Sum*.
   c. Enter next value for *FailTime*.
4. If *NumTimes* ≠ 0 then
   a. Calculate *MeanFailTime* = *Sum* / *NumTimes*.
   b. Display *MeanFailTime* and *NumTimes*.
   Else
       Display a 'No Data' message.

Here Statements 3a, 3b, and 3c are to be repeated as long as the value of *FailTime* is not a data flag entered by the user to signal the end of data. When it is, so that the value of the boolean expression "*FailTime* is not the end-of-data flag" becomes false, repetition terminates, and execution continues with Statement 4. In the Pascal program in Figure 4.8 that implements this algorithm, a negative fail time is used to signal the end of data, and the repetition structure in Step 3 is implemented as a **WHILE** statement controlled by the boolean expression `FailTime >= 0`.

 FIGURE 4.8 Mean time to failure.

```
PROGRAM CalculateMeanFailTime( input, output );
{*************************************************************************

    Input (keyboard): A list of fail times.
    Purpose:          Read a list of fail times, count them, and
                      calculate the mean time to failure.  Any
                      negative number serves to signal the end of data.
    Output (screen):  User prompts, number of fail times read, and
                      their mean or a message indicating that no
                      failure times were entered.


*************************************************************************}
```

FIGURE 4.8   Mean time to failure. (cont.)

```
VAR
    NumTimes : integer;        {number of scores}
    Sum,                       {sum of the scores}
    FailTime,                  {current score being processed}
    MeanFailTime : real;       {mean of the scores}

BEGIN
    writeln( '*** Enter a negative fail time to signal the end of input.' );
    writeln;
    Sum := 0;
    NumTimes := 0;
    write( 'Fail Time:  ' );
    readln( FailTime );
    WHILE FailTime >= 0 DO
        BEGIN
            NumTimes := NumTimes + 1;
            Sum := Sum + FailTime;
            write( 'Fail Time:  ' );
            readln( FailTime )
        END {WHILE};
    writeln;
    IF NumTimes > 0 THEN
        BEGIN
            MeanFailTime := Sum / NumTimes;
            writeln( NumTimes:1, ' failure times with mean = ',
                     MeanFailTime:5:2 )
        END {IF}
    ELSE
        writeln( 'No fail times were entered' )
END.
```

Sample run:

```
*** Enter a negative fail time to signal the end of input.

Fail Time:   127
Fail Time:   123.5
Fail Time:   155.4
Fail Time:   99
Fail Time:   117.3
Fail Time:   201.5
Fail Time:   -999

6 failure times with mean = 137.28
```

4.6   Program Testing and Debugging Techniques: An Example

In Section 2.4 we noted that three types of errors may occur when developing a program to solve a problem: syntax or compile-time errors, run-time errors, and logical errors. **Syntax errors,** such as incorrect punctuation, unbalanced parentheses, and misspelled key words, are detected during the program's compilation, and an appropriate error message is usually displayed. **Run-time errors,** such as division by zero and integer overflow, are detected during the program's execution, and again, a suitable error message is often displayed. These two types of errors are, for the most part, relatively easy to correct, since the system error messages often indicate the type of error and where it occurred. **Logical errors,** on the other hand, are usually more difficult to detect, since they arise in the design of the algorithm or in coding the algorithm as a program, and in most cases, no error messages are displayed to assist the programmer in identifying such errors.

The Programming Pointers at the ends of the chapters of this book include warnings about some of the more common errors. As programs become increasingly complex, however, the logical errors that occur may be more subtle and consequently more difficult to identify and correct. In this section we consider a program that contains logical errors and describe techniques that are useful in detecting them.

An Example

Suppose that as a programming exercise, students were asked to write a program to read a list of positive integers representing employee salaries in thousands of dollars and determine the salary range, that is, the difference between the largest salary and the smallest. The following program heading and declaration part were given, and the students were asked to write the statement part of the program:

```
PROGRAM SalaryRange( input, output );
{***************************************************************

    Input (keyboard):  A list of salaries in thousands of dollars.
    Purpose:           Read the list of salaries and determine the
                       salary range.
                       Note:  A zero value for the salary is
                       used to signal the end of data.
    Output (screen):   User prompts, labels, and the salary range.


 ***************************************************************}

VAR
    Salary,                {the current salary being processed}
    MaxSalary,             {largest salary read so far}
    MinSalary : integer;   {smallest salary read so far}
```

One attempted solution was the following (where the lines have been numbered for easy reference):

```
{1}    BEGIN
{2}        writeln( 'Enter salaries in thousands of dollars (0 to stop).' );
{3}        MaxSalary := 0;            {initialize maximum salary very small}
{4}        MinSalary := maxint;      {and minimum salary very large}
{5}        WHILE Salary <> 0 DO
```

```
{6}          BEGIN
{7}             write( 'Enter salary: ' );
{8}             readln( Salary );
{9}             IF Salary > MaxSalary THEN
{10}               MaxSalary := Salary
{11}            ELSE IF Salary < MinSalary THEN
{12}               MinSalary := Salary
{13}         END {WHILE};
{14}     writeln;
{15}     writeln( 'Salary range = ', MaxSalary - MinSalary : 1, ' thousand' )
{16} END.
```

Execution of the program produced

```
Enter salaries in thousands of dollars (0 to stop).
Salary range = 32767 thousand
```

Since the user was not allowed to enter any data, it is clear that the body of the while loop was not entered. This suggests that the boolean expression Salary <> 0 that controls repetition was initially false, thus causing immediate termination.

This is in fact what happened. Since the student did not ensure that Salary had been assigned a value before the WHILE statement in Line 5 was encountered, Salary had an undefined value when the boolean expression Salary <> 0 was evaluated. (The student did not heed the warning in Potential Problem 11 in the Programming Pointers of Chapter 3!) The particular system in which the program was executed used a value of 0 for Salary, making this boolean expression false and causing the while loop to terminate immediately.

To remedy the problem, the student inserted the statement Salary := 1 ahead of the WHILE statement to force an entrance into the while loop:

```
{1}  BEGIN
{2}     writeln( 'Enter salaries in thousands of dollars (0 to stop).' );
{3}     MaxSalary := 0;         {initialize maximum salary very small}
{4}     MinSalary := maxint;    {and minimum salary very large}
{5}     Salary := 1;
{6}     WHILE Salary <> 0 DO
{7}        BEGIN
{8}           write( 'Enter salary: ' );
{9}           readln( Salary );
{10}          IF Salary > MaxSalary THEN
{11}             MaxSalary := Salary
{12}          ELSE IF Salary < MinSalary THEN
{13}             MinSalary := Salary
{14}        END {WHILE};
{15}     writeln;
{16}     writeln( 'Salary range = ', MaxSalary - MinSalary : 1, ' thousand' )
{17} END.
```

This "quick and dirty patch" fixed the problem of premature termination of the while loop, and execution of this revised program produced

```
Enter salaries in thousands of dollars (0 to stop).
Enter salary:  10
Enter salary:  7
Enter salary:  15
Enter salary:  0
Salary range = 15 thousand
```

Data values were read and processed, terminating when the end-of-data flag 0 was read. The correct salary range for this set of data is $8000, however, and not $15000 as computed by the program.

Trace Tables

In the Exercises of Section 2.6, **trace tables** were used to trace the execution of an algorithm. These trace tables may also be used to locate logical errors in a program by tracing manually the segment of the program that is suspect. This technique is also known as **desk checking** and consists of recording in a table the values of all or certain key variables in the program segment, step by step. In this example, the following trace table for the while loop might be obtained:

Statements	Salary	MaxSalary	MinSalary	
	1	0	32767	← Initial values
6	1	0	32767 ⎫	
7–9	10	0	32767 ⎬ First pass through the loop	
10–11	10	10	32767 ⎭	
6	10	10	32767 ⎫	
7–9	7	10	32767 ⎬ Second pass through the loop	
12–13	7	10	7 ⎭	
6	7	10	7 ⎫	
7–9	15	15	7 ⎬ Third pass through the loop	
10–11	15	15	7 ⎭	
6	15	15	7 ⎫	
7–9	15	15	7 ⎬ Fourth pass through the loop	
12–13	15	15	0 ⎭	

The last line in this trace table shows why the salary range was incorrect: the value of **MinSalary** became 0 on the last pass through the loop, and this occurred because the value 0 used to signal the end of data was read and processed as a salary.

Debugging

The execution of a program segment can also be traced automatically by using a special system debugger like the Turbo Pascal debugger described in Appendix G.5 or by inserting temporary output statements to display the values of key variables at selected stages of program execution. For example, we might insert the statement

```
writeln( 'Salary ', Salary );
```

after the **readln** statement to echo the data values as they are entered, and the statement

```
writeln( 'Max '; MaxSalary, ' Min ', MinSalary )
```

at the bottom of the loop to display the values of these variables at the end of each pass through the loop. (Note that a semicolon must also be appended to the statement preceding this last **writeln** statement.) The resulting output then is

```
Enter salaries in thousands of dollars (0 to stop).
Enter salary:   10
Salary 10
Max 10 Min 32767
Enter salary:   7
Salary 7
Max 10 Min 7
Enter salary:   15
Salary 15
Max 15 Min 7
Enter salary:   0
Salary 0
Max 15 Min 0
Salary range = 15 thousand
```

This technique must not be used indiscriminately, however, since incorrect placement of such temporary debugging statements may display output that is not helpful in locating the source of the error. Also, if too many such statements are used, so much output may be produced that it is difficult to isolate the error.

Modifying and Testing the Program

Either manual or automatic tracing of this program reveals that the source of difficulty is that the value 0 used to signal the end of data is processed as an actual salary. A first reaction might be to fix this error by using a nested **IF** statement:

```
IF Salary > 0 THEN
   IF Salary > MaxSalary THEN
      MaxSalary := Salary
   ELSE IF Salary < MinSalary THEN
      MinSalary := Salary
```

Patches like this one and the ones used earlier are not recommended, however, because they often fail to address the real source of the problem and make the program unnecessarily complicated and messy.

The real source of difficulty in the preceding example is that the student did not use the correct technique for reading and processing data. As we noted in the preceding section, when an end-of-data flag is used to signal the end of data, the correct approach is to read the first data value before the while loop is entered, to ensure that the boolean expression controlling repetition is evaluated correctly the first time. This would solve the problem in the student's first version of the program. Also, as we noted, subsequent data values should be read at the "bottom" of the while loop so that they are compared with the end-of-data flag *before* they are processed in the next pass through the loop.

Using this standard technique for reading and processing data, the student rewrote his program as follows:

```
{1}  BEGIN
{2}      writeln( 'Enter salaries in thousands of dollars (0 to stop).' );
{3}      MaxSalary := 0;          {initialize maximum salary very small}
{4}      MinSalary := maxint;     {and minimum salary very large
{5}      write( 'Enter salary: ' );
{6}      readln( Salary );
{7}      WHILE Salary <> 0 DO
{8}          BEGIN
{9}              IF Salary > MaxSalary THEN
{10}                 MaxSalary := Salary
{11}             ELSE IF Salary < MinSalary THEN
{12}                 MinSalary := Salary;
{13}             write( 'Enter salary: ' );
{14}             readln( Salary )
{15}         END {WHILE};
{16}     write;
{17}     writeln ('Salary range = ', MaxSalary - MinSalary : 1, ' thousand')
{18} END.
```

A sample run using the same data values now produces the correct output:

```
Enter salaries in thousands of dollars (0 to stop).
Enter salary:  10
Enter salary:  7
Enter salary:  15
Enter salary:  0
Salary range = 8 thousand
```

The student may now be tempted to conclude that the program is correct. However, to establish confidence in the correctness of a program, it is necessary to test it with several sets of data. For example, the following sample run reveals that the program still contains a logical error:

```
Enter salaries in thousands of dollars (0 to stop).
Enter salary:  7
Enter salary:  10
Enter salary:  15
Enter salary:  0
Salary range = -32752 thousand
```

Tracing the execution of the while loop produces the following:

Statements	Salary	MaxSalary	MinSalary	
	7	0	32767	← Initial values
7–8	7	7	32767 ⎫	
9–10	7	7	32767 ⎬	First pass through the loop
13–14	10	7	32767 ⎭	
7–8	10	7	32767 ⎫	
9–10	10	10	32767 ⎬	Second pass through the loop
13–14	15	10	32767 ⎭	
7–8	15	10	32767 ⎫	
9–10	15	15	32767 ⎬	Third pass through the loop
13–14	0	15	32767 ⎭	

This trace table reveals that the value of **MinSalary** never changes, suggesting that the statement

        MinSalary := Salary

is never executed. This is because the boolean expression **Salary > MaxSalary** is true for each data value, since these values are entered in increasing order; consequently the **ELSE IF** part of the **IF** statement is never executed. This error can be corrected by using two **IF** statements:

        IF Salary > MaxSalary THEN
           MaxSalary := Salary;
        IF Salary < MinSalary THEN
           MinSalary := Salary;

The resulting program is then correct but is not as efficient as it could be, since the boolean expressions in both of these **IF** statements must be evaluated on each pass through the loop. A more efficient alternative is described in Exercise 9 at the end of this section.

Summary

Logical errors may be very difficult to detect, especially as programs become more complex, and so it is important that test data be carefully selected so that each part of the program is thoroughly tested. The program should be executed with data values entered in several different orders, with both large and small data sets, with extreme values, and with "bad" data. For example, entering the salaries in increasing order revealed the existence of a logical error in the program considered earlier. Also, even though the last version of the program will produce correct output if legitimate data values are read, the output

        Salary range = -32767 thousand

would be produced if the value 0 were entered immediately. Although it may not be necessary to guard against invalid data input in student programs, those written for the public domain, especially programs used by computer novices, should be as **robust** as possible and should not "crash" or produce "garbage" results when unexpected data values are read.

When a logical error is detected, a trace table is an effective tool for locating the error. Once it has been found, the program must be corrected and then tested again. It may be necessary to repeat this cycle of testing, tracing, and correcting many times before the program produces correct results for a wide range of test data, allowing us to be reasonably confident of its correctness. It is not possible, however, to check a program with every possible set of data, and thus obscure bugs may still remain. In some applications, this may not be critical, but in others, for example, in programs used to guide a space shuttle, errors cannot be tolerated. Certain formal techniques have been developed for proving that a program is correct and will always execute correctly (assuming no system malfunction), but a study of these techniques is beyond the scope of this introductory text.

Exercises

1. Assuming that I, J, and K are integer variables, describe the output produced by each of the following program segments:

   (a)
   ```
   K := 5;
   I := -2;
   WHILE I <= K DO
      BEGIN
          I := I + 2;
          K := K - 1;
          writeln( I + K:2 )
      END   {WHILE};
   ```

   (b)
   ```
   Number := 4;
   WHILE Number >= 0 DO
      BEGIN
          Number := Number - 1;
          writeln( Number:1 );
          writeln
      END {WHILE};
   writeln ('*****');
   ```

2. Write a Pascal statement to

   (a) Print the value of **x** and decrease **x** by 0.5 as long as **x** is positive.
   (b) Read values for **a**, **b**, and **c** and print their sum, repeating this as long as none of **a**, **b**, or **c** is negative.
   (c) Print the squares of the first 100 positive integers in increasing order.
   (d) Print the cubes of the first 50 positive integers in decreasing order.
   (e) Print the square roots of the first 25 odd positive integers.
   (f) Calculate and print the squares of consecutive positive integers until the difference between a square and the preceding one is greater than 50.
   (g) Print a list of points (x, y) on the graph of $y = x^3 - 3x + 1$ for x ranging from -2 to 2 in steps of 0.1.

3. Describe the output produced by the following poorly indented program segment:

```
Number := 4;
WHILE Number > 0 DO
   Number := Number - 1;
   writeln (Number:1);
   writeln;
writeln ('*****');
```

4. Write a program to read data values as shown in the following table, calculate the miles per gallon in each case, and print the values with appropriate labels:

Miles Traveled	Gallons of Gasoline Used
231	14.8
248	15.1
302	12.8
147	9.25
88	7
265	13.3

5. Write a program to read several values representing miles, convert miles to kilometers (1 mile = 1.60935 kilometers), and print all values with appropriate labels.

6. A certain product is to sell for **UnitPrice** dollars. Write a program that reads values for **UnitPrice** and **TotalNumber** and then produces a table showing the total price of from 1 through **TotalNumber** units. The table should have a format like the following:

```
Number of Units     Total Price
================     ===========
       1               $ 1.50
       2               $ 3.00
       3               $ 4.50
       4               $ 6.00
       5               $ 7.50
```

7. Write a program that reads the exchange rate for converting English currency to U.S. currency and then reads several values for **Pounds**, **Shillings**, and **Pence** and converts the amount of currency represented into the equivalent amount of U.S. dollars and cents. Display all amounts with appropriate labels.

8. Proceed as in Exercise 7, but convert several values from U.S. currency to English currency.

9. (a) Write a program that solves the salary range problem discussed in Section 4.6 but is more efficient than those described in the text. (*Hint:* Initialize **MaxSalary** and **MinSalary** to the first data value.)

(b) For each of the following data sets, construct a trace table for the repetition structure used in your program and determine the salary range that will be computed by your program:

(i) 7, 15, 10, −1   **(ii)** 7, 10, 15, −1   **(iii)** 15, 10, 7, −1

(iv) 7, −1   **(v)** −1

10. Write a program to read a set of numbers, count them, and calculate and display the mean, variance, and standard deviation of the set of numbers. The **mean** and **variance** of numbers $x_1, x_2, \ldots, x_n$ can be calculated using the formulas

$$\text{mean} = \frac{1}{n} \sum_{i=1}^{n} x_i \qquad \text{variance} = \frac{1}{n} \sum_{i=1}^{n} x_i^2 - \frac{1}{n^2} \left(\sum_{i=1}^{n} x_i \right)^2$$

The **standard deviation** is the square root of the variance.

11. Write a program for the "divide-and-average" algorithm for approximating square roots (see Exercise 11 of Section 2.6). It should accept positive real values for the variables `PosReal`, `Approx`, and `Epsilon` and approximate the square root of `PosReal` by repeatedly replacing `Approx` by the average of `Approx` and `PosReal / Approx`, until `Approx` and `PosReal / Approx` differ in absolute value by less than `Epsilon`, where the value of `Epsilon` is small. Have the program display each of the successive values of `Approx`.

12. The sequence of **Fibonacci numbers** begins with the integers

$$1, 1, 2, 3, 5, 8, 13, 21, \ldots$$

where each number after the first two is the sum of the two preceding numbers. In this sequence, the ratios of consecutive Fibonacci numbers (1/1, 1/2, 2/3, 3/5, ...) approach the "golden ratio"

$$\frac{\sqrt{5} - 1}{2}$$

Write a program to calculate all the Fibonacci numbers smaller than 5000 and the decimal values of the ratios of consecutive Fibonacci numbers.

13. The Rinky Dooflingy Company (Exercise 13 of Section 2.6) currently sells 200 dooflingies per month at a profit of $300 per dooflingy. The company now spends $2000 per month on advertising and has fixed operating costs of $1000 per month that do not depend on the volume of sales. If the company doubles the amount spent on advertising, sales will increase by 20 percent. Write a program that prints under appropriate headings the amount spent on advertising, the number of sales made, and the net profit. Begin with the company's current status and successively double the amount spent on advertising until the net profit "goes over the hump," that is, begins to decline. The output should include the amounts up through the first time that the net profit begins to decline.

14. Write a program that accepts a positive integer and gives its prime factorization, that is, expresses the integer as a product of primes or indicates that it is a prime.

Programming Pointers

Program Design

1. *All programs can be written using the three control structures considered in this chapter: sequence, selection, and repetition.*

2. *Use constant identifiers in place of specific constants for values that may need to be changed when revising a program.* For example, the statements

```
Tax := 0.1963 * Wages;
```

and

```
NewBalance := OldBalance + 0.185 * OldBalance;
```

are better expressed without the magic numbers **0.1963** and **0.185** as

```
Tax := TaxRate * Wages;
```

and

```
NewBalance := OldBalance + InterestRate * OldBalance;
```

where **TaxRate** and **InterestRate** are constants defined by

```
CONST
    TaxRate = 0.1963;
    InterestRate = 0.185;
```

3. *Multialternative selection structures can be implemented more efficiently with an* IF–ELSE IF *construct than with a sequence of* IF *statements.* For example, using the statements

```
IF Score < 60 THEN
    Grade := 'F';
IF (Score >= 60) AND (Score < 70) THEN
    Grade := 'D';
IF (Score >= 70) AND (Score < 80) THEN
    Grade := 'C';
IF (Score >= 80) AND (Score < 90) THEN
    Grade := 'B';
IF (Score >= 90) THEN
    Grade := 'A';
```

is less efficient than

```
IF Score < 60 THEN
    Grade := 'F'
```

```
ELSE IF Score < 70 THEN
    Grade := 'D'
ELSE IF Score < 80 THEN
    Grade := 'C'
ELSE IF Score < 90 THEN
    Grade := 'B'
ELSE
    Grade := 'A';
```

In the first case, all of the **IF** statements are executed for each score processed, and three of the boolean expressions are compound expressions. In the second case, each boolean expression is simple, and not all of them are evaluated for each score; for example, for a score of 65, only the boolean expressions **Score < 60** and **Score < 70** are evaluated.

Potential Problems

1. *Semicolons must be used to separate the statements in a compound statement.* Since Pascal programs have no line structure, a missing semicolon at the end of a line will not be detected until the next line. For example, compiling the erroneous compound statement

```
BEGIN
    Number := Number + 1
    Sum := Sum + Number
END
```

produces the error message

```
Error 85: ";" expected
```

and positions the cursor at the beginning of the statement

```
Sum := Sum + Number
```

Since a statement may be continued from one line to the next, the absence of a semicolon at the end of the statement

```
Number := Number + 1
```

is not detected until the next line is examined, and **S** is not a symbol that can legally follow this statement.

2. *Each* **BEGIN** *must have a matching* **END**. A missing **END** may be rather difficult to detect. The compiler may even search to the end of the program for an **END** to match an earlier **BEGIN** and produce an error message such as

```
Error 85: ";" expected
```

3. *Parentheses must be used within boolean expressions to indicate those subexpressions that are to be evaluated first.* The precedence of operators that may appear in boolean expressions is

NOT	1 highest (performed first)
/, *, DIV, MOD, AND	2
+, -, OR, XOR	3
<, >, =, <=, >=, <>	4 lowest (performed last)

To illustrate, consider the statement

```
IF 1 < x AND x < 10 THEN
    writeln( x )
```

where **x** is of real type. The first operation performed in evaluating the boolean expression is the **AND** operation. However, the subexpression **x AND x** is not a valid boolean expression, because boolean operators cannot be applied to numeric quantities; thus an error message such as the following results:

```
Error 41: Operand types do not match operator
```

4. *When real quantities that are algebraically equal are compared with* =, *the result may be a false boolean expression, because most real numbers are not stored exactly.* For example, even though the two real expressions **x * (1/x)** and 1.0 are algebraically equal, the boolean expression **x * (1/x) = 1.0** is false for most real numbers **x**.

5. *In an* **IF** *statement containing an* **ELSE** *clause, there is no semicolon immediately before the* **ELSE**. A statement such as

```
IF x > 0 THEN
    writeln( x );
ELSE
    writeln( 2 * x );
```

results in an error. A semicolon immediately following **THEN** or **ELSE** as in

```
IF x > 0 THEN;
    writeln( x );
```

or

```
IF x > 0 THEN
    x := abs(x)
ELSE;
    writeln( x );
```

is syntactically correct but is almost surely a mistake, since it indicates an empty statement. In both of these examples, the statement `writeln( x )` is executed, regardless of whether or not **x** is positive.

6. *In a nested* **IF** *statement, each* **ELSE** *clause is matched with the nearest preceding unmatched* **IF**. For example, consider the following statements, which are given without indentation:

```
IF x > 0 THEN
IF y > 0 THEN
z := x + y
ELSE
z := x + abs(y);
w := x * y * z;
```

With which **IF** is the **ELSE** associated? According to the rule just stated, these statements are executed as

```
IF x > 0 THEN
   IF y > 0 THEN
      z := x + y
   ELSE
      z := x + abs(y);
w := x * y * z;
```

where the **ELSE** matches the **IF** in **IF y > 0**.

7. *The statement within a* **WHILE** *statement must eventually cause the boolean expression controlling repetition to become false (except as noted in footnote 2 on page 150).* An **infinite loop** is the result otherwise. For example, if **x** is a real variable, the statements

```
x := 0;
WHILE x <> 1.0 DO
   BEGIN
      writeln( x:3:1 );
      x := x + 0.3
   END {WHILE};
```

produce an infinite loop.

Output:
0.0
0.3
0.6
0.9
1.2
1.5
1.8
  .
  .
  .

Since the value of **x** is never equal to 1.0, repetition is not terminated. In view of Potential Problem 4, the statements

```
x := 0;
WHILE x <> 1.0 DO
   BEGIN
      writeln( x:3:1 );
      x := x + 0.2
   END {WHILE};
```

may also produce an infinite loop.

Output:
```
0.0
0.2
0.4
0.6
0.8
1.0
1.2
1.4
1.6
  .
  .
  .
```

Since x is initialized to 0 and 0.2 is added to x five times, x should have the value 1.0. But the boolean expression $x \neq 1.0$ may remain true, because most real values are not stored exactly.

8. *In a* WHILE *statement, the boolean expression is evaluated before execution of the statement within the* WHILE *statement.* Thus, the statement within a WHILE statement is not executed if the boolean expression is false.

9. *The* WHILE *statement controls repetition of only one statement.* For example, the statements

```
Count := 1;
WHILE Count <= 10 DO
   BEGIN
      writeln( Count:2, sqr(Count):5 );
      Count := Count + 1
   END {WHILE}
```

display a list of the integers from 1 through 10 and their squares. The statements

```
Count := 1;
WHILE Count <= 10 DO
   writeln( Count:1, sqr(Count):5 );
   Count := Count + 1
```

produce an infinite loop.

Output:
```
1     1
1     1
1     1
1     1
.     .
.     .
.     .
```

Program Style

In this text, we use the following conventions for formatting the statements considered in this chapter.

1. *In a compound statement,* BEGIN *and* END *are aligned, and the statements they enclose are indented.*

```
BEGIN
    statement-1;
        .
        .
        .
    statement-n
END
```

2. *For an* IF *statement,* IF ... THEN *is on one line, with its statement indented on the next line. If there is an* ELSE *clause,* ELSE *is on a separate line, aligned with* IF, *and its statement is indented on the next line.*

```
IF ... THEN
    statement-1
ELSE
    statement-2

IF ... THEN
    BEGIN
        statement-1;
            .
            .
            .
        statement-k
    END {IF}
ELSE
    BEGIN
        statement-k + 1;
            .
            .
            .
        statement-n
    END {ELSE}
```

An exception is made when an IF–ELSE IF *construct is used to implement a multialternative selection structure. In this case the format used is*

```
IF ... THEN
    statement-1
ELSE IF ... THEN
    statement-2
ELSE IF ... THEN
    statement-3
        .
        .
        .
ELSE
    statement-n
```

3. *In a* WHILE *statement,* WHILE ... DO *is on one line, with the body of the loop indented on the next line(s).*

```
WHILE ... DO
    statement


WHILE ... DO
    BEGIN
        statement-1;
            .
            .
            .
        statement-n
    END {WHILE}
```

4. *A comment of the form* {IF} *or* {WHILE} *is attached to the reserved word* END, *which marks the end of a compound statement that serves as one of the alternatives in an* IF *statement or as the body of a while loop, respectively.*

Standard Pascal

The basic control structures provided in this chapter are the same in both Turbo Pascal and standard Pascal; the only point of difference is in the use of boolean operators. In standard Pascal:

- The exclusive-or operator XOR is not provided.
- The boolean operators may not be applied bitwise to integer values.
- Short-circuit evaluation of boolean expressions cannot be assumed.

MODULAR DESIGN

> *Great things can be reduced to small things, and small things can be reduced to nothing.*
> **CHINESE PROVERB**

CHAPTER CONTENTS

The problems we have considered thus far have been simple enough that the algorithms for their complete solution were quite straightforward. As we noted in Chapter 2, more complex problems are best solved using a **top–down** approach that uses a **divide-and-conquer** strategy to divide a problem into a number of simpler subproblems. Each of these subproblems is then considered individually, and in some cases, it may be necessary to divide them further until the resulting subproblems are simple enough that algorithms for their solution can be easily designed. The complete algorithm for the original problem is then described in terms of these subalgorithms. **Subprograms** or **modules** can then be written to implement each of these subalgorithms, and these subprograms combined to give a complete program that solves the original problem. Because the program units in this **modular** style of programming are independent of one another, the programmer can write each module and test it without worrying about the details of other modules. This makes it considerably easier to locate an error when it arises, since the effects of these modules are easily isolated. Programs developed in this manner are usually easier to understand because each program unit can be studied independently of other program units.

In Pascal, subprograms are **procedures** and **functions,** and we begin this chapter by looking at procedures and how they aid in the design of modular programs. We then discuss functions and illustrate them with many examples. This is followed by a menu-driven checkbook-balancing program that demonstrates modular design and a program for checking academic standing that is developed in a top–down manner. Finally, we introduce **units,** another feature of Turbo Pascal that facilitates modular design.

5.1   Introduction to Procedures and Modular Design

In this section we illustrate modular design by considering the problem of converting a monetary amount from one currency system to another. This problem will be divided into simpler subproblems, and individual subprograms will be designed to solve each of these subproblems. To keep the example simple, we begin by considering only the problem of converting between U.S. and Canadian currencies. A program to solve this problem should accept an amount in either U.S. dollars or Canadian dollars and convert this amount to the equivalent amount in the other currency system.

Using a divide-and-conquer approach, we identify three simpler subproblems:

1. The user must be instructed how to use the program.
2. It must be possible to convert U.S. currency to Canadian currency.
3. It must be possible to convert Canadian currency to U.S. currency.

We will design separate subprograms for these subproblems, named **DisplayInstructions**, **ConvertUSTOCanadian**, and **ConvertCanadianToUS**, and these subprograms will be part of a larger program **CurrencyConverter**, called a **main program,** which controls their execution and uses them to solve the larger problem. The complete program will thus have the following structure:

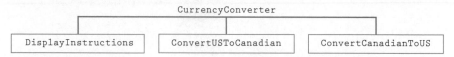

As we noted earlier, there are two types of subprograms in Pascal, **procedures** and **functions,** and since procedures are more general than functions, we begin by considering procedures. Functions are considered in Section 5.5.

The structure of a procedure is similar to that of a program (hence the name *subprogram*) in that it consists of three parts: a heading, a declaration part, and a statement part. Its syntax diagram is

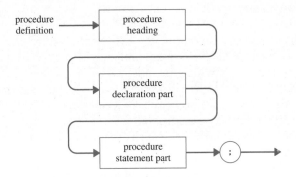

The general form of a procedure thus is

Procedure

> Procedure heading
> Procedure declaration part
> Procedure statement part

The simplest procedures are those that do not receive any information from other subprograms or from the main program and do not return any information to them. The procedure heading for such procedures has a very simple form:

Procedure Heading (Simple Form)

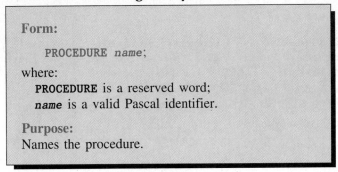

Form:

    PROCEDURE *name*;

where:
    PROCEDURE is a reserved word;
    name is a valid Pascal identifier.

Purpose:
Names the procedure.

For example, the procedure to display instructions in the currency conversion program does not require information from other parts of the program, and thus its heading is

```
PROCEDURE DisplayInstructions;
```

The statement part of a procedure has the same form as that of a Pascal program except that a semicolon rather than a period follows the reserved word **END** marking the end of the procedure definition. For example, the statement part of procedure `DisplayInstructions` is

```
BEGIN
   writeln( 'This program converts US currency to Canadian' );
   writeln( 'currency and vice versa.  Enter' );
   writeln( '1 to convert from U.S. to Canadian' );
   write  ( '2 to convert from Canadian to U.S.: ')
END {DisplayInstructions};
```

Thus, the complete procedure is

```
PROCEDURE DisplayInstructions;
{---------------------------------------------------------

   Purpose:         Display instructions to the user.
   Output (screen): Instructions for using the program.

-----------------------------------------------------------}

   BEGIN
      writeln( 'This program converts US currency to Canadian' );
      writeln( 'currency and vice versa.  Enter' );
      writeln( '1 to convert from U.S. to Canadian' );
      write  ( '2 to convert from Canadian to U.S.: ')
   END {DisplayInstructions};
```

The declaration part of a procedure is used to declare identifiers that are used only within that procedure. This declaration part has the same form as the that of a Pascal program. For example, the procedure `ConvertUSToCanadian` uses `Dollars` and `USToCanadian` as variables to store the dollar amount to be converted and the conversion rate, respectively, and so these identifiers must be declared in its declaration part:

```
VAR
   USToCanadian,     {conversion rate}
   Dollars : real;   {U.S. dollar amount to be converted}
```

The complete procedure is

```
PROCEDURE ConvertUSToCanadian;
{-----------------------------------------------------------------

   Input (keyboard): Amount in U.S. dollars.
   Purpose:          Convert U.S. currency to Canadian currency.
   Output (screen):  Prompts to the user and the amount in
                     Canadian dollars.

----------------------------------------------------------------}
```

```
VAR
    USToCanadian,       {conversion rate}
    Dollars : real;     {U.S. dollar amount to be converted}

BEGIN
    write( 'Enter the current U.S.-to-Candian conversion rate: ' );
    readln( USToCanadian );
    write( 'Enter U.S. dollars: ' );
    readln( Dollars );
    writeln( 'This is equivalent to ',
             USToCanadian * Dollars:4:2, ' Canadian dollars.' )
END {ConvertUSToCanadian};
```

The procedure `ConvertCanadianToUS` is similar and is given in Figure 5.1.

Variables declared within a procedure like `USToCanadian` and `Dollars` in procedure `ConvertUSToCanadian` have values only when this procedure is executed, and these values are accessible only within this procedure. Such variables are therefore said to be **local** to the procedure. The portion of a program in which a variable is accessible is called the **scope** of that variable. Thus the scope of local variables `USToCanadian` and `Dollars` is the procedure `ConvertUSToCanadian`.

One consequence of this scope rule for local variables is that the same identifier can be used without conflict in both a procedure and the main program or in two different procedures. For example, both the procedures `ConvertUSToCanadian` and `ConvertCanadianToUS` use the identifier `Dollars` to name the monetary value to be converted.

In a Pascal program, procedures are defined in the **subprogram section** of the declaration part of the main program. The subprogram section is usually placed immediately after the variable section (as required in standard Pascal).

A procedure is executed when it is activated by a **procedure reference statement.** For the procedures we have considered thus far, this statement has a simple form:

Procedure Reference Statement
(Simple Form)

Form:

    name;

where:
    name is the name of a procedure.

Purpose:
Activates the named procedure. Execution of the current program unit is suspended, and execution of the procedure begins. When the end of the procedure is reached, execution of the original program unit resumes with the statement following this procedure reference statement.

For example, the statement

```
DisplayInstructions;
```

can be used to activate or *call* the procedure **DisplayInstructions**.

Execution of a program containing procedures begins with the first statement in the statement part of the main program. Whenever a procedure reference statement is encountered, execution of the main program is suspended, and control is transferred to the procedure. When execution of the procedure is complete, control returns to the main program, and execution resumes with the statement following the procedure reference statement.

For example, execution of the currency conversion program of Figure 5.1 begins with the statements that prompt the user to enter the current date and then read the date entered. The next statement encountered is the procedure reference statement

```
DisplayInstructions;
```

which calls the procedure **DisplayInstructions**. Execution of the main program is then interrupted, and **DisplayIntructions** is executed. When the end of this procedure is reached, execution of the main program resumes with the statement

```
readln( CurrencyCode );
```

After the user enters a value, one of the two procedure reference statements

```
ConvertUSToCanadian
```

or

```
ConvertCanadianToUS
```

calls the appropriate procedure to carry out the conversions. Once again, execution of the main program is suspended, and control is transferred to the procedure. When the end of the procedure is reached, control returns to the main program, and execution resumes with the **writeln** statement that displays the transaction date.

FIGURE 5.1   Currency conversion—version 1.

```
PROGRAM CurrencyConversion1( input, output );
{*********************************************************************

   Input (keyboard): Current month, day, and year, an integer
                     indicating the type of currency, and a monetary
                     amount.
   Purpose:          Convert U.S. currency to Canadian currency or
                     vice versa.
   Output (screen):  Instructions to the user, a monetary amount,
                     and the date of the transaction.


*********************************************************************}
```

FIGURE 5.1 Currency conversion—version 1. (cont.)

```
VAR
    CurrentMonth,              {current month}
    CurrentDay,               {current day}
    CurrentYear,              {current year}
    CurrencyCode : integer; {indicates type of currency to be converted}

PROCEDURE DisplayInstructions;
{-----------------------------------------------------------------------

    Purpose:            Display instructions to the user.
    Output (screen): Instructions for using the program.


-----------------------------------------------------------------------}

    BEGIN
        writeln( 'This program converts US currency to Canadian' );
        writeln( 'currency and vice versa.  Enter' );
        writeln( '1 if amount is in U.S. currency');
        write  ( '2 if amount is Canadian currency: ')
    END {DisplayInstructions};

PROCEDURE ConvertUSToCanadian;
{-----------------------------------------------------------------------

    Input (keyboard): Amount in U.S. dollars.
    Purpose:           Convert U.S. currency to Canadian currency.
    Output (screen):  Prompts to the user and the amount in Canadian
                      dollars.


-----------------------------------------------------------------------}

    VAR
        USToCanadian,     { conversion rate }
        Dollars : real;   { U.S. dollar amount to be converted }

    BEGIN
        write( 'Enter the current U.S.-to-Canadian conversion rate: ' );
        readln( USToCanadian );
        write( 'Enter U.S. dollars: ' );
        readln( Dollars );
        writeln( 'This is equivalent to ',
                 USToCanadian * Dollars:4:2, ' Canadian dollars.' )
    END {ConvertUSToCanadian};

PROCEDURE ConvertCanadianToUS;
{-----------------------------------------------------------------------

    Input (keyboard): An amount in Canadian dollars.
    Purpose:           Convert Canadian currency to U.S. currency.
    Output (screen):  Prompts to the user and the amount in U.S.
                      dollars.


-----------------------------------------------------------------------}
```

FIGURE 5.1   Currency conversion—version 1. (cont.)

```
    VAR
        CanadianToUS,    {conversion rate}
        Dollars : real; {Canadian dollar amount to be converted}

    BEGIN
        write( 'Enter the current Canadian-to-U.S. conversion rate:  ' );
        readln( CanadianToUS );
        write( 'Enter Canadian dollars: ' );
        readln( Dollars );
        writeln( 'This is equivalent to ',
                  CanadianToUS * Dollars:4:2, ' U.S. dollars.' );
    END {ConvertCanadianToUS};

BEGIN {************************* main program *************************}
    write( 'Enter the current month, day, and year: ' );
    readln( CurrentMonth, CurrentDay, CurrentYear );
    DisplayInstructions;
    readln( CurrencyCode );
    IF CurrencyCode = 1 THEN
        ConvertUSToCanadian
    ELSE
        ConvertCanadianToUS;
    writeln( '*** TRANSACTION DATE: ', CurrentMonth:1, '-', CurrentDay:1,
              ', ', CurrentYear:1 )
END {CurrencyConversion1}.
```

Sample runs:

```
Enter the current month, day, and year: 12 29 1992
This program converts US currency to Canadian
currency and vice versa.  Enter
1 if amount is in U.S. currency
2 if amount is Canadian currency: 1
Enter the current U.S.-to-Canadian conversion rate: 1.13
Enter U.S. dollars: 125.00
This is equivalent to 141.25 Canadian dollars.
*** TRANSACTION DATE: 12-29, 1992


Enter the current month, day, and year: 12 29 1992
This program converts US currency to Canadian
currency and vice versa.  Enter
1 if amount is in U.S. currency
2 if amount is Canadian currency: 2
Enter the current Canadian-to-U.S. conversion rate:  0.885
Enter Canadian dollars: 250.00
This is equivalent to 221.25 U.S. dollars.
*** TRANSACTION DATE: 12-29, 1992
```

1. Extend the program in Figure 5.1 to allow conversions between other currency systems such as U. S. dollars and English pounds.

2. Write four procedures **PrintZero**, **PrintOne**, **PrintTwo**, and **PrintThree** to produce "stick numbers" like those on a calculator display for the digits 0, 1, 2, and 3, respectively:

   Use these procedures in a program that accepts numbers made up of these digits—for example, 123, 102, 20, 33, and 2323—and displays them in stick form, one digit above the next.

3. Extend the program in Exercise 2 to process all digits.

4. **(a)** Write a procedure that reads a radius of a circle and then calculates and displays its circumference and its area.
   (b) Write a procedure that reads the lengths of the sides of a rectangle and then calculates and displays its perimeter and its area.
   (c) Write a procedure that reads the lengths of three sides of a triangle and then calculates and displays its perimeter and its area. (The area of a triangle can be found by using **Hero's formula:**
   $$\sqrt{s(s-a)(s-b)(s-c)}$$
   where a, b, and c are the lengths of the sides and s is one half of the perimeter.)
   (d) Write a program that reads a code for a geometric shape (circle, rectangle, or triangle) and then calls the appropriate procedure from (a), (b), or (c) to calculate its circumference or perimeter and its area.

5. Write a program that allows the user to convert measurements from either minutes to hours or feet to meters (1 foot = 0.3048 meter) or from degrees Fahrenheit to degrees Celsius ($C = \frac{5}{9}(F - 32)$). Design the program so that it displays a **menu** of options, allows the user to select one of these options, and then calls an appropriate procedure that implements this option. A sample run of the program should proceed somewhat as follows:

```
Available options are
0. Display this menu.
1. Convert minutes to hours.
2. Convert feet to meters.
3. Convert degrees Fahrenheit to degrees Celsius.
4. Quit.
```

```
Enter an option (0 to see menu): 3
Enter degrees Fahrenheit: 212
This is equivalent to 100.0 degrees Celsius

Enter an option (0 to see menu): 5
*** 5 is not a valid option ***

Enter an option (0 to see menu): 0
Available options are
0. Display this menu.
1. Convert minutes to hours.
2. Convert feet to meters.
3. Convert degrees Fahrenheit to degrees Celsius.
4. Quit.

Enter an option (0 to see menu): 1
Enter minutes: 3600
This is equivalent to 60.0 hours

Enter an option (0 to see menu): 2
Enter number of feet: 1
This is equivalent to 0.3408 meters

Enter an option (0 to see menu): 4
```

5.2   Procedures with Parameters

The currency conversion problem that we considered in the preceding section
was solved using the simplest kinds of procedures, namely, those that do not
receive any information from or return any information to other parts of the program. A better solution to this problem can be designed using procedures that do
share information. In particular, the procedures **ConvertUSToCanadian** and
ConvertCanadianToUS perform essentially the same processing: Both accept as
input a conversion rate and a monetary amount; both calculate the equivalent
amount in the other currency system by multiplying the original amount by the
conversion rate; and both display the results. These two procedures can be combined into a single procedure if the main program reads a code indicating the kind
of currency to be converted, the conversion rate, and the monetary amount and then
shares these with the procedure. If this done, it is also easy to design the program
so that several amounts can be converted and the total of these amounts determined, a modification that would be somewhat awkward in the program of Figure
5.1. The following algorithms indicate how this can be done:

ALGORITHM FOR CURRENCY CONVERSION PROBLEM

(* Input: The current month, day, and year, a conversion code, a
              conversion rate, and several monetary amounts to be converted.
   Purpose: Convert U.S. currency to Canadian currency or vice versa and
              find total of all amounts.

Output: Instructions to the user, monetary amounts, date of the transactions, and total of amounts. *)

1. Enter the current month, day, and year.
2. Display instructions to the user.
3. Enter the code that indicates the currency type.
4. Enter the conversion rate for U.S. currency to Canadian.
5. Initialize a total to 0.
6. Enter the first amount to be converted (sentinel = 0 to stop).
7. While amount > 0 do the following:
   a. Pass the currency code, the conversion rate, and the monetary amount to subalgorithm *Convert* to display the equivalent amount in the other currency.
   b. Add amount to the running total.
   c. Read the next amount to be converted.
8. Display the transaction date and the total of the amounts.

SUBALGORITHM *Convert*

(* Accepts: A conversion *Code,* a conversion *Rate,* and a monetary *Amount.*
   Purpose: Convert *Amount* to an equivalent amount in another currency system using the conversion *Rate.*
   Output: The equivalent monetary amount. *)

If *Code* = 1 then do the following:
   Display *Rate* * *Amount* , 'Canadian Dollars'
Else
   Display (1 / *Rate*) * *Amount* , 'US Dollars'.

To implement the subalgorithm *Convert* as a procedure, it must be possible to pass the conversion code, the conversion rate, and the amount to be converted to the procedure from the main program, which will implement the main algorithm. This means that variables must be declared in this procedure to store these values. We cannot declare them within the procedure's declaration part, however, because as we observed in the preceding section, such variables are local to the procedure and cannot be assigned values from outside the procedure.

What is needed instead are special kinds of variables in a procedure to which values can be passed from outside the procedure. In Pascal, these special variables are called **formal parameters** and are declared in the procedure's heading. Parameters that can store values passed to them but that cannot return values are called **value parameters** or **in parameters** and are the kind of parameters we consider first. (Version 7.0 of Turbo Pascal also provides **constant parameters;** see Section H.2 of Appendix H.) Parameters that can both receive values and return values are called **variable** or **in-out parameters** and are considered later in this section.

Value (In) Parameters

Procedures that use parameters require a different heading than do those that do not. The following syntax diagram for a procedure heading specifies the general form:

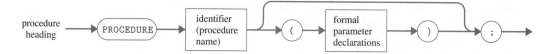

From this diagram, we see that a procedure heading can take two forms:

Procedure Heading

Form:

PROCEDURE *name*(*formal-parameter-declarations*);

where:
PROCEDURE is a reserved word;
name is a valid Pascal identifier;
formal-parameter-declarations declares the parameters of the procedure.

If the procedure has no parameters, the formal parameter declarations and the enclosing parentheses are omitted so that the heading has the simple form

PROCEDURE *name*;

Purpose:
Names the procedure and declares its parameters.

Declarations of formal value parameters have the form

    parameter-list : type

where **parameter-list** is a single variable or a list of variables separated by commas and **type** specifies their type. These declarations are separated by semicolons.

To illustrate, a procedure **Convert** to implement the subalgorithm for the currency conversion problem must have three value parameters:

Code: To store the currency code.
Rate: To store the conversion rate.
Amount: To store the monetary amounts.

An appropriate heading for this procedure thus is

```
PROCEDURE Convert( Code : integer;    {currency code}
                   Rate,              {conversion rate}
                   Amount : real );   {monetary amount}
        ↑
    procedure          formal parameter declarations
      name
```

When this procedure is called, values are passed from the main program to the formal parameters **Code**, **Rate**, and **Amount**. The procedure then uses these values in carrying out the required conversion as described in subalgorithm *Convert*. The complete procedure is

```
PROCEDURE Convert( Code : integer;   {currency code}
                   Rate,             {conversion rate}
                   Amount : real );  {monetary amount}
{----------------------------------------------------------------------

    Accepts:        Code, Rate, Amount.
    Purpose:        Convert monetary amount to another currency system.
    Output (screen): Equivalent monetary amount.


----------------------------------------------------------------------}

    VAR
        EquivAmount : real;   {equivalent amount in other currency system}

    BEGIN
        write( 'This is equivalent to ' );
        IF Code = 1 THEN
            BEGIN
                EquivAmount := Rate * Amount;
                writeln( EquivAmount:4:2, ' Canadian Dollars' )
            END {IF}
        ELSE
            BEGIN
                EquivAmount := (1.0 / Rate) * Amount;
                writeln( EquivAmount:4:2, ' U.S. Dollars' )
            END {ELSE}
    END {Convert};
```

Note that we have included comments to explain what the local variables represent—both formal parameters and those defined in the procedure's variable section—and to describe the procedure—what values are passed to it, what it does, and what output it produces. In this text we will include the following items in a procedure's documentation:

Accepts: Items passed to the procedure.
Purpose: A brief description of the processing done by the procedure.
Returns: Items returned by the procedure by means of variable parameters.
Input: Items whose values are input as the procedure executes.
Output: Items whose values are output as the procedure executes.

A procedure like **Convert** that uses parameters is called with a procedure reference statement that specifies not only the name of the procedure but also the values to be passed to the procedure:

Procedure Reference Statement

Form:

> name(*actual-parameter-list*);

where:
> **name** is the name of a procedure;
> **actual-parameter-list** is a single expression
> or a list of expressions separated by commas.

If the procedure has no parameters, the actual parameter list and the enclosing parentheses are omitted so that the statement has the simple form

> name;

Purpose:

Calls the named procedure. Execution of the current program unit is suspended; values of the actual parameters (if any) are passed to the corresponding formal parameters; and execution of the procedure begins. When the end of the procedure is reached, execution of the original program unit resumes with the statement following this procedure reference statement.

For example, the procedure **Convert** is called by the statement

```
Convert( CurrencyCode, ConversionRate, Money );
```

in the program of Figure 5.2. This statement causes the value of the actual parameters **CurrencyCode**, **ConversionRate**, and **Money** to be assigned to the formal parameters **Code**, **Rate**, and **Amount**, respectively, of the procedure **Convert**,

Formal parameters:	Code	Rate	Amount
	↑	↑	↑
Actual parameters:	CurrencyCode	ConversionRate	Money

and initiates execution of the procedure. When the end of the procedure is reached, execution resumes with the assignment statement **Total := Total + Money** following this procedure reference statement in the main program.

FIGURE 5.2   Currency conversion—version 2.

```
PROGRAM CurrencyConversion2( input, output );
{****************************************************************

    Input (keyboard): Current month, day, and year, an integer
                      indicating the type of currency, a conversion
                      rate, and several monetary amounts.
    Purpose:          Convert U.S. currency to Canadian currency or
                      vice versa.
    Output (screen):  Instructions to the user, monetary amounts, the
                      date of the transactions, and total of amounts.


****************************************************************}

VAR
    CurrentMonth,              {current month}
    CurrentDay,                {current day}
    CurrentYear,               {current year}
    CurrencyCode : integer;    {indicates type of currency to be converted}
    ConversionRate,            {the U.S. to Canadian conversion rate}
    Money,                     {monetary amount to be converted}
    Total : real;              {total of the amounts}

PROCEDURE DisplayInstructions;
{-----------------------------------------------------------------

    Purpose:          Display instructions to the user.
    Output (screen):  Instructions for using the program.

-----------------------------------------------------------------}

    BEGIN
        writeln( 'This program converts US currency to Canadian' );
        writeln( 'currency or vice versa and finds the total of all' );
        writeln( 'amounts. Enter 0 to signal that all amounts have been',
                 ' processed.' );
        writeln;
        writeln( 'Enter 1 if amounts entered are U.S. currency' );
        write  ( '      2 if amounts entered are Canadian currency: ' )
    END {DisplayInstructions};

PROCEDURE Convert( Code: integer;     {currency code}
                   Rate,              {conversion rate}
                   Amount : real );   {monetary amount}
{-----------------------------------------------------------------

    Accepts:          Code, Rate, Amount.
    Purpose:          Convert monetary amount to another currency system.
    Output (screen):  Equivalent monetary amount.

-----------------------------------------------------------------}
```

FIGURE 5.2   Currency conversion—version 2. (cont.)

```
    VAR
        EquivAmount : real;    {equivalent amount in other currency system}

    BEGIN
        write( 'This is equivalent to ' );
        IF Code = 1 THEN
            BEGIN
                EquivAmount := Rate * Amount;
                writeln( EquivAmount:4:2, ' Canadian Dollars' )
            END {IF}
        ELSE
            BEGIN
                EquivAmount := (1.0 / Rate) * Amount;
                writeln( EquivAmount:4:2, ' U.S. Dollars' )
            END {ELSE}
    END {Convert};

BEGIN {********************* main program **********************}
    write( 'Enter the current month, day, and year: ' );
    readln( CurrentMonth, CurrentDay, CurrentYear );
    DisplayInstructions;
    readln( CurrencyCode );
    write( 'Enter the U.S. to Canadian conversion rate: ' );
    readln( ConversionRate );
    Total := 0;

    write( 'Enter amount (0 to stop): ' );
    readln( Money );
    WHILE Money > 0 DO
        BEGIN
            Convert( CurrencyCode, ConversionRate, Money );
            Total := Total + Money;
            write( 'Enter amount (0 to stop): ' );
            readln( Money )
        END {WHILE};

    writeln( '*** TRANSACTION DATE: ', CurrentMonth:1, '-', CurrentDay:1,
            ', ', CurrentYear:1 );
    writeln( 'Total amount converted was $', Total:4:2 )
END {CurrentConversion2}.
```

Sample run:

```
Enter the current month, day, and year: 12 29 1992
This program converts US currency to Canadian
currency or vice versa and finds the total of all
amounts. Enter 0 to signal that all amounts have been processed.

Enter 1 if amounts entered are U.S. currency
      2 if amounts entered are Canadian currency: 1
Enter the U.S. to Canadian conversion rate: 1.13
```

FIGURE 5.2 Currency conversion—version 2. (cont.)

```
Enter amount (0 to stop): 5.00
This is equivalent to 5.65 Canadian Dollars
Enter amount (0 to stop): 125.00
This is equivalent to 141.25 Canadian Dollars
Enter amount (0 to stop): 200.00
This is equivalent to 226.00 Canadian Dollars
Enter amount (0 to stop): 0
*** TRANSACTION DATE: 12-29, 1992
Total amount converted was $330.00
```

Before a procedure like **Convert** is referenced, its formal parameters are undefined. At the time of reference, memory locations are associated with its value parameters, and the values of the corresponding actual parameters are copied into these locations. Thus, for the procedure **Convert**, the formal parameters **Code**, **Rate**, and **Amount** are undefined until the procedure reference statement

```
Convert( CurrencyCode, ConversionRate, Money );
```

is encountered. At this time, the values of the actual parameters **CurrencyCode**, **ConversionRate**, and **Money** are copied to **Code**, **Rate**, and **Amount**, respectively.

After execution of the procedure, value parameters once again become undefined, so that any values they had during execution of the procedure are lost and are not returned to the main program or subprogram that calls the procedure.

Variable (In–Out) Parameters

In the preceding currency conversion program, neither of the procedures returns any values to the main program. For some problems, however, it may be necessary for one or more of the values calculated by a procedure to be made available to other parts of the program. For example, a grocery store in Detroit, Michigan, might have both U.S. and Canadian customers, and to find the total receipts for the day, the Canadian amounts taken in must be converted to their U.S. equivalents. For another store in Windsor, Ontario, the owner may wish to convert all the U.S. receipts to their Canadian equivalents. This means that it must be possible for the subalgorithm *Convert* and the procedure that implements it not only to receive values but also to return values:

ALGORITHM FOR MODIFIED CURRENCY CONVERSION PROBLEM

(* Input: The current month, day, and year, a home currency indicator, a conversion rate, and several currency codes and monetary amounts.

  Purpose: Convert U.S. currency to Canadian currency or vice versa and find total of all amounts.

  Output: Instructions to the user, monetary amounts, date of the transactions, and total of all amounts. *)

1. Enter the current month, day, and year.
2. Display instructions to the user.
3. Enter the home currency code.
4. Enter the conversion rate for U.S. currency to Canadian.
5. Initialize a total to 0.
6. Enter the first currency code and monetary amount (0 to stop).
7. While amount > 0 do the following:
    a. If the currency code differs from the home currency code then
        (i) Pass the currency code, the conversion rate, and the monetary amount to the subalgorithm *Convert2,* which returns the converted amount.
        (ii) Add the converted amount to the running total.
     Else
        Add the amount to the running total.
    b. Read the next currency code and monetary amount (0 to stop).
8. Display the transaction date and the total of the amounts.

SUBALGORITHM *Convert2*

(* Accepts: A currency *Code,* a conversion *Rate,* and a monetary *Amount.*

  Purpose: Converts *Amount* to another currency system using the conversion *Rate.*

  Returns: The equivalent amount *EquivAmount.* *)

If *Code* = 1 then do the following:
    Calculate *EquivAmount* = *Rate* * *Amount.*
    Display *EquivAmount,* 'Canadian Dollars'.
Else
    Calculate *EquivAmount* = (1 / *Rate*) * *Amount.*
    Display *EquivAmount,* 'U.S. Dollars'.

As we noted earlier, a procedure must use **variable** or **in–out parameters** to return values to other parts of the program. Thus in the procedure that implements the preceding subalgorithm, the parameter that returns the converted monetary amounts must be a variable parameter. Declarations of formal variable parameters are preceded by the reserved word **VAR** to specify that they are variable rather than value parameters:

```
VAR parameter-list : type
```

where as before, each *parameter-list* is a single variable or a list of variables separated by commas and *type* specifies their type, and these declarations are separated by semicolons.

To illustrate, the procedure `Convert2`, which implements the preceding subalgorithm, must have three value parameters declared by

```
Code : integer;
Rate, Amount : real;
```

and one variable parameter declared by

```
VAR EquivAmount : real
```

An appropriate procedure heading thus is

```
PROCEDURE Convert2(    Code : integer;        {type of currency}
                       Rate,                  {conversion rate}
                       Amount : real;         {monetary amount to convert}
                  VAR EquivAmount : real );  {equivalent amount}
```

The complete procedure is given in the program in Figure 5.3, which implements the preceding algorithm and subalgorithm.

FIGURE 5.3   Currency conversion—version 3.

```
PROGRAM CurrencyConversion3( input, output );
{*****************************************************************

   Input (keyboard): Current month, day, and year, an integer
                     indicating the home currency type, a conversion
                     rate, and several conversion codes and monetary
                     amounts.
   Purpose:          Convert U.S. currency to Canadian currency or
                     vice versa and find total of all amounts.
   Output (screen):  Instructions to the user, converted monetary
                     amounts, the date of the transactions, and total
                     of amounts.

   *****************************************************************}

VAR
   CurrentMonth,              {current month}
   CurrentDay,                {current day}
   CurrentYear,               {current year}
   HomeCurrency,              {indicates type of home currency}
   CurrencyCode : integer;    {indicates currency type of monetary amounts}
   ConversionRate,            {the U.S. to Canadian conversion rate}
   Money,                     {monetary amount}
   ConvertedMoney,            {equivalent amount in other currency system}
   Total : real;              {total of the amounts}
```

FIGURE 5.3 Currency conversion—version 3. (cont.)

```
PROCEDURE DisplayInstructions;
{-----------------------------------------------------------------------

    Purpose:         Display instructions to the user.
    Output (screen): Instructions for using the program.

-----------------------------------------------------------------------}

    BEGIN
        writeln( 'This program converts US currency to Canadian' );
        writeln( 'currency or vice versa and finds the total of all' );
        writeln( 'amounts. Enter 0 to signal that all amounts have been',
                 ' processed.' );
        writeln;
        writeln( 'Enter 1 if home currency is U.S. currency' );
        write  ( '      2 if it is Canadian currency: ' )
    END {DisplayInstructions};

PROCEDURE Convert2(    Code : integer;          {type of currency}
                       Rate,                     {conversion rate}
                       Amount : real;            {monetary amount to convert}
                   VAR EquivAmount : real ); {equivalent amount}
{-----------------------------------------------------------------------

    Accepts:         Code, Rate, Amount.
    Purpose:         Convert monetary amount to another currency system.
    Returns:         EquivAmount.
    Output (screen): EquivAmount.

-----------------------------------------------------------------------}

    BEGIN
        write( 'This is equivalent to ' );
        IF Code = 1 THEN
            BEGIN
                EquivAmount := Rate * Amount;
                writeln( EquivAmount:4:2, ' Canadian Dollars' )
            END {IF}
        ELSE
            BEGIN
                EquivAmount := (1.0 / Rate) * Amount;
                writeln( EquivAmount:4:2, ' U.S. Dollars' )
            END {ELSE}
    END {Convert2};

BEGIN {********************* main program **********************}
    write( 'Enter the current month, day, and year: ' );
    readln( CurrentMonth, CurrentDay, CurrentYear );
    DisplayInstructions;
    readln( HomeCurrency );
    write( 'Enter the U.S. to Canadian conversion rate: ' );
    readln( ConversionRate );
    Total := 0;
```

FIGURE 5.3 Currency conversion—version 3. (cont.)

```
write( 'Enter currency type and amount (0 0 to stop): ' );
readln( CurrencyCode, Money );
WHILE Money > 0 DO
   BEGIN
      IF CurrencyCode <> HomeCurrency THEN
         BEGIN
            Convert2( CurrencyCode, ConversionRate, Money,
                      ConvertedMoney );
            Total := Total + ConvertedMoney
         END {IF}
      ELSE
         Total := Total + Money;
      write( 'Enter currency type and amount (0 0 to stop): ' );
      readln( CurrencyCode, Money )
   END {WHILE};

writeln( '*** TRANSACTION DATE: ', CurrentMonth:1, '-', CurrentDay:1,
         ', ', CurrentYear:1 );
writeln( 'Total amount in home currency was $', Total:4:2 )
END {CurrencyConversion3}.
```

Sample run:

```
Enter the current month, day, and year: 12 29 1992
This program converts US currency to Canadian
currency or vice versa and finds the total of all
amounts. Enter 0 to signal that all amounts have been processed.

Enter 1 if home currency is U.S. currency
      2 if it is Canadian currency: 1
Enter the U.S. to Canadian conversion rate: 1.13
Enter currency type and amount (0 0 to stop): 2 5.00
This is equivalent to 4.42 U.S. Dollars
Enter currency type and amount (0 0 to stop): 1 10.00
Enter currency type and amount (0 0 to stop): 1 20.00
Enter currency type and amount (0 0 to stop): 2 15.00
This is equivalent to 13.27 U.S. Dollars
Enter currency type and amount (0 0 to stop): 0 0
*** TRANSACTION DATE: 12-29, 1992
Total amount in home currency was $47.70
```

In this program, the declarations of the four variables **CurrencyCode**, **ConversionRate**, **Money**, and **ConvertedMoney** associate memory locations with these variables:

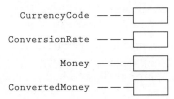

When the procedure reference statement

```
Convert( CurrencyCode, ConversionRate, Money, ConvertedMoney )
```

is executed, *new memory locations are associated with the formal value parameters* **Code**, **Rate**, and **Amount** of procedure **Convert**, and the values of **CurrencyCode**, **ConversionRate**, and **Money** are copied into these locations. No new memory location is obtained for the formal variable parameter **EquivAmount**; instead, this *variable parameter is associated with the existing memory location of the corresponding actual parameter* **ConvertedMoney**.

Actual Parameters	Memory Locations	Formal Parameters
CurrencyCode — — ⎯	2 ⎯⎯⎯⎯▶ 2	⎯⎯⎯⎯ Code
ConversionRate — — ⎯	1.13 ⎯⎯⎯▶1.13	⎯⎯⎯⎯ Rate
Money — — ⎯	5.00 ⎯⎯⎯▶5.00	⎯⎯⎯⎯ Amount
ConvertedMoney — — — — — — ⎯	⬚	⎯⎯⎯⎯⎯⎯⎯ EquivAmount

When the procedure **Convert2** is executed, a value is calculated for **EquivAmount**, and because **ConvertedMoney** is associated with the same memory location as **EquivAmount**, this value is also the value of **ConvertedMoney**.

Actual Parameters	Memory Locations	Formal Parameters
CurrencyCode — — ⎯	2 ⎯⎯⎯⎯▶ 2	⎯⎯⎯ Code
ConversionRate — — ⎯	1.13 ⎯⎯⎯▶1.13	⎯⎯⎯ Rate
Money — — ⎯	5.00 ⎯⎯⎯▶5.00	⎯⎯⎯ Amount
ConvertedMoney — — — — — ⎯	4.42	⎯⎯⎯⎯⎯⎯ EquivAmount

Because the memory locations associated with **CurrencyCode**, **ConversionRate**, and **Money** are distinct from those for **Code**, **Rate**, and **Amount**, changes to **Code**, **Rate**, and **Amount** in procedure **Convert2** cannot change the values of **CurrencyCode**, **ConversionRate**, and **Money**. When execution of the procedure is completed, the association of memory locations with **Code**, **Rate**, **Amount**, and **EquivAmount** is terminated, and these formal parameters become undefined:

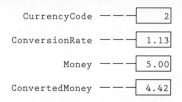

When a procedure is referenced, the number of actual parameters must be the same as the number of formal parameters, and the type of each parameter must be the same as the type of the corresponding formal parameter. One exception is that an actual parameter of integer type may be associated with a value parameter of real type. Thus, in a program in which variables **N1**, **N2**, and **N3** have been declared to be of integer type and **R1**, **R2**, and **R3** of real type, the procedure **Convert2** can be called with either of the following statements:

```
Convert2( N1, N2, N3, R1 )
Convert2( N1, N2 / 4, 7.5, R1 )
```

The following would not be valid, however, for the reasons indicated:

`Convert2( N1, R1, R2 )`	(The number of actual parameters does not agree with the number of formal parameters.)
`Convert2( N1, R1, R2, R3 / 5.1 )`	(The expression **R3 / 5.1** may not be associated with the *variable* parameter **EquivAmount**.)
`Convert( N1, R1, R2, N2 )`	(The **integer** actual parameter **N2** may not be associated with the real *variable* parameter **EquivAmount**.)

Rules for Parameter Association

The following rules summarize the relation between actual and formal parameters:

1. There must be the same number of formal parameters as there are actual parameters.
2. The types of associated formal and actual parameters must agree; however, an actual parameter of **integer** type may be associated with a formal *value* parameter of **real** type, but not with a formal *variable* parameter.
3. An actual parameter associated with a *variable* formal parameter must be a variable; it may not be a constant or an expression.

5.3   More Examples of Procedures

Example 1: Displaying a Date

Problem.   Modify the program in Figures 5.3 so that the transaction date entered by the user during execution of the main program is displayed in the form *mm/dd/yy,* where *mm* and *dd* are two-digit integers representing the month and the day, respectively, and *yy* is the last two digits of the year. For examples, the values 7, 4, 1976 are to be displayed as

```
07/04/76
```

and the values 12, 25, 1905 as

```
12/25/05
```

We could simply replace the last **writeln** statement in the main program by a set of statements that produce output in the required form, but the details of formatting this output are not really part of the conversion problem and would obscure the logical flow of the program. Thus we will isolate these details in a separate procedure **DisplayDate** to which the month, day, and year are passed. Also, this will make it possible to use this procedure in other programs that may require dates to be formatted in this manner.

Since the month, day, and year must be passed to the procedure **DisplayDate**, this procedure must have three formal parameters of **integer** type. And since these parameters are used only to pass values to the procedure, they will be value parameters. Thus, an appropriate heading is

```
PROCEDURE DisplayDate( Month,              {month number}
                       Day,                {day number}
                       Year : integer );   {the year}
```

Two digits are to be displayed for each of **Month**, **Day**, and **Year**. The last two digits of the year can be obtained by using the statement

```
Year := Year MOD 100;
```

If any of the values of **Month**, **Day**, and **Year** is less than 10, it will be necessary to first display a leading zero; for example,

```
IF Month < 10 THEN
   write( '0' );
write( Month:1, '/' );
```

The complete procedure is

```
PROCEDURE DisplayDate( Month,              {month number}
                       Day,                {day number}
                       Year : integer );   {the year}
{-------------------------------------------------------------

   Accepts:         Month, Day, Year.
   Purpose:         Display the date in the form mm/dd/yy.
   Output (screen): The date in a special format.

-------------------------------------------------------------}

BEGIN
   IF Month < 10 THEN
      write( '0' );
   write( Month:1, '/' );
   IF Day < 10 THEN
      write( '0' );
   write( Day:1, '/' );
   Year := Year MOD 100;
   IF Year < 10 THEN
      write( '0' );
   writeln( Year:1 )
END {DisplayDate};
```

Figure 5.4 shows the modified currency conversion program with this procedure added.

 FIGURE 5.4   Currency conversion—version 4.

```
PROGRAM CurrencyConversion4( input, output );
{***********************************************************************

    Input (keyboard): Current month, day, and year, an integer
                      indicating the home currency type, a conversion
                      rate, and several conversion codes and monetary
                      amounts.
    Purpose:          Convert U.S. currency to Canadian currency or
                      vice versa and find total of all amounts.
    Output (screen):  Instructions to the user, converted monetary
                      amounts, the date of the transactions, and total
                      of amounts.

    ***********************************************************************}

VAR
    CurrentMonth,            {current month}
    CurrentDay,              {current day}
    CurrentYear,             {current year}
    HomeCurrency,            {indicates type of home currency}
    CurrencyCode : integer;  {indicates currency type of monetary amounts}
    ConversionRate,          {the U.S. to Canadian conversion rate}
    Money,                   {monetary amount}
    ConvertedMoney,          {equivalent amount in other currency system}
    Total : real;            {total of the amounts}

PROCEDURE DisplayInstructions;
        .
        .
        .

PROCEDURE Convert2(     Code : integer;        {type of currency}
                        Rate,                  {conversion rate}
                        Amount : real;         {monetary amount to convert}
                    VAR EquivAmount : real );  {equivalent amount}
        .
        .
        .

PROCEDURE DisplayDate( Month,               {month number}
                       Day,                 {day number}
                       Year : integer );    {the year}
{-------------------------------------------------------------------

    Accepts:  Month, Day, Year.
    Purpose:  Display the date in the form mm/dd/yy.
    Output :  The date in a special format.


    -------------------------------------------------------------------}
```

FIGURE 5.4   Currency conversion—version 4. (cont.)

```
   BEGIN
      IF Month < 10 THEN
         write( '0' );
      write( Month:1, '/' );
      IF Day < 10 THEN
         write( '0' );
      write( Day:1, '/' );
      Year := Year MOD 100;
      IF Year < 10 THEN
         write( '0' );
      writeln( Year:1 )
   END {DisplayDate};


BEGIN {*********************** main program ***********************}
   write( 'Enter the current month, day, and year: ' );
   readln( CurrentMonth, CurrentDay, CurrentYear );
   DisplayInstructions;
   readln( HomeCurrency );
   write( 'Enter the U.S. to Canadian conversion rate: ' );
   readln( ConversionRate );
   Total := 0;

   write( 'Enter currency type and amount (0 0 to stop): ' );
   readln( CurrencyCode, Money );
   WHILE Money > 0 DO
      BEGIN
         IF CurrencyCode <> HomeCurrency THEN
            BEGIN
               Convert2( CurrencyCode, ConversionRate, Money,
                         ConvertedMoney );
               Total := Total + ConvertedMoney
            END {IF}
         ELSE
            Total := Total + Money;
         write( 'Enter currency type and amount (0 0 to stop): ' );
         readln( CurrencyCode, Money )
      END {WHILE};

   write( '*** TRANSACTION DATE: ' );
   DisplayDate( CurrentMonth, CurrentDay, CurrentYear );
   writeln( 'Total amount in home currency was $', Total:4:2 )
END {main program}.
```

Sample run:

```
Enter the current month, day, and year: 12 29 1992
This program converts US currency to Canadian
currency or vice versa and finds the total of all
amounts. Enter 0 to signal that all amounts have been processed.
```

FIGURE 5.4 Currency conversion—version 4. (cont.)

```
Enter 1 if home currency is U.S. currency
      2 if it is Canadian currency: 1
Enter the U.S. to Canadian conversion rate: 1.13
Enter currency type and amount (0 0 to stop): 2 5.00
This is equivalent to 4.42 U.S. Dollars
Enter currency type and amount (0 0 to stop): 1 10.00
Enter currency type and amount (0 0 to stop): 1 20.00
Enter currency type and amount (0 0 to stop): 2 15.00
This is equivalent to 13.27 U.S. Dollars
Enter currency type and amount (0 0 to stop): 0 0
*** TRANSACTION DATE: 12/29/92
Total amount in home currency was $47.70
```

When procedure **DisplayDate** is referenced, memory locations are associated with the value parameters **Month**, **Day**, and **Year**, and the values of the corresponding actual parameters **CurrentMonth**, **CurrentDay**, and **CurrentYear** are copied into these locations:

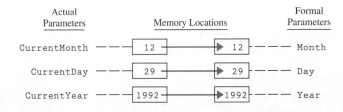

After execution of the procedure, these value parameters once again become undefined, so that any values they had during execution of the procedure are lost and are not returned to the main program or subprogram that calls the procedure. In particular, this means that although the statement

```
Year := Year MOD 100;
```

in **DisplayDate** changes the value of the formal parameter **Year**, it does not change the value of the corresponding actual parameter **CurrentYear**.

Example 2: Making Change

Problem. Design and test a procedure that reads the amount of a purchase and the amount given in payment and then computes and displays the change in dollars, half-dollars, quarters, dimes, nickels, and pennies.

A procedure to make change will have two value parameters, **Purchase** and **Payment**, of **real** type, whose values will be passed from the main program. It will also have variable parameters, **Dollars**, **Halves**, **Quarters**, **Dimes**, **Nickels**, and **Pennies** of **integer** type, whose values must be returned to the main program. An appropriate procedure heading is therefore

```
PROCEDURE MakeChange(       Purchase,            {amount of purchase}
                            Payment : real;      {amount of payment}
                        VAR Dollars, Halves,     {number of bills and}
                            Quarters, Dimes,     {coins to be given}
                            Nickels, Pennies
                                : integer );  {in change}
```

In addition, a local variable **Change** is needed to store intermediate results; this variable is declared in the declaration part of this procedure:

```
VAR
    Change : integer;
```

In the statement part of procedure **MakeChange**, **Change** is initially calculated by

```
Change := round( 100 * (Payment - Purchase) );
```

(The function **round** is used because the real values **Payment** and **Purchase** may not be stored exactly.) The number of dollars that must be given in change is then calculated by the statement

```
Dollars := Change DIV 100;
```

and the remaining change less than one dollar is given by

```
Change := Change MOD 100;
```

Similar calculations are used to determine the number of half-dollars, quarters, dimes, nickels, and pennies. The complete procedure is

```
PROCEDURE MakeChange(       Purchase,            {amount of purchase}
                            Payment : real;      {amount of payment}
                        VAR Dollars, Halves,     {number of bills and}
                            Quarters, Dimes,     {coins to be given}
                            Nickels, Pennies     {in change}
                                : integer );
{--------------------------------------------------------------------

    Accepts:  Amount of Purchase and amount of Payment.
    Purpose:  Determine various denominations of change for a given
              purchase and payment.
    Returns:  Number of each denomination to be given in change.

--------------------------------------------------------------------}

VAR
    Change : integer;    {amount of change}
```

```
BEGIN
    Change := round( 100 * (Payment - Purchase) );
    Dollars := Change DIV 100;
    Change := Change MOD 100;
    Halves := Change DIV 50;
    Change := Change MOD 50;
    Quarters := Change DIV 25;
    Change := Change MOD 25;
    Dimes := Change DIV 10;
    Change := Change MOD 10;
    Nickels := Change DIV 5;
    Pennies := Change MOD 5
END {MakeChange};
```

To test this procedure we might write a **test driver** program like that in Figure 5.5, that simply reads in the two amounts `AmountPurchased` and `AmountPaid` and calls procedure `MakeChange` to calculate the change that must be given. The main program then displays the amounts returned by `MakeChange`.

FIGURE 5.5 Making change.

```
PROGRAM ChangeMaker( input, output );
{******************************************************************

    Input (keyboard): Amount of a purchase and amount paid.
    Purpose:          Test procedure MakeChange that determines
                      change to be returned.
    Output (screen):  Prompts, labels, and change in dollars, halves,
                      quarters, dimes, nickels, and pennies.

******************************************************************}

VAR
    AmountPurchased,            {purchase made}
    AmountPaid : real;          {payment received (>= AmountPurchased)}
    NumberOfDollars,            {number of bills}
    NumberOfHalves,             { and}
    NumberOfQuarters,           {  :  }
    NumberOfDimes,              {coins}
    NumberOfNickels,            {  :  }
    NumberOfPennies : integer;  {to be returned in change}
```

FIGURE 5.5 Making change. (cont.)

```
PROCEDURE MakeChange(     Purchase,          {amount of purchase}
                         Payment : real;    {amount of payment}
                     VAR Dollars, Halves,   {number of bills and}
                         Quarters, Dimes,    {coins to be given}
                         Nickels, Pennies   {in change}
                             : integer );
{-----------------------------------------------------------------

   Accepts:   Amount of Purchase and amount of Payment.
   Purpose:   Determine various denominations of change
              for a given purchase and payment.
   Returns:   Number of each denomination to be given in change.


------------------------------------------------------------------}

   VAR
      Change : integer;   {amount of change}

   BEGIN
      Change := round( 100 * (Payment - Purchase) );
      Dollars := Change DIV 100;
      Change := Change MOD 100;
      Halves := Change DIV 50;
      Change := Change MOD 50;
      Quarters := Change DIV 25;
      Change := Change MOD 25;
      Dimes := Change DIV 10;
      Change := Change MOD 10;
      Nickels := Change DIV 5;
      Pennies := Change MOD 5
   END {MakeChange};

BEGIN {*********************** main program ***********************}
   write( 'Amount purchased and amount paid (0 0 to stop)?  ' );
   readln( AmountPurchased, AmountPaid );
   WHILE AmountPurchased > 0 DO
      BEGIN
         MakeChange( AmountPurchased, AmountPaid, NumberOfDollars,
                  NumberOfHalves, NumberOfQuarters, NumberOfDimes,
                  NumberOfNickels,NumberOfPennies );
         writeln( 'Change returned:' );
         writeln( NumberOfDollars:1, ' Dollars' );
         writeln( NumberOfHalves:1, ' Halves' );
         writeln( NumberOfQuarters:1, ' Quarters' );
         writeln( NumberOfDimes:1, ' Dimes' );
         writeln( NumberOfNickels:1, ' Nickels' );
         writeln( NumberOfPennies:1, ' Pennies' );
         writeln;
         write( 'Amount purchased and amount paid (0 0 to stop)?  ' );
         readln( AmountPurchased, AmountPaid )
      END {WHILE}
END {main program}.
```

FIGURE 5.5   Making change. (cont.)

Sample run:

```
Amount purchased and amount paid (0 0 to stop)?  1.01 2.00
Change tendered:
0 Dollars
1 Halves
1 Quarters
2 Dimes
0 Nickels
4 Pennies

Amount purchased and amount paid (0 0 to stop)?  1.09 3.00
Change tendered:
1 Dollars
1 Halves
1 Quarters
1 Dimes
1 Nickels
1 Pennies

Amount purchased and amount paid (0 0 to stop)?  9.99 10.00
Change tendered:
0 Dollars
0 Halves
0 Quarters
0 Dimes
0 Nickels
1 Pennies

Amount purchased and amount paid (0 0 to stop)?  0 0
```

5.4 Example of Modular Programming: Menu-Driven Checkbook-Balancing Program

In the introduction to this chapter, we claimed that one of the advantages of procedures is that they enable a programmer to develop programs in a **modular** fashion. This means that the major tasks to be performed by the program can be identified and individual procedures for these tasks can then be designed and tested. Programs written in this manner are not only easier to develop and test and easier to understand, but are also easier to modify, since individual modules can be added, deleted, or altered. In this section we demonstrate this technique of modular programming by developing a simple checkbook-balancing program.

Problem: Checkbook Reconciliation

A checkbook register is a record of the activity in a checking account. Whenever an amount is deposited in the account, it is recorded in the register and the account balance is updated by adding this amount to it. Whenever a check is written, the amount of the check, together with a service charge (if any), is recorded and subtracted from the balance. Each month a bank statement is mailed to customers that shows (among other things), the beginning balance in the account, the number of deposits, the number of checks written, the total of all check amounts, the total of all deposits, the total service charges, and the final balance. We wish to develop a program to assist with reconciling the checkbook register with such a statement, that is, to check if the information recorded in the register agrees with that shown on the statement.

Specification

The input to the program will consist of information obtained from the checkbook register, and the output will consist of items shown on the bank statement. Thus we have the following specification for this problem:

Input:	Initial balance
	Check amounts
	Amounts of deposits
Output:	Initial balance
	Number of checks processed
	Total amount of checks
	Number of deposits
	Total deposits
	Total service charges
	Final balance

Design Plan

Three main tasks must be performed:

1. Process deposits.
2. Process checks.
3. Print a summary of the transactions.

To make the program easy to use, we will design it as a **menu-driven program,** which will allow the user to select the appropriate task to be performed. Each of the possible options in this menu will be implemented as a procedure that will be called when the corresponding menu item is selected. In addition to these three procedures, another procedure will be designed to display the menu of options to the user, and another will be used to initialize certain variables used in the program. The following **structure diagram** thus summarizes the structure of the program:

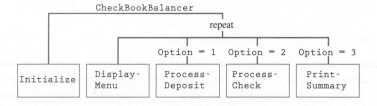

VARIABLES FOR CHECKBOOK-BALANCING PROGRAM

`InitialBalance`	Beginning balance in the checking account.
`Balance`	Current balance in the checking account.
`TotalDeposits`	Sum of all deposits for the month.
`TotalChecks`	Sum of all checks processed.
`TotalServiceCharges`	Total check-processing charges.
`NumberOfDeposits`	Total number of deposits made.
`NumberOfChecks`	Total number of checks written.
`Option`	Option selected by the user from the menu.

ALGORITHM FOR MAIN PROGRAM

(* Input: User-selected options, initial account balance, amounts of
deposits, amounts of checks.

Purpose: Read options entered by the user, and call the appropriate
subalgorithms to perform the processing selected.

Output: Menu of options, summary of month's activity. *)

1. Call subalgorithm **Initialize**.
2. Call subalgorithm **DisplayMenu**.
3. Read the first **Option**.
4. While **Option** ≠ 0 do the following:
   a. If **Option** = 1 then
        Call subalgorithm **DisplayMenu**.
      Else if **Option** = 2 then
        Call subalgorithm **ProcessDeposits**.
      Else if **Option** = 3 then
        Call subalgorithm **ProcessChecks**.
      Else if **Option** = 4 then
        Call subalgorithm **PrintSummary**.
      Else
        Display an "Invalid Option" message.
   b. Read the next **Option**.

SUBALGORITHM Initialize

(* Input: The **InitialBalance**.

Purpose: Get initial balance and initialize key variables.

Returns: **InitialBalance** and **Balance**; the initial value 0 for
TotalDeposits, **TotalChecks**, **TotalServiceCharges**,
NumberOfDeposits, and **NumberOfChecks**. *)

1. Read the **InitialBalance**.
2. Set **Balance** equal to **InitialBalance**.
3. Set each of **TotalDeposits**, **TotalChecks**, **TotalServiceCharges**,
NumberOfDeposits, and **NumberOfChecks** equal to 0.

SUBALGORITHM `DisplayMenu`

(* Purpose: Display a menu of options to the user.
   Output: Menu of options. *)

Display the following list of options:
   0: Stop processing
   1: Display this menu.
   2: Process a deposit.
   3: Process a check.
   4. Print a summary of transactions.

SUBALGORITHM `ProcessDeposit`

(* Accepts: Current `Balance, TotalDeposits`, and `NumberOfDeposits`.
   Input: Amount of `Deposit`.
   Purpose: Process a deposit by updating the values of `Balance`,
               `TotalDeposits`, and `NumberOfDeposits`.
   Returns: Updated values of `Balance, TotalDeposits`, and
               `NumberOfDeposits`. *)

1. Read `Deposit`.
2. Add `Deposit` to `Balance`.
3. Add `Deposit` to `TotalDeposits`.
4. Increment `NumberOfDeposits` by 1.

SUBALGORITHM `ProcessCheck`

(* Accepts: Current `Balance, TotalChecks, TotalServiceCharges`, and
               `NumberOfChecks`.
   Input: Amount of `Check`.
   Purpose: Process a check by updating the values of `Balance`,
               `TotalChecks, TotalServiceCharges`, and `NumberOfChecks`.
   Returns: Updated values of `Balance, TotalChecks`,
               `TotalServiceCharges`, and `NumberOfChecks`. *)

1. Read `Check`.
2. Subtract `Check` and `CheckCharge` from `Balance`.
3. Add `Check` to `TotalChecks`.
4. Add `CheckCharge` to `TotalServiceCharges`.
5. Increment `NumberOfChecks` by 1.

SUBALGORITHM `PrintSummary`

(* Accepts: `InitialBalance, Balance, TotalDeposits, TotalChecks`,
               `TotalServiceCharges, NumberOfDeposits, NumberOfChecks`.
   Purpose: Display summary of monthly transactions.
   Output: `InitialBalance, Balance, TotalDeposits, TotalChecks`,
               `TotalServiceCharges, NumberOfDeposits, NumberOfChecks`. *)

Display the values of `InitialBalance, TotalDeposits, TotalChecks`,
`TotalServiceCharges, Balance, NumberOfDeposits`, and `NumberOfChecks`.

Coding and Testing

For the procedure `Initialize`, all of the parameters must be variable parameters, since each of the values must be returned. An appropriate procedure heading is

```
PROCEDURE Initialize ( VAR InitialBalance,      {beginning balance}
                           Balance,             {current balance}
                           TotalDeposits,       {sum of all deposits}
                           TotalChecks,         {sum of all checks}
                           TotalServiceCharges  {sum of service charges}
                             : real;
                       VAR NumberOfDeposits,    {total # of deposits}
                           NumberOfChecks       {total # of checks}
                             : integer );
```

Note that although in previous examples we used different names for the actual parameters and the corresponding formal parameters, this is not necessary. In a problem like this in which all the procedures process the same quantities, it makes sense to use the same variable names throughout the program.

The procedure `DisplayMenu` simply displays the menu of options available to the user; no information is passed to or from it. Its heading thus requires no formal parameters:

```
PROCEDURE DisplayMenu;
```

The parameters for procedure `ProcessDeposit` must be in–out parameters, that is, variable parameters, because the current values for `Balance`, `TotalDeposits`, and `NumberOfDeposits` will be passed to this procedure, which must then update them and return the new values. Similarly, each of the parameters for procedure `ProcessCheck` must be variable parameters. Appropriate headings for these procedures are therefore

```
PROCEDURE ProcessDeposit ( VAR Balance,         {current balance}
                               TotalDeposits,   {sum of all deposits}
                                 : real;
                           VAR NumberOfDeposits {total # of deposits}
                                 : integer );
PROCEDURE ProcessCheck ( VAR Balance,           {current balance}
                             TotalChecks,        {sum of all checks}
                             TotalServiceCharges {sum of service charges}
                               : real;
                         VAR NumberOfChecks      {total # of checks}
                               : integer );
```

The procedure `PrintSummary` displays information that is passed to it. Its formal parameters are thus in parameters, that is, value parameters, so that its heading is

```
PROCEDURE PrintSummary( InitialBalance,      {beginning balance}
                        Balance,             {current balance}
                        TotalDeposits,       {sum of all deposits}
                        TotalChecks,         {sum of all checks}
                        TotalServiceCharges {sum of service charges}
                          : real;
                        NumberOfDeposits,    {total # of deposits}
                        NumberOfChecks       {total # of checks}
                          : integer );
```

Figure 5.6 shows the complete program with complete procedures. Although the final program is given here, it could well have been developed in a stepwise manner by writing and testing only some of the procedures before writing the others. In this case, undeveloped procedures could simply have empty statement parts:

```
BEGIN
END {ProcessCheck};
```

Usually, however, they would be **procedure stubs** that at least signal execution of these procedures:

```
BEGIN
   writeln( 'Executing ProcessCheck' )
END {ProcessCheck};
```

and they might also produce temporary printouts to assist in checking the procedures.

FIGURE 5.6 Balancing a checkbook.

```
PROGRAM CheckbookBalancer( input, output );
{*********************************************************************

   Input (keyboard):   User-selected options, initial account balance,
                       amounts of deposits, amounts of checks.
   Purpose:            This is a menu-driven program for reconciling
                       a checkbook with a monthly statement.
   Output (screen):    User prompts, menu of options, summary of
                       month's activities.

   *********************************************************************}

VAR
   InitialBalance,                 {beginning balance in checking account}
   Balance,                        {current balance}
   TotalDeposits,                  {sum of all deposits for the month}
   TotalChecks,                    {sum of all checks processed}
   TotalServiceCharges : real;     {total check-processing charges}
   NumberOfDeposits,               {total number of deposits made}
   NumberOfChecks,                 {          and checks written}
   Option : integer;               {option selected by user}
```

FIGURE 5.6   Balancing a checkbook. (cont.)

```
PROCEDURE Initialize( VAR InitialBalance,        {beginning balance}
                          Balance,               {current balance}
                          TotalDeposits,         {sum of all deposits}
                          TotalChecks,           {sum of all checks}
                          TotalServiceCharges    {sum of service charges}
                              : real;
                      VAR NumberOfDeposits,       {total # of deposits}
                          NumberOfChecks          {total # of checks}
                              : integer );
{------------------------------------------------------------------

    Input (keyboard):   InitialBalance.
    Purpose:            Get initial balance from user and initialize
                        variables.
    Returns:            InitialBalance, Balance (= InitialBalance),
                        0 values for TotalDeposits, TotalChecks,
                        TotalServiceCharges, NumberOfDeposits, and
                        NumberOfChecks.
    Output (screen):    User prompts.

-------------------------------------------------------------------}

    BEGIN
        write( 'Enter beginning balance:  $' );
        readln( InitialBalance );
        writeln;
        Balance := InitialBalance;
        TotalDeposits := 0;
        TotalChecks := 0;
        TotalServiceCharges := 0;
        NumberOfDeposits := 0;
        NumberOfChecks := 0
    END {Initialize};

PROCEDURE DisplayMenu;
{------------------------------------------------------------------

    Purpose:         Display the menu of options.
    Output (screen): Menu of options.

-------------------------------------------------------------------}

    BEGIN
        writeln( 'Options available are:' );
        writeln( '0.  Quit processing' );
        writeln( '1.  Display this menu' );
        writeln( '2.  Process a deposit' );
        writeln( '3.  Process a check' );
        writeln ('4.  Print summary of month''s activities' );
    END {DisplayMenu};
```

FIGURE 5.6   Balancing a checkbook. (cont.)

```
PROCEDURE ProcessDeposit( VAR Balance,           {current balance}
                              TotalDeposits      {sum of all deposits}
                                : real;
                              VAR NumberOfDeposits  {total # of deposits}
                                : integer );
{-----------------------------------------------------------------------

   Accepts:          Current Balance, TotalDeposits, and
                     NumberOfDeposits.
   Input (keyboard): Amount of deposit.
   Purpose:          Process a deposit by updating the Balance,
                     TotalDeposits, and NumberOfDeposits.
   Output (screen):  User prompt.
   Returns:          Updated values of Balance, TotalDeposits, and
                     NumberOfDeposits.


-----------------------------------------------------------------------}

   VAR
      Deposit : real;             {amount of deposit}

   BEGIN
      write( 'Enter deposit:  $' );
      readln( Deposit );
      Balance := Balance + Deposit;
      TotalDeposits := TotalDeposits + Deposit;
      NumberOfDeposits := NumberOfDeposits + 1
   END {ProcessDeposit};

PROCEDURE ProcessCheck( VAR Balance,             {current balance}
                            TotalChecks,         {sum of all checks}
                            TotalServiceCharges  {sum of service charges}
                              : real;
                            VAR NumberOfChecks   {total # of checks}
                              : integer );
{-----------------------------------------------------------------------

   Accepts:          Current Balance, TotalChecks, TotalServiceCharges,
                     and NumberOfChecks.
   Input (keyboard): Amount of check.
   Purpose:          Process a check by updating the Balance,
                     TotalChecks, and NumberOfChecks.  A fee
                     CheckCharge is charged for processing each check.
   Output (screen):  User prompt.
   Returns:          Updated values of Balance, TotalChecks,
                     TotalServiceCharges, and NumberOfChecks.


-----------------------------------------------------------------------}
```

FIGURE 5.6 Balancing a checkbook. (cont.)

```
CONST
    CheckCharge = 0.20;      {per check processing charge}

VAR
    Check : real;            {amount of check}

BEGIN
    write( 'Enter check:  $' );
    readln( Check );
    Balance := Balance - Check - CheckCharge;
    TotalChecks := TotalChecks + Check;
    TotalServiceCharges := TotalServiceCharges + CheckCharge;
    NumberOfChecks := NumberOfChecks + 1
END {ProcessCheck};

PROCEDURE PrintSummary( InitialBalance,       {beginning balance}
                        Balance,              {current balance}
                        TotalDeposits,        {sum of all deposits}
                        TotalChecks,          {sum of all checks}
                        TotalServiceCharges {sum of service charges}
                          : real;
                        NumberOfDeposits,     {total # of deposits}
                        NumberOfChecks        {total # of checks}
                          : integer );
{-----------------------------------------------------------------

    Accepts:        InitialBalance, Balance, TotalDeposits,
                    TotalChecks, TotalServiceCharges,
                    NumberOfDeposits, and NumberOfChecks.
    Purpose:        Display a summary of month's transactions.
    Output (screen): A summary showing the values of the parameters.

-----------------------------------------------------------------}

BEGIN
    writeln;
    writeln( 'Initial Balance . . . . . . . . $', InitialBalance:8:2 );
    writeln( 'Total Deposits . . . . . . . . $', TotalDeposits:8:2 );
    writeln( 'Total Checks . . . . . . . . . $', TotalChecks:8:2 );
    writeln( 'Total Service Charges . . . . $',
                                        TotalServiceCharges:8:2 );
    writeln( 'Final Balance . . . . . . . . $', Balance:8:2 );
    writeln( 'Number of Deposits:  ', NumberOfDeposits:1 );
    writeln( 'Number of Checks:    ', NumberOfChecks:1 )
END {PrintSummary};
```

FIGURE 5.6   Balancing a checkbook. (cont.)

```
BEGIN {*********************** main program ***********************}
   Initialize( InitialBalance, Balance, TotalDeposits, TotalChecks,
              TotalServiceCharges, NumberOfDeposits, NumberOfChecks );
   DisplayMenu;
   writeln;
   write( 'Enter Option:  ' );
   readln( Option );
   WHILE Option <> 0 DO
      BEGIN
         IF Option = 1 THEN
            DisplayMenu
         ELSE IF Option = 2 THEN
            ProcessDeposit( Balance, TotalDeposits, NumberOfDeposits )
         ELSE IF Option = 3 THEN
            ProcessCheck( Balance, TotalChecks, TotalServiceCharges,
                         NumberOfChecks )
         ELSE IF Option = 4 THEN
            PrintSummary( InitialBalance, Balance, TotalDeposits,
                         TotalChecks, TotalServiceCharges,
                         NumberOfDeposits, NumberOfChecks )
         ELSE
            writeln( '*** Invalid Option ***' );
         writeln;
         write( 'Enter Option:  ' );
         readln( Option )
      END {WHILE}
END {main program}.
```

Sample run:

```
Enter beginning balance:  $357.40

Options available are:
0.  Quit processing
1.  Display this menu
2.  Process a deposit
3.  Process a check
4.  Print summary of month's activities

Enter Option:  1
Options available are:
0.  Quit processing
1.  Display this menu
2.  Process a deposit
3.  Process a check
4.  Print summary of month's activities

Enter Option:  2
Enter deposit:  $250.00
```

FIGURE 5.6   Balancing a checkbook. (cont.)

```
Enter Option:  3
Enter check:  $35.00

Enter Option:  3
Enter check:  $14.00

Enter Option:  4

Initial Balance  . . . . . . . . $  357.40
Total Deposits . . . . . . . . . $  250.00
Total Checks . . . . . . . . . . $   49.00
Total Service Charges  . . . . . $    0.40
Final Balance  . . . . . . . . . $  558.00
Number of Deposits:  1
Number of Checks:    2

Enter Option:  0
```

Maintenance

A major advantage of the modular design of a program such as this is that it is relatively easy to modify when necessary. For example, if the bank changes the amount charged for processing checks, we know immediately that procedure **ProcessCheck** is the one to modify; we simply change the value of **CheckCharge** to the new value. Similarly, if a charge is to be made for processing deposits, procedure **ProcessDeposit** is the one requiring modification. Some changes may require modification of more than one procedure, but the task is still considerably easier than in a nonmodular program, since one can usually determine which procedures require change and which ones must be added or deleted. For example, suppose we wish to modify the program to handle cash withdrawals as well, such as those from an automatic teller machine for which no processing charge is made. We could design a new procedure **ProcessATM** with variable parameters **Balance**, **TotalATMs**, and **NumberOfATMs**. To incorporate this procedure into the program, we need only do the following:

1. Add a call to procedure **ProcessATM** in the **IF—ELSE IF** construct with a new option number 5 (or perhaps renumber **PrintSummary** with 5 and use 4 for **ProcessATM**).
2. Add another **writeln** statement in procedure **DisplayMenu** to display the new option.
3. Modify the heading of the reference to procedure **Initialize** to include **TotalATMS** and **NumberOfATMs** as variable parameters and add statements to **Initialize** to set these to 0.
4. Modify the heading of and the reference to procedure **PrintSummary** to include **TotalATMS** and **NumberOfATMs** as parameters and statements in **PrintSummary** to display their values.

Exercises

1. Consider the following program skeleton:

```
PROGRAM Demo( input, output );

CONST
    pi = 3.14159;
    two = 2;
    Initial = 'N';

VAR
    Month, Day, Year, p, q : integer;
    Hours, Rate, Amount, u, v : real;
    Code, Class : char;

PROCEDURE Calculate(     a : real;
                     VAR b : real;
                         m : integer;
                     VAR k, n : integer;
                     VAR c : char );
                         .
                         .
                         .
```

Determine whether each of the following statements can be used in the statement part of the program. If it cannot be used, explain why.

(a) `Calculate( u, v, two, p, q, Code );`
(b) `Calculate( pi, u, two, p, v, Class );`
(c) `Calculate( Hours, pi, two, Day, Year, Class );`
(d) `Calculate( '16', Hours, pi, 13, Year, Class );`
(e) `Calculate( pi * Hours, pi, two, Day, Year, Class );`
(f) `Calculate( pi, pi * Hours, two, Day, Year, Class );`
(g) `WHILE u > 0 DO`
       `Calculate( u, v, two, p, q, Code );`
(h) `Calculate( 0, Hours, (p + 1) / 2, Day, Year, Code )`
(i) `Calculate( sqrt( Amount ), Rate, 7, p, q, Initial );`
(j) `WHILE Amount > 0 DO`
       `Calculate( two, Amount, Day, p + q, Day, Class );`
(k) `writeln( Calculate( u, v, two, p, q, Code ) ) ;`

2. Write a procedure **DisplayMonth** that displays the name of a month whose number is passed to it.

3. Write a procedure that accepts a time in military format and displays it in the corresponding usual representation in hours, minutes, and A.M./P.M. For example, a time of 0100 should be displayed as 1:00 A.M., and 1545 as 3:45 P.M.

4. Write a procedure that accepts a time in the usual representation of hours, minutes, and a boolean value that indicates whether this is A.M. (true) or P.M. (false) and displays the corresponding military time.

5. Write a procedure **CalculateWages** that calculates and returns the wages for a given number of hours worked and a given hourly pay rate. Hours over 40 should be paid at 1.5 times the regular hourly rate.

6. Write a procedure **Switch** that interchanges the values of its parameters. For example, if **a** has the value **3** and **b** has the value **4**, then the reference **Switch(a, b)** causes **a** to have the value **4** and **b** the value **3**.

7. Write a program that reads two positive integers **n** and **b** and then calls a procedure **ChangeBase** to calculate and display the base-**b** representation of **n**. Assume that **b** is not greater than 10. (See Exercise 13 of Section 1.2 for one method for converting from base 10 to another base. Displaying the digits in reverse order as generated by this method is acceptable.)

8. Write a program that reads a positive integer **n** and then calls a procedure **Hexadecimal** to display the base-16 representation of **n**. The symbols A, B, C, D, E, and F should be displayed for 10, 11, 12, 13, 14, and 15, respectively. (See Exercise 13 of Section 1.2 and the preceding exercise.)

9. (a) Write a procedure **ConvertLength** that accepts a real **Value** and two characters or strings, **InUnits** and **OutUnits**, and then converts **Value** given in **InUnits** to the equivalent metric value in **OutUnits** and displays this value. The procedure should carry out the following conversions:

InUnits	OutUnits	
I	C	(inches to centimeters; 1 in = 2.54001 cm)
F	C	(feet to centimeters; 1 in = 30.4801 cm)
F	M	(feet to meters; 1 ft. = 0.304801 m)
Y	M	(yards to meters; 1 yd = 0.914402 m)
M	K	(miles to kilometers; 1 mi = 1.60935 km)

(b) Write a driver program that reads several values to be converted and the units and then calls this procedure to carry out the specified conversion. What happens if you enter units other than those listed?

(c) Write a procedure **ConvertWeight** that carries out the following conversions:

InUnits	OutUnits	
O	G	(ounces to grams; 1 ounce = 28.349527 g)
P	K	(pounds to kilograms; 1 pound = 0.453592 kg)

(d) Write a procedure **ConvertVolume** that carries out the following conversions:

InUnits	OutUnits	
P	L	(pints to liters; 1 pint = 0.473167 L)
Q	L	(quarts to liters; 1 quart = 0.946333 L)
G	L	(gallons to liters; 1 gallon = 3.78533 L)

(e) Write a menu-driven program to test the three procedures **ConvertLength**, **ConvertWeight**, and **ConvertVolume**. It should allow the user to select one of three options according to whether lengths, weights, or volumes are to be converted, read the value to be converted and the units, and then call the appropriate procedure to carry out the conversion.

10. With **polar coordinates** (r, θ) of a point P, the first polar coordinate r is the distance from the origin to P, and the second polar coordinate θ is the angle from the positive x axis to the ray joining the origin with P.

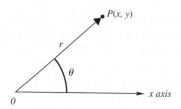

The formulas that relate polar coordinates of a point to its **rectangular coordinates** (x, y) are

$$x = r \cos \theta$$
$$y = r \sin \theta$$

Write a procedure **Convert** that converts polar coordinates to rectangular coordinates. Use it in a program that reads the polar coordinates for several points and calls **Convert**, which calculates and returns the rectangular coordinates for each point. The main program should display both pairs of coordinates.

11. Write a procedure **CalculateTaxes** that calculates and returns the amount of city income tax and the amount of federal income tax to be withheld from an employee's pay for one pay period. Assume that city income tax withheld is computed by taking 1.15 percent of gross pay on the first $15,000 earned per year and that federal income tax withheld is computed by taking the gross pay less $15 for each dependent claimed and multiplying by 20 percent.

   Use this procedure in a program that for each of several employees reads the employee's number, number of dependents, hourly pay rate, city income tax withheld to date, federal income tax withheld to date, and hours worked for this period and then calls procedure **CalculateTaxes** to find the amount of taxes to be withheld. The main program should then display the employee number, gross pay and net pay for this pay period, the amount of city income tax and the amount of federal income tax withheld for this pay period, and the total amounts withheld through this pay period.

12. The **greatest common divisor** of two integers a and b, GCD(a, b), not both of which are zero, is the largest positive integer that divides both a and b. The **Euclidean algorithm** for finding this greatest common divisor of a and b is as follows: Divide a by b to obtain the integer quotient q and remainder r, so that $a = bq + r$. (If $b = 0$, GCD$(a, b) = a$.) Then GCD$(a, b) = $ GCD(b, r). Replace a with b and b with r, and repeat this procedure. Since the remainders are

decreasing, eventually a remainder of 0 will result. The last nonzero remainder is GCD(a, b). For example,

$$1260 = 198 \cdot 6 + 72 \qquad \text{GCD}(1260, 198) = \text{GCD}(198, 72)$$
$$198 = 72 \cdot 2 + 54 \qquad\qquad\qquad\quad = \text{GCD}(72, 54)$$
$$72 = 54 \cdot 1 + 18 \qquad\qquad\qquad\quad = \text{GCD}(54, 18)$$
$$54 = 18 \cdot 3 + 0 \qquad\qquad\qquad\quad\; = 18$$

(*Note:* If either a or b is negative, replace it with its absolute value.) The **least common multiple** of a and b, LCM(a, b), is the smallest nonnegative integer that is a multiple of both a and b and can be calculated using

$$\text{LCM}(a, b) = \frac{|a \cdot b|}{\text{GCD}(a, b)}$$

Write a program that reads two integers and then calls a procedure that calculates and returns their greatest common divisor and their least common multiple. The main program should then display the two integers together with their greatest common divisor and their least common multiple.

13. Modify the checkbook-balancing program in Figure 5.6 to process ATM transactions as described in the text. Although there is no charge for making a deposit using an ATM, there is a 20 cent charge for each withdrawal.

5.5 Functions

As we noted in the introduction, there are two kinds of subprograms in Pascal, procedures and functions. In this section we describe functions, how they are defined and used in a Pascal program.

As we have seen, Pascal provides several **predefined functions,** such as **sqr**, **round**, and **odd**. Recall that to use any of these functions to calculate a function value in an expression, one need only give the function name followed by the actual parameter, enclosed in parentheses. For example, the statements

```
writeln( sqr(x) );

Alpha := round( 100 * Beta ) / 100;

IF odd( Number ) THEN
   writeln( Number );
```

display the square of **x**, assign to **Alpha** the value of **Beta** rounded to the nearest hundredth, and display the value of **Number**, provided it is an odd integer.

In some programs it is convenient to define additional functions. Such **programmer-defined functions** are possible in Pascal, and once defined, they are used in the same way as the predefined functions.

Like procedures, functions are defined in the subprogram section of a program and consist of a heading, a declaration part, and a statement part. The syntax diagram for a function definition is

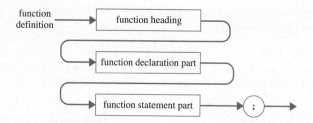

The general form a function thus is

Function

> Function heading
> Function declaration part
> Function statement part

The syntax diagram for a function heading is

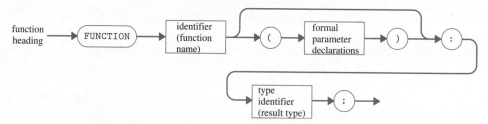

From this diagram, we see that a function heading has the following form:

Function Heading

Form:

    FUNCTION name(formal-parameter-declarations)
                        : result-type;

where:
   FUNCTION is a reserved word;
   name is a valid Pascal identifier;
   formal-parameter-declarations declares the parameters of
      the function;
   result-type is the type of the function value.

If the function has no parameters, the formal parameter declarations and the enclosing parentheses are omitted, so that the heading has the simple form

    FUNCTION name : result-type;

Purpose:
Names the function and declares its parameters and the type of the result.

The name of the function may be any legal Pascal identifier, and the value of the function is returned via this name. The type of this function value may be any of the standard data types considered thus far, **integer**, **real**, **char**, **string**, or **boolean** (or enumerated, subrange, or pointer types considered later). The formal parameter declarations have the same form as for a procedure heading.

The declaration and statement parts of a function definition have the same forms as for procedures, with the additional stipulation that at least one of the statements in the statement part must assign a value to the identifier that names the function.

Example: Cubes of Numbers

To illustrate, suppose that we wish to supplement the predefined function **sqr** by defining a function that computes the cube of a real number, that is, one that computes

$$f(x) = x^3$$

This function will have a single formal parameter of real type, and the result type will also be real. Thus an appropriate heading is

```
FUNCTION Cube( x : real ) : real;
```

and the complete function definition is

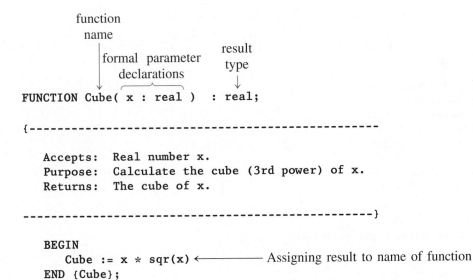

```
FUNCTION Cube( x : real )   : real;

{-------------------------------------------------------

   Accepts:  Real number x.
   Purpose:  Calculate the cube (3rd power) of x.
   Returns:  The cube of x.

-------------------------------------------------------}

   BEGIN
      Cube := x * sqr(x) ←——————— Assigning result to name of function
   END {Cube};
```

If this function definition is placed in the subprogram section of the declaration part of a program, the function **Cube** can then be referenced in the statement part of the program (or in later functions and procedures) in the same manner as are the predefined Pascal functions. The simple program in Figure 5.7 provides an illustration.

FIGURE 5.7   Printing a table of cubes.

```pascal
PROGRAM TableOfCubes( input, output );
{**********************************************************************

    Input (keyboard): A range of real numbers and a step size.
    Purpose:          Calculate a table of cubes of numbers in a
                      specified range.
    Output (screen):  User prompts, labels, a table of numbers and
                      their cubes.

**********************************************************************}
VAR
    Lower, Upper,    {bounds on range of values}
    Step,            {increment}
    Number : real;   {actual argument}

FUNCTION Cube( x : real ) : real;
{-----------------------------------------------------

    Accepts:  Real number x.
    Purpose:  Calculate the cube (3rd power) of x.
    Returns:  The cube of x.

-----------------------------------------------------}

    BEGIN
       Cube := x * sqr(x)
    END {Cube};

BEGIN {********************* main program *********************}
    write( 'Enter range of values and step size: ' );
    readln( Lower, Upper, Step );
    writeln;
    writeln( 'number   its cube' );
    writeln( '======   ========' );
    Number := Lower;
    WHILE Number <= Upper DO
       BEGIN
           writeln( Number:5:2, Cube(Number):12:4 );
           Number := Number + Step
       END {WHILE}
END {main program}.
```

Sample run:

```
Enter range of values and step size: 1 4 0.5

number    its cube
======    ========
 1.00       1.0000
 1.50       3.3750
 2.00       8.0000
 2.50      15.6250
 3.00      27.0000
 3.50      42.8750
 4.00      64.0000
```

Example: Rounding Amounts to the Nearest Cent

Several of the sample programs and exercises in the preceding chapters calculated wages. In these examples, and in most programs involving monetary calculations, the amounts should be rounded to the nearest cent. A function to do this is the following:

```
FUNCTION RoundCents( Amount : real )   {amount to be rounded}
                        : real;
{-------------------------------------------------------

     Accepts:  A real Amount.
     Purpose:  Round Amount to the nearest cent.
     Returns:  Rounded value of Amount.

-------------------------------------------------------

     BEGIN
        RoundCents := round( 100 * Amount ) / 100
     END {RoundCents};
```

A statement such as

```
GrossPay := RoundCents( Wages );
```

can be used to reference this function.

Example: Maximum of Two Integers

As another example, consider a function to find the maximum of two integers. If we name the function **Maximum** and its formal parameters **Number1** and **Number2**, then the function definition is

```
FUNCTION Maximum( Number1, Number2 : integer ) : integer;
{-------------------------------------------------------

     Accepts:  Two integers Number1 and Number2.
     Purpose:  Find the maximum of two integers.
     Returns:  Maximum of Number1 and Number2.

-------------------------------------------------------}
     BEGIN
        IF Number1 >= Number2 THEN
           Maximum := Number1
        ELSE
           Maximum := Number2
     END {Maximum};
```

Example: Pass–Fail Grades

In the preceding examples, the type of the function was the same as the type of its parameters, real for **Cube** and for **RoundCents** and integer for **Maximum**. This need not be the case, however. To illustrate, consider a function to assign a pass (P) or fail (F) grade according to whether a student's average is above or below some pass–fail line. If we name the function **PFGrade** and its formal parameters **Average** and **PFLine**, the function definition is given by

```
FUNCTION PFGrade( Average,          {an average score}
                  PFLine : real )   {pass-fail line}
                    : char;
{---------------------------------------------------------

   Accepts:   Real values Average and PFLine.
   Purpose:   Calculate a pass-fail grade of 'P' if
              Average >= PFLine, 'F' if Average < PFLine.
   Returns:   The pass-fail grade.

--------------------------------------------------------}

   BEGIN
      IF Average >= PFLine THEN
         PFGrade := 'P'
      ELSE
         PFGrade := 'F'
   END {PFGrade};
```

Note that this function has real parameters but that its value is of character type. The program in Figure 5.8 reads several students' averages and for each calls this function to determine whether the student passed or failed.

FIGURE 5.8 Determining pass-fail grades.

```
PROGRAM PassFailChecker( input, output );
{*****************************************************************

   Input (keyboard): A pass-fail line and several students' averages.
   Purpose:          Determine the pass-fail grade for each student
                     based on their averages.
   Output (screen):  User prompts, labels, and pass-fail grades.

*****************************************************************}

VAR
   Average,              {student's average}
   PFLine : real;        {pass/fail line}
   Grade : char;         {P/F grade assigned}

FUNCTION PFGrade( Average,          {an average score}
                  PFLine : real )   {pass-fail line}
                    : char;
{---------------------------------------------------------

   Accepts:   Real values Average and PFLine.
   Purpose:   Calculate a pass-fail grade of 'P' if
              Average >= PFLine, 'F' if Average < PFLine.
   Returns:   The pass-fail grade.

--------------------------------------------------------}
```

FIGURE 5.8   Determining pass-fail grades. (cont.)

```
    BEGIN
       IF Average >= PFLine THEN
          PFGrade := 'P'
       ELSE
          PFGrade := 'F'
    END {PFGrade};

BEGIN {****************** main program ******************}
    write( 'Enter pass-fail line:  ' );
    readln( PFLine );
    writeln( 'Enter a negative average to stop the program' );
    writeln;
    write( 'Student''s average? ' );
    readln( Average );
    WHILE Average >= 0 DO
       BEGIN
          Grade := PFGrade( Average, PFLine );
          writeln( '          Grade is  ', Grade );
          write( 'Student''s average? ' );
          readln( Average )
       END {WHILE}
END {main program}.
```

Sample run:

```
Enter pass-fail line:  60
Enter a negative average to stop the program

Student's average? 90
          Grade is  P
Student's average? 60
          Grade is  P
Student's average? 59.5
          Grade is  F
Student's average? 40
          Grade is  F
Student's average? -1
```

Example: Sum of Digits

Some function definitions may require using local variables other than the formal parameters to calculate the function value. To illustrate, suppose we wish to calculate the sum of the digits that make up a number. Such check sums are often used to detect errors in account numbers, stock numbers, id numbers, and so on. For example, an automatic teller machine may require that all valid id numbers have the property that the sum of their digits be divisible by 9 and will check whether id numbers entered by customers satisfy this condition. The following function can be used to find the sum of a number's digits:

```
FUNCTION CheckSum( Num : integer )    {number to be checked}
                          : integer;
{-------------------------------------------------------------

   Accepts:  An integer Number.
   Purpose:  Calculate the sum of the digits of a number.
   Returns:  Sum of Number's digits.


   -----------------------------------------------------------}

   VAR
      Sum : integer;

   BEGIN
      Sum := 0;
      WHILE Number <> 0 DO
         BEGIN
            Sum := Sum + Number MOD 10;
            Number := Number DIV 10
         END {WHILE};
      CheckSum := Sum
   END {CheckSum};
```

In this function, the local variable Sum is needed to accumulate the sum of the digits. The statement

```
   CheckSum := CheckSum + Number MOD 10;
```

can*not* be used because it contains an illegal function reference on the right side.

Functions Versus Procedures

Functions and procedures have many similarities:

1. The definition of each appears in the subprogram section of the declaration part of a program and in each case consists of a heading, a declaration part, and a statement part, followed by a semicolon.
2. Each of them is an independent program unit. Parameters, constants, and variables declared within a function or procedure are local to that function or procedure; they are accessible only within that subprogram.
3. When a function or procedure is referenced, the number of actual parameters must be the same as the number of formal parameters, and the types of actual parameters must agree with the types of corresponding formal parameters, with one exception: An actual parameter of integer type may be associated with a *value* parameter of real type.

There are also a number of differences between functions and procedures:

1. Whereas a procedure is referenced by a procedure reference statement, a function is referenced by using its name in an expression.
2. Since a value must be associated with a function name, a type must also be associated with it. Thus, the heading of a function must include a type identifier

that specifies the type of the result. No value is associated with the name of a procedure, however, and hence, no type is associated with it.

3. Functions usually return a single value to the main program or subprogram that references them. Procedures often return more than one value, or they may return no value at all but simply perform some task such as an output operation.

4. Values are returned from procedures by using variable parameters, but the value of a function is returned by assigning it to the function name within the statement part of the function definition. (Functions may also return values via parameters, but this is usually not done.)

Exercises

1. Consider the following program skeleton:

```
PROGRAM Demo( input, output );

CONST
    pi = 3.14159;
    two = 2;

VAR
    Month, Day, Year, p, q : integer;
    Hours, Rate, Amount, u, v : real;
    Code, Class : char;

FUNCTION f( x, y : real;
            d : integer ) : real;
         .
         .
         .

PROCEDURE Calculate(      a : real;
                      VAR b : real;
                          m : integer;
                      VAR k, n : integer;
                      VAR c : char );
         .
         .
         .
```

Determine whether each of the following statements can be used in the statement part of the program. If it cannot be used, explain why.

(a) `Amount := f( pi, Rate, Month );`
(b) `Rate := f( Hours, Day, two );`
(c) `writeln( f( 0, 0, 0 ) );`
(d) `f( Hours, Rate, Month );`
(e) `Calculate( u, v, p, two, Day, Code );`
(f) `Hours := two * f( pi, Amount ) / (2.71828 * Rate);`
(g) `Amount := f( pi * Hours, (2.71828 + Day) / Rate, two );`
(h) `IF Month = two THEN`
      `Year := f( Hours, f (Rate, pi, two ), Day );`

    (i)   IF u > 0 THEN

```
          Amount := Calculate( u, v, two, p, q, Code );
```

    (j)   IF Calculate(0, u, 1, p, Year, Class) > 0 THEN

```
          writeln( 'Okay' );
```

    (k) WHILE Amount > 0 DO

```
          Calculate( two, Amount, Day, p + q, Day, Class );
```

    (l) WHILE f(Amount, 0, 0) > 0 DO

```
          Amount := f( Amount, 0, Code );
```

    (m) Calculate(f(u, v, Day), Rate, 7, p, q, Code);

    (n) Calculate(Rate, f(u, v, Day), 7, p, q, Code);

    (o) Amount := f(a, b, Day);

2. Write a function **Range** that calculates the range between two integers, that is, the larger integer minus the smaller integer.

3. Write a function **Wages** that calculates and returns the wages for a given number of hours worked and a given hourly pay rate. Hours over 40 should be paid at 1.5 times the regular hourly rate.

4. Write a function that converts a temperature given in degrees Celsius to degrees Fahrenheit. (The conversion formula is $F = \frac{9}{5}C + 32$.)

5. Write a boolean-valued function **IsADigit** that determines whether a character is one of the digits 0 through 9.

6. Write a function **Binary** that converts a boolean value into its binary equivalent (false $\leftrightarrow$ 0, true $\leftrightarrow$ 1).

7. Write a function **RoundOff** that accepts a real value **Amount** and an integer value **NumPlaces** and returns the value of **Amount** rounded to the specified number of places. For example, the function references **RoundOff(10.536, 0)**, **RoundOff(10.536, 1)**, **RoundOff(10.536, 2)** should give the values 11.0, 10.5, and 10.54, respectively.

8. The number of bacteria in a culture can be estimated by

$$N \cdot e^{kt}$$

where N is the initial population, k is a rate constant, and t is time. Write a function to calculate the number of bacteria present at time t for given values of k and N; use it in a program that reads values for the initial population, the rate constant, and the time (e.g., 1000, 0.15, 100) and displays the number of bacteria at that time.

9. (a) Write a function **NumberGrade** that accepts a letter grade and returns the corresponding numeric value (A = 4.0, B = 3.0, C = 2.0, D = 1.0, F = 0.0).

    (b) Use the function **NumberGrade** in a program that reads several letter grades for students and calculates each student's average grade as the average of the numeric values of these letter grades.

(c) Write a function that accepts a number grade and returns the equivalent letter grade.

(d) Add this function to the program of part (b), and use it to find each student's average letter grade.

10. **(a)** Write a function **NumberGrade** that accepts a letter grade and one of the characters '+', '−', or a blank, and returns the corresponding numeric value, determined as follows: A = 4.0, A− = 3.7, B+ = 3.3, B = 3.0, B− = 2.7, C+ = 2.3, C = 2.0, C− = 1.7, D+ = 1.3, D = 1.0, D− = 0.7, F = 0.0.

(b) Use the function **NumberGrade** in a program that reads several letter grades for students and calculates each student's average grade as the average of the numeric values of these letter grades.

(c) Write a procedure that accepts a number grade in the range 0.0 through 4.0 and returns the equivalent letter grade together with a '+', '−', or blank. To determine the grade, find which of the values 0.0 , 0.7, 1.0, 1.3, 1.7, 2.0, 2.3, 2.7, 3.0, 3.3, 3.7, or 4.0 is nearest the numeric grade, and then use the letter equivalents given in part (a).

(d) Add this procedure to the program of part (b), and use it to find each student's average letter grade.

11. Write a character-valued function **LetterGrade** that assigns a letter grade to an integer score using the following grading scale

$$90–100: A$$
$$80–89: B$$
$$70–79: C$$
$$60–69: D$$
$$\text{Below } 60: F$$

Test the function with a program that reads several scores and displays the corresponding letter grades.

12. Write two boolean-valued functions that have formal parameters p and q of boolean type and that compute the values of the logical expressions

$$\sim p \wedge \sim q \quad (\text{not } p \text{ and not } q)$$

and

$$\sim(p \vee q) \quad (\text{not } (p \text{ or } q))$$

Write a program that prints truth values for these expressions, using these functions to compute the values.

13. A **prime number** is an integer $n > 1$ whose only positive divisors are 1 and n itself. Write a boolean-valued function that determines whether n is a prime number. Use it in a program that reads several integers, uses the function to determine whether each is prime, and displays each number with the appropriate label "is prime" or "is not prime."

5.6   Scope Rules

In a program that contains procedures and/or functions, there may be several points at which entities (variables, constants, procedures, functions, types) are declared—in the declaration part of the main program, in formal parameter declarations of procedure and function headings, or in declaration parts within procedures and functions. The portion of the program in which any of these items is *visible,* that is, where it is accessible and can be used, is called its **scope.** In this section, we state several rules that govern the scopes of objects in programs.

Fundamental Scope Principle

There is one general principle that describes the scope of an entity:

Fundamental Scope Principle

> The scope of an entity is the program or subprogram in which it is declared.

Scope Rule for Local Entities

One scope rule that follows from the fundamental scope principle applies to things that are declared within a procedure or function, that is, to the formal parameters that appear in its heading and to the constants, variables, procedure names, and function names in its declaration part (and type identifiers, described in Chapter 8):

Scope Rule 1

> An item declared within a procedure or function is not accessible outside that procedure or function.

To illustrate this rule we consider the problem of calculating depreciation. One of the methods of calculating depreciation is the *sum-of-the-years-digits* method. In this method, if a given *Amount* is to be depreciated over *NumYears* years, then the amount depreciated in the kth year is given by

$$\frac{(NumYears - k + 1) * Amount}{1 + 2 + \cdots + NumYears}$$

The program in Figure 5.9 reads values for **Amount**, **NumYears**, and **k**, uses the function **Sum** to calculate $1 + 2 + \cdots +$ **NumYears**, and then calculates and displays the amount that can be depreciated in the **k**th year, repeating this until the user terminates execution.

FIGURE 5.9 Calculating depreciation—Scope Rule 1.

```
PROGRAM Depreciation1( input, output );
{*******************************************************************

    Input (keyboard): User responses, Amounts to be depreciated,
                      and year numbers.
    Purpose:          Calculate the amount that can be depreciated in a
                      given year for a given amount and a given number
                      of years, using the sum-of-the-years-digits
                      method of depreciation.
    Output (screen):  User prompts and depreciation amounts.


*******************************************************************}

VAR
    Amount : real;      {amount to be depreciated}
    NumYears,           {number of years over which to depreciate it}
    k : integer;        {year for which depreciation to be calculated}
    Response : char;    {user response}

FUNCTION Sum( n : integer ) : integer;
{-----------------------------------------------------------------

    Accepts:  Integer n.
    Purpose:  Calculate 1 + 2 + ... + n.
    Returns:  Value of this sum.


-----------------------------------------------------------------}

    VAR
        TempSum,        {used to accumulate the sum}
        k : integer;    {index running from 1 through n}

    BEGIN
        k := 1;
        TempSum := 0;
        WHILE k <= n DO
            BEGIN
                TempSum := TempSum + k;
                k := k + 1
            END {WHILE};
        Sum := TempSum
    END {Sum};
```

FIGURE 5.9   Calculating depreciation—Scope Rule 1. (cont.)

```
BEGIN {********************** main program **********************}
   writeln( 'This program calculates depreciation using the ' );
   writeln( 'sum-of-the-years-digits method.' );
   write( 'Do you wish to continue (Y or N)? ' );
   readln( Response );
   WHILE Response = 'Y' DO
      BEGIN
         writeln( 'Enter amount to be depreciated, number of years,' );
         write( 'and year in which to calculate depreciation: ' );
         readln( Amount, NumYears, k );
         writeln( 'Amount depreciated in year ', k:1, ' is $',
                 (NumYears - k + 1) * Amount / Sum(NumYears) : 6:2 );
         writeln;
         write( 'More data (Y or N)? ' );
         readln( Response )
      END {WHILE}
END {main program}.
```

The scope of the formal parameter n and the variables TempSum and k declared within the function Sum is the function Sum; according to Scope Rule 1, they are not accessible outside this function. Such variables are said to be **local** to the function; their values can be accessed only within the function and are not available outside it.

Scope Rule for Global Entities

Any item declared in the declaration part of the main program or listed in the program heading is said to be **global,** because it is accessible throughout the entire program, except within subprograms in which a local entity has the same name as the global entity.

Scope Rule 2

> A global entity is accessible throughout the main program and in any subprogram in which no local entity has the same name as the global item.

For example, in the program in Figure 5.9, the variables Amount, NumYears, k, and Response as well as the function Sum are global entities. All of them are accessible to the main program, and all but k are accessible to the function Sum. The global variable k is not accessible within Sum because k is the name of a local variable within Sum. Reference to the variable k within the function Sum yields the value of the local variable k, whereas a reference to k outside the function gives the value of the global variable k. Thus the same identifier k names two different variables that are associated with two different memory locations.

Although global variables can be used to share data between the main program and subprograms or between subprograms, it is usually unwise to do so, since this practice reduces the independence of the various subprograms and thus makes modular programming more difficult. Changing the value of a global variable in one part of the program has the dangerous **side effect** of changing the value of that variable throughout the entire program, including all subprograms. Consequently, it is difficult to determine the value of that variable at any particular point in the program.

Scope Rule for Nested Subprograms

Scope Rule 2 applies to items in a main program and their accessibility in a subprogram. Recall that functions and procedures have declaration parts in which other functions and/or procedures may be defined. Scope Rule 3 applies to such nested functions and procedures.

Scope Rule 3

> An entity declared in a subprogram can be accessed by any subprogram defined within it, provided that no entity with the same name is declared in the internal subprogram.

To illustrate this scope rule, we extend the program of Figure 5.9 to display complete depreciation tables rather than simply to display the amount depreciated in a specific year. The program in Figure 5.10 calls procedure `GetData` to obtain values for `Amount` and `NumYears` and then calls procedure `PrintDepreciationTable`, which displays a table showing the amount to be depreciated for each of `k` years, beginning with the year `CurrentYear`. The relationship among these program components is indicated by the diagram in Figure 5.11, which shows clearly the nesting of the function `Sum` within procedure `PrintDepreciationTable` and `PrintDepreciationTable` within the main program.

 FIGURE 5.10 Calculating depreciation—Scope Rule 3.

```
PROGRAM Depreciation2( input, output );
{******************************************************************

    Input (keyboard): User responses, Amounts to be depreciated,
                      and number of years.
    Purpose:          Calculate and display depreciation tables,
                      using the sum-of-the-years-digits method of
                      depreciation.
    Output (screen):  User prompts and a depreciation table.


    ******************************************************************}
```

FIGURE 5.10   Calculating depreciation—Scope Rule 3. (cont.)

```
VAR
   Amount : real;        {amount to be depreciated}
   NumYears : integer; {number of years over which to depreciate it}
   Response : char;      {user response}

PROCEDURE GetData( VAR Amount : real;            {amount to be depreciated}
                   VAR NumYears : integer ); {number of years}
{-----------------------------------------------------------------------

      Input (keyboard):  Amount to depreciate and number of years.
      Purpose:           Read and return the Amount to be depreciated
                         and the number of years over which the
                         depreciation is to be carried out.
      Returns:           Amount and NumYears.

-----------------------------------------------------------------------}

   VAR
      Response : char;           {user response}

   BEGIN
      write( 'Enter amount to be depreciated, and the number',
             ' of years: ' );
      readln( Amount, NumYears );
      write( 'Is the data okay (Y or N)? ' );
      readln( Response );
      WHILE Response <> 'Y' DO
         BEGIN
            write( 'Amount, # years? ' );
            readln( Amount, NumYears );
            write( 'Okay? ' );
            readln( Response )
         END {WHILE}
   END {GetData};

PROCEDURE PrintDepreciationTable
                      ( Amount : real;            {amount being depreciated}
                        NumYears : integer ); {number of years}
{-----------------------------------------------------------------------

      Accepts:           Amount and NumYears.
      Purpose:           Calculate and display a depreciation table for
                         a specified amount over the given number of
                         years using the sum-of-the-years-digits method.
      Output (screen):   Depreciation table.

-----------------------------------------------------------------------}

   CONST
      CurrentYear = 1992;        {the current year}

   VAR
      SumOfYears,                {1 + 2 +  . . .  + NumYears}
      k : integer;               {index -- year number}
      Depreciation : real;       {amount to depreciate in k-th year}
```

FIGURE 5.10   Calculating depreciation—Scope Rule 3. (cont.)

```
FUNCTION Sum( n : integer ) : integer;
{-----------------------------------------------------------------------


    Accepts:   Integer n.
    Purpose:   Calculate 1 + 2 +  . . .  + n.
    Returns:   Value of this sum.


    -------------------------------------------------------------------}


    VAR
        TempSum,            {used to accumulate the sum}
        k : integer;       {index running from 1 through n}

    BEGIN
        k := 1;
        TempSum := 0;
        WHILE k <= n DO
            BEGIN
                TempSum := TempSum + k;
                k := k + 1
            END {WHILE};
        Sum := TempSum
    END {Sum};

BEGIN {PrintDepreciationTable}
    SumOfYears := Sum(NumYears);
    writeln( 'Year Depreciation' );
    writeln( '==== ============' );
    k := 0;
    WHILE k < NumYears DO
        BEGIN
            Depreciation := (NumYears - k) * Amount / SumOfYears;
            writeln( CurrentYear + k : 3, Depreciation:12:2 );
            k := k + 1
        END {WHILE}
END {PrintDepreciationTable};

BEGIN {********************** main program **********************}
    writeln( 'This program depreciation using the ' );
    writeln( 'sum-of-the-years-digits method.' );
    write( 'Do you wish to continue (Y or N)? ' );
    readln( Response );
    WHILE Response = 'Y' DO
        BEGIN
            GetData( Amount, NumYears );
            PrintDepreciationTable( Amount, NumYears );
            writeln;
            write( 'More data (Y or N)? ' );
            readln (Response)
        END {WHILE}
END {main program}.
```

FIGURE 5.11   Structure of depreciation program.

```
PROGRAM Depreciation2

    parameters:  input, output
    VAR Amount, NumYears, Response
    PROCEDURE GetData

        parameters:  Amount, NumYears
        VAR Response
        BEGIN
            .
            .
            .
        END {GetData};

    PROCEDURE PrintDepreciationTable

        parameters:  Amount, NumYears
        CONST CurrentYear
        VAR SumOfYears, k, Depreciation
        FUNCTION Sum

            parameters:  n
            VAR TempSum, k
            BEGIN
                .
                .
                .
            END {Sum};

        BEGIN
            .
            .
            .
            SumOfYears := Sum( NumYears );
            .
            .
            .
            Depreciation := (NumYears - k) * Amount / SumOfYears;
            .
            .
            .
        END {PrintDepreciationTable};

BEGIN {****************** main program ******************}
    .
    .
    .
    GetData( Amount, NumYears );
    PrintDepreciationTable( Amount, NumYears );
    .
    .
    .
END {main program}.
```

Scope Rule 3 states that an entity declared in a subprogram can be accessed in a subprogram contained in it, provided that no entity with the same name is declared locally in the internal subprogram. Thus, in this example, the local constant `CurrentYear` and local variables `Amount`, `NumYears`, `SumOfYears`, and `Depreciation` of the procedure `PrintDepreciationTable` are accessible within this procedure as well as within the function `Sum`. The local variable `k` in `PrintDepreciationTable`, however, is not accessible to the function `Sum`, because `Sum` has its own local variable `k`.

According to Scope Rule 2, the global variable `Response` (as well as the files `input` and `output`) is accessible to the procedure `PrintDepreciationTable` and thus also to the function `Sum`. On the other hand, the global variable `Response` is not accessible to the procedure `GetData`, since `Response` is a local variable within `GetData`. Similarly, the global variables `Amount` and `NumYears` are not accessible to either `GetData` or `PrintDepreciationTable`. (Their values, of course, are made available to these procedures through their formal parameters.)

It should be noted in this example that the function `Sum` is not accessible to the main program or to the procedure `GetData`, since it is defined within the procedure `PrintDepreciationTable`. This is undesirable if sums need to be calculated in the main program, because the function `Sum` is not available. In this case it would make sense to define all of the subprograms `GetData`, `Sum`, and `PrintDepreciationTable` in the main program so that the program has the structure shown in Figure 5.12.

FIGURE 5.12 Restructured depreciation program.

PROGRAM Depreciation2

```
parameters:  input, output
VAR Amount, NumYears, Response
PROCEDURE GetData

    parameters:  Amount, NumYears
    VAR Response
    BEGIN
        .
        .
        .
    END {GetData};

FUNCTION Sum

    parameters:  n
    VAR TempSum, k
    BEGIN
        .
        .
        .
    END {Sum};
```

FIGURE 5.12 Restructured depreciation program. (cont.)

```
PROCEDURE PrintDepreciationTable

    parameters:  Amount, NumYears
    CONST CurrentYear
    VAR SumOfYears, k, Depreciation

    BEGIN
        .
        .

        SumOfYears := Sum( NumYears );
        .
        .

        Depreciation := (NumYears - k) * Amount / SumOfYears;
        .
        .

    END {PrintDepreciationTable};

BEGIN {***************** main program ******************}
    .
    .

    GetData( Amount, NumYears );
    PrintDepreciationTable( Amount, NumYears );
    .
    .

END {main program}.
```

Scope Rule for Subprograms at the Same Level

Since the function Sum in the program in Figure 5.12 is referenced by the procedure PrintDepreciationTable, its definition must precede that of PrintDepreciationTable. In general, a function or procedure must be defined before it can be referenced by another function or procedure at the same level.

Scope Rule 4

> If *SubA* and *SubB* are subprograms defined in the same program or subprogram and if *SubA* is referenced by *SubB*, then *SubA* must be defined before *SubB*.

According to this scope rule, the program structure in Figure 5.12 is an acceptable alternative to that in Figure 5.11 because the subprograms are arranged in the order GetData, Sum, PrintDepreciationTable. Other acceptable orderings of these procedures and functions are Sum, GetData, PrintDepreciationTable, and Sum, PrintDepreciationTable, GetData. However, the ordering PrintDepreciationTable, Sum, GetData would not be valid, since PrintDepreciationTable references Sum, thus violating Scope Rule 4.

1. Consider the following program skeleton:

```
PROGRAM ScopeRules( input, output);

   VAR
      a, b : integer;

   FUNCTION F( x : real ) : real;

      VAR b, c : integer;

      BEGIN
         .
         .
         .
      END {F};

   PROCEDURE P1( d : real );

      VAR e, f : integer;

      PROCEDURE P2( a : real );

         VAR e, g : integer;

         BEGIN {P2}
            .
            .
            .
         END {P2};

      BEGIN {P1}
         .
         .
         .
      END {P1};

   BEGIN {***** main program *****}
      .
      .
      .
   END {main program}.
```

Answer the following true or false:

(a) The variable **a** declared in the main program is a global variable.

(b) The variable **a** declared in the main program is accessible within function **F**.

(c) The variable **a** declared in the main program is accessible within procedure **P2**.

(d) The function **F** is accessible within procedure **P2**.

(e) The variable **g** is accessible only within procedure **P2**.

(f) The statement **b** := **c** within the statement part of **F** would assign the value of **c** to the global variable **b**.

(g) The statement `writeln( F(f) )` may be used in the statement part of **P1**.

(h) The statement `P2(3)` may be used in the statement part of **P1**.

(i) The variable **f** is accessible within **P2**.

(j) The statement `P2(b)` may be used in the statement part of the main program.

(k) The statement `P1(F(a))` may be used in the statement part of the main program.

2. Describe the output produced by the following program, or explain why an error occurs:

```
PROGRAM Exercise2( output );

FUNCTION Product( x : integer ) : integer;

   BEGIN
      Product := 3 * x
   END {Product};

FUNCTION Sum( x : integer ) : integer;

   FUNCTION Product( a : integer ) : integer;

      BEGIN {Product}
         Product := 4 * a
      END {Product};

   BEGIN {Sum}
      Sum := 5 + Product(x)
   END {Sum};

BEGIN {***** main program *****}
   writeln( Product(2):5, Sum(2):5 );
   writeln( Sum(Product(3)):5, Product(Sum(3)):5 )
END {main program}.
```

3. Describe the output produced by the following program, or explain why an error occurs:

```
PROGRAM Exercise3( output );

VAR
   Num, i : integer;
```

```
PROCEDURE P( VAR Num : integer );

   BEGIN
      i := i + 1;
      Num := 2 * Num
   END {P};

BEGIN {***** main program *****}
   i := 1;
   Num := 3;
   WHILE i <= 4 DO
      BEGIN
         writeln( i:3, Num:3 );
         P( Num );
         writeln( i:3, Num:3 );
         i := i + 1
      END {WHILE}
END {main program}.
```

4. Describe the output produced by the following program, or explain why an error occurs:

```
PROGRAM Exercise4( output );

VAR
   Num, HalfNum : integer;

PROCEDURE Double( VAR Num : integer );

   BEGIN
      Num := 2 * Num
   END {Double};

BEGIN {***** main program *****}
   Num := 4;
   HalfNum := 2;
   writeln( HalfNum:3 );
   writeln( Num:3 );
   Double( HalfNum );
   writeln( HalfNum:3 );
   writeln( Num:3 )
END {main program}.
```

5.7 Top–Down Design

At several places in this text we have indicated that large and complex problems can best be solved using **top–down design.** In this approach, a divide-and-conquer strategy is used in which the original problem is divided into a number of simpler subproblems. Each of these subproblems can then be solved independently, perhaps using this same divide-and-conquer strategy to divide them into still simpler subproblems. This refinement process continues until subproblems are obtained that are simple enough that algorithms can be easily developed to solve them. Procedures and functions are then written to implement these algorithms, and these subprograms are combined in a program that solves the original problem. Because this software engineering technique is so important and because we have now considered procedures and functions in detail, we shall demonstrate the use of this approach to solve a relatively complex problem.

Problem: Academic Eligibility

Suppose that the athletic department at a certain university wants a program for its secretarial staff that can be used to determine the academic eligibility of its athletes for the next academic year. This eligibility check is made at the end of each of the first three years of the student's academic career. Eligibility is determined by two criteria: the number of hours that the student has successfully completed and the student's cumulative grade point average (GPA). To maintain eligibility, a student must have a completed at least 25 hours with a minimum GPA of 1.7 by the end of the first year. At the end of the second year, 50 hours must have been completed with a cumulative GPA of 1.85 or higher, and at the end of the third year, 85 hours must have been completed with a minimum cumulative GPA of 1.95.

Specification

The program should display the student's number, class, cumulative hours, GPA for the current year, and cumulative GPA, as well as an indication of the student's eligibility. At the end of this report, the program should also display the total number of students processed, the number who are eligible, and the average current GPA for all students. The information to be supplied to the program is the student's number, class level, hours accumulated, cumulative GPA, and hours and grades for courses taken during the current year. Thus we have the following input and output specifications for this problem:

Input: Student's number
Class level (1, 2, or 3)
Cumulative hours
Cumulative GPA
Hours and grades for each course completed in the current year

Output: Student's number
Class level
Current GPA
Updated cumulative hours and cumulative GPA
Indication of eligibility
Number of students processed
Number of students eligible
Average of all current GPAs

Design Plan

Using top–down design to develop this program, we begin by identifying three main tasks needed to solve it, describing them in fairly general terms:

1. **Instruct**. Since the program will be used by personnel who are generally not regular users of a computer system, some instructions must be displayed each time the program is used.
2. **CheckStudent**. The second task is to accept the given information for each student, calculate the relevant statistics, and determine eligibility.
3. **PrintSummary**. The final task is to generate and display the desired summary statistics after all the student information has been processed.

It is helpful to display these tasks and their relationship to one another in a **structure diagram** like the following:

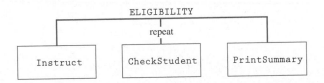

Typically, one or more of these first-level tasks are still quite complex and so must be divided into subtasks. In this example, the tasks **Instruct** and **PrintSummary** are straightforward, but the task **CheckStudent**, which is central to the entire program, is more complex and requires further analysis. We can identify three main subtasks in **CheckStudent**:

1. **ReadAndCalculate**. Read information about a student and calculate relevant statistics.
2. **CheckEligibility**. Determine a student's eligibility based on the statistics calculated in **ReadAndCalculate**.
3. **Report**. Report information about a student, including eligibility status.

The following refinement of the earlier structure diagram summarizes this analysis:

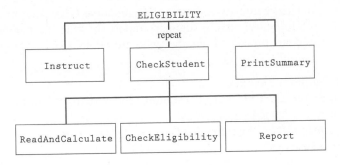

A student's eligibility is based on two criteria: an hours condition and a GPA condition. This means that two third-level subtasks of **CheckEligibility** can be identified:

1. **HoursCheck**. Check if a student's cumulative hours satisfies the hours condition.
2. **GPACheck**. Check if a student's cumulative GPA satisfies the GPA condition.

The final refinement of the structure diagram for the program thus is

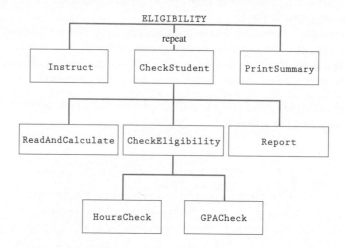

The next step in the design plan is to develop algorithms for each of these tasks and subtasks:

ALGORITHM FOR MAIN PROGRAM

(* Input: For each of several students, the student's number, class level, cumulative hours, cumulative GPA, hours and grades for current courses.

Purpose: Determine academic eligibility of individual students according to two criteria—cumulative hours and cumulative GPA—and display several summary statistics for all students processed.

Output: For each student, the student's number, class level, current GPA, updated cumulative hours and cumulative GPA, and an indication of eligibility; also, a summary report showing the number of students processed, number who are eligible, and average of all current GPAs. *)

1. Call subalgorithm **Instruct**.
2. Initialize **StudentCount**, **EligibleCount**, and **SumOfGPAs** to 0.
3. While there are students to process:
       Call subalgorithm **CheckStudent**.
4. Call **PrintSummary**.

SUBALGORITHM Instruct

(* Purpose: Display instructions to the user.
   Output: User instructions. *)

A series of output statements that inform the user of the purpose of the program and provide instructions for entering the data.

SUBALGORITHM `CheckStudent`

(* Accepts: `StudentCount`, `EligibleCount`, and `SumOfGPAs`.

Purpose: Read student information, determine eligibility, and maintain counts of the number of students processed and the number eligible, and a sum of current GPAs.

Returns: `StudentCount`, `EligibleCount`, and `SumOfGPAs`. *)

1. Call subalgorithm `ReadAndCalculate`.
2. Call subalgorithm `CheckEligibility`.
3. Call subalgorithm `Report`.

SUBALGORITHM `PrintSummary`

(* Accepts: `StudentCount`, `EligibleCount`, and `SumOfGPAs`.

Purpose: Display summary statistics.

Output: Number of students processed, average current GPA for all students, and the number found to be eligible. *)

1. Display `StudentCount`.
2. If `StudentCount` is not zero
   a. Calculate and display the average current GPA for all students.
   b. Display `EligibleCount`.

SUBALGORITHM `ReadAndCalculate`

(* Input: A student's number (`Snumb`), `Class`, cumulative hours (`CumHours`), and cumulative GPA (`CumGPA`), `Hours` and `Grade` for each current course.

Purpose: Read information about a student, and calculate current GPA (`CurrGPA`), update cumulative hours, cumulative GPA, count of students processed, and sum of cumulative GPAs for all students.

Returns: `Snumb`, `Class`, `CumHours`, `CumGPA`, `CurrGPA`, `StudentCount`, `SumOfGPAs`. *)

1. Read `Snumb`, `Class`, `CumHours`, and `CumGPA` for student.
2. Calculate the number of honor points the student already has earned:

`OldHonorPoints = CumHours * CumGPA`.

3. Initialize `NewHours` and `NewHonorPoints` to 0.
4. Read `Hours` of credit and numeric `Grade` for first course taken by student.
5. While the end-of-data flag has not been read do the following:
   a. Add `Hours` to `NewHours`.
   b. Add `Hours * Grade` to `NewHonorPoints`.
   c. Read `Hours` of credit and numeric `Grade` for next course.
6. Calculate student's current GPA (`CurrGPA`): 0 if student took no new courses; else

`CurrGPA = NewHonorPoints / NewHours`

7. Update cumulative hours for student by adding `NewHours` to `CumHours`.

8. Calculate student's cumulative GPA:

$$\text{CumGPA} = \frac{\text{OldHonorPoints} + \text{NewHonorPoints}}{\text{CumHours}}$$

9. Increment **StudentCount** by 1 and add **CurrGPA** to **SumOfGPAs**.

SUBALGORITHM CheckEligibility

(* Accepts: A student's **Class**, **CumHours**, **CumGPA**, and **EligibleCount**, the number of students determined to be eligible.

Purpose: Check if student's cumulative hours (**CumHours**) and cumulative GPA (**CumGPA**) satisfy the hours and GPA conditions for eligibility.

Returns: The student's eligibility status (**Eligible**) and updated value of **EligibleCount**. *)

If **Class** is not one of 1, 2, or 3 then
Display an illegal-class-code message.
Else do the following:

1. Call subalgorithm **HoursCheck** to determine whether student satisfies the hour's condition for eligibility.
2. Call subalgorithm **GPACheck** to determine whether student satisfies the GPA condition for eligibility.
3. If student is eligible, increment **EligibleCount** by 1.

SUBALGORITHM Report

(* Accepts: A student's **Snumb**, **Class**, **CumHours**, **CurrGPA**, **CumGPA**, and **Eligible**.

Purpose: Display statistics and eligibility status for a given student.

Output: **Snumb**, **Class**, **CumHours**, **CumGPA**, **CurrGPA**, and eligibility status. *)

A series of output statements to display the required information in an acceptable format.

SUBALGORITHM HoursCheck

(* Accepts: A student's **Class** and **CumHours**.

Purpose: Check if student satisfies the hours condition for eligibility.

Returns: True if student meets the hours criterion and false otherwise. *)

If **Class** = 1 then
Set **HoursCheck** to true if **CumHours** ≥ hours required for freshman eligibility.
Else if **Class** = 2 then
Set **HoursCheck** to true if **CumHours** ≥ hours required for sophomore eligibility.
Else if **Class** = 3 then
Set **HoursCheck** to true if **CumHours** ≥ hours required for junior eligibility.

SUBALGORITHM GPACheck

(* Accepts: A student's **Class** and **CumGPA**.
   Purpose: Check if student satisfies the GPA condition for eligibility.
   Returns: True if student meets the GPA criterion and false otherwise. *)

If **Class** = 1 then
   Set **GPACheck** to true if **CumGPA** ≥ GPA required for freshman eligibility.
Else if **Class** = 2 then
   Set **GPACheck** to true if **CumGPA** ≥ GPA required for sophomore eligibility.
Else if **Class** = 3 then
   Set **GPACheck** to true if **CumGPA** ≥ GPA required for junior eligibility.

Coding and Testing

The three main tasks we have identified can be implemented as three procedures, **Instruct**, **CheckStudent**, and **PrintSummary**. Since the procedure **Instruct** simply displays instructions to the user, it requires no information from other parts of the program. The procedure **PrintSummary** requires the total number of students processed (**StudentCount**), the total number who are eligible to participate in athletics (**EligibleCount**), and the sum of all the current GPAs (**SumOfGPAs**). These values must be calculated by the procedure **CheckStudent** and shared with **PrintSummary**. Thus, the entire program has the form

```
PROGRAM Eligibility( input, output );

VAR
    StudentCount, EligibleCount : integer;
    SumOfGPAs : real;
    Response : CHAR;

PROCEDURE Instruct;
    .
    .
    .

PROCEDURE CheckStudent( VAR StudentCount,      {number of students}
                            EligibleCount :    {number eligible}
                                integer;
                            VAR SumOfGPAs :     {sum of all GPAs}
                                real );
    .
    .
    .

PROCEDURE PrintSummary( StudentCount,          {number of students}
                            EligibleCount :    {number eligible}
                                integer;
                            SumOfGPAs :         {sum of all GPAs}
                                real );
    .
    .
    .
```

```
BEGIN {******************** main program ********************}
   Instruct;
   StudentCount := 0;
   EligibleCount := 0;
   SumOfGPAs := 0;
   write( 'Do you have students to check (Y or N)? ' );
   readln( Response );
   WHILE Response <> 'N' DO
      BEGIN
         CheckStudent( StudentCount, EligibleCount, SumOfGPAs );
         writeln;
         write( 'More (Y or N)? ' );
         readln( Response )
      END {WHILE};
   PrintSummary( StudentCount, EligibleCount, SumOfGPAs )
END {main program}.
```

Since **CheckStudent** is central to the entire program, we will code it first. The three second-level subtasks of **CheckStudent** can be implemented as procedures **ReadAndCalculate**, **CheckEligibility**, and **Report**. Implementing subalgorithm **ReadAndCalculate** as a procedure is straightforward. Note that because the values of **Snumb**, **Class**, **CumHours**, **CumGPA**, **CurrGPA**, **StudentCount**, and **SumOfGPAs** must be shared with other parts of the program, they must be variable parameters of this procedure.

Once the procedure **ReadAndCalculate** has been written, it can be incorporated into the program and tested before the other procedures are developed, as shown in Figure 5.13. We simply insert procedure stubs in the statement part of each undeveloped procedure to display a simple message indicating that the procedure has been called. In this program, the procedures **Instruct**, **PrintSummary**, and **CheckEligibility** contain such program stubs to signal their execution, and **Report** produces a temporary printout to enable us to check the correctness of **ReadAndCalculate**. The procedure **ReadAndCalculate** is in its final form, as is the statement part of the main program.

 FIGURE 5.13 Determining eligibility—first version.

```
PROGRAM Eligibility( input, output );
{*************************************************************************
   Input (keyboard): For each of several students, the student's
                     number, class level, cumulative hours, cumulative
                     GPA, hours and grades for current courses.
   Purpose:          Determine academic eligibility of individual
                     students according to two criteria--cumulative
                     hours and cumulative GPA--and display several
                     summary statistics for all students processed.
   Output (screen):  User prompts, messages, and for each student,
                     the student's number, current GPA, updated
                     cumulative hours and cumulative GPA, and
                     indication of eligibility; also, a summary
                     report showing the number of students processed,
                     number who are eligible, and average of all
                     current GPAs.

**************************************************************************}
```

FIGURE 5.13 Determining eligibility—first version. (cont.)

```
VAR
    StudentCount,              {number of students processed}
    EligibleCount : integer;   {number found to be eligible}
    SumOfGpas : real;          {sum of current GPAs of all students}
    Response : char;           {user response}

PROCEDURE Instruct;
{-----------------------------------------------------------------------

   Purpose:          Display instructions to the user.
   Output (screen): User instructions.

----------------------------------------------------------------------}

   BEGIN
      writeln( '********** Instruct called **********' )
   END {Instruct};

PROCEDURE CheckStudent
              ( VAR StudentCount,              {number of students}
                    EligibleCount : integer; {number found to be eligible}
                VAR SumOfGPAs : real );        {sum of all GPAs}
{-----------------------------------------------------------------------

   Accepts:  StudentCount, EligibleCount, and SumOfGPAs.
   Purpose:  Read student information, determine eligibility,
             and maintain counts of number processed and number
             eligible, and a sum of current GPAs.
   Returns:  StudentCount, EligibleCount, and SumOfGPAs.

----------------------------------------------------------------------}

   VAR
      Snumb,                 {student number}
      Class : integer;       {student's class level -- 1, 2, or 3}
      CumHours,              {cumulative hours}
      CumGPA,                {cumulative grade point average}
      CurrGPA : real;        {current grade point average}
      Eligible : boolean;    {true if student eligible, else false}

   PROCEDURE ReadAndCalculate
                 ( VAR Snumb, Class,             {student's number and class}
                       StudentCount : integer; {count of students}
                   VAR CumHours, CumGPA,         {cumulative hours and GPA}
                       CurrGPA,                  {current GPA}
                       SumOfGPAs : real );       {sum of all GPAs}
```

FIGURE 5.13   Determining eligibility—first version. (cont.)

```
{---------------------------------------------------------------------

    Input (keyboard): A student's number (Snumb), Class, cumulative
                      hours (CumHours), and cumulative GPA (CumGPA),
                      Hours and Grade for each current course.
    Purpose:          Read information about a student and calculate
                      current GPA (CurrGPA), update cumulative hours,
                      cumulative GPA, count of students processed,
                      and sum of cumulative GPAs for all students.
    Returns:          Snumb, Class, CumHours, CumGPA, CurrGPA,
                      StudentCount, SumOfGPAs.
    Output (screen):  User prompts.


---------------------------------------------------------------------}

    VAR
        Hours,                   {hours of credit for a course}
        Grade,                   {numeric grade for that course}
        NewHours,                {total hours earned during current year}
        NewHonorPts,             {honor points earned in current year}
        OldHonorPts : real;      {honor points earned in past years}

    BEGIN
        writeln( 'Enter student number, class, cum. hours, cum. GPA:' );
        readln( Snumb, Class, CumHours, CumGPA );
        OldHonorPts := CumHours * CumGPA;
        NewHours := 0;
        NewHonorPts := 0;
        write( 'Hours and grade? ' );
        readln( Hours, Grade );
        WHILE Hours > 0 DO
            BEGIN
                NewHours := NewHours + Hours;
                NewHonorPts := NewHonorPts + Hours * Grade;
                write( 'Hours and grade? ' );
                readln( Hours, Grade )
            END {WHILE};
        IF NewHours = 0 THEN
            CurrGPA := 0
        ELSE
            CurrGPA := NewHonorPts / NewHours;
        SumOfGPAs := SumOfGPAs + CurrGPA
        CumHours := CumHours + NewHours;
        CumGPA := (OldHonorPts + NewHonorPts) / CumHours;
        StudentCount := StudentCount + 1;
    END {ReadAndCalculate};

PROCEDURE CheckEligibility
            (    Class : integer;            {student's class,}
                 CumHours, CumGPA : real;    {cumulative hours, & GPA}
            VAR Eligible : boolean;          {eligibility indicator}
            VAR EligibleCount : integer );   {number eligible}
```

FIGURE 5.13 Determining eligibility—first version. (cont.)

```
{-------------------------------------------------------------------

    Accepts:   A student's Class, CumHours and CumGPA.
    Purpose:   Check if student's cumulative hours (CumHours) and
               cumulative GPA (CumGPA) satisfy the hours and GPA
               conditions for eligibility.
    Returns:   The student's eligibility status (Eligible) and
               updated value of EligibleCount, the number of
               students determined to be eligible.

-------------------------------------------------------------------}

  BEGIN
      writeln( '********** CheckEligibility called ***********' )
  END {CheckEligibility};

PROCEDURE Report
          (    Snumb, Class : integer;    {student's number, class,}
               CumHours,                  {cumulative hours,}
               CurrGPA, CumGPA : real );  {current and cumulative GPA}
{-------------------------------------------------------------------

    Accepts:        A student's Snumb, Class, CumHours, CurrGPA, and
                    CumGPA.
    Purpose:        Display statistics and eligibility status for a
                    given student.
    Output (screen): Snumb, Class, CumHours, CumGPA, CurrGPA, and
                    eligibility status.

-------------------------------------------------------------------}

  BEGIN
      writeln( '********** Report called ***********' );
      {***** Temporary printout *****}
      writeln( 'Snumb:  ', Snumb:1 );
      writeln( 'Class:  ', Class:1 );
      writeln( 'Cum. hours:  ', CumHours:4:2 );
      writeln( 'Curr. GPA:  ', CurrGPA:4:2 );
      writeln( 'Cum. GPA:  ', CumGPA:4:2 )
  END {Report};

BEGIN {CheckStudent}
   ReadAndCalculate( Snumb, Class, StudentCount, CumHours, CumGPA,
                     CurrGPA, SumOfGPAs );
   CheckEligibility( Class, CumHours, CumGPA, Eligible, EligibleCount );
   Report( Snumb, Class, CumHours, CurrGPA, CumGPA )
END {CheckStudent};
```

FIGURE 5.13   Determining eligibility—first version. (cont.)

```
PROCEDURE PrintSummary
            ( StudentCount,              {number of students}
              EligibleCount : integer; {number found to be eligible}
              SumOfGPAs : real );        {sum of all GPAs}
   {-------------------------------------------------------------------

      Accepts:        StudentCount, EligibleCount, and SumOfGpas.
      Purpose:        Display summary statistics.
      Output (screen): Number of students processed, average current
                      GPA for all students, and the number found to
                      be eligible.

      -------------------------------------------------------------------}

   BEGIN
      writeln( '********** PrintSummary called ***********' )
   END {PrintSummary};

BEGIN {******************** main program ********************}
   Instruct;
   StudentCount := 0;
   EligibleCount := 0;
   SumOfGPAs := 0;
   write( 'Do you have students to check (Y or N)? ' );
   readln( Response );
   WHILE Response <> 'N' DO
      BEGIN
         CheckStudent( StudentCount, EligibleCount, SumOfGPAs );
         writeln;
         write( 'More (Y or N)? ' );
         readln( Response )
      END {WHILE};
   PrintSummary( StudentCount, EligibleCount, SumOfGPAs )
END {main program}.
```

Sample run:

```
********** Instruct called **********
Do you have students to check (Y or N)? Y
Enter student number, class, cum. hours, cum. GPA:
1234 1 0 0
Hours and grade? 5 3.0
Hours and grade? 4 3.0
Hours and grade? 3.5 3.0
Hours and grade? 4 3.0
Hours and grade? 3 3.0
Hours and grade? 2 3.0
Hours and grade? 0 0
********** CheckEligibility called **********
```

FIGURE 5.13 Determining eligibility—first version. (cont.)

```
********** Report called ***********
Snumb:  1234
Class:  1
Cum. hours:  21.50
Curr. GPA:  3.00
Cum. GPA:  3.00

More (Y or N)? N
********** PrintSummary called **********
```

The sample run in the preceding figure is a part of the testing that must be done to ensure that the procedure **ReadAndCalculate** is correct. Such **unit testing** should be performed on each subprogram as it is developed and added to the program. When a subprogram has been thoroughly tested, we can proceed to develop and test other subprograms. This process continues until all of the algorithms in the design plan have been coded, tested, and added to the program.

In this example, once we are convinced of the correctness of **ReadAndCalculate**, we may turn to writing the other procedures. The subtasks **HoursCheck** and **GPACheck** of the procedure **CheckEligibility** can be conveniently implemented as boolean-valued functions **HoursCheck** and **GPACheck** that return the value **true** or **false**, depending on whether the student satisfies the corresponding eligibility criteria. Replacing the temporary version of **CheckEligibility** in the preceding program produces the refined program in Figure 5.14. Note that we have also modified the temporary version of **Report** and the reference to it in order to display the value of **Eligible**.

 FIGURE 5.14 Determining eligibility—refinement.

```
PROGRAM Eligibility( input, output );

         .
         .
         .

    PROCEDURE CheckEligibility
              (     Class :  integer;        {student's class,}
                    CumHours, CumGPA : real; {cumulative hours, & GPA}
                VAR Eligible : boolean;      {eligibility indicator}
                VAR EligibleCount : integer ); {number eligible}
      {-----------------------------------------------------------------

         Accepts:  A student's Class, CumHours and CumGPA, and the number
                   (EligibleCount) of students determined to be eligible.
         Purpose:  Check if student's cumulative hours (CumHours) and
                   cumulative GPA (CumGPA) satisfy the hours and GPA
                   conditions for eligibility.
         Returns:  The student's eligibility status (Eligible) and
                   updated value of EligibleCount.

      -------------------------------------------------------------------}
```

FIGURE 5.14   Determining eligibility—refinement. (cont.)

```
FUNCTION HoursCheck( Class : integer;      {student's class}
                     CumHours : real )     {and cumulative hours}
                            : boolean;
{-----------------------------------------------------------------

    Accepts:   A student's Class and CumHours.
    Purpose:   Check if student satisfies the hours condition for
               eligibility.
    Returns:   True if student meets the hours criterion and
               false otherwise.

-----------------------------------------------------------------}

    CONST
       FreshmanHours = 25;
       SophomoreHours = 50;
       JuniorHours = 85;

    BEGIN
       IF Class = 1 THEN
          HoursCheck := CumHours >= FreshmanHours
       ELSE IF Class = 2 THEN
          HoursCheck := CumHours >= SophomoreHours
       ELSE IF Class = 3 THEN
          HoursCheck := CumHours >= JuniorHours
    END {HoursCheck};

FUNCTION GPACheck( Class : integer;      {student's class}
                   CumGPA : real )       {and cumulative GPA}
                          : boolean;
{-----------------------------------------------------------------

    Accepts:   A student's Class and CumGPA.
    Purpose:   Check if student satisfies the GPA condition for
               eligibility.
    Returns:   True if student meets the GPA criterion and
               false otherwise.

-----------------------------------------------------------------}

    CONST
       FreshmanGPA = 1.7;
       SophomoreGPA = 1.85;
       JuniorGPA = 1.95;

    BEGIN
       IF Class = 1 THEN
          GPACheck := CumGPA >= FreshmanGPA
       ELSE IF Class = 2 THEN
          GPACheck := CumGPA >= SophomoreGPA
       ELSE IF Class = 3 THEN
          GPACheck := CumGPA>= JuniorGPA
    END {GPACheck};
```

FIGURE 5.14   Determining eligibility—refinement. (cont.)

```
    BEGIN {CheckEligibility}
       IF (Class < 1) OR (Class > 3) THEN
          BEGIN
             writeln( '*** Illegal class code ***' );
             Eligible := false
          END {IF}
       ELSE
          Eligible := HoursCheck( Class, CumHours )
                      AND GPACheck( Class, CumGPA );
       IF Eligible THEN
          EligibleCount := EligibleCount + 1
    END {CheckEligibility};


    PROCEDURE Report
            (    Snumb, Class : integer;    {student's number, class,}
                 CumHours,                  {cumulative hours,}
                 CurrGPA, CumGPA : real;    {current and cumulative GPA}
                 Eligible : boolean );      {eligibility indicator}
    {-----------------------------------------------------------------

       Accepts:        A student's Snumb, Class, CumHours, CurrGPA, CumGPA,
                       and Eligible (eligibility indicator).
       Purpose:        Display statistics and eligibility status for a
                       given student.
       Output (screen): Snumb, Class, CumHours, CumGPA, CurrGPA, and
                       eligibility status.


    -----------------------------------------------------------------}

    BEGIN
       writeln( '********** Report called **********' );
       {***** Temporary printout *****}
       writeln( 'Snumb:  ', Snumb:1 );
       writeln( 'Class:  ', Class:1 );
       writeln( 'Cum. hours:  ', CumHours:4:2 );
       writeln( 'Curr. GPA:  ', CurrGPA:4:2 );
       writeln( 'Cum. GPA:  ', CumGPA:4:2 );
       writeln( 'Eligible:  ', Eligible )
    END {Report};


BEGIN {CheckStudent}
    ReadAndCalculate( Snumb, Class, StudentCount, CumHours, CumGPA,
                      CurrGPA, SumOfGPAs );
    CheckEligibility( Class, CumHours, CumGPA, Eligible, EligibleCount );
    Report( Snumb, Class, CumHours, CurrGPA, CumGPA, Eligible )
END {CheckStudent};


         .
         .
         .

END {main program}.
```

FIGURE 5.14   Determining eligibility—refinement. (cont.)

Sample run:

```
*********** Instruct called ***********
Do you have students to check (Y or N)? Y
Enter student number, class, cum. hours, cum. GPA:
1234 1 0 0
Hours and grade? 5 3.0
Hours and grade? 4 3.0
Hours and grade? 3.5 3.0
Hours and grade? 4 3.0
Hours and grade? 3 3.0
Hours and grade? 2 3.0
Hours and grade? 0 0
********** Report called ***********
Snumb:   1234
Class:   1
Cum. hours:  21.50
Curr. GPA:   3.00
Cum. GPA:    3.00
Eligible:   FALSE

More (Y or N)? Y
Enter student number, class, cum. hours, cum. GPA:
5555 5 0 0
Hours and grade? 3 3.0
Hours and grade? 0 0
*** Illegal class code ***
********** Report called ***********
Snumb:   5555
Class:   5
Cum. hours:  3.00
Curr. GPA:   3.00
Cum. GPA:    3.00
Eligible:   FALSE

More (Y or N)? N
********** PrintSummary called ***********
```

Testing of the newly added procedure **CheckEligibility** indicates that this procedure is correct. Thus we can proceed to writing the remaining procedures **Report**, **Instruct**, and **PrintSummary**. We develop and test each of these procedures individually and add them to the program. The final version of the program is shown in Figure 5.15.

Each of the subprograms were tested as they were developed and added to the program. Although each of them was tested individually, it must also be determined that these subprograms were integrated into the program correctly, that is, that they interact with one another correctly, passing the required information to and from one another. This type of testing is called **integration testing.**

When all of the subprograms have been developed and integrated into the program, the complete program should be tested to determine that the overall system functions correctly. This is known as **system testing.**

FIGURE 5.15 Determining eligibility—final version.

```
PROGRAM Eligibility( input, output );
{*********************************************************************

    Input (keyboard): For each of several students, the student's
                      number, class level, cumulative hours, cumulative
                      GPA, hours and grades for current courses.
    Purpose:          Determine academic eligibility of individual
                      students according to two criteria -- cumulative
                      hours and cumulative GPA -- and display several
                      summary statistics for all students processed.
    Output (screen):  User prompts, messages, and for each student,
                      the student's number, class, current GPA, updated
                      cumulative hours and cumulative GPA, and
                      indication of eligibility; also, a summary
                      report showing the number of students processed,
                      number who are eligible, and average of all
                      current GPAs.

*********************************************************************}

VAR
    StudentCount,               {number of students processed}
    EligibleCount : integer;    {number found to be eligible}
    SumOfGPAs : real;           {sum of current GPAs of all students}
    Response : char;            {user response}

PROCEDURE Instruct;
{-------------------------------------------------------------------

    Purpose:          Display instructions to the user.
    Output (screen):  User instructions.

-------------------------------------------------------------------}

    BEGIN
        writeln( 'You will first be asked to enter the student''s' );
        writeln( 'number, class, cumulative hours, and cumulative GPA.' );
        writeln( 'Enter these with at least one space separating them.' );
        writeln;
        writeln( 'You will then be asked to enter the number of hours and' );
        writeln( 'the numeric grade earned for each of the courses the' );
        writeln( 'student took during the current year.  Separate the' );
        writeln( 'number of hours from the grade by at least one space.' );
        writeln( 'Enter 0 for hours and grades when you are finished' );
        writeln( 'entering the information for each student.' );
        writeln;
        writeln
    END {Instruct};
```

FIGURE 5.15   Determining eligibility—final version. (cont.)

```
PROCEDURE CheckStudent
          ( VAR StudentCount,                {number of students}
                EligibleCount : integer; {number found to be eligible}
              VAR SumOfGPAs : real );        {Sum of all GPAs}
{----------------------------------------------------------------------

   Accepts:   StudentCount, EligibleCount, and SumOfGPAs.
   Purpose:   Read student information, determine eligibility,
              and maintain counts of number processed and number
              eligible, and a sum of current GPAs.
   Returns:   StudentCount, EligibleCount, and SumOfGPAs.


-----------------------------------------------------------------------}

   VAR
      Snumb,                    {student number}
      Class : integer;          {student's class level -- 1, 2, or 3}
      CumHours,                 {cumulative hours}
      CumGPA,                   {cumulative grade point average}
      CurrGPA : real;           {current grade point average}
      Eligible : boolean;       {true if student eligible, else false}

   PROCEDURE ReadAndCalculate
             ( VAR Snumb,  Class,          {student's number and class}
                   StudentCount : integer; {count of students}
                 VAR CumHours, CumGPA,      {cumulative hours and GPA}
                   CurrGPA,                 {current GPA}
                   SumOfGPAs : real );      {sum of all GPAs}
   {----------------------------------------------------------------------

      Input (keyboard): A student's number (Snumb), Class, cumulative
                        hours (CumHours), and cumulative GPA (CumGPA),
                        Hours and Grade for each current course.
      Purpose:          Read information about a student and calculate
                        current GPA (CurrGPA), update cumulative hours,
                        cumulative GPA, count of students processed,
                        and sum of cumulative GPAs for all students.
      Returns:          Snumb, Class, CumHours, CumGPA, CurrGPA,
                        StudentCount, SumOfGPAs.
      Output (screen):  User prompts.


   -----------------------------------------------------------------------}

      VAR
         Hours,                    {hours of credit for a course}
         Grade,                    {numeric grade for that course}
         NewHours,                 {total hours earned during current year}
         NewHonorPts,              {honor points earned in current year}
         OldHonorPts : real;       {honor points earned in past years}
```

FIGURE 5.15   Determining eligibility—final version. (cont.)

```
BEGIN
    writeln( 'Enter student number, class, cum. hours, cum. GPA:' );
    readln( Snumb, Class, CumHours, CumGPA );
    OldHonorPts := CumHours * CumGPA;
    NewHours := 0;
    NewHonorPts := 0;
    write( 'Hours and grade? ' );
    readln( Hours, Grade );
    WHILE Hours > 0 DO
        BEGIN
            NewHours := NewHours + Hours;
            NewHonorPts := NewHonorPts + Hours * Grade;
            write( 'Hours and grade? ' );
            readln( Hours, Grade )
        END {WHILE};
    IF NewHours = 0 THEN
        CurrGPA := 0
    ELSE
        CurrGPA := NewHonorPts / NewHours;
    CumHours := CumHours + NewHours;
    CumGPA := (OldHonorPts + NewHonorPts) / CumHours;
    StudentCount := StudentCount + 1;
    SumOfGPAs := SumOfGPAs + CurrGPA
END {ReadAndCalculate};

PROCEDURE CheckEligibility
            (      Class :  integer;          {student's class,}
                   CumHours, CumGPA : real;   {cumulative hours, & GPA}
               VAR Eligible : boolean;        {eligibility indicator}
               VAR EligibleCount : integer ); {number eligible}
{-----------------------------------------------------------------

  Accepts:  A student's Class, CumHours and CumGPA, and the number
            (EligibleCount) of students determined to be eligible.
  Purpose:  Check if student's cumulative hours (CumHours) and
            cumulative GPA (CumGPA) satisfy the hours and GPA
            conditions for eligibility.
  Returns:  The student's eligibility status (Eligible) and
            updated value of EligibleCount.

------------------------------------------------------------------}

    FUNCTION HoursCheck( Class : integer;     {student's class}
                         CumHours : real )    {and cumulative hours}
                         : boolean;
    {--------------------------------------------------------------

      Accepts:  A student's Class and CumHours.
      Purpose:  Check if student satisfies the hours condition for
                eligibility.
      Returns:  True if student meets the hours criterion and
                false otherwise.

    ----------------------------------------------------------------}
```

FIGURE 5.15   Determining eligibility—final version. (cont.)

```
CONST
    FreshmanHours = 25;
    SophomoreHours = 50;
    JuniorHours = 85;

BEGIN
    IF Class = 1 THEN
        HoursCheck := CumHours >= FreshmanHours
    ELSE IF Class = 2 THEN
        HoursCheck := CumHours >= SophomoreHours
    ELSE IF Class = 3 THEN
        HoursCheck := CumHours >= JuniorHours
END {HoursCheck};

FUNCTION GPACheck( Class : integer;      {student's class}
                   CumGPA : real )       {and cumulative GPA}
                        : boolean;
{---------------------------------------------------------------------

    Accepts:   A student's Class and CumGPA.
    Purpose:   Check if student satisfies the GPA condition for
               eligibility.
    Returns:   True if student meets the GPA criterion and
               false otherwise.

    --------------------------------------------------------------------}

    CONST
        FreshmanGPA = 1.7;
        SophomoreGPA = 1.85;
        JuniorGPA = 1.95;

    BEGIN
        IF Class = 1 THEN
            GPACheck := CumGPA >= FreshmanGPA
        ELSE IF Class = 2 THEN
            GPACheck := CumGPA >= SophomoreGPA
        ELSE IF Class = 3 THEN
            GPACheck := CumGPA >= JuniorGPA
    END {GPACheck};

BEGIN {CheckEligibility}
    IF (Class < 1) OR (Class > 3) THEN
        BEGIN
            writeln( '*** Illegal class code ***' );
            Eligible := false
        END {IF}
    ELSE
        Eligible := HoursCheck( Class, CumHours )
                    AND GPACheck( Class, CumGPA );
    IF Eligible THEN
        EligibleCount := EligibleCount + 1
END {CheckEligibility};
```

FIGURE 5.15 Determining eligibility—final version. (cont.)

```
PROCEDURE Report
        (   Snumb, Class : integer;    {student's number, class,}
            CumHours,                  {cumulative hours,}
            CurrGPA, CumGPA : real;    {current and cumulative GPA}
            Eligible : boolean );      {eligibility indicator}
  {-------------------------------------------------------------------

      Accepts:        A student's Snumb, Class, CumHours, CurrGPA,
                      CumGPA, and Eligible (eligibility indicator).

      Purpose:        Display statistics and eligibility status for a
                      given student.
      Output (screen): Snumb, Class, CumHours, CumGPA, CurrGPA, and
                      eligibility status.

  -------------------------------------------------------------------}

  BEGIN
      writeln;
      writeln( '***** Report for student ', Snumb:1, ' *****' );
      writeln( 'Class:        ', Class:1 );
      writeln( 'Cum. hours:   ', CumHours:4:2 );
      writeln( 'Curr. GPA:    ', CurrGPA:4:2 );
      writeln( 'Cum. GPA:     ', CumGPA:4:2 );
      IF Eligible THEN
          writeln( 'ELIGIBLE' )
      ELSE
          writeln( '*** NOT ELIGIBLE ***' );
      writeln( '*********************************' );
      writeln
  END {Report};

BEGIN {CheckStudent}
    ReadAndCalculate( Snumb, Class, StudentCount, CumHours, CumGPA,
                      CurrGPA, SumOfGPAs );
    CheckEligibility( Class, CumHours, CumGPA, Eligible,
                      EligibleCount );
    Report( Snumb, Class, CumHours, CurrGPA, CumGPA, Eligible )
END {CheckStudent};

PROCEDURE PrintSummary
        ( StudentCount,               {number of students}
          EligibleCount : integer;    {number found to be eligible}
          SumOfGPAs : real );         {sum of all GPAs}
  {-------------------------------------------------------------------

      Accepts:        StudentCount, EligibleCount, and SumOfGPAs.
      Purpose:        Display summary statistics.
      Output (screen): Number of students processed, average current
                      GPA for all students, and the number found to
                      be eligible.

  -------------------------------------------------------------------}
```

FIGURE 5.15   Determining eligibility—final version. (cont.)

```
BEGIN
    writeln;
    writeln;
    writeln( '****************************************************' );
    writeln( '*                   SUMMARY STATISTICS             *' );
    writeln( '****************************************************' );
    writeln;
    writeln( 'NUMBER OF STUDENTS PROCESSED:      ', StudentCount:1 );
    IF StudentCount > 0 THEN
        BEGIN
            writeln( 'AVERAGE CURRENT GPA OF STUDENTS:   ',
                     SumOfGPAs / StudentCount :4:2 );
            writeln( 'NUMBER FOUND TO BE ELIGIBLE;       ', EligibleCount:1 )
        END {IF}
END {PrintSummary};

BEGIN {******************* main program *******************}
    Instruct;
    StudentCount := 0;
    EligibleCount := 0;
    SumOfGPAs := 0;
    write( 'Do you have students to check (Y or N)? ' );
    readln( Response );
    WHILE Response <> 'N' DO
        BEGIN
            CheckStudent( StudentCount, EligibleCount, SumOfGPAs );
            writeln;
            write( 'More (Y or N)? ' );
            readln( Response )
        END {WHILE};
    PrintSummary( StudentCount, EligibleCount, SumOfGPAs )
END {main program}.
```

Sample run:

```
You will first be asked to enter the student's
number, class, cumulative hours, and cumulative GPA.
Enter these with at least one space separating them.

You will then be asked to enter the number of hours and
the numeric grade earned for each of the courses the
student took during the current year.  Separate the
number of hours from the grade by at least one space.
Enter 0 for hours and grades when you are finished
entering the information for each student.
```

FIGURE 5.15   Determining eligibility—final version. (cont.)

```
Do you have students to check (Y or N)? Y
Enter student number, class, cum. hours, cum. GPA:
1234 1 0 0
Hours and grade? 5 3.0
Hours and grade? 4 3.0
Hours and grade? 3.5 3.0
Hours and grade? 4 3.0
Hours and grade? 3 3.0
Hours and grade? 2 3.0
Hours and grade? 0 0

***** Report for student 1234 *****
Class:       1
Cum. hours:  21.50
Curr. GPA:   3.00
Cum. GPA:    3.00
*** NOT ELIGIBLE ***
**********************************


More (Y or N)? Y
Enter student number, class, cum. hours, cum. GPA:
3333 2 30 3.3
Hours and grade? 5 3.3
Hours and grade? 5 4.0
Hours and grade? 5 2.7
Hours and grade? 5 3.0
Hours and grade? 3 3.7
Hours and grade? 0 0

***** Report for student 3333 *****
Class:       2
Cum. hours:  53.00
Curr. GPA:   3.31
Cum. GPA:    3.30
ELIGIBLE
**********************************


More (Y or N)? Y
Enter student number, class, cum. hours, cum. GPA:
4444 3 60 2.0
Hours and grade? 5 1.0
Hours and grade? 5 1.3
Hours and grade? 4 0.7
Hours and grade? 3 0.7
Hours and grade? 5 1.0
Hours and grade? 0 0
```

FIGURE 5.15   Determining eligibility—final version. (cont.)

```
***** Report for student 4444 *****
Class:        3
Cum. hours:   82.00
Curr. GPA:    0.97
Cum. GPA:     1.72
*** NOT ELIGIBLE ***
********************************


More (Y or N)? N


*************************************************************
*                  SUMMARY STATISTICS                      *
*************************************************************

NUMBER OF STUDENTS PROCESSED:    3
AVERAGE CURRENT GPA OF STUDENTS:  2.43
NUMBER FOUND TO BE ELIGIBLE;      1
```

Exercises

1. A loan officer at a bank needs a program to determine whether a loan applicant qualifies for various kinds of loans: automobile loans, home-improvement loans, home mortgages, and so on. The criteria for eligibility must be established for each kind of loan; for example, eligibility for a home mortgage might require that the applicant have a down payment that is at least 20 percent of the purchase price of the home, must have been employed for at least five years, must have an annual income that is at least 40 percent of the purchase price, and other credit obligations must not exceed 20 percent of annual income.

   (a) Develop a specification of the problem, including establishing criteria for the various kinds of loans. For this you might obtain the information from a local bank or other sources.
   (b) Develop a top–down design plan for a program for this loan-eligibility problem.
   (c) Code and test the subprograms and the complete program that implement the design plan.

2. Use a top–down design strategy to develop a menu-driven program that computes any of the following five quantities, given values for the other four:

   Amount: Original amount (in dollars) deposited in a savings account or, in the case of a loan, the original amount borrowed.
   Balance: The final amount (in dollars).
   Payment: Periodic payment made some specified number of times per year.

IntRate: Annual interest rate (percent).
Years: Number of years.

In each case, the user also enters the number of times per year that payments are made and indicates whether these payments are loan payments or deposits into a savings account.

3. A **complex number** is a number of the form $a + bi$, where a and b are real numbers and $i^2 = -1$. Using a top–down approach, develop a menu-driven program that reads two complex numbers (where $a + bi$ is entered simply as the pair of real numbers a and b) and allows the user to select one of the operations of addition, subtraction, multiplication, or division to be performed. The program should then call an appropriate procedure to perform the specified arithmetic operation and display the result in the form $a + bi$. The four operations are defined as follows:

$$(a + bi) + (c + di) = (a + c) + (b + d)i$$

$$(a + bi) - (c + di) = (a - c) + (b - d)i$$

$$(a + bi) * (c + di) = (ac - bd) + (ad + bc)i$$

$$(a + bi) / (c + di) = \left(\frac{ac + bd}{c^2 + d^2}\right) + \left(\frac{bc - ad}{c^2 + d^2}\right)i$$

provided that c and d are not both zero in the case of division.

5.8   Units

In Section 5.4, we considered the problem of designing a program to balance a checkbook, and in the preceding section, we developed a program for determining academic eligibility. Because of the complexity of these problems, we constructed each program in a modular fashion using procedures and functions rather than writing a single large program that would have been more difficult to develop and whose structure would have been more difficult to understand. Procedures and functions are part of almost every high-level language, but Turbo Pascal also includes an even more powerful tool for designing a modular programs, the **unit.** In this section we show how units are constructed and how the items they contain can be imported into programs and used in these programs.

What Is a Unit?

A unit is essentially a program whose contents can be used by another program. More precisely, a unit may contain definitions of constants, variables, types, procedures, and functions, all of which may be imported into another unit or into a program by including in that program a **USES clause** of the following form:

USES Clause

Form:

> USES *unit-name*;

where:
  USES is a reserved word;
  unit-name is a the name of a unit.

Purpose:
Makes available to the program the items defined
in the specified unit.

As we will see later, a unit may also contain an initialization part that is executed before any program that uses the unit.

Turbo Pascal provides the following standard units:[1]

Crt   Intended for specific kinds of input/output such as windowing, moving the cursor to a specified point on the screen, and setting text or background color.

Dos   Contains several useful operating system and file-handling routines such as getting the current date or time, determining the amount of free space on a disk, and searching for a file in a list of directories.

Graph   A collection of graphics routines including procedures for drawing lines, circles, ellipses, rectangles, and various other figures.

Overlay Contains routines for managing overlays, which are programs that occupy a common area of memory.

Printer Declares the file variable **Lst**, which if included as the first parameter in a **write** or **writeln** statement will direct the output of that statement to the printer.

System Contains all of the predefined procedures and functions of Turbo Pascal. Its contents are automatically imported into every program, and it is therefore not necessary to include **System** in a **USES** clause.

To use any of the items in the units, we need only include the name of the unit in a **USES** clause at the beginning of the program.

To illustrate, suppose we wish to modify the checkbook-balancing program of Figure 5.6 so that the menu of options is displayed in a small colored window on the screen, as shown in Figure 5.16. We can accomplish this quite easily using the procedures in the standard unit **Crt**. To make these procedures accessible in the program we would add the **USES** clause

    USES Crt;

after the program heading.

---

[1] Two other units, **Graph3** and the unit **Turbo3**, make available the set of graphics routines and other items from Version 3.0 of Turbo Pascal that are no longer supported in later versions.

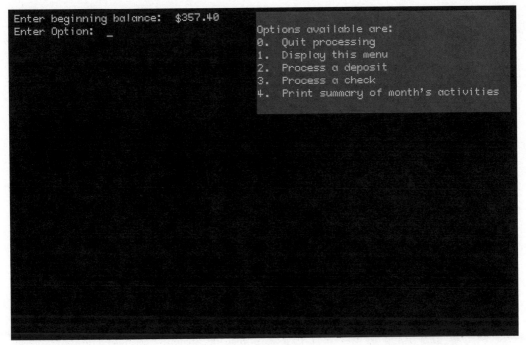

FIGURE 5.16 Windowing.

The following list gives a few of the procedures contained in `Crt`:

`ClrScr`	Clears the current window and positions the cursor at the upper left corner.
`GoTOXY( X, Y )`	Positions the cursor at the point in the current window whose coordinates are **X** (column number) and **Y** (row number).
`TextBackGround( Color )`	Sets the background color of the current window to `Color`, which may be any of `Black`, `Blue`, `Green`, `Cyan`, `Red`, `Magenta`, `Brown`, `LightGray`, `DarkGray`, `LightBlue`, `LightGreen`, `LightCyan`, `LightRed`, `LightMagenta`, `Yellow`, `White`, or any of the equivalent integer constants 0, 1, 2, . . . , 15, respectively.
`TextColor( Color )`	Sets the foreground color of the current window to `Color`.
`Window( X1, Y1, X2, Y2)`	Defines a text window in the screen whose upper left corner has coordinates **X1** and **Y1** and whose lower right corner has coordinates **X2** and **Y2**. The upper left corner of the screen has coordinates (1, 1), and the lower right has coordinates (80, 25) in 25-line mode or (80, 43) in 43-line mode.

We can use these procedures in the checkbook-balancing program to have the screen appear as in Figure 5.16. We need only add the statements

```
Window( 40, 1, 80, 8 );
TextBackground( LightGray );
ClrScr;
GotoXY( 1, 2 );
```

at the beginning of procedure **DisplayMenu** and

```
Window( 1, 1, 80, 25 );
TextBackGround( Black );
```

at the end. The first set of statements defines the small light gray rectangle at the upper right of the screen, clears its contents, and positions the cursor at the second line in this window. The output produced by the **writeln** statements in **DisplayMenu** appears in this window. The second set of statements then makes the default window the active window again and resets the background color to black.

In addition to providing standard units like **Crt**, Turbo Pascal also allows users to construct their own units. For example, we might wish to rename procedures **ProcessDeposit** and **ProcessCheck** from the checkbook-balancing program in Figure 5.6 as **ProcessCredit** and **ProcessDebit**, respectively, and package them and perhaps others as well in a unit so they can be used in developing other financial and accounting programs. The complete unit is given in Figure 5.17, but to understand it, we must first examine the structure of units in more detail.

The Structure of a Unit

A unit has three parts: a heading that names the unit, an interface part that describes the processing done by this unit, and an implementation part that specifies how this processing is carried out. A unit thus has the form

Unit

> Unit heading
> Interface part
> Implementation part

Unit Heading.   Every unit must begin with a **unit heading** of the following form:

Unit Heading

> **Form:**
>
>   UNIT *name*;
>
> where:
>   **UNIT** is a reserved word;
>   *name* is a valid Pascal identifier.
>
> **Purpose:**
> Names the unit.

It is the name specified in the heading that is used to reference the unit in a USES clause.

The name under which a unit is saved on disk should consist of the first eight or fewer letters of the unit's name followed by the extension .PAS; thus, a unit named TransProcessing would be filed under the name TRANSPRO.PAS. (The U compiler directive can be used to file a unit under a different name, as described in Appendix G. Also, compiling a unit to disk saves the object code under a name of the form *name*.TPU, for example, TRANSPRO.TPU.)

Interface Part. The **interface** or **definition part** of a unit is so named because it serves as an interface between the user and the unit. It contains all the information necessary to understand what the unit does and how to use it. It has the following form:

Interface Part

Form:

    INTERFACE

    USES clause
    Declaration part

where:
    INTERFACE is a reserved word;
    the USES clause has the same form as in a program and is optional;
    the declaration part has the usual form, except that subprogram sections contain only headings of the procedures and functions defined in this unit.

Purpose:
Specifies the contents of the unit. Any of the items specified in the USES clause or in the declaration part are accessible to other units and programs.

Since it only specifies *what* the unit is to do (not how it does it), the interface part has no statement part. This is also the reason that its declaration part has a modified structure. Although its constant and variable sections (as well as its type and label sections described later) have the usual forms, its subprogram sections contain only procedure and function headings that name the procedures and functions and their parameters, but there are no statement parts for these subprograms. It usually also contains documentation that specifies what the subprograms in this unit are to do.

Implementation Part. The **implementation part** of a unit is so named because it implements the procedures and functions that were specified in the interface part. It is this part that describes *how* the unit does its processing. The implementation part has the following form:

Implementation Part

Form:

        IMPLEMENTATION

        USES clause
        Declaration part
        Initialization part.

where:
   IMPLEMENTATION is a reserved word;
   the **USES** clause has the same form as in a program and is optional;
   the declaration part has the same form as in a program. Its subprogram sections must contain the complete definitions for those procedures and functions whose headings are given in the interface part. The formal parameter lists may be omitted from these headings, but if they are included, they must match those in the interface part.
   The initialization part may be trivial, consisting simply of the reserved word **END**, or it may have the same form as the statement part of a program. Note that in either case a period follows the initialization part to mark the end of the unit.

Purpose:
Defines the actual procedures and functions specified in the interface part of the unit. It may also import or declare items needed in these definitions, but these are *private* to the unit; that is, they are not accessible to other units or programs. If the initialization part is nontrivial, the statements in it are executed before those in any program or other unit in which this unit is used.

Note that all of the items declared in or imported into the implementation part are not accessible outside the unit. Whereas the information in the interface part is *public* information, that in the implementation part is *private* information.

Example: Transaction Processing

The purpose of the program in Figure 5.6 was to help reconcile a checkbook register with a monthly statement. It used two main procedures, **ProcessDeposit** and **ProcessCheck**, to process transactions. To make it possible to use these procedures in other financial and accounting programs, we might rename them **ProcessCredit** and **ProcessDebit**, respectively, and package them (and perhaps others) in a separate unit **TransProcessing** like that shown in Figure 5.17.

```
UNIT TransProcessing;
{****************************************************************

   Unit containing items intended for use in financial and
   accounting programs.
   EXPORTS:    Procedures:    ProcessCredit
                              ProcessDebit


   ***************************************************************}


INTERFACE

PROCEDURE ProcessCredit
              ( VAR Balance,           {current balance}
                    TotalCredits       {sum of credit transactions}
                        : real;
                VAR NumberOfCredits    {number of credit transactions}
                        : integer );
{------------------------------------------------------------------

   Accepts:          Current Balance, total of all credit
                     transactions (TotalCredits), and the number
                     of credit transactions (NumberOfCredits).
   Input (keyboard): Amount of a credit transaction.
   Purpose:          Process a credit transaction by updating
                     the balance and the total and number of
                     credit transactions.
   Output (screen):  User prompt.
   Returns:          Updated values of Balance, TotalCredits, and
                     NumberOfCredits.

------------------------------------------------------------------}


PROCEDURE ProcessDebit
              ( VAR Balance,           {current balance}
                    TotalDebits,       {sum of debit transactions}
                    TotalServiceCharges {sum of all service charges}
                        : real;
                VAR NumberOfDebits     {number of debit transactions}
                        : integer );
{------------------------------------------------------------------

   Accepts:          Current Balance, total of all debit
                     transactions (TotalDebits), total of service
                     charges (TotalServiceCharges), and the number
                     of debit transactions (NumberOfDebits).
   Input (keyboard): Amount of a debit transaction.
   Purpose:          Process a debit transaction by updating
                     the balance, the total and number of debit
                     transactions, and total service charge.
   Output (screen):  User prompt.
   Returns:          Updated values of Balance, TotalDebits,
                     TotalServiceCharges, and NumberOfDebits.

------------------------------------------------------------------}
```

FIGURE 5.17   Transaction processing unit. (cont.)

```
IMPLEMENTATION

PROCEDURE ProcessDebit;

   CONST
      ServiceCharge = 0.20;     {processing charge}

   VAR
      Debit : real;              {amount of debit}

   BEGIN
      write( 'Enter debit:   $' );
      readln( Debit );
      Balance := Balance - Debit - ServiceCharge;
      TotalDebits := TotalDebits + Debit;
      TotalServiceCharges := TotalServiceCharges + ServiceCharge;
      NumberOfDebits := NumberOfDebits + 1
   END {ProcessDebit};

PROCEDURE ProcessCredit;

   VAR
      Credit : real;             {amount of credit}

   BEGIN
      write( 'Enter credit:   $' );
      readln( Credit );
      Balance := Balance + Credit;
      TotalCredits := TotalCredits + Credit;
      NumberOfCredits := NumberOfCredits + 1
   END {ProcessCredit};

END {TransProcessing}.
```

Once this unit has been compiled, a program or another unit can use items from it simply by including its name in a USES clause. For example, the check-book-balancing program of Figure 5.6 can be simplified as shown in Figure 5.18 by using the procedures ProcessCredit and ProcessDebit from the unit TransProcessing in place of ProcessDeposit and ProcessCheck, respectively. To make these available to the program, we add the USES clause

```
      USES TransProcessing;
```

FIGURE 5.18 Balancing a checkbook—version 2.

```
PROGRAM CheckbookBalancer( input, output );
{***************************************************************

    Input (keyboard):  User-selected options, amounts of deposits,
                       amounts of checks.
    Purpose:           This is a menu-driven program for reconciling
                       a checkbook with a monthly statement.
    Output (screen):   User prompts, menu of options, summary of
                       month's activities.
    Uses:              Procedures ProcessCredit and ProcessDebit
                       from the unit TransProcessing.


***************************************************************}

USES TransProcessing;

CONST
    NumberOfOptions = 5;        {# of options in menu}

VAR
    InitialBalance,             {beginning balance in checking account}
    Balance,                    {current balance}
    TotalDeposits,              {sum of all deposits for the month}
    TotalChecks,                {sum of all checks processed}
    TotalServiceCharges:: real; {total check-processing charges}
    NumberOfDeposits,           {total number of deposits made}
    NumberOfChecks,             {           and checks written}
    Option : integer;           {option selected by user}

PROCEDURE Initialize( VAR InitialBalance,      {beginning balance}
                          Balance,             {current balance}
                          TotalDeposits,       {sum of all deposits}
                          TotalChecks,         {sum of all checks}
                          TotalServiceCharges  {total service charges}
                            : real;
                      VAR NumberOfDeposits,    {total # of deposits}
                          NumberOfChecks       {total # of checks}
                            : integer );
{-----------------------------------------------------------------

    Input (keyboard):  InitialBalance.
    Purpose:           Get initial balance from user and initialize
                       variables.
    Returns:           InitialBalance, Balance (= InitialBalance),
                       0 values for TotalDeposits, TotalChecks,
                       TotalServiceCharges, NumberOfDeposits, and
                       NumberOfChecks.


-----------------------------------------------------------------}
```

FIGURE 5.18   Balancing a checkbook—version 2. (cont.)

```
  BEGIN
     write( 'Enter beginning balance:   $' );
     readln( InitialBalance );
     writeln;
     Balance := InitialBalance;
     TotalDeposits := 0;
     TotalChecks := 0;
     TotalServiceCharges := 0;
     NumberOfDeposits := 0;
     NumberOfChecks := 0
  END {Initialize};


PROCEDURE DisplayMenu;
{-------------------------------------------------------------------------


  Purpose:          Display the menu of options.
  Output (screen):  Menu of options.


------------------------------------------------------------------------->}
  BEGIN
     writeln( 'Options available are:' );
     writeln( '0.  Quit processing' );
     writeln( '1.  Display this menu' );
     writeln( '2.  Process a deposit' );
     writeln( '3.  Process a check' );
     writeln( '4.  Print summary of month''s activities' );
  END {DisplayMenu};

PROCEDURE PrintSummary( InitialBalance, Balance, TotalDeposits,
                        TotalChecks, TotalServiceCharges:: real;
                        NumberOfDeposits, NumberOfChecks:: integer );
{-------------------------------------------------------------------------


  Accepts:          InitialBalance, Balance, TotalDeposits,
                    TotalChecks, TotalServiceCharges,
                    NumberOfDeposits, and NumberOfChecks.
  Purpose:          Display a summary of month's transactions.
  Output (screen):  A summary showing the values of the parameters.


------------------------------------------------------------------------->}

  BEGIN
     writeln;
     writeln( 'Initial Balance  . . . . . . . . $', InitialBalance:8:2 );
     writeln( 'Total Deposits . . . . . . . . . $', TotalDeposits:8:2 );
     writeln( 'Total Checks . . . . . . . . . . $', TotalChecks:8:2 );
     writeln( 'Total Service Charges  . . . . . $',
                                          TotalServiceCharges:8:2 );
     writeln( 'Final Balance  . . . . . . . . . $', Balance:8:2 );
     writeln( 'Number of Deposits:  ', NumberOfDeposits:1 );
     writeln( 'Number of Checks:    ', NumberOfChecks:1 )
  END {PrintSummary};
```

FIGURE 5.18   Balancing a checkbook—version 2. (cont.)

```
BEGIN {*********************** main program ********************}
   Initialize( InitialBalance, Balance, TotalDeposits, TotalChecks,
               TotalServiceCharges, NumberOfDeposits, NumberOfChecks );
   DisplayMenu;
   writeln;
   write( 'Enter Option:  ' );
   readln( Option );
   WHILE Option <> 0 DO
      BEGIN
         IF Option = 1 THEN
            DisplayMenu
         ELSE IF Option = 2 THEN
            ProcessCredit( Balance, TotalDeposits, NumberOfDeposits )
         ELSE IF Option = 3 THEN
            ProcessDebit( Balance, TotalChecks, TotalServiceCharges,
                          NumberOfChecks )
         ELSE IF Option = 4 THEN
            PrintSummary( InitialBalance, Balance, TotalDeposits,
                          TotalChecks, TotalServiceCharges,
                          NumberOfDeposits, NumberOfChecks )
         ELSE
            writeln( '*** Invalid Option ***' );
         writeln;
         write( 'Enter Option:  ' );
         readln( Option )
      END {WHILE}
END {main program}.
```

Why Use Units?

There are several benefits from using units. One that the preceding example demonstrates is that a unit extends the language by making available additional items—procedures, functions, constants, variables, and types—to any program or other unit. There is no need for the programmer to "reinvent the wheel" each time these items are needed.

Several other benefits result from separating units from programs that use them and from separating a unit itself into an interface part and an implementation part. To use the items in a unit, the programmer needs to know only the information in the interface part; the implementation details are of no concern. A copy of the interface part and other relevant documentation can be provided to the user in either a file or a manual, but source code for the implementation part need not be made available. The implementation details can remain "hidden" in the machine code of the compiled unit that is provided to the user. This **information hiding** makes it possible to use the unit without being concerned about these details. For example, one can use the unit **TransProcessing** without understanding the details of how a particular transaction is processed by the procedures in this unit. Information hiding is one of the important benefits that results from using units.

Another benefit that results from this separation of programs and units is that they can be compiled separately. **Separate compilation** makes it possible to change the implementation part of a unit and recompile only the unit; programs or other units that use the unit need not be changed or recompiled. For example, if procedure **ProcessCredit** in the implementation part of the unit **TransProcessing** (but not its heading in the interface part) were changed, then only the unit must be recompiled, but the preceding program need not be. Such changes in the implementation part of a unit, if made properly, should be transparent to users of this unit. Changes to the interface part of the unit, however, require recompilation of both the unit and all programs and other units that use it.

A third important benefit of using units is that they introduce another level of modularity into software design. Procedures and functions are designed to perform particular tasks, and units allow these subprograms that perform related tasks to be grouped together into independent units. This is especially useful in large programming projects that involve several programmers. These programmers can jointly develop the interface parts of the various units needed in the project. Some members of the programming team can then develop the implementation parts of these modules independently while other programmers write applications that use the modules as specified in their interface parts. The interface parts serve, therefore, as a well-defined interface between these units and their users. Separate units can be developed and tested independently, perhaps by different programmers or teams of programmers. The interface parts of these modules provide a well-defined interface between the units, their developers, and users of these units.

Exercises

1. Modify the checkbook-balancing program in Figure 5.6 to process ATM transactions as described at the end of Section 5.4. Although there is no charge for making a deposit using an ATM, there is a 20 cent charge for each withdrawal. The procedure **ProcessATM** should use procedures **ProcessCredit** and **ProcessDebit** from the unit **TransProcessing** for processing deposits and withdrawals.

2. If an amount A is invested and earns interest at an annual rate R with interest compounded k times per year, then the accumulated value after n years is given by

$$A\left(1 + \frac{r}{k}\right)^{n*k}$$

   (a) Add a function **AccumulatedValue** to the unit **TransProcessing** that calculates accumulated values using this formula.
   (b) Write a program that reads an amount to be deposited in a savings account, an annual interest rate, the number of times interest is compounded, and the number of years that interest is earned and determines the amount accumulated in this account, assuming no additional deposits or withdrawals are made. The program should import the function **AccumulatedValue** from **TransProcessing** and use it to carry out the interest calculations.

3. Design a unit for converting various units of measurements. Include, at least, procedures for converting minutes to hours, feet to meters, and degrees Fahren-

heit to degrees Celsius. Then redo Exercise 5 of Section 5.1, importing items from this unit as needed.

4. Design a unit that contains three procedures, **ReadBoole**, **WriteBoole**, and **WritelnBoole**. A procedure reference of the form **Read-Boole(*boolean-variable*)** should read the string **'TRUE'** or **'FALSE'** (or any string formed by using lowercase letters for some of the letters) and return the corresponding boolean value for ***boolean-variable***. References of the form **WriteBoole(*boolean-variable*)** and **WritelnBoole (*boolean-variable*)** should produce the same output as **write (*boolean-variable*)** and **writeln(*boolean-variable*)**, respectively.

5. Design a unit for processing complex numbers as described in Exercise 3 of Section 5.7.

described in earlier chapters for programs, procedures, and functions should be followed for units as well.

Programming Pointers

Program Design

1. *(From Wirth) "We recommend to choose function identifiers which are nouns. The noun then denotes the function's result. Boolean functions are appropriately labeled by an adjective. In contrast, regular procedures should be designated by a verb describing their action."*

2. *Programs for solving complex problems should be designed in a modular fashion.*

   - *A problem should be divided into simpler subproblems so that a function or procedure can be written to solve each of these subproblems.*
   - *Local identifiers should be used within subprograms to avoid conflict with identifiers in other program units and to make the program as modular as possible.*
   - *Formal parameters in subprograms should be declared as value parameters (or as constant parameters in Turbo Pascal 7.0; see Section H.2 of Appendix H) whenever appropriate so that subprograms cannot unexpectedly change the values of the actual parameters.*

3. *A number of benefits result from using units:*

   - *They extend the language by making additional items available to any program.*
   - *The items in a unit can be used without being concerned about the details of their implementation.*
   - *Programs and units can be compiled separately. Changing the implementation part of a unit requires compilation of only the unit.*
   - *Units provide another level of modularity in software design; related subprograms and other items can be grouped together into independent units.*

Potential Problems

1. *When a procedure or function is referenced, the number of parameters must be the same as the number of formal parameters in the procedure or function heading, and the type of each actual parameter must be compatible with the type of the corresponding formal parameter.* For example, consider the function with the heading

       FUNCTION Maximum(Number1, Number2 : integer) : integer;

   The statements

       Larger1 := Maximum(k, m, n);

   and

       Larger2 := Maximum(Number, 3.75);

   are incorrect. In the first case, the number of actual parameters does not agree with the number of formal parameters, and in the second, the real value 3.75 cannot be assigned to the integer parameter `Number`.

2. *Parameters that are to return values from a procedure must be declared as variable parameters using the indicator* VAR. *The actual parameters that correspond to variable formal parameters must be variables; they may not be constants or expressions.* For example, the procedure heading

       PROCEDURE FindTaxes(Income : real;
                            VAR NetIncome, Tax : real);

   can return only values of `NetIncome` and `Tax` to the calling program unit, and it cannot be called by the statement

       FindTaxes(Salary, 3525.67, IncomeTax)

   because the constant `3525.67` cannot be associated with the variable parameter `NetIncome`.

3. *Formal parameters in procedures and functions are defined only during execution of that procedure or function; they are undefined both before and after execution.* Any attempt to use these parameters outside the function or procedure is an error.

4. *The scope of a local entity is the program unit in which is it declared.* For example, for the procedure

       PROCEDURE Calculate(x : integer; y : real);

           VAR
             a, b : integer;
                 .
                 .
                 .

   the local variables `x`, `y`, `a`, and `b` cannot be accessed outside the procedure `Calculate`.

5. *Using global variables to share information between different program units (the main program and subprograms) should usually be avoided, since changing the value of such a variable in one program unit changes its value in all program units.* This may make it difficult to determine the value of such a variable at any point in the program because its values may have been changed by any of the program units.

6. *A procedure or function must be defined before it is referenced.* For example, if the procedure **FindTaxes** references the procedure **Calculate**, then **Calculate** must be defined before **FindTaxes**.

```
PROCEDURE Calculate . . .;
        .
        .
        .
PROCEDURE FindTaxes . . .;
        .
        .
        .
```

7. *Procedures and functions that have formal parameters cannot be referenced without corresponding actual parameters.* An error commonly made by beginning programmers is illustrated by the following attempt to define the function **Sum** (which calculates the sum $1 + 2 + \cdots + n$):

```
FUNCTION Sum( n : integer ) : integer;

    VAR
        k : integer;

    BEGIN
        Sum := 0;
        k := 1;
        WHILE k <= n DO
            BEGIN
                Sum := Sum + k;
                k := k + 1
            END {WHILE}
    END {Sum};
```

In this example, the statement

```
Sum := Sum + k
```

is not valid because the right side of this assignment statement contains a reference to the function **Sum** with no actual parameters. Instead, a local variable within **Sum** should be initialized

```
TempSum := 0;
```

and used in the loop:

```
WHILE k <= n DO
   BEGIN
      TempSum := TempSum + k;
      k := k + 1
   END {WHILE};
```

The final value of `TempSum` is then assigned to the function:

```
Sum := TempSum
```

See the program in Figure 5.9 for the complete function.

8. *A* **USES** *clause must follow the heading of any program (or unit) that uses items from a unit and must contain the names of all units from which the units are imported into the program.* Attempting to use an item from a unit not listed in a **USES** clause will produce the error message

```
Error 3: Unknown identifier
```

Program Style

1. *Procedures and functions should be documented in the same way that programs are.* The documentation should include specifications and descriptions of

- The items *accepted by* the subprogram.
- The items *input to* the subprogram.
- The *purpose* of the subprogram.
- The items *returned by* the subprogram.
- The items *output by* the subprogram.

2. *Procedures and functions are separate program units, and the program format should reflect this.* In this text we

- Insert a blank line before and after each procedure and function definition to separate it from other program units.
- Indent the declarations and statements within each subprogram.
- Follow the stylistic standards for programs described in earlier chapters when writing subprograms.

3. *Units should be documented in much the same way that programs are.* The documentation for a unit should describe clearly, precisely, and completely what the contents of the unit are and how to use the items in it, any special algorithms it implements, and other useful information such as the author and when it was last modified.

4. *All guidelines for programming style apply to units.* The stylistic standards described in earlier chapters for programs, procedures, and functions should be followed for units as well.

Standard Pascal

Only one feature of Turbo Pascal described in this chapter is not availabe in standard Pascal:

- Units are not supported.

DATA FILES

> . . . *it became increasingly apparent to me that, over the years, Federal agencies have amassed vast amounts of information about virtually every American citizen. This fact, coupled with technological advances in data collecting and dissemination, raised the possibility that information about individuals conceivably could be used for other than legitimate purposes and without the prior knowledge or consent of the individuals involved.*
> PRESIDENT GERALD R. FORD

> *The rights of the people to be secure in their persons, houses, papers, and effects against unreasonable searches and seizures, shall not be violated.* . . .
> FOURTH AMENDMENT OF THE U. S. CONSTITUTION

CHAPTER CONTENTS

The second phase in the development of a program or system of programs to solve a problem is formulating a design plan. As noted in Section 2.2, two important aspects of design are selecting appropriate structures to organize and store the data and devising algorithms and modules to process the data. Up to now we have focused more on the second aspect than on the first. Chapter 4 dealt with structured algorithms and programs, and Chapter 5 with the modular design of programs using procedures and functions. However, the data themselves and how they are organized is just as important as how they are processed. Often the amount of data or where they are stored makes it impractical to enter them interactively during program execution. In other applications, the data items are related to one another, and so using simple variables to store the individual items is awkward. Processing collections of related data items requires using **data structures,** and we consider several of these in later chapters—arrays in Chapters 9 and 11, strings in Chapter 10, records in Chapter 12, sets in Chapter 14, and other structures such as stacks, queues, linked lists, and binary trees in other chapters.

In this chapter we consider how data can be stored in and retrieved from **files.** Files are the basic building blocks of **databases,** some of which store vast amounts of data that may be linked together in rather complicated ways. Database design and management is an important area of computer science, and a study of files is an obvious prerequisite to understanding its basic principles and methodologies.

In our introduction to input/output in Chapter 3, we observed that these operations are carried out using files. We have thus far used only the standard system files **input** and **output** that are associated with the standard system input device (keyboard) and output device (screen), respectively. These are examples of a special kind of file called *text files,* which are studied in this chapter. Other kinds of files are considered in Chapter 15.

6.1   Input/Output Procedures

Up to now we have used **read**, **readln**, **write**, and **writeln** statements to perform input/output. These statements are in fact procedure reference statements that call the predefined Pascal procedures **read**, **readln**, **write**, and **writeln**, respectively. The input/output lists are in fact the parameter lists for these predefined procedures. These procedures have the special property that references to them may include any number of parameters.

Procedure **writeln**

The **writeln** procedure is called with a statement of the form

```
writeln( output-list )
```

where *output-list* is an expression or a list of expressions separated by commas. Execution of such a statement displays the values of the expressions on a single line and then advances to a new line. For example, if the value of the integer variable **Number** is 27, the statements

```
writeln( 'Square of ', Number, ' is ', sqr(Number) );
writeln( 'and its square root is ', sqrt(Number) )
```

produce as output:

```
Square_of_27_is_729_____
and_its_square_root_is___5.1961524227E+00
```

Recall that the format of the output can be specified by appending a format descriptor of the form *:w* or *:w:d* to the items in the output list. For example, the statements

```
writeln( 'Square of ', Number:2, ' is ', sqr(Number):4 );
writeln( 'and its square root is ', sqrt(Number):8:3 )
```

produce as output

```
Square_of_27_is__729_____
and_its_square_root_is____5.196
```

The **writeln** procedure may also be called with no output list:

```
writeln
```

and in this case the parentheses are also omitted. This statement serves merely to advance to the next line.

Procedure **write**

The **write** procedure is called with a statement of the form

```
write( output-list )
```

where the output list has the same form as for the **writeln** statement; format descriptors may be used as just described. When this statement is executed, the values are displayed on the current line, but there is no advance to a new line. Consequently, any subsequent output will be displayed on this same line. For example, the statements

```
write( 'The first 3 squares are:' );
write( 1:3 );
write( 4:3 );
write( 9:3 );
writeln( ' *****' );
writeln( '*****' )
```

produce as output

```
The_first_3_squares_are:__1__4__9_*****_
*****_____
```

Procedure `readln`

The `readln` procedure is called with a statement of the form

        readln(*input-list*)

where *input-list* is a variable or a list of variables of integer, real, or character type, separated by commas. When this statement is executed, values are read from the standard system file **input** and assigned to the variables in the input list. In a batch mode of operation, these values are typically obtained from a data file that accompanies the program. In an interactive mode, execution of the program is suspended while the user enters values for the variables. In this text, most of the examples illustrate interactive input.

For example, when the statements

```
writeln( 'Enter employee number, hours worked, and hourly rate:' );
readln( EmpNumber, Hours, HourlyRate )
```

are executed, the prompt

   Enter employee number, hours worked, and hourly rate:

is displayed, and execution of the program is interrupted. The user must enter values for the three variables before execution of the program can resume. To assign the values 3123, 38.5, and 7.50 to **EmpNumber**, **Hours**, and **HourlyRate**, respectively, where **EmpNumber** is of **integer** type and **Hours** and **HourlyRate** are of **real** type, the appropriate input is as follows (where ⏎ denotes the **RETURN** key):

   3123 38.5 7.50⏎

The File `input`

The values that are read are actually obtained from the standard system file **input**. Values are copied into this file sequentially as they are entered, and each time a line of input is terminated by depressing the **RETURN** key, an **end-of-line mark** is placed in the file. In Turbo Pascal, this end-of-line mark actually is a pair of characters: a carriage-return (CR) character (ASCII code 13) followed by a line-feed (LF) character (ASCII code 10). Thus, if the user enters

   3123 38.5 7.50
   3164 40.0 8.75

the contents of the file **input** are

   | 3 | 1 | 2 | 3 | | 3 | 8 | . | 5 | | 7 | . | 5 | 0 | ← | ↓ | 3 | 1 | 6 | 4 | | 4 | 0 | . | 0 | | 8 | . | 7 | 5 | ← | ↓ |

where we have used ← ↓ to denote the double-character end-of-line mark.

As values are read from this file by a **readln** statement, a data pointer, which is initially positioned at the beginning of the file, advances through the file. If we indicate the data pointer by ↑, then the initial status of the file **input** is

In Turbo Pascal, when a value for the **integer** variable **EmpNumber** is read from this file, any leading blanks, tabs, and end-of-line marks are skipped and characters are then read until a blank, tab, end-of-line mark, or the end of the file is reached. The resulting string of characters is then converted to an integer value and assigned to **EmpNumber**, provided such conversion is possible. Thus, for the statement

```
readln( EmpNumber, Hours, HourlyRate )
```

the value read for **EmpNumber** is 3123, and the data pointer is advanced to the blank that follows the last digit of this number.

If the string of input characters cannot be converted to an integer value because it contains illegal characters, an input/output error occurs, and program execution is terminated.

A value must now be read for the **real** variable **Hours**. Again, leading blanks, tabs, and end-of-line marks are ignored, and characters are read until a blank, tab, or end-of-line mark is encountered or the end of the file is reached. If the resulting string of characters represents a valid real number in either decimal or exponential form, it is converted to a real value and assigned to the appropriate real variable. Thus the value read for **Hours** is **38.5**, and the data pointer advances to the blank following the last digit of this number.

Similarly, the value **7.50** is read for the **real** variable **HourlyRate**, and the data pointer is advanced to the end-of-line mark.

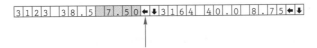

The **readln** procedure then advances the data pointer past this end-of-line mark

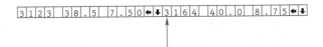

so that the values read for variables in subsequent **readln** statements begin at this point.

For the statement

```
readln( EmpNumber, Hours, HourlyRate )
```

the values might be entered one per line:

3123↵
38.5↵
7.50↵
3164↵
40.0↵
8.75↵

In this case, the contents of the file **input** are

The value read for **EmpNumber** is **3123**, and the data pointer advances to the end-of-line mark following the last digit of this number.

Next, a value must be read for **Hours**; the end-of-line mark is ignored, so that the value **38.5** is read and assigned to **Hours** and the data pointer is advanced.

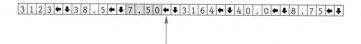

Similarly, the value **7.50** is read and assigned to **HourlyRate**, and the data pointer is advanced.

Because values have been read and assigned to each variable in the input list, the **readln** procedure now advances the data pointer past this end-of-line mark.

Suppose that the preceding data values are entered as

3123␣38.5␣7.50␣3164↵
40.0␣␣8.75↵

so that the contents of the file **input** are

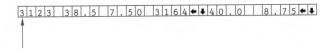

When the statement

    `readln( EmpNumber, Hours, HourlyRate )`

is executed, the values **3123**, **38.5**, and **7.50** are read and assigned to **EmpNumber**, **Hours**, and **HourlyRate**, respectively, as before. Because values have been read for each of the variables in the input list, the **readln** procedure now causes the data pointer to advance past the next end-of-line mark

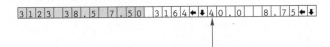

so that the value **3164** is not read. Subsequent input continues from this point. If the statement

    `readln( EmpNumber, Hours, HourlyRate )`

is executed again, the character string read for **EmpNumber** is **40.0**, and the data pointer advances to the blank following this string:

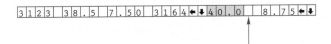

but an error occurs and execution terminates, since an integer may not contain a decimal point. The error message displayed is

    `Error 106: Invalid numeric format.`

Real values may also be entered in exponential form. For example, if the first real values in the preceding example are entered as **0.385E2** and **75E-1**, the same values can be written and assigned as before:

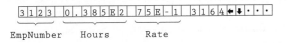

Procedure read

The **read** procedure can also be used for input. It is called with a statement of the form

    `read( input-list )`

where *input-list* is a variable or a list of variables separated by commas. The **read** procedure is similar to the **readln** procedure except that the **read** procedure does *not* advance the data pointer past an end-of-line mark after values have been read for the variables in the input list. To illustrate, consider the statement

    read(EmpNumber, Hours, HourlyRate)

and suppose that the data is entered as described previously:

    3123 38.5 7.50 3164↵
    40.0 8.75↵

As in the case of the **readln** statement, the values read for **EmpNumber**, **Hours**, and **HourlyRate**, are **3123**, **38.5**, and **7.50**, respectively. For the **read** statement, however, the data pointer is not advanced past the end-of-line mark.

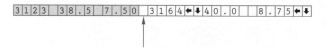

Thus if the statement

    read(EmpNumber, Hours, HourlyRate)

is executed again, the value **3164** is read for **EmpNumber**, **40.0** for **Hours** (the end-of-line mark preceding this number is ignored), and **8.75** for **HourlyRate**, and the data pointer is advanced to the end-of-line mark following this last value.

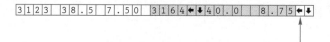

A second distinction between the **read** and **readln** procedures is that **readln**, but not **read**, may be called without an input list:

    readln

Note that in this case the parentheses are also omitted. Execution of this statement advances the data pointer past the next end-of-line mark so that subsequent input begins with a new line. It may thus be used to skip a line of input or to skip over values that remain in the current line or as we noted in Section 3.5, to suspend execution so that output to the screen can be examined.

Reading Strings

When a value is read for a numeric variable in Turbo Pascal, leading blanks, leading tabs, and leading end-of-line marks are ignored, and characters are read until a blank, tab, end-of-line mark, or the end of the file is encountered. When a value is read for a string variable, characters are read, beginning at the current position in the input file and continuing until an end-of-line mark is reached or the end of the file is encountered. Because blanks and tabs are legitimate characters, they are read as part of the string value; end-of-line marks are not read, however, since they serve to terminate the input. If the resulting string consists of 255 or fewer characters, it is assigned to the string variable; otherwise, the string is truncated, and only the first 255 characters are retained. (The default maximum length for string variables is 255; other maximum lengths can be specified as described in Chapter 10.)

As we noted in Section 3.5, the simplest way to read values for string variables is to use one **readln** statement for each variable and enter the values on separate lines. For example, to read values for the string variables **EmpName** and **DeptName**, we might use the statements

```
readln( EmpName );
readln( DeptName );
```

and enter the data as

<u>John_Q._Doe</u>↵
<u>Sales</u>↵

so that the file **input** contains

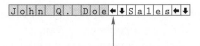

When the first **readln** statement is executed, the string **John Q. Doe** is read and assigned to **EmpName**, and the data pointer advances to the first end-of-line mark:

The **readln** procedure then advances this data pointer past the end-of-line mark:

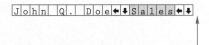

The string **Sales** is thus read and assigned to **DeptName**, and the data pointer is advanced past the next end-of-line mark:

It is important to note that the statement

```
readln( EmpName, DeptName )
```

cannot be used to read these values. With this statement, the string **John Q. Doe** is read and assigned to **EmpName**, and the data pointer is advanced to the first end-of-line mark:

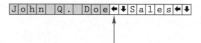

No additional characters will be read for **DeptName** because the data pointer is already positioned at an end-of-line mark; consequently, an **empty string** is assigned to **EmpName**.

The same difficulty occurs if the **read** procedure is used to read values for string variables. For example, consider the statements

```
read (EmpName);
read (DeptName);
```

When the first statement is executed, input characters are read until an end-of-line mark is encountered:

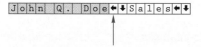

Because the data pointer is once again stuck at an end-of-line mark, no more characters will be read for **DeptName**, so that it is assigned an empty string.

Reading Character Data

When a value is read for a character variable, the next character is read and assigned to the variable, and the data pointer is advanced one position. Since blanks are legitimate characters, they are not ignored but, rather, are read and assigned as values for character variables. Similarly, the carriage-return and line-feed characters that comprise an end-of-line mark are not ignored but, rather, are read and interpreted as values for character variables.

To illustrate, consider the statement

```
read( Ch1, Ch2, Ch3, Ch4 )
```

where **Ch1**, **Ch2**, **Ch3**, and **Ch4**, are of type **char**. Suppose that the following data is entered:

AB_CD↵

so that the file **input** has the contents

When this statement is executed, the characters **A** and **B** are read and assigned to **Ch1** and **Ch2**, respectively; a blank is read and assigned to **Ch3**; **C** is read and assigned to **Ch4**; and the data pointer is advanced to the next character.

If characters are entered one per line

A↵
B↵
C↵
D↵

the contents of the file **input** are

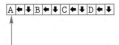

When the preceding **read** statement is executed, the value read for **Ch1** is **A**. The next character read is the carriage-return character and is assigned to **Ch2**. Similarly, the line-feed character is read and assigned to **Ch3**, the letter **B** is read and assigned to **Ch4**, and the data pointer is advanced to the next character.

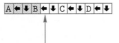

    If we wish to assign **A**, **B**, **C**, and **D** to the character variables **Ch1**, **Ch2**, **Ch3**, and **Ch4**, respectively, by using the statement

```
read( Ch1, Ch2, Ch3, Ch4 )
```

the data should be entered on a single line with no intervening blanks:

ABCD↵

When this statement is executed, the data pointer is positioned at the end-of-line mark following the **D**.

Subsequent reading of values begins at this point. Thus, if a value is read for a character variable, the carriage-return character is read and assigned to this variable.

Reading Mixed Data

Because of the differences in the way numeric, string, and character values are read, some care must be taken when the input data consists of some combination of these types.

To illustrate, suppose we wish to read values for the variables declared by

```
VAR
    EmpNumber : integer;
    EmpName, DeptName : string;
    Gender : char;
    Hours, Rate : real;
```

and that we wish to enter these values in the order **EmpNumber**, **EmpName**, **Gender**, **DeptName**, **Hours**, and **Rate**. One easy way to do this to use the statements

```
readln( EmpNumber );
readln( EmpName );
readln( Gender );
readln( DeptName );
readln( Hours, Rate );
```

and enter the data as

3123↵
John Q. Doe↵
M↵
Sales↵
38.5 7.50↵

so that the file **input** contains

`3│1│2│3│←│↓│J│o│h│n│ │Q│.│ │D│o│e│←│↓│M│←│↓│S│a│l│e│s│←│↓│3│8│.│5│ │7│.│5│0│←│↓`

The first statement reads the character string '**3123**', stopping when the end-of-line mark is encountered, converts this string to the integer **3123** and assigns it to **EmpName**. The **readln** procedure then advances the data pointer past this end-of-line mark.

`3│1│2│3│←│↓│J│o│h│n│ │Q│.│ │D│o│e│←│↓│M│←│↓│S│a│l│e│s│←│↓│3│8│.│5│ │7│.│5│0│←│↓`

The string read for **EmpName** is **John Q. Doe**, and after this value is read and assigned, the **readln** procedure advances the data pointer past the end-of-line mark that terminated the string:

`3│1│2│3│←│↓│J│o│h│n│ │Q│.│ │D│o│e│←│↓│M│←│↓│S│a│l│e│s│←│↓│3│8│.│5│ │7│.│5│0│←│↓`

The single character M is then read and assigned to `Gender`, and `readln` advances the data pointer to the next line:

After the string `'Sales'` is read and assigned to `DeptName`, the data pointer is positioned at the beginning of the fifth line:

Finally, the values **38.5** and **7.50** are read and assigned to the real variables `Hours` and `Rate`, and the data pointer is advanced past the end-of-line mark used to terminate the value of `Rate`.

There are other ways in which these values for `EmpNumber`, `EmpName`, `Gender`, `DeptCode`, `Hours`, and `Rate` could be read and entered. For example, we could use the statements

```
readln( EmpNumber );
readln( EmpName );
readln( Gender, DeptName );
readln( Hours, Rate );
```

with the values for `Gender` and `DeptName` entered on the same line:

```
3123↵
John Q. Doe↵
MSales↵
38.5 7.50↵
```

If we also enter the employee number and name on the same data line

```
3123 John Q. Doe↵
MSales↵
38.5 7.50↵
```

so that the data file has the form

then after the value **3123** is read for `EmpNumber`, the data pointer is positioned at the blank that terminates this value.

This blank will be read as the first character in the value for the string variable EmpName. This can be avoided by reading and assigning this extra blank to some character variable SkipChar before the value for EmpName is read:

```
readln( EmpNumber, SkipChar, EmpName );
readln( Gender, DeptName );
readln( Hours, Rate );
```

To read the preceding values with a single readln statement, we would need to skip over the space that terminates the value of EmpNumber so it is not read as the first character for EmpName and the end-of-line mark that terminates the value of EmpName, so that neither the carriage-return character nor the line line-feed character is read as the value for Gender:

```
readln( EmpNumber, SkipChar, EmpName, SkipChar, SkipChar,
        Gender, DeptName, Hours, Rate );
```

Summary

The following points summarize some of the important points regarding the input of numeric, string, and character values in Turbo Pascal:

1. Leading blanks, leading tabs, and leading end-of-line marks are ignored in reading numeric values.
2. Numeric values must be followed by a blank, tab, end-of-line mark, or the end of the file to indicate the end of the numeric value. After the value has been read, the data pointer is positioned at this terminating character.
3. Values for string variables begin at the current position of the data pointer.
4. String values must be followed by an end-of-line mark (or the end of the file) to indicate the end of the string. After the value is read, the data pointer is positioned at this end-of-line mark.
5. The value read for a character variable is the single character at the current position of the data pointer. After this value is read, the data pointer is advanced to the next character.

Exercises

1. Suppose that Num1, Num2, Num3, and Num4 are integer variables and that for each of the following read and readln statements, the following data is entered:

   <u>1</u>___<u>-2</u>_<u>3</u>↵
   <u>4</u>_<u>-5</u>_<u>6</u>↵
   <u>7</u>_____<u>-8</u>_____<u>9</u>↵

   What values will be assigned to these variables when each of the following statements is executed?

   (a) read(Num1, Num2, Num3, Num4);

   (b) readln(Num1, Num2, Num3, Num4);

(c) `read( Num1, Num2 );`
`read( Num3 );`
`read( Num4 );`

(d) `readln( Num1, Num2 );`
`readln( Num3, Num4 );`

(e) `readln;`
`readln( Num1, Num2, Num3, Num4 );`

2. Assume the following declarations:

```
VAR
    N1, N2, N3 : integer;
    R1, R2, R3 : real;
    C1, C2, C3, C4 : char;
    S1, S2, S3 : string;
```

and that for each of the following **read** and **readln** statements, this data is entered:

```
123_45.6↵
X78_-909.8_7↵
-65_$__432.10↵
CAT_DOG↵
HORSE↵
```

List the values that are assigned to each of the variables in the input list, or explain why an error occurs:

(a) `readln( N1, R1 );`
`read( C1, N2 );`
`readln( R2 );`
`read( C2, N3, C3, C4, R3);`
`readln( S1 );`
`readln( S2 );`

(b) `readln( N1 );`
`readln( C1, C2, R1, R2 );`
`readln( N2, N3, C3, S1 );`
`readln( S2 );`
`readln( S3 );`

(c) `read( N1, R1 );`
`readln( C1, C2, C3, N2, R2, C4, R3 );`
`readln( N3 );`
`readln( S1, S2, S3 );`

(d) `readln;`
`read( C1, N1, R1, R2 );`
`read( N2, C2, C3, R3 );`

(e) `readln( N1, R1, C1, C2 );`
`readln( C3, N2, S1 );`
`readln( C4, S2 );`

(f) readln(N1, R1, S1, C1, C2, S2, N2, C3, C4, R2, S3);

(g) read(N1, R1);
readln;
readln(C1, C2, C3, R2);
readln(R3);
readln(S1);
readln(S2);

(h) readln(N1, R1);
readln(C1, N2, N3, R2);
readln(R3, C4, S1);

3. Assume the following declarations:

```
VAR
    N1, N2, N3 : integer;
    R1, R2, R3 : real;
    C1, C2, C3, C4 : char;
    S1, S2, S3 : string;
```

and that the contents of the file **input** are

| |5|4| |3|2|E|1|←|↓|-|6|.|7|8| |$|9|0|←|↓|←|↓| |1|←|↓|

List the values that are assigned to each of the variables in the input list for each of the following statements, or explain why an error occurs. Also, show the position of the data pointer after each of the sequences of statements is executed:

(a) read(N1, R1, R2, S1, N2);

(b) read(N1, R1, R2, C1, C2, C3, N2, N3);

(c) readln(N1, S1);
readln(C1, R1, C2, C3, C4, N2, R2);

(d) read(N1);
read(C1);
read(C2);
read(C3);
read(C4);
read(R1);
read(R2);
read(S1);
read(R3);

(e) readln(R1);
readln(R2);
readln(R3);

(f) `read( C1, C2, C3, S1 );`
   `readln;`
   `readln( S2 );`

(g) `readln( R1, R2 );`
   `readln( C1, C2, R3, C3, C4, N1, N2 );`

(h) `read( R1, C1, S1 );`
   `readln( R2, C2, S2 );`

6.2   Text Files

Up to this point, we have assumed that the data for the sample programs was entered by the user during program execution. In this interactive mode, the data values are copied into the standard system file **input**, and values are obtained from this file by the **read** or **readln** procedures. In general, any collection of data items that are input to or output by a program is called a **file.** It is possible to create a file before a program is executed and then to read values from this file during execution. There are several reasons that this may be desirable. It may be inconvenient for the user to enter the data each time the program is executed, especially if the data set is large; also, as described in Programming Pointer 8 at the end of this chapter, interactive input can be somewhat difficult. These problems can be avoided by preparing a data file in advance and designing the program to read the values from this file. In this section, we introduce **text files** and describe how input and output using such files are carried out.

Files are usually stored on magnetic disk or magnetic tape or some other form of external (secondary) memory. Information is stored on disks in tracks arranged in concentric circles and is written to or read from a disk using a **disk drive.** This device transfers information by means of a read/write head that is positioned over one of the tracks of the rotating disks. Magnetic tape stores information for computer processing in somewhat the same way that an audio tape stores sound information. Information can be written to or read from a tape using a device called a **tape drive.**

Input Files

To illustrate how text files can be processed by Pascal programs, we consider the problem of processing employee wage information. Some employee information, such as the employee number and hourly pay rate, remains unchanged for long periods of time, and so it is preferable to avoid entering this information each time that programs for processing it are executed. Consequently, a file containing data such as the following might be created to store this permanent employee information:

```
3123   7.50
3164   8.75
3185   9.35
3202  10.50
3559   6.35
        •
        •
        •
4813  11.60
```

This file might be created using a text editor and stored in secondary memory. It might also be produced by a program that writes output to a file using the techniques described later in this section.

In this file, the information for each employee appears on a separate line, and one or more blanks separate the items in that line. A text file, like the standard system file **input**, is a sequence of characters, and thus this file should be viewed as having the form

```
3 1 2 3     7 . 5 0 ← ↓ 3 1 6 4     8 . 7 5 ← ↓  · · ·  ← ↓ 4 8 1 3     1 1 . 6 0 ← ↓ ▼
```

where ▼ denotes an **end-of-file mark.** If the file is prepared by using a text editor or is an output file produced by some program, this mark is usually placed at the end of the file automatically, after the last data line has been entered. In an interactive mode, that is, when the file is **input**, the user must enter the special control character **Ctrl-z** from the keyboard to mark the end of the file.

Declaring Text Files

In Pascal, text files are accessed using **file variables** of type **text**. The type identifier **text** is quite different from those considered up to now. The data types **integer**, **shortint**, **longint**, **byte**, **word**, **real**, **single**, **double**, **extended**, **comp**, **boolean**, and **char** are called **simple data types** because a data value of one of these types consists of a single item that cannot be subdivided. The type **text**, however, is a **structured data type** in which a data value is a collection of items (as is type **string**, as we shall see in Chapter 10). For example, to process the text file containing the permanent employee information, we might use the file variable **EmpFile** declared by

```
VAR
    EmpFile : text;
```

The names of all files used in a program, including the standard files **input** and **output**, should appear in the file list of the program heading to indicate what files the program uses. In our example, **EmpFile** will be used and should, therefore, be listed in the program heading:

```
PROGRAM Payroll( input, EmpFile, output );
```

Opening an Input File

Before a file can be used in a Turbo Pascal program, the procedure `assign` must be called:

Procedure `assign`

Form of reference:

```
assign( file-variable, file-name )
```

where:
   file-variable denotes the text file being opened;
   file-name is the name of a data file stored on disk.

Action:
Associates the *file-variable* used to refer to the file within the program with the actual data file *file-name* stored on disk. If *file-name* is the empty string, the standard file **input** will be associated with *file-variable*.

Before the contents of a file can be read, the file must be *opened for input*; that is, a data pointer must be positioned at the beginning of the file. This is done by using the predefined Pascal procedure `reset`.

Procedure `reset`

Form of reference:

```
reset( file-variable )
```

where:
   file-variable denotes the text file being opened.

Action:
Opens the specified file so that values can be read from it. The data pointer is positioned at the beginning of the file.

Thus, for our example, the statement

```
assign( EmpFile, 'A:EMPLOY.DAT' );
```

associates the file **EMPLOY.DAT** on the disk in drive **A** with the file variable **EmpFile**. The statement

```
reset( EmpFile );
```

then opens the employee information file for input, positioning the data pointer at the beginning of the file.

3 1 2 3   7 . 5 0 ←↓ 3 1 6 4   8 . 7 5 ←↓ ··· ←↓ 4 8 1 3   1 1 . 6 0 ←↓▼

The data pointer is advanced sequentially through the file as the items are read, in the same manner as described for the file **input** in the preceding section.

Reading from a File

The values in a text file are read by using the standard input procedures **readln** and **read**.

Input Procedures

Form of reference:

>   readln(*file-variable*, *input-list*)

or

>   read(*file-variable*, *input-list*)

or

>   readln(*file-variable*)

where:

  file-variable denotes the text file from which the values are to be read;

  input-list is a single variable or a list of variables separated by commas.

Action:

Reads values for the variables in the input list from the specified file. **Readln** advances to the next line in the file after values have been obtained for all of the variables; **read** causes no such advance. The last form of reference to **readln** in which the input list is empty simply causes an advance to a new line in the file.

When an input statement is executed, sequences of characters are read from the specified file and, if necessary, are converted to values of the same type as those of the variables for which values are being read. These values are then assigned to the variables in the input list. After each value is read, the data pointer is advanced in the same manner as described earlier for the standard file **input**. Thus, for the employee information file **EmpFile**, the statement

```
readln( EmpFile, EmpNumber, HourlyRate );
```

reads values for the integer variable **EmpNumber** and the real variable **HourlyRate** from **EmpFile**. The data pointer is then advanced so that it is positioned after the next end-of-line mark. The first execution of this statement therefore assigns the value **3123** to `EmpNumber` and the value **7.50** to `HourlyRate` and then advances the data pointer past the first end-of-line mark.

End-of-File While Loops: The eof Function

The end of a file can be detected by using the boolean-valued function `eof`.

Function eof

> **Form of reference:**
>
>   eof(*file-variable*)
>
> or
>
>   eof
>
> where:
>   *file-variable* denotes the text file being
>   checked.
>
> **Returns:**
> The boolean value **true** if the data pointer is positioned at the end-of-file mark and **false** otherwise. In the second form, the standard system file **input** is assumed; it is thus equivalent to `eof( input )`.

The `eof` function can be used in a boolean expression to construct an **end-of-file while loop;** for example,

```
WHILE NOT eof( EmpFile ) DO
   BEGIN
      readln( EmpFile, EmpNumber, HourlyRate );
                      .
                      .
                      .
   END {WHILE};
```

Note that unlike the sentinel-controlled while loops described in Section 4.5, only one input statement is used in an end-of-file while loop, and it is at the beginning of the loop:

End-of-File While Loop

While not end-of-file do:
  Read a data value.
  Process the data value.

Sentinel-Controlled While Loop

Read first data value.
While data value $\neq$ sentinel value do:
  Process the data value.
  Read the next data value.

The program in Figure 6.1 uses an end-of-file while loop to read the contents of **EmpFile** and calculate the average hourly rate of all employees. After the last values, **4813** and **11.60**, are read from the file and assigned to **EmpNumber** and **HourlyRate**, respectively, the **readln** procedure advances the data pointer past the last end-of-line mark so that it is positioned at the end-of-file mark. The **eof** function now returns the value true, and execution of the while loop is terminated.

FIGURE 6.1   Reading an employee file.

```
PROGRAM AverageHourlyRate( input, EmpFile, output );
{**********************************************************************

    Input (EmpFile): Employee numbers and hourly rates.
    Function:        Display the contents of a file containing
                     employee numbers and hourly rates,  Also,
                     determine the average hourly rate for all
                     employees.
    Output (screen): An echo of the contents of EmpFile, and the
                     average hourly rate.

    **********************************************************************}

CONST
    EmpFileName = 'FIL6-1.DAT';   {name of employee file}

VAR
    EmpFile : text;               {the employee file}
    EmpNumber,                    {employee number}
    Count : integer;              {counts number of employees}
    HourlyRate,                   {hourly pay rate}
    Sum : real;                   {sum of hourly pay rates}

BEGIN
    assign( EmpFile, EmpFileName );
    reset( EmpFile );
    Count := 0;
    Sum := 0;
    writeln( 'Contents of employee file:' );
    writeln( 'Employee  Hourly Rate' );
    writeln( '========  ===========' );
    WHILE NOT eof( EmpFile ) DO
        BEGIN
            readln( EmpFile, EmpNumber, HourlyRate );
            writeln( EmpNumber:7, HourlyRate:12:2 );
            Count := Count + 1;
            Sum := Sum + HourlyRate
        END {WHILE};
    writeln;
    IF Count > 0 THEN
        writeln( 'Average hourly rate is $', Sum / Count :4:2 )
    ELSE
        writeln( 'No employees listed in the file' )
END.
```

FIGURE 6.1   Reading an employee file. (cont.)

Sample run:

```
Contents of employee file:
Employee  Hourly Rate
========  ===========
   3123        7.50
   3164        8.75
   3185        9.35
   3202       10.50
   3559        6.35
   3600       10.85
   4013        7.15
   4409        9.15
   4723        8.75
   4813       11.60


Average hourly rate is $9.00
```

Care must be taken to avoid attempting to read beyond the end of the file. To illustrate, if the **readln** statement in this program is replaced with

    read(EmpFile, EmpNumber, HourlyRate);

an error will result. After the last data values, **4813** and **11.60**, are read, the data pointer is positioned at the end-of-line mark following these values.

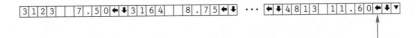

Since it is not positioned at the end-of-file mark, **eof(EmpFile)** is false. Consequently, the **read** statement is executed again, and an attempt is made to read another value for **EmpNumber**. Since this is to be a numeric value, the leading end-of-line mark is skipped, and the data pointer advances to the end-of-file mark:

In Turbo Pascal, when the end-of-file mark is encountered while attempting to read a value for a numeric variable, the value 0 is assigned to that variable. Thus, in this example, **EmpNumber** and **HourlyRate** are assigned the values 0 and 0.0, respectively; **Count** is incremented by 1; and the value of **Sum** is not changed, since **HourlyRate** has the value 0. Since **eof(EmpFile)** is now true, the while loop is terminated. The output produced is

    Average hourly rate is $8.18

which is not correct because `Count` is incremented by 1 on the last pass through the loop, even though no values for `EmpNumber` and `HourlyRate` were read from the file.

Output Files

It is also possible to write to a user-defined text file so that the output can be stored for later processing. For example, suppose that all the employees listed in `EmpFile` are granted a 5 percent raise and that we wish to generate a new employee file, `NewEmpFile`, with the new hourly rates. In this case, the file variable `NewEmpFile` should also be listed in the program heading and declared to be of type `text`:

```
PROGRAM Payroll (input, EmpFile, output, NewEmpFile );
    .
    .
    .
VAR
    EmpFile,
    NewEmpFile : text;
```

Opening a File for Output

Before data can be written to a text file, the `assign` procedure must be used to associate the file variable with the actual name of a file on disk, and the file must be opened for output by using one of the predefined procedures `rewrite` or `append`.

Procedure `rewrite`

Form of reference:

    `rewrite(` *file-variable* `)`

where:
  file-variable denotes the text file being
    opened.

Action:
Creates an empty file with the specified name and opens the file so that values can be written to it. Any previous contents of the file are destroyed.

Procedure `append`

Form of reference:

    `append(` *file-variable* `)`

where:
  file-variable denotes the text file being
    opened.

> **Action:**
> Opens the file with the specified name for output
> and positions the data pointer at the end of the file
> so that values can be appended to it.

In our example program, we would thus include the statement

```
rewrite( NewEmpFile );
```

Writing to a File

Output may be directed to a text file by using the standard output procedures `write` and `writeln`.

Output Procedures

> **Form of reference:**
>
>   writeln(*file-variable, output-list*)
>
> or
>
>   write(*file-variable, output-list*)
>
> or
>
>   writeln(*file-variable*)
>
> where:
>   *file-variable* denotes the text file to which the values are
>   to be written;
>   *output-list* is a single expression or a list of expressions
>   separated by commas.
>
> **Action:**
> Writes values of the expressions in the output list to the specified
> file. **Writeln** advances to the next line in the file after values of
> all of the expressions have been written; **write** causes no such
> advance. The last form of reference to **writeln** in which the
> output list is empty simply causes an advance to a new line in
> the file.

In our example, the statement

```
writeln( NewEmpFile, EmpNumber:5, NewHourlyRate:6:2 )
```

is used in the program in Figure 6.2 to write the values of **EmpNumber** and **NewHourlyRate**, followed by an end-of-line mark, to the text file **NewEmpFile**.

A **writeln** statement of the form

```
writeln( file-variable )
```

in which the output list is omitted produces an advance to a new line in the specified text file. Such a statement can thus be used to write blank lines to this file.

Closing a File

After output to a file is completed, the file must be closed by calling the procedure **close**.

Procedure **close**

Form of reference:

> close(*file-variable*)

where:

> *file-variable* denotes the file being closed.

Action:
Closes the file with the specified name. It also disassociates the file variable from the file name associated with it by the **assign** procedure.

Close can also be used to close files opened for input so that the file variable can be associated with a different file. In the case of output files, calling **close** ensures that the output, which is temporarily stored in an output buffer, is transferred to the file. Thus, in our example program, after all values have been written, the statement

```
close( NewEmpFile)
```

closes the file.

FIGURE 6.2   Generating a new employee file.

```
PROGRAM IncreaseHourlyRates( EmpFile, NewEmpFile );
{*********************************************************************

    Input (EmpFile):    Employee numbers and hourly rates.
    Function:           Read employee numbers and hourly rates from
                        Empfile and generate NewEmpFile in which all
                        hourly rates are increased by a specified
                        percentage.
    Output (NewEmpFile): Employee numbers and new hourly rates.


*********************************************************************}
```

FIGURE 6.2 Generating a new employee file. (cont.)

```
CONST
    EmpFileName = 'FILA6-2.DAT';        {name of employee file}
    NewEmpFileName = 'FILB6-2.DAT';     {name of new employee file}
    Increase = 0.05;                     {percentage increase}

VAR
    EmpFile,                             {the original employee file}
    NewEmpFile : text;                   {the new file to be produced}
    EmpNumber : integer;                 {employee number}
    HourlyRate,                          {hourly pay rate}
    NewHourlyRate : real;                {new hourly rate}

BEGIN
    assign( EmpFile, EmpFileName );
    assign( NewEmpFile, NewEmpFileName );
    reset( EmpFile );
    rewrite( NewEmpFile );
    WHILE NOT eof( EmpFile ) DO
        BEGIN
            readln( EmpFile, EmpNumber, HourlyRate );
            NewHourlyRate := (1 + Increase) * HourlyRate;
            writeln( NewEmpFile, EmpNumber:5, NewHourlyRate:6:2 )
        END {WHILE};
    close( NewEmpFile )
END.
```

Listing of `FILA6-2.DAT`:

```
3123   7.50
3164   8.75
3185   9.35
3202 10.50
3559   6.35
3600 10.85
4013   7.15
4409   9.15
4723   8.75
4813 11.60
```

Listing of `FILB6-2.DAT`:

```
3123   7.87
3164   9.19
3185   9.82
3202 11.02
3559   6.67
3600 11.39
4013   7.51
4409   9.61
4723   9.19
4813 12.18
```

Files as Parameters

File variables, like simple variables, may be used as parameters in user-defined procedures and functions. In this case, they *must be variable parameters,* since allowing them to be value parameters would require assigning the value of one file variable to another file variable, and this is not allowed in Pascal.

To demonstrate the use of file variables as parameters, consider the following problem:

Problem. Wages are to be calculated for employees whose employee numbers and hourly rates are contained in the file **EmpFile** described earlier. For each of these employees, this information is to be read from the file, but the hours worked are to be entered by the user during program execution, since this value is usually not the same for all pay periods. The total of all employees' wages is also to be calculated and displayed.

The program in Figure 6.3 solves this problem. The actual name of the employee file is entered by the user during execution and is assigned to the string variable `EmpFileName`, and the statement

```
assign( EmpFile, EmpFileName );
```

then associates this file with the file variable `EmpFile`. The file is then opened by the statement

```
reset( EmpFile );
```

Procedure `GetEmployeeInfo` is called repeatedly to obtain an employee number and hourly rate from this file. One of its formal parameters is a a file variable `InFile` of type `text` which denotes the file from which this information is to be obtained. Since the corresponding actual parameter in the statement that calls this procedure in the main program is the file variable `EmpFile`, `GetEmployeeInfo` actually reads this information from the file `EmpFile`. It then prompts the user to enter the hours worked for this employee and returns this value, together with the employee's number and hourly rate, to the main program, which then calls procedure `CalculateWages` to determine the wages for this employee. When the end-of-file mark in `EmpFile` is encountered, the `eof` function returns true, causing the repetition to terminate, and the main program then displays the total wages for all employees.

 FIGURE 6.3 Calculating payroll—version 1.

```
PROGRAM Payroll( input, EmpFile, output );
{*******************************************************************

    Input (EmpFile):   Employee numbers and hourly rates.
    Input (keyboard):  Name of Employee file and hours worked for
                       each employee.
    Function:          Calculate wages for several employees whose
                       employee numbers and hourly rates are read from
                       the file EmpFile and whose hours are entered by
                       the user during execution.  Total wages for this
                       payroll is also calculated.
    Output (screen):   User prompt, employee number, hourly rate,
                       and wages.

*******************************************************************}
VAR
    EmpFileName : string;      {actual file name of employee file}
    EmpFile : text;            {the permanent employee file}
    EmpNumber : integer;       {employee number}
    Hours,                     {hours worked}
    HourlyRate,                {hourly pay rate}
    Wages,                     {total wages for employee}
    TotalPayroll : real;       {total wages for this payroll}
```

FIGURE 6.3   Calculating payroll—version 1. (cont.)

```
PROCEDURE GetEmployeeInfo( VAR InFile : Text;          {input file}
                          VAR EmpNumber : integer;     {employee number}
                          VAR HourlyRate,              {hourly rate}
                              Hours : real );          {hours worked}
{-----------------------------------------------------------------

     Accepts:          File variable InFile.
     Input (InFile):   Employee number and hourly rate.
     Input (keyboard): Hours worked.
     Purpose:          Reads an employee number EmpNumber and
                       HourlyRate from a text file InFile; the
                       Hours worked is entered by the user.
     Returns:          EmpNumber, HourlyRate, and Hours.

-------------------------------------------------------------------}

   BEGIN
      readln( InFile, EmpNumber, HourlyRate );
      write( 'Hours worked for ', EmpNumber:1,':  ' );
      readln( Hours )
   END {GetEmployeeInfo};

   PROCEDURE CalculateWages(     Hours,               (hours worked)
                                 HourlyRate : real;   (hourly rate)
                             VAR Wages,               (employee's wages)
                                 TotalPayroll : real ); (total emp. wages)
{-----------------------------------------------------------------

     Accepts:  Hours and HourlyRate.
     Purpose:  Calculate Wages for employee who has worked the
               given number of Hours at the given HourlyRate.
               Hours above HoursLimit are paid at OvertimeFactor
               times the hourly rate.  Total wages for this payroll
               are also accumulated.  The function RoundCents is
               used to round wages to the nearest cent.
     Returns:  Wages and TotalPayroll.

-------------------------------------------------------------------}

   CONST
      OvertimeFactor = 1.5; {overtime multiplication factor}
      HoursLimit = 40.0;    {overtime hours limit}

   VAR
      RegWages,             {regular wages}
      OverWages : real;     {overtime pay}

   FUNCTION RoundCents( Amount : real ) : real;
      {-----------------------------------------------------------

        Accepts:  An Amount.
        Purpose:  Round Amount to the nearest cent.
        Returns:  Rounded amount.

      -------------------------------------------------------------}
```

FIGURE 6.3   Calculating payroll—version 1. (cont.)

```
      BEGIN
          RoundCents := round( 100 * Amount ) / 100
      END {RoundCents};

   BEGIN {CalculateWages}
      IF Hours > HoursLimit THEN
          BEGIN {Overtime}
              RegWages := RoundCents( HourlyRate * HoursLimit );
              OverWages :=
                  RoundCents( OvertimeFactor * HourlyRate
                              * (Hours - HoursLimit) )
          END {Overtime}
      ELSE
          BEGIN {No overtime}
              RegWages := RoundCents( HourlyRate * Hours );
              OverWages := 0
          END {No overtime};
      Wages := RegWages + OverWages;
      TotalPayroll := TotalPayroll + Wages
   END {CalculateWages};

BEGIN {**************** main program ****************}
   write( 'Enter name of employee file: ' );
   readln( EmpFileName );
   assign( EmpFile, EmpFileName );
   reset( EmpFile );
   TotalPayroll := 0;
   WHILE NOT eof( EmpFile ) DO
      BEGIN
          GetEmployeeInfo( EmpFile, EmpNumber, HourlyRate, Hours );
          writeln( 'Hourly rate:   $', HourlyRate:4:2 );
          CalculateWages( Hours, HourlyRate, Wages, TotalPayroll );
          writeln( 'Wages:  $', Wages:4:2 );
          writeln
      END {WHILE};
   writeln;
   writeln( 'Total wages = $', TotalPayroll:4:2 )
END {main program}.
```

Sample Run:

```
Hours worked for 3123:   38.5
Hourly rate:    $7.50
Wages:  $288.75


Hours worked for 3164:   40.0
Hourly rate:    $8.75
Wages:  $350.00


Hours worked for 3185:   43.5
Hourly rate:    $9.35
Wages:  $423.09
```

Listing of FIL6-3.DAT:

```
3123   7.50
3164   8.75
3185   9.35
3202  10.50
3559   6.35
3600  10.85
4013   7.15
4409   9.15
4723   8.75
4813  11.60
```

FIGURE 6.3   Calculating payroll—version 1. (cont.)

```
Hours worked for 3202:   45
Hourly rate:   $10.50
Wages:  $498.75

Hours worked for 3559:   39
Hourly rate:   $6.35
Wages:  $247.65

Hours worked for 3600:   0
Hourly rate:   $10.85
Wages:  $0.00

Hours worked for 4013:   20
Hourly rate:   $7.15
Wages:  $143.00

Hours worked for 4409:   50
Hourly rate:   $9.15
Wages:  $503.25

Hours worked for 4723:   40
Hourly rate:   $8.75
Wages:  $350.00

Hours worked for 4813:   44
Hourly rate:   $11.60
Wages:  $533.60

Total wages = $3338.09
```

The End-of-Line Function `eoln`

The preceding examples used the boolean-valued function **eof** to detect the end-of-file mark. End-of-line marks can be detected by using the boolean-valued function **eoln**.

Function `eoln`

Form of reference:

    eoln(*file-variable*)

or

    eoln

where:
  file-variable denotes the text file being
    checked.

Returns:
The boolean value **true** if the data pointer is positioned at an end-of-line mark and **false** otherwise. In the second form, the standard system file **input** is assumed; it is thus equivalent to **eoln(input)**.

To illustrate the use of the **eoln** function, consider the problem of calculating the average length of the lines in a file. Each line of the input file **InFile** must be read, character by character, and each character counted, up to the end-of-line mark. When the end of the line is encountered, a line counter must be incremented by 1, and a new line begun. Finally, when the end of the file is reached, the character count can be divided by the line count to obtain the average line length.

To read and count the characters in a line of **InFile**, we use an input loop whose repetition is controlled by the boolean expression **NOT eoln(InFile)**:

```
WHILE NOT eoln( InFile ) DO
    BEGIN
        read( InFile, Character );
        CharCount := CharCount + 1
    END {WHILE NOT eoln};
```

When an end-of-line mark is reached, the function **eoln** returns the value true, and execution of the preceding while loop is terminated. A line counter must now be incremented by 1,

```
LineCount := LineCount + 1;
```

and the data pointer in **InFile** must be advanced to a new line. For this we can use a **readln** statement with no input list:

```
readln( InFile )
```

This processing can be repeated for each line of **InFile** by placing these statements in an end-of-file while loop controlled by the boolean expression **NOT eof(InFile)**. The complete program, together with a listing of **InFile**, is shown in Figure 6.4.

FIGURE 6.4 Calculate average line length for a file.

```
PROGRAM AverageLineLength( InFile, output );
{*****************************************************************

    Input (InFile):    Several lines of text.
    Input (keyboard): Name of input file.
    Purpose:          Read the file InFile and determine the average
                      length of the lines in the file.
    Output (screen):  User prompt and average line length.


*****************************************************************}
VAR
    InFile : text;         {the input file}
    FileName : string;     {actual name of InFile}
    Character : char;      {character read from InFile}
    CharCount,             {count of characters}
    LineCount : integer;   {number of lines in file}
```

FIGURE 6.4   Calculate average line length for a file. (cont.)

```
BEGIN
   write( 'Enter name of input file: ' );
   readln( FileName );
   assign( InFile, FileName );
   reset( InFile );
   CharCount := 0;
   LineCount := 0;
   WHILE NOT eof( InFile ) DO
      BEGIN
         WHILE NOT eoln( InFile ) DO
            BEGIN
               read( InFile, Character );
               CharCount := CharCount + 1
            END {WHILE NOT eoln};
         LineCount := LineCount + 1;
         readln( InFile )
      END {WHILE NOT eof};
   writeln;
   writeln( 'Average line length = ', CharCount/LineCount:5:2 )
END.
```

Listing of `FIL6-4.DAT`:

```
Fourscore and seven years ago,
our fathers brought
forth
on this continent a new nation
conceived in liberty
and dedicated to the proposition
that
all men
are created equal.
```

Sample run:

```
Enter name of input file: FIL6-4.DAT

Average line length = 18.33
```

6.3   PART OF THE PICTURE: Databases

Data stored more or less permanently in a computer is called a **database,** and the software that allows users to access and modify these data is called a **database management system.** Databases, like crabgrass, are almost everywhere, and we come into contact with them in a variety of situations:

- When we purchase groceries at most supermarkets, a scanner reads the universal product code and searches a database to determine the name of the item and its price so that this information can be printed on the register tape. The inventory information stored in this database may also be updated to reflect the sale of this item.

- When we charge a purchase using a bank card, a database of credit information must be searched to locate our account number and to determine whether this charge should be approved. If it is, the amount of the purchase is recorded for billing purposes, and the amount of available credit is reduced.

- When we make travel arrangements, we might use the databases maintained by airlines, hotel chains, and rental car agencies. For example, an airline reservation system maintains a database of information about flight schedules, number of seats available in various fare categories, seat assignments, type of aircraft, and so on.

- A computerized card catalog that is common in large libraries is a database that contains information about the library holdings and allows the user to search for books and articles by title, author, and subject area, to determine whether a given book is available for loan, and so on.

As we noted in Section 2.6, the ubiquity of databases makes many people worry about an invasion of their privacy. In a recent article, one information technology professional expressed her concern as follows:

> The violation of personal privacy, which today is possible through the use of customer data bases, ISDN source telephone number recognition, personnel files, insurance records, and so on, is staggering.
>
> Even if you pay cash, you cannot shop at some stores without giving your home phone number. From your number, the merchant can determine your name and address.
>
> If you are a credit card user, your credit card vendor can compile a list of your favorite restaurants, the trips you have taken, the hotels you have stayed at and the gifts you purchased while traveling. The hotel companies' databases will know that you requested an iron, a makeup mirror and extra towels, that you ordered room service for two and that you had an 8 A.M. wake-up call.
>
> If you call to make a catalog purchase and get a busy signal, the vendor may call you back. You don't even have to leave a message. The new ISDN source-routing tags source phone numbers and registers them, so the company's phone switch can later retrieve and display them. . . .
>
> All of that information is in the hands of total strangers. You, as an individual, have no way of knowing the level of integrity of the people handling your information. Moreover, the firms with which you do business have no way of knowing the level of integrity of their employees. . . .
>
> I like people and I like to interact with them, but there is virtually no way to do this without being put in a database somewhere.
>
> As a professional, I feel strongly that we need to build provisions into the databases we create to flag those subscribers, customers and clients who choose not to be included in mailings, who choose not to have their names sold and so on. And, of course, we must give those individuals the opportunity to designate their preference . . . we can actively build in the security and take the measures required to safeguard one another's privacy.[1]

---

[1] Corinne Chaves, "The Death of Personal Privacy," in *Computerworld*, January 27, 1992, p. 25.

As we noted in the introduction, files are the basic building blocks of databases, and the study of files is therefore necessary to understanding the basic principles of database design and management. The files that make up the database may be very large, and the information contained in them may be interrelated and linked together in intricate ways. For example, a file that maintains credit information on consumers would contain names, addresses, phone numbers, records of loan applications, payment defaults, credit approvals and denials, records of charge accounts, balances in these accounts, balances in banks, credit unions, investments, and so on. Keeping such information up-to-date and accurate is a complex task, and news reports frequently tell of complaints from consumers about inaccuracies in their credit reports and their resulting poor credit ratings.

Files are usually stored on magnetic disks, tapes, or some other form of secondary memory, and accessing and retrieving data from such devices is slower than for data stored in internal memory. It is important, therefore, that data be organized in such a way that any item of information can be located as efficiently as possible and the data stored in this location retrieved, displayed, and perhaps updated with more current information. In this section we describe some of the structures used to organize the data stored in a file and some of the techniques used to access them.

The basic operation required to retrieve information from a file is searching the file to determine where that information is stored. Each search is based on some **key,** that is, part of the information stored in the records of the file. The records are next examined to locate a particular record or perhaps several records that contain this key. For example, a person's social security number might be the search key for a file whose records contain credit information about individuals. If the file is being searched to locate the records of all persons living in a particular city, the key field will be the name of that city. Or if all records of customers having charge accounts with that company are to be retrieved, the search key might be the name of a particular company. We will consider the searching problem in detail in Chapter 9 and the information retrieval problem in Chapter 12.

The types of files considered in this chapter, and the only types of files supported in standard Pascal, are **sequential files.** In sequential files, the components of the file, also called **records,** can be accessed only sequentially; that is, to access any record in the file, one must pass through all of the records that precede it. It obviously takes more time, therefore, to access a record near the end of the file than one near the beginning. This contrasts with **direct** or **random access files** in which each component can be accessed directly just by specifying its location in the file. For such files, the time required to access any records is the same as that required for any other records. Direct access files are considered in Chapter 14.

Exercises

For descriptions of the files **InventoryFile** and **UserIdFile**, see Appendix E.

1. Suppose that **InFile** contains the following:

```
I_think_that_I_shall_never_see
A_poem_lovely_as_a_tree_____

------------------------------
_____-JOYCE_KILMER_(1914)
```

and that a program begins with

```
PROGRAM Echo( InFile, output );

VAR
    Character : char;
    InFile : text;
```

What output will be produced by each of the following statement parts?

(a)
```
BEGIN
    assign( InFile, 'EXER1.DAT' );
    reset( InFile );
    WHILE NOT eof( InFile ) DO
       BEGIN
          WHILE NOT eoln( InFile ) DO
             BEGIN
                read( InFile, Character );
                write( Character )
             END {WHILE NOT eoln};
          readln( InFile );
          writeln
       END {WHILE NOT eof}
END.
```

(b)
```
BEGIN
    assign( InFile, 'EXER1.DAT' );
    reset( InFile );
    WHILE NOT eof( InFile ) DO
       BEGIN
          WHILE NOT eoln( InFile ) DO
             BEGIN
                read( InFile, Character );
                write( Character )
             END {WHILE NOT eoln};
          readln( InFile )
       END {WHILE NOT eof}
END.
```

(c)
```
BEGIN
    assign( InFile, 'EXER1.DAT' );
    reset( InFile );
    WHILE NOT eof( InFile ) DO
       BEGIN
          WHILE NOT eoln( InFile ) DO
             BEGIN
                read( InFile, Character );
                write( Character )
             END {WHILE NOT eoln};
          writeln
       END {WHILE NOT eof}
END.
```

2. Write a program to copy one text file into another text file in which the lines are numbered 1, 2, 3, . . . with a number at the left of each line.

3. Write a program that reads a text file and counts the vowels in the file.

4. Write a program that reads a text file and counts the occurrences in the file of specified characters entered during execution of the program.

5. People from three different income levels, A, B, and C, rated each of two different products with a number from 0 through 10. Construct a text file in which each line contains the income level and product ratings for one respondent. Then write a program that reads this information and calculates

(a) For each income bracket, the average rating for Product 1.
(b) The number of persons in Income Bracket B who rated both products with a score of 5 or higher.
(c) The average rating for Product 2 by persons who rated Product 1 lower than 3.

Label all output and design the program so that it automatically counts the number of respondents.

6. Write a program to search `UserIdFile` to find and display the resources used to date for specified users whose identification numbers are entered during execution of the program.

7. Write a program to search `InventoryFile` to find an item with a specified item number. If a match is found, display the item number and the number currently in stock; otherwise, display a message indicating that it was not found.

8. At the end of each month, a report is produced that shows the status of each user's account in `UserIdFile.` Write a program to accept the current date and produce a report of the following form:

```
              USER ACCOUNTS--12/31/92

                       RESOURCE          RESOURCES
       USER-ID          LIMIT              USED
      --------------------------------------------------
       10101            $750               $381
       10102            $650               $599***
          .               .                  .
          .               .                  .
          .               .                  .
```

where the three asterisks (***) indicate that the user has already used 90 percent or more of the resources available to him or her.

9. Write a program that reads a text file and counts the characters in each line. The program should display the line number and the length of the shortest and longest lines in the file, as well as the average number of characters per line.

10. Write a program that reads a text file and writes it to another text file, but with leading blanks and blank lines removed. Run this program using as input files the last two Pascal programs you have written, and comment on whether you think indenting Pascal programs makes them more readable.

11. Write a file pagination program that reads a text file and prints it in blocks of 20 lines. If after printing a block of lines, there still are lines in the file, the program should allow the user to indicate whether more output is desired; if so, the next block should be printed; otherwise, execution of the program should terminate.

12. Write a program that reads a text file; counts the nonblank characters, the nonblank lines, the words, and the sentences; and calculates the average number of characters per word and the average number of words per sentence. You may assume the following: The file contains only letters, blanks, commas, periods, semicolons, and colons; a word is any sequence of letters that begins a line or is preceded by one or more blanks and that is terminated by a blank, comma, semicolon, colon, period, or the end of a line; and a sentence is terminated by a period.

Programming Pointers

Program Design

1. *Either an end-of-file while loop or a sentinel-controlled while loop may be used to read data.* These loops have the forms

End-of-File While Loop	Sentinel-Controlled While Loop

While not end-of-file do:
    Read a data value.
    Process the data value.
	Read first data value.
	While data value ≠ sentinel value do:
	    Process the data value.
	    Read the next data value.

For input from a file, an end-of-file while loop is the natural repetition structure to use, but for interactive input, a sentinel-controlled while loop often works better. (See the difficulties with interactive input described in Potential Problem 8.)

Potential Problems

1. *After values have been read for each variable in the input list, the* `readln` *procedure advances the data pointer past the next end-of-line mark.* Thus, if there are more values in a line of input data than there are variables in the input list, some data values will not be read. For example, suppose that `Number` is an `integer` variable, `xCoord` is a `real` variable, and the file `InFile` from which values are to be read contains

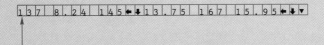

Then the statement

```
readln( InFile, Number, xCoord )
```

reads the value **137** for **Number** and **8.24** for **xCoord** and advances the data pointer past the end-of-line mark

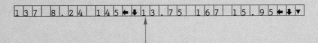

Consequently, the value **145** is skipped. Moreover, if this statement is executed again, an error occurs, because the string **13.75** read for **Number** cannot be converted to an integer.

2. *After values have been obtained for each variable in the input list, the* **read** *procedure leaves the data pointer at the position immediately following the last character read.* Thus, if the preceding **readln** statement is replaced with

```
read( InFile, Number, xCoord )
```

the value **137** will be read for **Number**, **8.24** for **xCoord**, and the data pointer will be positioned at the blank following the character **4**.

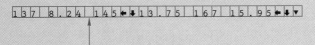

If the statement is executed again, the value **145** will be read and assigned to **Number**, the end-of-line mark will be ignored, and the value **13.75** will be read for **xCoord**. The data pointer is then positioned at the blank following the character **5**.

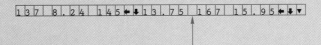

A potential problem in using the **read** statement occurs in attempting to read values at the end of the file. For example, consider the following input loop:

```
WHILE NOT eof( InFile ) DO
   BEGIN
      read( InFile, Number, xCoord );
          .
          .
          .
   END {WHILE};
```

where the file **InFile** contains

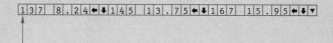

The values read and assigned to **Number** and **xCoord** are

Number	xCoord
137	8.24
145	13.75
167	15.95
0	0.0

After the third pair of values is obtained, the data pointer is positioned at the last end-of-line mark.

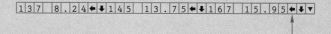

Because the data pointer is not positioned at the end-of-file mark, **eof(InFile)** is false, and so the **read** statement is executed again. The value **0** is assigned to **Number** and **0.0** to **xCoord**, and the data pointer is advanced to the end-of-file mark. Note that this problem does not occur if a **readln** statement is used, since after the last values **167** and **15.95** are read, the data pointer is advanced past the last end-of-line mark to the end-of-file mark. The boolean expression **eof(InFile)** is then true, and so execution of the while loop is terminated.

In a batch mode of operation, the end-of-file mark is automatically placed at the end of the file after the last data line has been entered. In an interactive mode, the user must enter the control character **Ctrl-z** from the keyboard to signal the end of the file.

3. *Leading blanks, leading tabs, and leading end-of-line marks are ignored when reading numeric values but not when reading values for character or string variables.* One consequence of this is that consecutive numeric values may be entered on separate lines. For example, if the data

123↵
456↵

is entered, the file **input** will contain

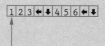

The statement

```
readln( Num1, Num2 )
```

where **Num1** and **Num2** are integer variables, reads the value **123** for **Num1** and advances the data pointer to the first end-of-line mark. This end-of-line mark is ignored when reading a value for **Num2** so that the value **456** is read. The **readln** procedure then advances the data pointer past the next end-of-line mark.

In contrast, if **Ch1**, **Ch2**, and **Ch3** are character variables and the data

$\underline{A} \triangleleft$
$\underline{B} \triangleleft$
$\underline{C} \triangleleft$

is entered so that the file **input** contains

the statements

```
readln( Ch1, Ch2 );
readln( Ch3 );
```

read and assign the letter **A** to **Ch1** and advance the data pointer to the first end-of-line mark. The carriage-return character is then read and assigned to **Ch2**. The data pointer is then advanced past the next end-of-line mark, so the character **B** is skipped, and the letter **C** is read for **Ch3**.

4. *Every numeric input value must be followed by a blank, a tab, an end-of-line mark, or an end-of-file mark.* When a value is read for a numeric variable, all characters up to the next blank, tab, end-of-line mark, or end-of-file mark are read. If the resulting string cannot be converted to a numeric value of the appropriate type, an error occurs and execution terminates.

5. *In reading a value for a numeric variable, if an end-of-file mark is encountered while skipping leading blanks, tabs, and end-of-line marks, 0 is assigned to that variable.*

6. *Characters are read for a string variable up to the next end-of-line or end-of-file mark. If the resulting string has too many characters (more than 255), it is truncated before it is assigned. If the data pointer is already positioned at an end-of-line mark or at the end-of-file mark, an empty string is assigned to the variable.*

One consequence of this last property is that a loop containing a **read** statement to read strings may not terminate. For example, suppose that **S** is of type **string**, and consider the loop:

```
WHILE NOT eof( InFile ) DO
   BEGIN
      read( S );
      writeln( S )
   END {WHILE};
```

where **InFile** contains

the string **ABC** is read and assigned to **S** and displayed, and the data pointer advances to the end-of-line mark.

Since **eof(InFile)** is not true, the loop is executed again. However, since the data pointer is at an end-of-line mark, an empty string is assigned to **S** and is displayed, but the data pointer is not advanced. Thus, an infinite loop results.

7. *Inadvertent trailing blanks in an input line or a blank input line may cause* **eof** *or* **eoln** *to remain false after all the other characters in that line have been read.* For example, suppose that the last two lines of a data file are

```
2771 8.75
ЬЬЬ
```

where Ь denotes a blank, and consider the following end-of-file while loop:

```
WHILE NOT eof( EmpFile ) DO
   BEGIN
      readln( EmpFile, EmpNumber, HourlyRate );
         .
         .
         .
   END {WHILE}
```

After the line **2771 8.75** is read, **eof(EmpFile)** is false because the data pointer is positioned at the first blank in the last line. Thus, the while loop is executed again, and an attempt is made to read two numeric values, but there are no more in the file, and so zero values are assigned to **EmpNumber** and **HourlyRate**.

8. *The data pointer in an input file always points to the next character to be read.* This "look-ahead" property of the data pointer is a common source of difficulty for beginning programmers. This is especially true for interactive input. To illustrate, consider the following statements:

```
WHILE NOT eof( input ) DO
   BEGIN
      writeln( 'Enter value: ' );
      readln( X );
      writeln( 'Value is ', X )
   END {WHILE};
```

When the **WHILE** statement is encountered, the boolean expression **eof(input)** cannot be evaluated, since the system file **input** is empty because no values have yet been copied into it from the keyboard. Before execution can proceed, the user must enter some value. After the value is entered from the keyboard and the **Enter** key is pressed, it is copied into file **input**, and only then can **eof(input)** be evaluated. To illustrate, suppose the user enters

    123↵

so the file **input** now contains

with the data pointer pointing at the first character. Since **eof(input)** is false, the while loop is entered, and the **write** statement is executed:

    123↵
    Enter value:

Thus, the prompt is displayed *after* the value has been entered! The value **123** is then obtained from the file **input** and assigned to **Number** by the **readln** procedure; the data pointer is advanced past the end-of-line mark;

and the **writeln** statement is executed, producing the following rather strange output:

    123↵
    Enter value: Value is 123

Since there is no character following this end-of-line mark, once again the boolean expression **eof(input)** cannot be evaluated, and so the process is repeated.

One way to get around this difficulty is to press the **Enter** key before entering each numeric value (and after entering it, of course). When the **Enter** key is pressed for the first time, an end-of-line mark will be placed at the beginning of the file **input**,

so that the expression **eof(input)** can be evaluated and the while loop entered:

    ↵
    Enter value:

This leading end-of-line mark will be ignored when reading the value entered by the user for **Number**.

```
↵
Enter value: 123↵
Value is 123
```

When the **Enter** key is pressed again,

```
↵
Enter value: 123↵
Value is 123
↵
```

the data pointer will be positioned at the end-of-line mark generated,

so that **eof(input)** can be evaluated and found to be false. Thus, the loop is repeated:

```
↵
Enter value: 123↵
Value is 123
↵
Enter value:
```

Entering the end-of-file character (**Ctrl-z**) will terminate the loop.

If **X** is a string variable in the preceding example, the first value assigned to **X** is the empty string, since the data pointer is positioned initially at the first end-of-line mark generated by depressing the **Enter** key. A sample of the output produced by this while loop is

```
↵
Enter value: Value is
ABCDE↵
Enter value: Value is ABCDE
HELLO↵
Enter value: Value is HELLO
^Z↵
```

where **^Z** is the character generated by depressing the **Ctrl** key and **Z** simultaneously.

If **X** is of type **char** in this example, the carriage-return character of the leading end-of-line marks will be read and processed:

```
↵
Enter value: A
Value is  ←—————— (carriage-return character is displayed)
↵
```

```
Enter value: B
Value is
⏎

Enter value:
    •
    •
    •
```

In summary, interactive input can be rather complicated, especially when the next character in the file **input** must be known so that some expression such as **eof(input)** or **eoln(input)** can be evaluated. In the preceding example, perhaps the best solution is to use a sentinel-controlled while loop:

```
write( 'Enter value: ' );
readln( X );
WHILE X <> EndData Do
    BEGIN
        writeln( 'Value is '; X )
        write( 'Enter value: ' );
        readln( X )
    END {WHILE};
```

9. *All file variables should appear in the file list of the program heading and must be declared to be of type* **text** *in the variable section of the program.*

10. *Before a user-defined text file can be used for input or output, it must be associated with an actual file name by using the procedure* **assign**. *If data is to be read from such a file, it must then be opened for input using the procedure* **reset**. *Similarly, before any data can be written to a user-defined text file, it must be opened for output by using the procedure* **rewrite** *or the procedure* **append**. But remember the following:

   ■ Each call to **reset** positions the data pointer at the beginning of the file.
   ■ Each call to **rewrite** creates an empty file, and any previous contents of the file are destroyed.

11. *Every output file should be closed using procedure* **close** *after output to it has been completed.* Failure to do so may cause some values to be left in the output buffer and not transferred to the file.

12. *File variables used as parameters must be variable parameters.*

Standard Pascal

There are a number of differences between Turbo Pascal and standard Pascal regarding input/output operations. In standard Pascal:

■ The end-of-line mark is read and interpreted as a blank.
■ The end of a numeric input value is indicated by any character that cannot be a part of a value of that type. It need not be followed by a blank, tab, or end-of-line mark.

- There is no predefined string type.
- All file variables associated with permanent files must be listed in the program heading. All file variables not listed in the program heading are associated with temporary files that are not saved after program execution is completed.
- Only the procedures `reset` and `rewrite` are provided for opening files, and no procedures are provided for closing files.

OTHER CONTROL STRUCTURES

We are all special cases.
ALBERT CAMUS

Progress might be a circle, rather than a straight line.
EBERHARD ZEIDLER

So, Naturalists observe, a flea
Hath smaller fleas that on him prey;
And these have smaller fleas to bite 'em
and so proceed ad infinitum.
JONATHAN SWIFT

CHAPTER CONTENTS

The basic control structures used in writing programs are **sequence, selection,** and **repetition.** In Chapter 4 we described compound statements in Pascal for implementing sequential structures. We also introduced the **IF** statement to implement selection structures and the **WHILE** statement to implement repetition structures. In this chapter we consider the **CASE** statement that can also be used to implement certain selection structures and the **FOR** and **REPEAT-UNTIL** statements to implement repetition structures. We also consider **recursion,** which is another technique for controlling the execution of subprograms.

7.1   Multialternative Selection Structure: The CASE Statement

Recall from Chapter 4 that an **IF** statement can be used to implement a selection structure in which exactly one of several alternative actions is selected and performed. In this statement, a selection is made by evaluating one or more boolean expressions, and because selection criteria can usually be formulated as boolean expressions, an **IF-ELSE IF** construct can be used to implement almost any multialternative selection structure. In this section we describe the **CASE** statement, which, although it is not as general as the **IF** statement, is useful for implementing some selection structures.

Form of the CASE Statement

The syntax diagram for a **CASE statement** is

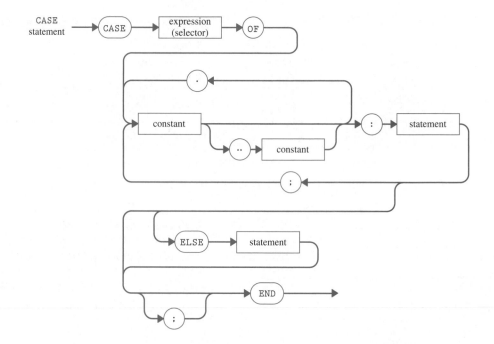

From this we see that a **CASE** statement has the following form:[1]

CASE Statement

Form:

```
CASE selector OF
    label-list-1 : statement-1;
    label-list-2 : statement-2;
                     .
                     .
                     .
    label-list-n : statement-n
    ELSE
                     statement-n + 1
END
```

where:

CASE, OF, ELSE, and END are reserved words;

the ELSE part is optional;

statement-1, statement-2, . . . , statement-n + 1 are Pascal statements;

selector is an expression of type **integer, shortint, byte, boolean,** or **char** (or of enumerated or subrange type, defined in Chapter 8);

each *label-list-i* is a list of one or more possible values of the selector or ranges of values of the form

first-value..last-value

Purpose:

When the **CASE** statement is executed, the *selector* is evaluated; if this value is in *label-list-i*, then *statement-i* is executed, and execution continues with the statement following the reserved word **END** that marks the end of the **CASE** statement. If the selector's value is not in any of the label lists, then the statement specified in the **ELSE** part is executed, and execution continues with the statement following the **CASE** statement. If the **ELSE** part is omitted, execution "falls through" the **CASE** statement if the selector's value is not in any of the label lists. Note that the values of the selector may not be real numbers or string constants having more than one character.

---

[1] Standard Pascal does not allow an ELSE part in a CASE statement or the use of ranges in the label lists. Also, it is an error if the selector's value is not in any of the label lists.

Examples of CASE Statements

As an example of a **CASE** statement, consider the problem of displaying the class name for a given numeric class code. If the value of the variable **ClassCode** is 1, 2, 3, or 4, then the following **CASE** statement displays the correct name:

```
CASE ClassCode OF
   1 : writeln( 'Freshman' );
   2 : writeln( 'Sophomore' );
   3 : writeln( 'Junior' );
   4 : writeln( 'Senior' )
   ELSE
       writeln( 'Illegal class code' )
END {CASE};
```

Occasionally, no action is required for certain values of the selector in a **CASE** statement. In such situations, these values may be placed in a label list for which the corresponding statement is empty. For example, a program to count aces and face cards might use the **CASE** statement

```
CASE Card OF
            'A' : ace := ace + 1;
  'J', 'Q', 'K' : face := face + 1;
  '2', '3', '4',
  '5', '6', '7',
  '8', '9', 'T' : {no action required}
   ELSE
       writeln( 'Illegal character' )
END {CASE};
```

where the **CASE** selector **CARD** is of type **char**. Note that using string constants such as **'ACE'**, **'JACK'**, **'QUEEN'**, and **'KING'** in a label list is not allowed.

Example: Assigning Letter Grades

The program in Figure 4.6 used an **IF** statement to implement the multialternative selection structure required to assign a letter grade to a student's average, as specified in the following table:

Average	Letter Grade
Average $\geq$ 90	A
$80 \leq$ average < 90	B
$70 \leq$ average < 80	C
$60 \leq$ average < 70	D
Average < 60	F

If we assume that the value of **Average** does not exceed 100, we can use a **CASE** statement to implement this five-way selection structure:

```
CASE trunc(Average) OF
    90..100  : Grade := 'A';
    80..89   : Grade := 'B';
    70..79   : Grade := 'C';
    60..69   : Grade := 'D';
       ELSE
                Grade := 'F'
END {CASE};
```

Note that the real quantity **Average** is converted to **integer** type by using the **trunc** function so that it can be used as a selector in a **CASE** statement.

The program in Figure 7.1 is the modification of that in Figure 4.6 obtained by replacing the **IF** statement by this **CASE** statement and using a while loop to process several sets of scores.

FIGURE 7.1   Grade assignment—version 4.

```
PROGRAM GradeAssignment4( input, output );
{*****************************************************************

    Input (keyboard): Triples of real numbers representing students' homework
                      average, average on tests, and final exam score.
    Purpose:          Compute final course averages using homework
                      average, average on tests, and final exam score;
                      letter grades are then assigned.
    Output (screen):  User prompts, the weighted averages, and the letter
                      grades.

    *****************************************************************}

CONST
    HWWeight = 0.2;        {weight factors for homework,}
    TestWeight = 0.5;      {    tests,}
    ExamWeight = 0.3;      {    and the exam}

VAR
    Homework, Tests, Exam, {homework, test, and exam averages}
    Average : real;        {final course average}
    Grade : char;          {grade assigned (A, B, C, D or F)}
```

FIGURE 7.1   Grade assignment—version 4. (cont.)

```
BEGIN
    write( 'Enter homework, test and exam scores (0''s to stop): ' );
    readln( Homework, Tests, Exam );
    WHILE Homework > 0 DO
        BEGIN
            Average := HWWeight * Homework + TestWeight * Tests
                    + ExamWeight * Exam;
            CASE trunc(Average) OF
                90...100 : Grade := 'A';
                  80..89 : Grade := 'B';
                  70..79 : Grade := 'C';
                  60..69 : Grade := 'D';
                    ELSE
                          Grade := 'F'
            END {CASE};
            writeln( 'Average = ', Average:5:1, ' Grade = ', Grade );
            writeln;
            write( 'Enter homework, test and exam scores (0''s to stop): ' );
            readln( Homework, Tests, Exam )
        END (* WHILE *)
END.
```

Sample run:

```
Enter homework, test and exam scores (0's to stop): 100 100 100
Average = 100.0 Grade = A

Enter homework, test and exam scores (0's to stop): 30 40 50
Average =  41.0 Grade = F

Enter homework, test and exam scores (0's to stop): 56.2 62.7 66.5
Average =  62.5 Grade = D

Enter homework, test and exam scores (0's to stop): 87.5 91.3 80
Average =  87.2 Grade = B

Enter homework, test and exam scores (0's to stop): 0 0 0
```

Exercises

    1. Write a CASE statement for each of the following:

        (a) If the value of the character variable TransCode is D, increase Balance by adding Amount to it; if TransCode is W, decrease Balance by subtracting Amount from it; if TransCode is P, display the value of Balance; any other value should result in a void transaction.

        (b) Display the name of a month or an error message for a given value of the integer variable Month. Display an error message if the value of Month is less than 1 or greater than 12.

(c) Assign the value to `Cost` corresponding to the value of the integer variable `Distance` given in the following table:

Distance	Cost
0 through 99	5.00
At least 100 but less than 300	8.00
At least 300 but less than 600	10.00
At least 600 but less than 1000	12.00

(d) Display the number of days in a month. (See Exercise 1[d] of Section 4.4 regarding the determination of leap years.)

2. Rewrite the while loop in the statement part of the checkbook-balancing program of Figure 5.6 using a **CASE** statement to process the various options.

3. Write the menu-driven program for converting measurements as described in Exercise 9 of Section 5.4, but use a **CASE** statement to process the various options.

4. Write a program that reads numbers representing TV channels and then uses a **CASE** statement to determine the call letters of the station that corresponds to each number or some message indicating that the channel is not used. Use the following channel numbers and call letters (or use those that are available in your locale):

   2: WCBS
   4: WNBC
   5: WNEW
   7: WABC
   9: WOR
   11: WPIX
   13: WNET

5. A wholesale office supply company discounts the price of each of its products depending on the number of units bought and the price per unit. The discount increases as the numbers of units bought and/or the unit price increases. These discounts are given in the following table:

Number Bought	Unit Price (dollars) 0–10.00	Unit Price (dollars) 10.01–100.00	Unit Price (dollars) 100.01–
1–9	0%	2%	5%
10–19	5%	7%	9%
20–49	9%	15%	21%
50–99	14%	23%	32%
100–	21%	32%	43%

Write a program that reads the number of units bought and the unit price and then calculates and prints the total full cost, the total amount of the discount, and the total discounted cost.

6. Locating avenues' addresses in mid-Manhattan is not easy; for example, the nearest cross street to 866 Third Avenue is 53rd Street, whereas the nearest cross street to 866 Second Avenue is 46th Street. To locate approximately the nearest numbered cross street for a given avenue address, the following algorithm can be used:

Cancel the last digit of the address, divide by 2, and add or subtract the number given in the following (abbreviated) table:

1st Ave.	Add 3
2nd Ave.	Add 3
3rd Ave.	Add 10
4th Ave.	Add 8
5th Ave. up to 200	Add 13
5th Ave. 200 up to 400	Add 16
6th Ave. (Ave. of the Americas)	Subtract 12
7th Ave.	Add 12
8th Ave.	Add 10
10th Ave.	Add 14

Write a program that reads an avenue address and then uses a **CASE** statement to determine the number of the nearest cross street, according to the preceding algorithm.

7. An airline vice-president in charge of operations needs to determine whether or not the current estimates of flight times are accurate. Since there is a larger possibility of variations due to weather and air traffic in the longer flights, he allows a larger error in the time estimates for them. He compares an actual flight time with the estimated flight time and considers the estimate to be too large, acceptable, or too small, as determined by the following table of acceptable error margins:

Estimated Flight Time in Minutes	Acceptable Error Margin in Minutes
0–29	1
30–59	2
60–89	3
90–119	4
120–179	6
180–239	8
240–359	13
360–	17

For example, if an estimated flight time is 106 minutes, the acceptable error margin is 4 minutes. Thus, the estimated flight time is too large if the actual flight time is less than 102 minutes, or the estimated flight time is too small if the actual flight time is greater than 110 minutes; otherwise, the estimate is acceptable. Write a program that reads an estimated flight time and an actual flight time, uses a **CASE** statement to determine the acceptable error according to this table, and then prints whether the estimated time is too large, acceptable, or too small. If the estimated flight time is either too large or too small, the program should also print the amount of the overestimate or underestimate.

7.2   Repetition Structure: The FOR Statement

In Chapter 4 we described the **WHILE** statement that is used to implement repetition structures called while loops. In such loops the body of the loop is executed repeatedly while some boolean expression remains true. Another repetition structure is a **for loop,** in which the body of the loop is executed for all values in some specified range. This kind of loop can be implemented in Pascal using a **FOR** statement.

The syntax diagram for a **FOR** statement is

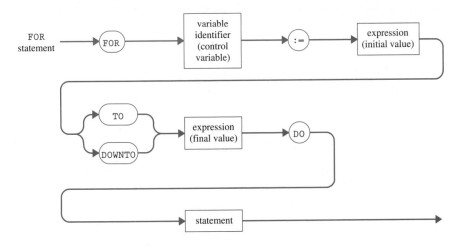

From this diagram we see that this statement has two forms:

FOR Statement

```
Forms:

    FOR control-variable := initial-value
    TO final-value DO
        statement

    FOR control-variable := initial-value
    DOWNTO final-value DO
        statement
```

where:

> **FOR**, **TO**, **DOWNTO**, and **DO** are reserved words;
>
> *statement* is a Pascal statement;
>
> the control variable, the initial value, and the final value must be of the same type, which may be **integer**, **shortint**, **longint**, **byte**, **word**, **char**, or **boolean** (or of enumerated or subrange types, as described in Chapter 8). For a **FOR** statement in a subprogram, the control variable must be a local variable.

Purpose:

When a **FOR** statement is executed, the specified statement, called the body of the loop, is executed once for each value of the control variable, from the initial value to the final value.[2] For the first form, if the initial value is greater than the final value and, for the second form, if the initial value is less than the final value, the body of the loop is not executed.

A **FOR** statement of the form

```
FOR control-variable := initial-value TO final-value DO
    statement
```

executes the specified *statement* for each value of the *control-variable* in the range from *initial-value* through *final-value*, provided that the initial value does not exceed the final value. More precisely, it implements the control structure:

If *initial-value* $\leq$ *final-value*, do the following:

1. Set *control-variable* equal to *initial-value*.
2. Execute the specified *statement* in the for loop.
3. While *control-variable* $\neq$ *final-value* do the following:
   a. Increment *control-variable* by 1.
   b. Execute the specified *statement* in the for loop.

From this we see that if *initial-value* $\leq$ *final-value*, then the control variable will run through the range of values *initial-value..final-value*, and the specified statement in the for loop, called its **body,** will be executed once for each of the values in this range (unless it modifies the value of the control variable, as described later).

To illustrate, consider the statement

```
FOR Number := 1 TO 10 DO
    writeln( Number:2, sqr(Number):5 );
```

where **Number** is of **integer** type. In this statement, **Number** is the control variable, the initial value is 1, and the final value is 10. When this statement is executed, the initial value 1 is assigned to **Number**, and the **writeln** statement is

---

[2] As described in the footnote on page 150, the **Break** and **Continue** procedures of Turbo Pascal 7.0 can be used to modify the execution pattern of for loops.

executed. Because the value of **Number** is not equal to the final volume **10**, it is incremented by **1**, and the **writeln** statement is executed again. This repetition continues as long as the value of the control variables **Number** is not equal to the final value **10**. Thus, the output produced by this statement is

```
 1     1
 2     4
 3     9
 4    16
 5    25
 6    36
 7    49
 8    64
 9    81
10   100
```

To repeat more than one statement using a **FOR** loop, we combine them into a single compound statement. For example, to double-space the preceding output, we might use

```
FOR Number := 1 TO 10 DO
   BEGIN
      writeln( Number:2, sqr(Number):5 );
      writeln
   END {FOR};
```

In the second form of the **FOR** statement,

```
FOR control-variable := initial-value DOWNTO final-value DO
   statement
```

the control variable is decremented rather than incremented. It thus implements the following control structure:

If *initial-value* ≥ *final-value*, do the following:

1. Set *control-variable* equal to *initial-value*.
2. Execute the specified *statement* in the for loop.
3. While *control-variable* ≠ *final-value* do the following:
      a. Decrement *control-variable* by 1.
      b. Execute the specified *statement* in the for loop.

Note that in this form of the **FOR** statement, **DOWNTO** is a single word.
To illustrate, consider the statement

```
FOR Number := 10 DOWNTO 1 DO
   writeln( Number:2, sqr(Number):5 );
```

Here the control variable **Number** is assigned the initial value **10** and the **writeln** statement is executed. Because this value is not equal to the final value **1**, the value of **Number** is decreased to **9** and the **writeln** statement is executed. This process continues as long as the value of **Number** is not equal to the final value 1. Thus, the output produced by this for loop is

```
10   100
 9    81
 8    64
 7    49
 6    36
 5    25
 4    16
 3     9
 2     4
 1     1
```

In the pseudocode descriptions of the control structures implemented by the two forms of the **FOR** statement, note that the first action is to compare the initial value with the final value to determine whether the range of values for the control variable is nonempty. In a **FOR-TO** statement, if the initial value is greater than the final value, the control variable is not set equal to the initial value and the body of the loop is never executed. This is also the case in the **FOR-DOWNTO** form if the initial value is less than the final value.

Example: A Table of Squares

The initial and/or final values in a **FOR** statement may be constants, or they may be the values of variables or expressions. To illustrate, consider the statements

```
write( 'Enter table size:    ' );
readln ( TableSize );
FOR Number := 1 TO TableSize DO
   writeln( Number:4, sqr(Number):8 );
```

The value entered for **TableSize** is the final value in this **FOR** statement. These statements are used in the program of Figure 7.2 to print a table of squares whose size is read during program execution.

FIGURE 7.2 Printing a table of squares.

```
PROGRAM TableOfSquares( input, output );
{*****************************************************************

   Input (keyboard): Number of rows in table.
   Purpose:          Print a table of integers and their squares.
   Output (screen):  User prompt and the table.


*****************************************************************}

VAR
   TableSize,           {number of rows in table}
   Number : integer;    {number whose square is calculated}
```

FIGURE 7.2   Printing a table of squares. (cont.)

```
BEGIN
   write( 'Enter table size:  ' );
   readln( TableSize );
   writeln;
   writeln( 'Number  Square' );
   writeln( '------  ------' );
   FOR Number := 1 TO TableSize DO
      writeln( Number:4, sqr(Number):8 )
END.
```

Sample run:

```
Enter table size:   10

Number  Square
------  ------
   1       1
   2       4
   3       9
   4      16
   5      25
   6      36
   7      49
   8      64
   9      81
  10     100
```

Some Rules for FOR Statements

There are a number of important rules that must be followed when using **FOR** statements:

1. *The initial and final values of the control variable are determined before repetition begins and cannot be changed during execution of the* **FOR** *statement.* Within the body of the for loop, the values of variables that specify these initial and final values may change, but this does not affect the number of repetitions. (See the example in Potential Problem 3 in the Programming Pointers at the end of this chapter.)
2. *The statement within a* **FOR** *statement may use the value of the control variable, but it should not modify this value.* (See the example in Potential Problem 4 in the Programming Pointers at the end of this chapter.)
3. *The control variable in a* **FOR** *statement must be declared within the program unit in which it is used.* A global variable or any variable declared in some larger program unit may not be used for this purpose.

Example: A Multiplication Table

The statement that appears within a **FOR** statement may itself be a **FOR** statement; that is, one **FOR** statement may be nested within another **FOR** statement. As an example, consider the program in Figure 7.3 that calculates and displays products of the form **X** * **Y** for **X** ranging from 1 through **LastX** and **Y** ranging from 1 through **LastY** for integers **LastX** and **LastY**. The table of products is generated by the **FOR** statement

```
FOR X := 1 TO LastX DO
    FOR Y := 1 TO LastY DO
        BEGIN
            Product := X * Y;
            writeln( X:2, ' *', Y:2, ' =', Product:3 )
        END {FOR}
```

In the sample run, both **LastX** and **LastY** are assigned the value 4. The control variable **X** is assigned its initial value 1, and the statement

```
FOR Y := 1 TO LastY DO
    BEGIN
        Product := X * Y;
        writeln( X:2, ' *', Y:2, ' =', Product:3 )
    END {FOR}
```

is executed. This calculates and displays the first four products, 1 * 1, 1 * 2, 1 * 3, and 1 * 4. The value of **X** is then incremented by 1, and the preceding **FOR** statement is executed again. This calculates and displays the next four products, 2 * 1, 2 * 2, 2 * 3, and 2 * 4. The control variable **X** is then incremented to 3, producing the next four products, 3 * 1, 3 * 2, 3 * 3, and 3 * 4, and finally **X** is incremented to 4, giving the last four products 4 * 1, 4 * 2, 4 * 3, and 4 * 4.

 FIGURE 7.3 Printing a multiplication table.

```
PROGRAM Products( input, output );
{***************************************************************

    Input (keyboard): Largest numbers to be multiplied.
    Purpose:          Calculate and display a list of products
                      of two numbers.
    Output (screen):  User prompt and a list of products.


***************************************************************}

VAR
    X, Y,                  {two numbers being multiplied}
    LastX, LastY,          {last values of X and Y, respectively}
    Product : integer;     {product of X and Y}
```

FIGURE 7.3   Printing a multiplication table. (cont.)

```
BEGIN
   write( 'Enter upper limits for factors of product:  ' );
   readln( LastX, LastY );
   writeln;
   FOR X := 1 TO LastX DO
      FOR Y := 1 TO LastY DO
         BEGIN
            Product := X * Y;
            writeln( X:2, ' *', Y:2, ' =', Product:3 )
         END {FOR}
END.
```

Sample run:

```
Enter upper limits for factors of product:  4 4

1 * 1 =   1
1 * 2 =   2
1 * 3 =   3
1 * 4 =   4
2 * 1 =   2
2 * 2 =   4
2 * 3 =   6
2 * 4 =   8
3 * 1 =   3
3 * 2 =   6
3 * 3 =   9
3 * 4 = 12
4 * 1 =   4
4 * 2 =   8
4 * 3 = 12
4 * 4 = 16
```

7.3   Repetition Structure: The REPEAT–UNTIL Statement

Recall that a while loop is a pretest or "test-at-the-top" loop in which the boolean expression that controls repetition is evaluated *before* the body of the loop is executed. Sometimes, however, it is appropriate to use a **posttest loop** or "test-at-the-bottom" loop like that pictured in the following diagram, in which the termination test is made *after* the body of the loop is executed:

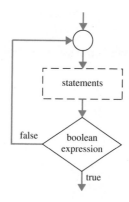

Such a posttest loop is also called a **REPEAT-UNTIL loop** and can be implemented in Pascal by using a **REPEAT-UNTIL statement.**

Form of a REPEAT-UNTIL Statement

The syntax diagram for a **REPEAT-UNTIL** statement is

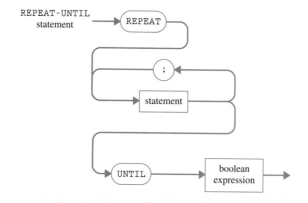

A **REPEAT-UNTIL** statement thus has the following form:

REPEAT-UNTIL Statement

Form:

```
REPEAT
    statement-1;
    statement-2;
        .
        .
        .
    statement-n
UNTIL boolean-expression
```

where:
    REPEAT and **UNTIL** are reserved words;
    boolean-expression is any boolean expression;
    statement-1, *statement-2*, ..., *statement-n* are Pascal
    statements.

Purpose:
The specified statements, *statement-1*, *statement-2*, ...,
statement-n, are executed. The boolean expression is then evaluated, and if it is false, these statements are executed again. This process of evaluating the boolean expression and executing the specified statements is repeated as long as the boolean expression is false.[3] When it becomes true, repetition is terminated.

Example: Calculating the Mean Time to Failure

To illustrate the use of **REPEAT-UNTIL** statements, we consider once again the problem of calculating the mean of a set of failure times, as described in Section 4.5. Since the number of scores is not known in advance, a program to solve this problem must read and count the data values before the mean can be calculated. The program in Figure 4.8 used the standard technique of signaling the end of data with an end-of-data flag. An alternative approach is to ask the user repeatedly if there are more data items, terminating when the response is no. And because there ordinarily will be at least one data item, it seems natural to check this termination condition at the bottom of the loop, that is, to use a repeat-until loop to read the data values.

This leads to the following modified algorithm:

ALGORITHM TO CALCULATE MEAN TIME TO FAILURE

(* Input: A collection of failure times and user responses.
   Purpose: Algorithm to read failure times, count them, and find the mean time to failure (*MeanFailTime*). *FailTime* represents the current failure time entered, *NumTimes* is the number of failure times, and *Sum* is their sum. Values are read until the user enters a value of 'N' or 'n' for *Response,* indicating that there are no more data values to be entered.
   Output: User prompts, *MeanFailTime,* and *NumTimes.* *)

1. Initialize *NumTimes* to 0 and *Sum* to 0.0.

---

[3] The **Break** and **Continue** procedures of Turbo Pascal 7.0 can be used to modify the normal pattern of execution of repeat–until loops. See Section H.1 of Appendix H.

2. Repeat the following:
   a. Read a value for *FailTime*.
   b. Increment *NumTimes* by 1.
   c. Add *FailTime* to *Sum*.
   d. Ask the user if there is more data and read *Response*.
   Until *Response* is 'N' or 'n'.
3. Calculate *MeanFailTime = Sum / NumTimes*.
4. Display *MeanFailTime* and *NumTimes*.

(Note that because a repeat-until loop always is executed at least once, at least one data value will be read. Consequently, the **IF** structure used in the algorithm in Section 4.5 to check if any data values have been entered is no longer needed.)

For this algorithm, the repetition structure in Step 2 can be implemented in Pascal by

```
REPEAT
    write( 'Fail Time:  ' );
    readln( FailTime );
    NumTimes := NumTimes + 1;
    Sum := Sum + FailTime;
    write( 'More fail times (Y or N)? ' );
    readln( Response )
UNTIL (Response = 'N') OR (Response = 'n');
```

This **REPEAT-UNTIL** statement is used in the program in Figure 7.4 that implements the preceding algorithm.

FIGURE 7.4 Mean time to failure—version 2.

```
PROGRAM CalculateMeanFailTime2( input, output );
{*******************************************************************

   Input (keyboard): A list of fail times and user's response to
                     'More fail times?' query.
   Purpose:          Read a list of fail times, count them, and
                     calculate the mean time to failure.
   Output (screen):  User prompts, number of fail times read, and
                     mean time to failure.

*******************************************************************}

VAR
    NumTimes : integer;          {number of fail times}
    Sum,                         {sum of the fail times}
    FailTime,                    {current fail time being processed}
    MeanFailTime : real;         {mean of the fail times}
    Response : char;             {user's response to 'More fail times?'}
```

FIGURE 7.4 Mean time to failure—version 2. (cont.)

```
BEGIN
   Sum := 0;
   NumTimes := 0;
   REPEAT
      write( 'Fail Time:  ' );
      readln( FailTime );
      NumTimes := NumTimes + 1;
      Sum := Sum + FailTime;
      write( 'More fail times (Y or N)? ' );
      readln( Response )
   UNTIL (Response = 'N') OR (Response = 'n');
   MeanFailTime := Sum / NumTimes;
   writeln;
   writeln( NumTimes:1, ' failure times with mean = ', MeanFailTime:5:2 )
END.
```

Sample run:

```
Fail Time:  127
More fail times (Y or N)? Y
Fail Time:  123.5
More fail times (Y or N)? Y
Fail Time:  155.4
More fail times (Y or N)? Y
Fail Time:  99
More fail times (Y or N)? Y
Fail Time:  117.3
More fail times (Y or N)? Y
Fail Time:  201.5
More fail times (Y or N)? N

6 failure times with mean = 137.28
```

7.4 Examples: Depreciation Tables, Compound Interest, Simulation

We have now considered all the statements provided in Pascal for implementing the basic control structures:

Control Structure	Pascal Implementation
Sequential	Compound statement
Selection	**IF** statement
	CASE statement
Repetition	**WHILE** statement
	FOR statement
	REPEAT-UNTIL statement

We have also introduced procedures and functions, which play an important role in the modular design of software. In this section we demonstrate how these are used by designing programs for three applications: (1) calculating depreciation tables, (2) calculating compound interest, and (3) simulating random phenomena.

Example 1: Depreciation Tables

Depreciation is a decrease in the value over time of some asset due to wear and tear, decay, declining price, and so on. For example, suppose that a company purchases a new computer system for $200,000 that will serve its needs for five years. After that time it can be sold at an estimated price of $50,000. Thus, the value of the computing equipment will have depreciated $150,000 over the five-year period.

The calculation of depreciation tables that display the value lost in each of several years is an important accounting problem, and there are several ways of calculating depreciation. One of the simplest methods is the **straight-line method** in which the amount to be depreciated is divided evenly over the specified number of years. For example, straight-line depreciation of $150,000 over a five-year period gives an annual depreciation of $150,000 / 5 = $30,000. An algorithm for calculating depreciation using this method is simple:

ALGORITHM FOR STRAIGHT-LINE DEPRECIATION

(* Input: An *Amount* and number of years (*NumYears*).
  Purpose: Depreciate *Amount* over *NumYears* using the straight-line method
            of calculating depreciation.
  Output: A depreciation table. *)

1. Calculate *Depreciation* = *Amount* / *NumYears*.
2. For *Year* ranging from 1 through *NumYears* do the following:
       Display *Year* and *Depreciation*.

Another common method of calculating depreciation is the **sum-of-the-years-digits method.** To illustrate it, consider again depreciating $150,000 over a five-year period. We first calculate the "sum of the years," 1 + 2 + 3 + 4 + 5 = 15. In the first year, 5/15 of $150,000 ($50,000) is depreciated; in the second year, 4/15 of $150,000 ($40,000) is depreciated; and so on, giving the following depreciation table:

Year	Depreciation
1	$50,000
2	$40,000
3	$30,000
4	$20,000
5	$10,000

An algorithm for calculating depreciation using this method is

---

ALGORITHM FOR SUM-OF-THE-YEARS-DIGITS DEPRECIATION

(* Input: An *Amount* and number of years (*NumYears*).
     Purpose: Depreciate *Amount* over *NumYears* years using the sum-of-the-years-digits method of calculating depreciation.
     Output: A depreciation table. *)

1. Calculate *Sum* = 1 + 2 + $\cdots$ + *NumYears*.
2. For *Year* ranging from 1 through *NumYears* do the following:
     a. Calculate

$$\textit{Depreciation} = (\textit{NumYears} - \textit{Year} + 1) * \textit{Amount} / \textit{Sum}$$

     b. Display *Year* and *Depreciation*.

A third method of calculating depreciation is the **double-declining balance method.** In this method, if an amount is to be depreciated over *n* years, 2/*n* times the undepreciated balance is depreciated annually. For example, in the depreciation of $150,000 over a five-year period using the double-declining balance method, 2/5 of $150,000 ($60,000) would be depreciated the first year, leaving an undepreciated balance of $90,000. In the second year, 2/5 of $90,000 ($36,000) would be depreciated, leaving an undepreciated balance of $54,000. Since only a fraction of the remaining balance is depreciated in each year, the entire amount will never be depreciated. Consequently, it is permissible to switch to the straight-line method at any time. Developing an algorithm for this method of calculating depreciation is left as an exercise.

The program in Figure 7.5 is a menu-driven program for calculating depreciation tables and has the structure shown in the following diagram:

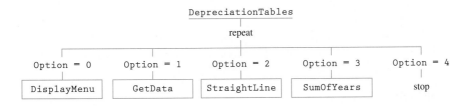

The user selects options from the menu, and a **CASE** statement is used to process these options:

```
CASE Option OF
    0 : DisplayMenu;
    1 : GetData( Amount, NumYears );
    2 : StraightLine( Amount, NumYears );
    3 : SumOfYears( Amount, NumYears );
    4 : {stop}
END {CASE}
```

Here `DisplayMenu`, `GetData`, `StraightLine`, and `SumOfYears` are procedures that carry out the operations selected by the user. A **REPEAT-UNTIL** statement is used to implement the repetition structure indicated in the structure diagram. Another **REPEAT-UNTIL** statement is used to force the user to enter a legal option number:

```
REPEAT
   write( 'Option? ' );
   readln( Option )
UNTIL (Option >= 0) AND (Option <= MaxOption);
```

Here `MaxOption` is the number (4) of the last option in the menu. Note also the use of **FOR** statements to calculate the sum of the years and to display depreciation tables in procedures `StraightLine` and `SumOfYears`.

FIGURE 7.5 Methods of depreciation.

```
PROGRAM DepreciationTables( input, output );
{*******************************************************************

   Input (keyboard): User-selected options, amounts to be depreciated,
                     and number of years.
   Purpose:          Calculate and display depreciation tables using
                     various methods of depreciation.
   Output (screen):  User prompts, menu of options, and depreciation
                     tables.


*******************************************************************}

CONST
   MaxOption = 4;            {maximum option number}

VAR
   Option,                   {option selected by the user}
   NumYears : integer;       {number of years over which to depreciate}
   Amount : real;            {amount to be depreciated}

PROCEDURE DisplayMenu;
{-------------------------------------------

   Purpose:  Display the menu of options

-----------------------------------------}
```

FIGURE 7.5   Methods of depreciation. (cont.)

```
BEGIN
   writeln;
   writeln( 'The following options are available:' );
   writeln( '0:  Display this menu' );
   writeln( '1:  Enter new amount and number of years' );
   writeln( '2:  Print depreciation table using straight-line method' );
   writeln( '3:  Print depreciation table using sum-of-years-digits',
                 ' method' );
   writeln( '4:  Stop' )
END {DisplayMenu};

PROCEDURE GetData( VAR Amount : real;          {amount to be depreciated}
                   VAR NumYears : integer ); {number of years}
{------------------------------------------------------------------------

   Input (keyboard): Amount and number of years.
   Purpose:          Read an Amount to be depreciated and the number
                     of years over which to depreciate it.
   Returns:          Amount and NumYears.
   Output (screen):  User prompts.

------------------------------------------------------------------------}

BEGIN
   write( 'Enter amount to be depreciated: ' );
   readln( Amount );
   write( 'Enter number of years: ' );
   readln( NumYears )
END {GetData};

PROCEDURE StraightLine( Amount : real;          {amount to be depreciated}
                        NumYears : integer ); {number of years}
{------------------------------------------------------------------------

   Accepts:          Amount and number of years.
   Purpose:          Calculate and display a depreciation table for Amount
                     over NumYears years using the straight-line method of
                     depreciation.
   Output (screen):  A depreciation table.

------------------------------------------------------------------------}

VAR
   Depreciation : real;          {annual depreciation}
   Year : integer;               {year number}
```

FIGURE 7.5 Methods of depreciation. (cont.)

```
  BEGIN
     Depreciation := Amount / NumYears;
     writeln;
     writeln( 'Year Depreciation' );
     writeln( '-----------------' );
     FOR Year := 1 TO NumYears DO
        writeln( Year : 3, Depreciation : 12:2 )
  END {StraightLine};

PROCEDURE SumOfYears( Amount : real;          {amount to be depreciated}
                     NumYears : integer ); {number of years}
{-------------------------------------------------------------------------

  Accepts:         Amount and number of years.
  Purpose:         Calculate and display a depreciation table for Amount
                   over NumYears years using the sum-of-the-years-digits
                   method of depreciation.
  Output (screen): A depreciation table.


--------------------------------------------------------------------------}

  VAR
     Depreciation : real;          {annual depreciation}
     Sum,                          {1 + 2 + ... + NumYears}
     Year : integer;               {index -- year number}

  BEGIN
     Sum := 0;
     FOR Year := 1 TO NumYears DO
        Sum := Sum + Year;

     writeln;
     writeln( 'Year Depreciation' );
     writeln( '-----------------' );
     FOR Year := 1 TO NumYears DO
        BEGIN
           Depreciation := (NumYears - Year + 1) * Amount / Sum;
           writeln( Year : 3, Depreciation : 12:2 )
        END {FOR}
  END {SumOfYears};
```

FIGURE 7.5   Methods of depreciation. (cont.)

```
BEGIN {*************** main program ***************}
   writeln( 'The following program allows you to print depreciation' );
   writeln( 'tables using various methods of depreciation.' );
   DisplayMenu;
   REPEAT
      writeln;
      REPEAT
         write( 'Option? ' );
         readln( Option )
      UNTIL (Option >= 0) AND (Option <= MaxOption);
      CASE Option OF
         0 : DisplayMenu;
         1 : GetData( Amount, NumYears );
         2 : StraightLine( Amount, NumYears );
         3 : SumOfYears( Amount, NumYears );
         4 : {stop}
      END {CASE}
   UNTIL Option = MaxOption
END {main program}.
```

Sample run:

```
The following program allows you to print depreciation
tables using various methods of depreciation.

The following options are available:
0:  Display this menu
1:  Enter new amount and number of years
2:  Print depreciation table using straight-line method
3:  Print depreciation table using sum-of-years-digits method
4:  Stop

Option? 0

The following options are available:
0:  Display this menu
1:  Enter new amount and number of years
2:  Print depreciation table using straight-line method
3:  Print depreciation table using sum-of-years-digits method
4:  Stop

Option? 1
Enter amount to be depreciated: 1500.00
Enter number of years: 5
```

FIGURE 7.5   Methods of depreciation. (cont.)

```
Option? 2

Year Depreciation
-----------------
   1        300.00
   2        300.00
   3        300.00
   4        300.00
   5        300.00

Option? 3

Year Depreciation
-----------------
   1        500.00
   2        400.00
   3        300.00
   4        200.00
   5        100.00

Option? 6      ← Illegal option
Option? 1
Enter amount to be depreciated: 1000.00
Enter number of years: 2

Option? 2

Year Depreciation
-----------------
   1        500.00
   2        500.00

Option? 4
```

Example 2: Compound Interest

Suppose that an amount is deposited in a savings account that earns interest compounded several times per year. We wish to determine the amount that will have accumulated in this account after a specified number of years, assuming that no additional deposits or withdrawals are made.

In developing a program to solve this problem, we use the following variables:

Amount:	Amount of initial deposit.
Rate:	Annual interest rate in decimal form.
NumTimes:	Number of times per year interest is compounded.
Years:	Number of years interest is accumulated.

Because the interest rate for each interest period is `Rate/NumTimes`, the interest earned during the first interest period is

```
Amount * (Rate/NumTimes)
```

so that the accumulated value after this first period is

```
Amount + Amount * (Rate/NumTimes)
```

which can also be written as

```
Amount * (1 + Rate/NumTimes)
```

Similarly, the accumulated value at the end of the second interest period will be

```
[Amount * (1 + Rate/NumTimes)] * (1 + Rate/NumTimes)
```

or simply

$$\texttt{Amount * (1 + Rate/NumTimes)}^2$$

In general, after **k** interest periods, the accumulated value will be

$$\texttt{Amount * (1 + Rate/NumTimes)}^k$$

In this problem there are `Years` * `NumTimes` interest periods, and thus the final accumulated value will be

$$\texttt{Amount * (1 + Rate/NumTimes)}^{\texttt{Years * NumTimes}}$$

The program in Figure 7.6 uses the function `AccumulatedValue` to evaluate this formula. It uses the function `Power` to carry out the necessary exponentiation. Note the use of a for loop in `Power` to calculate the value of x^n. A repeat-until loop is used in the main program to repeatedly accept new amounts, interest rates, number of times interest is compounded, and number of years.

   FIGURE 7.6   Compound interest.

```
PROGRAM CompoundInterest( input, output );
{*******************************************************************

    Input (keyboard): Amounts, interest rates, number of times interest is
                      compounded, and number of years.
    Purpose:          Calculate compound interest for various amounts,
                      interest rates, number of years, and number of times
                      interest is compounded.
    Output (screen):  User prompts and accumulated values.


*******************************************************************}
```

FIGURE 7.6   Compound interest. (cont.)

```
VAR
   Amount,                  {amount of initial deposit}
   Rate,                    {annual interest rate in decimal form}
   AccumValue : real;       {accumulated value}
   NumTimes,                {number of times per year interest is compounded}
   Years : integer;         {number of years interest is accumulated}
   Response : char;         {user's response to 'More Data (Y or N)?'}

FUNCTION Power( x : real;         {any real number}
               n : integer )  {any integer exponent}
               : real;
{-------------------------------------------------------------

   Accepts:  A real number x and an integer n.
   Purpose:  Calculate the n-th power of x.
   Returns:  n-th power of x.

-----------------------------------------------------------------}

   VAR
      i : integer;         {counter}
      Product : real;      {product of n x's}

   BEGIN
      IF x = 0 THEN
         Power := 0
      ELSE
         BEGIN
            Product := 1;
            FOR i := 1 to abs(n) DO
               Product := Product * x;
            IF n >= 0 THEN
               Power := Product
            ELSE
               Power := 1.0 / Product
         END {ELSE}
   END {Power};

FUNCTION AccumulatedValue( Amount,           {amount of deposit}
                           Rate : real;      {annual interest rate}
                           NumTimes,          {# times to compound interest}
                           Years : integer) {number of years}
                              : real;
{----------------------------------------------------------------------

   Accepts:  Amount, Rate, NumTimes, Years.
   Purpose:  Calculate the value accumulated if a given Amount earns
             interest at annual interest Rate and interest is compounded
             NumTimes per year for a given number of Years.
             It uses the function Power.
   Returns:  Accumulated value.

-------------------------------------------------------------------------}
```

FIGURE 7.6   Compound interest. (cont.)

```
  BEGIN
     AccumulatedValue :=
                    Amount * Power( 1 + Rate / NumTimes, Years * NumTimes )
  END {AccumulatedValue};

BEGIN {**************** main program ****************}
  REPEAT
     write( 'Enter amount deposited: $' );
     readln( Amount );
     write( 'Enter annual interest rate (in decimal form): ' );
     readln( Rate );
     write( 'Enter number of times per year interest is compounded: ' );
     readln( NumTimes );
     write( 'Enter number of years interest is to be accumulated: ' );
     readln( Years );
     AccumValue := AccumulatedValue( Amount, Rate, NumTimes, Years );
     writeln( 'Accumulated value is: $', AccumValue:8:2 );
     writeln;
     write( 'More data (Y or N)? ' );
     readln( Response )
  UNTIL (Response = 'N') OR (Response = 'n')
END {main program}.
```

Sample run:

```
Enter amount deposited: $100.00
Enter annual interest rate (in decimal form): 0.04
Enter number of times per year interest is compounded: 1
Enter number of years interest is to be accumulated: 1
Accumulated value is: $  104.00

More data (Y or N)? Y
Enter amount deposited: $100.00
Enter annual interest rate (in decimal form): 0.04
Enter number of times per year interest is compounded: 4
Enter number of years interest is to be accumulated: 1
Accumulated value is: $  104.06

More data (Y or N)? Y
Enter amount deposited: $100.00
Enter annual interest rate (in decimal form): 0.09
Enter number of times per year interest is compounded: 12
Enter number of years interest is to be accumulated: 5
Accumulated value is: $  156.57

More data (Y or N)? N
```

Example 3: Simulation

The term **simulation** refers to modeling a dynamic process and using this model to study the behavior of the process. The behavior of some **deterministic** processes can be modeled with an equation or a set of equations. For example, processes that involve exponential growth or decay are commonly modeled with an equation of the form

$$A(t) = A_0 e^{kt}$$

where $A(t)$ is the amount of some substance A present at time t, A_0 is the initial amount of the substance, and k is a rate constant.

In many problems, however, the process being studied involves **randomness,** for example, Brownian motion, the arrival of airplanes at an airport, the number of defective parts manufactured by a machine, and so on. Computer programs that simulate such processes use a **random number generator,** which produces a number selected from some fixed range in such a way that a sequence of these numbers tends to be uniformly distributed over the given range. Although it is not possible to develop an algorithm that produces truly random numbers, there are some methods that produce sequences of **pseudorandom numbers** that are adequate for most purposes.

Turbo Pascal provides such a random number generator **Random**. A reference to this function of the form

```
Random
```

with no parameters returns a random real number in the range 0 to 1. A reference of the form

```
Random (k)
```

where k is a positive integer returns a random integer in the range 0 to k. This function can also be used to generate random numbers in other ranges. For example, the expression

```
a + (b - a) * Random
```

can be used to generate random real numbers in the range **a** to **b**, and the expression

```
m + trunc( n * Random )
```

can be used to generate random integers in the range **m** through **m + n - 1**.

To illustrate, suppose we wish to model the random process of tossing a pair of dice. Using the preceding expression for generating random integers, we might define the following function:

```
FUNCTION RandomInteger( m, n : integer ) : integer;
{------------------------------------------------------------------

   Accepts:  Two integers m and n.
   Purpose:  Generate an integer randomly selected from
             m, m + 1, . . . , m + n - 1. It uses the function
             Random that generates a random real number in the
             interval from 0 to 1.
   Returns:  A random integer.

----------------------------------------------------------------->}

   BEGIN
      RandomInteger := m + Random( n )
   END {RandomInteger};
```

and then use the statements

```
   Die1 := RandomInteger( 1, 6 );
   Die2 := RandomInteger( 1, 6 );
   Pair := Die1 + Die2;
```

to simulate one roll of two dice; the value of **Pair** is the total number of dots showing.

If the random number generator is suitably constructed, the relative frequency of each value from 2 through 12 for **Pair** should correspond to the probability of that number occurring on one throw of a pair of dice. These probabilities (rounded to three decimal places) are given in the following table:

Outcome	Probability
2	0.028
3	0.056
4	0.083
5	0.111
6	0.139
7	0.167
8	0.139
9	0.111
10	0.083
11	0.056
12	0.028

The program in Figure 7.7 reads an integer indicating the number of times that two dice are to be tossed and then repeatedly asks the user to enter a possible outcome of a roll of the dice and displays the relative frequency of this outcome. A repeat-until loop is used to implement this repetition structure. For each outcome, a for loop is used to produce the required number of dice rolls. The program uses the predefined function **Random** to generate random integers and the predefined procedure **Randomize** to initialize the random number generator so that a different sequence of numbers will be generated each time the program is run.

 FIGURE 7.7   Dice-roll simulation.

```
PROGRAM DiceRoll( input, output );
{*********************************************************************

    Input (keyboard): Number of dice rolls, number of spots to count,
                      and user's response to 'More rolls?' query.
    Purpose:          Use a random number generator to simulate
                      rolling a pair of dice several times, counting
                      the number of times a specified number of spots
                      occurs.
    Output (screen):  User prompts, and the relative frequency of
                      the number of spots.

*********************************************************************}

VAR
    Spots,              {number of spots to be counted}
    Count,              {number of times Spots occurred}
    NumRolls,           {number of rolls of dice}
    Die1, Die2,         {number of spots on die #1, #2, respectively}
    Pair,               {sum of Die1 and Die2 = total # of spots on the dice}
    Roll : integer;     {counts dice rolls}
    Response : char;    {user response}

FUNCTION RandomInteger( m, n : integer ) : integer;
{-----------------------------------------------------------------

    Accepts:  Two integers m and n.
    Purpose:  Generate an integer randomly selected from
              m, m + 1, . . . , m + n - 1. It uses the function
              Random that generates a random real number in the
              interval from 0 to 1.
    Returns:  A random integer.

-----------------------------------------------------------------}

    BEGIN
        RandomInteger := m + Random(n)
    END {Random Integer};
```

FIGURE 7.7   Dice-roll simulation. (cont.)

```
BEGIN {*************** main program ***************}
   write( 'Number of times to roll the dice: ' );
   readln( NumRolls );
   Randomize;
   REPEAT
      write( 'Number of spots to count: ' );
      readln( Spots );
      Count := 0;
      FOR Roll := 1 TO NumRolls DO
         BEGIN
            Die1 := RandomInteger( 1, 6 );
            Die2 := RandomInteger( 1, 6 );
            Pair := Die1 + Die2;
            IF Pair = Spots THEN
               Count := Count + 1
         END {FOR};
      writeln( 'Relative frequency of ', Spots:1,
               ' was ',Count / NumRolls:5:3 );
      writeln;
      write( 'More rolls (Y or N)? ' );
      readln( Response)
   UNTIL (Response = 'n') OR (Response = 'N')
END {main program}.
```

Sample run:

```
Number of times to roll the dice: 1000
Number of spots to count: 6
Relative frequency of 6 was 0.139

More rolls (Y or N)? Y
Number of spots to count: 7
Relative frequency of 7 was 0.171

More rolls (Y or N)? Y
Number of spots to count: 11
Relative frequency of 11 was 0.047

More rolls (Y or N)? N
```

Most random number generators generate random numbers having a **uniform distribution,** but they can also be used to generate random numbers having other distributions. The **normal distribution** is especially important because it models many physical processes. For example, the heights and weights of people, the lifetime of light bulbs, the tensile strength of steel produced by a machine, and, in general, the variations in parts produced in almost any manufacturing process have normal distributions. The normal distribution has the familiar bell-shaped curve

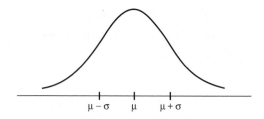

where μ is the mean of the distribution, σ is the standard deviation, and approximately two-thirds of the area under the curve lies between $\mu - \sigma$ and $\mu + \sigma$.

A normal distribution having $\mu = 0$ and $\sigma = 1$ is called a **standard normal distribution,** and random numbers having approximately this distribution can be generated quite easily from a uniform distribution, with the following algorithm:

ALGORITHM FOR THE STANDARD NORMAL DISTRIBUTION

(* Purpose: Generate random numbers having an approximate standard
               normal distribution from a uniform distribution.

   Returns: A random number Z from a standard normal distribution. *)

1. Set *Sum* equal to 0.
2. Do the following 12 times:
   a. Generate a random number X from a uniform distribution.
   b. Add X to *Sum.*
3. Calculate $Z = Sum - 6$.

The numbers Z generated by this algorithm have an approximate standard normal distribution. To generate random numbers Y having a normal distribution with mean μ and standard deviation σ, we simply add the following step to the algorithm:

4. Calculate $Y = \mu + \sigma * Z$.

Implementing this algorithm as a program is left as an exercise.

Exercises

1. Describe the output produced by each of the following program segments:

    (a)
```
FOR I := -2 TO 3 DO
    writeln( I:1, ' squared = ', sqr(I):1 );
```

    (b)
```
FOR I := 1 TO 5 DO
    BEGIN
        write( I:1 );
        FOR J := I DOWNTO 1 DO
            writeln( J:1 )
    END {FOR I};
```

```
(c) K := 5;
    FOR I := -2 to 3 DO
        BEGIN
            writeln( I + K : 2 );
            K := 1
        END {FOR};

(d) FOR I := 1 TO 3 DO
        FOR J := 1 TO 3 DO
            FOR K := 1 TO J DO
                writeln( I:1, J:1, K:2 );

(e) FOR I := 1 TO 3 DO
        FOR J := 1 TO 3 DO
            BEGIN
                FOR K := I TO J DO
                    write( I:1, J:1, K:1 );
                writeln
            END {FOR J};

(f) I := 0;
    REPEAT
        K := I * I * I - 3 * I + 1;
        writeln( I:3, K:3 )
    UNTIL I > 2;

(g) I := 0;
    REPEAT
        J := I * I * I;
        write( I:3 );
        REPEAT
            K := I + 2 * J;
            write( J:3, K:3 );
            J := J + 2
        UNTIL K > 10;
        writeln;
        I   := I + 1
    UNTIL J > 5;
```

2. Write a program that uses a for loop to generate the table of prices described in Exercise 6 of Section 4.6. Use a repeat-until loop to process the given data sets.

3. Write a program that reads a positive integer n and then uses a for loop to generate the first n Fibonacci numbers (see Exercise 12 of Section 4.6).

4. Suppose that at a given time, genotypes AA, AB, and BB appear in the proportions x, y, and z, respectively, where $x = 0.25$, $y = 0.5$, and $z = 0.25$. If individuals of type AA cannot reproduce, the probability that one parent will donate gene A to an offspring is

$$p = \frac{1}{2}\left(\frac{y}{y + z}\right)$$

since $y / (y + z)$ is the probability that the parent is of type AB and $1/2$ is the probability that such a parent will donate gene A. Then the proportions x', y', and z' of AA, AB, and BB, respectively, in the succeeding generation are given by

$$x' = p^2, \qquad y' = 2p(1 - p), \qquad z' = (1 - p)^2$$

and the new probability is given by

$$p' = \frac{1}{2}\left(\frac{y'}{y' + z'}\right)$$

Write a program to calculate and print the generation number and the proportions of AA, AB, and BB under appropriate headings for 30 generations. (Note that the proportions of AA and AB should approach 0, since gene A will gradually disappear.)

5. For a positive integer n, **n factorial** is denoted by $n!$ and is defined to be the product of the integers from 1 through n; 0! is defined as 1. A for loop is the natural repetition structure to use in calculating factorials. Write a program that reads several nonnegative integers and calculates and displays the factorial of each. Use a function to calculate the factorials.

6. Write a program that uses nested for loops to print the following multiplication table:

```
      1   2   3   4   5   6   7   8   9
  1   1
  2   2   4
  3   3   6   9
  4   4   8  12  16
  5   5  10  15  20  25
  6   6  12  18  24  30  36
  7   7  14  21  28  35  42  49
  8   8  16  24  32  40  48  56  64
  9   9  18  27  36  45  54  63  72  81
```

7. In the program of Figure 4.7, the following statements were used to find the smallest value of *Number* for which the sum $1 + 2 + \cdots + $ *Number* is greater than *Limit*:

```
Number := 0;
Sum := 0;
WHILE Sum <= Limit DO
   BEGIN
      Number := Number + 1;
      Sum := Sum + Number
   END {WHILE};
```

Now suppose that the while loop is replaced by a repeat-until loop:

```
Number := 0;
Sum := 0;
REPEAT
   Number := Number + 1;
   Sum := Sum + Number
UNTIL Sum > Limit;
```

Make two trace tables, one for each of these program segments, each of which displays the values of **Number** and **Sum** for the following values of **Limit**:
(a) 10   **(b)** 0   **(c)** −1

8. The number of digits in an integer can be found by counting how many times the absolute value of the integer must be divided by 10 before a quotient of 0 results. Write two program segments to count the digits in a given integer, one of which uses a posttest loop and another of which uses a pretest loop. Make trace tables for each program segment, assuming that the given integer is
(a) 1234   **(b)** −12   **(c)** 5   **(d)** 0
Which of the two versions seems more natural, and why?

9. Exercise 13 of Section 1.2 describes the method of repeated division for converting a nonnegative integer n from base 10 to another base b. Since this method requires at least one division by b to produce the digits in the base-b representation, a repeat-until loop is a natural repetition structure to use. Write a program to accept various integers and bases and display the digits of the base-b representation (in reverse order) for each integer. You may assume that each base is in the range 2 through 10.

10. Proceed as in Exercise 9 but convert integers from base 10 to hexadecimal (base 16). Use a **CASE** statement to display the symbols A, B, C, D, E, and F for 10, 11, 12, 13, 14, and 15, respectively.

11. Write a program that reads the amount of a loan, an annual interest rate, and a monthly payment and then displays in a table with appropriate headings the payment number, the interest for that month, the balance remaining after that payment, and the total interest paid to date. (The monthly interest is $R / 12$ percent of the unpaid balance after the payment is subtracted, where R is the annual interest rate.) Use a procedure to generate these tables. Design the program so it can process several different loan amounts, interest rates, and monthly payments, including at least the following triples of values: $100, 18 percent, $10 and $500, 12 percent, $25. (*Note:* In general, the last payment will not be the same as the monthly payment; the program should show the exact amount of the last payment due.)

12. Proceed as in Exercise 11, but with the following modifications: During program execution, have the user enter a payment amount and a day of the month on which this payment was made (see Exercise 1[d] of Section 7.1). The monthly interest is to be calculated on the *average daily balance* for that month. (Assume, for simplicity, that the billing date is the first of the month.)

For example, if the balance on June 1 is $500 and a payment of $20 is received on June 12, the interest will be computed on (500 ∗ 11 + 480 ∗ 19)/30 dollars, which represents the average daily balance for that month.

13. Suppose that on January 1, April 1, July 1, and October 1 of each year, some fixed *Amount* is invested and earns interest at some annual interest rate *R* compounded quarterly (that is, *R* / 4 percent is added at the end of each quarter). Write a program that reads a number of years and calculates and displays a table showing the year, the yearly dividend (total interest earned for that year), and the total savings accumulated through that year. Design the program to process several different inputs and to call a procedure to display the table for each input.

A *possible modification/addition to your program:* Instead of investing *Amount* dollars each quarter, invest *Amount* / 3 dollars on the first of each month. Then in each quarter, the first payment earns interest for three months (*R* / 4 percent), the second for two months (*R* / 6 percent), and the third for one month (*R* / 12 percent).

14. The proper divisors of an integer *n* are the positive divisors less than *n*. A positive integer is said to be a **deficient, perfect,** or **abundant** number if the sum of its proper divisors is less than, equal to, or greater than the number, respectively. For example, 8 is deficient because its proper divisors are 1, 2, and 4, and 1 + 2 + 4 < 8; 6 is perfect, because 1 + 2 + 3 = 6; 12 is abundant, because 1 + 2 + 3 + 4 + 6 > 12. Write a program that classifies *n* as being deficient, perfect, or abundant for *n* = 20 to 30, then for *n* = 490 to 500, and finally for *n* = 8120 to 8130. *Extra:* Find the smallest odd abundant number. *Warning:* An attempt to find an odd perfect number will probably fail because none has yet been found, but it has not been proved that such numbers do not exist.

15. **(a)** Develop an algorithm for the third method of calculating depreciation (double-declining balance combined with straight-line), described in Example 1 of this section.
    (b) Modify the program in Figure 7.5 so that it includes this third method of calculating depreciation as one of the options. Also modify the output so that the year numbers in all of the depreciation tables begin with the current year rather than with year number 1.

Simulation Exercises

16. A coin is tossed repeatedly, and a payoff of 2^n dollars is made, where *n* is the number of the toss on which the first head appears. For example, TTH pays $8, TH pays $4, and H pays $2. Write a program to simulate playing the game several times and to print the average payoff for these games.

17. Suppose that a gambler places a wager of $5 on the following game: A pair of dice is tossed, and if the result is odd, the gambler loses his wager. If the result is even, a card is drawn from a standard deck of fifty-two playing cards. If the card drawn is an ace, 3, 5, 7, or 9, the gambler wins the value of the card (with

aces counting as 1); otherwise, he loses. What will be the average winnings for this game? Write a program to simulate the game.

18. Johann VanDerDoe, centerfielder for the Klavin Klodhoppers, has the following lifetime hitting percentages:

Out	63.4%
Walk	10.3%
Single	19.0%
Double	4.9%
Triple	1.1%
Home run	1.3%

Write a program to simulate a large number of times at bat for Johann, for example, 1000, counting the number of outs, walks, singles, and so on, and calculating his

$$\text{batting average} = \frac{\text{number of hits}}{\text{number of times at bat} - \text{number of walks}}$$

19. The classic **drunkard's walk problem** is as follows: Over an 8-block line, the home of an intoxicated chap is at block 8, and a pub is at block 1. Our poor friend starts at block n, $1 < n < 8$, and wanders at random, one block at a time, either toward or away from home. At any intersection, he moves toward the pub with a certain probability, say 2/3, and toward home with a certain probability, say 1/3. Having gotten either home or to the pub, he remains there. Write a program to simulate 500 trips in which he starts at block 2, another 500 in which he starts at block 3, and so forth up to block 7. For each starting point, calculate and print the percentage of time he ends up at home and the average number of blocks he walked on each trip.

20. A slab of material is used to shield a nuclear reactor, and a particle entering the shield follows a random path by moving forward, backward, left, or right with equal likelihood, in jumps of one unit. A change of direction is interpreted as a collision with an atom in this shield. Suppose that after 10 such collisions, the particle's energy is dissipated and it dies within the shield, provided that it has not already passed back inside the reactor or outside through the shield. Write a program to simulate particles entering this shield and determine what percentage of them reaches the outside.

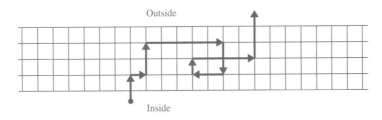

21. Consider a quarter circle inscribed in a square whose sides have length 1:

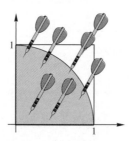

Imagine throwing q darts at this square and counting the total number p that hit within the quarter circle. For a large number of throws, we would expect

$$\frac{p}{q} \sim \frac{\text{area of quarter circle}}{\text{area of square}} = \frac{\pi}{4}$$

Write a program to approximate π using this method. To simulate throwing the darts, generate two random numbers X and Y and consider point (X, Y) as being where the dart hits.

22. The famous **Buffon Needle problem** is as follows: A board is ruled with equidistant parallel lines, and a needle of length equal to the distance between these lines is dropped at random on the board. Write a program to simulate this experiment and estimate the probability p that the needle crosses one of these lines. Display the values of p and $2 / p$. (The value of $2 / p$ should be approximately equal to a well-known constant. What constant is it?)

7.5   PART OF THE PICTURE: Numeric Computation

Mathematical models are used to solve problems in a wide variety of areas, including science, engineering, business, and the social sciences. Many of these models consist of ordinary algebraic equations, differential equations, systems of equations, and so on, and the solution of the problem is obtained by finding solutions of these equations. Methods for solving such equations that can be implemented in a computer program are called **numerical methods,** and the development and analysis of such numerical methods is an important area of study in computer science.

Some of the major types of problems in which numerical methods are routinely used include

1. *Curve fitting.* In many applications, the solution of a problem often requires analyzing data consisting of pairs of values to determine whether the items in these pairs are related. For example, a sociologist might wish to determine whether there is a linear relationship between educational level and income level.
2. *Solving equations.* Such problems deal with finding the value of a variable that satisfies a given equation.

3. *Integration.* The solution of many problems such as finding area under a curve, determining total revenue generated by sales of an item, calculating probabilities of certain events, and calculating work done by a force require the evaluation of an integral. Often these integrals can be evaluated only by using numerical techniques.

4. *Differential equations.* Differential equations involve one or more derivatives of functions and play an important role in many different applications. Several effective and efficient numerical methods for solving these equations have been developed.

5. *Solving linear systems.* Linear systems consist of several equations, each of which has several unknowns. A solution of such a system is a collection of values for these unknowns that satisfies all of the equations simultaneously.

In this section, we consider simple numerical methods for three of these areas: curve fitting, solving equations, and integration. The numerical methods for all of these problems involve iteration: For curve fitting, several sums of data values must be calculated; for equation solving, a sequence of approximations to the solution is generated; for integration, the sum of a sequence of numbers must be calculated. Numerical methods for solving differential equations are described in the exercises, and numerical methods for solving linear systems will be considered in Chapter 11.

1. Curve Fitting: Least Squares Line

Suppose the following table contains a small part of the data collected in a survey designed to determine what relationship (if any) exists between the annual income of a student's parents and the composite score earned by the student on a series of college entrance exams:

Income ($ thousands)	Composite Score
20.0	761
31.5	817
50.0	874
71.8	917
91.3	1018

The plot of this data in Figure 7.8 indicates a linear relationship between income and score. We wish to find the equation of the line that "best fits" this data.

In general, whenever the relation between two quantities x and y appears to be roughly linear, that is, when a plot of the points (x, y) indicates that they tend to fall along a straight line, one can ask for the equation

$$y = mx + b$$

of a best-fitting line for these points. This equation (called a **regression equation**) can then be used to predict the value of y by evaluating the equation for a given value of x.

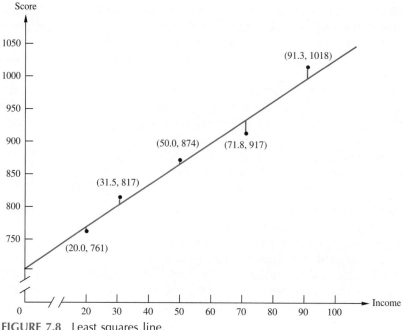

FIGURE 7.8   Least squares line.

A standard method for finding the **regression coefficients** m and b is the **method of least squares,** so named because it produces the line $y = mx + b$, for which the sum of the squares of the deviations of the observed y values from the predicted y values (using the equation) is as small as possible (see Figure 7.8); that is, values of m and b are found to minimize the sum

$$\sum_{i=1}^{n} [y_i - (mx_i + b)]^2 =$$

$$[y_1 - (mx_1 + b)]^2 + [y_2 - (mx_2 + b)]^2 + \ldots + [y_n - (mx_n + b)]^2$$

Using the methods of calculus for minimizing a function of two variables, one obtains the following formulas for the slope m and the y intercept b:

$$\text{slope} = m = \frac{(\Sigma xy) - (\Sigma x)\bar{y}}{(\Sigma x^2) - (\Sigma x)\bar{x}}$$

$$y \text{ intercept} = b = \bar{y} - m\bar{x}$$

where Σx is the sum of the x values.
          Σx^2 is the sum of the squares of the x values.
          Σxy is the sum of the products xy of corresponding x and y values.
          $\bar{x}$ and $\bar{y}$ are the means of the x and y values, respectively.

The program in Figure 7.9 uses these formulas to find the equation of the least squares line for a given set of data points. Note that in this program a sentinel-controlled while loop is used to read the data values and to calculate the necessary sums. It implements the following algorithm:

ALGORITHM FOR LEAST SQUARES LINE

(* Input: A collection of data points (x, y).

   Function: Find the equation of the least squares line for a set of n data points (x, y). *Slope* is its slope, and *YIntercept* is its y intercept. *SumX, SumY, SumX2,* and *SumXY* are the sums of the xs, the ys, the squares of the xs, and the products $x * y$, respectively. *XMean* and *YMean* are the means of the xs and the ys, respectively.

   Output: The equation of the least squares line. *)

1. Initialize n, *SumX, SumY, SumX2,* and *SumXY* all to 0.
2. Read the first data point x, y.
3. While x is not the end-of-data sentinel, do the following:
   a. Increment n by 1.
   b. Add x to *SumX*.
   c. Add x^2 to *SumX2*.
   d. Add y to *SumY*.
   e. Add $x * y$ to *SumXY*.
   f. Read the next data point x, y.
4. If $n > 0$ then
   a. Calculate

$$XMean = \frac{SumX}{n}$$

   and

$$YMean = \frac{SumY}{n}$$

   b. Calculate

$$Slope = \frac{SumXY - SumX * YMean}{SumX2 - SumX * XMean}$$

   and

$$YIntercept = YMean - Slope * XMean$$

   c. Display *Slope* and *YIntercept*.
   Else
   Display a message that no data points were read.

FIGURE 7.9 Least squares line.

```
PROGRAM LeastSquaresLine( input, output );
{******************************************************************

    Input (keyboard): A set of data points.
    Purpose:          Find the equation of the least squares line
                      for the set of data points.
    Output (screen):  User prompts and equation of least squares line.

*******************************************************************}

CONST
    Sentinel = -9999;   {data sentinel}

VAR
    n : integer;        {number of data points}
    x, y,               {an observed data point}
    SumX,               {sum of the xs}
    SumY,               {sum of the ys}
    SumX2,              {sum of the squares of the xs}
    SumXY,              {sum of the products x*y}
    XMean,              {mean of the xs}
    YMean,              {mean of the ys}
    Slope,              {slope of the least squares line}
    YIntercept : real;  {y intercept of the line}

BEGIN
    {Initialize n and sums to 0}
    n := 0;
    SumX := 0;
    SumX2 := 0;
    SumY := 0;
    SumXY := 0;

    {Read and count the data points and accumulate the necessary sums}
    writeln( 'Enter ', Sentinel:1, ' for x and any value for y ',
             'to signal the end of data.' );
    writeln;
    write( 'Data point? ' );
    readln( x, y );
    WHILE x <> Sentinel DO
        BEGIN
            n := n + 1;
            SumX := SumX + x;
            SumY := SumY + Y;
            SumX2 := SumX2 + sqr(x);
            SumXY := SumXY + x * y;
            write( 'Data point? ' );
            readln( x, y );
        END {WHILE};
```

FIGURE 7.9 Least squares line. (cont.)

```
{Find equation of least squares line,
 unless no data points were entered}
writeln;
IF n > 0 THEN
   BEGIN
      XMean := SumX / n;
      YMean := SumY / n;
      Slope := (SumXY - SumX * YMean) / (SumX2 - SumX * XMean);
      YIntercept := YMean - Slope * XMean ;
      writeln( 'Equation of least squares line is y = mx + b, where');
      writeln( 'Slope = m = ', Slope:8:4 );
      writeln( 'Y intercept = b = ', YIntercept:8:4 )
   END {IF}
ELSE
   writeln( 'No data points were entered' )
END.
```

Sample run:

```
Enter -9999 for x and any value for y to signal the end of data.

Data point? 20     761
Data point? 31.5   817
Data point? 50     874
Data point? 71.8   917
Data point? 91.3   1018
Data point? -9999 0

Equation of least squares line is y = mx + b, where
Slope = m =    3.3366
Y intercept = b = 700.8283
```

2. Solving Equations

In many applications, it is necessary to solve an equation of the form

$$f(x) = 0$$

For some functions f, it may be very difficult or even impossible to find an exact solution. Examples include the equation

$$50 \cdot 10^{-9}(e^{40v} - 1) + v - 20 = 0$$

which may arise in a problem of determining the dc operating point in an electrical circuit, or the equation

$$A - P\frac{(1 + r)^n - 1}{r(1 + r)^n} = 0$$

which can be solved to find the monthly interest rate r for a loan amount A, where P is the payment to be made for a period of n months.

For such equations, an iterative numerical method is used to find an approximate solution. One method that may be used is called the **bisection method.** In this method, one begins with two numbers a and b where the function values $f(a)$ and $f(b)$ have opposite signs. If f is continuous between $x = a$ and $x = b$—that is, if there is no break in the graph of $y = f(x)$ between these two values—then the graph of f must cross the x axis at least once between $x = a$ and $x = b$, and thus there must be at least one solution of the equation $f(x) = 0$ between a and b. To locate one of these solutions, we first bisect the interval $[a, b]$ and determine in which half f changes sign, thereby locating a smaller subinterval containing a solution of the equation. We bisect this subinterval and determine in which half of it f changes sign; this gives a still smaller subinterval containing a solution.

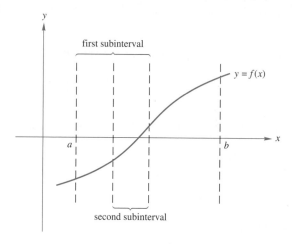

Repeating this process gives a sequence of subintervals, each of which contains a solution of the equation and has a length one-half that of the preceding interval. Note that at each step, the midpoint of a subinterval of length L is within $L/2$ of the exact solution:

The program in Figure 7.10 uses the bisection method to find an approximate solution of

$$f(x) = x^3 + x - 5 = 0$$

It begins with a repeat-until loop that asks the user to enter values of **a** and **b** for which **f(a)** and **f(b)** have opposite signs, terminating when such values are entered. It then generates and displays successive approximations to a solution using the bisection method, terminating when **L/2** is less than **DesiredAccuracy**, where **L** is the length of the subinterval containing a solution and **DesiredAccuracy** is a value entered by the user to specify how accurate the approximation should be. The midpoint of this subinterval is the approximate solution of the equation.

FIGURE 7.10 Bisection method.

```pascal
PROGRAM Bisection( input, output );
{*****************************************************************

    Input (keyboard): Desired accuracy of approximation, endpoints of
                      an interval containing a solution.
    Purpose:          Find an approximate solution of the equation
                                   f(x) = 0
                      in the given interval, using the bisection
                      method.  The approximate solution is to be within
                      DesiredAccuracy of the exact solution.
    Output (screen):  Prompts to the user and the approximate solution.


*****************************************************************}

VAR
    Left, Right,            {endpoints of current subinterval}
    MidPt,                  {midpoint of [Left, Right]}
    fMid,                   {value of f at MidPt}
    Len,                    {length of [Left, Right]}
    DesiredAccuracy : real; {accuracy desired}

FUNCTION f( x : real ) : real;
{--------------------------------------------------------------

    Accepts:  Real number x.
    Purpose:  Returns value of function at x; f is the function
              for which a solution of f(x) = 0 is being found.
    Returns:  Value of f at x.

--------------------------------------------------------------}

    BEGIN
        f := x*x*x + x - 5
    END {f};

BEGIN {*************** main program ****************}
    {Get interval containing solution and the
     desired accuracy for the approximate solution}
    REPEAT
        write( 'Enter endpoints of interval containing a solution: ' );
        readln( Left, Right )
    UNTIL f(Left) * f(Right) < 0;
    writeln;
    write( 'Enter desired accuracy for approximate solution: ' );
    readln( DesiredAccuracy );
    Len := Right - Left;
```

FIGURE 7.10 Bisection method. (cont.)

```
{ Iterate using bisection method while
  Len/2 is greater than Desired Accuracy. }

WHILE Len / 2 > DesiredAccuracy DO
   BEGIN
      MidPt := (Left + Right) / 2;
      fMid := f(MidPt);
      IF f(Left) * fMid < 0 THEN   {solution in left half}
         Right := MidPt
      ELSE                         {solution in right half}
         Left := MidPt;
      Len := Len / 2
   END {WHILE};
writeln;
writeln( MidPt:9:6, ' is an approximate solution of f(x) = 0 ',
         'to within ',  DesiredAccuracy:12 )
END {main program}.
```

Sample run:

```
Enter endpoints of interval containing a solution: 0 1
Enter endpoints of interval containing a solution: 1 2

Enter desired accuracy for approximate solution: 1E-4

 1.515991 is an approximate solution of f(x) = 0 to within  1.00000E-04
```

3. Numerical Integration

One problem in which numerical methods are often used is that of approximating an integral:

$$\int_a^b f(x)\,dx$$

For a nonnegative function f, this integral gives the area of the region bounded by the graph of $y = f(x)$, the x axis, and the vertical lines $x = a$ and $x = b$:

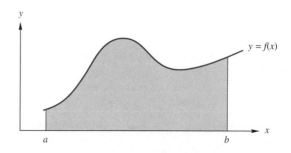

One simple method of approximating this area, called the *rectangle method,* is to divide the interval $[a, b]$ into n subintervals, each of length $\Delta x = (b - a) / n$, and then to form rectangles having these subintervals as bases and with altitudes given by the values of the function at the midpoints (or left or right endpoints) x_1, $x_2, \ldots, x_n$ of the subintervals. This is illustrated by the following diagram:

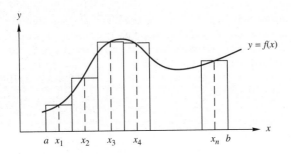

The sum of the areas of these rectangles

$$f(x_1)\Delta x + f(x_2)\Delta x + \cdots + f(x_n)\Delta x$$

which is the same as

$$[f(x_1) + f(x_2) + \cdots + f(x_n)]\Delta x$$

or, written more concisely using Σ (sigma) notation,

$$\left[\sum_{i=1}^{n} f(x_i)\right] \Delta x$$

is then an approximation to the area under the curve.

The preceding figure shows this method for a curve lying above the x axis. It may also be used to approximate the integral of a function whose graph falls below the x axis. In this case, the integral does not give the total area between the curve and the axis but, rather, gives the area of the region(s) above the axis minus the area of the region(s) below the axis.

The program in Figure 7.11 uses this rectangle method to approximate the area under the graph of $y = x^2 + 1$ from $x = a$ to $x = b$. The endpoints a and b of the interval of integration and the number n of subintervals are read during execution.

FIGURE 7.11 Numerical integration.

```
PROGRAM Integrate( input, output );
{*****************************************************************

    Input (keyboard): Interval endpoints a and b and the number n of
                      subintervals.
    Purpose:          Approximate the integral of a function f from
                      x = a to x = b using the rectangle method with
                      altitudes chosen at the midpoints of the
                      subintervals.
    Output (screen):  Prompts to the user and approximate values of
                      the integral.


*****************************************************************}

VAR
    a, b,                  {endpoints of interval}
    x,                     {the midpoint of one of the subintervals}
    Deltax,                {the length of the subintervals}
    Sum : real;            {the approximating sum}
    n,                     {number of subintervals used}
    i : integer;           {counter}
    Response : char;       {user response}

FUNCTION f( x : real ) : real;
{-------------------------------------------------------------------

    Accepts:  Real number x.
    Purpose:  This is the integrand, the function for which the
              integral is being approximated.
    Returns:  The value of the function at x.


-------------------------------------------------------------------}

    BEGIN
        f := x * x + 1
    END {f};
```

FIGURE 7.11 Numerical integration. (cont.)

```
BEGIN {*************** main program ****************}
   REPEAT
      write( 'Enter interval endpoints: ' );
      readln( a, b );
      REPEAT
         write( 'Enter number of subintervals: ' );
         readln( n );
         Deltax := (b - a) / n;
         Sum := 0;
         x := a + Deltax / 2;
         FOR i := 1 TO n DO
            BEGIN
               Sum := Sum + f(x);
               x := x + Deltax
            END {FOR};
         Sum := Deltax * Sum;
         writeln( 'Approximate area using ', n:1,
                  ' subintervals is ', Sum:8:4 );
         write( 'Different number of subintervals (Y or N)? ' );
         readln( Response )
      UNTIL (Response = 'N') OR (Response = 'n');
      writeln;
      write( 'Change the interval (Y or N)? ' );
      readln( Response )
   UNTIL (Response = 'N') OR (Response = 'n')
END {main program}.
```

Sample run:

```
Enter interval endpoints: 0 1
Enter number of subintervals: 20
Approximate area using 20 subintervals is    1.3331
Different number of subintervals (Y or N)? Y
Enter number of subintervals: 100
Approximate area using 100 subintervals is    1.3333
Different number of subintervals (Y or N)? N

Change the interval (Y or N)? Y
Enter interval endpoints: -1 2
Enter number of subintervals: 10
Approximate area using 10 subintervals is    5.9775
Different number of subintervals (Y or N)? Y
Enter number of subintervals: 20
Approximate area using 20 subintervals is    5.9944
Different number of subintervals (Y or N)? Y
Enter number of subintervals: 50
Approximate area using 50 subintervals is    5.9991
Different number of subintervals (Y or N)? N

Change the interval (Y or N)? N
```

Exercises

1. The infinite series

$$\sum_{k=0}^{\infty} \frac{1}{k!}$$

converges to the number e, whose approximate value is 2.71828. (See Exercise 5 of Section 7.4 for a definition of $k!$, the factorial of k.) The *n*th *partial sum* of such a series is the sum of the first *n* terms of the series; for example,

$$\frac{1}{0!} + \frac{1}{1!} + \frac{1}{2!} + \frac{1}{3!}$$

is the fourth partial sum. Write a program to calculate and print the first 10 partial sums of this series.

2. In this section we considered the problem of fitting a line to a set of data points. In some situations, a better fit is obtained by using an exponential function

$$y = ae^{bx}$$

One common method for determining the constants a and b is to take logarithms of both sides of the exponential equation to obtain

$$\ln y = \ln a + bx$$

and then use the method of least squares to find values of the constants b and $\ln a$. Write a program that uses this method to fit an exponential curve to a set of data points. Run it for the values in the following table, which gives barometric pressure readings, in millimeters of mercury, at various altitudes:

Altitude (meters) x	Barometric Pressure (millimeters) y
0	760
500	714
1000	673
1500	631
2000	594
2500	563

3. Related to the least squares method is the problem of determining whether there is a linear relationship between two quantities x and y. One statistical measure used in this connection is the *correlation coefficient*. It is equal to 1 if there is a perfect positive linear relationship between x and y, that is, if y increases linearly as x increases. If there is a perfect negative linear relationship between x and y, that is, if y decreases linearly as x increases, then the correlation coefficient has the value -1. A value of zero for the correlation coefficient indicates that there is no linear relationship between x and y, and

nonzero values between -1 and 1 indicate a partial linear relationship between the two quantities. The correlation coefficient for a set of n pairs of x and y values is calculated by

$$\frac{n(\Sigma xy) - (\Sigma x)(\Sigma y)}{\sqrt{(n\Sigma x^2 - (\Sigma x)^2)(n\Sigma y^2 - (\Sigma y)^2)}}$$

where Σx is the sum of the x values.
            Σy is the sum of the y values.
            Σx^2 is the sum of the squares of the x values.
            Σy^2 is the sum of the squares of the y values.
            Σxy is the sum of the products xy of corresponding x and y values.

Write a program to calculate the correlation coefficient of a set of data points. Run it for the data points used in the sample run in Figure 7.9 and for several data sets of your own.

4. Another method for finding an approximate solution of an equation $f(x) = 0$ is **Newton's method.** This method consists of taking an initial approximation x_1 to the solution and constructing the tangent line to the graph of f at point $P_1(x_1, f(x_1))$. The point x_2 at which this tangent line crosses the x axis is the second approximation to the solution. Another tangent line may be constructed at point $P_2(x_2, f(x_2))$, and the point x_3 where this tangent line crosses the x axis is the third approximation. For many functions, this sequence of approximations $x_1, x_2, x_3, \ldots$ converges to the solution, provided that the first approximation is sufficiently close to the solution. The following diagram illustrates Newton's method:

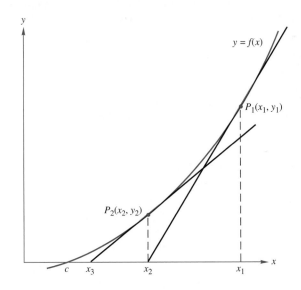

If x_n is an approximation to the solution of $f(x) = 0$, then the formula for obtaining the next approximation x_{n+1} by Newton's method is

$$x_{n+1} = x_n - \frac{f(x_n)}{f'(x_n)}$$

where f' is the derivative of f. Note that Newton's method will fail if $f'(x_n)$ is 0 at some approximation x_n. Write a program to find an approximate solution of an equation $f(x) = 0$ using Newton's method. The process should terminate when the difference $|x_{n+1} - x_n|$ between two successive approximations is sufficiently small or when the number of iterations exceeds some upper limit. Display the sequence of successive approximations.

5. The Cawker City Cookie Company can purchase a new microcomputer for $4440, or by paying $141.19 per month for the next 36 months. You are to determine what annual interest rate is being charged in the monthly payment plan.

The equation that governs this calculation is the *annuity formula*

$$A = P \cdot \left(\frac{(1 + R)^N - 1}{R(1 + R)^N} \right)$$

where A is the amount borrowed, P is the monthly payment, R is the monthly interest rate (annual rate/12), and N is the number of payments. In this problem, this equation is to be solved for R. Write a program that uses the bisection method or Newton's method (see Exercise 4) to find an approximate solution of the equation

$$A - P \cdot \left(\frac{(1 + x)^N - 1}{x(1 + x)^N} \right) = 0$$

6. In this section we considered the numerical approximation of integrals using rectangles. As the following figure indicates, a better approximation can usually be obtained by using trapezoids rather than rectangles:

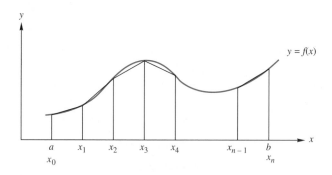

The sum of the areas of these trapezoids is given by

$$\sum_{i=1}^{n} [f(x_{i-1}) + f(x_i)] \frac{\Delta x}{2}$$

which can also be written

$$\frac{\Delta x}{2} [f(x_0) + 2f(x_1) + 2f(x_2) + \cdots + 2f(x_{n-1}) + f(x_n)]$$

or

$$\Delta x \left[\frac{f(a) + f(b)}{2} + \sum_{i=1}^{n-1} f(x_i) \right]$$

Write a program to approximate an integral using this *trapezoidal method.*

7. Another method of numerical integration that generally produces better approximations than does the rectangle method described in this section or the trapezoidal method described in Exercise 6 is based on the use of parabolas and is known as *Simpson's rule.* In this method, the interval [a, b] is divided into an even number *n* of subintervals, each of length Δx, and the sum

$$\frac{\Delta x}{3} [f(x_0) + 4f(x_1) + 2f(x_2) + 4f(x_3)$$

$$+ 2(f(x_4) + \cdots + 2f(x_{n-2}) + 4f(x_{n-1}) + f(x_n)]$$

is used to approximate the integral of *f* over the interval [a, b]. Write a program to approximate an integral using Simpson's rule.

8. A method of approximating π by throwing darts at a quarter circle inscribed in a square was described in Exercise 21 of Section 7.4. This method can be generalized to find the area under the graph of any function and is known as a *Monte Carlo* method of approximating integrals. To illustrate it, consider a rectangle that has base [a, b] and height *m*, where $m \geq f(x)$ for all *x* in [a, b]:

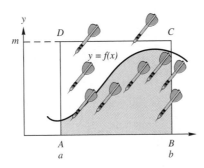

Imagine throwing *q* darts at rectangle *ABCD* and counting the total number *p* that hit the shaded region. For a large number of throws, we would expect

$$\frac{p}{q} \sim \frac{\text{area of shaded region}}{\text{area of rectangle } ABCD}$$

Write a program to calculate areas using this Monte Carlo method. To simulate throwing the darts, generate two random numbers, *X* from [a, b] and *Y* from [0, m], and consider point (*X*, *Y*) as being where the dart hits.

9. Consider a first-order differential equation

$$y' = f(x, y)$$

satisfying the initial condition

$$y(x_0) = y_0$$

One method of obtaining an approximate solution over some interval $[a, b]$ where $a = x_0$, known as **Euler's method,** is as follows:

1. Select an x increment Δx.
2. For $n = 0, 1, 2, \ldots$, do the following:
   a. Set $x_{n+1} = x_n + \Delta x$.
   b. Find the point $P_{n+1}(x_{n+1}, y_{n+1})$ on the line through $P_n(x_n, y_n)$ with slope $f(x_n, y_n)$:

   $$y_{n+1} = y_n + f(x_n, y_n)\,\Delta x$$

   c. Display y_{n+1}, which is the approximate value of y at x_{n+1}.

The following diagram illustrates:

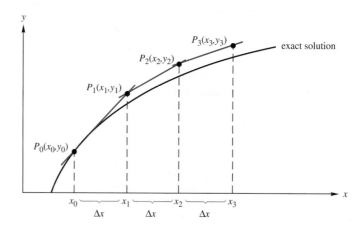

Write a program that uses Euler's method to obtain an approximate solution for

$$y' = 2xy$$
$$y(0) = 1$$

Execute the program with $a = 0$, $b = .5$, $\Delta x = .2$, and then with $a = 0$, $b = .5$, $\Delta x = .05$. Compare the results with those obtained using the exact solution $y = e^{x^2}$.

10. One of the most popular and most accurate numerical methods for solving a first-order differential equation (see Exercise 9) is the following **Runge–Kutta method:**

   1. Select an x increment Δx.
   2. The approximate solution y_{n+1} at $x_{n+1} = x_0 + (n + 1)\Delta x$ for $n = 0, 1, 2, \ldots$, is given by

   $$y_{n+1} = y_n + \frac{1}{6}(K_1 + 2K_2 + 2K_3 + K_4)$$

where $K_1 = \Delta x \cdot f(x_n, y_n)$

$$K_2 = \Delta x \cdot f\left(x_n + \frac{\Delta x}{2}, y_n + \frac{K_1}{2}\right)$$

$$K_3 = \Delta x \cdot f\left(x_n + \frac{\Delta x}{2}, y_n + \frac{K_2}{2}\right)$$

$$K_4 = \Delta x \cdot f(x_n + \Delta x, y_n + K_3)$$

Write a program to implement this Runge–Kutta method to obtain an approximate solution of the differential equation given in Exercise 9.

7.6 Introduction to Recursion

When a procedure or function is referenced, execution of the calling program unit is interrupted, and execution of the subprogram begins. Then, when execution of the subprogram is completed, execution of the calling program unit is resumed. Its "execution environment" is restored to what it was before execution was interrupted. This restoration is possible because the values of all local variables, constants, parameters, and all other items that make up the execution environment are stored before execution of the subprogram begins. When execution of the subprogram is completed, these values can be retrieved, the execution environment of the calling program unit can be re-created, and execution can be resumed at the point at which it was interrupted. Thus subprogram references can be viewed as a control mechanism that interrupts execution of the calling program unit, saves the execution environment, initiates execution of the subprogram, and, upon completion of the subprogram, restores the execution environment of the calling program unit and resumes its execution.

All of the examples of function and procedure references considered thus far have involved a main program referencing a subprogram or one subprogram referencing another subprogram. In fact, a procedure or function may even reference itself, a phenomenon known as **recursion,** and in this section, we show how recursion is implemented in Pascal.

To illustrate the basic idea of recursion, we consider the problem of calculating the factorial function. The first definition of the factorial $n!$ of a nonnegative integer n that one usually learns is

$$n! = 1 \times 2 \times \cdots \times n, \text{ for } n > 0$$

and that $0!$ is 1. In calculating a sequence of consecutive factorials, however, it would be foolish to calculate each one using this definition, that is, to multiply together the numbers from 1 through n each time; for example,

$$0! = 1$$
$$1! = 1$$
$$2! = 1 \times 2 = 2$$
$$3! = 1 \times 2 \times 3 = 6$$
$$4! = 1 \times 2 \times 3 \times 4 = 24$$
$$5! = 1 \times 2 \times 3 \times 4 \times 5 = 120$$

.

.

.

It is clear that once one factorial has been calculated, it can be used to calculate the next one; for example, given the value 4! = 24, we can use this value to calculate 5! simply by multiplying the value of 4! by 5:

$$5! = 4! \times 5 = 24 \times 5 = 120$$

and this value can then be used to calculate 6!:

$$6! = 5! \times 6 = 120 \times 6 = 720$$

and so on. Indeed, to calculate $n!$ for any positive integer n, we need only know the value of 0!,

$$0! = 1$$

and the fundamental relation between one factorial and the next:

$$n! = n \times (n - 1)!$$

This approach to calculating factorials leads to the following recursive definition of $n!$:

$$0! = 1$$
$$\text{For } n > 0, \; n! = n \times (n - 1)!$$

Another classic example of a function that can be calculated recursively is the power function that calculates x^n, where x is a real value and n is a nonnegative integer. The first definition of x^n that one learns is usually an iterative (nonrecursive) one:

$$x^n = \underbrace{x \times x \times \cdots \times x}_{n \; x\text{'s}}$$

and later one learns that x^0 is defined to be 1. (For convenience, we assume here that x^0 is 1 also when x is 0, although in this case, it is usually left undefined.)

In calculating a sequence of consecutive powers of some number, however, it would again be foolish to calculate each one using this definition, that is, to multiply the number by itself the required number of times; for example,

$$3.0^0 = 1$$
$$3.0^1 = 3.0$$
$$3.0^2 = 3.0 \times 3.0 = 9.0$$
$$3.0^3 = 3.0 \times 3.0 \times 3.0 = 27.0$$
$$3.0^4 = 3.0 \times 3.0 \times 3.0 \times 3.0 = 81.0$$
$$3.0^5 = 3.0 \times 3.0 \times 3.0 \times 3.0 \times 3.0 = 243.0$$

.

.

.

Once again, the value of this function for a given integer can be used to calculate the value of the function for the next integer. For example, to calculate 3.0^4, we can simply multiply the value of 3.0^3 by 3.0:

$$3.0^4 = 3.0 \times 3.0^3 = 3.0 \times 27.0 = 81.0$$

Similarly, we can use the value of 3.0^4 to calculate 3.0^5:

$$3.0^5 = 3.0 \times 3.0^4 = 3.0 \times 81.0 = 243.0$$

and so on. We need only know the value of 3.0^0,

$$3.0^0 = 1$$

and the fundamental relation between one power of 3.0 and the next:

$$3.0^n = 3.0 \times 3.0^{n-1}$$

This suggests the following recursive definition of x^n:

$$x^0 = 1$$
$$\text{For } n > 0, \ x^n = x \times x^{n-1}$$

In general, a function is said to be **defined recursively** if its definition consists of two parts:

1. An **anchor** or **base case,** in which the value of the function is specified for one or more values of the parameter(s).
2. An **inductive** or **recursive step,** in which the function's value for the current values of the parameter(s) is defined in terms of previously defined function value(s) and parameter values.

We have seen two examples of such recursive definitions of functions, the factorial function

$$0! = 1 \qquad \qquad \text{(the anchor or base case)}$$
$$\text{For } n > 0, \ n! = n \times (n-1)! \qquad \text{(the inductive or recursive step)}$$

and the power function

$$x^0 = 1 \qquad \qquad \text{(the anchor or base case)}$$
$$\text{For } n > 0, \ x^n = x \times x^{n-1} \qquad \text{(the inductive or recursive step)}$$

In each definition, the first statement specifies a particular value of the function, and the second statement defines its value for n in terms of its value for $n - 1$.

As we noted in these examples, such recursive definitions are useful in calculating function values $f(n)$ for a sequence of consecutive values of n. Using them to calculate any one particular value, however, requires computing earlier values. For example, consider using the recursive definition of the factorial function to calculate 5!. We must first calculate 4! because 5! is defined as the product of 5 and 4!. But to calculate 4! we must calculate 3! because 4! is defined as $4 \times 3!$. And to calculate 3!, we must apply the inductive step of the definition again, $3! = 3 \times 2!$, then again to find 2!, which is defined as $2! = 2 \times 1!$, and once again to find $1! = 1 \times 0!$. Now we have finally reached the anchor case:

$$5! = 5 \times 4!$$
$$\downarrow$$
$$4! = 4 \times 3!$$
$$\downarrow$$
$$3! = 3 \times 2!$$
$$\downarrow$$
$$2! = 2 \times 1!$$
$$\downarrow$$
$$1! = 1 \times 0!$$
$$\downarrow$$
$$0! = 1$$

Since the value of 0! is given, we can now backtrack to find the value of 1!,

$$5! = 5 \times 4!$$
$$\downarrow$$
$$4! = 4 \times 3!$$
$$\downarrow$$
$$3! = 3 \times 2!$$
$$\downarrow$$
$$2! = 2 \times 1!$$
$$\downarrow$$
$$1! = 1 \times 0! = 1 \times 1 = 1$$
$$\downarrow \nearrow$$
$$0! = 1$$

then backtrack again to find the value of 2!,

$$5! = 5 \times 4!$$
$$\downarrow$$
$$4! = 4 \times 3!$$
$$\downarrow$$
$$3! = 3 \times 2!$$
$$\downarrow$$
$$2! = 2 \times 1! = 2 \times 1 = 2$$
$$\downarrow \nwarrow$$
$$1! = 1 \times 0! = 1 \times 1 = 1$$
$$\downarrow \nearrow$$
$$0! = 1$$

and so on until we eventually obtain the value 120 for 5!

$$5! = 5 \times 4! = 5 \times 24 = 120$$
$$\downarrow \nwarrow$$
$$4! = 4 \times 3! = 4 \times 6 = 24$$
$$\downarrow \nwarrow$$
$$3! = 3 \times 2! = 3 \times 2 = 6$$
$$\downarrow \nwarrow$$
$$2! = 2 \times 1! = 2 \times 1 = 2$$
$$\downarrow \nwarrow$$
$$1! = 1 \times 0! = 1 \times 1 = 1$$
$$\downarrow \nearrow$$
$$0! = 1$$

As this example demonstrates, calculating function values by hand using recursive definitions may require considerable bookkeeping to record information at the various levels of the recursive evaluation so that after the anchor case is reached, this information can be used to backtrack from one level to the preceding one. Fortunately, most modern high-level languages, including Pascal, support recursive functions and procedures, and all of the necessary bookkeeping and backtracking is done automatically by the computer.

To illustrate, consider the factorial function again. The recursive definition of this function can be implemented as a recursive function in Pascal in a straightforward manner:

```
FUNCTION Factorial( n : integer ) : integer;
{--------------------------------------------------

   Accepts:    Nonnegative integer n.
   Purpose:    Compute n! recursively.
   Returns:    Factorial of n.


------------------------------------------------}

   BEGIN
      IF n = 0 THEN                          {anchor}
         Factorial := 1
      ELSE
         Factorial := n * Factorial( n - 1 ) {inductive step}
   END {Factorial};
```

When this function is referenced, the inductive step

```
   ELSE
      Factorial := n * Factorial( n - 1 )
```

causes the function to reference itself repeatedly, each time with a smaller parameter, until the anchor case

```
   IF n = 0 THEN
      Factorial := 1
```

is reached.

For example, consider the reference **Factorial(5)** to calculate 5!. Since the value of **n**, which is **5**, is not **0**, the inductive step generates another reference to **Factorial** with parameter **n - 1 = 4**. Before execution of the original function reference is suspended, the current value **5** of the parameter **n** is saved so that the value of **n** can be restored when execution resumes. This might be pictured as follows:

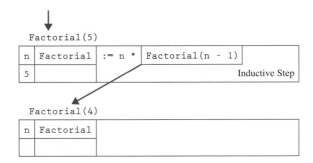

Since the value **4** of **n** in this function reference is not **0**, the inductive step in this second reference to **Factorial** generates another reference to **Factorial** with parameter **3**. Once again, the value **4** of **n** is saved so that it can be restored later:

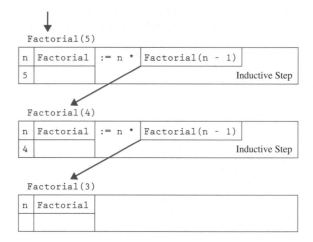

The inductive step in this function reference with parameter $n = 3$ generates another reference to **Factorial** with parameter **2**, which in turn generates another reference with parameter **1**, which in turn generates another reference with parameter **0**.

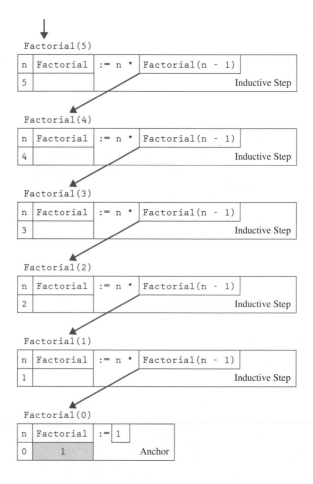

Because the anchor condition is now satisfied in this last function reference, no additional references are generated; instead the value 1 is assigned to **Factorial(0)**.

The function reference with parameter **0** is thus completed, and the value 1 is returned as the value for **Factorial(0)**. Execution of the preceding function is resumed. The value of the parameter **n** is restored, and the expression **n * Factorial(n - 1)** = 1 * **Factorial(0)** = 1 * 1 = 1 is calculated and returned as the value of **Factorial(1)**:

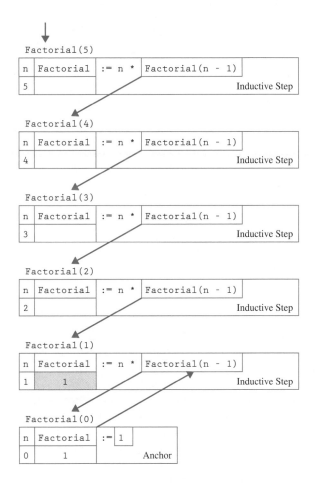

Execution of **Factorial** with parameter 1 is thus complete, and execution of the preceding reference is resumed. The value of **n** is restored, and the value of **n * Factorial(n - 1)** = 2 * **Factorial(1)** = 2 * 1 = 2 is calculated for **Factorial(2)**:

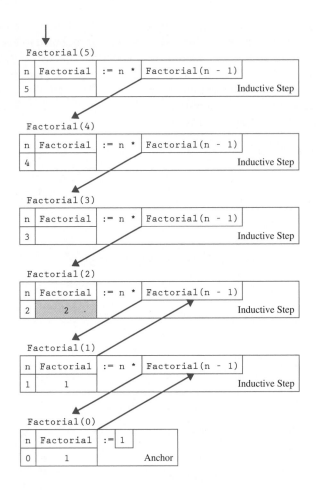

Execution of the preceding reference to **Factorial** is resumed; the value **3** of the parameter **n** is restored; and the expression **n * Factorial(n - 1)** = 3 * **Factorial(2)** = 3 * 2 = **6** is computed for **Factorial(3)**. This completes the reference to **Factorial** with parameter **3**, and execution of the preceding references resumes. The value **4** is restored to the parameter **n**, and the value **n * Factorial(n - 1)** = 4 * **Factorial(3)** = 4 * 6 = **24** is computed for **Factorial(4)**. Since this completes the function reference with parameter **4**, execution of the original function reference resumes. The value **5** is restored to the parameter **n**, and the value **n * Factorial(n - 1)** = 5 * **Factorial(4)** = 5 * 24 = **120** is computed for **Factorial(5)**:

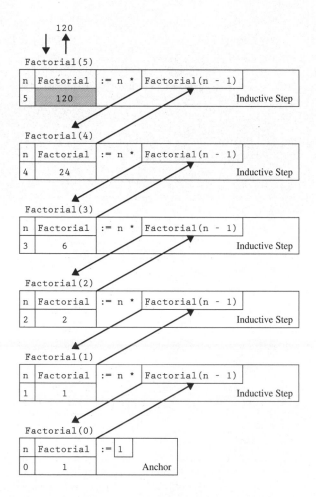

The value **120** is thus returned as the value for **Factorial(5)**.

As a second example of a recursive function, consider the exponentiation operation that we earlier defined recursively by

$x^0 = 1$ (anchor)

If $n > 0$, $x^n = x * x^{n-1}$ (inductive step)

Like the factorial function, this definition leads naturally to a recursive Pascal function:

```
FUNCTION Power( x : real; n : integer ) : real;
{--------------------------------------------------

    Accepts:  Real number x and integer n >= 0.
    Purpose:  Compute n-th power of x recursively.
    Returns:  n-th power of x.

------------------------------------------------}
```

```
BEGIN
   IF n = 0 THEN                                    {anchor}
      Power := 1
   ELSE
      Power := x * Power( x, n - 1 ) {inductive step}
END {Power};
```

The following diagram pictures the five levels of function references generated by
the initial reference **Power(3.0, 4)**:

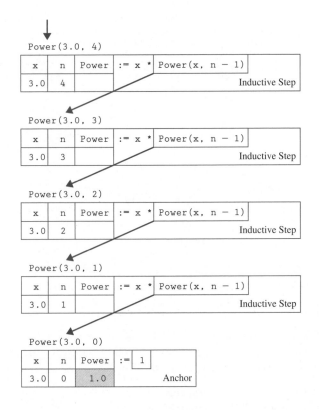

In the function reference with actual parameters **3.0** and **0**, the value **1.0** is
assigned to **Power**. The fifth function reference is thus completed; control returns
to the preceding reference; and the values **3.0** and **1** are restored to **x** and
n, respectively. This fourth reference is then completed by calculating **x** *
Power(x, n - 1) = **3.0** * **Power(3.0, 0)** = **3.0** * **1.0** = **3.0** as the value
of **Power(3.0, 1)**, and this value is returned to the previous function reference.
Eventually control returns to the original function reference; the values **3.0** and **4**
are restored to the parameters **x** and **n**, respectively; the expression **x** * **Power(x,
n - 1)** = **3.0** * **Power(3.0, 3)** = **3.0** * **27.0** = **81.0** is evaluated; and this
value **81.0** is returned as the value for the initial function reference **Power(3.0,
4)**. The following diagram summarizes:

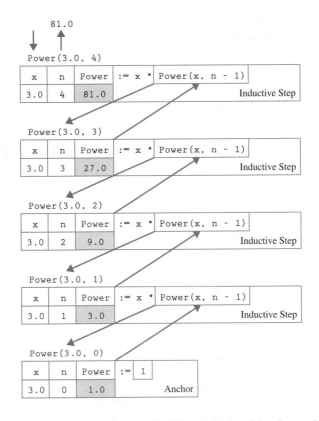

Procedures may also be recursive. To illustrate, consider the problem of printing the digits of a nonnegative integer in order from right to left. Although this problem can easily be solved without recursion (as the exercises ask you to do), it can also be solved by a recursive procedure.

The recursive approach to solving this problem is motivated by considering how the problem would be solved by hand. To write the digits of the number 6385 in reverse order, we first look at the last digit 5 and write it. Next we look to the left and consider the number formed by the remaining digits and process it *in exactly the same way* (inductive step). We continue in this way until we reach the left end of the number (anchor step). Viewed in this way, the processing is recursive and leads naturally to the following recursive procedure for solving this problem:

```
PROCEDURE PrintReverse( Number : integer );
{-----------------------------------------------------------

   Accepts:  An integer Number >= 0.
   Purpose:  Recursively display the digits of Number
             in reverse order .
   Output:   Reversal of Number.


------------------------------------------------------------}

   VAR
      LeftDigits : integer;   {leftmost digits of Number}
```

```
BEGIN
   write( Number MOD 10 : 1 );
   LeftDigits := Number DIV 10;
   IF LeftDigits = 0 THEN     {anchor}
      writeln
   ELSE                          {inductive step}
      PrintReverse( LeftDigits )
END {PrintReverse};
```

To show how this procedure carries out its processing, we will trace the execution of the procedure reference `PrintReverse(6285)`. The statement

```
write( Number MOD 10 :1 );
```

displays the rightmost digit, and the number that remains when this last digit is removed is calculated by the statement

```
LeftDigits := Number DIV 10;
```

Since the value of `LeftDigits` is not `0`, the inductive step generates a new procedure call with parameter `LeftDigits = 628`, as pictured in the following diagram:

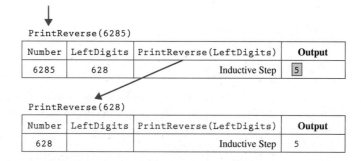

The new procedure reference with parameter `628`, displays the rightmost digit `8`, calculates `LeftDigits = 62`, and the inductive step generates another procedure reference with parameter `62`:

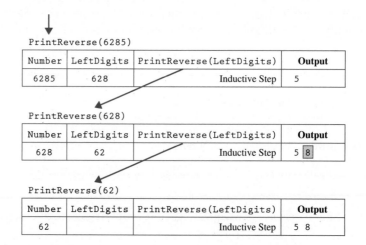

This reference displays the rightmost digit **2** and generates another procedure reference with parameter **LeftDigits** = **6**, and this reference displays the digit **6** and generates another reference with parameter **LeftDigits** = **0**:

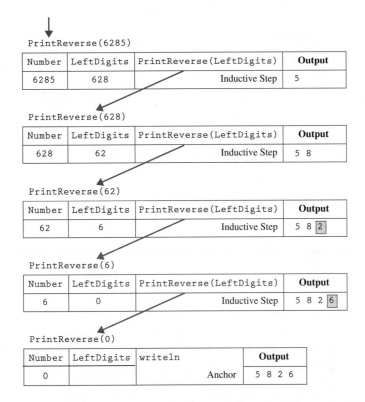

Since the anchor case has now been reached, this last procedure reference executes the **writeln** statement, which terminates output on the current line. Execution of the preceding reference to procedure **PrintReverse** is resumed. Since the procedure reference in the inductive step was at the end of the procedure, no additional processing is done, and control simply returns to the preceding reference. The earlier references to **PrintReverse** terminate in the same way. The following diagram summarizes this execution trace of **PrintReverse(6285)**:

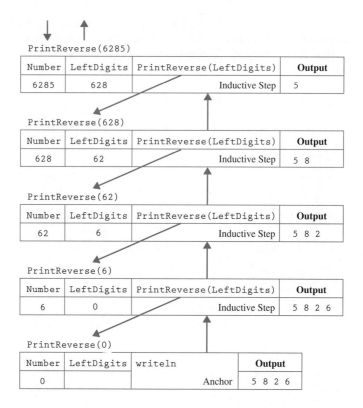

Many problems can be solved with equal ease using either a recursive or a nonrecursive algorithm. For example, the factorial and power functions were implemented in this section as recursive functions, but these functions can be written nonrecursively just as easily. Nonrecursive functions and procedures may execute more rapidly and utilize memory more efficiently than do the corresponding recursive subprograms. Thus, if an algorithm can be described either recursively or nonrecursively with little difference in effort, it is usually better to use the nonrecursive formulation.

For some problems, such as the Towers of Hanoi problem described in the next section, recursion is the most natural and straightforward technique. For these problems, nonrecursive algorithms may not be obvious, may be more difficult to develop, and may be less readable than recursive ones are. For such problems, the simplicity of the recursive algorithms compensates for any inefficiency. Unless the programs are to be executed many times, the extra effort required to develop nonrecursive solutions is not warranted. Recursion is also appropriate when the problem's data is organized in a data structure that is defined recursively. Such data structures are considered in Chapter 16.

The examples of recursion in this section have illustrated direct recursion, in which a function or procedure references itself directly. Indirect recursion occurs when a subprogram references other subprograms, and some chain of subprogram references eventually results in a reference to the first subprogram again. For example, function *A* may reference function *B,* which calls procedure *C,* which references *A* again. The implementation of indirect recursion in Pascal is discussed in Appendix F.

1. Consider the following procedure P:

```
PROCEDURE P( Num : integer );
   BEGIN
      IF (1 <= Num) AND (Num <= 8) THEN
         BEGIN
            P( Num - 1 );
            write( Num:1 )
         END {IF}
      ELSE
         writeln
   END {P};
```

  (a) What output is produced by each of the following procedure calls?
     (i) P(3)   **(ii)** P(7)   **(iii)** P(10)
  (b) If Num - 1 is replaced by Num + 1 in the procedure, what output will be
     produced by the procedure calls in (a)?
  (c) If the **write** statement and the recursive call to P are interchanged, what
     output will be produced by the calls in (a)?
  (d) If a copy of the **write** statement is inserted before the recursive call to P,
     what output will be produced by the calls in (a)?

2. Given the following function F, use the method illustrated in this section to
trace the sequence of function calls and returns in evaluating F(1, 5) and
F(8, 3).

```
FUNCTION F( Num1, Num2 : integer ) : integer;
   BEGIN
      IF Num1 > Num2 THEN
         F := 0
      ELSE IF Num2 = Num1 + 1 THEN
         F := 1
      ELSE
         F := F( Num1 + 1, Num2 - 1 ) + 2
   END {F};
```

3. Consider the following procedure Q:

```
PROCEDURE Q( Num1, Num2 : integer );
   BEGIN
      IF Num2 <= 0 THEN
         writeln
      ELSE
         BEGIN
            Q( Num1 - 1, Num2 - 1 );
            write( Num1:1 );
            Q( Num1 + 1, Num2 - 1 )
         END {ELSE}
   END {Q};
```

  (a) What output is produced by the procedure call Q(14, 4)? (*Hint*: First try
     Q(14, 2), then Q(14, 3).)

(b) How many lines of output are produced by the call `Q(14, 10)`?

(c) If the `write` statement is moved before the first recursive call to `Q`, what output will be produced by `Q(14, 4)`?

4. Determine what is calculated by the following recursive functions. For parts (a)–(d), assume $n \geq 0$.

(a)
```
FUNCTION F( n : integer ) : integer;
    BEGIN
        IF n = 0 THEN
            F := 3
        ELSE
            F := n * F( n - 1 )
    END {F};
```

(b)
```
FUNCTION F( x : real; n : integer ) : real;
    BEGIN
        IF n = 0 THEN
            F := 0
        ELSE
            F := x + F( x, n - 1 )
    END {F};
```

(c)
```
FUNCTION F( n : integer ) : integer;
    BEGIN
        IF n < 2 THEN
            F := 0
        ELSE
            F := 1 + F( n DIV 2 )
    END {F};
```

(d)
```
FUNCTION F( n : integer ) : integer;
    BEGIN
        IF n = 0 THEN
            F := 0
        ELSE
            F := F( n DIV 10 ) + n MOD 10
    END {F};
```

(e)
```
FUNCTION F( n : integer ) : integer;
    BEGIN
        IF n < 0 THEN
            F := F( -n )
        ELSE IF n < 10 THEN
            F := n
        ELSE
            F := F( n DIV 10 )
    END {F};
```

5. Write nonrecursive versions of the functions in Exercise 4.

6. Write a nonrecursive version of the recursive procedure `PrintReverse` in the text.

7. Write a test driver for one of the functions in Exercise 4. Add output statements to the function to trace its actions as it executes. For example, the trace displayed for `F(21)` for the function `F` in part (c) should have a form like

```
F(21) = 1 + F(10)
    F(10) = 1 + F(5)
        F(5) = 1 + F(2)
            F(2) = 1 + F(1)
                F(1) returns 0
            F(2) returns 1
        F(5) returns 2
    F(10) returns 3
F(21) returns 4
```

where the indentation level reflects the depth of the recursion. (*Hint*: This can be accomplished by using a global variable `Level` that is incremented when the function is entered and decremented when it is exited.)

8. Write a test driver for the procedure `PrintReverse` in this section, and add output statements to the procedure to trace its actions as it executes. For example, the trace displayed for `PrintReverse(9254)` might have a form like

```
PrintReverse(9254):  Output 4, then call PrintReverse(925).
    PrintReverse(925):  Output 5, then call PrintReverse(92).
        PrintReverse(92):  Output 2, then call PrintReverse(9).
            PrintReverse(9):  Output 9, then call PrintReverse(0).
                PrintReverse(0) returns.
            PrintReverse(9) returns.
        PrintReverse(92) returns.
    PrintReverse(925) returns.
PrintReverse(9254) returns.
```

where the indentation level reflects the depth of the recursion. (See the hint in Exercise 7.)

9. (a) Write a recursive function that returns the number of digits in a nonnegative integer.
   (b) Write a program to test the function of part (a).

10. (a) Write a recursive procedure to convert an integer from base 10 to base b (see Exercise 9 of Section 7.4).
   (b) Write a program to test the function of part (a).

11. The Euclidean algorithm for finding the greatest common divisor of two integers a and b, GCD(a, b), not both of which are zero, was described in Exercise 12 of Section 5.4.
   (a) Write a recursive greatest common divisor function that implements this algorithm.
   (b) Write a program that uses the function of part (a) to find the greatest common divisors of several pairs of numbers.

12. Proceed as in Exercise 11, but write a nonrecursive function.

13. Binomial coefficients can be defined recursively as follows:

$$\left.\begin{array}{c}\dbinom{n}{0} = 1 \\[2mm] \dbinom{n}{n} = 1\end{array}\right\} \quad \text{(anchor)}$$

$$\text{For } 0 < k < n, \quad \binom{n}{k} = \binom{n-1}{k-1} + \binom{n-1}{k} \quad \text{(inductive step)}$$

  (a) Write a recursive function or procedure to calculate binomial coefficients.

  (b) Use your recursive subprogram in a program that reads values for n and k and displays the value of $\dbinom{n}{k}$, using the subprogram to obtain this value.

14. Binomial coefficients can also be defined as follows:

$$\binom{n}{k} = \frac{n!}{k!(n-k)!}$$

Write a nonrecursive function or procedure for calculating binomial coefficients using this definition.

15. (a) Write a recursive procedure that displays a nonnegative integer with commas in the correct locations. For example, it should display 20131 as 20,131.

  (b) Write a program to test the procedure of part (a).

16. Consider a network of streets laid out in a rectangular grid, for example,

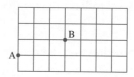

In a *northeast path* from one point in the grid to another, one may walk only to the north (up) and to the east (right). For example, there are four northeast paths from A to B in the preceding grid:

Write a program that uses a recursive function or procedure to count the number of northeast paths from one point to another in a rectangular grid.

17. Write a recursive procedure to find the prime factorization of a positive integer, that is, to express the integer as a product of primes or indicate that it is a prime. Display the prime factors in descending order.

7.7 PART OF THE PICTURE: Artificial Intelligence

Artificial intelligence (AI) is the part of computer science concerned with designing computer systems that exhibit characteristics associated with human intelligence; for example, learning, deductive reasoning, problem solving, language understanding, and the recognition of visual images. Because of the nature of its subject matter, it is necessarily interdisciplinary in its approach, using ideas and techniques drawn from philosophy, psychology, linguistics, mathematics, physics, electrical engineering, and computer science. The history of research in AI is marked by some controversy, occasioned at least in part by grandiose claims made early in its history about what AI could and would accomplish. Although many of these goals have not been reached, progress has been made in a number of areas. The discipline continues to change and grow as applications in new areas are studied. Currently, areas studied in AI include

- *Search techniques:* Searching large data sets in problems such as airline scheduling and routing problems in which the number of possible search paths is so large that it is not feasible to examine them all.
- *Game playing:* Devising programs that solve puzzles and play board games such as ticktacktoe, chess, and checkers.
- *Automated reasoning:* Making logical inferences like those needed to prove mathematical theorems or discover new results; in general, attempting to automate the process of reasoning.
- *Computational linguistics:* Using computational techniques to generate languages and analyze their structures such as in the design of lexical analyzers, parsers, and code generators.
- *Natural language processing:* Recognizing and translating natural languages such as English. Applications include the design of style and spelling checkers, verification of authorship, and intelligent user interfaces for complex software such as database management systems.
- *Expert systems:* Designing systems that use a knowledge base of information obtained from a human expert in some area and logical rules to answer questions, analyze problems, and provide advice, much as a human expert would. Successful expert systems include MYCIN for medical consultations, DENDRAL for chemical inference, PROSPECTOR for dealing with geological data, and XCON to configure computer systems.
- *Pattern recognition:* Recognizing speech, handwriting, patterns of amino acids in DNA strands, and so on.
- *Computer vision:* Designing machines that can accept input in visual form and can recognize and classify the images they receive.
- *Robotics:* Attempting to build machines that have sensing capabilities (vision, force, touch), can manipulate objects (grasp them, pick them up, put them down), and solve various object- and space-oriented problems (moving without bumping into things, fitting parts together).

Recursion is an important technique used in many of these areas of AI. In fact, it is the basic control structure in the programming language LISP, which is one of the major programming languages in AI. In this section we consider one problem from the area of game playing that can easily be solved using recursion, but for which a nonrecursive solution is quite difficult.

The **Towers of Hanoi** problem is to solve the puzzle shown in the following figure, in which one must move the disks from the left peg to the right peg according to the following rules:

1. When a disk is moved, it must be placed on one of the three pegs.
2. Only one disk may be moved at a time, and it must be the top disk on one of the pegs.
3. A larger disk may never be placed on top of a smaller one.

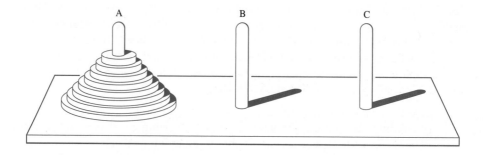

The following *game tree* shows the various configurations that are possible in the problem with two disks; the highlighted path in the tree shows a solution to the two-disk problem:

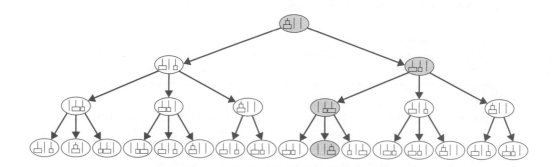

Legend has it that the priests in the Temple of Bramah were given a puzzle consisting of a golden platform with the three golden needles on which were placed sixty-four golden disks. Time was to end when they had successfully finished moving the disks to another needle, following the preceding rules. (*Query:* If the priests moved one disk per second and began their work in year 0, when would time end?)

Novices usually find the puzzle easy to solve for a small number of disks, but they have more difficulty as the number of disks grows to seven, eight, and beyond. To a computer scientist, however, the Towers of Hanoi puzzle is easy:

If there is one disk, move it from Peg A to Peg C; thus the puzzle can be solved for $n = 1$ disk.

Assuming that a solution exists for $n - 1$ disks, a solution for n disks can easily be obtained recursively:

1. Move the topmost $n - 1$ disks from Peg A to Peg B, using C as an auxiliary peg.
2. Move the large disk remaining on Peg A to Peg C.
3. Move the $n - 1$ disks from Peg B to Peg C, using Peg A as an auxiliary peg.

This scheme is implemented by the recursive procedure **Move** in the program of Figure 7.12, which solves the Towers of Hanoi puzzle:

FIGURE 7.12   Towers of Hanoi.

```
PROGRAM TowersOfHanoi( input, output );
{***************************************************************

    Input (keyboard):  Number of disks.
    Purpose:           Solve the Towers of Hanoi puzzle recursively,
                       using procedure Move.
    Output (screen):   User prompts and a sequence of moves that
                       solves the puzzle.


***************************************************************}

CONST
    Peg1 = 'A';
    Peg2 = 'B';
    Peg3 = 'C';

VAR
    NumDisks : integer;      {number of disks}

PROCEDURE Move( n : integer; StartPeg, AuxPeg, EndPeg : char );
{-------------------------------------------------------------

    Accepts:         Positive integer n, representing the number
                     of disks, and three characters representing
                     pegs of the Tower of Hanoi puzzle: StartPeg,
                     AuxPeg, and EndPeg.
    Purpose:         Move n disks from StartPeg to EndPeg using
                     AuxPeg as an auxiliary peg.
    Output (screen): A sequence of moves that solves the puzzle.

-------------------------------------------------------------}
```

FIGURE 7.12   Towers of Hanoi. (cont.)

```
    BEGIN
       IF n = 1 THEN                          {anchor}
          writeln( 'Move disk from ', StartPeg, ' to ', EndPeg)

       ELSE                                   {inductive step}
          BEGIN
             {Move n - 1 pegs from StartPeg to AuxPeg
              using EndPeg as an auxiliary peg}
             Move( n - 1, StartPeg, EndPeg, AuxPeg );

             {Move disk from StartPeg to EndPeg}
             Move( 1, StartPeg, ' ', EndPeg );

             {Move n - 1 pegs from AuxPeg to EndPeg
              using StartPeg as an auxiliary peg}
             Move( n - 1, AuxPeg, StartPeg, EndPeg )
          END {ELSE}
    END {Move};

BEGIN {*********** main program *************}
   write( '# of disks:  ' );
   readln( NumDisks );
   Move( NumDisks, Peg1, Peg2, Peg3 );
END {main program}.
```

Sample run:

```
# of disks:  4
Move disk from A to B
Move disk from A to C
Move disk from B to C
Move disk from A to B
Move disk from C to A
Move disk from C to B
Move disk from A to B
Move disk from A to C
Move disk from B to C
Move disk from B to A
Move disk from C to A
Move disk from B to C
Move disk from A to B
Move disk from A to C
Move disk from B to C
```

Exercises

1. Trace the execution of **Move(4, 'A' , 'B' , 'C')** far enough to produce the first five moves. Does your answer agree with the program output in Figure 7.12? Do the same for **Move(5, 'A', 'B', 'C')**.

2. Modify the program in Figure 7.12 so that it displays a picture of each move rather than a verbal description.

*7.8   Functions and Procedures as Parameters

Example 2 in Section 7.5 considered the problem of approximating the integral of a function f on an interval $[a, b]$:

$$\int_a^b f(x) \, dx$$

As we noted there, for a nonnegative function f, this integral gives the area of the region bounded by the graph of $y = f(x)$, the x axis, and the vertical lines $x = a$ and $x = b$. In the program of Figure 7.11, the statement part of the main program carried out the computations necessary to approximate this integral. A more flexible arrangement would be to incorporate these computations into a subprogram `ApproxIntegral`, one of whose parameters is the function whose integral is being approximated. Pascal does allow **function parameters** and **procedure parameters,** and in this section we describe how they are used.

The subprogram `ApproxIntegral` must have as its formal parameters the endpoints **a** and **b** of the interval and the number **n** of subintervals into which this interval is divided, which are ordinary value parameters, and a function parameter **f**. When `ApproxIntegral` is referenced, actual parameters of **real** type are associated with the formal parameters **a** and **b**; an actual parameter of **integer** type is associated with the formal parameter **n**; and an actual function is associated with the formal parameter **f**.

Function parameters are designated as such by a function heading (without the closing semicolon) within the formal parameter list. In Turbo Pascal, an appropriate heading for `ApproxIntegral` is

```
FUNCTION ApproxIntegral( f : RealFunction;
                         a, b : real; n : integer) : real;
```

where `RealFunction` would be a type identifier defined in a **type section** in the declaration part of the program. In this example, the type section might have the form

```
TYPE
    RealFunction = FUNCTION( x : real ) : real;
```

The type identifier `RealFunction` can then be used to specify that the value of a formal parameter (or variable or other identifier) is a function having one parameter of type **real** and whose value is of type **real**.

The program in Figure 7.13 is a modification of the one in Figure 7.11 that contains this type section and the complete function `ApproxIntegral`. It calculates the approximate area under the graph defined by the function `Poly(x)`. In Turbo Pascal, whenever a function or procedure is used as a parameter, it is necessary to satisfy the *far call requirement.* In this program we do this by attaching the compiler directive **FAR**; to the heading of function **Poly**. An alternative is to turn on the **Force far calls** option in the **Compiler Options** of the Turbo Pascal integrated environment or to include the compiler directive {**$F+**} in the program (see Appendix E for more details).

 FIGURE 7.13 Numerical integration—function parameters.

```
PROGRAM Integrate2( input, output );
{*******************************************************************

    Input (keyboard): Interval endpoints a and b and the number n of
                      subintervals.
    Purpose:          Approximate the integral of a function f from
                      x = a to x = b using the rectangle method with
                      altitudes chosen at the midpoints of the
                      subintervals.
    Output (screen):  Prompts to the user and approximate values of
                      the integral.

*******************************************************************}

TYPE
   RealFunction = FUNCTION( x : real ) : real;

VAR
   a, b : real;           {endpoints of interval}
   n : integer;           {number of subintervals used}
   Response : char;       {user response}

FUNCTION Poly( x : real ) : real; FAR;
{-------------------------------------------------------------------

    Accepts:  Real number x.
    Purpose:  This is the integrand, the function for which the
              integral is being approximated.
    Returns:  The value of the function at x.

-------------------------------------------------------------------}

   BEGIN
      Poly := x * x + 1
   END {Poly};
```

FIGURE 7.13 Numerical integration—function parameters. (cont.)

```
FUNCTION ApproxIntegral( f : RealFunction;
                                {function parameter; the integrand}
                         a, b : real;
                                {endpoints of interval}
                         n : integer )  : real;
                                {number of  subintervals}
{------------------------------------------------------------

   Accepts:  Function parameter f, real numbers a and b, integer n.
   Purpose:  Approximate the integral of f over the interval [a, b]
             using the rectangle method with n subintervals.
   Returns:  The approximate integral of f over [a, b].

-------------------------------------------------------------------}

   VAR
      x,                   {the midpoint of one of the subintervals}
      Deltax,              {the length of the subintervals}
      Sum : real;          {the approximating sum}
      i : integer;         {counter}

   BEGIN
      Deltax := (b - a) / n;
      Sum := 0;
      x := a + Deltax / 2;
      FOR i := 1 TO n DO
         BEGIN
            Sum := Sum + f(x);
            x := x + Deltax
         END {FOR};
      ApproxIntegral := Deltax * Sum
   END {ApproxIntegral};

BEGIN {*************** main program ****************}
   REPEAT
      write( 'Enter interval endpoints: ' );
      readln( a, b );
      REPEAT
         write( 'Enter number of subintervals: ' );
         readln( n );
         writeln( 'Approximate area using ', n:1, ' subintervals is ',
                  ApproxIntegral( Poly, a, b, n ):8:4 );
         write( 'Different number of subintervals (Y or N)? ' );
         readln( Response )
      UNTIL (Response = 'N') OR (Response = 'n');
      writeln;
      write( 'Change the interval (Y or N)? ' );
      readln( Response )
   UNTIL (Response = 'N') OR (Response = 'n')
END {main program}.
```

Procedures may also be used as parameters in subprograms. In this case, an appropriate type section to define a type identifier representing a procedure type would have the form

```
TYPE
    proc-type = PROCEDURE( formal-parameter-declarations );
```

The identifier *proc-type* could then be used to declare that the type of a formal parameter in some subprogram is to be a procedure having the specified formal parameter list.

Programming Pointers

Program Design

1. *Multialternative selection structures in which the selection is based on the value of some integer or character variable are sometimes better implemented with a* CASE *statement than with an* IF *statement.* The CASE implementation may be more readable than the IF implementation. For example, classifying the value of a **char** variable **Ch** as an arithmetic operator (+, -, *, /), a relational operator (<, >, =), or a punctuation symbol (semicolon, colon, comma, or period), by using the CASE statement

```
CASE Ch OF
    '+', '-', '*', '/' : writeln( 'Arithmetic operator' );
            '<', '>', '=' : writeln( 'Relational operator' );
    ';', ':', ',', '.' : writeln( 'Punctuation' )
END {CASE};
```

looks cleaner than does an implementation using an IF statement:

```
IF (Ch = '+') OR (Ch = '-')
    OR (Ch = '*') OR (Ch = '/') THEN
        writeln( 'Arithmetic operator' )
ELSE IF (Ch = '<') OR (Ch = '>') OR (Ch = '=') THEN
        writeln( 'Relational operator' )
ELSE IF (Ch = ';') OR (Ch = ':')
    OR (Ch = ',') OR (Ch = '.') THEN
        writeln( 'Punctuation' );
```

2. *Repetition structures can be implemented in Pascal using the* WHILE, FOR, *and* REPEAT-UNTIL *statements, and it is important to select the one that best implements the repetition structure required in a given problem.* Some guidelines for selecting the appropriate statement are

   ■ *The* WHILE *statement is usually the best choice for implementing repetition structures that are controlled by boolean expressions.* Since the boolean expression appears at the top of the loop, one can see immediately what the termination test is. This also ensures that the body of the loop will not be entered inadvertently if the boolean expression is false initially.

■ *The* FOR *statement is appropriate for implementing repetition structures in which the number of repetitions can be determined before the loop is entered.*

■ *The* REPEAT-UNTIL *statement is appropriate for implementing repetition structures in which the body of the loop must be executed at least once.*

Potential Problems

1. *Each* CASE *statement must be terminated with the reserved word* END. As we noted in Potential Problem 2 of the Programming Pointers of Chapter 4, a missing END may be difficult to detect. The compiler may even search to the end of the program for an END to match an earlier BEGIN or CASE.

2. *The selector in a* CASE *statement must be of integer, character, or boolean type (or enumerated or subrange type; see Chapter 8).* In particular, the values of the selector in label lists may not be string constants like 'JACK', 'QUEEN', and 'KING' that contain more than one character.

3. *The initial value and the final value of a* FOR *statement cannot be modified within the body of the loop.* The values of variables that specify these initial and/or final values may change within the loop body, but this does not change the number of repetitions. For example, the statements

```
k := 5;
FOR i := 1 TO k DO
   BEGIN
      writeln( k );
      k := k - 1
   END {FOR};
```

produce the output

```
5
4
3
2
1
```

4. *The control variable in a* FOR *statement should not be modified within the body of the for loop, since it is intended to run through a specified range of consecutive values.* Strange or undesirable results may be produced otherwise. To illustrate, the statement

```
FOR i := 1 TO 4 DO
   BEGIN
      writeln( i );
      i := i - 1
   END {FOR};
```

produces the output

```
1
3
```

The statement

```
FOR i := 1 TO 4 DO
   BEGIN
      writeln( i );
      i := i - 1
   END {FOR};
```

results in an **infinite loop** and produces the output

```
1
1
1
1
.
.
.
```

The output produced by the statement

```
FOR i := 1 TO 4 DO
   BEGIN
      writeln( i );
      i := i + 2
   END {FOR};
```

is

```
1
4
7
10
.
.
.
```

This loop also is infinite, since the value of the control variable **i** is never equal to the final value **4**.

5. *A control variable for a* **FOR** *statement must be declared within the program unit in which it is used.* A global variable or any variable declared in some larger program unit may not be used for this purpose.

6. *The* **REPEAT-UNTIL** *statement controls repetition of all statements between* **REPEAT** *and* **UNTIL**, *but* **FOR** *and* **WHILE** *statements control repetition of only one statement.* For example, the statements

```
FOR i := 1 TO 10 DO
   J := sqr( i );
   writeln( J );
```

produce only one line of output:

```
100
```

The body of the for loop contains only the assignment statement `J := sqr( i )` and not the output statement `writeln( J )` (even though the indentation suggests that it does). If both statements are to be included within the **FOR** statement, they must be combined into a single compound statement.

```
FOR i := 1 TO 10 DO
   BEGIN
      J := sqr( i );
      writeln( J )
   END {FOR};
```

7. *The statements within a* **REPEAT-UNTIL** *statement must eventually cause the boolean expression in the* **UNTIL** *clause to become true (but see footnote 3 on page 343).* Otherwise, an infinite loop is the result. For example, the statements

```
x := 0;
REPEAT
   writeln( x:4:1 );
   x := x + 0.3
UNTIL x = 1.0;
```

produce an infinite loop:

Output:

```
0.0
0.3
0.6
0.9
1.2
1.5
1.8
 .
 .
 .
```

Since the value of **x** is never equal to 1.0, repetition is not terminated. Also, since comparisons of two algebraically equal real values with = may not be evaluated as true, the statements

```
x := 0;
REPEAT
   writeln( x:4:1 );
   x := x + 0.2
UNTIL x = 1.0;
```

may also produce an infinite loop:

Output:

```
0.0
0.2
0.4
0.6
0.8
1.0
1.2
1.4
1.6
 .
 .
 .
```

Since x is initialized to 0 and 0.1 is added to x five times, x should have the value 1.0. But the boolean expression $x = 1.0$ may be false, because most real values are not stored exactly.

8. *In a while loop, the boolean expression that controls repetition is evaluated before execution of the body of the loop. In a repeat-until loop, the boolean expression that controls repetition is evaluated after execution of the body of the loop.* Thus, the body of a while loop will not be executed if the boolean expression is false, but the statements within a repeat-until loop are always executed at least once.

9. *In a while loop, repetition continues as long as the boolean expression that controls repetition is true. In a repeat-until loop, repetition continues as long as the boolean expression that controls repetition is false.* In Turbo Pascal 7.0, however, the **Break** procedure can be called within the body of a loop to cause an early termination.

Program Style

In this text, we use the following conventions for formatting the control statements considered in this chapter:

1. *In* **CASE** *statements,* **CASE** *is aligned with its corresponding* **END***; the lines within the* **CASE** *statement are indented; and the colons or the label lists are aligned.*

```
CASE selector OF
   label-list-1 : statement-1;
                .
                .
                .
   label-list-n : statement-n
   ELSE
                   statement-n + 1
END {CASE}
```

2. *In a* **REPEAT-UNTIL** *statement,* **REPEAT** *is aligned with its corresponding* **UNTIL***, and the body of the loop is indented.*

```
REPEAT
    statement-1;
        .
        .
        .
    statement-n
UNTIL . . .
```

3. *In a* **FOR** *statement,* **FOR . . . DO** *is on one line, with the body of the loop indented on the next line(s):*

```
FOR . . . DO
    statement


FOR . . . DO
    BEGIN
        statement-1;
            .
            .
            .
        statement-n
    END {FOR}
```

4. *A comment of the form* {CASE}, {IF}, {WHILE}, {FOR}, *and so on, is attached to the reserved word* **END** *that marks the end of a* **CASE** *statement, the end of a compound statement in an* **IF** *statement, the body of a while loop, or the body of a for loop, respectively.*

Standard Pascal

Several features of Turbo Pascal described in this chapter are not supported in standard Pascal:

- A **CASE** statement may not have an **ELSE** part.
- Ranges of values may not be specified in the form *first-value..last-value* in the label lists of a **CASE** statement.
- It is an error if the value of the selector in a **CASE** statement is not in any of the label lists.
- The value of the control variable cannot be changed within the body of a for loop.
- The value of the control variable is undefined after execution of a for loop is completed.
- **Random** is not a predefined function.
- **Randomize** is not a predefined procedure.
- The form of the declaration of a function or procedure that is a parameter of another subprogram is different.

ORDINAL DATA TYPES: ENUMERATED AND SUBRANGE

God created the integers; all the rest is the work of man.
LEOPOLD KRONECKER

The old order changeth, yielding place to new.
ALFRED, LORD TENNYSON

CHAPTER CONTENTS

In Chapter 2 we considered in some detail the program development process, and in Section 2.2 we discussed the design phase of this process. In the design phase we select appropriate structures to organize and store the data to be processed and develop algorithms to process the data. In the first seven chapters of this text, the emphasis was on the Pascal statements and control structures that are used to implement algorithms. We placed less emphasis on the data, considering only the four predefined Pascal data types, `integer`, `real`, `boolean`, and `char` and the additional types `byte`, `shortint`, `word`, `longint`, `single`, `double`, `extended`, and `comp` provided in Turbo Pascal. Pascal does, however, provide other predefined data types and also allows the user to define certain new data types. In this chapter we begin our study of these other data types.

8.1   PART OF THE PICTURE: Data Structures and Data Types

A **data type** consists of a collection of values together with basic operations and relations that are defined on these values. For example, the type `integer` in Pascal (and the other integer types `byte`, `shortint`, `word`, and `longint` in Turbo Pascal) consists of a subset of the mathematical set of integers, { . . . , −3, −2, −1, 0, 1, 2, 3, . . .}, the basic arithmetic operations +, -, *, /, **DIV**, and **MOD**, and the relations <, >, =, <>, <=, and >=. The type `real` (and the related real types `single`, `double`, `extended`, and `comp` in Turbo Pascal) consists of a subset of the set of real numbers together with the usual arithmetic operations and relations. The type `boolean` consists of only two values, `true` and `false`, and the basic operations are **NOT**, **AND**, and **OR**. Values of type `char` may be any character in the Pascal character set, and the basic operations are the relations used to compare characters.

These data types are called **simple** because a datum of one of these types is atomic; that is, it consists of a single item that cannot be subdivided. In addition to these simple data types, Pascal provides **structured** data types such as `text` and `string` in Turbo Pascal, in which a datum is a collection of items, and a **pointer** type used for data values that are memory addresses. Figure 8.1 shows the various Pascal data types. The structured data types and pointer types are discussed in later chapters.

A simple data type is said to be an **ordinal** type if the values of that type are ordered so that each one except the first has an immediate predecessor and each one except the last has an immediate successor. Integer types are ordinal types, since integer values are ordered by the natural ordering . . . , −2, −1, 0, 1, 2, ... The type `boolean` is an ordinal type with the ordering `false`, `true`. The type `char` is also an ordinal type in which the ordering is that established by the numeric codes for the Pascal character set (see Section 4.2). Real types are not ordinal types, however, because a given real number does not have an immediate predecessor or an immediate successor.

In many programs, the data types provided in Pascal are adequate for organizing and processing the data. In some problems, however, the nature of the data or the way the data values are related require other kinds of data structures and data types. Most modern programming languages, including Pascal, allow the definition of new data types, thus providing programmer-defined extensions to the language. The definition of a new data type must, of course, include a specification of the

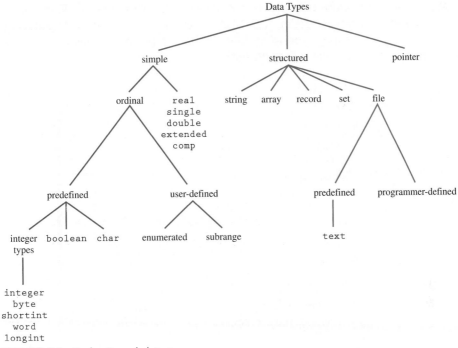

FIGURE 8.1 Turbo Pascal data types.

values of that data type and definitions of the basic operations and relations appropriate to that type.

Such programmer-defined types may be either simple or structured. In Pascal, simple ordinal types can be defined either as subranges of other ordinal types or as enumerated types. Subrange and enumerated types are considered in this chapter, and structured data types are considered in Chapters 9 and following.

8.2 The Type Section

The declaration part of a program consists of five kinds of sections:

Declaration Part

Form:

label section
constant section
type section
variable section
subprogram section

Purpose:
Define the labels, named constants, types, variables, and subprograms to be used in the program.

We previously described the constant, variable, and subprogram sections, and we now consider the type section. (The label section is described in Appendix F.)

The type section is used to declare new data types or to rename previously defined types. It has the following form:

Type Section

> Form:
>
> ```
> TYPE
>     name-1 = type-1;
>     name-2 = type-2;
>         .
>         .
>         .
>     name-m = type-m;
> ```
>
> where:
>   **TYPE** is a reserved word;
>   each **name-i** is a legal identifier;
>   each **type-i** is a predefined Pascal data type or
>   a user-defined type.
>
> Purpose:
> Each **name-i** names the data type given by **type-i**.

For example, the type section

```
TYPE
    Symbol = char;
    Logical = boolean;
```

declares **Symbol** and **Logical** to be synonyms for **char** and **boolean**, respectively. In the variable section we can then declare variables to be of type **Symbol** or **Logical**:

```
VAR
    Code, Class : Symbol;
    p, q, r : Logical;
```

Of course, the standard identifiers **char** and **boolean** may still be used in place of, or in addition to, the names **Symbol** and **Logical**, respectively.

The scope rules given in Section 5.6 apply also to data types. Recall that Scope Rule 1 states that an item declared within a subprogram is not accessible outside that subprogram. Thus, the data type **FloatingPoint** declared in the function **Power** by

```
FUNCTION Power( x : real; n : integer ) : real;

    TYPE
        FloatingPoint = real;
```

```
VAR
    Prod : FloatingPoint;
            .
            .
            .
```

may be used only to declare the types of local variables such as **Prod** within the function **Power**. It is not accessible outside this function.

Scope Rule 2 states that a global entity is accessible within any subprogram in which no local item has the same name. Thus *any type defined in the type section of the main program is accessible within any subprogram that does not use the same identifier to name a local item.* This is one instance in which the use of global items is often necessary, since data types may not be used as parameters for subprograms. For example, suppose that the type section

```
TYPE
    Symbol = char;
    Logical = boolean;
```

appears in the declaration part of the main program, and consider the following procedure skeleton:

```
PROCEDURE Gamma( x, y : Logical; VAR c : Symbol );

    CONST
        Symbol = 'A';

    TYPE
        Bit = Logical;
            .
            .
            .
```

Since the identifier **Logical** is not used to name an item within procedure **Gamma**, the global data type **Logical** may be used within **Gamma**. Thus parameters **x** and **y** may be declared of type **Logical**, and **Bit** may be declared as a synonym for **Logical** (and hence also for **boolean**). The identifier **Symbol** is used locally as the name of a constant in procedure **Gamma**; hence the global data type **Symbol** cannot be used in the declaration part of **Gamma.** Note, however, that it may be used to declare the type of parameter **c**, because this declaration occurs before the local constant **Symbol** is defined within **Gamma**.

Scope Rule 3 asserts that entities declared in a subprogram can be accessed within any subprogram contained in it, provided that no local item in the internal subprogram has the same name. Like the other scope rules, this rule also applies to data types.

8.3 Enumerated Data Types

Programmer-defined ordinal types can be divided into two classes: **enumerated** and **subrange.** Enumerated data types are considered in this section and subrange types in the next.

Defining an Enumerated Type

The form of an enumerated type definition is as follows:

Enumerated Type Definition

Form:

   (*ident-1*, *ident-2*, . . ., *ident-n*)

where:
    each *ident-i* is a legal Pascal identifier;
    no *ident-i* may appear in more than one enu-
      merated type definition.

Purpose:
Define a data type whose values are the identifiers
ident-1, *ident-2*, . . . , *ident-n*.

For example,

```
( Sunday, Monday, Tuesday, Wednesday, Thursday, Friday, Saturday )
```

defines an enumerated data type whose values are the identifiers **Sunday**, **Monday**, **Tuesday**, **Wednesday**, **Thursday**, **Friday**, and **Saturday**. Note, however, that neither of (**12531, 14405, 21724, 30081**) or (**A-, B+, B-, 'FAIL'**) is a legal type definition because the items listed are not valid identifiers.

The values of an enumerated data type are ordered by the listing of the values in the definition of that type. Thus, in this example, the predecessor of **Wednesday** is **Tuesday**, and **Thursday** is the successor of **Wednesday**; **Sunday** has no predecessor, and **Saturday** has no successor.

The listing of values that defines an enumerated type can be associated with a type identifier in the type section; for example,

```
TYPE
    DaysOfWeek = ( Sunday, Monday, Tuesday, Wednesday,
                   Thursday, Friday, Saturday );
```

This type identifier can then be used to specify the types of variables, formal parameters, and function values:

```
VAR
    Day : DaysOfWeek;
      .
      .
      .

FUNCTION Convert( x, y : integer ) : DaysOfWeek;
      .
      .
      .
```

```
PROCEDURE Schedule( Day : DaysOfWeek; VAR NumberOfDay : integer );
    .
    .
    .
```

It is also possible to use the listing of values that define an enumerated type in the variable section to specify the type of a variable, for example,

```
VAR
    Day : ( Sunday, Monday, Tuesday, Wednesday,
            Thursday, Friday, Saturday );
```

Such listings cannot be used, however, in function and procedure headings. Instead, *type identifiers must be used to declare the types of formal parameters and function values.*

Operations on Enumerated Types

Values of an enumerated type may be compared using the relational operators = and <>. For example,

```
IF (Day <> Sunday) AND (Day <> Saturday) THEN
    writeln( 'Weekday' );
```

Since the values of an enumerated type are ordered, they may also be compared by using <, >, <=, and >=. For example, the preceding **IF** statement can also be written as

```
IF (Monday <= Day) AND (Day < Saturday) THEN
    writeln( 'Weekday' );
```

Enumerated-type variables may also be used as control variables in **FOR** statements such as

```
FOR Day := Monday TO Friday DO
    BEGIN
        TotalHours := TotalHours + HoursWorked
    END {FOR};
```

The predefined Pascal functions **pred** and **succ** may be used to find the predecessor and successor, respectively, of a value of any ordinal type. The following table gives several examples:

Function Reference	Value
pred(Monday)	Sunday
succ(Friday)	Saturday
succ(3)	4
pred(17)	16
pred('G')	'F'
succ('W')	'X'
succ(false)	true
pred(true)	false
pred(Sunday)	undefined
succ(Saturday)	undefined

Note that the function **pred** is not defined if its parameter is the first element of the ordinal type being considered, nor is **succ** if its parameter is the last element.[1] Such references are errors.

The predefined procedures **Inc** and **Dec** provided in Turbo Pascal that we described in Section 3.4 may be used with any ordinal types. The following table gives several examples:

Old Value of x	Procedure Reference	New Value of x
Monday	Dec(x)	Sunday
Friday	Inc(x)	Saturday
Wednesday	Inc(x, 3)	Saturday
Wednesday	Dec(x, 3)	Saturday
3	Inc(x)	4
-17	Dec(x, 5)	-22
false	Inc(x)	true
true	Dec(x)	false
Sunday	Dec(x)	Undefined
Saturday	Inc(x)	Undefined

Note that **Dec(x)** is undefined if **x** is the first element of an ordinal type, as is **Inc(x)** if **x** is the last element.

Another predefined function used for processing ordinal data is **ord**. This function returns the **ordinal number** of an element in the ordering for that type, with position numbering beginning with 0. Thus, for the data type **DaysOfWeek**,

ord(Sunday) = 0, and ord(Tuesday) = 2

For the enumerated date type **FaceCard** defined by

---

[1] The functions Low and High in Turbo Pascal 7.0 can be used to find the first and last elements. For example, Low(DaysOfWeek) = Sunday and High(DaysOfWeek) = Saturday. See Section H.3 of Appendix H.

```
TYPE
    FaceCard = ( Jack, Queen, King );
```

$ord(Jack) = 0$, $ord(Queen) = 1$, and $ord(King) = 2$.

For an integer **n**, **ord(n)** has the value **n**. Thus

```
ord(7) = 7
ord(-3) = -3
```

For **boolean** type, **ord(false)** = 0 and **ord(true)** = 1. For **char** data, the ordinal number of a character is its numeric code. For ASCII code, **ord('A')** = 65, **ord('Z')** = 90, and **ord('2')** = 50 (see the tables of ASCII codes in Appendix A).

For **char** data, the function **chr** is the inverse of **ord**. This function has an integer parameter, and its value is the character whose ordinal number is that integer, provided that there is such a character. Thus **chr(65)** = 'A' and **chr(50)** = '2'. Note that for any element **c** of type **char**

```
chr(ord(c)) = c
```

and if **n** is the ordinal number of some character, then

```
ord(chr(n)) = n
```

One application of the functions **chr** and **ord** is in converting numerals to numbers and vice versa, as described in the exercises.

Conversion between other ordinal types is possible using **type casting,** in which a type identifier is used as a function. If *type-ident* is an ordinal type identifier and *expr* is an expression of some ordinal type, then

```
type-ident(expr)
```

is the value of type *type-ident* that has the same ordinal value as *expr*. The following table gives several examples:

Type cast	Value
DaysOfWeek(1)	Monday
FaceCard(0)	Jack
boolean(1)	true
DaysOfWeek(false)	Sunday
FaceCard(Monday)	Queen
integer(King)	2
char(65)	A

It should be clear that the predefined functions **ord** and **chr** are special cases of type casting (using type identifiers **integer** and **char**, respectively).

Values of an enumerated type cannot be read from the keyboard or displayed on the screen; in fact, they cannot be read from or written to any text file. Instead, special input/output procedures must be written for enumerated types. For output, this can be accomplished by means of a **CASE** statement to select an appropriate string to be displayed for each value of the enumerated type. The input of an enumerated type value is usually accomplished by having the user enter a character string corresponding to that value. Enough of this string is then examined, character by character, to determine what enumerated type value should be assigned to the input variable. The procedures **PrintDay** and **ReadDay** in the following example illustrate these techniques for the input and output of values of type **DaysOfWeek**.

Example: A Unit for the Data Type DaysOfWeek

In Turbo Pascal, data types may be defined in units and may be imported from them by programs and other units. To illustrate, it might be convenient to have a unit for processing a particular type like **DaysOfWeek**. We might write a unit like that in Figure 8.2, which defines the enumerated type **DaysOfWeek** and input/output procedures for this type.

 FIGURE 8.2   Unit for the data type **DaysOfWeek**.

```
UNIT DaysIO;

{***********************************************************************

   Unit defines the enumeration type DaysOfWeek.
   EXPORTS:    Type:        DaysOfWeek
               Procedures:  PrintDay
                            ReadDay

***********************************************************************}

INTERFACE

TYPE
   DaysOfWeek = ( Sunday, Monday, Tuesday, Wednesday,
                  Thursday, Friday, Saturday );

PROCEDURE PrintDay( Day : DaysOfWeek );
{-----------------------------------------------------------

   Accepts:        A value Day of the enumerated type
                   DaysOfWeek.
   Output (screen): A string corresponding to Day.

-----------------------------------------------------------}
```

FIGURE 8.2   Unit for the data type **DaysOfWeek**. (cont.)

```
PROCEDURE ReadDay( VAR Day : DaysOfWeek );
{------------------------------------------------------------

    Input (keyboard): A character string corresponding to
                      a value of type DaysOfWeek.
    Returns:          A value for the input variable Day.


------------------------------------------------------------}


IMPLEMENTATION

PROCEDURE PrintDay;

    BEGIN
       CASE Day OF
          Sunday     : write( 'Sunday' );
          Monday     : write( 'Monday' );
          Tuesday    : write( 'Tuesday' );
          Wednesday  : write( 'Wednesday' );
          Thursday   : write( 'Thursday' );
          Friday     : write( 'Friday' );
          Saturday   : write( 'Saturday' )
       END {CASE}
    END {PrintDay};

PROCEDURE ReadDay

    VAR
       Ch1, Ch2 : char;     {first two characters of input string}

    BEGIN
       Read( Ch1 );
       CASE Ch1 OF
          'M', 'm' : Day := Monday;
          'W', 'w' : Day := Wednesday;
          'F', 'f' : Day := Friday;
          'S', 's' : BEGIN
                        read( Ch2 ):
                        CASE Ch2 OF
                           'U', 'u' : Day := Sunday;
                           'A', 'a' : Day := Saturday
                        ELSE
                                   writeln( 'Illegal input' )
                        END {CASE Ch2}
                     END;
```

FIGURE 8.2   Unit for the data type **DaysOfWeek**. (cont.)

```
        'T', 't' : BEGIN
                      read( Ch2 ):
                      CASE Ch2 OF
                         'U', 'u' : Day := Tuesday;
                         'H', 'h' : Day := Thursday
                         ELSE
                                       writeln( 'Illegal input' )
                      END {CASE Ch2}
                   END;
         ELSE
                      writeln( 'Illegal input' )
      END {CASE Ch1};
      readln
   END {ReadDay};

END {DaysIO}
```

The enumerated type **DaysOfWeek** and procedures **PrintDay** and **ReadDay** can be imported from the unit into any program or other unit. The program in Figure 8.3 illustrates. It is a modification of the program in Figure 6.3 to read an employee number and an hourly rate from a permanent text file and to calculate wages. The **USES** clause

```
     USES DaysIO;
```

makes the contents of **DaysIO** accessible to the program. The procedure **GetEmployeeInfo** declares the local variable **Day** to be of type **DaysOfWeek** and uses the for loop

```
     FOR Day := Sunday TO Saturday DO
        BEGIN
           PrintDay( Day );
           write( ': ' );
           readln( DayHours );
           WeekHours := WeekHours + DayHours
        END {FOR}
```

to display each value of **Day** from **Sunday** to **Saturday**, read the number of hours worked on that day, and accumulate these hours.

FIGURE 8.3 Calculating payroll—version 5.

```
PROGRAM Payroll ( input, EmpFile, output );
(***************************************************************

    Input (EmpFile):  Employee numbers and hourly rates.
    Input (keyboard): Hours worked on each day.
    Purpose:          Calculate wages for several employees whose
                      employee numbers and hourly rates are read
                      from the file EmpFile and whose hours are
                      entered by the user during execution.  Total
                      wages for this payroll are also calculated.
    Output (screen):  User prompts, names of days, hours worked,
                      hourly rates, wages, and total of all wages.


****************************************************************)

USES DaysIO;

VAR
    EmpFileName : string;      {actual file name of employee file}
    EmpFile : text;           {the permanent employee file}
    EmpNumber : integer;      {employee number}
    Hours,                    {hours worked}
    HourlyRate,               {hourly pay rate}
    Wages,                    {total wages for employee}
    TotalPayroll : real;      {total wages for this payroll}

PROCEDURE GetEmployeeInfo
             ( VAR EmpFile : Text;        {the input file}
               VAR EmpNumber : integer;  {employee's number}
               VAR HourlyRate,            {hourly rate, and}
                   WeekHours : real );   {number of hours worked}
{-------------------------------------------------------------

    Input (file):     EmpNumber and HourlyRate from EmpFile.
    Input (keyboard): Hours worked.
    Purpose:          Read the employee number EmpNumber and
                      HourlyRate from a text file InFile; Hours
                      worked for each day are entered by the user
                      and the total WeekHours is calculated.  The
                      procedure PrintDay is used to print names of
                      days.
    Returns:          EmpNumber, HourlyRate, HourlyRate, and
                      WeekHours.
    Output (screen):  User prompts, employee numbers, and names
                      of days.

-------------------------------------------------------------}
```

FIGURE 8.3   Calculating payroll—version 5. (cont.)

```
VAR
    Day : DaysOfWeek;      {day of the week}
    DayHours : real;       {hours worked each day}

BEGIN
    readln( EmpFile, EmpNumber, HourlyRate );
    writeln( 'Hours worked for ', EmpNumber:1, ' on' );
    WeekHours := 0;
    FOR Day := Sunday TO Saturday DO
        BEGIN
            PrintDay( Day );
            write( ': ' );
            readln( DayHours );
            WeekHours := WeekHours + DayHours
        END {FOR}
END {GetEmployeeInfo};

PROCEDURE CalculateWages
                   (     Hours,                    {hours worked}
                         HourlyRate : real;        {and hourly pay rate}
                     VAR Wages,                     {employee's wages}
                         TotalPayroll : real ); {total of all wages}
{------------------------------------------------------------------
```

```
    Accepts:  Hours and HourlyRate.
    Purpose:  Calculate Wages for an employee who has worked the
              given number of Hours at the given HourlyRate. Hours
              above HoursLimit are paid at OvertimeFactor times
              the hourly rate.  Total wages for this payroll are
              also accumulated.  The function RoundCents is used to
              round wages to the nearest cent.
    Returns:  Wages and TotalPayroll.


-------------------------------------------------------------------}
```

```
    CONST
        OvertimeFactor = 1.5; {overtime multiplication factor}
        HoursLimit = 40.0;    {overtime hours limit}

    VAR
        RegWages,              {regular wages}
        OverWages : real;      {overtime pay}

    FUNCTION RoundCents( Amount : real ) : real;
    {-------------------------------------------------------------

        Accepts:  A real Amount.
        Purpose:  Round Amount to the nearest cent.
        Returns:  Rounded value of Amount.


    -------------------------------------------------------------}
```

FIGURE 8.3 Calculating payroll—version 5. (cont.)

```
      BEGIN
         RoundCents := round( 100 * Amount ) / 100
      END {RoundCents};

   BEGIN {CalculateWages}
      IF Hours > HoursLimit THEN
         BEGIN {Overtime}
            RegWages := RoundCents( HourlyRate * HoursLimit );
            OverWages :=
               RoundCents( OvertimeFactor * HourlyRate
                           * (Hours - HoursLimit) )
         END {Overtime}
      ELSE
         BEGIN {No overtime}
            RegWages := RoundCents( HourlyRate * Hours );
            OverWages := 0
         END {No overtime};
      Wages := RegWages + OverWages;
      TotalPayroll := TotalPayroll + Wages
   END {CalculateWages};

BEGIN {*************** main program ***************}
   write( 'Enter name of employee file: ' );
   readln( EmpFileName );
   assign( EmpFile, EmpFileName );
   reset( EmpFile );
   TotalPayroll := 0;
   WHILE NOT eof( EmpFile ) DO
      BEGIN
         GetEmployeeInfo( EmpFile, EmpNumber, HourlyRate, Hours) ;
         writeln( 'Hours worked:  ', Hours:4:2 );
         writeln( 'Hourly rate:   $', HourlyRate:4:2 );
         CalculateWages( Hours, HourlyRate, Wages, TotalPayroll );
         writeln( 'Wages:  $', Wages:4:2 );
         writeln
      END {WHILE};
   writeln;
   writeln( 'Total wages = $', TotalPayroll:4:2 )
END {main program}.
```

Listing of FIL8-3.DAT:

```
3123   7.50
3164   8.75
3185   9.35
3202  10.50
```

Sample run:

```
Enter name of employee file: FIL8-3.DAT
```

FIGURE 8.3   Calculating payroll—version 5. (cont.)

```
Hours worked for 3123 on
Sunday: 0
Monday: 8
Tuesday: 8
Wednesday: 8
Thursday: 8
Friday: 8
Saturday: 0
Hours worked:   40.00
Hourly rate:    $7.50
Wages:   $300.00

Hours worked for 3164 on
Sunday: 0
Monday: 7.5
Tuesday: 9.25
Wednesday: 8
Thursday: 8
Friday: 10
Saturday: 0
Hours worked:   42.75
Hourly rate:    $8.75
Wages:   $386.09

Hours worked for 3185 on
Sunday: 0
Monday: 8
Tuesday: 8
Wednesday: 9
Thursday: 8.5
Friday: 6
Saturday: 4
Hours worked:   43.50
Hourly rate:    $9.35
Wages:   $423.09

Hours worked for 3202 on
Sunday: 0
Monday: 0
Tuesday: 0
Wednesday: 0
Thursday: 8
Friday: 8
Saturday: 0
Hours worked:   16.00
Hourly rate:    $10.50
Wages:   $168.00


Total wages = $1277.18
```

8.4   Subrange Data Types

In the preceding sections we considered the predefined ordinal data types `integer`, `boolean`, and `char` and enumerated types. The set of values of each of these types is ordered. In some cases it may be convenient to use a data type that is a **subrange** of such a set.

Defining a Subrange Type

The definition of a subrange type has the following form:

Subrange Type Definition

Form:

> *first-value..last-value*

where:
> *first-value* and *last-value* are values of some ordinal type called the **base type** and *first-value* ≤ *last-value*.

Purpose:
Define a data type whose values are all values *x* of the associated base type such that

> *first-value* ≤ *x* ≤ *last-value*

Subrange definitions may be used in the variable section of a program unit to declare the type of a variable, or they may be associated with a type identifier in the type section. To illustrate, consider the following:

```
TYPE
    DaysOfWeek = ( Sunday, Monday, Tuesday, Wednesday,
                   Thursday, Friday, Saturday );
    Weekdays = Monday..Friday;
    Cardinal = 0..maxint;
    Digit = '0'..'9';

VAR
    SchoolDay : Weekdays;
    n : Cardinal;
    DaysInMonth : 28..31;
    Cents : 0..99;

FUNCTION F( n : integer ) : Cardinal;
        .
        .
        .


PROCEDURE Schedule( Day : Weekdays; VAR Code : Digit );
        .
        .
        .
```

Note that although the same value may not be listed in two different enumerated type definitions, it is permissible to use a value in two different subrange definitions.

A constant value to be assigned to a variable or a function of a subrange type is checked at compile time to determine whether this value is in the specified range. If such **range checking** indicates that a value is out of range, an error message to that effect is displayed. *In Turbo Pascal, however, no range checking is done on values of expressions during program execution unless the range-checking compiler option is enabled* (or equivalently, the program contains the compiler directive `{$R+}`).

The rules that govern the use of an ordinal type also apply to any subrange of that type. For example, because an integer value may be assigned to a real variable, it also is permissible to assign a value of type `Cardinal` to a real variable in the preceding example. In general, two simple data types are said to be **compatible** if they are the same type, one is a subrange of the other, or both are subranges of the same base type. If **A** and **B** are two compatible data types, then wherever **A** may be used, **B** may also be used. Thus, in the preceding example, the function reference

```
F( DaysInMonth )
```

is valid, since the type `28..31` of the actual parameter `DaysInMonth` is a subrange of type `integer` and is therefore compatible with the integer formal parameter **n**. The assignment statement

```
Cents := F( DaysInMonth );
```

also is valid, since both the type `Cardinal` of function **F** and the type `0..99` of `Cents` are subranges of type `integer` and hence are compatible.

The main use of subrange types is to specify index types for arrays, as described in the next chapter. They can also be used to ensure that input data values are in a specified range, provided, of course, that range checking is enabled; in this case, program execution will be terminated if an out-of-range error occurs. The following example illustrates.

Example: An Octal Calculator

Suppose that we wish to develop a program to implement an octal (base-8) calculator. The input to this program will be two octal numerals and an operator, +, -, *, DIV, or MOD, and the output will be the octal value obtained by applying the specified operator to the input values.

The input numerals are strings of characters, each of which must be in the range '0'..'7'. An appropriate data type for these characters is thus a subrange of `char`:

```
OctalDigit = '0'..'7';
```

The program in Figure 8.4 uses this subrange data type to validate the input of each character. Note the error that results in the second sample run when an illegal character is entered. Since the program is designed to process only nonnegative integers, an appropriate data type to declare the numeric equivalents of the input values is a subrange of **integer**:

```
Cardinal = 0..maxint;
```

Procedure **ReadOctal** reads the octal numerals and converts them to the corresponding decimal equivalents of type **Cardinal**. **WriteOctal** is a recursive procedure that displays the octal equivalent of a decimal **Value** of type **Cardinal**; since each of the digits that is generated by repeatedly dividing **Value** by 8 is one of the numbers 0, 1, 2, 3, 4, 5, 6, or 7, an appropriate data type for these digits is the subrange

```
0..7
```

of **Cardinal** (and thus also a subrange of type **integer**).

   FIGURE 8.4   An octal calculator.

```
PROGRAM OctalCalculator( input, output );
(***********************************************************************

    Input (keyboard): Strings representing octal numerals.
    Purpose:          Read pairs of octal numerals and operators, perform
                      the indicated operations, and display the results
                      in octal.
    Output (screen):  Instructions to the user, prompts, and octal
                      numerals.

***********************************************************************)

TYPE
    OctalDigit = '0'..'7';
    Cardinal = 0..maxint;

VAR
    Num1, Num2 : Cardinal;   {decimal equivalents of octal input values}
    Result : integer;        {result of applying operator to Num1 and Num2}
    Operator,                {arithmetic operator}
    Response : char;         {user response}

PROCEDURE ReadOctal( VAR Value : Cardinal );
{---------------------------------------------------------------------

    Input (keyboard): A string representing an octal numeral.
    Purpose:          Read an octal numeral and convert it to decimal.
    Return:           The decimal Value.

---------------------------------------------------------------------}
```

FIGURE 8.4   An octal calculator. (cont.)

```
    VAR
        Ch : OctalDigit;    {an input character representing an octal digit}

    BEGIN
        Value := 0;
        WHILE NOT eoln DO
            BEGIN
                read( Ch );
                Value := 8 * Value + ord(Ch) - ord('0')
            END {WHILE};
        readln
    END {ReadOctal};

PROCEDURE WriteOctal( Value : Cardinal );
{------------------------------------------------------------------------

    Accepts:        A decimal Value.
    Purpose:        Display the octal equivalent of Value.    Note
                    that this is a recursive procedure.
    Output (screen): An octal numeral.


-------------------------------------------------------------------------}

    VAR
        Digit : 0..7;       {an octal digit -- numeric}

    BEGIN
        Digit := Value MOD 8;
        Value := Value DIV 8;
        IF Value > 0 THEN
            WriteOctal( Value );
        Write( Digit:1 )
    END {WriteOctal};

BEGIN {************** main program **************}
    writeln( 'This program implements an octal calculator.' );
    writeln( 'Input values must be nonnegative and must be valid octal' );
    writeln( 'numerals (or execution will terminate).  Legal operators ' );
    writeln( 'are +, -, *, D(IV), and M(OD). ' );
    REPEAT
        write( 'Enter first octal number: ' );
        ReadOctal( Num1 );
        write( 'Enter second octal number: ' );
        ReadOctal( Num2 );
        write( 'Enter operator: ' );
        readln( Operator );
        CASE Operator OF
            '+' : Result := Num1 + Num2;
            '-' : Result := Num1 - Num2;
            '*' : Result := Num1 * Num2;
            'D' : Result := Num1 DIV Num2;
            'M' : Result := Num1 MOD Num2
        END {CASE};
```

FIGURE 8.4   An octal calculator. (cont.)

```
      write( 'Result = ' );
      IF Result < 0 THEN
         BEGIN
            write( '-' );
            Result := ABS(Result)
         END {IF};
      WriteOctal( Result );
      writeln; writeln;
      write ( 'More values to process (Y or N)? ' );
      readln( Response )
   UNTIL (Response = 'n') OR (Response = 'N')
END {OctalCalculator}.
```

Sample run #1:

```
This program implements an octal calculator.
Input values must be nonnegative and must be valid octal
numerals (or execution will terminate).  Legal operators
are +, -, *, D(IV), and M(OD).
Enter first octal number: 751
Enter second octal number: 27
Enter operator: +
Result = 1000

More values to process (Y or N)? Y
Enter first octal number: 751
Enter second octal number: 27
Enter operator: -
Result = 722

More values to process (Y or N)? Y
Enter first octal number: 751
Enter second octal number: 27
Enter operator: *
Result = 25757

More values to process (Y or N)? Y
Enter first octal number: 751
Enter second octal number: 27
Enter operator: DIV
Result = 25

More values to process (Y or N)? Y
Enter first octal number: 751
Enter second octal number: 27
Enter operator: MOD
Result = 6

More values to process (Y or N)? N
```

FIGURE 8.4   An octal calculator. (cont.)

Sample run #2:

```
This program implements an octal calculator.
Input values must be nonnegative and must be valid octal
numerals (or execution will terminate).  Legal operators
are +, -, *, D(IV), and M(OD).
Enter first octal number: 178

Error 201: Range check error.
```

Exercises

1. **(a)** Write a type section that defines the enumerated type `MonthAbbrev`, whose values are abbreviations of the months of the year and consist of the first three letters of the months' names; also, define the subrange type `MonthNumber` consisting of the integers 1, 2, 3, . . . , 12.
   (b) Write a function whose parameter is the number of a month and whose value is the corresponding value of type `MonthAbbrev`.

2. **(a)** Write a type section that defines type `Numeral` to be the subrange of character type consisting of the characters '0', '1', '2', . . . , '9' and the type `Number` to be the subrange of integers consisting of the values 0, 1, 2, . . . , 9.
   (b) Write a function whose parameter is a variable of type `Numeral` and whose value is the corresponding numeric value. (*Hint:* Use the function `ord`.)
   (c) Write another function whose parameter is an integer in the range 0 through 9 and whose value is the corresponding numeral. (*Hint:* Use the functions `ord` and `chr`.)

3. For the enumerated type `MonthAbbrev` of Exercise 1, find the values of the following expressions:

   (a) `Jan < Aug`   **(b)** `Sep <= Sep`
   (c) `succ(Sep)`   **(d)** `pred(Apr)`
   (e) `succ(succ(Aug))`   **(f)** `pred(pred(Aug))`
   (g) `succ(pred(Mar))`   **(h)** `succ(pred(Jan))`
   (i) `ord(Jun)`   **(j)** `ord(Sep) - ord(Jan)`
   (k) `ord(succ(May)) - ord(May)`   **(l)** `chr(ord(Sep) + ord('0'))`

4. Write a function or procedure whose parameters are a nonnegative integer **n** and a month abbreviation `Abbrev`, like that in Exercise 1, and finds the "nth successor" of `Abbrev`. The 0th successor of `Abbrev` is `Abbrev` itself; for n > 0, the nth successor of `Abbrev` is the nth month following `Abbrev`. For example, the fourth successor of `Aug` is `Dec`, and the sixth successor of `Aug` is `Feb`.

5. Repeat Exercise 4, but define the function or procedure recursively.

6. Using the enumerated type **DaysOfWeek** in the text, write a program to read a customer's account number and current balance; then for each weekday (Monday through Friday) read a series of transactions by that customer of the form **D** (deposit) or **W** (withdrawal), followed by an amount, and update the balance with this amount. Display the new balance after all transactions for the week have been processed.

7. **(a)** Write a function whose parameters are a month of type **MonthAbbrev** (see Exercise 1) and a year in the range from 1538 through 1999 and whose value is the number of days in the month. Remember that February has 28 days, except in a leap year, when it has 29. A leap year is one in which the year number is divisible by 4, except for centesimal years (those ending in 00); these centesimal years are not leap years unless the year number is divisible by 400. Thus 1950 and 1900 are not leap years, but 1960 and 1600 are.

   (b) Use the function of part (a) in a program to read two dates in the form *mm dd yyyy* (such as **7 4 1776** and **1 1 1992**), and calculate the number of days that have elapsed between the two dates.

Programming Pointers

Program Design

1. *It usually is best to associate type identifiers with user-defined types.* For example, rather than simply putting a definition of an enumerated type in a variable declaration such as

   ```
   VAR
        Class : ( freshman, sophomore, junior, senior, special );
   ```

   it is better to associate this enumerated type with a type identifier and then to use it to specify the types of variables:

   ```
   TYPE
        ClassType = ( freshman, sophomore, junior, senior, special );

   VAR
        Class : ClassType;
   ```

   A major advantage of this second approach is that **ClassType** can then be used to specify the types of parameters in subprogram headings and the result types of functions; type identifiers must be used in these cases.

2. *Use enumerated types to improve program readability, making the program easier to understand and use.* For example, using enumerated values like

   ```
   ( red, yellow, blue, green, black, white, tan, brown, gray )
   ```

   to represent colors in a program instead of cryptic codes 1, 2, 3, 4, 5, 6, 7, 8, 9 obviously makes the program easier to read and understand.

3. *Make sure that range checking is enabled, especially when developing and debugging progams that use subrange types.* Potential Problem 2 in the next chapter illustrates the "strange" things that may happen otherwise. Since range checking does increase the execution time of a program, it may be desirable to disable it in applications in which program performance is critical, but this should not be done until the program has been thoroughly tested.

Potential Problems

1. *Type identifiers must be used to declare formal parameters in a subprogram and the type of a function.* One may not list the values of an ordinal type in a function or procedure heading to specify the type of a parameter or the type of a function value. For example, the heading

   ```
   FUNCTION CardValue( Card : ( Jack, Queen, King ) ) : 11..13;
   ```

   is not valid. The enumerated type (Jack, Queen, King) and the subrange type 11..13 must be associated with type identifiers such as

   ```
   TYPE
       FaceCard = ( Jack, Queen, King );
       FaceValue = 11..13;
   ```

   in a program unit that contains the function definition, and these type identifiers used in the heading:

   ```
   FUNCTION CardValue( Card : FaceCard ) : FaceValue;
   ```

2. *The scope rules given in Section 5.6 apply to type identifiers.*

3. *Values listed in an enumerated type definition must be legal identifiers and may not appear in any other enumerated type definition within that program unit.* For example, the declaration

   ```
   TYPE
       PassengerType = ( first-class, coach, standby );
   ```

   is not allowed because **first-class** is not a legal identifier. The declarations

   ```
   TYPE
       Weekdays = ( Monday, Tuesday, Wednesday, Thursday, Friday );
       VacationDays = ( Friday, Saturday, Sunday, Monday );
   ```

   are not allowed because the same identifier may not be used in both of these type definitions.

4. *The function* pred(x) *is undefined if* x *is the first value of an ordinal type;* succ(x) *is undefined if* x *is the the last value.* Thus some care is required when using these functions to decrement or increment a value of an enumerated type. To demonstrate, consider the following alternative to the for loop in procedure **GetEmployeeInfo** of the program in Figure 8.3:

```
Day := Sunday;
WHILE Day <= Saturday DO
    BEGIN
        PrintDay( Day );
        write( ': ' );
        readln( DayHours );
        WeekHours := WeekHours + DayHours;
        Day := succ( Day )
    END {WHILE}
```

An out-of-range error results when the value of Day is **Saturday** because **succ(Saturday)** is undefined, since **Saturday** is the last value of the data type **DaysOfWeek**.

5. *Values of an enumerated data type cannot be input from or output to text files, including the standard files* **input** *and* output. It is necessary to use procedures like **ReadDay** and **PrintDay** in Figure 8.2 to convert between enumerated type values and values that can be read or written.

6. *If a variable or a function is declared to be of some subrange type, an attempt to assign it a value that is not in this subrange is an error (provided that range checking is enabled).* For example, if **x** and **y** are declared by

```
VAR
    x, y : 1..10;
```

the statement

```
FOR x := 1 TO 10 DO
    BEGIN
        y := x * x;
        writeln( y )
    END {FOR};
```

will result in an error when **x** reaches the value 4, because the value of **x** * **x** is then outside the range **1..10** and cannot be assigned to **y**.

Standard Pascal

There are a few differences between Turbo Pascal and standard Pascal regarding ordinal types. Standard Pascal:

- Does not provide procedures **Inc** and **Dec**.
- Does not support type casting.
- Does perform range checking of subrange values.

ONE-DIMENSIONAL ARRAYS

With silver bells, and cockle shells,
And pretty maids all in a row.
MOTHER GOOSE

There is nothing more difficult to take in hand, more perilous to conduct, or
more uncertain in its success, than to take the lead in the introduction of a
new order of things.
NICCOLO MACHIAVELLI, *The Prince*

CHAPTER CONTENTS

The simple data types we have considered thus far represent single values. In many situations, however, it is necessary to process a collection of values that are related in some way, for example, a list of test scores, a collection of measurements resulting from some experiment, or a sales-tax table. Processing such collections using only simple data types can be extremely cumbersome, and for this reason, most high-level languages include special features for structuring such data. As we noted in Chapter 8, Turbo Pascal provides five structured data types: arrays, strings, files, records, and sets. In this chapter we consider arrays, their implementation in Pascal, and how they can be used to process lists.

9.1   Introduction to Arrays; Indexed Variables

In many of our examples, we processed a collection of data values by reading the data items one at a time and processing each item individually, for example, reading a test score and assigning it to a variable, counting it, and adding it to a running sum. When the value was no longer needed, a new value was read for the same variable, counted, and added to the running sum. This process was repeated again and again. For many problems, however, the collection of data items must be processed several times. The following example illustrates.

Problem

Suppose that a program is to be developed to

1. Read a list of test scores.
2. Find their mean.
3. Print a list of scores greater than the mean.
4. Sort the list so the scores are in ascending order.

The following are two possible solutions.

Solution 1: Use One Variable for Each Test Score. Suppose, for example, that there are 100 test scores. We might use 100 different variables, **Score1**, **Score2**, . . . , **Score100**, thus creating 100 different memory locations to store the test scores:

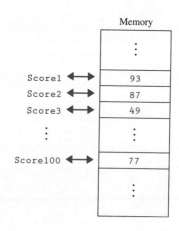

Although this approach may be practical if we have only a few data values to process, it is obviously cumbersome and awkward for large data sets, as the following program skeleton vividly demonstrates:

```
PROGRAM ProcessScores( input, output );

VAR
    Score1, Score2, Score3, Score4, Score5,
    Score6, Score7, Score8, Score9, Score10,
              .
              .
              .
    Score96, Score97, Score98, Score99, Score100 : integer;
    Mean : real;

BEGIN
    { Read the scores }
    read( Score1 );
    read( Score2 );
    read( Score3 );
            .
            .
            .
    read( Score100 );

    { Calculate the mean score }
    Mean := (Score1 + Score2 + Score3 + Score4 +
              Score5 + Score6 + Score7 + Score8 +
                        .
                        .
                        .
              Score97 + Score98 + Score99 + Score100) / 100;
    writeln( 'Mean =', Mean:6:2 );

    { Display scores above the mean }
    IF Score1 > Mean THEN
       writeln( Score1:5 );
    IF Score2 > Mean THEN
       writeln( Score2:5 );
    IF Score3 > Mean THEN
       writeln( Score3:5 );
                .
                .
                .
    IF Score100 > Mean THEN
       writeln( Score100:5 );

    { After more than 450 lines of code, sort them?
        There must be a better way! }

END.
```

Solution 2: Use a Data File. If we do not use 100 different memory locations to store the test scores, then we are forced to read the scores several times. Reentering the scores again and again so that the required processing can be carried out is obviously not practical. Instead, we can prepare a data file containing the scores and read the scores from it, as described in Chapter 6, closing and reopening the file for input each time we need to read through the list of scores.

```
PROGRAM ProcessScores( input, ScoresFile, output );

VAR
   Score, NumScores, i : integer;
   Sum, Mean : real;
   ScoresFile : text;

BEGIN
   { Read and count the test scores }
   assign( ScoresFile, 'SCORES.DAT' );
   reset( ScoresFile );
   NumScores := 0;
   WHILE NOT eof( ScoresFile ) DO
      BEGIN
         NumScores := NumScores + 1;
         readln( ScoresFile, Score )
      END {WHILE};

   { Calculate the mean score }
   reset( ScoresFile );
   Sum := 0;
   FOR i := 1 TO NumScores DO
      BEGIN
         readln( ScoresFile, Score );
         Sum := Sum + Score
      END {FOR};
   Mean := Sum / NumScores;
   writeln( 'Mean =', Mean:6:2 );

   { Display scores above the mean }
   reset( ScoresFile );
   FOR i := 1 TO NumScores DO
      BEGIN
         readln( ScoresFile, Score );
         IF Score > Mean THEN
            writeln( Score:5 )
      END {FOR};

   { Sort them???   Hm-m-m-m }

END.
```

Although this program is more manageable than that in Solution 1, it is still not a good solution to the problem because files are usually stored in secondary memory, and retrieving data from secondary memory is rather slow.

Arrays

To solve this problem efficiently, we need a data structure to store and organize the entire collection of test scores, as in Solution 2. However, because file input/output is slow, we need the scores stored in main memory, as in Solution 1. Also, many kinds of list processing such as sorting cannot be done efficiently if the data items can be retrieved only **sequentially,** that is, when an item can be accessed only by searching from the beginning of the list. What is needed instead is a **direct access** structure that allows a data item to be stored or retrieved directly by specifying its location in the structure, so that it takes no longer to access the item in location 100 than to access the item in location 5. And we prefer that the structure be stored in main memory so that storage and retrieval are fast. One such data structure is an **array,** in which a fixed number of data items, all of the same type, are organized in a sequence and each item can be accessed directly by specifying its position in this sequence.

If an array is to be used in a Pascal program to solve the test scores problem, a block of memory cells must be reserved. This block must be large enough to store the elements of the array. A simple declaration that does this is

```
VAR
    Score : ARRAY[1..100] OF integer;
```

This declaration instructs the compiler to establish an array with the name `Score`, consisting of 100 memory locations in which values of type `integer` can be stored:

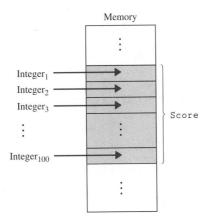

In the program we can then refer to this entire array of integers by using the **array variable `Score`,** but we can also access each individual element of the array by using an **indexed variable,** formed by appending an **index** enclosed in brackets to the array variable. This index specifies the position of an array element. Thus `Score[1]` refers to the first element of the array `Score`, `Score[2]` to the second element, and so on. The array declaration

```
VAR
    Score : ARRAY[1..100] OF integer;
```

thus not only reserves a block of memory locations in which to store the elements of the array **Score**, but it also associates the indexed variables **Score[1]**, **Score[2]**, **Score[3]**, . . . , **Score[100]** with these locations:

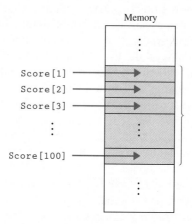

Each indexed variable names an individual memory location and hence can be used in much the same way as an ordinary variable can. For example, the assignment statement

```
Score[4] := 83
```

stores the value 83 in the fourth location of the array **Score**, and the output statement

```
writeln( Score[10]:5 )
```

displays the value stored in the tenth location of **Score**.

An important feature of this indexed notation for arrays is that the index may be a variable. For example, the statement

```
IF Score[n] > 90 THEN
   writeln( Score[n]:3, ' = A' )
```

retrieves the nth item of the array **Score**, compares it with 90, and prints it with a letter grade of A if it exceeds 90. The index may even be an expression, as in

```
IF Score[i] > Score[i + 1] THEN
   BEGIN
      Temp:= Score[i];
      Score[i] := Score[i + 1];
      Score[i + 1] := Temp
   END {IF};
```

This statement interchanges the contents of **Score[i]** and **Score[i + 1]** if the first is greater than the second.

Using an array reference in which the index is a variable or an expression within a loop that changes the value of the index on each pass through the loop is a convenient way to process each item in the array. Thus

```
FOR n := 1 TO 100 DO
   IF Score[n] > 90 THEN
      writeln( Score[n]:3, ' = A' );
```

retrieves each item of the array **Score** in sequence, beginning with **Score[1]**, compares it with 90, and prints it with a letter grade of A if it exceeds 90. It is equivalent to the following sequence of **IF** statements:

```
IF Score[1] > 90 THEN
   writeln( Score[1]:3, ' = A' );
IF Score[2] > 90 THEN
   writeln( Score[2]:3, ' = A' );
IF Score[3] > 90 THEN
   writeln( Score[3]:3, ' = A' );
                    .
                    .
                    .
IF Score[100] > 90 THEN
   writeln( Score[100]:3, ' = A' );
```

Figure 9.1 illustrates.

Arrays such as **Score** involve only a single index and so are commonly called **one-dimensional arrays.** Pascal programs, however, may process arrays of more than one dimension, in which case each element of the array is designated by attaching the appropriate number of indices to the array name. In this chapter we confine our attention to one-dimensional arrays; we will consider multidimensional arrays in Chapter 11.

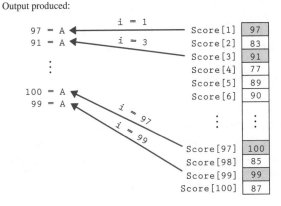

FIGURE 9.1 Processing an array of records.

Array Declarations

The name of a one-dimensional array, the type of its components, and the type of its index are declared by using an **array declaration** of the form shown in the following syntax diagram. (Note that an array declaration may include the specification **packed,** which directs the compiler to store the data in a special compact format. The word **PACKED** has no effect in Turbo Pascal, since items are automatically packed whenever possible.)

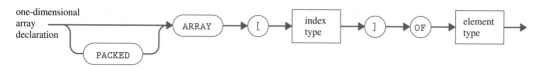

From this syntax diagram we see that an array declaration has the following form:

Array Declaration

Form:

   ARRAY[*index-type*] OF *element-type*

where:
   ARRAY and **OF** are reserved words;
   index-type may be any ordinal type;
   element-type may be any type.

Purpose:
Specifies that *index-type* is the type of the indices and that *element-type* is the type of the elements in an array.

For example, the array declaration

```
ARRAY[1..10] OF real
```

specifies a one-dimensional array whose index may be any of the values 1, 2, 3, . . . , 10 and whose elements are of type **real**. The array declaration

```
ARRAY['A'..'Z'] OF integer
```

specifies a one-dimensional array whose index may be any of the characters A, B, . . ., Z and each of whose twenty-six elements is an integer.

Although array declarations may appear in the variable section of a program's declaration part to specify the type of an array, it is preferable to associate them with type identifiers, as in

```
CONST
   NumLimit = 100;
```

```
TYPE
   xRange = -5..10;
   Letter = 'A'..'Z';
   RealArray = ARRAY[xRange] OF real;
   ArrayOfNumbers = ARRAY[0..NumLimit] OF 1..999;
   FrequencyArray = ARRAY[Letter] OF integer;
   Line = ARRAY[1..80] OF char;
```

These type identifiers can then be used to declare the types of array variables such as

```
VAR
   Coordinate : RealArray;
   Number : ArrayOfNumbers;
   CharCount : FrequencyArray;
   TextLine : Line;
```

They may also be used to declare the types of formal parameters, as in

```
PROCEDURE Sort( VAR List : ArrayOfNumbers );
```

Note that the array declaration **ARRAY[0..NumLimit] OF 1..999** cannot be used to specify the type of the parameter **List**. *Like all formal parameters, the type of a formal array parameter must be specified by a type identifier.*[1]

Array Initialization

In Turbo Pascal, an array variable may be initialized as a typed constant by using a declaration of the form

```
CONST
   array-name : array-type = ( list-of-array-elements );
```

For example, the declarations

```
TYPE
   DigitType = 0..9;
   NumeralType = '0'..'9';
   NumeralArray = ARRAY[DigitType] OF NumeralType;

CONST
   Numeral : NumeralArray = ( '0', '1', '2', '3', '4',
                              '5', '6', '7', '8', '9' );
```

initialize the array **Numeral** with **Numeral[0]** = **'0'**, **Numeral[1]** = **'1'**, . . . **Numeral[9]** = **'9'**. For arrays of characters, an alternative form of constant section can also be used:

```
CONST
   Numeral : NumeralArray = '0123456789';
```

---

[1] See the footnote on page 457. Also see Section H.3 of Appendix H.

Address Translation

As we have noted, each element of an array is directly accessible. This direct access is accomplished by means of **address translation.** The first cell in the memory block is used to store the first array element. Its address is called the **base address** of the array, and the address of any other array element is calculated in terms of this base address. For example, if the base address for the array **Score** is b and each score can be stored in a single memory cell, then the address of **Score[1]** is b, the address of **Score[2]** is $b + 1$, that for **Score[3]** is $b + 2$, and in general, the address of **Score[i]** is $b + i - 1$.

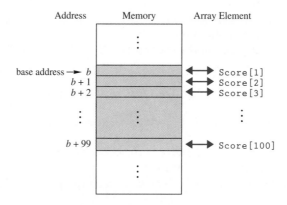

If w memory cells are required for each element, then **Score[1]** will be stored in w consecutive cells beginning at the cell with address b, **Score[2]** in a block beginning at address $b + w$, and in general, **Score[i]** in a block of size w beginning at address $b + (i - 1) * w$. Each time an array element is accessed using an indexed variable, this address translation must be performed by the system software and/or hardware to determine the location of that element in memory.

9.2 List Processing Using One-Dimensional Arrays

Many problems involve processing lists: a list of test scores, a list of names, a list of employee records, and so on. Such processing includes displaying all the items in the list, inserting new items, deleting items, searching the list for a specified item, and sorting the list so that the items are in a certain order. Since most programming languages do not provide a predefined list type (LISP, an acronym for LISt Processing, is one exception), lists must be processed using some other structure. This is commonly done using an array to store the list, storing the ith list item in the ith position of the array.

Examples

To illustrate list processing, suppose we wish to process a list of test scores, as in the example of the preceding section. If we declare the array **Score** by

```
CONST
   ScoresLimit = 100;
```

```
TYPE
   ListOfScores = ARRAY[1..ScoresLimit] OF integer;

VAR
   Score : ListOfScores;
```

we can read the scores into the array **Score** by using an input statement in a repetition structure. For example, we might use a **FOR** statement

```
FOR i := 1 to ScoresLimit DO
   read( Score[i] );
```

where the type of the control variable **i** is compatible with the subrange type **1..ScoresLimit** specified for the array indices in the array declaration. A **WHILE** statement

```
i := 1;
WHILE i <= ScoresLimit DO
   BEGIN
      read( Score[i] );
      i := i + 1
   END {WHILE};
```

or a **REPEAT-UNTIL** statement

```
i := 1;
REPEAT
   read( Score[i] );
   i := i + 1
UNTIL i > ScoresLimit;
```

could also be used. If the number of scores to be processed is not always the same, we might declare an integer variable **NumScores** and use only part of the array:

```
VAR
   Score : ListOfScores;
   NumScores : integer;
```

The statements

```
readln( NumScores );
IF NumScores > ScoresLimit THEN
   writeln( 'At most ', ScoresLimit:1,
            ' scores can be processed' )
ELSE
   FOR i := 1 TO NumScores DO
      read( Score[i] );
```

might then be used to read and store the test scores in the first **NumScores** locations of the array **Score**. Note that after a value is read for **NumScores**, a check is made to ensure that this value is not too large. If the range-checking compiler option is enabled (see Section 8.4), an error results if an attempt is made to use an index that is out of range. If range checking is not performed, unexpected results may occur if an index is out of range (see Potential Problem 2 at the end of this chapter). Thus, it is usually best to have range checking activated when using arrays.

If the value 15 is read for `NumScores`, the **read** statement will be executed fifteen times, and values will be assigned to the first fifteen positions `Score[1]`, `Score[2]`, . . . , `Score[15]` of the array. The rest of the array, `Score[16]`, . . . , `Score[100]`, is unchanged; these array elements retain their previous values.

The items in a list may be displayed by placing an output statement in a repetition structure. For example, the statement

```
FOR i := 1 TO NumScores DO
    writeln( Score[i]:3 );
```

displays the first `NumScores` entries of the list `Score` on separate lines, one per line. The statement

```
FOR i := 1 TO NumScores DO
    write( Score[i]:3 );
```

displays these entries on the same line. Note that subsequent output will also appear on this same line. This can be avoided by following the **FOR** statement with a **writeln** statement having no output list:

```
FOR i := 1 TO NumScores DO
    write( Score[i]:3 );
writeln;
```

Other kinds of list processing are also easy using repetition structures. For example, the mean of the scores in the list `Score` can be calculated by

```
Sum := 0;
FOR i := 1 TO NumScores DO
    Sum := Sum + Score[i];
MeanScore := Sum / NumScores;
writeln( 'Mean of the scores is: ', MeanScore:3:1 );
```

To display the scores that are greater than the mean, we can use the statement

```
FOR i := 1 TO NumScores DO
    IF Score[i] > Mean THEN
        writeln( Score[i]:3 )
```

The program in Figure 9.2 uses these statements to solve the first part of the problem stated in the preceding section. It reads a list of up to 100 scores, calculates their mean, and displays a list of scores greater than the mean. The sorting part of the problem is solved in Section 9.4.

FIGURE 9.2 Processing a list of test scores.

```
PROGRAM TestScores( input, output );
{**********************************************************************

    Input (keyboard):  A list of test scores.
    Purpose:           Read a list of test scores, calculate their mean,
                       and print a list of scores greater than the mean.
    Output (screen):   User prompts, messages, mean of test scores,
                       and a list of scores greater than the mean.


**********************************************************************}

CONST
    ScoresLimit = 100;      {maximum number of scores}

TYPE
    ListOfScores = ARRAY[1..ScoresLimit] OF integer;

VAR
    Score : ListOfScores;   {list of scores}
    NumScores,              {number of scores}
    i,                      {index}
    Sum : integer;          {sum of the scores}
    MeanScore : real;       {mean of the scores}

BEGIN
    write( 'Enter number of scores:  ' );
    readln( NumScores );
    IF NumScores > ScoresLimit THEN
        writeln( 'At most ', ScoresLimit:1, ' scores can be processed' )
    ELSE
        BEGIN
            { Read the scores and store them in array Score }

            writeln( 'Enter the scores, as many per line as desired.' );
            FOR i := 1 TO NumScores DO
                read( Score[i] );

            { Calculate the mean of the scores }

            Sum := 0;
            FOR i := 1 TO NumScores DO
                Sum := Sum + Score[i];
            MeanScore := Sum / NumScores;
            writeln( 'Mean of the scores is ', MeanScore:3:1 );
```

FIGURE 9.2   Processing a list of test scores. (cont.)

```
        { Print list of scores greater than the mean }

        writeln;
        writeln( 'List of scores greater than the mean:' );
        FOR i := 1 TO NumScores DO
            IF Score[i] > MeanScore THEN
                writeln( Score[i]:3 )
      END {ELSE}
END.
```

Sample run:

```
Enter number of scores:   15
Enter the scores, as many per line as desired.
88 77 56 89 100 99 55 35 78 65
69 83 71 38 95
Mean of the scores is 73.2

List of scores greater than the mean:
 88
 77
 89
100
 99
 78
 83
 95
```

In most of our examples of arrays, the indices have been positive integers, ranging from 1 through some upper limit. This is probably the most common index type, but as we noted in the preceding section, the type of the index may be any ordinal type. For example, the declarations

```
TYPE
    DaysOfWeek = ( Sunday, Monday, Tuesday, Wednesday,
                    Thursday, Friday, Saturday );
    DaysArray = ARRAY[DaysOfWeek] OF real;

VAR
    HoursWorked : DaysArray;
```

establish a one-dimensional array **HoursWorked** with seven locations, each of which can store a real number:

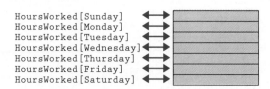

Real values can be read into these seven locations by the statement

```
FOR Day := Sunday TO Saturday DO
   read( HoursWorked[Day] );
```

where the index `Day` is of type `DaysOfWeek`. In general, the type of the indices in any array reference must be compatible with that specified in the array declaration, and the type of values stored in the array must be compatible with the element type. Recall that two **types** are **compatible** if they are the same, one is a subrange of the other, or both are subranges of the same underlying type.

The examples in the next section illustrate the use of arrays with nonnumeric indices. In the first example, an array indexed by a subrange of characters is used to store the number of occurrences of these characters in a text file. The second example uses an array indexed by an enumerated type `ClassName` to store the sum of test scores for students in various classes.

Array Assignment

Sometimes it is necessary to copy the elements of one array into a second array. Suppose, for example, that arrays `Alpha` and `Beta` are declared by

```
TYPE
   RealList = ARRAY[1..5] OF real;

VAR
   Alpha, Beta : RealList;
```

If values have been assigned to the array `Alpha`, they can be copied to the array `Beta` by the statement

```
FOR i := 1 to 5 DO
   Beta[i] := Alpha[i];
```

The elements of the array `Alpha` to the array `Beta` can be assigned more simply, however, by using the assignment statement

```
Beta := Alpha;
```

In general, one array may be assigned to another array only when they have the **same type** and the array components are not files. This means that they must be declared in the same type declaration or by the same type identifier or by **equivalent** type identifiers. Two type identifiers are equivalent if their definitions can be traced back to a common *type identifier*. For example, consider the following type definitions:

```
TYPE
   Aarray = ARRAY[1..5] OF real;
   Barray = Aarray;
   Carray = Aarray;
   Darray = Barray;
   Earray = ARRAY[1..5] OF real;
```

The type identifiers **Barray** and **Carray** are equivalent to **Aarray** and to each other, since they are synonyms for the type identifier **Aarray**. Similarly, **Darray** is a synonym for **Barray** and is therefore equivalent to **Barray**. The type identifiers **Aarray**, **Barray**, **Carray**, and **Darray** are equivalent because their definitions can be traced back to a common *type identifier* (**Aarray**). Note, however, that even though the definitions of **Aarray** and **Earray** are identical, these type identifiers are not equivalent because they are not defined using a common type *identifier*. Thus, if arrays **A**, **A1**, **B**, **C**, **D**, and **E** are declared by

```
VAR
    A, A1 : Aarray;
    B : Barray;
    C : Carray;
    D : Darray;
    E : Earray;
```

the array assignment statements

```
A1 := A;
B := A;
B := C;
B := D;
C := D;
```

all are valid because **A**, **A1**, **B**, **C**, and **D** all have the same type, but the assignment statement

```
A := E;
```

is not valid.

Arrays as Parameters

Arrays may also be used as parameters for functions and procedures, but the value of a function may not be an array. To illustrate, consider the following function:

```
FUNCTION Mean( VAR Item : ListType;        {a list of items}
               NumItems : integer )   {number of items}
               : real;
{------------------------------------------------------------

   Accepts: A list of NumItems numbers stored in an array Item.
   Returns: The mean of the numbers.

   ------------------------------------------------------------}

VAR
    i : integer; {index}
    Sum : real;  {sum of the numbers}
```

```
BEGIN
   IF NumItems = 0 THEN
      BEGIN
         writeln( 'No elements -- returning mean of 0' );
         Mean := 0
      END {IF}
   ELSE
      BEGIN
         Sum := 0;
         FOR i := 1 TO NumItems DO
            Sum := Sum + Item[i];
         Mean := Sum / NumItems
      END {ELSE}
END {Mean};
```

Because the types of formal parameters must be specified by type identifiers, an array declaration such as **ARRAY[1..100] OF integer** cannot be used to specify the type of the formal parameter **Item**.[2]

When this function is referenced, the type of each actual parameter that is an array must be the same as the type of the corresponding formal parameter. Thus, to reference this function in the program of Figure 9.2 with the statement

```
MeanScore := Mean( Score, NumScores );
```

it would be necessary to set the type identifier **ListType** equal to the type identifier **ListOfScores** in the main program:

```
TYPE
   ListOfScores = ARRAY[1..ScoresLimit] OF integer;
   ListType = ListOfScores;
```

or to use the same type identifier, either **ListOfScores** or **ListType**, both in the main program and in the heading of this function.

In this function **Mean**, the array **Item** is a variable parameter, although this is not required. If it were a value parameter, however, then a reference to this function would require copying the elements of the actual array into **Item**. This would produce two copies of the same list of values and would therefore not be an efficient use of memory. Moreover, the process of copying the elements of one array into another is time-consuming.

An array must be a variable parameter if the subprogram is to return the array to the program unit that calls it. For example, a procedure to read a list of items into an array **Item**, count the number of elements that were read, and return both this array and the count to the main program must declare both the array and the count as variable parameters:

---

[2] Turbo Pascal 7.0 allows **open-array parameters** whose declarations have the form *array-param* : ARRAY OF *element-type*. The corresponding actual array may have any legal index type, but *array-param* will have index type 0..*n* - 1, where *n* is the number of elements in the actual array. See Section H.4 of Appendix H for a discussion of open-array parameters.

```
PROCEDURE ReadList( VAR Item : ListType;      {list of items}
                    VAR Count : integer );    {number of items read}
{------------------------------------------------------------------

   Input (keyboard): A list of elements.
   Purpose:          Read list elements into array Item and
                     count the elements.
   Returns:          The array Item and the Count of the elements.

------------------------------------------------------------------}

   VAR
      Response : char; {user response}

   BEGIN
      writeln( 'Enter the list of items, as many per line as desired.' );
      writeln( 'Note: At most ', ListLimit:1,' items can be read.' );
      writeln;
      Count := 0;
      REPEAT
         write( 'Items: ' );
         WHILE NOT eoln DO
            BEGIN
               Count := Count + 1;
               read( Item[Count] )
            END {WHILE}
         readln;
         write( 'More (Y or N)?' );
         readln( Response )
      UNTIL (Response <> 'Y') AND (Response <> 'y')
   END {ReadList};
```

Some Limitations

The examples in this section indicate that arrays are very useful for processing lists. The array implementation of lists does have its drawbacks, however. One is that whereas a list need not have a fixed length, an array must have a fixed number of elements. This means that it is possible to declare the array to have exactly the right size for storing the list only if the list is static, that is, if its size never changes. The common approach otherwise is to estimate the maximum size of the list and to declare the array to have this number of components. However, if we declare the array too small, we run the risk of an error resulting from indices that are out of range, or we may lose some of the list elements because there is no room for them in the array. If we make the array too large, then we may be wasting a considerable part of the memory allocated to it.

Another weakness of the array implementation of lists is that although algorithms for the insertion and deletion operations are quite easy to write (as the exercises ask you to do), they are not very efficient. For example, inserting the new value 75 at position 6 in the following list of ten integers

23, 34, 48, 55, 68, 80, 82, 84, 91, 97

requires shifting the array elements in positions 6 through 10 into positions 7 through 11 to make room for the new value:

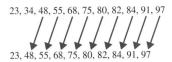

Deleting an item from the list also requires moving array elements; for example, to remove the second number in the list, we must shift the array elements in positions 3 through 11 into positions 2 through 10 to "close the gap":

23, 34, 48, 55, 68, 75, 80, 82, 84, 91, 97

23, 48, 55, 68, 75, 80, 82, 84, 91, 97

If insertions and deletions are restricted to the ends of the list, then array implementations that do not require moving array elements are possible. Two important special cases are stacks and queues. A **stack** is a list in which elements may be inserted (**pushed**) and deleted (**popped**) at only one end, called the **top** of the stack. If elements may be inserted only at one end (the **rear**) and deleted only at the other (the **front**), the list is called a **queue.** Array-based implementations of stacks and queues are described in the exercises at the end of the next section and are considered in detail in Chapter 13.

In summary, arrays work very well for static lists and reasonably well for lists whose maximum sizes can be estimated and for which insertions and deletions are infrequent or are restricted to the ends of the list. **Dynamic** lists whose sizes may vary greatly during processing and those in which items are frequently inserted and/or deleted anywhere in the list are better implemented using a linked structure, as described in Chapter 16.

9.3 Examples: Frequency Distributions; Class Averages

Example 1: Frequency Distributions

Consider the problem of reading text, counting the occurrences of each of the letters 'a' through 'z', and summarizing this information in a **frequency distribution.**

To solve this problem, we use an array **Frequency** to store the number of occurrences of each letter:

Frequency: **Frequency[ch]** is the number of occurrences of character **ch**.

Thus, **Frequency['A']** is the number of occurrences of **A** or **a** in the text file; **Frequency['B']** is the number of occurrences of **B** or **b**; and so on. An algorithm for solving this problem is

ALGORITHM TO GENERATE A FREQUENCY DISTRIBUTION

(* Input: Text from a file.
   Purpose: Count the number of times each letter appears in the text.
   Output: Frequency of occurrences of each letter. *)

1. Initialize array *Frequency* to all zeros.
2. While there is more data, do the following:
     a. Read a character *ch* from the file.
     b. Convert *ch* to uppercase.
     c. If *ch* is one of the letters 'A' through 'Z' then
         Increment *Frequency*[*ch*] by 1.
3. For *ch* ranging from 'A' to 'Z'
     Display *Frequency*[*ch*].

The program in Figure 9.3 implements this algorithm and uses an array **Frequency** declared by

```
TYPE
    Letter = 'A'..'Z';
    CharCountArray = ARRAY[Letter] OF integer;

VAR
    Frequency : CharCountArray;
```

The program uses the function **upcase** provided in Turbo Pascal to convert the indices to uppercase.

FIGURE 9.3   Generating a frequency distribution.

```
PROGRAM LetterCount( input, TextFile, output );
{**********************************************************************

    Input (file):    Several lines of text.
    Purpose:         Count the occurrences of each of the letters A, B,
                     ..., Z (or their lowercase equivalents a, b, ..., z)
                     in several lines of text.  The array Frequency
                     indexed by the subrange 'A'..'Z' is used for this.
                     If Ch is any one of these 26 letters, Frequency[Ch]
                     is the number of occurrences of Ch.
    Output (screen): Messages and the elements of array Frequency.

**********************************************************************}

TYPE
    Letter = 'A'..'Z';
    CharCountArray = ARRAY[Letter] OF integer;
```

FIGURE 9.3 Generating a frequency distribution. (cont.)

```
VAR
    TextFile : text;            {file of text}
    TextFileName : string;      {actual name of text file}
    Frequency : CharCountArray; {frequencies of letters}
    Ch : char;                  {character from text line}

BEGIN
    {First initialize all frequencies to 0}

    FOR Ch := 'A' TO 'Z' DO
        Frequency[Ch] := 0;

    {Read the lines of text and count occurrences of letters}

    write( 'Enter name of text file: ' );
    readln( TextFileName );
    assign( TextFile, TextFileName );
    reset( TextFile );
    WHILE NOT eof( TextFile ) DO
        BEGIN
            read( TextFile, Ch );
            Ch := upcase(Ch);
            IF ('A' <= Ch) AND (Ch <= 'Z') THEN
                Frequency[Ch] := Frequency[Ch] + 1;
        END {WHILE};

    {Print the frequencies}

    writeln;
    writeln( 'In the text processed, the letters A - Z occurred with' );
    writeln( 'the following frequencies:' );
    writeln;
    FOR Ch := 'A' TO 'Z' DO
        writeln( 'Frequency of ', Ch, ':  ', Frequency[Ch]:2 )
END {main program}.
```

Listing of FIL9-3.DAT:

```
These two lines of text are being used to test this program.
THE QUICK BROWN FOX JUMPED OVER THE LAZY DOGS AND RAN AWAY.
```

Sample run:

```
Enter name of text file: FIL9-3.DAT
In the text processed, the letters A - Z occurred with
the following frequencies:
```

FIGURE 9.3 Generating a frequency distribution. (cont.)

```
Frequency of A:    7
Frequency of B:    2
Frequency of C:    1
Frequency of D:    4
Frequency of E:   12
Frequency of F:    2
Frequency of G:    3
Frequency of H:    4
Frequency of I:    4
Frequency of J:    1
Frequency of K:    1
Frequency of L:    2
Frequency of M:    2
Frequency of N:    5
Frequency of O:    8
Frequency of P:    2
Frequency of Q:    1
Frequency of R:    6
Frequency of S:    6
Frequency of T:   10
Frequency of U:    3
Frequency of V:    1
Frequency of W:    3
Frequency of X:    2
Frequency of Y:    2
Frequency of Z:    1
```

A **bar graph** or **histogram** is often used to display frequency distributions graphically. Each item is represented by a bar whose length corresponds to the number of occurrences of that item. Thus, the frequency distribution produced by the sample run in the preceding program could be represented by the bar graph

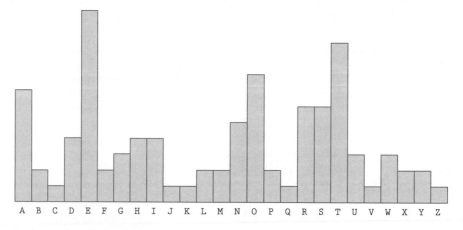

The program in Figure 9.4 is a modification of the preceding program. Procedure **PlotBarGraph** is used to display a bar graph.

FIGURE 9.4   Generating a bar graph.

```pascal
PROGRAM LetterCount( input, TextFile, output );
{*******************************************************************

    Input (file):    Several lines of text.
    Purpose:         Count the occurrences of each of the letters A, B,
                     ..., Z (or their lowercase equivalents a, b, ..., z)
                     in several lines of text. The array Frequency
                     indexed by the subrange 'A'..'Z' is used for this.
                     If Ch is any one of these 26 letters, Frequency[Ch]
                     is the number of occurrences of Ch.
    Output (screen): Messages and the bar graph.


*******************************************************************}

TYPE
   Letter = 'A'..'Z';
   CharCountArray = ARRAY[Letter] OF integer;

VAR
   TextFile : text;                 {file of text}
   TextFileName : string;           {actual name of text file}
   Frequency : CharCountArray;      {frequencies of letters}
   Ch : char;                       {character from text line}

PROCEDURE PlotBarGraph( Frequency : CharCountArray );
{-------------------------------------------------------------------

    Accepts:         Array Frequency of frequency counts of
                     characters.
    Purpose:         Display a bar graph of frequency distribution.
    Output (screen) : Bar graph.


-------------------------------------------------------------------}

   VAR
      Ch : char;    {index}
      i : integer; {loop counter}

   BEGIN
      FOR Ch := 'A' TO 'Z' DO
         BEGIN
            write( Ch, ':' );
            FOR i := 1 TO Frequency[Ch] DO
               write( '#' );
            writeln
         END {FOR}
   END {PlotBarGraph};
```

FIGURE 9.4   Generating a bar graph. (cont.)

```
BEGIN {****************** main program ******************}

   {First initialize all frequencies to 0}

   FOR Ch := 'A' TO 'Z' DO
      Frequency[Ch] := 0;

   {Read the lines of text and count occurrences of letters}

   write( 'Enter name of text file: ' );
   readln( TextFileName );
   writeln;
   assign( TextFile, TextFileName );
   reset( TextFile );
   WHILE NOT eof( TextFile ) DO
      BEGIN
         read( TextFile, Ch );
         Ch := upcase(Ch);
         IF ('A' <= Ch) AND (Ch <= 'Z') THEN
            Frequency[Ch] := Frequency[Ch] + 1;
      END {WHILE};

   {Plot the bar graph of these frequencies}

   PlotBarGraph( Frequency )

END {main program}.
```

Bar graph generated using FIL9-3.DAT of Figure 9.3:

```
A:#######
B:##
C:#
D:####
E:###########
F:##
G:###
H:####
I:####
J:#
K:#
L:##
M:##
N:#####
O:########
P:##
Q:#
R:#####
S:#####
T:##########
U:###
V:#
W:###
X:##
Y:##
Z:#
```

Example 2: Class Averages

Consider the problem of calculating the average test score received by students in each of the four classes freshman, sophomore, junior, and senior. For each student, a score must be read together with a class code of 1, 2, 3, or 4, representing the class to which the student belongs. For each class we must calculate the average score received by the students in that class.

Since there are four classes, we can use an array **Number** with four elements to record the number of students in the classes and another array **SumOfScores** to record the sum of the scores received by students in the various classes. These arrays could be indexed **1..4**, but to illustrate the use of arrays indexed by an enumerated type, we will use

```
ClassName = ( Freshman, Sophomore, Junior, Senior )
```

for indices. We thus will use the following arrays:

Number: **Number[Class]** is the number of students in the class specified by the index **Class**, which is of type **ClassName**.

SumOfScores: **SumOfScores[Class]** is the sum of the test scores for all students in the class specified by the value of **Class**.

There are three main tasks to be performed in solving this problem. The first is to initialize the arrays **Number** and **SumOfScores** to 0. The second task is to read and tabulate the pairs of class codes and test scores in the arrays **Number** and **SumOfScores**. Finally, after all the data has been read, the class averages must be calculated and displayed. The following diagram summarizes the structure of the program in Figure 9.5 that solves this problem:

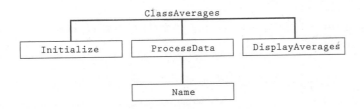

Initialization consists simply of setting to 0 each of the elements of the arrays **Number** and **SumOfScores**. In the program this is done by calling the procedure **Initialize**.

An algorithm for the second task is

ProcessData

(∗ Algorithm to read pairs of class codes (1, 2, 3, 4) and test scores and tabulate these in the arrays *Number* and *SumOfScores* whose indices are of type *ClassName*. ∗)

1. Read *ClassCode* and *Score*.

2. While there is more data, do the following:
   a. If *ClassCode* is less than 1 or greater than 4
      Display an illegal class code message,
      Otherwise do the following:
         i. Convert *ClassCode* to *Class* of type *ClassName*.
         ii. Add 1 to *Number*[*Class*].
         iii. Add *Score* to *SumOfScores*[*Class*].
   b. Read next *ClassCode* and *Score*.

The procedure **ProcessData** in the program implements this algorithm. **ClassCode** is converted to **Class**, whose type is the enumerated type **ClassName**, by using the function **Name**.

An algorithm for the third task is straightforward:

DisplayAverages

(∗ Algorithm to calculate and display the class averages. ∗)

1. Print suitable headings for the output.
2. For *Class* ranging from *Freshman* to *Senior,* do the following:
   a. Write the class number.
   b. If *Number*[*Class*] is 0
      Display a message that there were no test scores for this class
      Otherwise
      Display *SumOfScores*[*Class*] / *Number*[*Class*].

This algorithm is implemented by the procedure **DisplayAverages** in the program in Figure 9.5.

FIGURE 9.5 Calculating class averages.

```
PROGRAM ClassAverages( input, output );
{****************************************************************

   Input (keyboard): Pairs of class codes and scores, user responses.
   Purpose:          Calculate the average score received on a test
                     by students in each of four classes:
                     Freshman (1), Sophomore (2), Junior (3) and
                     Senior (4).
   Output (screen):  User prompts; average score for each class.

****************************************************************}
TYPE
   ClassName = ( Freshman, Sophomore, Junior, Senior );
   ClassList = ARRAY[ClassName] OF integer;
```

FIGURE 9.5   Calculating class averages. (cont.)

```
VAR
   Number,                        {Number[Class] = # of students in Class}
   SumOfScores : ClassList;   {SumOfScores[Class] = sum of scores for
                                   students in Class}


PROCEDURE Initialize( VAR Number,        {numbers of students}
                          SumOfScores    {sums of student scores}
                          : ClassList );
{------------------------------------------------------------------

   Purpose:  Initialize the arrays Number and SumOfScores to zero.
   Returns:  Arrays Number and SumOfScores.


-------------------------------------------------------------------}

   VAR
      Class : ClassName;        {index}


   BEGIN
      FOR Class := Freshman TO Senior DO
         BEGIN
            Number[Class] := 0;
            SumOfScores[Class] := 0
         END {FOR}
   END {Initialize};

PROCEDURE ProcessData( VAR Number,        {numbers of students}
                           SumOfScores    {sums of student scores}
                           : ClassList );
{------------------------------------------------------------------

   Input (keyboard): Pairs of class codes and scores.
   Purpose:          Read pairs of class codes and scores, and for
                     each pair, increment the appropriate counter
                     Number[Class] by 1, and add the test score to
                     SumOfScores[Class], the sum  of scores for
                     this class.
   Returns:          The arrays Number and SumOfScores.
   Output (screen):  User prompts.


-------------------------------------------------------------------}

   TYPE
      ClassNumber = 1..4;

   VAR
      ClassCode : integer;    {class code}
      Class : ClassName;      {class name corresponding to class code}
      Score : integer;        {student's test score}
```

FIGURE 9.5 Calculating class averages. (cont.)

```
FUNCTION Name(ClassCode : ClassNumber) : ClassName;
{-------------------------------------------------------------------

    Accepts:   ClassCode.
    Purpose:   Convert class code (1, 2, 3, 4) to the
               corresponding value of enumerated type ClassName.
    Returns:   A value of type ClassName.


-------------------------------------------------------------------}

    BEGIN
       CASE ClassCode OF
          1 : Name := Freshman;
          2 : Name := Sophomore;
          3 : Name := Junior;
          4 : Name := Senior
       END {CASE}
    END {Name};

BEGIN {ProcessData}
    writeln( 'Enter the class codes and the test scores in pairs,' );
    writeln( 'as many per line as desired.  Enter 0''s to signal' );
    writeln( 'the end of data.' );
    writeln;
    read( ClassCode, Score );
    WHILE ClassCode <> 0 DO
       BEGIN
          IF (ClassCode < 1) OR (ClassCode > 4) THEN
             writeln( '** Illegal class code **' )
          ELSE
             BEGIN
                Class := Name( ClassCode );
                Number[Class] := Number[Class] + 1;
                SumOfScores[Class] := SumOfScores[Class] + Score
             END {ELSE};
          read( ClassCode, Score )
       END {WHILE}
END {ProcessData};

PROCEDURE DisplayAverages( VAR Number,         {numbers of students}
                              SumOfScores   {sums of student scores}
                              : ClassList );
{-------------------------------------------------------------------

    Accepts:        Arrays Number and SumOfScores.
    Purpose:        Calculate and display the average score for each
                    of the four classes.
    Output (screen): Averages of test scores.


-------------------------------------------------------------------}
```

FIGURE 9.5   Calculating class averages. (cont.)

```
VAR
    Class : ClassName;     {index}

BEGIN
    writeln;
    writeln( 'CLASS #  AVE. SCORE' );
    writeln( '=======  ==========' );
    FOR Class := Freshman TO Senior DO
        BEGIN
            write( 1 + ord(Class):4 );
            IF Number[Class] = 0 THEN
                writeln( '      No scores' )
            ELSE
                writeln( SumOfScores[Class] / Number[Class]:11:1 )
        END {FOR}
END {DisplayAverages};

BEGIN {************** main program **************}
    Initialize( Number, SumOfScores );
    ProcessData( Number, SumOfScores );
    DisplayAverages( Number, SumOfScores )
END {main program}.
```

Sample run:

```
Enter the class codes and the test scores in pairs
as many per line as desired.  Enter 0's to signal
the end of data.

1 95   1 88   3 77   4 100  4 67   1 58   3 62   3 99
3 87   4 72   4 58   1 66   4 89
0 0

CLASS #  AVE. SCORE
=======  ==========
   1       76.8
   2     No scores
   3       81.2
   4       77.2
```

Exercises

1. Assume that the following declarations have been made:

```
TYPE
    Color = ( red, yellow, blue, green, white, black );
    ColorArray = ARRAY[Color] OF real;
    LittleArray = ARRAY[1..10] OF integer;
    CharCountArrray = ARRAY['A'..'F'] OF integer;
```

```
VAR
   Price : ColorArray;
   Number : LittleArray;
   LetterCount : CharCountArray;
   i : integer;
   Ch : char;
   Col : Color;
```

For each of the following, tell what value (if any) will be assigned to each array element, or explain why an error occurs:

(a) FOR i := 1 TO 10 DO
      Number[i] := i DIV 2;

(b) FOR i := 1 TO 6 DO
      Number[i] := i * i;
   FOR i := 7 TO 10 DO
      Number[i] := Number[i - 5];

(c) i := 0;
   WHILE i <> 10 DO
      BEGIN
         IF i MOD 3 = 0 THEN
            Number[i] := 0
         ELSE
            Number[i] := i;
         i := i + 1
      END {WHILE};

(d) Number[1] := 1;
   i := 2;
   REPEAT
      Number[i] := 2 * Number[i - 1];
      i := i + 1
   UNTIL i = 10;

(e) FOR Ch := 'A' TO 'F' DO
      IF Ch = 'A' THEN
         LetterCount[Ch] := 1;
      ELSE
         LetterCount[Ch] := LetterCount[pred(Ch)] + 1;

(f) FOR Col := yellow TO white DO
      Price[Col] := 13.95;

(g) FOR Col := red TO black DO
      CASE Col OF
         red, blue   : Price[Col] := 19.95;
         yellow   : Price[Col] := 12.75;
         green, black : Price[Col] := 14.50;
         white   :
      END {CASE};

2. For each of the following, write appropriate declarations and statements to create the specified array:

(a) An array whose indices are the integers from 0 through 5 and in which each element is the same as the index.

(b) An array whose indices are the integers from −5 through 5 and for which the elements are the indices in reverse order.

(c) An array whose indices are the uppercase letters and in which each element is the same as the index.

(d) An array whose indices are the integers from 1 through 20 and for which an array element has the value true if the corresponding index is even, and false otherwise.

(e) An array whose indices are the uppercase letters and for which each element is the letter preceding the index, except that the array element corresponding to A is Z.

(f) An array whose indices are the uppercase letters and in which each array element is the number of the position of the corresponding index in the sequence A, B, C, . . . , Z.

(g) An array whose indices are the lowercase letters and in which an array element has the value true if the index is a vowel, and false otherwise.

(h) An array whose indices are the names of the five subjects mathematics, chemistry, speech, history, and economics and in which the array elements are the letter grades received: A in mathematics and speech, B in chemistry, F in history, and C in economics.

3. Assuming that values of type **integer** and **char** are stored in one memory word and values of type **real** require two memory words, indicate with a diagram like that in Section 9.1 where each element of an array **A** of the following type will be stored if the base address of **A** is *b;* also give the general address translation formula for **A[i]**.

(a) `ARRAY[1..5] OF integer;`

(b) `ARRAY[1..5] OF real;`

(c) `ARRAY[-5..5] OF char;`

(d) `ARRAY['A'..'Z'] OF integer;` (*Hint:* Use the **ord** function.)

4. Write a function **Max** that finds the largest value in an integer array **Number** of type **NumberArray** having **NumElements** components.

5. Write a procedure to locate and return the smallest and largest integers in an array **Number** as described in Exercise 4 and their positions in the array. It should also find and return the range of the numbers, that is, the difference between the largest number and the smallest.

6. Write a procedure **Insert** for inserting an item at a specified position in a list implemented as an array and a procedure **Delete** for deleting an item at a specified position.

7. The Cawker City Candy Company records the number of cases of candy produced each day over a four-week period. Write a program that reads these production numbers and stores them in an array. The program should then accept from the user a week number and a day number and should display the production level for that day. Assume that each week consists of five workdays.

8. The Cawker City Candy Company maintains two warehouses, one in Chicago and one in Detroit, each of which stocks at most 25 different items. Write a program that first reads the product numbers of items stored in the Chicago warehouse and stores them in an array **Chicago**, and then repeats this for the items stored in the Detroit warehouse, storing these product numbers in an array **Detroit**. The program should then find and display the **intersection** of these two lists of numbers, that is, the collection of product numbers common to both lists. The lists should not be assumed to have the same number of elements.

9. Repeat Exercise 8 but find and display the **union** of the two lists, that is, the collection of product numbers that are elements of at least one of the lists.

10. If $\bar{x}$ denotes the mean of the numbers $x_1, x_2, \ldots, x_n$, the **variance** is the average of the squares of the deviations of the numbers from the mean:

$$\text{Variance} = \frac{1}{n} \sum_{i=1}^{n} (x_i - \bar{x})^2$$

and the **standard deviation** is the square root of the variance. Write a program that reads a list of real numbers, counts them, and then calculates their mean, variance, and standard deviation. Display with appropriate labels the number of values read and their mean, variance, and standard deviation. Use functions or procedures to calculate the mean, variance, and standard deviation.

11. Letter grades are sometimes assigned to numeric scores by using the grading scheme commonly called "grading on the curve." In this scheme, a letter grade is assigned to a numeric score according to the following table:

x = Numeric Score	Letter Grade
$x < m - \dfrac{3}{2}\sigma$	F
$m - \dfrac{3}{2}\sigma \leq x < m - \dfrac{1}{2}\sigma$	D
$m - \dfrac{1}{2}\sigma \leq x < m + \dfrac{1}{2}\sigma$	C
$m + \dfrac{1}{2}\sigma \leq x < m + \dfrac{3}{2}\sigma$	B
$m + \dfrac{3}{2}\sigma \leq x$	A

where *m* is the mean score and σ (sigma) is the standard deviation. Extend the program in Exercise 10 to read a list of real numbers representing numeric scores, calculate their mean and standard deviation, and display the letter grade corresponding to each numeric score.

12. Peter the postman became bored one night, and to break the monotony of the night shift, he carried out an experiment with a row of mailboxes in the post office. These mailboxes were numbered 1 through 150, and beginning with mailbox 2, he opened the doors of all the even-numbered mailboxes. Next, beginning with mailbox 3, he went to every third mailbox, opening its door if it was closed and closing it if it was open. Then he repeated this procedure with every fourth mailbox, then every fifth mailbox, and so on. When he finished, he was surprised at the distribution of closed mailboxes. Write a program to determine which ones these were.

13. One possible implementation of a stack is to use an array `Stack` indexed `1..StackLimit`, with the top of the stack at position 1 of the array.

(**a**) Why isn't this a good implementation?

(**b**) A better implementation is to let the stack grow from position 1 toward position `StackLimit` and to maintain an integer variable `Top` to "point" to the current top of the stack. Write procedures for the push and pop operations in this implementation.

(**c**) Use the procedures of part (b) in a program that reads a command I (Insert) or D (Delete); for I, read an integer and push it onto the stack and, for D, pop an integer from the stack and display it.

14. For a queue, we might imitate the array implementation of a stack in Exercise 13, using an array `Queue` indexed `1..QueueLimit` and maintaining two "pointers," `Front` to the item at the front of the queue and `Rear` to the item at the rear. To add an item to the queue, simply increment `Rear` by 1 and store the item in `Queue[Rear]`; to remove an item, simply increment `Front` by 1.

(**a**) Describe the inadequacies of this implementation. Consider, for example, an integer array with five elements and the following sequence of queue operations: Insert 37, Insert 82, Insert 59, Delete an item, Delete an item, Insert 66, Insert 13, Insert 48.

(**b**) A better implementation is to think of the array as being circular, with the first element following the last. For this, index the array beginning with 0 and increment `Front` and `Rear` using addition `MOD QueueLimit`. Write procedures for the insertion and deletion operations, assuming this implementation. Use these procedures in a program that reads a command I (Insert) or D (Delete); for I, read an integer and add it to the queue and, for D, remove an integer from the queue and display it.

15. A **prime number** is an integer greater than 1 whose only positive divisors are 1 and the integer itself. One method for finding all the prime numbers in the range from 1 through *n* is known as the **Sieve of Eratosthenes.** Consider the list of numbers from 2 through *n*. Two is the first prime number, but the multiples of 2 (4, 6, 8, . . .) are not, and so they are crossed out in the list. The first number after 2 that was not crossed out is 3, the next prime. We then cross out from the list all higher multiples of 3 (6, 9, 12, . . .). The next number not crossed out is 5, the next prime, and so we cross out all higher multiples of 5 (10, 15, 20, . . .). We repeat this procedure until we reach the first number in the list that has not been crossed out and whose square is greater than n. All the numbers that remain in the list are the primes from 2 through n. Write a program that uses this sieve method to find all the prime numbers from 2 through n. Run it for $n = 50$ and for $n = 500$.

16. Write a program to add two large integers with up to 300 digits. One approach is to treat each number as a list, each of whose elements is a block of digits of the number. For example, the integer 179,534,672,198 might be stored with `Block[1]` = 198, `Block[2]` = 672, `Block[3]` = 534, and `Block[4]` = 179. Then add the integers (lists) element by element, carrying from one element to the next when necessary.

17. Proceeding as in Exercise 16, write a program to multiply two large integers of length up to 300 digits.

18. Develop a recursive procedure to generate all of the $n!$ permutations of the set $\{1, 2, . . . , n\}$. (*Hint:* The permutations of $\{1, 2, . . . , k\}$ can be obtained by considering each permutation of $\{1, 2, . . . , k - 1\}$ as an ordered list and inserting k into each of the k possible positions in this list, including at the front and at the rear.) For example, the permutations of $\{1, 2\}$ are (1, 2) and (2, 1). Inserting 3 into each of the three possible positions of the first permutation yields the permutations (3, 1, 2), (1, 3, 2), and (1, 2, 3) of $\{1, 2, 3\}$, and using the second permutation gives (3, 2, 1), (2, 3, 1), and (2, 1, 3). Write a program to test your procedure.

 ## 9.4   PART OF THE PICTURE: Sorting and Searching

Sorting and searching are two problems that have received a great deal of study because they are important to many different applications. Over the years literally hundreds of sorting and searching algorithms have been developed. In fact, entire books have been written about these problems, for example, *The Art of Computer Programming, Volume 3: Sorting and Searching,* written by Donald Knuth. **Sorting** is the problem of arranging the items in a list so that they are in either ascending or descending order, and **searching** is the problem of examining a collection of data to determine whether or not it contains some specified item. In this section, we will look at two sorting algorithms and two searching algorithms. Others are described in the exercises and in Chapter 15.

Sorting: Simple Selection Sort

One of the simplest sorting methods is known as **simple selection sort.** Although it is not an efficient sorting method for large lists, it does perform reasonably well for small lists, and it is easy to understand. More efficient sorting schemes are described in the exercises at the end of this section.

The basic idea of a selection sort of a list is to make a number of passes through the list or a part of the list and, on each pass, to select one item to be correctly positioned. For example, on each pass through a sublist, the smallest item in this sublist might be found and then moved to its proper location.

To illustrate, suppose that the following list is to be sorted into ascending order:

$$67 , 33 , 21 , 84 , 49 , 50 , 75$$

We first scan the list to locate the smallest item and find it in position 3:

$$67 , 33 , \boxed{21} , 84 , 49 , 50 , 75$$

We interchange this item with the first item and thus properly position the smallest item at the beginning of the list:

$$\boxed{21} , 33 , 67 , 84 , 49 , 50 , 75$$

Next we scan the sublist consisting of the items from position 2 on to find the smallest item

$$21 , \boxed{33} , 67 , 84 , 49 , 50 , 75$$

and exchange it with the second item (itself in this case) and thus properly position the next-to-smallest item in position 2:

$$21 , \boxed{33} , 67 , 84 , 49 , 50 , 75$$

We continue in this manner, locating the smallest item in the sublist of items from position 3 on and interchanging it with the third item, then properly positioning the smallest item in the sublist of items from position 4 on, and so on until we eventually do this for the sublist consisting of the last two items:

$$21 , 33 , \boxed{49} , 84 , 67 , 50 , 75$$

$$21 , 33 , 49 , \boxed{50} , 67 , 84 , 75$$

$$21 , 33 , 49 , 50 , \boxed{67} , 84 , 75$$

$$21 , 33 , 49 , 50 , 67 , \boxed{75} , 84$$

Positioning the smallest item in this last sublist obviously also positions the last item correctly and thus completes the sort.

An algorithm for this simple selection sort is

SIMPLE SELECTION SORT ALGORITHM

(* Accepts: A list of items $X[1]$, . . . , $X[n]$.
  Purpose: Sort the list into ascending order.
  Returns: The sorted list. *)

For i ranging from 1 to $n - 1$, do the following:
    (* On the ith pass, first find the smallest item in the sublist
    $X[i]$, . . . , $X[n]$. *)

a. Set *SmallPos* equal to *i*.
b. Set *Smallest* equal to *X*[*SmallPos*].
c. For *j* ranging from *i* + 1 to *n* do the following:
   If *X*[*j*] < *Smallest* then   (∗ smaller item found ∗)
      i. Set *SmallPos* equal to *j*.
      ii. Set *Smallest* equal to *X*[*SmallPos*].

(∗ Now interchange this smallest item with the item at the beginning of this sublist. ∗)

d. Set *X*[*SmallPos*] equal to *X*[*i*].
e. Set *X*[*i*] equal to *Smallest*.

The program in Figure 9.6 implements this algorithm as procedure **SelectionSort**. It reads a list of up to 100 items, using procedure **ReadList** given in the preceding section, sorts them using selection sort, and then displays the sorted list.

FIGURE 9.6   Selection sort.

```
PROGRAM Sort( input, output );
{***********************************************************************

    Input (keyboard): List of items and user responses.
    Purpose:          Read and count a list of items Item[1], Item[2],
                      ..., Item[n], sort them in ascending order,
                      and then display the sorted list.
    Output (screen):  User prompts and a sorted list of items.

***********************************************************************}
CONST
    ListLimit = 100;   {maximum # of items in the list}

TYPE
    ListElementType = integer;
    ListType = ARRAY[1..ListLimit] of ListElementType;

VAR
    NumItems : integer;    {number of items}
    Item : ListType;       {list of items to be sorted}

PROCEDURE ReadList( VAR Item : ListType;    {list of items to be read}
                    VAR Count : integer );  {number of items}
{------------------------------------------------------------------

    Input (keyboard): List elements.
    Purpose:          Read list elements into array Item and Count
                      the elements read.
    Returns:          Array Item and Count.
    Output (screen):  User prompts.

-------------------------------------------------------------------}
```

FIGURE 9.6 Selection sort. (cont.)

```
VAR
    Response : char;   {user response}

BEGIN
    writeln( 'Enter the list of items, as many per line as desired.' );
    writeln( 'Note:  At most ', ListLimit:1, ' items can be read.' );
    writeln;
    Count := 0;
    REPEAT
        write( 'Items:  ' );
        WHILE NOT eoln DO
            BEGIN
                Count := Count + 1;
                read( Item[Count] )
            END {WHILE};
        readln;
        write( 'More (Y or N)?  ' );
        readln( Response )
    UNTIL Response <> 'Y'
END {ReadList};

PROCEDURE SelectionSort( VAR Item : ListType;   {list to be sorted}
                             n : integer );     {number of items}


{------------------------------------------------------------------

    Accepts:  A list of n items stored in an array Item.
    Purpose:  Sort Item[1], ..., Item[n] into ascending order
              using the simple selection sort algorithm.
    Returns:  The sorted list.

--------------------------------------------------------------------}

VAR
    Smallest : ListElementType;   {smallest item in current sublist}
    SmallPos,                     {position of Smallest}
    i, j : integer;               {indices}

BEGIN
    FOR i := 1 TO n - 1 DO
        BEGIN

            { find smallest item in sublist Item[i], ... , Item[n] }

            SmallPos := i;
            Smallest := Item[SmallPos];
            FOR j := i + 1 TO n DO
                IF Item[j] < Smallest THEN   { smaller item found }
                    BEGIN
                        SmallPos := j;
                        Smallest := Item[j]
                    END {IF};
```

FIGURE 9.6   Selection sort. (cont.)

```
              { interchange smallest item with Item[i] at beginning
                of sublist }

              Item[SmallPos] := Item[i];
              Item[i] := Smallest
         END {FOR i }
   END {SelectionSort};

PROCEDURE PrintItems( VAR Item : ListType;        {list of items}
                          NumItems : integer ); {number of items}
{-------------------------------------------------------------------

   Accepts:        List of NumItems items stored in array Item.
   Purpose:        Display the list of items.
   Output (screen): Items in list.


   ------------------------------------------------------------------}

   VAR
      i : integer;        {index}

   BEGIN
      writeln;
      writeln( 'Sorted list of ', Numitems:1, ' items:' );
      writeln;
      FOR i := 1 TO NumItems DO
         writeln( Item[i] )
   END {PrintItems};

BEGIN {*************** main program ***************}
   ReadList( Item, ListLimit, NumItems );
   SelectionSort( Item, NumItems );
   PrintItems( Item, NumItems )
END {main}.
```

Sample run:

```
Enter the list of items, as many per line as desired.
Note:  At most 100 items can be read.

Items:  55 88 34 84 21
More (Y or N)?  Y
Items:  99 5 83 71
More (Y or N)?  N
```

FIGURE 9.6 Selection sort. (cont.)

`Sorted list of 9 items:`

       5
      21
      34
      55
      71
      83
      84
      88

Sorting: Quicksort

The **quicksort** method of sorting is more efficient than simple selection sort. It is in fact one of the fastest methods of sorting and is most often implemented by a recursive algorithm. The basic idea of quicksort is to choose some element called a **pivot** and then perform a sequence of exchanges so that all elements that are less than this pivot are to its left and all elements that are greater than the pivot are to its right. This correctly positions the pivot and divides the (sub)list into two smaller sublists, each of which may then be sorted independently in the *same* way. This **divide-and-conquer** strategy leads naturally to a recursive sorting algorithm.

To illustrate this splitting of a list into two sublists, consider the following list of integers:

50, 30, 20, 80, 90, 70, 95, 85, 10, 15, 75, 25

If we select the first number as the pivot, we must rearrange the list so that 30, 20, 10, 15, and 25 are placed before 50, and 80, 90, 70, 95, 85, and 75 are placed after it. To carry out this rearrangement, we search from the right end of the list for an element less than 50 and from the left end for an item greater than 50.

50, 30, 20, 80, 90, 70, 95, 85, 10, 15, 75, 25

This locates the two numbers 25 and 80, which we now interchange to obtain

50, 30, 20, 25, 90, 70, 95, 85, 10, 15, 75, 80

We then resume the search from the right for a number less than 50 and from the left for a number greater than 50:

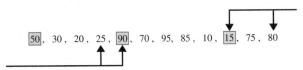

50, 30, 20, 25, 90, 70, 95, 85, 10, 15, 75, 80

This locates the numbers 15 and 90, which are then interchanged:

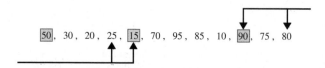

A continuation of the searches locates 10 and 70:

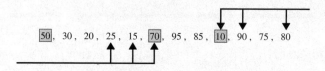

Interchanging these gives

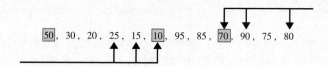

When we resume our search from the right for a number less than 50, we locate the value 10, which was found on the previous left-to-right search. This signals the end of the two searches, and we interchange 50 and 10, giving

10 , 30 , 20 , 25 , 15 , 50 , 95 , 85 , 70 , 90 , 75 , 80

The two underlined sublists now have the required properties: All elements in the first sublist are less than 50, and all those in the right sublist are greater than 50. Consequently, 50 has been properly positioned.

Both the left sublist

10, 30, 20, 25, 15

and the right sublist

95, 85, 70, 90, 75, 80

can now be sorted independently. Each must be split by choosing and correctly positioning one pivot element (the first) in each of them. For this, a procedure is needed to split a list of items in the array positions given by two parameters **Low** and **High**, denoting the beginning and end positions of the sublist, respectively. If we assume that the type **ListType** has been defined as in the program of Figure 9.6, then the following procedure carries out the desired splitting of the (sub)list **X[Low]**, . . . , **X[High]**:

```
PROCEDURE Split( VAR X : ListType; Low, High : integer;
                 VAR Mid : integer );
{-----------------------------------------------------------------------

   Accepts:   A list of items stored in locations Low..High of the
              array X.
   Purpose:   Rearrange X[Low], ..., X[High] so that one item is
              properly positioned.
   Returns:   The rearranged list and the final position Mid of that
              item.


-----------------------------------------------------------------------}

   VAR
      Left,                        {index for searching from the left}
      Right : integer;             {index for searching from the right}
      TempItem : ListElementType;  {temporary item used for interchange}

   BEGIN
      {Initialize indices for left and right searches}
      Left := Low;
      Right := High;

      {Carry out the searches}
      WHILE Left < Right DO         {While searches haven't met}
         BEGIN
            {Search from the right}
            WHILE X[Right] > X[Low] DO
               Right := Right - 1;

            {Search from the left}
            WHILE (Left < Right) AND (X[Left] <= X[Low]) DO
               Left := Left + 1;

            {Interchange items if searches have not met}
            IF Left < Right THEN
               BEGIN
                  TempItem := X[Left];
                  X[Left] := X[Right];
                  X[Right] := TempItem
               END {IF}
         END {WHILE};

      {End of searches; place selected item in proper position}
      Mid := Right;
      TempItem := X[Mid];
      X[Mid] := X[Low];
      X[Low] := TempItem
   END {Split};
```

A recursive procedure to sort a list is now easy to write:

```
PROCEDURE QuickSort( VAR X : ListType; Low, High : integer );
{----------------------------------------------------------------

   Accepts:  A list of items stored in locations Low..High of the
             array X.
   Purpose:  Sort X[Low], ..., X[High] into ascending order using
             quicksort.
   Returns:  The sorted list.


------------------------------------------------------------------}

   VAR
      Mid : integer;     {final position for selected item}

   BEGIN
      IF Low < High THEN       {list has more than one item}
         BEGIN
            Split( X, Low, High, Mid );    {split into two sublists}
            QuickSort( X, Low, Mid - 1 );  {sort first sublist}
            QuickSort( A, Mid + 1, High )  {sort second sublist}
         END {IF}
   END {QuickSort};
```

This procedure is called with a statement of the form

```
        QuickSort( Item, 1, NumItems )
```

where **NumItems** is the number of elements in the list **Item** to be sorted.

To demonstrate this procedure, suppose that the following list of integers is to be sorted:

8, 2, 13, 5, 14, 3, 6

The following table traces the action of **Quicksort** as it sorts this list. An underlined (sub)list in the first column indicates the current (sub)list being sorted, and the boxes indicate items correctly positioned in the list; each indentation represents a recursive call to **Quicksort** with the underlined sublist and the values shown for **Low** and **High** as parameters. A program that uses **Quicksort** to sort a list can be found in Example 9.4 of Appendix E.

(Sub)List Being Sorted	Low	High	Mid	Action
<u>8, 2, 13, 5, 14, 3, 6</u>	1	7		Call **Quicksort** with original list.
<u>3, 2, 6, 5, 8 , 14, 13</u>			5	**Split** positions 8 in location 5.
<u>3, 2, 6, 5,</u> 8 , 14, 13	1	4		Call **Quicksort** with left sublist.

(Sub)List Being Sorted	Low	High	Mid	Action
2, ⌐3⌐, 6, 5, ⌐8⌐, 14, 13			2	**Split** positions 3 in location 2.
2, ⌐3⌐, 6, 5, ⌐8⌐, 14, 13	1	1		Call **Quicksort** with left (one-element) sublist. **Low ≮ High**, so sublist is already sorted. Return to previous reference to **Quicksort**.
⌐2⌐, ⌐3⌐, 6, 5, ⌐8⌐, 14, 13	1	4	2	Left sublist is now sorted.
⌐2⌐, ⌐3⌐, 6, 5, ⌐8⌐, 14, 13	3	4		Now call **Quicksort** with right sublist.
⌐2⌐, ⌐3⌐, ⌐5⌐, 6, ⌐8⌐, 14, 13			3	**Split** positions 5 in location 3.
⌐2⌐, ⌐3⌐, ⌐5⌐, 6, ⌐8⌐, 14, 13	4	3		Call **Quicksort** with left (empty) sublist. **Low ≮ High**, so sublist is already sorted. Return to previous reference to **Quicksort**.
⌐2⌐, ⌐3⌐, ⌐5⌐, 6, ⌐8⌐, 14, 13	3	4	3	Left (empty) sublist has been sorted.
⌐2⌐, ⌐3⌐, ⌐5⌐, 6, ⌐8⌐, 14, 13	4	4		Call **Quicksort** with right (one-element) sublist. **Low ≮ High**, so sublist is already sorted. Return to previous reference to **Quicksort**.
⌐2⌐, ⌐3⌐, ⌐5⌐, ⌐6⌐, ⌐8⌐, 14, 13	3	4	3	Right sublist has been sorted, so return to previous reference to **Quicksort**.
⌐2⌐, ⌐3⌐, 5, 6, ⌐8⌐, 14, 13	1	4	2	Right sublist has been sorted, so return to previous (original) reference to **Quicksort**.
2, 3, 5, 6, ⌐8⌐, 14, 13	1	7	5	Left sublist has been sorted.
⌐2, 3, 5, 6⌐, ⌐8⌐, 14, 13	6	7		Now call **Quicksort** with right sublist.
⌐2, 3, 5, 6⌐, ⌐8⌐, ⌐13⌐, 14			6	**Split** positions 13 in location 6.
⌐2, 3, 5, 6⌐, ⌐8⌐, ⌐13⌐, 14	7	6		Call **Quicksort** with left (empty) sublist. **Low ≮ High**, so sublist is already sorted. Return to previous reference to **Quicksort**.
⌐2, 3, 5, 6⌐, ⌐8⌐, ⌐13⌐, 14	6	7	6	Left sublist has been sorted.
⌐2, 3, 5, 6⌐, ⌐8⌐, ⌐13⌐, 14			7	Call **Quicksort** with right (one-element) sublist. **Low ≮ High**, so sublist is already sorted. Return to previous reference to **Quicksort**.
⌐2, 3, 5, 6⌐, ⌐8⌐, ⌐13, 14⌐	6	7	6	Right sublist has been sorted, so return to previous (original) reference to **Quicksort**.
⌐2, 3, 5, 6, 8, 13, 14⌐	1	7	5	Original reference to **Quicksort** is complete, so entire list has been sorted.

Searching: Linear Search

Another important problem in data processing is **searching** a collection of data items for a specified item and retrieving some information associated with that item. For example, we search a telephone directory for a specific name in order to retrieve the phone number listed with that name, a dictionary for a word in order to retrieve its meaning, and a file of student records in order to find the record of a student with a specified student number.

A **linear search** of a list begins with the first item in a list and searches sequentially until either the desired item is found or the end of the list is reached. The following algorithm describes this method of searching:

LINEAR SEARCH ALGORITHM

(∗ Accepts: A list $X[1]$, $X[2]$, . . . , $X[n]$ and an item being sought
                 (*ItemSought*).
  Purpose: Linear-search the list for *ItemSought*.
  Returns: *Found* is set to true and *Location* to the position of *ItemSought* if
                 the search is successful; otherwise, *Found* is set to false. ∗)

1. Set *Location* equal to 1.
2. Set *Found* to false.
3. While *Location* $\leq n$ and not *Found* do the following:
    If *ItemSought* = $X[Location]$ then
        Set *Found* to true.
    Else
        Increment *Location* by 1.

This linear search technique can be used for any list; it does not require that the elements of the list have any special organization or arrangement. This means that if the item for which we are searching is not in the list, the entire list must be searched to determine this. If, however, the list of items has been sorted, then a more efficient version of linear search may be used. If the list has been arranged in increasing order, we need only examine list elements until either the item is found or we encounter a list element that is greater than the item. All the list elements that follow will also be greater than the item for which we are searching. The following algorithm incorporates this modification:

LINEAR SEARCH ALGORITHM FOR ORDERED LISTS

(∗ Accepts: A list $X[1]$, $X[2]$, . . . $X[n]$ that has been ordered so the
                 elements are in ascending order and an item being sought
                 (*ItemSought*).
  Purpose: Linear-search this ordered list for *ItemSought*.
  Returns: *Found* is set to true and *Location* to the position of *ItemSought* if
                 the search is successful; otherwise, *Found* is set to false. ∗)

1. Set *Location* equal to 1.
2. Set *DoneSearching* to false.
3. While *Location* ≤ *n* and not *DoneSearching* do the following:
    If *ItemSought* ≥ *X*[*Location*] then
        Set *DoneSearching* to true.
    Else
        Increment *Location* by 1.
4. If *DoneSearching* and *ItemSought* = *X*[*Location*] then
        set *Found* to true
    Else
        set *Found* to false.

Searching: Binary Search

Although linear search may be an adequate method for small data sets, a more efficient technique is needed for large collections. If the list to be searched has been sorted, the **binary search** algorithm may be used. With this method, we first examine the middle item in the list; if it is the desired entry, the search is successful. Otherwise, we determine whether the item for which we are searching is in the first half or the second half of the list and then repeat this process, using the middle entry of that sublist.

To illustrate, suppose that the list to be searched is

1331
1373
1555
1624
1682
1755
1889
2002
2335
2665
3103

and that we are looking for 1889. We first examine the middle number, 1755, in the sixth position. This is not the item for which we are searching, but because 1889 is greater than 1755, we can disregard the first half of the list and concentrate on the second half:

1889
2002
2335
2665
3103

The middle number in this sublist is 2335 and the desired item 1889 is less than 2335, so we discard the second half of this sublist and concentrate on the first half:

1889
2002

Since there is no middle number in this half, we examine the number immediately preceding the middle position, that is, 1889. In this example we have located the desired entry with only three comparisons rather than seven, as required in a linear search.

In general, the algorithm for binary search is as follows:

BINARY SEARCH ALGORITHM

(∗ Accepts: A list $X[1]$, $X[2]$, . . . , $X[n]$ that has been ordered so the elements are in ascending order and an item being sought (*ItemSought*).

Purpose: Binary-search this ordered list for *ItemSought*.

Returns: *Found* is set to true and *Location* to the position of *ItemSought* if the search is successful; otherwise, *Found* is set to false. ∗)

1. Initialize *First* to 1 and *Last* to *NumItems*. These represent the positions of the first and last items of the list or sublist being searched.
2. Initialize *Found* to false.
3. While *First* <= *Last* and not *Found,* do the following:
   a. Find the middle position in the sublist by setting *Middle* equal to the integer quotient of (*First* + *Last*) divided by 2.
   b. Compare *ItemSought* with *X[Middle]*. There are three possibilities:
      (i)   *ItemSought* < *X[Middle]*: *ItemSought* is in the first half of the sublist; set *Last* equal to *Middle* − 1.
      (ii) *ItemSought* > *X[Middle]*: *ItemSought* is in the last half of the sublist; set *First* equal to *Middle* + 1.
      (iii) *ItemSought* = *X[Middle]*: *ItemSought* has been found; set *Location* equal to *Middle* and *Found* to true.

Figure 9.7 is a program for information retrieval. It reads student numbers, class codes, and test scores for a group of students and stores these in three arrays:

`Snumb`:	`Snumb[i]` is the ith student number.
`Class`:	`Class[i]` is the class code for the ith student.
`TestScore`:	`TestScore[i]` is the test score for the ith student.

The user can then enter a student's number, and the program will retrieve and display the class code and test score for that student. Since the data triples in the file are arranged so that the student numbers are in ascending order, these numbers also are in ascending order in the array **Snumb**. Consequently, binary search can be used to search this array for the given student's number.

The structure of this program is summarized by the following structure diagram:

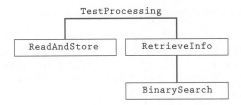

The procedure **ReadAndStore** reads the student numbers, section letters, and test scores from a file and stores them in the arrays **Snumb**, **Class**, and **TestScore**, respectively. The procedure **RetrieveInfo** then repeatedly accepts a student's number from the user and retrieves the class code and test score for that student. It uses the procedure **BinarySearch** to search the array **Snumb**.

FIGURE 9.7   Student information retrieval.

```
PROGRAM StudentInfoRetrieval( input, StuInfoFile, output );
{************************************************************************

    Input (file):      A list of student numbers, class codes, and test
                       scores.
    Input (keyboard):  Student numbers.
    Purpose:           Read student numbers, class codes, and test
                       scores from StuInfoFile with student numbers in
                       ascending order and store them in an array.
                       A student number can then be input, the list
                       searched using a binary search, and the
                       corresponding class code and test score
                       displayed.
    Output (screen):   User prompts, class codes, test scores

    ************************************************************************}

CONST
    ListLimit = 100;   {maximum number of items in the list}

TYPE
    ListElementType = integer;
    ListType = ARRAY[1..ListLimit] OF ListElementType;

VAR
    Snumb,                 {Snumb[i] = i-th student number}
    Class,                 {Class[i] = class code for i-th student}
    TestScore : ListType;  {TestScore[i] = test score for i-th student}
    NumScores : integer;   {number of test scores}
    StuInfoFile : text;    {file from which student data is read}
```

FIGURE 9.7   Student information retrieval. (cont.)

```
PROCEDURE ReadAndStore
                ( VAR Snumb,                 {list of student numbers}
                      Class,                 {list of class codes}
                      TestScore : ListType; {list of test scores}
                  VAR Count : integer );     {number of items in lists}
{-----------------------------------------------------------------------

   Input (file): Student numbers, class codes, and test scores.
   Purpose:      Read the items from StuInfoFile and store them in
                 the arrays Snumb, Class, and TestScore.
   Returns:      Arrays Snumb, Class, and TestScore.


-----------------------------------------------------------------------}

   VAR
      StuInfoFileName : string; {actual name of student info. file}

   BEGIN
      write( 'Enter name of file containing student information: ');
      readln( StuInfoFileName );
      assign( StuInfoFile, StuInfoFileName );
      reset( StuInfoFile );
      Count := 0;
      WHILE NOT eof( StuInfoFile ) DO
         BEGIN
            Count := Count + 1;
            readln( StuInfoFile, Snumb[Count], Class[Count],
               TestScore[Count] )
         END {WHILE}
   END {ReadAndStore};

PROCEDURE RetrieveInfo
                ( VAR Snumb,                 {list of student numbers}
                      Class,                 {list of class codes}
                      TestScore : ListType; {list of test scores}
                  VAR NumItems : integer ); {number of items in lists}
{-----------------------------------------------------------------------

   Accepts:        Arrays Snumb, Class, and TestScores, and the number
                   NumItems of list elements stored in each array.
   Input (keyboard): A student number.
   Purpose:        Accept a student number and then search the
                   list Snumb for it.  If it is found, the class
                   code and test score for that student are
                   displayed.
   Output (screen): Class codes and test scores.


-----------------------------------------------------------------------}
```

FIGURE 9.7   Student information retrieval. (cont.)

```
VAR
    SnumbDesired : ListElementType; {student number to search for}
    Found : boolean;                {indicates if search was successful}
    Location : integer;             {location of number in the list}

PROCEDURE BinarySearch
                ( VAR X : ListType;                        {ordered list}
                    n : integer;                           {# of list items}
                    ItemSought : ListElementType; {search item}
                VAR Found : boolean;                       {indicates if found}
                VAR Location : integer );                  {position if found }
{-----------------------------------------------------------------------

    Accepts:  The ordered list X, n = number of items in the list,
              and ItemSought = item for which to search.
    Purpose:  Search the list X for ItemSought using binary search.
    Returns:  If ItemSought is found in the list a value of true
              is returned for Found and the Location of the item;
              otherwise, Found is false.

-------------------------------------------------------------------------}

    VAR
        First,             {first position in sublist being searched}
        Last,              {last position in sublist}
        Middle : integer;  {middle position in sublist}

    BEGIN
        First := 1;
        Last := NumItems;
        Found := false;
        WHILE (First <= Last) AND (NOT Found) DO
            BEGIN
                Middle := (First + Last) DIV 2;
                IF ItemSought < X[Middle] THEN
                    Last := Middle - 1
                ELSE IF ItemSought > X[Middle] THEN
                    First := Middle + 1
                ELSE
                    BEGIN
                        Location := Middle;
                        Found := TRUE
                    END {ELSE}
            END {WHILE}
    END {BinarySearch};

BEGIN {RetrieveInfo}
    writeln( 'To stop searching, enter student number of 0.' );
    write( 'Student number?  ' );
    readln( SnumbDesired );
```

FIGURE 9.7 Student information retrieval. (cont.)

```
    WHILE SnumbDesired <> 0 DO
        BEGIN
            BinarySearch( Snumb, NumScores, SnumbDesired,
                          Found, Location );
            IF Found THEN
                BEGIN
                    writeln( 'Student ', SnumbDesired:1, ' is in class ',
                             Class[Location]:1 );
                    writeln( 'His/her test score was ',
                             TestScore[Location]:1 )
                END {IF Found}
            ELSE
                writeln( 'Student ', SnumbDesired:1, ' not found' );
            writeln;
            write( 'Student number?  ' );
            readln( SnumbDesired )
        END {WHILE}
  END {RetrieveInfo};

BEGIN {************* main program *************}
   ReadAndStore (Snumb, Class, TestScore, NumScores);
   RetrieveInfo (Snumb, Class, TestScore, NumScores)
END {main program}.
```

Listing of FIL9-7.DAT:

```
1111 1  99
2222 2 100
3333 3  77
4444 1  55
5555 2  87
6666 1  63
7777 3  93
```

Sample run:

```
Enter name of file containing student information: FIL9-7.DAT
To stop searching, enter student number of 0.
Student number?  1111
Student 1111 is in class 1
His/her test score was 99

Student number?  5555
Student 5555 is in class 2
His/her test score was 87

Student number?  8888
Student 8888 not found

Student number?  3333
Student 3333 is in class 3
His/her test score was 77

Student number?  0
```

1. For each of the following arrays X, show X after each of the first four passes of simple selection sort:

(a)

i	1	2	3	4	5	6	7	8
$X[i]$	30	50	80	10	60	20	70	40

(b)

i	1	2	3	4	5	6	7	8
$X[i]$	20	40	70	60	80	50	30	10

(c)

i	1	2	3	4	5	6	7	8
$X[i]$	80	70	60	50	40	30	20	10

(d)

i	1	2	3	4	5	6	7	8
$X[i]$	10	20	30	40	50	60	70	80

2. One variation of simple selection sort for a list stored in an array $X[1], \ldots, X[n]$ is to locate both the smallest and the largest elements while scanning the list and to position them at the beginning and the end of the list, respectively. On the next scan, this process is repeated for the sublist $X[2], \ldots, X[n-1]$, and so on.

   (a)–(d) Using the arrays X in Exercise 1, show X after each of the first four passes of this double-ended simple selection sort.

   (e) Write an algorithm to implement this double-ended selection sort.

3. Write a recursive procedure that implements simple selection sort.

4. For the following array X, show the contents of X after the procedure reference `Split( X, 1, 10, SplitPos )` is executed, and give the value of the array index `SplitPos`:

i	1	2	3	4	5	6	7	8	9	10
$X[i]$	45	20	50	30	80	10	60	70	40	90

5. Construct a trace table like that in the text to trace the action of `QuickSort` as it sorts the following lists:

   (a) 5, 1, 6, 4, 3, 2   (b) 1, 2, 3, 6, 5, 4
   (c) 6, 5, 4, 3, 2, 1   (d) 1, 2, 3, 4, 5, 6

6. One of the lists in Exercise 5 shows why the condition `Left < Right` is needed to control the search from the left in procedure `Split`. Which is it? What would happen if this condition were omitted?

7. **Insertion sort** is an efficient sorting method for small data sets. It begins with the first item, x_1, then inserts x_2 into this one-item list in the correct position to

form a sorted two-element list, then inserts x_3 into this two-element list in the correct position, and so on. For example, to sort the list 7, 1, 5, 2, 3, 4, 6, 0, the steps are as follows (the element being inserted is highlighted):

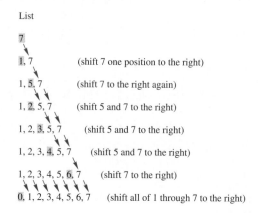

List

7

1, 7   (shift 7 one position to the right)

1, 5, 7   (shift 7 to the right again)

1, 2, 5, 7   (shift 5 and 7 to the right)

1, 2, 3, 5, 7   (shift 5 and 7 to the right)

1, 2, 3, 4, 5, 7   (shift 5 and 7 to the right)

1, 2, 3, 4, 5, 6, 7   (shift 7 to the right)

0, 1, 2, 3, 4, 5, 6, 7 (shift all of 1 through 7 to the right)

Write a program to sort a list of items, using this insertion sort method.

8. The investment company of Shyster and Shyster has been recording the trading price of a particular stock over a 15-day period. Write a program that reads these prices and sorts them into increasing order, using the insertion sort scheme described in the preceding exercise. The program should display the trading range, that is, the lowest and the highest prices recorded, and also the median price.

9. Insertion sort (see Exercise 7) performs best for small lists or partially sorted lists. **Shell sort** (named after Donald Shell) is a more efficient scheme that uses insertion sort to sort small sublists to produce larger partially ordered sublists. Specifically, one begins with a "gap" of a certain size g and then uses insertion sort to sort sublists of elements that are g apart, first $X[1]$, $X[1 + g]$, $X[1 + 2g]$, . . . , then the sublist $X[2]$, $X[2 + g]$, $X[2 + 2g]$, . . . , then $X[3]$, $X[3 + g]$, $X[3 + 2g]$, . . . , and so on. Next the size of the gap g is reduced, and the process is repeated. This continues until the gap g is 1, and the final insertion sort results in the sorted list. Write a program to sort a list of items using this Shell sort method, beginning with a gap g of the form $\dfrac{3^k - 1}{2}$

for some integer k and dividing it by 3 at each stage.

10. The procedure **QuickSort** always sorts the left sublist before the right. Its performance will improve slightly if the shorter of the two sublists is sorted first. Modify **QuickSort** to sort the shorter sublist first.

11. Another improvement of the quicksort method is to use some other sorting algorithm to sort small sublists. For example, insertion sort is usually better than quicksort when the list has fewer than 20 items. Modify the quicksort scheme to use insertion sort (see Exercise 7) if the sublist has fewer than **LBound** items for some constant **LBound**, and otherwise, use quicksort.

12. The procedure `Split` in the quicksort method of sorting always selects the first element of the sublist to position. Another common practice is to use the "median-of-three" rule, in which the median of the three numbers `X[Low]`, `X[Middle]`, and `X[High]` is selected, where `Middle = (Low + High) DIV 2`. (The median of three numbers *a, b,* and *c,* arranged in ascending order, is the middle number *b.*) Modify `Split` to use this median-of-three rule.

13. Write a procedure to implement the linear search algorithm given in the text.

14. The Cawker City Candy Company manufactures different kinds of candy, each identified by a product number. Write a program that reads in two arrays, `Number` and `Price`, where `Number[1]` and `Price[1]` are the product number and unit price for the first item, `Number[2]` and `Price[2]` are the product number and unit price for the second item, and so on. The program should then allow the user to select one of the following options:

    (a) Retrieve and display the price of a product whose number is entered by the user. (Use the linear search procedure developed in Exercise 13 to determine the index in the array `Number` of the specified item.)

    (b) Print a table displaying the product number and the price of each item.

15. Write a recursive procedure to implement the binary search algorithm described in this section.

9.5   PART OF THE PICTURE: Analysis of Algorithms

As the preceding section demonstrates, there may be several different algorithms for solving a particular problem. In these situations, it is important to be able to compare the performance of these algorithms. Thus in this section we will look more carefully at how algorithms are analyzed and at some of the techniques for measuring their efficiency.

An algorithm's efficiency is usually measured according to two criteria. The first is **space utilization,** the amount of memory required to store the data, and the second is **time efficiency,** the amount of time required to process the data. Unfortunately, it usually is not possible to minimize both the space and the time requirements. Algorithms that require the least memory are often slower than those that use more memory. Thus the programmer is often faced with a trade-off between space efficiency and time efficiency. An algorithm's time efficiency is usually considered the more important of the two, and in this section we consider how it can be measured.

The execution time of an algorithm is influenced by several factors. Obviously, one factor is the size of the input, since the number of input items usually affects the time required to process these items. For example, the time it takes to sort a list of items surely depends on the number of items in the list. Thus the execution time T of an algorithm must be expressed as a function $T(n)$ of the size n of the input.

The kind of instructions and the speed with which the machine can execute them also influence execution time. These factors, however, depend on the particular computer being used; consequently, we cannot expect to express meaningfully the value of $T(n)$ in real time units such as seconds. Instead, $T(n)$ will be an approximate count of the number of instructions executed.

In many cases, T may depend not only on the size of the input but also on the arrangement of the input items. For example, it may take less time to sort a list of items that are nearly in order initially than to sort a list in which the items are in reverse order. Thus we might attempt to measure T in the **worst case** or in the **best case,** or we might attempt to compute the **average** value of T over all possible cases. The best-case performance of an algorithm is usually not very informative, and the average performance is often quite difficult to determine; thus $T(n)$ is commonly taken as a measure of the algorithm's performance in the worst case.

Another factor that influences computing time is the quality of the source code that implements the algorithm and the quality of the machine code generated from this source code by a compiler. Some languages are better suited than others for certain algorithms; some programmers write better programs than others; and some compilers generate more efficient code than others. This means, in particular, that $T(n)$ cannot be computed as the number of machine instructions executed, and instead it is taken to be the number of times that the instructions in the *algorithm* are executed.

To illustrate how the computing time of an algorithm is measured, we first examine the two methods for searching a list described in the preceding section, linear search and binary search. There we claimed that binary search is more efficient than linear search, and we now substantiate this claim.

Recall that a linear search is carried out by examining each element in a list sequentially, beginning with the first element, until either the desired item is found or the end of the list is reached. The following algorithm for linear search was given in the preceding section:

LINEAR SEARCH ALGORITHM

(∗ Accepts: A list $X[1]$, $X[2]$, . . . , $X[n]$ and an item being sought
                    (*ItemSought*).
   Purpose: Linear-search the list for *ItemSought.*
   Returns: *Found* is set to true and *Location* to the position of *ItemSought* if
                    the search is successful; otherwise, *Found* is set to false. ∗)

(1) Set *Location* equal to 1.
(2) Set *Found* to false.
(3) While *Location* $\leq n$ and not *Found* do the following:
(4)   If *ItemSought* = $X[Location]$ then
(5)   Set *Found* to true.
(6)   Else
            Increment *Location* by 1.

(The statements have been renumbered for easy reference.)

The worst case for the linear search algorithm obviously occurs when *Item-Sought* is not in the list; thus, to measure the performance of this algorithm, we count the number of times that each statement is executed in this case. Clearly, Statements 1 and 2 are executed only once. The boolean expression in Statement 3 is evaluated $n + 1$ times, once for each value of *Location* from 1 through $n + 1$. Statements 4 and 6 are executed n times, once on each pass through the while loop, and Statement 5 is never executed, since *ItemSought* is not in the list. The following table summarizes these statement counts:

Statement	# of times executed
1	1
2	1
3	$n + 1$
4	n
5	0
6	n
Total:	$3n + 3$

Thus the total number of statements executed, expressed as a function of the size n of input, is

$$T(n) = 3n + 3$$

For sufficiently large values of n ($n >= 3$), we see that

$$T(n) \leq 4n$$

and so we say that $T(n)$ has **order of magnitude n** and denote this using the "big Oh" notation:

$$T(n) = O(n)$$

In general, the execution time $T(n)$ of an algorithm is said to have **order of magnitude $g(n)$,** denoted

$$T(n) = O(g(n))$$

if there exists some constant C so that

$$T(n) \leq C \cdot g(n)$$

for all sufficiently large values of n.

The binary search algorithm for ordered lists is as follows:

BINARY SEARCH ALGORITHM

(* Accepts: A list $X[1]$, $X[2]$, . . . $X[n]$ that has been ordered so the elements are in ascending order and an item being sought (*ItemSought*).

Purpose: Binary-search this ordered list for *ItemSought.*

Returns: *Found* is set to true and *Location* to the position of *ItemSought* if the search is successful; otherwise, *Found* is set to false. *)

(1) Set *First* equal to 1.
(2) Set *Last* equal to *n.*
(3) Set *Found* to false.
(4) While *First* <= *Last* and not *Found,* do the following:
(5)   a. Calculate *Location* = (*First* + *Last*) DIV 2.
(6)   b. If *ItemSought* < *X*[*Location*] then
(7)   Set *Last* equal to *Location* − 1.
(8)   Else if *ItemSought* > *X*[*Location*] then
(9)   Set *First* equal to *Location* + 1.
(10)   Else
             Set *Found* equal to true.

In this algorithm, it is clear that Statements 1, 2, and 3 are executed exactly once, and to determine the worst-case performance, we must determine the number of times the loop composed of Statements 4 through 10 is executed when *ItemSought* is not in the list. This is not as easy to determine as it is for linear search, and so we first consider some particular values of *n.*

First, consider a list containing only one element *X*[1], and suppose that *ItemSought* is greater than *X*[1]. After Statements 1, 2, and 3 are executed, the boolean expression in Statement 4 is evaluated and found to be true (*First* = 1, *Last* = 1, and *Found* = false). Thus the body of the while loop is executed; Statement 5 calculates the value 1 for *Location,* and Statements 8 and 9 set *First* equal to 2. The boolean expression in Statement 4 is then evaluated again and found to be false (*First* = 2, *Last* = 1), causing repetition to terminate. Thus we see that for *n* = 1, one pass through the loop is made, and one additional evaluation of the boolean expression is made to terminate repetition.

Next, consider a list of size *n* = 2, *X*[1], *X*[2], and suppose that *ItemSought* is greater than both elements of this list. A first pass through the loop sets *First* equal to 2 so that the sublist yet to be searched is reduced from two elements to one, *X*[2]. As we have just seen, a list of size 1 requires one pass through the loop and one more evaluation of the boolean expression in Statement 4 to terminate repetition. Thus, for *n* = 2, the loop is executed twice and Statement 4 one additional time.

Now consider a list of size *n* = 4, *X*[1], *X*[2], *X*[3], *X*[4], with *ItemSought* greater than each list element. A first pass through the loop reduces the list to one of size 2, *X*[3], *X*[4]. We have just determined that two passes are required to search a list of two elements, and thus we see that for a list of size 4, the loop is executed three times, and the boolean expression in Statement 4 is evaluated one additional time.

Continuing this analysis with values 8, 16, . . . for *n,* we obtain the following table:

n	Number of Passes Through the Loop
$1 = 2^0$	1
$2 = 2^1$	2
$4 = 2^2$	3
$8 = 2^3$	4
.	.
.	.
.	.
2^k	$k + 1$

Thus we see that a list of size 2^k requires $k + 1 = \log_2(2^k) + 1$ passes through the loop. In general, a list of size n requires no more than $\log_2 n + 1$ passes through the loop.

Since only Statements 5, 8, and 9 are executed in the worst case and Statement 4 is executed one more time than the number of loop repetitions, we obtain the following (approximate) counts for executions of the statements in the binary search algorithm:

Statement	# of times executed
1	1
2	1
3	1
4	$\log_2 n + 2$
5	$\log_2 n + 1$
6	0
7	0
8	$\log_2 n + 1$
9	$\log_2 n + 1$
10	0
Total:	$4\log_2 n + 8$

Thus we see that in the worst case, the computing time of binary search is $T(n) = 4 \log_2 n + 8$, and since

$$T(n) \leq 5\log_2 n$$

for large n ($n >= 2^8$), we see that $T(n)$ has order of magnitude $\log_2 n$,

$$T(n) = O(\log_2 n)$$

In summary, we have the following measures of worst-case performance of the linear search and binary search algorithms (which also measure the average-case performance):

Linear search: $O(n)$
Binary search: $O(\log_2 n)$

Since the function $\log_2 n$ grows less rapidly than n as the number n of inputs increases, it follows that binary search is more efficient than linear search for large lists. For small lists, however, linear search may, and in fact does, outperform binary search. Empirical studies indicate that linear search is more efficient than binary search for lists of up to twenty elements. Moreover, binary search can be used only for ordered lists; consequently, it may be necessary to sort the list before it can be used.

The computing time of simple selection sort is $O(n^2)$, where n is the size of the list. To see this, consider again the algorithm for this sorting scheme given in the preceding section:

SIMPLE SELECTION SORT ALGORITHM

(* Accepts: A list of items $X[1],\ \ldots,\ X[n]$
    Function: Sort the list into ascending order.
    Returns: The sorted list. *)

(1) For $i = 1$ to $n - 1$ do the following:
       (* On the ith pass, first find the smallest element in the sublist
       $X[i],\ \ldots\ X[n]$. *)
(2)   a. Set *SmallPos* equal to i.
(3)   b. Set *Smallest* equal to $X[SmallPos]$.
(4)   c. For $j = i + 1$ to n do the following:
(5)   If $X[j] < Smallest$ then (* smaller element found *)
(6)   i. Set *SmallPos* equal to j.
(7)   ii. Set *Smallest* equal to $X[SmallPos]$.
       (* Now interchange this smallest element with the
       element at the beginning of this sublist. *)
(8)   d. Set $X[SmallPos]$ equal to $X[i]$.
(9)   e. Set $X[i]$ equal to *Smallest*.

It should be clear from the preceding examples that the order of magnitude of an algorithm is determined by the statements executed most often, and for simple selection sort these are Statements 5 through 7 in the innermost loop. On the first pass through the outer loop with $i = 1$, these statements are executed $n - 1$ times. On the second pass with $i = 2$, they are executed $n - 2$ times, and so on. Thus these statements are executed a total of $(n - 1) + (n - 2) + \cdots + 1$ times. One of the standard summation formulas in mathematics states that

$$1 + 2 + \ \ldots\ + k = \frac{k(k + 1)}{2}$$

or in the usual summation notation,

$$\sum_{i=1}^{k} i = \frac{k(k + 1)}{2}$$

Thus we see that Statements 5 through 7 are executed a total of $n(n-1)/2 = (n^2 - n)/2$ times, from which it follows that the computing time of selection sort is given by $T(n) = O(n^2)$.

Although the worst-case computing time for quicksort is $O(n^2)$, its average computing time is $O(n \cdot \log_2 n)$. A rigorous derivation of these times is considerably more difficult than for simple selection sort, and we leave it for more advanced courses in analysis of algorithms.

Besides $O(\log_2 n)$, $O(n)$, $O(n \cdot \log_2 n)$, and $O(n^2)$, other computing times that frequently arise in algorithm analysis are $O(\log_2(\log_2 n))$, $O(n^3)$, and $O(2^n)$. The following table displays values of these functions for several values of n:

$\log_2(\log_2 n)$	$\log_2 n$	n	$n \cdot \log_2 n$	n^2	n^3	2^n
—	0	1	0	1	1	2
0	1	2	2	4	8	4
1	2	4	8	16	64	16
1.58	3	8	24	64	512	256
2	4	16	64	256	4096	65536
2.32	5	32	160	1024	32768	4294967296
2.6	6	64	384	4096	2.6×10^5	1.85×10^{19}
3	8	256	2.05×10^3	6.55×10^4	1.68×10^7	1.16×10^{77}
3.32	10	1024	1.02×10^4	1.05×10^6	1.07×10^9	1.8×10^{308}
4.32	20	1048576	2.1×10^7	1.1×10^{12}	1.15×10^{18}	6.7×10^{315652}

Graphs of these functions are shown in Figure 9.8.

It should be clear from the preceding table and the graphs in Figure 9.8 that algorithms with exponential computing times are practical only for solving problems in which the number of inputs is small. To emphasize this, suppose that each instruction in some algorithm can be executed in one microsecond (.000001 second). The following table shows the time required to execute $f(n)$ instructions for the preceding seven functions f with $n = 256$ inputs:

Function	Time
$\log_2(\log_2 n)$	.000003 seconds
$\log_2 n$	.000008 seconds
n	.0025 seconds
$n \cdot \log_2 n$	.002 seconds
n^2	.065 seconds
n^3	17 seconds
2^n	3.7×10^{61} centuries

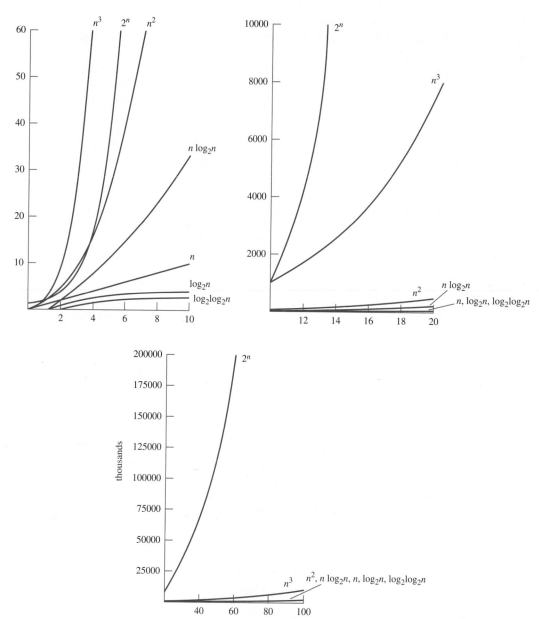

FIGURE 9.8 Computing times.

Exercises

1. Which of the orders of magnitude given in this section is the best O notation to describe the following computing times?

(a) $T(n) = n^3 + 100n \cdot \log_2 n + 5000$

(b) $T(n) = 2^n + n^{99} + 7$

(c) $T(n) = \dfrac{n^2 - 1}{n + 1} + 8 \log_2 n$

(d) $T(n) = 1 + 2 + 4 + \cdots + 2^{n-1}$

2. What would it mean to say that an algorithm has computing time $T(n) = O(1)$? Give an example of such an algorithm.

3. For each of the following segments, determine which of the orders of magnitude given in this section is the best O notation for expressing the worst-case computing time as a function of n:

(a) {Calculate mean}
```
n := 0;
Sum := 0;
readln( x );
WHILE x <> -999 DO
   BEGIN
      n := n  + 1;
      Sum := Sum  + x;
      readln( x )
   END {FOR};
Mean := Sum / n;
```

(b) {Calculate array sums}
```
Sum1 := 0;
FOR i := 1 TO n  DO
   Sum1 := Sum1 + A[i];
Sum2 := 0;
FOR j := 1 TO n  DO
   Sum2 := Sum2 + B[j];
```

(c) {Print sums of array elements}
```
FOR i := 1 TO n  DO
   BEGIN
      FOR j := 1 TO n  DO
         write( A[i] + B[j] : 3 );
      writeln
   END {FOR i};
```

(d) {Print sums of array elements}
```
FOR i := 1 TO n  DO
   BEGIN
      FOR j := 1 TO n  DO
         BEGIN
            FOR k := 1 TO n  DO
               write( A[i] + B[j] + C[k] : 3 );
            writeln
         END {FOR j};
      writeln
   END {FOR i};
```

(e) {Bubble sort}
```
FOR i := 1 TO n - 1 DO
  BEGIN
    FOR j := i TO n - 1 DO
      IF X[j] > X[j + 1] THEN
        BEGIN
          Temp := X[j];
          X[j] := X[j + 1];
          X[j + 1] := Temp
        END {IF}
  END {FOR};
```

(f) {Repeated division}
```
WHILE n >= 1 DO
  n := n DIV 2;
```

(g) {Repeated multiplication}
```
x := 1;
FOR i := 1 TO n - 1 DO
  BEGIN
    FOR j := 1 TO x DO
      writeln( j );
    x := 2 * x
  END {FOR};
```

Programming Pointers

Program Design

1. *Array types should be associated with type identifiers in the* TYPE *section.* For example, rather than simply putting a definition of an array type in a variable declaration such as

```
VAR
    Score : ARRAY[1..ScoresLimit] OF integer;
```

it is better to associate this array type with a type identifier and then to use it to specify the types of variables:

```
TYPE
    ListOfScores = ARRAY[1..ScoresLimit] OF integer;

VAR
    Score : ListOfScores;
```

ListOfScores can then also be used to specify the types of parameters in subprogram headings, where type identifiers are required (but see footnote 2 on page 457).

2. *It is appropriate to use an array when a complete list of data values must be stored in main memory for processing.* Using an array when it is not necessary, however, ties up a block of memory locations, and the address translation required for array references slows down execution.

3. *To utilize memory efficiently, it is usually advisable to specify as variable parameters the formal parameters of functions and procedures that represent arrays (especially if they are large).* If value parameters are used for arrays, two copies of the array will be stored in memory; also, the elements of the actual array must be copied to that of the subprogram, and this is quite time-consuming for large arrays.

Potential Problems

1. *An array cannot be read/written by simply including the array name in an input/output list.* Rather, it is necessary to read or write each element of the array, as in

```
FOR i := 1 TO NumScores DO
    writeln( Score[i] );
```

2. *Array indices must stay within the range specified in the array declarations. Also, make sure that range checking is enabled, especially when developing and debugging programs that use arrays.* Out-of-range errors occur most often when a variable being used as an index takes on a value outside the range specified for the index in the array declaration. To illustrate, consider the following declarations:

```
CONST
    ListLimit = 10;
    EndOfDataFlag = -999;

TYPE
    ListOfNumbers = ARRAY[1..ListLimit] OF integer;

VAR
    Number : ListOfNumbers;
    i, Value : integer;
```

and consider the following statements designed to read and count the elements of this array:

```
i := 0;
read( Value );
WHILE Value <> EndOfDataFlag DO
    BEGIN
        i := i + 1;
        Number[i] := Value;
        read( Value )
    END {WHILE};
```

These statements correctly read values for the entries of **Number**, provided that there are no more than ten values preceding the end-of-data flag. But if there are more than ten values, an error will result when the value of **i** reaches 11, because an attempt is made to read a value for **Number[11]**. If range checking is in effect, an error message will be displayed, and execution terminated.

As this example demonstrates, it is important to check **boundary conditions** when processing the elements of arrays, that is, to check to make sure that the index is not out of range. Thus, the preceding set of statements could better be written as

```
i := 0;
read( Value );
WHILE (Value <> EndOfDataFlag) AND (i < 10) DO
    BEGIN
        i := i + 1;
        Number[i] := Value;
        read( Value )
    END {WHILE};
```

If range checking has not been turned on, strange results may be obtained when an index is allowed to get out of bounds. In this case, the memory location that is being accessed is typically determined by simply counting forward or backward from the base address of the array. This is illustrated by the program in Figure 9.9. Here **A**, **B**, and **C** are arrays declared by

```
CONST
    ArrayLimit = 4;

TYPE
    SmallArray = ARRAY[1..ArrayLimit] OF integer;

VAR
    A, B, C : SmallArray;
```

and the illegal array references **B[-2]** and **B[7]** access the memory locations associated with **A[2]** and **C[3]**:

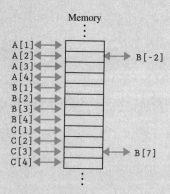

Thus modifying **B[-2]** and **B[7]** changes **A[2]** and **C[3]**, respectively. This change is obviously undesirable. An array reference such as **B[500]** that is very much out of range may even cause a program instruction to be modified! Consequently, *it is important to ensure that indices do not get out of range.*

FIGURE 9.9 Why array indices must stay in bounds.

```pascal
PROGRAM OutOfRangeIndices( output );
{*************************************************************************

    Purpose:          Demonstrate what may result when indices get out
                      of range and range-checking is turned off.
    Output (screen): Arrays A, B, and C.


*************************************************************************}

CONST
    ArrayLimit = 4;

TYPE
    SmallArray = ARRAY[1..ArrayLimit] OF integer;

VAR
    A, B, C : SmallArray;
    below,                    {index below lower limit}
    above : integer;          {index above upper limit}

PROCEDURE PrintArray( Name : char;  X : SmallArray);
{----------------------------------------------------------------------

    Accepts:          Name of an array and the array X.
    Output (screen): The array's name and the elements of the array X


----------------------------------------------------------------------}

    VAR
       i : integer;              {index}

    BEGIN
       write( Name, '=' );
       FOR i := 1 TO ArrayLimit DO
          write( X[i]:5 );
       writeln
    END {PrintArray};

BEGIN {********** main program **********}
    { Initialize the arrays }
    A[1] := 1; A[2] := 2;  A[3] := 3;  A[4] := 4;
    B[1] := 5; B[2] := 6;  B[3] := 7;  B[4] := 8;
    C[1] := 9; C[2] := 10; C[3] := 11; C[4] := 12;

    { Display the original arrays }

    PrintArray( 'A', A );
    PrintArray( 'B', B );
    PrintArray( 'C', C );
```

FIGURE 9.9   Why array indices must stay in bounds. (cont.)

```
{ Reference array B with a subscript that is out of bounds }

below := -2;
B[below] := -999;
above := 7;
B[above] := 999;

{ Display each of the arrays again }

writeln;
PrintArray( 'A', A );
PrintArray( 'B', B );
PrintArray( 'C', C )
END {main program}.
```

Sample run:

```
A =   1    2    3    4
B =   5    6    7    8
C =   9   10   11   12

A =   1 -999    3    4
B =   5    6    7    8
C =   9   10  999   12
```

3. *When reading the elements of an array of characters, remember that end-of-line marks are read as pairs of characters*—a carriage-return (CR) character followed by a line-feed (LF) character.

4. *Assignment of one array to another requires that the arrays have the same type.* This means that they must be declared by the same or by equivalent type *identifiers*.

5. *All of the elements of an array have the type specified in the array declaration.* For example, for the array **Number** in Potential Problem 2, each of the indexed variables **Number[1]**, **Number[2]**, **Number[3]**, . . . , is an **integer** variable and cannot be assigned a **real** value or a value of any type not compatible with type **integer**.

Standard Pascal

There are only a few variations between how Turbo Pascal and standard Pascal process arrays. In standard Pascal:

- Range checking is performed.
- Arrays may not be initialized in constant sections.

STRINGS

An average English word is four letters and a half. By hard, honest labor I've dug all the large words out of my vocabulary and shaved it down till the average is three and a half. . . .
MARK TWAIN

CHAPTER CONTENTS

The word *compute* usually suggests arithmetic operations performed on numeric data; thus, computers are sometimes thought to be mere "number crunchers," devices whose only function is to process numeric information. We know that this is not the case, however, for in Chapter 1 we considered coding schemes used to represent character as well as boolean information, and in subsequent chapters we introduced some of Pascal's capabilities for processing character, string, and boolean data. In this chapter we describe in detail how strings are processed in Turbo Pascal.

10.1   The String ADT

As we noted in Chapter 8, a *data type* consists of a collection of values together with basic operations and relations that are defined on these values. When the data and the basic operations and relations are being studied independent of any implementation, the data type is said to be an **abstract data type** (commonly abbreviated as **ADT**). Viewed as an ADT, strings are finite sequences of characters drawn from some given character set. The basic operations on strings depend on the particular application, but in almost every instance they include

> Assignment of a string value to a string variable.
> Relational operators to compare string values.
> Input/output operations to read and display string values.

Other basic operations that are useful in text-editing and word-processing applications include

Length:	Count the characters in a string.
Concatenate:	Join strings together.
Copy:	Copy a substring from a given string, beginning at a specified position.
Position:	Locate one string within another.
Insert:	Insert one string into another.
Delete:	Delete part of a string.

Because an ADT consists of two parts, a collection of data values and a collection of basic operations and relations, its **implementation** also must consist of two parts:

1. **Storage structures** to store the data values.
2. **Algorithms** for the basic operations and relations.

10.2   The Predefined Data Type `string` in Turbo Pascal

Although standard Pascal does not provide a predefined string data type, many versions of Pascal do include it. In particular, we have seen that Turbo Pascal does provide a string type, and in this section we examine this data type in detail.

Type Declarations

In Turbo Pascal, a string type declaration can have one of two forms:

String Declaration

Forms:

   `string[limit];`   or   `string;`

where:
   limit is a constant.

Purpose:
Specifies that *limit* is the maximum number of
characters in a string value of this type. In the second form where the length specifier is omitted, a
default maximum string length of 255 is assumed.

For example, the declarations

```
CONST
    StringLimit = 20;

VAR
    Name, Department : string[StringLimit];
    Color : string[5];
    Sentence : string;
```

specify that **Name** and **Department** are string variables whose values will be strings
containing at most 20 characters, **Color** is a string variable whose values will have
at most 5 characters, and **Sentence** is a string variable whose value may be any
string containing 255 or fewer characters. In any case, the value of a string variable
may be an **empty string** consisting of no characters and denoted by the string
constant ′ ′, a pair of consecutive single quotes.

Note that a type specifier of the form **string[L]** *is not a type identifier* and
thus may not be used to specify the type of a parameter in a subprogram heading.
For example, to declare a formal parameter in a procedure **P** to have type
string[5], it is necessary to associate this type specifier with a type identifier in
a program unit that contains this procedure, for example,

```
TYPE
    String5 = string[5];
```

and then use this type identifier in the procedure heading:

```
PROCEDURE P( . . .; param : String5; . . . );
```

(Turbo Pascal 7.0 also allows **open-string parameters.** See Section H.5 of Appendix H.)

Storage Structure

Because strings are finite sequences of characters, it is natural to use arrays of characters to store strings, with each array element storing a single character of the string. In Turbo Pascal, when the compiler encounters a string declaration of the form

```
string-var : string[L];
```

it associates with *string-var* an array named *string-var* of type **char** indexed **0..L** and uses this array to store the value of *string-var*. If there are *n* characters in this value ($n \le L$), they will be stored in positions 1, 2, . . . , *n* of this array. Position 0 stores **chr(*n*)**, the character whose ASCII code is *n*.

For example, the declaration

```
VAR
    Name : string[20];
```

associates with **Name** an array named **Name** of type **char** with index type **0..20**. If the string **'William Smith'** is assigned to **Name**, the characters of this string are stored in locations 1, 2, . . . , 13 of the array:

i	0	1	2	3	4	5	6	7	8	9	10	11	12	13	14	15	16	17	18	19	20
Name[i]	←	W	i	l	l	i	a	m		S	m	i	t	h	?	?	?	?	?	?	?

The question marks in locations 14, 15, . . . , 20 indicate unused locations in the array. The character ← in position 0 is **chr(13)**, the carriage-return character whose ASCII code is 13, the length of the string. Thus **ord(Name[0])** is the length of the string assigned to **Name**.

Because an array is used to store a string, an indexed variable may be used to access the individual characters in the string. For example, **Name[1]** is the letter **'W'** and **Name[2]** is the letter **'i'**. The for loop

```
FOR i := 9 TO 13 DO
    write( Name[i] );
```

or equivalently,

```
FOR i := 9 TO ord( Name[0] ) DO
    write( Name[i] );
```

displays the rightmost characters in the value of **Name**, beginning at position 9:

```
Smith
```

The statement

```
Name[1] := 'J';
```

changes the value of **Name** to

```
Jilliam Smith
```

Note that changing the value of a string variable by changing individual characters as in the last example does not change the current length. To illustrate, suppose that **Name** has the value **'William Smith'** and thus has length 13, and consider the statements

```
Name[14] := 'e';
Name[15] := 'r';
Name[16] := 's';
```

Although these statements store characters in positions 14, 15, and 16 of the array **Name**, the value of **Name[0]**, and hence the current length of **Name**, does not change. The output statement

```
writeln( Name );
```

thus produces as output

```
William Smith
```

If the statement

```
Name[0] := chr(16);
```

were included in the preceding assignment statements to change the current length of **Name** to 16, the value displayed by the **writeln** statement would be

```
William Smithers
```

This method of modifying a string by using indexed variables to change individual characters is not the usual method, since such modifications can usually be performed more easily using the operations, functions, and procedures that implement the basic string operations. For example, appending characters to a string can better be done by using concatenation:

```
Name := Name + 'ers';
```

In this case, the current length of **Name** is automatically increased.

Implementations of the Basic Operations

In the preceding section we listed some of the basic operations and relations on strings: assignment, comparison, input/output, length, concatenate, copy, position, insert, and delete. In the following descriptions of how these are implemented in Turbo Pascal, we will assume that *strexp, strexp-1, strexp-2, . . . , strexp-n* are string expressions of any string type or of type **char** (or are packed arrays of characters, as described in the Standard Pascal section at the end of this chapter).

Assignment.   An assignment statement may be used to assign a value to a string variable:

```
strvar := strexp
```

For example, if **Color** is of type **string[5]**, the statement

```
Color := 'green';
```

assigns the string **'green'** to **Color**. The length of the value being assigned may be less than the declared length of the string variable. For example,

```
Color := 'red';
```

assigns the stirng **'red'** to **Color**, and its length becomes 3. Thus we see that the lengths of strings vary *dynamically*. If the length of the value being assigned is greater than the declared length of the variable, the value is truncated to the size specified for the variable, and the leftmost characters are assigned; thus, the statement

```
Color := 'chartreuse';
```

assigns the value **'chart'** to **Color**.

Comparison.   Two string values may be compared with the relational operators **<**, **>**, **=**, **<=**, **>=**, and **<>**. Boolean expressions of the form

```
strexp-1 relop strexp-2
```

where **relop** is one of the relational operators, are evaluated by comparing **strexp-1** and **strexp-2**, character by character, using their ASCII codes, as described in Section 4.2. For example, a boolean expression of the form

```
strexp-1 < strexp-2
```

is true if the first character of **strexp-1** is less than the first character of **strexp-2** (that is, the ASCII code of **strexp-1**'s first character is less than the ASCII code of **strexp-2**'s first character). Thus,

```
'cat' < 'dog'
```

is true, since **'c'** < **'d'** is true. If the first characters of **strexp-1** and **strexp-2** are the same, the second characters are compared; if these characters are the same, the third characters are compared, and so on. Thus,

```
'cat' < 'cow'
```

is true, since **'a'** is less than **'o'**. Similarly,

```
'June' > 'July'
```

is true, since '**n**' is greater than '**l**'. If the two strings have different lengths, they are compared as though the shorter string is padded with blanks to make it have the same length as the longer string. For example, the boolean expression

>   '**cat**' **<** '**cattle**'

or equivalently,

>   '**cat**ᵇᵇᵇ' **<** '**cattle**'

(where ᵇ denotes a blank) is true because a blank character precedes all letters.

Input/Output.   As we saw in Chapter 6, strings can be read from and written to text files. When a value is read for a string variable, characters are read, beginning at the current position of the data pointer and continuing until an end-of-line mark or the end-of-file mark is encountered. If the length of the resulting string is greater than the declared length of the string variable, the string is truncated, and only the leftmost characters are retained.

As we have noted several times, the simplest way to read values for string variables is to use one **readln** statement for each variable and enter the values on separate lines. For example, to read values for the string variables **Name** and **Department**, we might use the statements

```
readln( Name );
readln( Department );
```

and enter the data as

>   **William Smith**↵
>   **Research and Development**↵

so that the file **input** contains

The first **readln** statement reads the string '**William Smith**', assigns it to **Name**, and advances the data pointer past the end-of-line mark:

The string '**Research and Development**' is then read, and truncated to length 20 so that the string '**Research and Develop**' is assigned to **Department**.

It is not possible to read and assign these values with a single **readln** statement,

```
readln( Name, Department )
```

With this statement, the string `'William Smith'` is read and assigned to `Name`, and the data pointer to advanced to the first end-of-line mark, as before. However, an empty string is assigned to `Department`, since no additional characters will be read because the data pointer is already positioned at an end-of-line mark. The same values would be assigned if two consecutive `read` statements were used:

```
read( Name );
read( Department );
```

When the first statement is executed, the string `'William Smith'` is read and assigned to `Name` as before, and the data pointer is once again stuck at an end-of-line mark so that an empty string is assigned to `Department`.

When a string is displayed or written to a text file using the `write` or `writeln` procedures, the size of the output field is the current length of the string. Thus, if `Name` and `Department` have the values assigned by the two preceding `read` statements, the statement

```
writeln( Name, Department, '***' );
```

displays the value of `Name` in a field of width 13, the value of `Department` in a field of width 0, and the string `***` in a field of width 3:

<u>William Smith</u>***

If format descriptors are used, a string value is right justified in the specified field; if the field is too small, it is automatically enlarged to accommodate the value. Thus, the statement

```
writeln( Name:1, '***':5 );
```

produces the output

<u>William Smith </u>***

Length.   In our discussion of the storage structure for strings, we noted that for a string variable *strvar*, *strvar*[0] is the character whose ASCII code is the length of the string value assigned to *strvar*; thus `ord(`*strvar*`[0])` is the length of this string value. Turbo Pascal also provides the function `length` which may be used to find the length of any string expression. A reference to this function has the form

```
length( strexp )
```

and returns the current length of *strexp*.

Concatenation.   The concatenation of a string `Str1` with a string `Str2` is obtained by appending `Str2` to `Str1`. For example, if `Str1` is the string `'list'` and `Str2` is `'en'`, the concatenation of `Str1` with `Str2` is

```
'listen'
```

and the concatenation of `Str2` with `Str1` is

'enlist'

Turbo Pascal provides both a concatenation operation and a concatenation function `concat`. The concatenation operation is denoted by `+`. Thus,

'Pasc' + 'al'

produces the string `'Pascal'`. A reference to the function `concat` has the form

concat(*strexp-1*, *strexp-2*, . . . , *strexp-n*)

and returns the string formed by concatenating *strexp-1*, *strexp-2*, . . . , *strexp-n* in this order. For example, if `FirstName` and `LastName` are of type `string` and have the values

FirstName := 'THOMAS';
LastName := 'JEFFERSON';

then the function reference

concat(FirstName, '***', LastName)

returns the value

'THOMAS***JEFFERSON'

Note that `concat( `*strexp-1*`, `*strexp-2*`, . . . , `*strexp-n*` )` has the same value as an expression of the form

strexp-1 + *strexp-2* + · · · + *strexp-n*

Copy. The copy or substring operation retrieves a (sub)string of a specified length from a given string, beginning at some specified position. For example, if `Str` is the string `'ABCDEFG'`, the substring of `Str` of length 3 beginning at position 2 is

'BCD'

The copy operation is implemented in Turbo Pascal by the function `copy`, which is referenced with an expression of the form

copy(*strexp*, *index*, *size*)

and returns a substring of the specified *size* from the string *strexp*, beginning at position *index*. For example, if `LastName` has the value `'JEFFERSON'`, the function reference

copy(LastName, 2, 5)

returns the value

'EFFER'

and

    copy(LastName, 7, length(LastName) - 7)

returns the value

'SON'

Position.   The position or index operation determines the starting location of the first occurrence of one string within a second string, or it gives the value 0 if the first string does not appear in the second string. The predefined function **pos** implements this operation in Turbo Pascal. A reference to function **pos** has the form

    pos(*strexp-1, strexp-2*)

and returns the starting location of the first occurrence of *strexp-1* in *strexp-2* or the value 0 if *strexp-1* does not appear in *strexp-2*. For example,

    pos('SO', LastName)

has the value 7, and

    pos('E', LastName)

the value 2, whereas

    pos('so', LastName)

has the value 0.

Insert.   The insert operation modifies a string by inserting another string into it at a specified position. For example, inserting **Str1 = 'XY'** into the string **Str2 = 'abc'** at position 3 changes **Str2** to 'abXYc'; inserting it at position 1 changes **Str2** to 'XYabc'.
    The insert operation is implemented in Turbo Pascal by the procedure **insert**, which is referenced with a statement of the form

    insert(*strexp, strvar, position*)

and modifies the string variable *strvar* by inserting the value of the string expression *strexp* at the specified *position*. For example,

    insert(' P', LastName, 5)

changes the value of **LastName** from 'JEFFERSON' to

'JEFF PERSON'

Delete. The delete operation modifies a string by deleting from it a substring of a specified length at a specified position. For example, deleting the substring of length 3 at position 2 from `Str = 'compute'` changes `Str` to `'cute'`.

The delete operation is implemented in Turbo Pascal by the procedure `delete`, which is referenced with a statement of the form

```
delete( strvar, position, size )
```

This procedure modifies the string variable *strvar* by removing a substring of the specified *size*, starting at the specified *position*. For example,

```
delete( FirstName, 5, 2 )
```

changes the value of `FirstName` from `'THOMAS'` to

```
'THOM'
```

Other String-Processing Procedures. Turbo Pascal also provides the procedures `str` and `val` for converting values between numeric and string types. `Str` is called with a statement of the form

```
str( numexp, strvar )
```

and converts the value of the numeric expression *numexp* to a string of characters and assigns this string to the string variable *strvar*. The format of this character string is exactly the same as that produced by the output statement

```
write( numexp )
```

For example, if `S1`, `S2`, and `S3` are of type `string` and `Num` is an integer variable with value 5, the statements

```
str( 1234, S1 );
str( Num - 10, S2 );
str( 123.456, S3 );
```

assign the string `'1234'` to `S1`, the string `'-5'` to `S2`, and the string `'1.2345600000E+02'` to `S3`. Format descriptors may also be attached to the numeric expression, in which case the conversion is carried out as specified by these descriptors. For example, the statements

```
str( Num - 10 : 5, S2 );
str( 123.456 : 4 : 2 , S3 );
```

assign `S2` the value `'ƀƀƀ-5'` and `S3` the value `'123.46'`.

The procedure `val` is used to convert strings representing numbers into the corresponding numeric values. It is called with a statement of the form

```
val( strexp, numvar, errorcode )
```

where *strexp* is a string expression, *numvar* is an integer or real variable, and *errorcode* is an integer variable. When it is executed, this statement converts *strexp* to the corresponding numeric value, if possible, and assigns this value to *numvar*. Conversion is possible only if the value of *strexp* is a string of characters representing a valid integer. In this case, *errorcode* is assigned the value 0; otherwise, it is assigned the position of the first character in the string that prevented conversion. For example, if `I` and `Code` are integer variables and `Numeral` is a string variable with value `'12'`, the statement

```
val( Numeral + '34', I, Code );
```

assigns `I` the value 1234 and `Code` the value 0, while

```
val( '123ABC', I, Code );
```

assigns `Code` the value 4 and leaves `I` undefined.

10.3   Examples: Text Editing; Sorting Names

Example 1: Text Editing

The preparation of textual material such as letters, books, and computer programs often involves the insertion, deletion, and replacement of parts of the text. The software of most computer systems includes an **editor** that makes these operations easy. These and other text-editing operations are often implemented using the basic string operations, as illustrated in the text-editor program in Figure 10.1.

A level-one algorithm for this text editor is

TEXT-EDITING ALGORITHM

1. Open the input file *TextFile* and a new file *EditedFile* for the edited output.
2. Display instructions and the list of available editing commands to the user.
3. Read the first line from *TextFile*.
4. Repeat the following:
     a. Get an editing command from the user.
     b. Process the editing command.
   Until the user selects the "Quit" option.
5. Copy the rest of *TextFile* to *EditedFile*.

The heart of the algorithm is processing the editing commands in Step 4b, but the availability of the string-processing functions and procedures makes this quite straightforward. The sample run in Figure 10.1 displays the menu of editing commands:

```
I(nsert)    : insert a substring
D(elete)    : delete a substring
R(eplace)   : replace one substring with another
L(ength)    : determine the length of current line
P(osition)  : find position of a substring
N(ewLine)   : get next line of text
Q(uit)      : quit editing
```

The I, D, L, and P options are implemented easily using the string-processing subprograms insert, delete, length, and pos, respectively. Algorithms for the other editing commands are also straightforward:

N(ewLine):

(∗ Stop editing the current line and get the next line. ∗)

1. Write the edited line to *EditedFile*.
2. Read the next line from *TextFile*.

Q(uit):

(∗ Terminate editing of the file. ∗)

1. Write the edited line to *EditedFile*.
2. While the end of *TextFile* has not been reached, do the following:
   a. Read the next line from *TextFile*.
   b. Write the line to *EditedFile*.

R(eplace):

(∗ Replace a substring *Sub1* in the string *Str* with string *Sub2*. ∗)

1. Determine the length *Len* of *Sub1*.
2. Find the *Position* of the first occurrence of *Sub1* in *Str*.
3. If *Position* > 0 (∗ *Sub1* is found in *Str* ∗) then do the following:
   a. Delete the *Len* characters from *Str* beginning at *Position*.
   b. Insert *Sub2* into *Str* at *Position*.

This program in Figure 10.1 uses these algorithms to solve the text-editing problem. It reads the lines in **TextFile** one at a time and stores them in the string variable **Line** of type **string[StringLimit]**, where **StringLimit** is defined to be 80, the upper limit on the length of lines in **TextFile**. The predefined string-processing operations, functions, and procedures are used to carry out the required editing operations.

FIGURE 10.1   Text editing.

```
PROGRAM TextEditor( input, TextFile, output, EditedFile) ;
{******************************************************************
```

Input (file):	A text file TextFile.
Input (keyboard):	Editing commands entered by the user.
Purpose:	Perform several basic text-editing operations on lines of text read from TextFile; after editing has been completed, each line is written to a new file EditedFile. Text-editing commands include the following:

```
                         Insert   : insert a substring in a line
                         Delete   : delete a substring from a line
                         Replace  : replace one substring in a line with
                                    another
                         Length   : determine the length of a line
                         Position : find the position of a substring in
                                    a line
                         NewLine  : get next line of text
                         Quit     : quit editing
```

Output (screen):	A menu of editing commands, user prompts, unedited and edited lines of text.
Output (file):	Text file EditedFile.

```
    ******************************************************************}

CONST
   StringLimit = 80;

TYPE
   StringType = string[StringLimit];

VAR
   TextFile,                   {file of original text}
   EditedFile : text;          {file of edited text}
   TextFileName,               {actual name of text file}
   EditedFileName,             {actual name of edited file}
   Line : StringType;          {line of text to be edited}
   Command : char;             {editing command}
   Str1, Str2 : StringType;    {strings used in editing}
   Position,                   {position of a string in Line}
   Len : integer;              {length of some string}

PROCEDURE PrintCommands;
{------------------------------------------------------------------
```

Input:	None.
Purpose:	Display a menu of editing commands.
Output (screen):	Menu of editing commands.

```
------------------------------------------------------------------}
```

FIGURE 10.1 Text editing. (cont.)

```
    BEGIN
        writeln( 'Editing commands are:' );
        writeln( '        I(nsert)    : insert a substring' );
        writeln( '        D(elete)    : delete a substring' );
        writeln( '        R(eplace)   : replace one substring with another' );
        writeln( '        L(ength)    : determine the length of current line' );
        writeln( '        P(osition)  : find position of a substring' );
        writeln( '        N(ewLine)   : get next line of text' );
        writeln( '        Q(uit)      : quit editing' )
    END {PrintCommands};

PROCEDURE Replace( Sub1, Sub2 : StringType; VAR Str : StringType );
{------------------------------------------------------------------

    Accepts: Strings Sub1 and Sub2.
    Purpose: Replace substring Sub1 with string Sub2 in string Str.
    Returns: String Str.

-------------------------------------------------------------------}

    VAR
        Position : integer;    {position where replacement to be made}

    BEGIN
        Position := pos( Sub1, Str );
        IF Position > 0 THEN
            BEGIN
                delete( Str, Position, length(Sub1) );
                insert( Sub2, Str, Position )
            END {IF}
    END {Replace};

BEGIN {*************** main program ***************}
    write( 'Enter name of text file to be edited: ' );
    readln( TextFileName );
    assign( TextFile, TextFileName );
    reset( TextFile );
    write( 'Enter name of file to contain the edited text: ' );
    readln( EditedFileName );
    assign( EditedFile, EditedFileName );
    rewrite( EditedFile );
    PrintCommands;
    writeln( 'Enter a 1-character editing command following the prompt >' );
    writeln;
    readln( TextFile, Line );
    writeln( Line );
```

FIGURE 10.1   Text editing. (cont.)

```
REPEAT
    write( '>' );
    readln( Command );
    CASE Command OF
        'L','l' : writeln( 'Length = ' pel^, length(Line):1 );
        'P','p' : BEGIN
                        write( 'Position of?  ' );
                        readln( Str1 );
                        writeln( '      is ', pos( Str1, Line ) )
                  END {Position};
        'I','i' : BEGIN
                        write( 'Insert what?  ' );
                        readln( Str1 );
                        write( ' At position?  ' );
                        readln( Position );
                        insert( Str1, Line, Position );
                        writeln( Line )
                  END {Insert};
        'D','d' : BEGIN
                        write( 'Delete where?  ' );
                        readln( Position );
                        write( 'How many characters?  ' );
                        readln( Len );
                        delete( Line, Position, Len );
                        writeln( Line )
                  END {Delete};
        'R','r' : BEGIN
                        write( 'Replace what?  ' );
                        readln( Str1 );
                        write( '   With what?  ' );
                        readln( Str2 );
                        Replace( Str1, Str2, Line );
                        writeln( Line )
                  END {Replace};

        'N','n' : BEGIN
                        writeln( EditedFile, Line );
                        IF NOT eof( TextFile ) THEN
                            BEGIN
                                writeln( 'Next Line:' );
                                readln( TextFile, Line );
                                writeln( Line )
                            END {IF}
                        ELSE
                            Command := 'Q'
                  END {NewLine};
```

FIGURE 10.1 Text editing. (cont.)

```
        'Q','q' : BEGIN
                        writeln( EditedFile, Line );
                        WHILE NOT eof( TextFile ) DO
                            BEGIN
                                readln( TextFile, Line );
                                writeln( EditedFile, Line )
                            END {WHILE};
                        END {Quit}
        ELSE
                        BEGIN
                            writeln;
                            writeln( '--- Illegal command ---' );
                            PrintCommands;
                            writeln( Line )
                        END {ELSE}
            END {CASE}
    UNTIL (Command IN ['Q','q'] );
    close( TextFile );
    close( EditedFile );
    writeln;
    writeln( '--- Editing complete ---' )
END {main program}.
```

Listing of `FIL10-1A.DAT` used in sample run:

```
Foursscore and five years ago, our mothers
brought forth on continent
a new nation conceived in liberty and and dedicated
to the preposition that all men
are created equal.
```

Sample run:

```
Enter name of textfile to be edited: FIL10-1A.DAT
Enter name of file to contain the edited text: FIL10-1B.DAT
Editing commands are:
      I(nsert)    : insert a substring
      D(elete)    : delete a substring
      R(eplace)   : replace one substring with another
      L(ength)    : determine the length of current line
      P(osition)  : find position of a substring
      N(ewLine)   : get next line of text
      Q(uit)      : quit editing
Enter a 1-character editing command following the prompt >
```

FIGURE 10.1 Text editing. (cont.)

```
Foursscore and five years ago, our mothers
>D
Delete where?   5
How many characters?   1
Fourscore and five years ago, our mothers
>R
Replace what?   five
   With what?   seven
Fourscore and seven years ago, our mothers
>R
Replace what?   mo
   With what?   fa
Fourscore and seven years ago, our fathers
>N
Next Line:
brought forth on continent
>P
Position of?   con
     is 18
>I
Insert what?   this
 At position?   17
brought forth on this continent
>N
Next Line:
a new nation conceived in liberty and and dedicated
>P
Position of?   and
     is 35
>D
Delete where?   35
How many characters?   4
a new nation conceived in liberty and dedicated
>N
Next Line:
to the preposition that all men
>R
Replace what?   pre
   With what?   pro
to the proposition that all men
>N
Next Line:
are created equal.
>Q

--- Editing complete ---
```

FIGURE 10.1   Text editing. (cont.)

Listing of `FIL10-1B.DAT` produced:

```
Fourscore and seven years ago, our fathers
brought forth on this continent
a new nation conceived in liberty and dedicated
to the proposition that all men
are created equal.
```

Example 2: Sorting Names

Suppose that a list of names, each consisting of a first name followed by a blank followed by a last name, is to be read from a data file. The names in this list are then to be displayed in the form *last-name, first-name,* with the last names in alphabetical order.

The list of names to be read and processed can be stored in an array **Name** whose elements are strings. Since a string is an array of characters, the array **Name** will in fact be an *array of arrays.* If the names are stored in this array in the format *last-name, first-name,* they can be sorted using one of the sorting algorithms described in Section 9.4 and then displayed. This is summarized in the following algorithm:

ALGORITHM TO SORT A LIST OF NAMES

(∗ Input: A list of names.
   Purpose: Read a list of names and sort them so the last names are in
                alphabetical order.
   Output: The sorted list of names. ∗)

1. Repeat the following until all the names have been read or the array *Name* is filled:
    a. Read *TempName* and extract *FirstName* and *LastName* from it.
    b. Attach a comma followed by a blank to *LastName*.
    c. Concatenate *LastName* with *FirstName* and store the resulting string in the next location of array *Name*.
2. Alphabetize the array *Name* using some sorting method.
3. Display the sorted list of names in the desired format.

The program in Figure 10.2 implements this algorithm. Each name is read and the function **pos** is used to locate the blank separating the first and last names. The procedure **copy** is then used to extract **FirstName** and **LastName** as required in Step 1a, and the concatenation operation is used to carry out the operations described in Steps 1b and 1c and the selection sort algorithm is used in Step 2.

FIGURE 10.2 Sorting a list of names.

```pascal
PROGRAM NameSort( input, output );
{*****************************************************************

    Input (keyboard): A list of names.
    Purpose:          Read a list of first and last names, sort them
                      so the last names are in alphabetical order,
                      and display them in the form:
                                Last-name, First-name.
    Output (screen):  User prompts and the sorted list of names.

*****************************************************************}

CONST
    StringLimit = 30;   {limit on lengths of strings}
    ListLimit = 100;    {limit on length of list}

TYPE
    StringType = string[StringLimit];
    List = ARRAY[1..ListLimit] of StringType;
    ItemType = StringType;

VAR
    Name : List;        {list of names}
    i,                  {index}
    NumNames : integer; {number of names in list}

PROCEDURE ReverseAndStoreNames( VAR Name : List;       {list of names}
                                VAR Count : integer ); {number of names}
{------------------------------------------------------------------------

    Input (keyboard): List of names.
    Purpose:          Read and count names, reverse them so they
                      have the form
                              Last-Name, First-Name
                      and store these reversed names in the array Name.
    Returns:          Array Name and the Count of the names.
    Output (screen):  User prompt and an error message.

------------------------------------------------------------------------}

    VAR
        TempName,                  {temporary variable for name}
        FirstName,                 {first name}
        LastName : StringType;     {last name}
        BlankPos : integer;        {position of blank in name}

    BEGIN
        {Read names, reverse and store them}
        writeln( 'Enter the names in the form Firstname Lastname,' );
        writeln( '1 name per line.  Enter STOP to stop.' );
        writeln;
        Count := 0;
        readln( TempName );
```

FIGURE 10.2   Sorting a list of names. (cont.)

```
        WHILE TempName <> 'STOP' DO
          IF Count < ListLimit THEN
              BEGIN
                {Form last-name, first-name and store in Name}
                BlankPos := pos( ' ', TempName, );
                FirstName := copy( TempName, 1, BlankPos - 1 );
                LastName := copy( TempName, BlankPos + 1,
                                  length(TempName) - BlankPos );
                Count := Count + 1;
                Name[Count] := LastName + ', ' + FirstName;
                readln( TempName );
              END {IF}
          ELSE
              BEGIN
                writeln( '*** Too many names -- processing first ',
                         ListLimit:1, ' names ***' );
                TempName[1] := '*'   {force end of data}
              END {ELSE}
      END {ReverseAndStoreNames};

PROCEDURE SelectionSort( VAR Item : List;          {list of items}
                             NumItems : integer ); {number of items}
{--------------------------------------------------------------------

   Accepts:  List Item and number (NumItems) of items.
   Purpose:  Sort Item[1], ..., Item[NumItems] into ascending order
             using the simple selection sort algorithm.
   Returns:  Sorted array Item.


---------------------------------------------------------------------}

   VAR
      Smallest : ItemType;      {smallest item in current sublist}
      SmallPos,                 {position of Smallest}
      i, j : integer;           {indices}

   BEGIN
      FOR i := 1 TO NumItems - 1 DO
         BEGIN

            {find smallest item in sublist Item[i], ..., Item[NumItems]}
            SmallPos := i;
            Smallest := Item[SmallPos];
            FOR j := i + 1 TO NumItems DO
               IF Item[j] < Smallest THEN   {smaller item found}
                  BEGIN
                     SmallPos := j;
                     Smallest := Item[j]
                  END {IF};
```

FIGURE 10.2   Sorting a list of names. (cont.)

```
              {interchange smallest item with Item[i] at beginning
                      of sublist}
              Item[SmallPos] := Item[i];
              Item[i] := Smallest
           END {FOR i}
   END {SelectionSort};

BEGIN {************** main program **************}
   ReverseAndStoreNames(Name, NumNames) ;
   SelectionSort( Name, NumNames );
   writeln;
   writeln( 'Sorted list of names:' );
   FOR i := 1 TO NumNames DO
      writeln( Name[i] )
END {main program}.
```

Sample run:

```
Enter the names in the form Firstname Lastname,
1 name per line.  Enter STOP to stop.

John Doe
Mary Smith
Fred Jones
Jesse James
Merry Christmas
STOP

Sorted list of names:
Christmas, Merry
Doe, John
James, Jesse
Jones, Fred
Smith, Mary
```

Exercises

1. Write a procedure to convert a string of lowercase and uppercase letters into all lowercase letters.

2. Write a program to count the occurrences of a specified string in several lines of text.

3. Write a program to count all double-letter occurrences in a given line of text.

4. Write a program to determine whether a specified string occurs in a given string and, if so, print an asterisk (*) under the first position of each occurrence.

5. The local chapter of the Know-Nothing party maintains a file of names and addresses of its contributors. Each line of the file contains the following items of information in the order indicated:

> Last name: a string of length at most 12
> First name: a string of length at most 10
> Middle initial: a character
> Street address: a string of length at most 15
> City and state: a string of length at most 20
> Zip code: a string of length at most 10

and all of the items in each line are separated by some delimiter such as #; for example,

```
Doe#John#Q#123 SomeStreet#AnyTown, AnyState#12345
```

Write a program that reads each line of the file and produces a mailing label having the format

```
John Q. Doe
123 SomeStreet
AnyTown, AnyState 12345
```

6. Write a program to print "personalized" contest letters like those frequently received in the mail. It might have a format like that of the following sample, with the underlined locations filled in with appropriate data:

```
Mr. John Q. Doe
123 SomeStreet
AnyTown, AnyState 12345

Dear Mr. Doe:

    How would you like to see a brand new Cadillac parked in
front of 123 SomeStreet in AnyTown, AnyState? Impossible, you
say?  No, it isn't, Mr. Doe.  Simply keep the enclosed raffle
ticket and validate it by sending a $100.00 tax-deductible
political contribution and 10 labels from Shyster & Sons
chewing tobacco.  Not only will you become eligible for the
drawing to be conducted on February 29 by the independent
firm of G. Y. P. Shyster, but you will also be helping to
reelect Sam Shyster. That's all there is to it, John.  You
may be a winner!!!
```

7. Write a program that permits the input of a name consisting of a first name, a middle name or initial, and a last name, in that order, and then prints the last name, followed by a comma and then the first and middle initials, each followed by a period. For example, the input **John H. Doe** should produce **Doe, J. H.**

8. There are 3 teaspoons in a tablespoon, 4 tablespoons in a quarter of a cup, 2 cups in a pint, and 2 pints in a quart. Write a program to convert units in cooking. The program should call for the input of the amount, the units, and

the new units desired. For example, the input **0.5 CUPS TEASPOONS** asks for the conversion of one-half cup to teaspoons.

9. Write a program to convert ordinary Hindu–Arabic numerals into Roman numerals and vice versa (I = 1, V = 5, X = 10, L = 50, C = 100, D = 500, and M = 1,000).

10. The game of Hangman is played by two persons. One person selects a word and the other person tries to guess the word by guessing individual letters. Design a program to play Hangman. You might store a list of words in an array or file and have the program randomly select a word for the user to guess (see Section 7.4).

11. A string is said to be a **palindrome** if it does not change when the order of characters in the string is reversed. For example,

MADAM
463364
ABLE WAS I ERE I SAW ELBA

are palindromes. Write a program to read a string and then determine whether it is a palindrome.

12. Repeat Exercise 11, but this time use a recursive procedure to determine whether a string is a palindrome.

13. Graphs of equations also can be plotted using the computer. For example, Figure 10.3 shows computer-generated plots of

$$Y = X^2 \text{ for } -3 \le X \le 3$$

and

$$Y = X^3 \text{ for } -2 \le X \le 2$$

using an X increment of 0.25 in each case. Note that for convenience, the X axis has been printed vertically and the Y axis horizontally.

Write a program to produce a similar plot of a given equation, using a packed character array with the number of array elements equal to the width of the page. For each X value, set all of the array elements equal to blanks, or equal to the marks comprising the Y axis if $X = 0$; then set one array element equal to the X axis mark and another equal to the plotting character; the position of this latter array element should correspond to the Y coordinate of the point on the graph for that X value.

14. Write a program that accepts two strings and determines whether one string is an anagram of the other, that is, whether one string is a permutation of the characters in the other string. For example, "dear" is an anagram of "read," as is "dare."

15. Modify the program in Figure 10.2 so that instead of displaying the sorted list of names, it accepts last names from the user and then searches the list to find all names for which this is the last name.

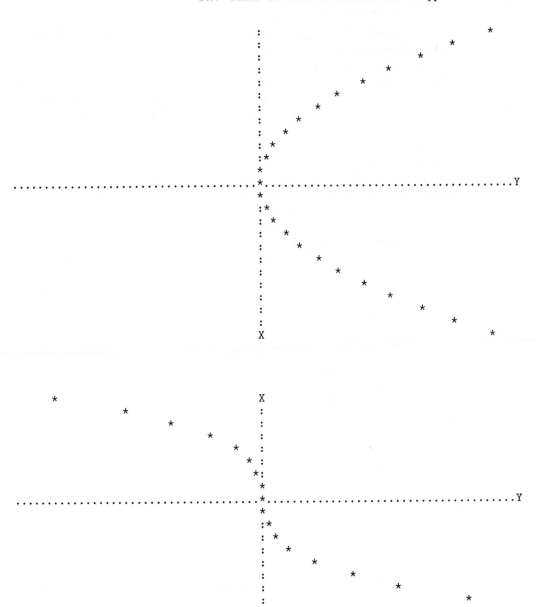

FIGURE 10.3   Plots of $Y = X^2$ and $Y = X^3$.

16. Proceed as in Exercise 15, but have the program accept complete names from the user, and then binary-search the list to determine whether this name is in the list.

10.4   PART OF THE PICTURE: Data Encryption

The basic string operations length, position, concatenate, copy, insert, and delete are the operations most useful in text-editing applications like those of the preceding section. There are, however, some important kinds of string processing that require other operations. One such application is data encryption, in which the important basic operations are *substitution* and *permutation.*

Encryption refers to the coding of information in order to keep it secret. The string of characters comprising the information is transformed into another string that is a coded form of the information. This is called a **cryptogram** or **ciphertext** and may be safely stored or transmitted. At a later time it can be deciphered by reversing the encrypting process to recover the original information, which is called **plaintext.**

Data encryption has been used to send secret military and political messages from the days of Julius Caesar to the present. More recent situations in which the transmission of secret data was crucial include the Washington–Moscow hotline of the cold-war era, electronic funds transfer, electronic mail, and database security. Less serious applications include the Captain Midnight secret decoder rings that could be obtained in the 1950s for twenty-five cents and two Ovaltine labels, puzzles appearing in the daily newspaper, and a number of other frivolous applications.

The simplest encryption schemes are based on the string operation of **substitution,** in which each character in the plaintext string is replaced by some other character according to a fixed rule. For example, the **Caesar cipher** scheme consists of replacing each letter by the letter that appears k positions later in the alphabet for some integer k. (The alphabet is thought of as being arranged in a circle, with A following Z.) In the original Caesar cipher, k was 3, so that each occurrence of A in the plaintext was replaced by D, each B by E, . . . , each Y by B, and each Z by C. For example, we would encrypt the string 'IDESOFMARCH' as follows:

The following program implements this encryption scheme.

 FIGURE 10.4 Encrypting a message.

```
PROGRAM Encrypt( input, output );
{*****************************************************************

   Input (keyboard):   A message string and an encryption key.
   Purpose:            Encrypt a message using a Caesar-cipher
                       scheme.
   Output (screen):    Prompts to the user and the cryptogram.


*****************************************************************}

CONST
   StringLimit = 80;   {limit on length of strings}

TYPE
   StringType = string[StringLimit];
```

FIGURE 10.4   Encrypting a message. (cont.)

```
VAR
   Message,                       {message to be encrypted}
   Cryptogram : StringType;       {encrypted message}
   Response : char;               {user response}

PROCEDURE CaesarCipher
                  (     Message : StringType;       {message to encrypt}
                   VAR Cryptogram : StringType );  {encrypted message}
{------------------------------------------------------------------

   Accepts:   String Message.
   Purpose:   Encrypt Message by converting each character of the
              message to its numeric code, adding an integer to this
              code, and convert the resulting number back to a
              character.
   Returns:   Encrypted string Cryptogram.

-------------------------------------------------------------------}

   VAR
      NewCode,                     {new code for character}
      Key : integer;               {encryption key}
      i : integer;                 {index}

   BEGIN
      REPEAT
         write( 'Enter positive integer to use as encryption key: ' );
         readln( Key )
      UNTIL Key > 0;
      Cryptogram := Message;
      FOR i := 1 TO length(Cryptogram) DO
         BEGIN
            NewCode := ord(Cryptogram[i]) + Key;
            IF NewCode >= 127 THEN
               NewCode := 32 + NewCode MOD 127;
            Cryptogram[i] := chr(NewCode)
         END {FOR};
   END {CaesarCipher};

BEGIN {*************** main program ***************}
   REPEAT
      writeln( 'Enter message to be encrypted:' );
      readln( Message );
      CaesarCipher( Message, Cryptogram );
      writeln;
      writeln( 'Encrypted message:' );
      writeln( Cryptogram );
      writeln;
      write( 'More messages (Y or N)? ' );
      readln( Response )
   UNTIL (Response = 'N') or (Response = 'n')
END {main program}.
```

FIGURE 10.4   Encrypting a message. (cont.)

Sample run:

```
Enter message to be encrypted:
IDESOFMARCH
Enter positive integer to use as encryption key: 3

Encrypted message:
LGHVRIPDUFK

More messages (Y or N)? Y
Enter message to be encrypted:
THEREDCOATSARECOMING
Enter positive integer to use as encryption key: 5

Encrypted message:
YMJWJIHTFYXFWJHTRNSL

More messages (Y or N)? N
```

To decode the message, the receiver simply replaces each character in the cryptogram by the character k positions earlier in the alphabet. This is obviously not a very secure scheme, since it is easy to "break the code" by simply trying the twenty-six possible values for the key k.

An improved substitution operation is to use a *keyword* to specify several different displacements of letters rather than the single offset k of the Caesar cipher. In this **Vignère cipher** scheme, a keyword is added character by character to the plaintext string, where each letter is represented by its position in the character set and addition is carried out mod 26. For example, if the positions of A, B, C, ..., Z are given by 0, 1, 2, ..., 25, respectively, and the keyword is DAGGER, the message 'IDESOFMARCH' is encrypted as follows:

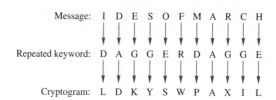

The receiver recovers the message by subtracting the characters in this keyword from those in the cryptogram.

A different substitution operation is to use a **substitution table,** for example:

Original character:	A	B	C	D	E	F	G	H	I	J	K	L	M
Substitute character:	Q	W	E	R	T	Y	U	I	O	P	A	S	D

	N	O	P	Q	R	S	T	U	V	W	X	Y	Z
	F	G	H	J	K	L	Z	X	C	V	B	N	M

The string 'IDESOFMARCH' would then be encoded using this substitution table as follows:

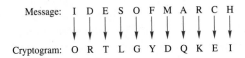

Message: I   D   E   S   O   F   M   A   R   C   H

Cryptogram: O   R   T   L   G   Y   D   Q   K   E   I

To decode the cryptogram, the receiver simply uses the substitution table in reverse.

Since there are 26! (approximately 10^{28}) possible substitution tables, this scheme is considerably more secure than the simple Caesar cipher scheme. Experienced cryptographers can easily break the code, however, by analyzing frequency counts of certain letters and combinations of letters.

Another basic string operation in some encryption schemes is **permutation,** in which the characters in the plaintext or in blocks of the plaintext are rearranged. For example, we might divide the message into blocks (substrings) of size 3 and permute the characters in each block as follows:

Original position: 1   2   3
Permuted position: 3   1   2

Thus the message 'IDESOFMARCH' would be encrypted (after the addition of a randomly selected character X so that the string length is a multiple of the block length) as

Message: I D E S O F M A R C H X

Cryptogram: D E I O F S A R M H X C

To decode the cryptogram, the receiver must know the key permutation and its inverse:

Original position: 1   2   3
Permuted position: 2   3   1

Many modern encryption schemes use both of these techniques by combining several substitution and permutation operations. Perhaps the best known is the **Data Encryption Standard (DES)** developed in the early 1970s by researchers at the IBM Corporation. The scheme is described in *Federal Information Processing Standards Publication 46* (FIPS Pub 46)[1] and in the second edition of our text *Data Structures and Program Design in Pascal.*[2] It consists essentially of a permutation followed by a sequence of sixteen substitutions and a final permutation. The substitution operations are similar to those in earlier examples. Some are obtained by the addition of keywords (sixteen different ones), and others use substitution tables.

DES was adopted in 1977 by the National Institute of Standards and Technology (formerly the National Bureau of Standards) as the standard encryption

---

[1] Copies of this publication can be obtained from the National Institute of Standards and Technology of the U. S. Department of Commerce.

[2] Larry Nyhoff and Sanford Leestma, *Data Structures and Program Design in Pascal,* 2nd ed. (New York: Macmillan, 1992).

scheme for sensitive federal documents. It has been the subject of some controversy, however, because of questions about its security. In fact, two Israeli scientists, E. Biham and A. Shamir (one of the developers of the popular public-key encryption scheme described later) recently announced a mathematical technique that makes it possible to break the DES code under certain circumstances.

Each of the preceding encryption schemes requires that both the sender and the receiver know the encryption key or keys. This means that although the cryptogram may be transmitted through some public channel such as a telephone line that is not secure, the keys must be transmitted in some secure manner, for example, by a courier. This problem of maintaining secrecy of the key is compounded when it must be shared by several persons.

Recently developed encryption schemes eliminate this problem by using two keys, one for encryption and one for decryption. These schemes are called **public-key encryption schemes** because the encryption key is made public by the receiver to all those who transmit messages to him or her; the decryption key, however, is known only to the receiver. The security of these schemes depends on its being nearly impossible to determine the decryption key if one knows only the encryption key.

In 1978, R. L. Rivest, A. Shamir, and L. Adelman proposed one method of implementing a public-key encryption scheme.[3] The public key is a pair (e, n) of integers, and one encrypts a message string M by first dividing M into blocks M_1, $M_2, \ldots, M_k$ and converting each block M_i of characters to an integer P_i in the range 0 through $n - 1$ (for example, by concatenating the ASCII codes of the characters). M is then encrypted by raising each block to the power e and reducing modulo n:

Message: $M = M_1 M_2 \cdots M_k \rightarrow P_1 P_2 \cdots P_k$

Cryptogram: $C = C_1 C_2 \cdots C_k$, where $C_i = P_i^e \text{ MOD } n$

The cryptogram C is decrypted by raising each block C_i to the power d and reducing modulo n, where d is a secret decryption key.

To illustrate, suppose that characters are converted to numeric values using the codes $0, 1, 2, \ldots, 25$ for the letters A, B, C, $\ldots$, Z, respectively, and that $(17, 2773)$ is the public encryption key. To encrypt the message $M =$ 'IDESOFMARCH' using the RSA algorithm, we divide M into two-character blocks $M_1, M_2, \ldots, M_6$ (after appending a randomly selected character X) and represent each block M_i as an integer P_i in the range 0 through $2773 - 1 = 2772$ by concatenating the numeric codes of the characters that comprise the block:

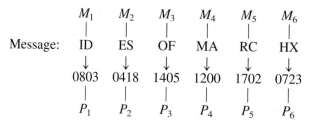

[3] R. L. Rivest, A. Shamir, and L. Adelman, "A Method for Obtaining Digital Signatures and Public-Key Cryptosystems," *Communications of the ACM*, February 1978, pp. 120–126.

Each of these blocks P_i is then encrypted by calculating $C_i = P_i^{17}$ MOD 2773:

Cryptogram: 0779   1983   2641   1444   0052   0802
$\qquad\qquad\quad$ | $\quad$ | $\quad$ | $\quad$ | $\quad$ | $\quad$ |
$\qquad\qquad\quad C_1 \quad\; C_2 \quad\; C_3 \quad\; C_4 \quad\; C_5 \quad\; C_6$

For this encryption key, the corresponding decrypting key is $d = 157$. Thus, we decode the cryptogram by calculating C_i^{157} MOD 2773 for each block C_i. For the preceding cryptogram this gives

Decoded cryptogram: 0803   0418   1405   1200   1702   0723

which is the numeric form of the original message.

The number n used in this scheme is the product of two large "random" primes p and q,

$$n = p \cdot q$$

In the preceding example, we used the small primes 47 and 59 to simplify the computations, but Rivest, Shamir, and Adelman suggest that p and q have several hundred digits. The decrypting key d is then selected to be some large integer that is relatively prime to both $p - 1$ and $q - 1$; that is, one that has no factors in common with either number. In our example, $d = 157$ has this property. The number e is then selected to have the property that

$$e \cdot d \text{ MOD } ((p - 1) \cdot (q - 1)) \text{ is equal to } 1$$

To break this code, one must be able to determine the value of d from the values of n and e. Because of the manner in which d and e are selected, this is possible if n can be factored into a product of primes. Thus, the security of the RSA encryption scheme is based on the difficulty of determining the prime factors of a large integer. Even with the best factorization algorithms known today, this is a prohibitively time-consuming task. A study a few years ago gave the following table displaying some estimated times, assuming that each operation required one microsecond:

Number of Digits in Number Being Factored	Time
50	4 hours
75	104 days
100	74 years
200	4 billion years
300	5×10^{15} years
500	4×10^{25} years

Although research on factorization continues, no efficient algorithms have been found that significantly reduce the times in the preceding table. Improved algorithms and the use of high-speed computers have made factorization possible in less time than the table shows, but not significantly less for large numbers. This public-key encryption scheme thus appears (so far) to be quite secure and is being endorsed by a growing number of major computer vendors; and the adoption of a public-key encryption standard is being considered by the National Institute of Standards and Technology.

Exercises

1. A pure permutation encryption scheme is very insecure. Explain why by describing how an encryption scheme that merely permutes the bits in an n-bit string can easily be cracked by studying how certain basic bit strings are encrypted. Show this for $n = 4$.

2. Using the character codes 0, 1, . . . , 25 given in the text and the message 'PUBLIC':

   (a) Find the cryptogram produced by the Caesar cipher scheme with key = 3.
   (b) Find the cryptogram produced by the Vignère cipher scheme with keyword 'AND'.
   (c) Find the cryptogram produced using the substitution table given in the text.
   (d) Find the cryptogram produced using the permutation given in the text:

   Original position: 1 2 3
   Permuted position: 3 1 2

   (e) Find the cryptogram produced using the RSA scheme with encryption key $(e, n) = (5, 2881)$.
   (f) One decrypting key for the RSA scheme in part (e) is $d = 1109$. Use it to decode the cryptogram obtained in part (e).

3. Modify the program in Figure 10.4 by adding a procedure to decode a cryptogram produced by the Caesar cipher scheme.

4. Write a program to encrypt and decrypt a message using the Vignère cipher scheme.

5. Write a program to encrypt and decrypt a message using a substitution table.

6. Write a program to encrypt and decrypt a message using a permutation scheme.

7. Write a program that implements the RSA scheme (with integer values in the range allowed by your version of Pascal).

8. The Morse code is a standard encoding scheme that uses substitutions similar to those in the scheme described in this section. The substitutions used in this case are shown in the following table. Write a program to read a message either in plaintext or in Morse code and then to encode or decode the message.

A ·—	M ——	Y —·——
B —···	N —·	Z ——··
C —·—·	O ———	1 ·————
D —··	P ·——·	2 ··———
E ·	Q ——·—	3 ···——
F ··—·	R ·—·	4 ····—
G ——·	S ···	5 ·····
H ····	T —	6 —····
I ··	U ··—	7 ——···
J ·———	V ···—	8 ———··
K —·—	W ·——	9 ————·
L ·—··	X —··—	0 —————

Since strings are stored as arrays of characters, some of the programming pointers in the preceding chapter are relevant here also. See the Programming Pointers section at the end of Chapter 9 for additional details.

Program Design

1. *String types should be associated with type identifiers in the* **TYPE** *section.*

Potential Problems

1. *A value assigned a string variable will be truncated if its length is greater than the declared length of the variable.* In this case, only the leftmost characters are assigned.

2. *Characters are read for a string variable up to the next end-of-line or end-of-file mark. If the length of the resulting string is greater than the declared length of the variable, the string is truncated before it is assigned. If the data pointer is already positioned at an end-of-line mark or at the end-of-file mark, an empty string is assigned to the variable.* As noted in Potential Problem 8 of the Programming Pointers of Chapter 6, one consequence of this last property is that a loop containing a **read** statement to read strings may not terminate. The simplest way to read values for string variables is to use one **readln** statement for each variable and enter the values on separate lines.

3. *Position 0 of the array associated with a string variable stores* chr(L), *where L is the current length of the value assigned to the variable.* Modifying the value stored in this position will make it impossible for some of the string functions and procedures to process this string correctly. For example, suppose that **S** is declared by

```
VAR
   S : string[10];
```

and is assigned a value by

```
S := 'ABCDE';
```

If the value of S[0] is changed,

```
S[0] := 10;
```

then the statement writeln(S) may produce as output

ABCDE♠# ¶↑

4. *Modifying the value of a string variable by changing individual characters does not change the current length (unless the character in position 0 is modified as in the preceding programming pointer).* In particular, reading a value for a string variable by reading characters into the positions of the array associated with it does not set the length equal to the number of characters read. For example, if string variable S is declared to be of type string[10], if the statements

```
FOR i := 1 To 10 DO
   read( S[i] );
readln;
```

are executed and the user enters

ABCDEFGHIJ↵

the characters read are assigned to S[1], S[2], . . . , S[10], but S[0] is undefined, so the string S has an undefined length:

i	0	1	2	3	4	5	6	7	8	9	10
S[i]	?	A	B	C	D	E	F	G	H	I	J

Since the length of S is undefined, the statement

```
writeln( S );
```

would display an empty string if the "garbage" value stored in S[0] is the NUL character with ASCII code 0, but it might display the string of length 32

ABCDEFGHIJ!@#$%^&*()♥♦♣♠↑∅∩αβγ ≤ ä

if S[0] is a blank.

5. *When accessing the individual positions in the array associated with a string variable by using indexed variables, range checking is performed as described for arrays in general.* This means that if a constant index is out of range, that is, if the index is less than 0 or greater than the declared length of the string, an error results. If the index is an expression, however, no range checking is carried out unless the range-checking option has been turned on; memory locations before or after those assigned to the array are accessed as described in Potential Problem 2 of the Programming Pointers of Chapter 9.

Standard Pascal

Many of the string-processing features of Turbo Pasca described in this chapter are not supported in standard Pascal. In standard Pascal:

- There is no predefined string type. Rather, strings are processed using packed arrays of characters. More precisely, definitions of string types have the form

  ```
  CONST
      StringLimit = 10 ;    {limit on lengths of strings}

  TYPE
      StringType = PACKED ARRAY[0..StringlImit] OF char;
  ```

  where **StringLimit** specifies the lengths of strings to be assigned to variables of this type. Such packed string declarations are also allowed in Turbo Pascal to provide compatibility with standard Pascal, and a variable of packed string type may be assigned to a variable of type **string**. Specifying an array in Turbo Pascal to be packed is not necessary, however, since several array elements are packed into a single memory word whenever possible.
- Predefined procedure **pack** is provided to convert an unpacked array into a packed array and procedure **unpack** may be used to unpack a packed array.
- Strings have a fixed length. For example, if **S** is of type **StringType**, then all values assigned to **S** must have length 10. For example, the string **'ABCDEF'** cannot be assigned to or read as a value for **S**; it must be padded with blanks to make it have the correct length:

  ```
  S := 'ABCDEF␢␢␢␢';
  ```

- The default field width used to display strings is the declared length. For example, the statement

  ```
  writeln( S, '***' );
  ```

  produces as output

  ```
  ABCDEF␢␢␢␢***
  ```

- If format descriptors are used to display strings, truncation occurs if the field width is too small. Thus, the statements

  ```
  writeln( S:5, '***' );
  writeln( S:8, '***' );
  ```

  produce as output

  ```
  ABCDÉ***
  ABCDEF␢␢***
  ```

- No predefined procedure for reading strings is provided.
- Strings being compared with the relational operators =, <, >, <>, <=, and >= must have the same length.
- There are no predefined string-processing operations, functions, or procedures.

MULTIDIMENSIONAL ARRAYS

11

Everyone knows how laborious the usual Method is of attaining to Arts and Sciences; whereas by this Contrivance, the most ignorant Person at a reasonable Charge, and with a little bodily Labour, may write Books in Philosophy, Poetry, Politicks, Law, Mathematicks, and Theology, without the least Assistance from Genius or Study. He then led me to the Frame, about the sides whereof all his Pupils stood in Ranks. It was Twenty Foot square . . . linked by slender Wires. These Bits . . . were covered on every Square with Paper pasted upon them; and on These Papers were written all the Words of their Language. . . .

The Professor then desired me to observe, for he was going to set his Engine at work. The Pupils at this Command took each of them hold of an Iron Handle, whereof there were Forty fixed round the Edges of the Frame; and giving them a sudden Turn, the whole Disposition of the Words was entirely changed. . . .
JONATHAN SWIFT, *Gulliver's Travels*

CHAPTER CONTENTS

In Chapter 9 we considered one-dimensional arrays and used them to process lists. We also observed that Pascal allows arrays of more than one dimension and that two-dimensional arrays are useful when the data being processed can be arranged in rows and columns. Similarly, a three-dimensional array is appropriate when the data can be arranged in rows, columns, and ranks. When there are several characteristics associated with the data, still higher dimensions may be useful, with each dimension corresponding to one of these characteristics. In this chapter we consider how such multidimensional arrays are processed in Pascal programs.

11.1   Introduction to Multidimensional Arrays; Multiply Indexed Variables

There are many problems in which the data being processed can be naturally organized as a table. For example, suppose that water temperatures are recorded four times a day at each of three locations near the discharge outlet of the cooling system of a nuclear power plant. These temperature readings can be arranged in a table having four rows and three columns:

Time	Location 1	2	3
1	65.5	68.7	62.0
2	68.8	68.9	64.5
3	70.4	69.4	66.3
4	68.5	69.1	65.8

In this table, the three temperature readings at time 1 are in the first row, the three temperatures at time 2 are in the second row, and so on.

These twelve data items can be conveniently stored in a **two-dimensional array.** The array declaration

```
CONST
    MaxTimes = 4;
    MaxLocations = 3;

TYPE
    TemperatureTable = ARRAY[1..MaxTimes, 1..MaxLocations]
                       OF real;
VAR
    TempTab : TemperatureTable;
```

reserves twelve memory locations for these data items. The doubly indexed variable

```
    TempTab[2, 3]
```

then refers to the entry in the second row and third column of the table, that is, to the temperature 64.5 recorded at time 2 at location 3. In general,

```
    TempTab[i, j]
```

refers to the entry in the ith row and jth column, that is, to the temperature recorded at time i at location j.

As another example, suppose that seat reservations for a small commuter airplane are recorded by marking an ''X'' on a seating diagram for the airplane. The rows are numbered 1, 2, 3, . . . , 12, and in each row are seats labeled A, B, C, and D. This seating diagram can be arranged as a table having 12 rows and 4 columns in which each entry is either a blank or an X indicating an empty seat or an assigned seat, respectively.

```
   A B C D
12 X
11 X X X X
10 X X
 9 X   X X
 8 X X   X
 7       X
 6       X
 5 X X X X
 4 X X
 3 X   X X
 2 X     X
 1
```

This table can be represented by a two-dimensional array whose components are of type **char**, whose first index is the subrange **1..12** of type **integer**, and whose second index is the subrange **'A'..'D'** of type **char**. The following declaration can be used to declare this array:

```
CONST
    MaxRows = 12;

TYPE
    SeatingDiagram = ARRAY[1..MaxRows, 'A'..'D'] OF char;

VAR
    Seat : SeatingDiagram;
```

A value of **'X'** for the doubly indexed variable **Seat[5, 'D']** indicates that seat 5D has been assigned.

To illustrate the use of an array with more than two dimensions, suppose that the temperatures in the first example are recorded for one week, so that seven temperature tables are collected:

Time	Location 1	2	3	
1	66.5	69.4	68.4	
2	68.4	71.2	69.3	Saturday
3	70.1	71.9	70.2	
4	69.5	70.0	69.4	

Time	Location 1	2	3	
1	63.7	66.2	64.3	
2	64.0	66.8	64.9	Monday
			66.3	
			65.8	

Time	Location 1	2	3	
1	65.5	68.7	62.0	
2	68.8	68.9	64.5	Sunday
3	70.4	69.4	66.3	
4	68.5	69.1	65.8	

A **three-dimensional array** `Temp` declared by

```
CONST
   MaxTimes = 4;
   MaxLocations = 3;

TYPE
   Days = ( Sunday, Monday, Tuesday, Wednesday,
            Thursday, Friday, Saturday );
   ThreeDimTempArray =
            ARRAY[Days, 1..MaxTimes, 1..MaxLocations] OF real;

VAR
   Temp : ThreeDimTempArray;
```

can be used to store these 84 temperature readings. The value of the triply indexed variable

```
Temp[Monday, 1, 3]
```

is the temperature recorded on Monday at time 1 at location 3, that is, the value 64.3 in the second table, first row, and third column. In general,

```
Temp[Day, Time, Loc]
```

is the temperature recorded on day **Day** at time **Time** at location **Loc**.

In some problems, even higher-dimensional arrays may be useful. For example, suppose that a retailer maintains an inventory of jeans. He carries several different brands of jeans and for each brand stocks a variety of styles, waist sizes, and inseam lengths. A four-dimensional array can be used to record the inventory, with each element of the array being the number of jeans of a particular brand, style, waist size, and inseam length currently in stock. The first index represents the brand; thus it might be of type

```
BrandType = ( Levi, Wrangler, CalvinKlein, Lee, BigYank );
```

The second index represents styles and is of type

```
StyleType = 'A'..'F';
```

The third and fourth indices represent waist size and inseam length, respectively. Their types might be given by

```
WaistSize = 28..40;
Inseam = 28..36;
```

In a Pascal program for maintaining this inventory, the following type section is thus appropriate:

```
TYPE
    BrandType = ( Levi, Wrangler, CalvinKlein, Lee, BigYank );
    StyleType = 'A'..'F';
    WaistSize = 28..40;
    Inseam = 28..36;
    JeansArray = ARRAY[BrandType, StyleType, WaistSize, Inseam]
                 OF integer;
```

The four-dimensional array **JeansInStock** having indices of the types just described can be declared by

```
VAR
    JeansInStock : JeansArray;
```

The value of the quadruply indexed variable

```
JeansInStock[Levi, 'B', 32, 31]
```

is the number of Levi style B, 32×31 jeans in stock. The statement

```
JeansInStock[b, s, w, i] := JeansInStock[b, s, w, i] - 1;
```

records the sale of one pair of jeans of brand **b**, style **s**, waist size **w**, and inseam length **i**.

As the following syntax diagram for array declarations indicates, Pascal places no limit on the number of dimensions of an array, but the type of each index must be specified:

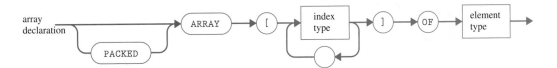

From this we see that the general form of an array declaration is

Array Declaration

Form:

ARRAY[*index-type-1, index-type-2, ..., index-type-n*]
  OF *element-type*

where:
  ARRAY and **OF** are reserved words;
  each *index-type-i* must be an ordinal type;
  element-type may be any type;
  PACKED may precede the word **ARRAY** to declare a packed
    array.

> **Purpose:**
> Specifies that *index-type-1*, *index-type-2*, . . . , *index-type-n* are the types of the indices and *element-type* is the type of the elements in an *n*-dimensional array.

An equivalent method of declaring a multidimensional array is as an **array of arrays,** that is, an array whose elements are other arrays. The array **Name** of strings in Example 2 of Section 10.4 was in fact such an array of arrays, since a string type is implemented as an array of characters. As another example, reconsider the seating diagram for a small airliner. The seating diagram can be thought of as a list of 12 rows; thus, from this perspective, the diagram can be viewed as a one-dimensional array with 12 elements:

Each element of this array represents a list of 4 seats and is thus an array itself. The entire seating diagram can be viewed therefore as a one-dimensional array whose components are also one-dimensional arrays.

Pascal allows array declarations to be given in a form that reflects this perspective. If we define the types **SeatRows** and **ArrayOfSeatRows** by

```
CONST
   MaxRows = 12;

TYPE
   SeatRows = ARRAY['A'..'D'] OF char;
   ArrayOfSeatRows = ARRAY[1..MaxRows] OF SeatRows;

VAR
   Seat : ArrayOfSeatRows;
```

or

```
CONST
   MaxRows = 12;
```

```
TYPE
   ArrayOfSeatRows =
      ARRAY[1..MaxRows] OF ARRAY['A'..'D'] OF char;

VAR
   Seat : ArrayOfSeatRows;
```

the singly indexed variable

```
Seat[2]
```

refers to the second row of seats in this diagram:

```
  A B C D
2 X     X
```

The doubly indexed variable

```
Seat[2]['D']
```

or, equivalently,

```
Seat[2, 'D']
```

then refers to the seat labeled **D** in this row, and the fact that its value is **'X'** indicates that this seat has been assigned. In general, if **i** is an integer in the range 1 through 12 and **Ch** is a character variable whose value is one of **'A'**, **'B'**, **'C'**, or **'D'**,

```
Seat[i][Ch]      or      Seat[i, Ch]
```

refers to the seat in row **i** and column **Ch**.

The array of temperature tables considered earlier can also be thought of as an array of arrays. In particular, since one temperature table was recorded for each day, the entire three-dimensional array can be viewed as a list of temperature tables, that is, as a one-dimensional array whose components are two-dimensional arrays. If we adopt this point of view, we are led to the array declarations

```
CONST
   MaxTimes = 4;
   MaxLocations = 3;

TYPE
   DaysOfWeek = ( Sunday, Monday, Tuesday, Wednesday,
                  Thursday, Friday, Saturday );
   TemperatureTables =
                  ARRAY[1..MaxTimes, 1..MaxLocations] OF real;
   ListOfTemperatureTables =
                  ARRAY[DaysOfWeek] OF TemperatureTables;

VAR
   Temp : ListOfTemperatureTables;
```

The singly indexed variable

```
Temp[Monday]
```

then refers to the temperature table recorded on Monday; that is, `Temp[Monday]` is the two-dimensional array

	Location		
Time	1	2	3
1	63.7	66.2	64.3
2	64.0	66.8	64.9
3	72.7	69.9	66.3
4	66.6	68.0	65.8

To access the temperature 64.3 at time 1 at location 3 in this table, we could use the notation

```
Temp[Monday][1, 3]
```

or, equivalently,

```
Temp[Monday, 1, 3]
```

Note that as in the seating diagram example, each row in a temperature table can be viewed as a one-dimensional array of temperatures, and each table can therefore be viewed as a one-dimensional array of temperature arrays. The doubly indexed variable

```
Temp[Monday][1]
```

then refers to the first row in the temperature table for Monday,

63.7	66.2	64.3

and

```
Temp[Monday][1][3]
```

denotes the third temperature in this row,

64.3

as do all of the following:

```
Temp[Monday, 1, 3]
```

```
Temp[Monday][1, 3]
```

```
Temp[Monday, 1][3]
```

In Chapter 9 we saw that Turbo Pascal allows one-dimensional arrays to be initialized in constant sections. Multidimensional arrays may also be initialized using this same technique. For example, to initialize the 4×3 array **TempTab**, we could replace its declaration in the variable section by the following constant section:

```
CONST
   TempTab : TemperatureTable =
                  ( (65.5, 68.7, 62.0),
                    (68.8, 68.9, 64.5),
                    (70.4, 69.4, 66.3),
                    (68.5, 69.1, 65.8) );
```

Note that the list used to initialize **TempTab** has four elements, each of which is a triple of numbers: the three values in the first row followed by the three values in the second row, then those in the third row, and finally those in the fourth row. Note that this is precisely the form required for initializing a one-dimensional array having four elements, each of which is a one-dimensional array having three elements. This is as expected, since **TemperatureTable** could equivalently be defined as

```
TemperatureTable = ARRAY[1..4] OF ARRAY[1..3] OF real;
```

Higher-dimensional arrays may also be initialized. For example, to initialize the three-dimensional array **Temp**, we think of the type identifier **ThreeDimTempArray** as being defined by

```
ThreeDimTempArray = ARRAY[DaysOfWeek] OF
                        ARRAY[1..MaxTimes] OF
                            ARRAY[1..MaxLocations] OF real;
```

The following constant section can then be used to initialize **Temp**:

```
CONST
   Temp : ThreeDimTempArray =
               ( ( (65.5, 68.7, 62.0),
                   (68.8, 68.9, 64.5),
                   (70.4, 69.4, 66.3),
                   (68.5, 69.1, 65.8) ),
                 ( (63.7, 66.2, 64.3),
                   (64.0, 66.8, 64.9),
                   (.........., 66.3),
                   (.........., 65.8) ),
                         .
                         .
                         .
                 ( (66.5, 69.4, 68.4),
                   (68.4, 71.2, 69.3),
                   (70.1, 71.9, 70.2),
                   (69.5, 70.0, 69.4) ) );
```

11.2   Processing Multidimensional Arrays

In the preceding section we gave several examples of multidimensional arrays and showed how such arrays are declared in a Pascal program. We also noted that any element of the array can be accessed directly by using a multiply indexed variable consisting of the array name followed by the indices that indicate that item's location in the array. In this section we consider the processing of multidimensional arrays, including the input and output of arrays or parts of arrays, copying the elements of one array into another array, and using multidimensional arrays as parameters in subprograms.

As we observed in Chapter 9, the most natural order for processing the elements of a one-dimensional array is the usual sequential order from first item to last. For multidimensional arrays there are several different orders in which the indices may be varied when processing the array elements.

Two-dimensional arrays are often used when the data can be organized as a table consisting of rows and columns. This suggests two natural orders for processing the entries of a two-dimensional array, **rowwise** and **columnwise.** Rowwise processing means that the array elements in the first row are processed first, then those in the second row, and so on, as shown in Figure 11.1(a) for the 3 × 4 array **A.** In columnwise processing, the entries in the first column are processed first, then those in the second column, and so on, as illustrated in Figure 11.1(b).

For arrays of three or more dimensions, several kinds of processing are possible. For example, Figure 11.2 shows one common pattern for a three-dimensional array made up of three 2 × 4 tables.

The elements of a multidimensional array can be read by using nested repetition structures; we simply place an input statement within a pair of nested for (or while or repeat-until) loops, each of whose control variables controls one of the

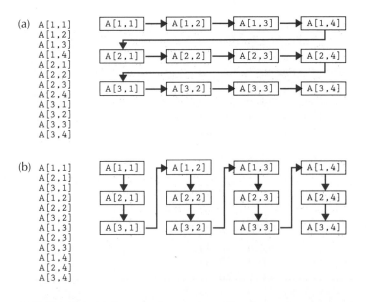

FIGURE 11.1   (a) Rowwise processing; (b) columnwise processing.

```
B[1,1,1]
B[1,1,2]
B[1,1,3]
B[1,1,4]
B[1,2,1]
B[1,2,2]
B[1,2,3]
B[1,2,4]
B[2,1,1]
B[2,1,2]
B[2,1,3]
B[2,1,4]
B[2,2,1]
B[2,2,2]
B[2,2,3]
B[2,2,4]
B[3,1,1]
B[3,1,2]
B[3,1,3]
B[3,1,4]
B[3,2,1]
B[3,2,2]
B[3,2,3]
B[3,2,4]
```

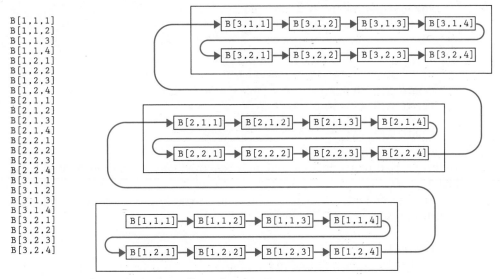

FIGURE 11.2   Processing a three-dimensional array.

indices of the array. For example, to read the twelve entries of a 3 × 4 integer array
A in rowwise order so that it has the value

$$\begin{bmatrix} 22 & 37 & 0 & 0 \\ 0 & 1 & 17 & 32 \\ 6 & 18 & 4 & 12 \end{bmatrix}$$

we could use the nested **FOR** statements

```
FOR row := 1 TO 3 DO
   FOR column := 1 TO 4 DO
      read( A[row, column] );
```

When these statements are executed, the outer for loop sets the value of the control
variable **row** to 1, and the inner for loop is then executed, using 1 as the value for
row; the effect, therefore, is the same as executing

```
FOR column := 1 TO 4 DO
   read( A[1, column] );
```

which is equivalent to the following four **read** statements:

```
read( A[1, 1] );
read( A[1, 2] );
read( A[1, 3] );
read( A[1, 4] );
```

The first pass through the outer for loop thus reads values for the first row of **A**, so
that the first four values entered must be **22, 37, 0**, and **0**.

Now the outer for loop sets the value of the control variable **row** to **2**, and the
inner for loop is executed again:

```
FOR column := 1 TO 4 DO
   read( A[2, column] );
```

which is equivalent to the four **read** statements

```
read( A[2, 1] );
read( A[2, 2] );
read( A[2, 3] );
read( A[2, 4] );
```

so that the next four values entered must be those in the second row of **A**: **0**, **1**, **17**, and **32**.

Finally, the outer for loop sets the value of **row** to **3**, and the inner for loop is executed again:

```
FOR column := 1 TO 4 DO
   read( A[3, column] );
```

which has the same effect as

```
read( A[3, 1] );
read( A[3, 2] );
read( A[3, 3] );
read( A[3, 4] );
```

for which the values in the third row of **A** must be entered: **6**, **18**, **4**, and **12**. Thus the entries in this table must be entered in the order

22 37 0 0 0 1 17 32 6 18 4 12

for rowwise processing or, perhaps better,

```
22 37  0  0
 0  1 17 32
 6 18  4 12
```

to emphasize the rowwise arrangement. Note that if **readln** had been used instead of **read**, it would have been necessary to enter the values one per line, thus requiring twelve separate lines of data.

Columnwise input is also possible. We need only reverse the order of the two for loops

```
FOR column := 1 TO 4 DO
   FOR row := 1 TO 3 DO
      read( A[row, column] );
```

and enter the values in the order **22, 0, 6, 37, 1, 18, 0, 17, 4, 0, 32, 12.**

Special care must be taken when reading values for a character array. To illustrate, consider the 3 × 3 table

$$\begin{bmatrix} A & B & C \\ D & E & F \\ G & H & I \end{bmatrix}$$

To read these nine characters into the 3×3 character array **CharArray** in rowwise order, we could use the statements

```
FOR row := 1 TO 3 DO
   FOR column := 1 TO 3 DO
      read( CharArray[row, column] );
```

and enter all the data items on one line:

A̲B̲C̲D̲E̲F̲G̲H̲I̲⤶

But the data cannot be entered on separate lines because the carriage-return and line-feed characters that comprise an end-of-line character are read and stored in the array. Thus, if the characters are entered as

A̲B̲C̲⤶
D̲E̲F̲⤶
G̲H̲I̲⤶

then the table actually stored in the array **CharArray** is

$$\begin{bmatrix} A & B & C \\ \leftarrow & \downarrow & D \\ E & F & \leftarrow \end{bmatrix}$$

because the carriage-return character (denoted by $\leftarrow$) is read for **CharArray[2, 1]** and **CharArray[3, 3]**, and the line-feed character (denoted by $\downarrow$) is read for **CharArray[2, 2]**. If the preceding nested **FOR** statements are changed to

```
FOR row := 1 TO 3 DO
   BEGIN
      FOR column := 1 TO 3 DO
         read( CharArray[row, column] );
      readln
   END {FOR};
```

the data can be entered as

A̲B̲C̲⤶
D̲E̲F̲⤶
G̲H̲I̲⤶

because in this case the **readln** statement with no input list advances the data pointer past the next end-of-line mark.

The elements of an array can be displayed by using repetition structures similar to those used for input. For example, the statement

```
FOR row := 1 TO 3 DO
   BEGIN
      FOR column := 1 TO 4 DO
         write( A[row, column]:4 );
      writeln;
   END {FOR};
```

where **A** is the integer array considered earlier, produces as output

```
 22  37   0   0
  0   1  17  32
  6  18   4  12
```

Note that the **write** statement displays the values in each row on the same line and that a **writeln** statement is used to terminate this line.

These same input/output techniques can be applied to higher-dimensional arrays. For example, values can be read into the three-dimensional array **B** in the order indicated in Figure 11.2 by the nested **FOR** statements

```
FOR table := 1 TO 3 DO
   FOR row := 1 TO 2 DO
      FOR column := 1 TO 4 DO
         read( B[table, row, column] );
```

Other types of array processing can also be carried out using nested repetition structures. To illustrate, consider the 4×3 array **TempTab** used in Section 11.1 to store the following table of temperature readings:

| Time | Location | | |
	1	2	3
1	65.5	68.7	62.0
2	68.8	68.9	64.5
3	70.4	69.4	66.3
4	68.5	69.1	65.8

To calculate the average temperature at each of the four times, it is necessary to calculate the sum of the entries in each row and to divide each of these sums by 3. The following program segment can be used to carry out this computation and to display the average temperature at each time:

```
FOR Time := 1 TO 4 DO
   BEGIN
      Sum := 0;
      For Loc := 1 TO 3 DO
         Sum := Sum + TempTab[Time, Loc];
      MeanTemp := Sum / 3;
      writeln( 'Mean temperature at time ',Time:1,
               ' is ', MeanTemp:3:1 )
   END {FOR};
```

Nested repetition structures can also be used to copy the entries of one array into another array. For example, if **A** and **B** are 5 × 10 arrays, the nested **FOR** statements

```
FOR row := 1 TO 5 DO
   FOR column := 1 TO 10 DO
      B[row, column] := A[row, column];
```

will copy the entries of **A** into the corresponding locations of array **B**, assuming, of course, that the element type of **A** is compatible with the element type of **B**. If **A** and **B** have the *same types* (see Section 9.2), this can be done more simply with the array assignment

```
B := A;
```

Multidimensional arrays may also be used as parameters for functions and procedures. The rules governing the use of arrays as parameters, which were described in detail in Section 9.2 for one-dimensional arrays, also apply to multidimensional arrays. These rules are summarized as follows:

1. The types of formal parameters in a function or procedure heading must be specified by type identifiers. Thus, for example, the array declaration **Grades : ARRAY[1..25, 1..4] OF real** may not be used to declare the type of a formal parameter in a procedure or function heading. It must be given in the form **Grades : Table**, where **Table** is a type identifier associated with **ARRAY[1..25, 1..4] OF real**.
2. The types of arrays used as actual parameters must be the same as the types of the corresponding arrays used as formal parameters.
3. The type of a function value may not be an array.

11.3   Examples: Automobile Sales, Inventory Control

Example 1: Automobile Sales

Suppose that a certain automobile dealership sells fifteen different models of automobiles and employs ten salesmen. A record of sales for each month can be represented by a table in which the first row contains the number of sales of each model by salesman 1, the second row contains the number of sales of each model by salesman 2, and so on. For example, suppose that the sales table for a certain month is the following:

0	0	2	0	5	6	3	0	10	0	3	2	5	7	5
5	1	9	0	0	2	3	2	1	1	3	1	5	3	0
0	0	0	1	0	0	0	0	0	0	2	0	8	2	3
1	1	1	0	2	2	2	1	1	0	2	0	3	0	12
5	3	2	0	0	2	5	5	7	0	0	2	0	0	2
2	2	1	0	1	1	0	0	6	8	0	0	0	2	0
3	2	5	0	1	2	0	4	8	0	0	2	2	2	1
3	0	7	1	3	5	2	4	4	3	5	1	7	2	4
0	2	6	1	0	5	2	1	4	3	0	0	4	0	5
4	0	2	0	3	2	1	0	9	0	1	4	5	4	8

A program is to be written to produce a monthly sales report, displaying the monthly sales table in the form

SALESMAN:		MODEL 1	2	3	4	5	6	7	8	9	10	11	12	13	14	15
1	:	0	0	2	0	5	6	3	0	10	0	3	2	5	7	5
2	:	5	1	9	0	0	2	3	2	1	1	3	1	5	3	0
3	:	0	0	0	1	0	0	0	0	0	0	2	0	8	2	3
4	:	1	1	1	0	2	2	2	1	1	0	2	0	3	0	12
5	:	5	3	2	0	0	2	5	5	7	0	0	2	0	0	2
6	:	2	2	1	0	1	1	0	0	6	8	0	0	0	2	0
7	:	3	2	5	0	1	2	0	4	8	0	0	2	2	2	1
8	:	3	0	7	1	3	5	2	4	4	3	5	1	7	2	4
9	:	0	2	6	1	0	5	2	1	4	3	0	0	4	0	5
10	:	4	0	2	0	3	2	1	0	9	0	1	4	5	4	8

and which also displays the total number of automobiles sold by each salesman and the total number of each model sold by all salesmen.

The input to the program is to be a sales table, as just described, and the output is to be a report of the indicated form. The required processing is given by the following algorithm:

ALGORITHM FOR SALES REPORT

(* Input: A sales table, number of rows, and number of columns.
   Purpose: Read a sales table and display a sales report consisting of the table, total sales for each salesman, and total sales for each model.
   Output: Sales table, total sales for each salesman and for each model. *)

1. Read the number of rows and the number of columns in the sales table.
2. Read the sales table into a two-dimensional array *Sales* so that each of the rows contains the sales information for one of the salesmen, and each of the columns contains the information for one of the models.
3. Print the array *Sales* with appropriate headings.
4. Calculate and print the totals of the entries in each of the rows. These totals are the sales totals for each of the salesmen.
5. Calculate and print the totals of the entries in each of the columns. These totals are the total sales for each of the models.

Each of the tasks listed in this algorithm can be implemented as a separate procedure so that the structure of the program that solves this problem is

In the preceding section we considered several examples of array input/output, and these can be easily adapted to give procedures **ReadTable** and **PrintSalesTable**. We also considered the problem of calculating the averages of rows in a temperature table, and the techniques used there can be used to develop procedures **FindSalesmanTotals** and **FindModelTotals**. The program in Figure 11.3 implements the preceding algorithm, using these four procedures to perform the required tasks.

FIGURE 11.3   Reporting automobile sales.

```
PROGRAM AutomobileSales( SalesFile, output );
{***************************************************************

    Input (file):    A sales table.
    Purpose:         Read a sales table and calculate total sales for
                     each salesman and total sales of each model
                     of automobile.
    Output (screen): Sales table, total sales per salesman, total
                     sales per model.


****************************************************************}

CONST
    RowLimit = 25;                  {limit on # of rows in table}
    ColumnLimit = 25;               {limit on # of columns in table}
    SalesFileName = 'FIL11-3.DAT';  {actual name of SalesFile}

TYPE
    Table = ARRAY[1..RowLimit, 1..ColumnLimit] OF integer;

VAR
    Rows,                   {number of rows (salesmen) in sales table}
    Columns : integer;      {number of columns (models) in sales table}
    Sales : Table;          {sales table}
    SalesFile : text;       {file containing the sales data}

PROCEDURE ReadTable( VAR Sales : Table;
                     VAR Rows, Columns : integer );
{---------------------------------------------------------------

    Input (file): Number of rows and columns in a sales table and
                  the table.
    Purpose:      Read the dimensions of a sales table and the
                  table itself from the file SalesFile.
    Returns:      Rows, Columns, and the Sales table.

----------------------------------------------------------------}

    VAR
        Man,                {row index -- salesman number}
        Model : integer;    {column index -- model number}
```

FIGURE 11.3 Reporting automobile sales. (cont.)

```
BEGIN
   assign( SalesFile, SalesFileName );
   reset( SalesFile );
   readln( SalesFile, Rows, Columns );
   FOR Man := 1 TO Rows DO
      FOR Model := 1 TO Columns DO
         read( SalesFile, Sales[Man, Model] )
END {ReadTable};

PROCEDURE PrintSalesTable( VAR Sales : Table;
                                 Rows, Columns : integer );
{-------------------------------------------------------------------

   Accepts:        A Sales table and the number of rows and
                   columns in the table.
   Purpose:        Display a sales table in a specified format.
   Output (screen): The sales table.


--------------------------------------------------------------------}

VAR
   Man,                  {salesman number}
   Model : integer;   {model number}

BEGIN
   writeln( 'MODEL' : 2 * Columns + 9 );
   write( 'SALESMAN:' );
   FOR Model := 1 TO Columns DO
      write( Model:4 );
   writeln;
   FOR Model := 1 TO 4 * Columns + 9 DO
      write( '-' );
   writeln;
   FOR Man := 1 TO Rows DO
      BEGIN
         write( Man:5, '   :' );
         FOR Model := 1 TO Columns DO
            write( Sales[Man, Model]:4 );
         writeln
      END {FOR}
END {PrintSalesTable};

PROCEDURE FindSalesmanTotals( VAR Sales : Table;
                                 Rows, Columns : integer);
{-------------------------------------------------------------------

   Accepts:        A Sales table and the number of rows and
                   columns in the table.
   Purpose:        Find and display sum of each row of sales table.
   Output (screen): Row sums and appropriate labels.


--------------------------------------------------------------------}
```

FIGURE 11.3   Reporting automobile sales. (cont.)

```pascal
    VAR
        Man,                    {row index -- salesman number}
        Model,                  {column index -- model number}
        RowTotal : integer;  {row total}

    BEGIN
        writeln;
        FOR Man := 1 TO Rows DO
            BEGIN
                RowTotal := 0;
                FOR Model := 1 TO Columns DO
                    RowTotal := RowTotal + Sales[Man, Model];
                writeln( 'Sales of salesman', Man:3, ':', RowTotal:4 )
            END {FOR}
    END {FindSalesmanTotals};

PROCEDURE FindModelTotals( VAR Sales : Table;
                            Rows, Columns : integer);
{-------------------------------------------------------------------

    Accepts:        A Sales table and the number of rows and
                    columns in the table.
    Purpose:        Find and display sum of each column of sales
                    table.
    Output (screen): Column sums and appropriate labels.

--------------------------------------------------------------------}


    VAR
        Man,                    {row index -- salesman number}
        Model,                  {column index -- model number}
        ColTotal : integer;  {column total}

    BEGIN
        writeln;
        FOR Model := 1 TO Columns DO
            BEGIN
                ColTotal := 0;
                FOR Man := 1 TO Rows DO
                    ColTotal := ColTotal + Sales[Man, Model];
                writeln( 'Sales of model   ', Model:3, ':', ColTotal:4 )
            END {FOR}
    END {FindModelTotals};

BEGIN {*************** main program ***************}
    ReadTable( Sales, Rows, Columns );
    PrintSalesTable( Sales, Rows, Columns );
    FindSalesmanTotals( Sales, Rows, Columns );
    FindModelTotals( Sales, Rows, Columns )
END {main program}.
```

FIGURE 11.3   Reporting automobile sales. (cont.)

Listing of FIL11-3.DAT used in sample run:

```
10 15
0  0  2  0  5  6  3  0 10  0  3  2  5  7  5
5  1  9  0  0  2  3  2  1  1  3  1  5  3  0
0  0  0  1  0  0  0  0  0  0  2  0  8  2  3
1  1  1  0  2  2  2  1  1  0  2  0  3  0 12
5  3  2  0  0  2  5  5  7  0  0  2  0  0  2
2  2  1  0  1  1  0  0  6  8  0  0  0  2  0
3  2  5  0  1  2  0  4  8  0  0  2  2  2  1
3  0  7  1  3  5  2  4  4  3  5  1  7  2  4
0  2  6  1  0  5  2  1  4  3  0  0  4  0  5
4  0  2  0  3  2  1  0  9  0  1  4  5  4  8
```

Sample run:

								MODEL							
SALESMAN:	1	2	3	4	5	6	7	8	9	10	11	12	13	14	15
1 :	0	0	2	0	5	6	3	0	10	0	3	2	5	7	5
2 :	5	1	9	0	0	2	3	2	1	1	3	1	5	3	0
3 :	0	0	0	1	0	0	0	0	0	0	2	0	8	2	3
4 :	1	1	1	0	2	2	2	1	1	0	2	0	3	0	12
5 :	5	3	2	0	0	2	5	5	7	0	0	2	0	0	2
6 :	2	2	1	0	1	1	0	0	6	8	0	0	0	2	0
7 :	3	2	5	0	1	2	0	4	8	0	0	2	2	2	1
8 :	3	0	7	1	3	5	2	4	4	3	5	1	7	2	4
9 :	0	2	6	1	0	5	2	1	4	3	0	0	4	0	5
10 :	4	0	2	0	3	2	1	0	9	0	1	4	5	4	8

```
Sales of salesman  1:  48
Sales of salesman  2:  36
Sales of salesman  3:  16
Sales of salesman  4:  28
Sales of salesman  5:  33
Sales of salesman  6:  23
Sales of salesman  7:  32
Sales of salesman  8:  51
Sales of salesman  9:  33
Sales of salesman 10:  43
```

FIGURE 11.3   Reporting automobile sales. (cont.)

```
Sales of model     1:   23
Sales of model     2:   11
Sales of model     3:   35
Sales of model     4:    3
Sales of model     5:   15
Sales of model     6:   27
Sales of model     7:   18
Sales of model     8:   17
Sales of model     9:   50
Sales of model    10:   15
Sales of model    11:   16
Sales of model    12:   12
Sales of model    13:   39
Sales of model    14:   22
Sales of model    15:   40
```

Example 2: Inventory Control

In Section 11.1 we noted that a four-dimensional array **JeansInStock** might be used in a program that maintains an inventory of jeans of various brands, styles, and sizes. In this example, the type of the first index for this array is an enumerated type:

```
BrandType = ( Levi, Wrangler, CalvinKlein, Lee, BigYank );
```

the type of the second index is a subrange of **char**:

```
StyleType = 'A'..'F';
```

and the types of the third and fourth indices are subranges of **integer**:

```
WaistSize = 28..40;
InseamSize = 28..36;
```

The information about the current inventory is stored in a file, which contains 390 lines of numbers. The first 78 lines describe the current inventory of Levi jeans; the next 78 describe the current inventory of Wrangler jean; and so on. Within each of these brand blocks of 78 lines, the first 13 lines pertain to style A, the next 13 to style B, and so on. Within each of these 13-line style blocks, the first line contains information about jeans with waist size 28; the second contains information about jeans with waist size 29; and so on. And each of these lines contains 9 numbers that represent the number of jeans in stock for inseam lengths 28, 29, . . . , 36. For example, the third line in the data file is

18 7 19 10 11 3 2 18 12

and from this we see that there are currently 11 Levi jeans of style A having waist size 30 and inseam 32.

The first task in solving this problem is to read this inventory information from the file and store it in the array `JeansInStock`. Because of the way in which this information is organized, nested for loops can be used to do this. The index of the outermost loop varies over the values of `BrandType`; the index of the second loop varies over the style type `'A'..'F'`; the index of the third loop varies over waist sizes; and the index of the innermost loop varies over the inseam sizes.

The procedure `Initialize` in the program in Figure 11.2 that solves this problem uses such nested for loops to load the initial inventory information into the array `JeansInStock`. It also initializes an array `BrandName` that is used to convert between values of the enumerated type `BrandType` and strings that name these brands.

Once the array `JeansInStock` has been initialized, the program must update the inventory information stored in this array, based on sales entered by the user. The procedure `UpdateInventory` reads the sales information entered by the user and does the necessary updating. It implements the following algorithm:

UpdateInventory

1. Read the brand name.
2. Convert this string to the corresponding value of type `BrandType`.
3. Read the style, waist size, and inseam.
4. Read the number `NumSold` of jeans sold.
5. Subtract `NumSold` from `JeansInStock[Brand, Style, Waist, Inseam]`.

Procedure `UpdateInventory` uses the procedure `Convert` to perform the conversion in Step 2. This procedure simply searches the array `BrandName` to find the index of type `BrandType` that corresponds to the brand name entered by the user.

After all the sales have been recorded, it is necessary to write the updated inventory information in array `JeansInStock` back to the data file. The procedure `WrapUp` in the program does this, using nested for loops much like those in the procedure `Initialize`.

The solution of the problem thus consists of three main procedures: `Initialize`, `UpdateInventory`, and `WrapUp`. The structure of the program in Figure 11.4 has the form

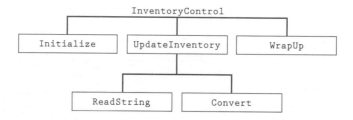

FIGURE 11.4   Maintaining an inventory.

```
PROGRAM InventoryControl( input, InventoryFile, output, NewInventoryFile );
{*****************************************************************

    Input (file):      An inventory array JeansArray.
    Input (keyboard): Sales information about jeans.
    Purpose:           This is an inventory control program that
                       demonstrates use of a four-dimensional array
                       with different types of indices.
    Output (screen):  User prompts.
    Output (file):     The updated inventory array JeansArray.


*****************************************************************}

CONST
    StringLimit = 11;                      {length of strings}
    FirstStyle = 'A'; LastStyle = 'F';     {first, last values of StyleType}
    SmallWaist = 28; LargeWaist = 40;      {first, last values of WaistSize}
    ShortInseam = 28; LongInseam = 36;     {first, last values of InseamSize}
    InvenFileName = 'FIL11-4A.DAT';        {acutal name of inventory file}
    NewInvenFileName = 'FIL11-4B.DAT';     {actual name of new inventory file}


TYPE
    BrandType = ( Levi, Wrangler, CalvinKlein, Lee, BigYank ) ;
    StyleType = FirstStyle..LastStyle;
    WaistSize = SmallWaist..LargeWaist;
    InseamSize = ShortInseam..LongInseam;
    JeansArray = ARRAY[BrandType, StyleType, WaistSize, InseamSize]
                 OF integer;
    StringType = string[StringLimit];
    BrandNameArray = ARRAY[BrandType] OF StringType;


VAR
    JeansInStock : JeansArray;         {array that maintains jeans inventory}
    BrandName : BrandNameArray;        {array of strings -- names of brands}
    InventoryFile,                     {original inventory file}
    NewInventoryFile : text;           {inventory file produced by program}
    Response : char;                   {user response}

PROCEDURE Initialize ( VAR InventoryFile : text;
                       VAR JeansInStock : JeansArray;
                       VAR BrandName : BrandNameArray);
{------------------------------------------------------------------

    Accepts:           File variable InventoryFile.
    Input (file):      Array JeansInStock.
    Purpose:           Initialize array JeansInStock from
                       InventoryFile and initialize the array
                       BrandName of names of brands.
    Returns:           Arrays JeansInStock and BrandName.
------------------------------------------------------------------}
```

FIGURE 11.4   Maintaining an inventory. (cont.)

```
VAR
    Brand : BrandType;      {index}
    Style : StyleType;      {   "   }
    Waist : WaistSize;      {   "   }
    Inseam : InseamSize;    {   "   }

BEGIN
    {Read array JeansInStock from InventoryFile}
    assign( InventoryFile, InvenFileName );
    reset( InventoryFile );
    FOR Brand := Levi TO BigYank DO
        FOR Style := FirstStyle TO LastStyle DO
            FOR Waist := SmallWaist TO LargeWaist DO
                FOR Inseam := ShortInseam TO LongInseam DO
                    read( InventoryFile,
                            JeansInStock[Brand, Style, Waist, Inseam] );

    {Initialize array of brand names}
    BrandName[Levi]         := 'LEVI';
    BrandName[Wrangler]     := 'WRANGLER';
    BrandName[CalvinKlein]  := 'CALVINKLEIN';
    BrandName[Lee]          := 'LEE';
    BrandName[BigYank]      := 'BIGYANK'
END {Initialize};

PROCEDURE UpdateInventory( VAR JeansInStock : JeansArray;
                            BrandName: BrandNameArray );
{--------------------------------------------------------------------

    Accepts:            Arrays JeansInStock and BrandName.
    Input (keyboard):   Sales information.
    Purpose:            Read sales information consisting of brand
                        name, style, waist size, inseam, and number
                        sold and then update the inventory
                        information in array JeansInStock.
    Returns:            Updated array JeansInStock.

-----------------------------------------------------------------------}

VAR
    Name : StringType;        {name of brand entered by user}
    NameFound : boolean;      {signals if name found in array BrandName}
    Brand : BrandType;        {index}
    Style : StyleType;        {index}
    Waist : WaistSize;        {index}
    Inseam : InseamSize;      {index}
    NumSold ,                 {number sold}
    InStock : integer;        {number in stock}
```

FIGURE 11.4   Maintaining an inventory. (cont.)

```
   PROCEDURE Convert(     Name : StringType;
                          BrandName : BrandNameArray;
                     VAR NameFound : boolean;
                     VAR Brand : BrandType);
{------------------------------------------------------------------

   Accepts:  String Name and array JeansInStock.
   Purpose:  Search the array BrandName to find the string Name
             and the corresponding index Brand of enumerated
             type BrandType.
   Returns:  NameFound, which is true or false according as the
             search is successful or not.  If search is
             successful, Brand is the location of Name in
             BrandName.


--------------------------------------------------------------------}

   VAR
      b: BrandType;    {index}

   BEGIN
      NameFound := false;
      FOR b := Levi TO BigYank DO
         IF BrandName[b] = Name THEN
            BEGIN
               Brand := b;
               NameFound := TRUE
            END {IF};
      IF NOT NameFound THEN
         writeln( '*** Not a legal brand name ***' )
   END {Convert};

BEGIN {UpdateInventory}
   REPEAT
      write( 'BRAND (use all CAPS)?  ' );
      Readln( Name );
      Convert( Name, BrandName, NameFound, Brand )
   UNTIL NameFound;
   write( 'Style (', FirstStyle, '-', LastStyle, ')?  ' );
   readln( Style );
   write( 'Waist size (', SmallWaist:1, '-', LargeWaist:1, ')?  ' );
   readln( Waist );
   write( 'Inseam (', ShortInseam:1, '-', LongInseam:1, ')?  ' );
   readln( Inseam );
   write( 'Number sold?  ' );
   readln( NumSold );
```

FIGURE 11.4 Maintaining an inventory. (cont.)

```
      InStock := JeansInStock[Brand, Style, Waist, Inseam] - NumSold;
      IF InStock < 0 THEN
         BEGIN
            writeln( 'Not enough in stock; backorder ', abs(InStock):1 );
            InStock := 0
         END {IF};
      JeansInStock[Brand, Style, Waist, Inseam] := InStock;
   END {UpdateInventory};

PROCEDURE WrapUp( VAR NewInventoryFile : text;
                 VAR JeansInStock : JeansArray );
{-------------------------------------------------------------------

   Accepts:        File variable NewInventoryFile and array
                   JeansInStock.
   Purpose:        Copy array JeansInStock to NewInventoryFile.
   Output (file):  Elements of array JeansInStock.


   ------------------------------------------------------------------}

   VAR
      Brand : BrandType;     {index}
      Style : StyleType;     {  "  }
      Waist : WaistSize;     {  "  }
      Inseam : InseamSize;   {  "  }

   BEGIN
      assign( NewInventoryFile, NewInvenFileName );
      rewrite( NewInventoryFile );
      FOR Brand := Levi TO BigYank DO
         FOR Style := FirstStyle TO LastStyle DO
            FOR Waist := SmallWaist TO LargeWaist DO
               BEGIN
                  FOR Inseam := ShortInseam TO LongInseam DO
                     write( NewInventoryFile,
                            JeansInStock[Brand, Style, Waist, Inseam]:3 );
                  writeln( NewInventoryFile )
               END {FOR}
   END {WrapUp};

BEGIN {*************** main program ***************}
   Initialize( InventoryFile, JeansInStock, BrandName );
   REPEAT
      UpdateInventory( JeansInStock, BrandName );
      writeln;
      write( 'More sales (Y or N)?  ' );
      readln( Response );
   UNTIL (Response <> 'Y') AND (Response <> 'y');
   WrapUp( NewInventoryfile, JeansInStock )
END {main program}.
```

FIGURE 11.4   Maintaining an inventory. (cont.)

Listing of `FIL11-4A.DAT`:

```
 3   3   0 12   1 12 19 17   0
 4  15  18   2 14   2   0 14 19
18   7  19 10 11   3   2 18 12
              .
              .
              .
12  18  11 12 16 14   9 12   9
```

Sample run:

```
BRAND (use all CAPS)?   LEVI
Style (A-F)?   A
Waist size (28-40)?   28
Inseam (28-36)?   28
Number sold?   10
Not enough in stock; backorder 7

More sales (Y or N)?   Y
BRAND (use all CAPS)?   BIGYANK
Style (A-F)?   F
Waist size (28-40)?   40
Inseam (28-36)?   36
Number sold?   1

More sales (Y or N)?   N
```

Listing of `FIL11-4B.DAT`:

```
 0   3   0 12   1 12 19 17   0
 4  15  18   2 14   2   0 14 19
18   7  19 10 11   3   2 18 12
              .
              .
              .
12  18  11 12 16 14   9 12   8
```

Exercises

1. Consider the following type declarations:

```
TYPE
    Color = ( red, yellow, blue, green, white, black );
    BigTable = ARRAY[1..50, 1..100] OF integer;
    PointTable = ARRAY[-10..10, -10..10] OF real;
    CharTable = ARRAY['A'..'Z', 'A'..'Z'] OF char;
    BooleanTable = ARRAY[boolean, boolean] OF boolean;
    BitArray = ARRAY[0..1, 0..1, 0..1, 0..1] OF 0..1;
    Shirt = ARRAY[Color, 14..18, 32..36] of integer;
    MixedArray =
        ARRAY[Color, 'A'..'F', 0..10, boolean] OF real;
    InStockArray = ARRAY['A'..'F'] OF ARRAY[Color] OF real;
    ShirtStock = ARRAY[1..5] OF Shirt;
```

How many elements can be stored in an array of each of the following types?

(a) `BigTable`   (b) `PointTable`   (c) `CharTable`
(d) `BooleanTable`   (e) `BitArray`   (f) `Shirt`
(g) `MixedArray`   (h) `InStockArray`   (i) `ShirtStock`

2. Assume that the following declarations have been made:

```
TYPE
    Array3X3 = ARRAY[1..3, 1..3] OF  integer;

VAR
    Matrix : Array3X3;
    i, j : integer;
```

For each of the following, tell what value (if any) is assigned to each array element, or explain why an error occurs:

(a)
```
FOR i := 1 TO 3 DO
    FOR j := 1 TO 3 DO
        Matrix[i, j] := i + j;
```

(b)
```
FOR i := 1 TO 3 DO
    FOR j := 3 DOWNTO 1 DO
        IF i = j THEN
            Matrix[i, j] := 0
        ELSE
            Matrix[i, j] := 1;
```

(c)
```
FOR i := 1 TO 3 DO
    FOR j := 1 TO 3 DO
        IF i < j THEN
            Matrix[i, j] := -1
        ELSE IF i = j THEN
            Matrix[i, j] := 0
        ELSE
            Matrix[i, j] := 1;
```

(d) FOR i := 1 TO 3 DO
    BEGIN
      FOR j := 1 TO i DO
        Matrix[i, j] := 0;
      FOR j := i + 1 TO 3 DO
        Matrix [i, j] := 2
    END {FOR};

3. Assume that the following declarations have been made:

    TYPE
      ArrayOfStrings = ARRAY[1..2] OF string[6];

    CONST
      TextLine : ArrayOfStrings = ('ABCDEF', 'GHIJKL');

For each of the following, tell what output will be produced or explain why an error occurs:

(a) FOR i := 1 TO 2 DO
    BEGIN
      FOR j := 1 TO 6 DO
        write(TextLine[i, j]);
      writeln
    END {FOR};

(b) FOR i := 1 TO 2 DO
    BEGIN
      FOR j := 1 TO 6 DO
        write(TextLine[i][j]);
      writeln
    END {FOR};

(c) FOR i := 1 TO 2 DO
    FOR j := 1 TO 6 DO
      write(TextLine[i][j]);

(d) FOR j := 1 TO 6 DO
    BEGIN
      FOR i := 1 TO 2 DO
        write(TextLine[i, j]);
      writeln
    END {FOR};

(e) FOR j := 1 TO 6 DO
    BEGIN
      FOR i := 1 TO 2 DO
        write(TextLine[j, i]);
      writeln
    END {FOR};

(f) FOR i := 1 TO 2 DO
    FOR j := 6 DOWNTO 1 DO
      write(TextLine[i, j]);

4. Modify the program segment on page 556 so that it calculates and displays the average temperature at each of the three locations.

5. In procedure **Convert** of the inventory control program in Figure 11.4, a for loop is used to search the array **BrandName** for the **Name** entered by the user. This means that the entire array is examined for each **Name**. Rewrite this program segment so the search terminates as soon as **Name** is found in the array. (*Hint:* Be careful not to "fall off the end" of the enumerated type **BrandType**. You may find it convenient to add a dummy last value in this type.)

6. Like one-dimensional arrays, multidimensional arrays are stored in a block of consecutive memory locations, and address translation formulas are used to determine the location in memory of each array element. To illustrate, consider an array **A** of type **ARRAY[1..3, 1..4] OF integer**, and assume that an integer can be stored in one memory word. If **A** is allocated memory in a rowwise manner and b is its base address, then the first row of **A**, **A[1, 1]**, **A[1, 2]**, **A[1, 3]**, **A[1, 4]**, is stored in words b, $b + 1$, $b + 2$, $b + 3$, the second row in words $b + 4$ through $b + 7$, and the third row in words $b + 8$ through $b + 11$.

Address	Memory	Array Element
	⋮	
b		A[1,1]
$b + 1$		A[1,2]
$b + 2$		A[1,3]
$b + 3$		A[1,4]
$b + 4$		A[2,1]
$b + 5$		A[2,2]
$b + 6$		A[2,3]
$b + 7$		A[2,4]
$b + 8$		A[3,1]
$b + 9$		A[3,2]
$b + 10$		A[3,3]
$b + 11$		A[3,4]
	⋮	

In general, **A[i, j]** is stored in word $b + 4(i - 1) + (j - 1)$.

(a) Give a similar diagram and formula for **A[i, j]**, assuming columnwise allocation.

(b) Give diagrams and formulas for both rowwise and columnwise allocation if **A** is of type **ARRAY[0..3, -1..1] OF integer**.

(c) Repeat part (b) for **A** of type **ARRAY[0..2, 4..7] OF real**, where real values require two words for storage.

7. A certain company has a product line that includes five items that sell for $100, $75, $120, $150, and $35. There are four salespersons working for this company, and the following table gives the sales report for a typical week:

Salesperson	Item Number				
Number	1	2	3	4	5
1	10	4	5	6	7
2	7	0	12	1	3
3	4	9	5	0	8
4	3	2	1	5	6

Write a program to

(a) Compute the total dollar sales for each salesperson.

(b) Compute the total commission for each salesperson if the commission rate is 10 percent.

(c) Find the total income for each salesperson for the week if each salesperson receives a fixed salary of $200 per week in addition to commission payments.

8. A car manufacturer has collected some data on the noise level (measured in decibels) produced at seven different speeds by six different models of cars that it produces. This data is summarized in the following table:

	Speed(mph)						
Car	20	30	40	50	60	70	80
1	88	90	94	102	111	122	134
2	75	77	80	86	94	103	113
3	80	83	85	94	100	111	121
4	68	71	76	85	96	110	125
5	77	84	91	98	105	112	119
6	81	85	90	96	102	109	120

Write a program that will display this table in a nice format and that will calculate and display the average noise level for each car model, the average noise level at each speed, and the overall average noise level.

9. A number of students from several different engineering sections performed the same experiment to determine the tensile strength of sheets made from two different alloys. Each of these strength measurements is a real number in the range 0 through 10. Write a program to read several lines of data, each consisting of a section number and the tensile strength of the two types of sheets recorded by a student in that section, and store these values in a two-dimensional array. Then calculate

(a) For each section, the average of the tensile strengths for each type of alloy.

(b) The number of persons in a given section who recorded strength measures of 5 or higher.

(c) The average of the tensile strengths recorded for alloy 2 by students who recorded a tensile strength lower than 3 for alloy 1.

10. Write a program to calculate and display the first ten rows of Pascal's triangle. The first part of the triangle has the form

$$
\begin{array}{ccccccccc}
 & & & & 1 & & & & \\
 & & & 1 & & 1 & & & \\
 & & 1 & & 2 & & 1 & & \\
 & 1 & & 3 & & 3 & & 1 & \\
1 & & 4 & & 6 & & 4 & & 1
\end{array}
$$

in which each row begins and ends with 1 and each of the other entries in a row is the sum of the two entries just above it. If this form for the output seems too challenging, you might display the triangle as

```
1
1  1
1  2  1
1  3  3  1
1  4  6  4  1
```

11. A demographic study of the metropolitan area around Dogpatch divided it into three regions, urban, suburban, and exurban, and published the following table showing the annual migration from one region to another (the numbers represent percentages):

↱	Urban	Suburban	Exurban
Urban	1.1	0.3	0.7
Suburban	0.1	1.2	0.3
Exurban	0.2	0.6	1.3

For example, 0.3 percent of the urbanites (0.003 times the current population) move to the suburbs each year. The diagonal entries represent internal growth rates. Using a two-dimensional array with an enumerated type for the indices to store this table, write a program to determine the population of each region after 10, 20, 30, 40, and 50 years. Assume that the current populations of the urban, suburban, and exurban regions are 2.1 million, 1.4 million, and 0.9 million, respectively.

12. Suppose that the prices for the fifteen automobile models in Example 1 of Section 11.3 are as follows:

Model #	Model Price
1	$ 7,450
2	$ 9,995
3	$26,500
4	$ 5,999
5	$10,400
6	$ 8,885
7	$11,700
8	$14,440
9	$17,900
10	$ 9,550
11	$10,500
12	$ 8,050
13	$ 7,990
14	$12,300
15	$ 6,999

Write a program to read this list of prices and the sales table given in Example 1 of Section 11.3, and calculate the total dollar sales for each salesman and the total dollar sales for all salesmen.

13. The inventory control program in Example 2 of Section 11.3 simply updates the array **JeansInStock** with sales figures entered during execution. Extend the program by adding other user options such as the following:

   (a) Search the array **JeansInStock** to determine how many of a particular kind of jeans are currently in stock.
   (b) Print a reorder list of all brand names, styles, and sizes of jeans for which the number in stock is below some specified reorder point.
   (c) Do the same as in (b), but print a list of jeans for which the number in stock is greater than some specified overstock point.

14. Write an inventory control program like that in Example 2 of Section 11.3 (see also the preceding exercise), but for an automobile dealership and using a five-dimensional array. The first index is the make of a car **(Chrysler, Dodge, Plymouth)**, the second is style **(TwoDoor, FourDoor, StationWagon, Van)**, the third is color **(blue, brown, green, red, silver, yellow)**, the fourth is the year of the vehicle (a small subrange of integers), and the fifth is a sales code **(A, B, C)**.

15. A magic square is an $n \times n$ matrix in which each of the integers 1, 2, 3, . . . , n^2 appears exactly once and all column sums, row sums, and diagonal sums are equal. For example, the following is a 5×5 magic square in which all the rows, columns, and diagonals add up to 65:

17	24	1	8	15
23	5	7	14	16
4	6	13	20	22
10	12	19	21	3
11	18	25	2	9

The following is a procedure for constructing an $n \times n$ magic square for any odd integer n. Place 1 in the middle of the top row. Then after integer k has been placed, move up one row and one column to the right to place the next integer $k + 1$, unless one of the following occurs:

(i) If a move takes you above the top row in the jth column, move to the bottom of the jth column and place the integer $k + 1$ there.

(ii) If a move takes you outside to the right of the square in the ith row, place $k + 1$ in the ith row at the left side.

(iii) If a move takes you to an already-filled square or if you move out of the square at the upper right-hand corner, place $k + 1$ immediately below k.

Write a program to construct an $n \times n$ magic square for any odd value of n.

16. The famous mathematician G. H. Hardy once mentioned to the brilliant young Indian mathematician Ramanujan that he had just ridden in a taxi whose number he considered to be very dull. Ramanujan promptly replied that on the contrary, the number was very interesting because it was the smallest positive integer that could be written as the sum of two cubes (that is, written in the form $x^3 + y^3$, with x and y integers) in two different ways. Write a program to find the number of Hardy's taxi.

17. Consider a square grid, with some cells empty and others containing an asterisk. Define two asterisks to be *contiguous* if they are adjacent to each other in the same row or in the same column. Now suppose we define a *blob* as follows:

(a) A blob contains at least one asterisk.

(b) If an asterisk is in a blob, then so is any asterisk that is contiguous to it.

(c) If a blob has more than two asterisks, then each asterisk in it is contiguous to at least one other asterisk in the blob.

For example, there are four blobs in the partial grid

*			*	*			*		*	*
							*		*	*

seven blobs in

*		*		*				*	*	*
					*				*	
*				*						

and only one in

		*	*	*		*	*	*	
				*			*		*
			*	*	*				

Write a program that uses a recursive function or procedure to count the number of blobs in a square grid. Input to the program should consist of the locations of the asterisks in the grid, and the program should display the grid and the blob count.

18. The game of Nim is played by two players. There are usually three piles of objects, and on his or her turn, each player is allowed to take any number (at least one) of objects from one pile. The player taking the last object loses. Write a program that allows the user to play Nim against the computer. You might have the computer play a perfect game, or you might design the program to "teach" the computer. One way for the computer to "learn" is to assign a value to every possible move, based on experience gained from playing games. The value of each possible move is stored in some array; initially, each value is 0. The value of each move in a winning sequence of moves is increased by 1, and those in a losing sequence are decreased by 1. At each stage, the computer selects the best possible move (that having the highest value).

19. Write a program that allows the user to play tic-tac-toe against the computer.

11.4 PART OF THE PICTURE: Numeric Computation

Matrix Multiplication

A two-dimensional array having m rows and n columns is called an $m \times n$ **matrix.** One important operation of matrix algebra is matrix multiplication, defined as follows: Suppose that *Mat1* is an $m \times n$ matrix and *Mat2* is an $n \times p$ matrix. The product *Prod* of *Mat1* with *Mat2* will then be an $m \times p$ matrix with the entry *Prod*[i, j], which appears in the ith row and the jth column given by

> *Prod*[i, j] = The sum of the products of the entries in row i of
> *Mat1* with the entries of column j of *Mat2*
> = *Mat1*[i, 1] * *Mat2*[1, j] + *Mat1*[i, 2] * *Mat2*[2, j]
> + ... + *Mat1*[i, n] * *Mat2*[n, j]

Note that the number of columns (n) in *Mat1* must equal the number of rows in *Mat2* for the product of *Mat1* with *Mat2* to be defined.

For example, suppose that *Mat1* is the 2×3 matrix

$$\begin{bmatrix} 1 & 0 & 2 \\ 3 & 0 & 4 \end{bmatrix}$$

and that *Mat2* is the 3×4 matrix

$$\begin{bmatrix} 4 & 2 & 5 & 3 \\ 6 & 4 & 1 & 8 \\ 9 & 0 & 0 & 2 \end{bmatrix}$$

Because the number of columns (3) in *Mat1* equals the number of rows in *Mat2*, the product matrix *Prod* is defined. The entry in the first row and first column, *Prod*[1, 1], is

$$1 * 4 + 0 * 6 + 2 * 9 = 22$$

Similarly, the entry $Prod[1, 2]$ in the first row and second column is

$$1 * 2 + 0 * 4 + 2 * 0 = 2$$

The complete product matrix $Prod$ is the 2×4 matrix given by

$$\begin{bmatrix} 22 & 2 & 5 & 7 \\ 48 & 6 & 15 & 17 \end{bmatrix}$$

In general, the algorithm for multiplying matrices is

MATRIX MULTIPLICATION ALGORITHM

(* Accepts: $Rows1 \times Cols1$ matrix $Mat1$ and $Rows2 \times Cols2$ matrix $Mat2$.
   Purpose: Compute the product $Mat1 * Mat2$. $Cols1$ must equal $Rows2$ for
             the product to be defined.
   Returns: The product matrix $Prod$, provided it is defined. *)

1. If $Cols1 \neq Rows2$, then the product $Prod = Mat1 * Mat2$ is not defined;
   terminate the algorithm. Otherwise proceed with the following steps:
2. For an index i ranging from 1 to the number of rows $Rows1$ of $Mat1$, do
   the following:
   For an index j ranging from 1 to the number of columns $Cols2$ of $Mat2$,
   do the following:
      a. Set Sum equal to 0.
      b. For an index k ranging from 1 to the number of columns $Cols1$ of
         $Mat1$ ($=$ the number of rows $Rows2$ of $Mat2$):
            Add $Mat1[i, k] * Mat2[k, j]$ to Sum.
      c. Set $Prod[i, j]$ equal to Sum.

The program in Figure 11.5 reads two matrices and uses this algorithm to calculate
and display their product.

FIGURE 11.5 Matrix multiplication.

```
PROGRAM MatrixMultiplication( input, output );
{*****************************************************************

   Input (keyboard):   Dimensions of two matrices and their entries.
   Purpose:            Calculate the product of the matrices.
   Output (screen):    Prompts to the user and the product matrix.


*****************************************************************}

CONST
   RowLimit = 20;      {limit on number of rows in a matrix}
   ColumnLimit = 20;   {limit on number of columns in a matrix}
```

FIGURE 11.5 Matrix multiplication. (cont.)

```
TYPE
    Matrix = ARRAY[1..RowLimit, 1..ColumnLimit] OF integer;

VAR
    Mat1, Mat2,                  {matrices being multiplied}
    Prod : Matrix;               {product of Mat1 with Mat2}
    Rows1, Cols1,                {dimensions of Mat1}
    Rows2, Cols2 : integer;      {dimensions of Mat2}
    ProductDefined : boolean;    {true if Cols1 = Rows2, else false}

PROCEDURE ReadMatrix( VAR Mat : Matrix; VAR Rows, Columns : integer );
{-------------------------------------------------------------------

    Input (keyboard): Dimension of a matrix Mat and its entries.
    Purpose:          Read number of rows and columns in a matrix
                      and then read a matrix of those dimensions.
    Returns:          Matrix Mat, number of Rows and Columns.

--------------------------------------------------------------------}

    VAR
        i, j : integer;    {row, column indices}

    BEGIN
        write( 'Enter number of rows & columns:  ' );
        readln( Rows, Columns );
        writeln( 'Enter the matrix rowwise:' );
        FOR i := 1 TO Rows DO
            FOR j := 1 TO Columns DO
                read( Mat[i,j] );
        readln
    END {ReadMatrix};

PROCEDURE PrintMatrix( VAR Mat : Matrix; Rows, Columns : integer );
{-------------------------------------------------------------------

    Accepts:         A matrix Mat and its number of Rows and Columns.
    Purpose:         Display a Rows X Columns matrix with integer
                     entries.
    Output (screen): Matrix Mat.

--------------------------------------------------------------------}

    CONST
        FieldWidth = 5;    {width of field used to display an entry}

    VAR
        i, j : integer;    {row, column indices}
```

FIGURE 11.5   Matrix multiplication. (cont.)

```
BEGIN
    writeln;
    FOR i := 1 TO Rows DO
        BEGIN
            FOR j := 1 TO Columns DO
                write( Mat[i,j]:FieldWidth );
            writeln;
            writeln
        END {FOR}
END {PrintMatrix};

PROCEDURE MatMultiply( VAR Mat1, Mat2, Prod : Matrix;
                            Rows1, Cols1, Rows2, Cols2 : integer;
                        VAR ProductDefined : boolean );
{------------------------------------------------------------------

    Accepts:    Rows1 X Cols1 matrix Mat1 and Rows2 X Cols2
                matrix Mat2.
    Purpose:    Multiply the Rows1 X Cols1 matrix Mat1 and the
                Rows2 X Cols2 matrix Mat2; Cols1 must equal Rows2
                for the product Prod to be defined.
    Returns:    Product matrix Prod and ProductDefined, which
                indicates if the product is defined.

------------------------------------------------------------------}

    VAR
        i, j, k,          {indices}
        Sum : integer;    {used to calculate product matrix}

BEGIN
    ProductDefined := (Cols1 = Rows2);
    IF ProductDefined THEN
        BEGIN
            FOR i := 1 TO Rows1 DO
                FOR j := 1 TO Cols2 DO
                    BEGIN
                        Sum := 0;
                        FOR k := 1 TO Cols1 DO
                            Sum := Sum + Mat1[i,k] * Mat2[k,j];
                        Prod[i,j] := Sum
                    END {FOR j}
        END {IF}
END {MatMultiply};
```

FIGURE 11.5   Matrix multiplication. (cont.)

```
BEGIN {*************** main program ***************}
   ReadMatrix( Mat1, Rows1, Cols1 );
   writeln( 'First Matrix:' );
   PrintMatrix( Mat1, Rows1, Cols1 );
   ReadMatrix( Mat2, Rows2, Cols2 );
   writeln( 'Second Matrix:' );
   PrintMatrix( Mat2, Rows2, Cols2 );
   MatMultiply( Mat1, Mat2, Prod, Rows1, Cols1, Rows2, Cols2,
                ProductDefined );
   IF ProductDefined THEN
      BEGIN
         writeln( 'Product:' );
         PrintMatrix( Prod, Rows1, Cols2 )
      END {IF}
   ELSE
      BEGIN
         writeln( 'Product undefined -- number of columns ', Cols1:1,
                  ' in first matrix' );
         writeln( ' is not equal to number of rows ', Rows2:1,
                  ' in second matrix' )
      END {ELSE}
END {main program}.
```

Sample run:

```
Enter number of rows & columns:  2 3
Enter the matrix rowwise:
1 0 2
3 0 4
First Matrix:

   1    0    2

   3    0    4

Enter number of rows & columns:  3 4
Enter the matrix rowwise:
4 2 5 3
6 4 1 8
9 0 0 2
Second Matrix:

   4    2    5    3

   6    4    1    8

   9    0    0    2

Product:

  22    2    5    7

  48    6   15   17
```

Solving Linear Systems

A linear system is a set of linear equations, each of which involves several unknowns; for example,

$$5x_1 - x_2 - 2x_3 = 11$$
$$-x_1 + 5x_2 - 2x_3 = 0$$
$$-2x_1 - 2x_2 + 7x_3 = 0$$

is a linear system of three equations involving the three unknowns x_1, x_2, and x_3. A solution of such a system is a collection of values for these unknowns that satisfies all of the equations simultaneously.

One method for solving a linear system is called **Gaussian elimination.** In this method, we first eliminate x_1 from the second equation by adding 1/5 times the first equation to the second equation and, from the third equation, by adding 2/5 times the first equation to the third equation. This yields the linear system

$$5x_1 - x_2 - 2x_3 = 11$$
$$4.8x_2 - 2.4x_3 = 2.2$$
$$-2.4x_2 + 6.2x_3 = 4.4$$

which is equivalent to the first system because it has the same solution as the original system. We next eliminate x_2 from the third equation by adding $2.4/4.8 = 1/2$ times the second equation to the third, giving the new equivalent linear system

$$5x_1 - x_2 - 2x_3 = 11$$
$$4.8x_2 - 2.4x_3 = 2.2$$
$$5x_3 = 5.5$$

Once the original system has been reduced to such a *triangular* form, it is easy to find the solution. It is clear from the last equation that the value of x_3 is

$$x_3 = \frac{5.5}{5} = 1.1$$

Substituting this value for x_3 in the second equation and solving for x_2 gives

$$x_2 = \frac{2.2 + 2.4(1.1)}{4.8} = 1.008$$

and substituting these values for x_2 and x_3 in the first equation gives

$$x_1 = \frac{11 + 1.008 + 2(1.1)}{5} = 2.842$$

The original linear system can also be written as a single matrix equation

$$Ax = b$$

where A is the 3×3 **coefficient matrix,** b is the 3×1 **constant vector,** and x is the 3×1 **vector of unknowns:**

$$A = \begin{bmatrix} 5 & -1 & -2 \\ -1 & 5 & -2 \\ -2 & -2 & 7 \end{bmatrix}, \quad x = \begin{bmatrix} x_1 \\ x_2 \\ x_3 \end{bmatrix}, \quad b = \begin{bmatrix} 11 \\ 0 \\ 0 \end{bmatrix}$$

The operations used to reduce the original linear system to triangular form use only the coefficient matrix A and the constant vector $\boldsymbol{b}$. Thus, if we combine these into a single matrix by adjoining $\boldsymbol{b}$ to A as a last column,

$$Aug = \begin{bmatrix} 5 & -1 & -2 & 11 \\ -1 & 5 & -2 & 0 \\ -2 & -2 & 7 & 0 \end{bmatrix}$$

we can carry out the operations on this new matrix, called the **augmented matrix**, without writing down the unknowns at each step. Thus we add $-Aug[2,1]/Aug[1,1] = 1/5$ times the first row of Aug to the second row and $-Aug[3,1]/Aug[1,1] = 2/5$ times the first row of Aug to the third row to obtain the new matrix

$$Aug = \begin{bmatrix} 5 & -1 & -2 & 11 \\ 0 & 4.8 & -2.4 & 2.2 \\ 0 & -2.4 & 6.2 & 4.4 \end{bmatrix}$$

Then adding $-Aug[3,2]/Aug[2,2] = 1/2$ times the second row to the third row gives the following *triangular* matrix, which corresponds to the final triangular system of equations:

$$Aug = \begin{bmatrix} 5 & -1 & -2 & 11 \\ 0 & 4.8 & -2.4 & 2.2 \\ 0 & 0 & 5 & 5.5 \end{bmatrix}$$

From this example, we see that the basic row operation performed at the ith step of the reduction process is:

For $k = i + 1, i + 2, \ldots, n$

Replace row_k by $\text{row}_k - \dfrac{Aug[k,i]}{Aug[i,i]} \times \text{row}_i$

Clearly, for this to be possible, the element $Aug[i, i]$, called a **pivot** element, must be nonzero. If it is not, we must interchange the ith row with a later row to produce a nonzero pivot.

An algorithm and a program for solving linear systems using Gaussian elimination is given in Example 11.4 in Appendix E. To minimize the effect of roundoff error in the computations, it selects as a pivot at each stage in the reduction the candidate that is largest in absolute value.

Exercises

1. Write and test a procedure to add two matrices. If A_{ij} and B_{ij} are the entries in the ith row and jth column of $m \times n$ matrices A and B, respectively, then $A_{ij} + B_{ij}$ is the entry in the ith row and jth column of the sum, which will also be an $m \times n$ matrix. For example,

$$\begin{bmatrix} 1 & 0 & 2 \\ -1 & 3 & 5 \end{bmatrix} + \begin{bmatrix} 4 & 2 & 1 \\ 7 & 0 & 3 \end{bmatrix} = \begin{bmatrix} 5 & 2 & 3 \\ 6 & 3 & 8 \end{bmatrix}$$

2. A certain company manufactures four electronic devices using five different components that cost $10.95, $6.30, $14.75, $11.25, and $5.00, respectively. The number of components used in each device is given in the following table:

Device Number	Component Number				
	1	**2**	**3**	**4**	**5**
1	10	4	5	6	7
2	7	0	12	1	3
3	4	9	5	0	8
4	3	2	1	5	6

Write a program that uses the procedure **MatMultiply** in the program of Figure 11.5 to

(a) Calculate the total cost of each device.
(b) Calculate the total cost of producing each device if the estimated labor cost for each device is 10 percent of the cost in part (a).

3. A company produces three different products. They are processed through four different departments, A, B, C, and D, and the following table gives the number of hours that each department spends on each product:

Product	A	B	C	D
1	20	10	15	13
2	18	11	11	10
3	28	0	16	17

The cost per hour of operation in each of the departments is as follows:

Department	A	B	C	D
Cost per hour	$140	$295	$225	$95

Write a program that uses the procedure **MatMultiply** in the program of Figure 11.5 to find the total cost of each of the products.

4. The vector-matrix equation

$$\begin{bmatrix} N \\ E \\ D \end{bmatrix} = \begin{bmatrix} \cos \alpha & -\sin \alpha & 0 \\ \sin \alpha & \cos \alpha & 0 \\ 0 & 0 & 1 \end{bmatrix} \begin{bmatrix} \cos \beta & 0 & \sin \beta \\ 0 & 1 & 0 \\ -\sin \beta & 0 & \cos \beta \end{bmatrix} \begin{bmatrix} 1 & 0 & 0 \\ 0 & \cos \gamma & -\sin \gamma \\ 0 & \sin \gamma & \cos \gamma \end{bmatrix} \begin{bmatrix} I \\ J \\ K \end{bmatrix}$$

is used to transform local coordinates (I, J, K) for a space vehicle to inertial coordinates (N, E, D). Write a program that reads values for α, β, and γ and a set of local coordinates (I, J, K) and then uses the procedure **MatMultiply** in the program of Figure 11.5 to determine the corresponding inertial coordinates.

5. A Markov chain is a system that moves through a discrete set of states in such a way that when the system is in state i there is probability P_{ij} that it will next move to state j. These probabilities are given by a transition matrix P, whose (i, j) entry is P_{ij}. It is easy to show that the (i, j) entry of P^n then gives the probability of starting in state i and ending in state j after n steps.

To illustrate, suppose there are two urns A and B containing a given number of balls. At each instant, a ball is chosen at random and is transferred to the other urn. This is a Markov chain if we take as a state the number of balls in urn A and let P_{ij} be the probability of a change from i balls in A to j balls in A. For example, for four balls, the transition matrix P is given by

$$\begin{bmatrix} 0 & 1 & 0 & 0 & 0 \\ 1/4 & 0 & 3/4 & 0 & 0 \\ 0 & 1/2 & 0 & 1/2 & 0 \\ 0 & 0 & 3/4 & 0 & 1/4 \\ 0 & 0 & 0 & 1 & 0 \end{bmatrix}$$

Write a program that reads a transition matrix P for such a Markov chain and calculates and displays the value of n and P^n for several values of n. (Use procedure `MatMultiply` in the program of Figure 11.5 to carry out the required matrix multiplications.)

6. A directed graph, or digraph, consists of a set of vertices and a set of directed arcs joining certain of these vertices. For example, the following diagram pictures a directed graph having five vertices numbered 1, 2, 3, 4, and 5, and seven directed arcs joining vertices 1 to 2, 1 to 4, 1 to 5, 3 to 1, 3 to itself, 4 to 3, and 5 to 1:

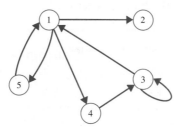

A directed graph having n vertices can be represented by its adjacency matrix, which is an $n \times n$ matrix, with the entry in the ith row and jth column a 1 if vertex i is joined to vertex j, and 0 otherwise. The adjacency matrix for this graph is

$$\begin{bmatrix} 0 & 1 & 0 & 1 & 1 \\ 0 & 0 & 0 & 0 & 0 \\ 1 & 0 & 1 & 0 & 0 \\ 0 & 0 & 1 & 0 & 0 \\ 1 & 0 & 0 & 0 & 0 \end{bmatrix}$$

If A is the adjacency matrix for a directed graph, the entry in the ith row and jth column of A^k gives the number of ways that vertex j can be reached from the vertex i by following k edges. Write a program to read the number of vertices in a directed graph and a collection of ordered pairs of vertices representing directed arcs, construct the adjacency matrix, and then find the number of ways that each vertex can be reached from every other vertex by following k edges for some value of k.

7. The inverse of an $n \times n$ matrix A is a matrix A^{-1} for which both the products $A * A^{-1}$ and $A^{-1} * A$ are equal to the identity matrix having 1s on the diagonal from the upper left to the lower right and 0s elsewhere. The inverse of matrix A can be calculated by solving the linear systems $Ax = b$ for each of the following constant vectors b:

$$\begin{bmatrix} 1 \\ 0 \\ 0 \\ \cdot \\ \cdot \\ \cdot \\ 0 \end{bmatrix} \begin{bmatrix} 0 \\ 1 \\ 0 \\ \cdot \\ \cdot \\ \cdot \\ 0 \end{bmatrix} \begin{bmatrix} 0 \\ 0 \\ 1 \\ \cdot \\ \cdot \\ \cdot \\ 0 \end{bmatrix} \cdots \begin{bmatrix} 0 \\ 0 \\ 0 \\ \cdot \\ \cdot \\ \cdot \\ 1 \end{bmatrix}$$

These solutions give the first, second, third, . . . , nth column of A^{-1}. Write a program that uses Gaussian elimination (see Example 11.4 of Appendix E) to solve these linear systems and thus calculate the approximate inverse of a matrix.

11.5 PART OF THE PICTURE: Computer Graphics

Plotting Graphs

The number and quality of software packages and hand-held calculators that can be used to generate high-resolution graphs of functions are increasing rapidly. For example, Figure 11.6(a) shows the graph of $y = x * \cos(x)$ for $-8 \le x \le 8$ as plotted on a CASIO fx-7000GA calculator, and Figure 11.6(b) shows the same graph as produced by the powerful software package Mathematica™.

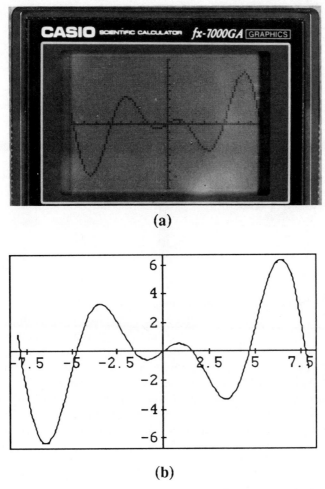

(a)

(b)

FIGURE 11.6 (a) Plot of $y = x * \cos(x)$ on a CASIO fx-7000GA calculator. (Photo by Randal Nyhof, Nyhof School Pictures) (b) Plot of $y = x * \cos(x)$ produced by Mathematica.

The window containing each of the plots shown in Figure 11.6 is simply a two-dimensional array of points (called *pixels*) on the screen, some of which (those corresponding to points on the graph of the function) are "on" (black) and the rest of which are "off" (white). The following enlarged view of the portion of the graphics window near the origin shows clearly the grid structure of this part of the window:

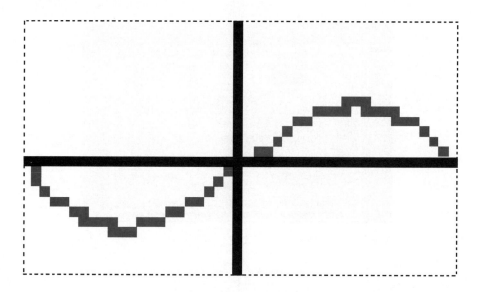

Such a graphics window can be modeled with a two-dimensional character array *Window,* each element of which corresponds to a point in the window. The rows of *Window* correspond to x values and the columns to y values. For each x value, the y value nearest the actual function value $y = f(x)$ is determined, and the point $Window[x, y]$ is set to some plotting character such as '*' ("on"); all other elements of *Window* are blank ("off").

The program in Example 11.5A of Appendix E uses a two-dimensional array in this way to plot graphs of functions. One sample run of that program produced the following plot for the function $f(x) = x * \cos x$:

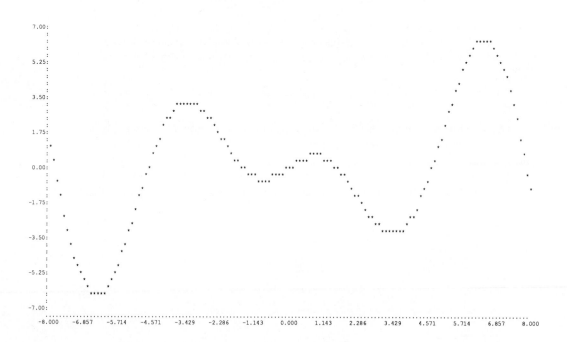

Density Plots

We have just seen how a function $y = f(x)$ of a single variable x can be plotted. Graphs of functions $z = f(x, y)$ of two variables x and y are surfaces in three dimensions and are considerably more difficult to display on a two-dimensional screen. Some software packages are able to generate good two-dimensional representations of many three-dimensional surfaces. For example, the following is a graph produced by Mathematica of the surface defined by

$$z = e^{-(x^2 + y^2)}$$

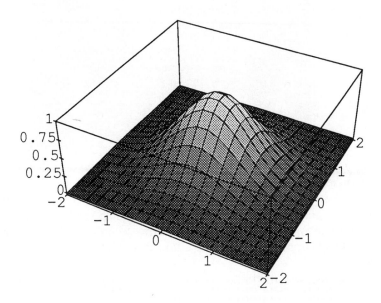

Note that in this representation, shading is used to represent the height of the function, with lighter shades for larger values and darker shades for smaller values. This shading, together with the curved grid lines and the enclosing box produces a visual illusion of a three-dimensional surface.

Another representation of a surface that also uses shading but not perspective is a **density plot,** obtained by projecting onto a plane a representation like the preceding one. The following is the density plot generated by Mathematica for this surface. The various densities of gray again indicate different heights of the function.

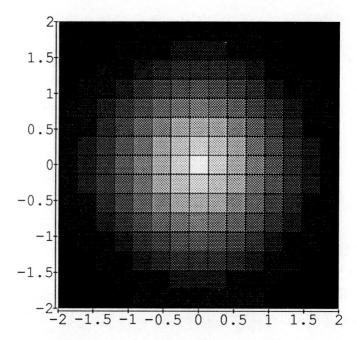

To generate a density plot, we can use a two-dimensional character array *Window* whose elements are different characters, more dense characters to produce darker shades of gray and less dense characters for lighter shades. The program in Example 11.5B of Appendix E uses such an array to produce density plots. One sample run of that program produced the following output for the function $f(x,y) = e^{-(x^2+y^2)}$:

The ideas in this example can be modified to display an image that is represented in digitized form and to enhance this image. This digitized representation might be a table of light intensities transmitted from a remote sensor such as a television camera in a satellite. This problem of visual image processing and enhancement is described in the exercises.

Exercises

1. Modify the program in Example 11.5A of Appendix E to plot graphs of parametric equations of the form

$$x = x(t), \ y = y(t), \ a \le t \le b$$

2. A **scatter plot** of a set of data pairs (x, y) of real numbers is obtained simply by plotting these points. Modify the program in Example 11.5A of Appendix E to produce a scatter plot of a set of data pairs read from a file. Execute your program using the data file **LeastSquaresFile** given in Appendix E.

3. At the end of this section, we noted that the ideas there can be modified to carry out *visual image processing* and *enhancement*. Make a file that represents light intensities of an image in digitized form, say, with intensities from 0 through 9. Write a program that reads these intensities from the file and then reconstructs and displays them using a different character for each intensity. This image might then be enhanced to sharpen the contrast. For example, "gray" areas might be removed by replacing all intensities in the range 0 through some value by 0 (light) and intensities greater than this value by 9 (dark). Design your program to accept a threshold value that distinguishes light from dark and then enhances the image in the manner described.

4. An alternative method for enhancing an image (see Exercise 3) is to accept three successive images of the same object and, if two or more of the intensities agree, to use that value; otherwise, the average of the three values is used. Modify the program of Exercise 3 to use this technique for enhancement.

5. The game of *Life,* invented by the mathematician John H. Conway, is intended to model life in a society of organisms. Consider a rectangular array of cells, each of which may contain an organism. If the array is assumed to extend indefinitely in both directions, each cell will have eight neighbors, the eight cells surrounding it. Births and deaths occur according to the following rules:

   (a) An organism is born in an empty cell that has exactly three neighbors.
   (b) An organism will die from isolation if it has fewer than two neighbors.
   (c) An organism will die from overcrowding if it has more than three neighbors.
   (d) All other organisms will survive to the next generation.

The following display shows the first five generations of a particular configuration of organisms:

Write a program to play the game of Life and investigate the patterns produced by various initial configurations. Some configurations die off rather quickly; others repeat after a certain number of generations; others change shape and size and may move across the array; and still others may produce "gliders" that detach themselves from the society and sail off into space.

Programming Pointers

Many of the programming pointers given for one-dimensional arrays at the end of Chapter 9 also apply to multidimensional arrays, and the reader should refer to those for an expanded discussion.

Program Design

1. *Array types should be associated with type identifiers in the* **TYPE** *section.*

2. *Use of a multidimensional array is appropriate when a table of data values, a list of tables, and so on must be stored in main memory for processing.* Using a multidimensional array when it is not necessary, however, can tie up a large block of memory locations. Moreover, the address translation required for array references slows execution. The amount of memory required to store a multidimensional array may be quite large, even though each index is restricted to a small range of values. For example, the three-dimensional array **ThreeD** declared by

```
TYPE
    ThreeDimArray = ARRAY[1..20, 1..20, 1..20] OF integer;

VAR
    ThreeD : ThreeDimArray;
```

requires $20 \times 20 \times 20 = 8000$ memory locations.

3. *To utilize memory efficiently, it is usually advisable to specify as variable parameters the formal parameters of functions and procedures that represent arrays (especially if they are large).*

Potential Problems

1. *Arrays cannot be read/written simply by including the array name in an input/ output list.* Rather, the individual array elements must be read/written.

2. *Array indices must stay within the ranges specified in the array declaration. Also, make sure that range checking is enabled, especially when developing and debugging progams that use arrays.* Out-of-range errors occur most often when a variable being used as an index takes on a value outside the range specified for the indices in the array declaration.

3. *When reading the elements of an array of characters, remember that end-of-line marks consist of two characters: a carriage-return character (*CR*) followed by a line-feed character (*LF*).*

4. *Assignment of one array to another requires that the arrays have the same type.* This means that they must be declared by the same or by equivalent *type identifiers.*

5. *All of the elements of an array must have the type specified in the array declaration.*

6. *When processing the elements of a multidimensional array using nested repetition structures, the structures must be arranged so that the indices vary in the intended order.* To illustrate, suppose that the two-dimensional array **Table** is declared by

```
TYPE
    Array3X4 = ARRAY[1..3, 1..4] OF integer;

VAR
    Table : Array3X4;
```

and the following data values are to be read into the array:

```
11 22 27 35 39 40 48 51 57 66 67 92
```

If these values are to be read and assigned in a rowwise manner so that the value of **Table** is the matrix

$$\begin{bmatrix} 11 & 22 & 27 & 35 \\ 39 & 40 & 48 & 51 \\ 57 & 66 & 67 & 92 \end{bmatrix}$$

then the following nested **FOR** statements are appropriate:

```
FOR row := 1 TO 3 DO
    FOR col := 1 TO 4 DO
        read( Table[row, col] );
```

If the value are to be read and assigned in a columnwise manner so that the value of **Table** is

$$\begin{bmatrix} 11 & 35 & 48 & 66 \\ 22 & 39 & 51 & 67 \\ 27 & 40 & 57 & 92 \end{bmatrix}$$

then the statements should be

```
FOR col := 1 TO 4 DO
  FOR row := 1 TO 3 DO
    read( Table[row, col] );
```

Standard Pascal

There are only a few differences between the way Turbo Pascal and standard Pascal process arrays. In standard Pascal:

■ Range checking is performed.
■ Arrays may not be initialized in constant sections.

RECORDS

12

Yea, from the table of my memory
I'll wipe away all trivial fond records.
WILLIAM SHAKESPEARE, *Hamlet*

CHAPTER CONTENTS

In Chapters 9 and 11, we introduced one of Pascal's structured data types, the array, which may be used to store elements of the same type. In many situations, however, we need to process items that are related in some way but that are not all of the same type. For example, a date consists of a month name (of string type), a day (of type 1..31), and a year (of type 1900..2000 perhaps); an employee record might contain, among other items, an employee name (string), age (integer), number of dependents (integer), and an hourly pay rate (real). Such related data items of different types can be organized in a **record.** In this chapter we consider how records are implemented and processed in Pascal.

12.1   Introduction to Records and Fields

A **record** is a data structure in which a collection of related data items of possibly different types may be stored. The positions in which these data items are stored are called the **fields** of the record. Thus, an employee record might contain a name field, an age field, a dependents field, and an hourly rate field.

Record Declarations

Records can be implemented in Pascal by using the structured data type **record.** The following syntax diagrams specify one form of a record declaration:

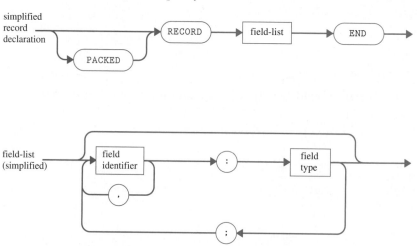

From this we see that a record declaration has the form

Record Declaration (Simplified)

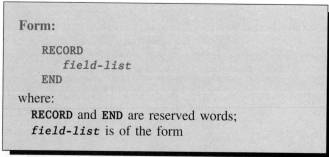

Form:

        RECORD
            field-list
        END

where:
    RECORD and **END** are reserved words;
    field-list is of the form

```
       list-1 : type-1;
       list-2 : type-2;
                   .
                   .
                   .
       list-m : type-m
```
with each *list-i* a single identifier or a list of
identifiers, separated by commas;
PACKED may precede the word **RECORD** to declare
a packed record.

Purpose:
Declares a record whose fields are named by the
identifiers in the *list-i*; *type-i* specifies the type
of each of these fields.

To illustrate, an employee record, as we have described it, could be declared by

```
RECORD
   Name : string[20];
   Age, Dependents : integer;
   HourlyRate : real
END;
```

Such record declarations, like those of other data types, may be used in the variable
section of a program's declaration part to specify the types of variables. But as with
other structured types, it is preferable to assign them to type identifiers in the type
section and then use these identifiers to declare record variables. For example,
consider

```
TYPE
   EmployeeRecord = RECORD
                     Name : string[20];
                     Age, Dependents : integer;
                     HourlyRate : real
                    END;
   BirthRecord = RECORD
                     Month : string[8];
                     Day : 1..31;
                     Year : 1900..2000
                  END;

VAR
   Employee : EmployeeRecord;
   Birth : BirthRecord;
```

The variable **Employee** may have as a value any record of type **EmployeeRecord**.
The first field of such a record is of type **string[20]** and is named with the field
identifier **Name**; the second and third fields are of type **integer** and have the

names **Age** and **Dependents**; and the fourth field is of type **real** and is named **HourlyRate**. The variable **Birth** may have as a value any record of type **BirthRecord**. The first field of this record is of type **string[8]** and is named **Month**; the second field is of subrange type **1..31** and is named **Day**; and the third field is of type **1900..2000** and is named **Year**. Typical values for **Employee** and **Birth** might be pictured as follows:

Name	Age	Dependents	HourlyRate
John Q. Doe	52	4	12.25

Month	Day	Year
January	15	1941

Accessing Fields in a Record

We have seen that each element of an array can be accessed directly using an indexed variable formed by attaching an index enclosed in brackets to the array name. In a similar manner, one can access each field of a record directly by using a **field-designated variable,** which we abbreviate to **fielded variable,** of the form

> *record-name.field-name*

in which a period followed by the field name is attached to the record name. Thus **Employee.Name** designates the first field of the record variable **Employee**. For the record displayed here, the value of **Employee.Name** would be the string **John♭Q.♭Doe** (where ♭ denotes a blank). Similarly, **Employee.Age**, **Employee.Dependents**, and **Employee.HourlyRate** refer to the second, third, and fourth fields and would have the values **52**, **4**, and **12.25**, respectively. If the second record is the value of the record variable **Birth**, then **Birth.Month** has the value **January**, **Birth.Day** has the value 15, and **Birth.Year** has the value 1941.

The scope of a field identifier is the record in which that identifier is declared. This means that the same identifier may not be used to specify two different fields within the same record, but an identifier that names a field may be used elsewhere in the program for some other purpose.

Nested Records

The fields that comprise a record may be of any data type; in particular, they may be other records. For example, the declarations

```
TYPE
   Date = RECORD
            Month : string[8];
            Day : 1..31;
            Year : 1900..2000
          END;
```

```
PersonnelRecord = RECORD
                     Name : string[20];
                     Birth : Date;
                     Age, Dependents : integer;
                     HourlyRate : real
                  END;

VAR
    Employee : PersonnelRecord;
```

specify that **Employee** may have as a value any record of type **PersonnelRecord**. Such a record consists of five fields: The first field is of type **string[20]** and is identified by **Name**; the second field is of type **Date** and is itself a record having three fields, **Month**, **Day**, and **Year**; the third and fourth fields are named **Age** and **Dependents** and are of type **integer**; and the fifth field is of type **real** and is named **HourlyRate**. A typical value for **Employee** might be pictured as follows:

	Birth					
Name	Month	Day	Year	Age	Dependents	HourlyRate
John Q. Doe	January	15	1941	52	4	12.25

The fields within such a **nested** (or **hierarchical**) **record** may be accessed by simply affixing a second field identifier to the name of the larger record. Thus, **Employee.Birth.Month** refers to the first field in the inner record of type **Date**; for this record, its value would be the string **January**. Similarly, the values of **Employee.Birth.Day** and **Employee.Birth.Year** would be 15 and 1941, respectively.

Record Initialization

In Turbo Pascal, a record variable may be initialized as a typed constant by using a declaration of the form

```
CONST
    record-name : record-type-identifier =
                     (list-of-field-constants);
```

where each field constant has the form

```
    field-name : field-value
```

and these field constants are separated by semicolons. For example, to initialize **Emp** of type **EmployeeRecord**, we can use the constant section

```
CONST
   Emp : EmployeeRecord =
              ( Name : 'John Q. Doe';
                Age : 48;
                Dependents : 4;
                HourlyRate : 12.25 );
```

To initialize the nested record **Employee** of type **PersonnelRecord**, we can use the constant section

```
CONST
   Employee : PersonnelRecord =
                  ( Name : 'John Q. Doe';
                    Birth : ( Month : 'January';
                              Day : 15;
                              Year : 1941 );
                    Age : 52;
                    Dependents : 4;
                    HourlyRate : 12.25 );
```

All the records considered in this section consist of a fixed number of fields, each of which has a fixed type. It is also possible to declare records in which some of the fields are fixed, but the number and types of other fields may vary. Thus, the number and types of fields in a variable of this record type may change during program execution. Such **variant records** are discussed in Section 12.6.

12.2   Processing Records

In the previous section we saw that records may be used to store several related data items that may be of different types and that each item or field in a record can be accessed with a fielded variable of the form

> *record-name.field-name*

In this section we discuss how values can be assigned to the fields within a record, how these values can be read and displayed, and how the value of one record variable can be copied to another.

Assigning Values to Fields in a Record

Both fielded variables and indexed variables serve to specify a particular item in a structure, and hence they are used in much the same way. To illustrate, consider the record type **ClassRecord** and the record variable **Student** declared by

```
CONST
   NumScores = 5;
   MaxScore = 100;

TYPE
   ListOfScores = ARRAY[1..NumScores] OF 0..MaxScore;
   ClassRecord = RECORD
                     Snumb : integer;
                     Name : string[20];
                     Gender : char;
                     TestScore : ListOfScores
                  END;

VAR
   Student : ClassRecord;
```

Because the fielded variable `Student.Snumb` is of `integer` type, it may be assigned an integer value in an assignment statement

```
Student.Snumb := 12345;
```

or by an input statement

```
readln( Student.Snumb );
```

and its value can be displayed by using an output statement

```
writeln( 'Student number: ', Student.Snumb );
```

Similarly, because `Student.TestScore` is an array, `Student.TestScore[1]` may be used to reference the first test score for this particular student.

Input and output of a record from or to a text file (including `input` and `output`) must be done by reading or displaying the value of each field in the record. For example, to read a value for the record variable `Student` from a text file `StudentFile`, the following statements might be used:

```
readln( StudentFile, Student.Snumb );
readln( StudentFile, Student.Name );
readln( StudentFile, Student.Gender );
FOR i := 1 TO NumScores DO
   read( StudentFile, Student.TestScore[i] );
readln( StudentFile );
```

Example: Processing Student Records

To illustrate record processing, suppose that a data file contains information about the students in a certain class, as just described: student number, first name, last name, gender, and five test scores:

```
12345
John Doe
M
44 55 78 83 72
15651
Mary Smith
F
94 85 62 66 83
22001
Pete Vandervan
M
34 44 29 51 47
       .
       .
       .
```

A program is to be developed to read this information and calculate and display the average of the test scores for each student.

Since the information in this file consists of students' numbers, names, gender, and test scores, it is natural to organize this information in records of type **ClassRecord**. The processing required to solve this problem is summarized in the following algorithm:

ALGORITHM TO PROCESS STUDENT RECORDS

(∗ Input (file): Student records.
    Purpose: Read student records from a file; calculate each student's average score; and display this average score together with other information in the student's record.
    Output: Student's number, name, gender, and average score. ∗)

1. Open the input file.
2. While the end of the file has not been reached, do the following:
    a. Read a student record.
    b. Calculate the average score for this student.
    c. Display student's number, name, gender, and average score.

The program in Figure 12.1 implements this algorithm. The procedure **ReadRecord** uses statements like those given earlier to read a value for the record variable **Student**. The function **Mean** of Section 9.2 is used to calculate the average test scores.

FIGURE 12.1 Processing student records—version 1.

```
PROGRAM StudentAverages1( input, StudentInfoFile, output );
{*******************************************************************

    Input (file):      Student records.
    Purpose:           Read student records, each of which includes
                       a student's number, name, gender, 5 test
                       scores; calculate the average of the test
                       scores; and display this average together with
                       other student information.  The student records
                       are read from the text file StudentInfoFile.
    Output (screen):   Student's number, name, gender, and test average.

*******************************************************************}
CONST
    StuInfoFileName = 'FIL12-1.DAT';   {actual name of file}
    NumScores = 5;                     {number of test scores}
    MaxScore = 100;                    {maximum test score}
```

FIGURE 12.1 Processing student records—version 1. (cont.)

```
TYPE
   ListOfScores = ARRAY[1..NumScores] OF 0..MaxScore;
   ClassRecord = RECORD
                      Snumb : integer;        {student's number,}
                      Name : string[20];      {name,}
                      Gender : char;          {gender, and}
                      TestScore : ListOfScores {list of test scores}
                  END;

VAR
   StudentInfoFile : text;  {file containing student records}
   Student : ClassRecord;   {record for current student}
   AveScore : real;         {average test score}

PROCEDURE ReadRecord( VAR StudentInfoFile : text;
                                           {file of student records}
                      VAR Student : ClassRecord );
                                           {one student's record}
{-------------------------------------------------------------------------

   Accepts:       File variable StudentInfoFile.
   Input (file): A student's record.
   Purpose:       Read a student's record Student from the text file
                  StudentInfoFile.
   Returns:       The record Student.

-------------------------------------------------------------------------}

   VAR
      i : integer;       {index}

   BEGIN
      readln( StudentInfoFile, Student.Snumb );
      readln( StudentInfoFile, Student.Name );
      readln( StudentInfoFile, Student.Gender );
      FOR i := 1 TO NumScores DO
         read( StudentInfoFile, Student.TestScore[i] );
      readln( StudentInfoFile )
   END {ReadRecord};

FUNCTION Mean( VAR Item : ListOfScores; NumItems : integer ) : real;
{-------------------------------------------------------------------------

   Accepts:   An array Item of numeric scores and integer NumItems.
   Purpose:   Find the mean of a list of NumItems numbers stored in
              the array Item.
   Returns:   The mean of the list.

-------------------------------------------------------------------------}
```

FIGURE 12.1 Processing student records—version 1. (cont.)

```
    VAR
        i,                  {index}
        Sum : integer;   {sum of the numbers}

    BEGIN
        IF NumItems = 0 THEN
            BEGIN
                writeln( 'No elements -- returning mean of 0' );
                Mean := 0
            END {IF}
        ELSE
            BEGIN
                Sum := 0;
                FOR i := 1 TO NumItems DO
                    Sum := Sum + Item[i];
                Mean := Sum / NumItems
            END {ELSE}
    END {Mean};

BEGIN {*************** main program ***************}
    assign( StudentInfoFile, StuInfoFileName );
    reset( StudentInfoFile );

    {Print headings}

    writeln( 'Student                          Test' );
    writeln( 'Number          Name      Gender  Average' );
    writeln( '======          ====      ======  =======' );

    WHILE NOT eof( StudentInfoFile ) DO
        BEGIN
            ReadRecord( StudentInfoFile, Student );
            AveScore := Mean( Student.TestScore, NumScores );
            writeln( Student.Snumb:5, Student.Name:17, Student.Gender:6,
                     AveScore:10:1 )
        END {WHILE}
END {main program}.
```

Listing of FIL12-1.DAT:

```
12345
John Doe
M
44 55 78 83 72
15651
Mary Smith
F
94 85 62 66 83
22001
Pete Vandervan
M
34 44 29 51 47
```

FIGURE 12.1   Processing student records—version 1. (cont.)

Sample run:

```
Student                         Test
Number          Name      Gender  Average
======          ====      ======  =======
12345         John Doe      M       66.4
15651        Mary Smith     F       78.0
22001      Pete Vandervan   M       41.0
```

Record Assignment

Sometimes it is necessary to copy the fields of one record into another record. This can be done with a series of assignment statements that copy the individual fields of one record to the fields of the other record; but if the records have the same type, it can be done more conveniently with a single assignment statement of the form

```
record-variable-1 := record-variable-2
```

The two record variables must have the same type, which means that they must be declared using the same or equivalent type identifiers (see Section 9.2).

Records as Parameters

Recall that the value of a function may not be a structured type; in particular, it may not be a record. Records may, however, be used as parameters of functions and procedures, and in this case, the corresponding actual and formal record parameters must have the same type.

Example: Equations of Lines

To illustrate the use of records as parameters for subprograms, consider the problem of finding the length of the segment joining two points in the plane and finding the equation of the line that passes through these points. The length of the segment joining point P_1 with coordinates (x_1, y_1) and point P_2 with coordinates (x_2, y_2) is given by

$$\sqrt{(x_2 - x_1)^2 + (y_2 - y_1)^2}$$

The **slope-intercept** form of the equation of the line through the points P_1 and P_2 is

$$y = mx + b$$

where m is the **slope** of the line and is calculated by

$$m = \frac{y_2 - y_1}{x_2 - x_1}$$

(provided that $x_1 \neq x_2$); and b is the **y-intercept** of the line; that is, $(0, b)$ is the point where the line crosses the y axis. Using the slope m, we can calculate b as

$$b = y_1 - mx_1$$

In case $x_1 = x_2$, there is no y-intercept and the slope is not defined; the line through P_1 and P_2 is the vertical line having the equation

$$x = x_1$$

The program in Figure 12.2 uses the function **Length** to calculate the length of the segment joining points P_1 and P_2, and calls the procedure **FindLine** to find the equation of the line passing through P_1 and P_2. Points are represented as records having two fields named **x** and **y** of real type, which represent the x and y coordinates, respectively:

```
Point = RECORD
          x, y : real  {x and y coordinates}
        END;
```

 FIGURE 12.2   Equations of lines.

```
PROGRAM PointsAndLines( input, output );
{***********************************************************************

   Input (keyboard): Coordinates of points.
   Purpose:          Read two points P1 and P2 represented as records,
                     calculate the length of the line segment joining
                     P1 and P2, and find the slope-intercept equation
                     of the line determined by P1 and P2.
   Output (screen):  User prompts, labels, length of line segment
                     joining two points, and slope-intercept of equation
                     of line through the points.


***********************************************************************}

TYPE
   Point = RECORD
             x, y : real  {x and y coordinates}
           END;

VAR
   P1, P2 : Point;   {2 points being processed}
   Response : char;  {user response}

FUNCTION Length( P1, P2 : Point ) : real;
{---------------------------------------------------------------------

   Accepts:   Records P1 and P2 of type Point.
   Purpose:   Calculate the length of the line segment joining the two
              points P1 and P2.
   Returns:   Length of segment joining P1 and P2.


---------------------------------------------------------------------}
```

FIGURE 12.2   Equations of lines. (cont.)

```
    BEGIN
        Length := sqrt( sqr( P2.x - P1.x ) + sqr( P2.y - P1.y ) )
    END {Length};

PROCEDURE FindLine( P1, P2 : Point );
{-------------------------------------------------------------------------

   Accepts:            Records P1 and P2 of type Point.
   Purpose:            Find the slope-intercept equation  y = mx + b of
                       the line passing though points P1 and P2.
   Output (screen): Length of segment joining P1 and P2.


-------------------------------------------------------------------------}

   VAR
      m,          {slope of line}
      b : real;   {y intercept of line}

   BEGIN
      IF P1.x = P2.x THEN
         writeln( 'Line is vertical line  x = ', P1.x:4:2 )
      ELSE
         BEGIN
            m := (P2.y - P1.y) / (P2.x - P1.x);
            b := P1.y - m * P1.x;
            writeln( 'Equation of line is y = ', m:4:2, 'x + ', b:4:2 )
         END {ELSE}
   END {FindLine};

BEGIN {*************** main program ***************}
   REPEAT
      write( 'Enter coordinates of points P1 and P2:  ' );
      readln( P1.x, P1.y, P2.x, P2.y);
      writeln( 'For points (', P1.x:4:2, ',', P1.y:4:2, ') and (',
               P2.x:4:2, ',', P2.y:4:2, '):' );
      writeln( 'Length of segment joining P1 & P2 is ',
               Length( P1,P2 ):4:2 );
      FindLine( P1, P2 );
      writeln;
      write( 'More (Y or N)?  ' );
      readln( Response )
   UNTIL Response <> 'Y'
END {main program}.
```

Sample run:

```
Enter coordinates of points P1 and P2:  0 0  1 1
For points (0.00,0.00) and (1.00,1.00):
Length of segment joining P1 & P2 is 1.41
Equation of line is y = 1.00x + 0.00
```

FIGURE 12.2   Equations of lines. (cont.)

```
More (Y or N)?  Y
Enter coordinates of points P1 and P2:  1 1   1 5
For points (1.00,1.00) and (1.00,5.00):
Length of segment joining P1 & P2 is 4.00
Line is vertical line  x = 1.00

More (Y or N)?  Y
Enter coordinates of points P1 and P2:  3.1 4.2   -5.3 7.2
For points (3.10,4.20) and (-5.30,7.20):
Length of segment joining P1 & P2 is 8.92
Equation of line is y = -0.36x + 5.31

More (Y or N)?  N
```

12.3   The WITH Statement

Writing out the complete fielded variable for each of a record's fields can be quite cumbersome. For example, consider again the record type **PersonnelRecord** of the preceding section:

```
TYPE
   Date = RECORD
                Month : string[8];
                Day : 1..31;
                Year : 1900..2000
            END;
   PersonnelRecord = RECORD
                         Name : string[20];
                         Birth : Date;
                         Age, Dependents : integer;
                         HourlyRate : real
                     END;

VAR
   CompanyName : string[20];
   Employee : PersonnelRecord;
   StartingDate : Date;
```

To display the values of **StartingDate** and **Employee**, we must display the values of each of their fields:

```
write( 'Date of first employment: ' );
writeln( StartingDate.Month,
        StartingDate.Day:3, ',', StartingDate.Year:5 );
writeln;
writeln( Employee.Name );
writeln( 'Birthday: ', Employee.Birth.Month,
        Employee.Birth.Day:3, ',', Employee.Birth.Year:5,
        ' Age = ', Employee.Age:1 );
```

```
writeln( '# of dependents: ', Employee.Dependents:1 );
writeln( 'Hourly pay rate : $', Employee.HourlyRate:4:2 );
```

To simplify references to the fields in a record, Pascal provides an option that makes it unnecessary to specify the record name each time that a field within that record is referenced. This is accomplished by using a **WITH statement** of the form

```
WITH record-name DO
    statement
```

The record name is automatically combined with each field identifier in the specified statement to form a complete fielded variable. For example, the statement

```
WITH StartingDate DO
    writeln( Month, Day:3, ',', Year:5 );
```

attaches the record name **StartingDate** to the field identifiers **Month**, **Day**, and **Year** to form the fielded variables **StartingDate.Month**, **StartingDate.Day**, and **StartingDate.Year**. It is thus equivalent to the statement

```
writeln( 'StartingDate.Month,
        StartingDate.Day:3, ',', StartingDate.Year:5 );
```

Identifiers in a **WITH** statement that are not field identifiers are not combined with the record name but, rather, are treated in the usual way. Thus, in the statement

```
WITH StartingDate DO
    writeln( Month, Day:3, ',', Year:5, CompanyName:30 );
```

the identifier **CompanyName** is not a field identifier in the record **StartingDate** and hence is not modified by the **WITH** statement. This statement is equivalent, therefore, to

```
writeln( StartingDate.Month, StartingDate.Day:3, ',',
        StartingDate.Year:5, CompanyName:30 );
```

Nested WITHs

WITH statements may also be **nested;** that is, one **WITH** statement may appear within another **WITH** statement. To illustrate, the preceding statements to display the value of the record variable **Employee** could be replaced by the **WITH** statement.

```
WITH Employee DO
    BEGIN
        writeln( Name );
        writeln( 'Birthday: ', Birth.Month, Birth.Day:3, ',',
                Birth.Year:5,  ' Age = ', Age:1 );
        writeln( '# of dependents: ', Dependents:1 );
        writeln( 'Hourly pay rate: $', HourlyRate:4:2 )
    END {WITH};
```

or nested **WITH** statements might be used:

```
WITH Employee DO
   BEGIN
      writeln( Name );
      WITH Birth DO
         writeln( 'Birthday: ', Month, Day:3, ',', Year:5,
                  ' Age = ', Age:1 );
      writeln( '# of dependents: ', Dependents:1 );
      writeln( 'Hourly pay rate: ', HourlyRate:4:2 )
   END {WITH};
```

In this case, the inner **WITH** statement first attaches the record name **Birth** to the field identifiers **Month**, **Day**, and **Year** to form the fielded variables **Birth.Month**, **Birth.Day**, and **Birth.Year**; but it does not attach **Birth** to the identifier **Age**, because **Age** is not a field identifier within the record **Birth**. The outer **WITH** statement then attaches the record name **Employee** to form the fielded variables **Employee.Name**, **Employee.Birth.Month**, **Employee.Birth.Day**, **Employee.Birth.Year**, and **Employee.Age**.

An extended form of the **WITH** statement allows several record names to be listed:

WITH Statement

Form:

WITH *record-name-1*, *record-name-2*, ..., *record-name-n* DO
   statement

where:

  WITH and **DO** are reserved words;

  record-name-1, *record-name-2*, . . . , *record-name-n* are records;

  statement is a Pascal statement.

Purpose:

When a **WITH** statement is encountered, each record name followed by a period is attached as a prefix to each field identifier in the specified statement that names a field within that record, forming a complete fielded variable. The record names are attached in the order *record-name-n*, . . . , *record-name-2*, *record-name-1*. The form is thus equivalent to

WITH *record-name-1* DO
  WITH *record-name-2* DO
     .
     .
     .
       WITH *record-name-n* DO
         statement

For example, the previous nested **WITH** statement could also be written as

```
WITH Employee, Birth DO
   BEGIN
      writeln( Name );
      writeln( 'Birthday: ', Month, Day:3, ',', Year:5,
               ' Age = ', Age:1);
      writeln( '# of dependents: ', Dependents:1 );
      writeln( 'Hourly pay rate: $', HourlyRate:4:2 )
   END {WITH};
```

Example: Processing Student Record—Version 2

The program in Figure 12.1 to read student records and display them together with an average test score can be simplified using **WITH** statements. Figure 12.3 shows the resulting program.

FIGURE 12.3   Processing student records—version 2.

```
PROGRAM StudentAverages2( input, StudentInfoFile, output );
{***********************************************************************

   Input (file):     Student records.
   Purpose:          Read student records, each of which includes
                     a student's number, name, gender, 5 test
                     scores; calculate the average of the test
                     scores; and display this average together with
                     other student information.  The student records
                     are read from the text file StudentInfoFile.
   Output (screen):  Student's number, name, gender, and test average.

***********************************************************************}

CONST
   StuInfoFileName = 'FIL12-3.DAT';   {actual name of file}
   NumScores = 5;                     {number of test scores}
   MaxScore = 100;                    {maximum test score}

TYPE
   ListOfScores = ARRAY[1..NumScores] OF 0..MaxScore;
   ClassRecord = RECORD
                    Snumb : integer;          {student's number,}
                    Name : string[20];        {name,}
                    Gender : char;            {gender, and}
                    TestScore :  ListOfScores {list of test scores}
                 END;
```

FIGURE 12.3   Processing student records—version 2. (cont.)

```
VAR
   StudentInfoFile : text;   {file containing student records}
   Student : ClassRecord;    {record for current student}
   AveScore : real;          {average test score}

PROCEDURE ReadRecord( VAR StudentInfoFile : text;
                                              {file of student records}
                      VAR Student : ClassRecord );
                                              {one student's record}
{-----------------------------------------------------------------------

   Input (file): A student's record.
   Purpose:      Read a student's record Student from the text file
                 StudentInfoFile.
   Returns:      The record Student.


-------------------------------------------------------------------------}

   VAR
      i : integer;      {index}

   BEGIN
      WITH Student DO
         BEGIN
            readln( StudentInfoFile, Snumb );
            readln( StudentInfoFile, Name );
            readln( StudentInfoFile, Gender );
            FOR i := 1 TO NumScores DO
                read( StudentInfoFile, TestScore[i] )
         END {WITH};
      readln( StudentInfoFile )
   END {ReadRecord};

FUNCTION Mean( VAR Item : ListOfScores; NumItems : integer ) : real;
{-----------------------------------------------------------------------

   Accepts:   An array Item of numeric scores and integer NumItems.
   Purpose:   Find the mean of a list of NumItems numbers stored in
              the array Item.
   Returns:   The mean of the list.

-------------------------------------------------------------------------}

   VAR
      i,                {index}
      Sum : integer;    {sum of the numbers}

   BEGIN
      IF NumItems = 0 THEN
         BEGIN
            writeln( 'No elements -- returning mean of 0' );
            Mean := 0
         END {IF}
```

FIGURE 12.3   Processing student records—version 2. (cont.)

```
      ELSE
         BEGIN
            Sum := 0;
            FOR i := 1 TO NumItems DO
               Sum := Sum + Item[i];
            Mean := Sum / NumItems
         END {ELSE}
   END {Mean};

BEGIN {*************** main program ***************}
   assign( StudentInfoFile, StuInfoFileName );
   reset( StudentInfoFile );

   {Print headings}

   writeln( 'Student                           Test' );
   writeln( 'Number         Name      Gender  Average' );
   writeln( '======         ====      ======  =======' );

   WHILE NOT eof( StudentInfoFile ) DO
      BEGIN
         ReadRecord( StudentInfoFile, Student );
         WITH Student DO
            BEGIN
               AveScore := Mean( TestScore, NumScores );
               writeln( Snumb:5, Name:17, Gender:6, AveScore:10:1 )
            END {WITH}
      END {WHILE}
END {main program}.
```

When Not to Use WITH

In some cases it may not be desirable to use **WITH** statements. For example, the statement

```
   readln( P1.x, P1.y, P2.x, P2.y );
```

in the program of Figure 12.2 to read coordinates of points **P1** and **P2** cannot be written as

```
   WITH P1, P2 DO
      readln( x, y, x, y );
```

since this would attach the record variable **P2** to the field identifiers **x** and **y** and is thus equivalent to

```
   readln( P2.x, P2.y, P2.x, P2.y );
```

which reads a value only for the record **P2** (twice). The statement could be written

```
WITH P1 DO
   readln( x, y, P2.x, P2.y );
```

or

```
WITH P1 DO
   read( x, y );
WITH P2 DO
   readln( x, y );
```

but neither of these seems better than the original. Similarly, replacing the statement

```
Length := sqrt( sqr( P2.x - P1.x ) + sqr( P2.y - P1.y ) )
```

with

```
WITH P1, P2 DO
   Length := sqrt( sqr( x - x ) + sqr( y - y ) )
```

is obviously incorrect, since it is equivalent to the statement

```
Length := sqrt( sqr( P2.x - P2.x ) + sqr( P2.y - P2.y ))
```

which would always assign 0 to **Length**.

12.4   Example: Grading on the Curve and Sorting an Array of Records

Consider the problem of assigning letter grades to students by using the grading scheme commonly called "grading on the curve." In this scheme, a letter grade is assigned to a numeric grade according to the following table:

x = Numeric Score	Letter Grade
$x < m - \dfrac{3}{2}\sigma$	F
$m - \dfrac{3}{2}\sigma \leq x < m - \dfrac{1}{2}\sigma$	D
$m - \dfrac{1}{2}\sigma \leq x < m + \dfrac{1}{2}\sigma$	C
$m + \dfrac{1}{2}\sigma \leq x < m + \dfrac{3}{2}\sigma$	B
$m + \dfrac{3}{2}\sigma \leq x$	A

where *m* is the mean numeric score and σ is the standard deviation (see Exercise 11 of Section 9.3).

For each student we have the following information: student number and name and three numeric scores, one for homework, another which is an average test score (computed as in the program of Figure 12.1 or 12.3), and a third for the final examination. The final numeric grade is a weighted average of these scores and is to be calculated by

$$.2 \times (\text{homework score}) + .5 \times (\text{average test score}) + .3 \times (\text{exam score})$$

The output is to be a list of student numbers, final numeric scores, and final letter grades, arranged so that the scores are in descending order.

One alternative for storing this information would be to use seven **parallel arrays,** one of **integer** type to store the student numbers, another of string type to store the names, four arrays of **real** type to store the numeric scores, and an array of **char** type to store the letter grades. However, since the fields of a record may be of different types, it is much more convenient to use a single array whose components are records containing these items of information.

In the program in Figure 12.4, the given information, together with the calculated numeric score and letter grade for each student, is stored in a record having the following structure:

```
StudentRecord = RECORD
                 Number : integer;        {student's number,}
                 Name : StringType;       {name,}
                 Scores : RECORD          {scores on}
                            Homework,        {homework,}
                            TestAve,         {tests, and}
                            Exam : real      {exam,}
                          END;
                 FinalNumScore : real;    {final numeric score,}
                 LetterGrade : char       {& final letter grade}
               END;
```

There is one record for each student, and the array **Student** is used to store these records so that **Student[i]** refers to the record of the *i*th student.

The structure of the program is displayed by the following structure diagram:

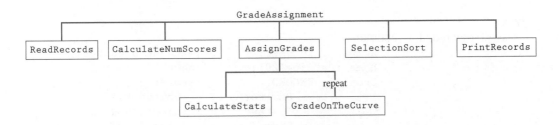

The procedure **ReadRecords** is first called to read each student's number, name, and three scores, storing these in the array **Student**. This array is then passed to the procedure **CalculateNumScores**, which calculates the final numeric score for each student and inserts it in the field **FinalNumScore** of his or her record. The array of records is then passed to the procedure **AssignGrades**, which inserts the final letter grade in the field **LetterGrade** of each record. The procedure **AssignGrades** uses the procedure **CalculateStats** to calculate the mean and standard deviation of the final scores needed by the function **GradeOnTheCurve**, which calculates the final letter grade. Finally, the program calls the procedure **SelectionSort** to arrange the records so that final numeric grades are in descending order and then calls the procedure **PrintRecords** to display the desired information. The procedure **SelectionSort** uses the selection sort algorithm described in Section 9.4, with the modification that entire records are interchanged when necessary.

FIGURE 12.4   Grading on the curve.

```
PROGRAM GradeAssignment( input, ScoresFile, output );
{***********************************************************************

   Input (file):   Student records.
   Purpose:        Read students' records, each of which contains a
                   student's number, name, and three numeric scores,
                   one for homework, another for tests, and a third
                   for the final exam.  Calculate the final numeric
                   grade as a weighted average of these scores using
                   the weighting constants HomeworkWeight, TestWeight,
                   and ExamWeight.  A letter grade is then calculated
                   by "grading on the curve."  A list of student
                   numbers with final numeric and letter grades is
                   then displayed with numeric grades in descending
                   order.  The student information is read from the
                   text file ScoresFile.
   Output (screen): A list of student numbers, final scores, and
                   final letter grades.

   ***********************************************************************}

CONST
   ScoresFileName = 'FIL12-4.DAT';  {actual file name}
   ListLimit = 100;                 {limit on number of records}

TYPE
   StudentRecord = RECORD
                    Number : integer;       {student's number,}
                    Name : string[20];      {name,}
                    Scores : RECORD         {scores on}
                         Homework,          {homework,}
                         TestAve,           {tests, and}
                         Exam : real        {exam,}
                    END;
                    FinalNumScore : real;   {final numeric score,}
                    LetterGrade : char      {& final letter grade}
                END;
   StudentRecordList = ARRAY[1..ListLimit] of StudentRecord;
```

FIGURE 12.4 Grading on the curve. (cont.)

```
VAR
   ScoresFile : text;              {file of student scores}
   Student : StudentRecordList;    {list of student records}
   NumStudents : integer;          {number of students}

PROCEDURE ReadRecords( VAR Student : StudentRecordList;
                                      {array of student records}
                       VAR Count : integer ); {number of records read}
{------------------------------------------------------------------

   Input (file): An array Student of student records.
   Purpose:      Read and count the list Student[1], Student[2], ...
                 Student[Count] of student records from the text file
                 ScoresFile.
   Returns:      The array Student and integer Count.

------------------------------------------------------------------}

   BEGIN
      assign( ScoresFile, ScoresFileName );
      reset( ScoresFile );
      Count := 0;
      WHILE NOT eof( ScoresFile ) DO
         BEGIN
            Count := Count + 1;
            WITH Student[Count], Scores DO
               BEGIN
                  readln( ScoresFile, Number );
                  readln( ScoresFile, Name );
                  readln( ScoresFile, Homework, TestAve, Exam )
               END {WITH}
         END {WHILE}
   END {ReadRecords};

PROCEDURE CalculateNumScores( VAR Student : StudentRecordList;
                                          {array of student records}
                              NumStudents : integer );
                                          {number of records}
{------------------------------------------------------------------

   Accepts:   An array Student of student records and the number
              NumStudents of records.
   Purpose:   Calculate final numeric grade for each student as a
              weighted average and insert it into his/her record.
   Returns:   The modified array Student.

------------------------------------------------------------------}

   CONST                         {weights for:}
      HomeWorkWeight = 0.2;       {homework,}
      TestWeight = 0.5;           {tests, and}
      ExamWeight = 0.3;           {exam}
```

FIGURE 12.4   Grading on the curve. (cont.)

```
    VAR
       i : integer;  {index}

    BEGIN
       FOR i := 1 TO NumStudents DO
          WITH Student[i], Scores DO
             FinalNumScore := HomeWorkWeight * Homework + TestWeight * TestAve
                               + ExamWeight * Exam
    END {CalculateNumScores};

PROCEDURE AssignGrades( VAR Student : StudentRecordList;
                                             {array of student records}
                        NumStudents : integer );
                                             {number of records}
{------------------------------------------------------------------------

   Accepts:   An array Student of student records and the number
              NumStudents of records.
   Purpose:   Insert letter grades in the students' records.
   Returns:   The modified array Student.

------------------------------------------------------------------------}

    VAR
       i : integer;                {index}
       Mean,                       {mean of final numeric scores}
       StandardDeviation : real;   {standard deviation of final scores}

    PROCEDURE CalculateStats( VAR Student : StudentRecordList;
                                                {array of student records}
                              NumStudents : integer;
                                                {number of records}
                              VAR Mean,  StandardDeviation : real );
                                                {mean & std. deviation}
    {-----------------------------------------------------------------

       Accepts:   An array Student of student records and the number
                  NumStudents of records.
       Purpose:   Find the mean and standard deviation of the students'
                  final numeric grades.
       Returns:   The mean and standard deviation.

    ------------------------------------------------------------------}

       VAR
          i : integer;           {index}
          Sum,                   {used to calculate necessary totals}
          Variance : real;       {variance of the scores}
```

FIGURE 12.4 Grading on the curve. (cont.)

```
    BEGIN

        {Find the mean}
        Sum := 0;
        FOR i := 1 TO NumStudents DO
            Sum := Sum + Student[i].FinalNumScore;
        Mean := Sum / NumStudents;

        {Find the variance and standard deviation}
        Sum := 0;
        FOR i := 1 TO NumStudents DO
            Sum := Sum + sqr( Student[i].FinalNumScore - Mean );
        Variance := Sum / NumStudents;
        StandardDeviation := sqrt( Variance )
    END {CalculateStats};

FUNCTION GradeOnTheCurve( Score, Mean, StDev : real ) : char;
{--------------------------------------------------------------------

    Accepts:    A student's Score, the Mean and standard deviation
                StDev of a set of scores.
    Purpose:    Use "grading on the curve" to assign letter grade to
                numeric Score.
    Returns:    A letter grade.

--------------------------------------------------------------------}

    BEGIN
        IF Score < (Mean - 1.5 * StDev) THEN
            GradeOnTheCurve := 'F'
        ELSE IF Score < (Mean - 0.5 * StDev) THEN
            GradeOnTheCurve := 'D'
        ELSE IF Score < (Mean + 0.5 * StDev) THEN
            GradeOnTheCurve := 'C'
        ELSE IF Score < (Mean + 1.5 * StDev) THEN
            GradeOnTheCurve := 'B'
        ELSE
            GradeOnTheCurve := 'A'
    END {GradeOnTheCurve};

BEGIN {AssignGrades}
    CalculateStats( Student, NumStudents, Mean, StandardDeviation );
    FOR i := 1 TO NumStudents DO
        WITH Student[i] DO
            LetterGrade :=
                GradeOnTheCurve( FinalNumScore, Mean, StandardDeviation )
END {AssignGrades};
```

FIGURE 12.4 Grading on the curve. (cont.)

```
PROCEDURE SelectionSort( VAR Student : StudentRecordList;
                                        {array of student records}
                         NumStudents : integer );
                                        {number of records}
{------------------------------------------------------------------------

    Accepts:   An array Student of student records and the number
               NumStudents of records.
    Purpose:   Sort Student[1], ..., Student[NumStudents] using the
               selection sort algorithm so that key fields FinalNumScore
               are in descending order.
    Returns:   The sorted array Student.

 ------------------------------------------------------------------------}

    VAR
       Largest : StudentRecord;    {record with largest key}
       LargePos,                   {position of Largest}
       i, j : integer;             {indices}

    BEGIN
       FOR i := 1 TO NumStudents - 1 DO
          BEGIN

             {find record with largest key in the sublist
                 Student[i], ..., Student[NumStudents]}
             LargePos := i;
             Largest := Student[LargePos];
             FOR j := i + 1 TO NumStudents DO
                IF Student[j].FinalNumScore > Largest.FinalNumScore THEN
                   BEGIN    {larger item found}
                      LargePos := j;
                      Largest := Student[j]
                   END {IF};

             {interchange record with largest key with Student[i]
                 at beginning of sublist}
             Student[LargePos] := Student[i];
             Student[i] := Largest
          END {FOR i}
    END {SelectionSort};

PROCEDURE PrintRecords( VAR Student : StudentRecordList;
                                        {array of student records}
                        NumStudents : integer );
                                        {number of records}
{------------------------------------------------------------------------

    Accepts:        An array Student of student records and the number
                    NumStudents of records.
    Purpose:        Print the final grades for all students.
    Output (screen): List of student numbers, final numeric scores,
                    and final letter grades.

 ------------------------------------------------------------------------}
```

FIGURE 12.4   Grading on the curve. (cont.)

```
    VAR
       i : integer;    {index}

    BEGIN
       writeln( 'Student    Final     Final' );
       writeln( 'Number     Score     Grade' );
       writeln( '======     =====     =====' );
       FOR i := 1 TO NumStudents DO
           WITH Student[i] DO
               writeln( Number:5, FinalNumScore:11:2, LetterGrade:8 )
    END {PrintRecords};

BEGIN {*************** main program ***************}
   ReadRecords( Student, NumStudents );
   CalculateNumScores( Student, NumStudents );
   AssignGrades( Student, NumStudents );
   SelectionSort( Student, NumStudents );
   PrintRecords( Student, NumStudents )
END {main}.
```

Listing of `FIL12-4.DAT`:

```
1234
John Doe
50 53 57
1441
Mary Smith
62 59 65
1531
Fred Jones
72 65 70
1554
Pete Vander
100 100 100
1638
Jane Doe
22 15 19
1734
Al Johnson
62 58 55
```

Sample run:

Student Number	Final Score	Final Grade
======	=====	=====
1554	100.00	A
1531	67.90	C
1441	61.40	C
1734	57.90	C
1234	53.60	C
1638	17.60	F

12.5   PART OF THE PICTURE: Databases

Information Retrieval

As we noted in Section 6.3, one important database operation is retrieving information from a data base. Since the information in a database is a collection of related items of different types, it is most easily processed using records.

To illustrate, suppose that the program in Figure 12.4 has been modified to produce a file of student information consisting of a student's number, name, homework score, average test score, an exam score, a final numeric score, and a final letter grade:

```
1234
John H. Doe
50 53 57 53.6
C
1441
Mary A. Smith
62 59 65 67.9
C
1531
Fred J. Jones
72 65 70 67.9
C
1554
Pete C. Vander
100 100 100 100.0
A
1638
Jane T. Doe
22 15 19 17.6
F
1734
Albert M. Johnson
62 58 55 57.9
F
  .
  .
  .
```

A record of type

```
StudentRecord = RECORD
               Number : integer;      {student's number,}
               Name : string[20];     {name,}
```

```
        Scores : RECORD              {scores on}
                   Homework,         {homework,}
                   TestAve,          {tests, and}
                   Exam : real       {exam,}
                 END;
        FinalNumScore : real;        {final numeric score,}
        LetterGrade : char           {& final letter grade}
      END;
```

can be used to store this information.

The basic operation in retrieving information is searching the database to determine where the information is stored. Each search is based on some **key field** in the file's records, which are examined to locate a record that contains this key. A linear search is generally too slow, and so a faster search technique like binary search is often used.

The program in Figure 12.5 reads records of type **StudentRecord** from the text file **StudentInfoFile**, using the procedure **ReadAndStoreRecords**, and stores them in the array **Student**. Since the records in **StudentInfoFile** are arranged so that the student numbers are in ascending order, the array **Student** also is ordered by student number. Thus, if the field **Number** is used for the key field, a binary search can be used to locate the record for a given student. If this record is found, the procedure **PrintARecord** is then called to display the information in this record.

 FIGURE 12.5   Information retrieval.

```
PROGRAM InformationRetrieval( input, StudentInfoFile, output );
{**********************************************************************

    Input (file):      Student records.
    Input (keyboard):  Student numbers.
    Purpose:           Copy the information in the file StudentInfoFile
                       into an array of records and then search this array
                       to retrieve information about a given student.
                       The file and thus the array also are assumed to be
                       sorted so student numbers are in order; a binary
                       search is then used to retrieve a student's record.
    Output (screen):   User prompts; information from student records.


************************************************************************}

CONST
   StuInfoFileName = 'FIL12-5.DAT';   {actual file name}
   ListLimit = 100;                   {limit on number of records}
```

FIGURE 12.5   Information retrieval. (cont.)

```
TYPE
   StudentRecord = RECORD
                       Number : integer;        {student's number,}
                       Name : string[20];       {name,}
                       Scores : RECORD          {scores on}
                                   Homework,        {homework,}
                                   TestAve,         {tests, and}
                                   Exam : real      {exam,}
                                END;
                       FinalNumScore : real;    {final numeric score,}
                       LetterGrade : char       {& final letter grade}
                    END;
   ArrayOfRecords = ARRAY[1..ListLimit] of StudentRecord;

VAR
   StudentInfoFile: text;       {file of student records}
   Student : ArrayOfRecords;    {array of student records}
   NumStudents,                 {number of students}
   Location,                    {location of specified record in the array}
   NumSought : integer;         {number of student to be searched for}
   Found : boolean;             {indicates if record is found}

PROCEDURE ReadAndStoreRecords
              ( VAR StudentInfoFile : text;   {file of student records}
                VAR Student: ArrayOfRecords;  {array of student records}
                VAR Count : integer );        {number of student records}
{-----------------------------------------------------------------------

   Accepts:      File variable StudentInfoFile.
   Input (file): An array Student of student records.
   Purpose:      Read and count the list Student[1], Student[2], ...
                 Student[Count] of student records from the text file
                 StudentInfoFile.
   Returns:      The array Student and integer Count.
------------------------------------------------------------------------}

   BEGIN
      assign( StudentInfoFile, StuInfoFileName );
      reset( StudentInfoFile );
      Count := 0;
      WHILE NOT eof( StudentInfoFile ) DO
         BEGIN
            Count := Count + 1;
            WITH Student[Count], Scores DO
               BEGIN
                  readln( StudentInfoFile, Number );
                  readln( StudentInfoFile, Name );
                  readln( StudentInfoFile, Homework, TestAve,
                          Exam, FinalNumScore );
                  readln( StudentInfoFile, LetterGrade )
               END {WITH}
         END {WHILE}
   END {ReadAndStoreRecords};
```

FIGURE 12.5   Information retrieval. (cont.)

```
PROCEDURE BinarySearch
        ( VAR Student : ArrayOfRecords;   {array of student records}
              n : integer;                {number of records}
              NumSought : integer;        {number to be searched for}
          VAR Loc : integer;              {location of record}
          VAR Found : boolean );          {indicates if search successful}
{------------------------------------------------------------------

   Accepts:  Array Student of student records, number n of records,
             and student number NumSought to be searched for.
   Purpose:  Binary search the array Student for the record containing
             a specified student number.
   Returns:  True is returned for Found if the search is successful
             and Loc is then the location of this record; else Found
             is set to false.

-------------------------------------------------------------------}

   VAR
       First, Last : integer;   {first and last positions of
                                 the sublist being searched}
   BEGIN
      Found := false;
      First := 1;
      Last := n;
      WHILE (First <= Last) AND NOT Found DO
          BEGIN
             Loc := (First + Last) DIV 2;
             WITH Student[Loc] DO
                IF NumSought < Number THEN
                   Last := Loc - 1
                ELSE IF NumSought > Number THEN
                   First := Loc + 1
                ELSE
                   Found := true
          END {WHILE}
   END {BinarySearch};

PROCEDURE PrintARecord( Student : StudentRecord ); {student record}
{------------------------------------------------------------------

   Accepts:         A Student record.
   Purpose:         Display the record.
   Output (screen): Values stored in the record Student.

-------------------------------------------------------------------}
```

FIGURE 12.5   Information retrieval. (cont.)

```
    BEGIN
        WITH Student, Scores DO
            BEGIN
                writeln( 'Student ', Number:5, ' ', Name );
                writeln( 'Homework  Test    Exam    Final  Letter' );
                writeln( ' Score      Score   Score   Score   Grade' );
                writeln( Homework:6:1, TestAve:9:1, Exam:7:1,
                         FinalNumScore:7:1, LetterGrade:5 );
                writeln( '======================================' )
            END {WITH}
    END {PrintARecord};

BEGIN {************** main program **************}
    ReadAndStoreRecords( StudentInfoFile, Student, NumStudents );
    write( 'Enter student number (0 to stop): ' );
    readln( NumSought );
    WHILE NumSought <> 0 DO
        BEGIN
            BinarySearch( Student, NumStudents, NumSought, Location, Found );
            IF Found THEN
                PrintARecord( Student[Location] )
            ELSE
                writeln( 'Student''s record not found' );
            writeln;
            write( 'Enter student number (0 to stop): ' );
            readln( NumSought )
        END {WHILE}
END {main program}.
```

Listing of FIL12-5.DAT:

```
1234
John H. Doe
50 53 57 53.6
C
1441
Mary A. Smith
62 59 65 67.9
C
1531
Fred J. Jones
72 65 70 67.9
C
1554
Pete C. Vander
100 100 100 100.0
A
1638
```

FIGURE 12.5 Information retrieval. (cont.)

```
Jane T. Doe
22 15 19 17.6
F
1734
Albert M. Johnson
62 58 55 57.9
F
```

Sample run:

```
Enter student number (0 to stop): 1234
Student   1234 John H. Doe
Homework  Test    Exam    Final  Letter
  Score      Score  Score   Score  Grade
  50.0       53.0   57.0    53.6     C
========================================

Enter student number (0 to stop): 1554
Student   1554 Pete C. Vander
Homework  Test    Exam    Final  Letter
  Score      Score  Score   Score  Grade
 100.0      100.0  100.0   100.0     A
========================================

Enter student number (0 to stop): 1638
Student   1638 Jane T. Doe
Homework  Test    Exam    Final  Letter
  Score      Score  Score   Score  Grade
  22.0       15.0   19.0    17.6     F
========================================

Enter student number (0 to stop): 0
```

12.6 Variant Records

As we noted in Section 12.1, records may have a **variant part** in addition to a **fixed part.** The number and types of the fields in the fixed part of a record variable do not change during program execution, but those in the variant part may change in number and/or in type. In this section we discuss such **variant records.**

Examples of Variant Records

To illustrate variant records, suppose that payroll information about employees at a certain company is to be processed. For all employees, this information includes the employee's name, age, number of dependents, and an indication of whether the employee is a city resident; in addition, other information is needed to determine an employee's pay. Some employees are factory workers who are paid on an hourly basis and those in certain departments are paid overtime. For these employees, the following record might be used to store this information:

```
FactoryEmployeeRecord = RECORD
                    Name : string[20];
                    Age, Dependents : integer;
                    Resident : boolean;
                    DeptCode : char;
                    HourlyRate : real
                END;
```

Office employees are salaried, and so the records for them might thus have the following structure:

```
OfficeEmployeeRecord = RECORD
                    Name : string[20];
                    Age, Dependents : integer;
                    Resident : boolean;
                    Salary : real
                END;
```

Salespersons receive a base pay plus a commission on their sales; in addition, they receive a mileage allowance. For them, an appropriate record structure might be

```
SalespersonRecord = RECORD
                    Name : string[20];
                    Age, Dependents : integer;
                    Resident : boolean;
                    BasePay, CommissionRate : real;
                    AutoAllowance : integer
                END;
```

All of these record structures can be incorporated into a single record by using a record with a variant part:

```
EmployeeRecord = RECORD
                    Name : string[20];
                    Age, Dependents : integer;
                    Resident : boolean;
                    CASE EmpCode : char OF
                        'F' : (DeptCode : char;
                            HourlyRate : real);
                        'O' : (Salary : real);
                        'S' : (BasePay, CommissionRate : real;
                            AutoAllowance : integer)
                END;
```

This record has a fixed part that is the same for all values of type **EmployeeRecord**, and this fixed part consists of the fields **Name**, **Age**, **Dependents**, **Resident**, and an additional field **EmpCode** used to distinguish between the three kinds of employees: factory (**F**), office (**O**), and salepersons (**S**). In addition to these fields, some values have **DeptCode** and **HourlyRate** fields; others have only a **Salary** field; and still others have **BasePay**, **CommissionRate**, and **AutoAllowance** fields. If **EmpCode** has the value **F**, then the fields **DeptCode** and **HourlyRate** are in effect; if **EmpCode** has the value **O**, then the field **Salary** is in effect; and if the value of **EmpCode** is **S**, then the **BasePay**, **CommissionRate**, and **AutoAllowance** fields are in effect.

The field **EmpCode** is called the **tag field** in this record. Its values are used to label the variant fields of the record and determine the structure of a particular value of type **EmployeeRecord**. Thus if the value of **EmpCode** is **F**, which labels the variant for a factory employee, the structure of the record is the same (except for the extra tag field) as one of type **FactoryEmployeeRecord**. If the value of **EmpCode** is **O**, which labels the variant for an office employee, the structure of the record is essentially that of type **OfficeEmployeeRecord**. Finally, if the value of **EmpCode** is **S**, which labels the variant for a salesperson, the structure is basically the same as that of type **SalespersonRecord**. Note that the variant part of a record follows the fixed part and that each variant field list is enclosed in parentheses.

In a variant record, several tag field values may label the same variant field list. For example, suppose that factory employees are classified according to the shift they work and these work shifts are coded as **A**, **B**, and **C**, so that the code for these employees may be any of these letters rather than simply **F**. In this situation the record declaration might be

```
EmployeeRecord = RECORD
                  Name : string[20];
                  Age, Dependents : integer;
                  Resident : boolean;
                  CASE EmpCode : char OF
                     'A','B','C' : (DeptCode : char;
                                    HourlyRate : real);
                           'O' : (Salary : real);
                           'S' : (BasePay,
                                   CommissionRate : real;
                                   AutoAllowance : integer);
             END;
```

It is also permissible for tag field values to label empty variant field lists. To illustrate, suppose that in addition to factory, office, and sales employees, the company maintains records for several other groups of individuals who are not currently on the payroll, for example, student interns and individuals on leave or temporarily laid off. These groups could be coded **I**, **L**, and **U**, and so on, and an empty variant used for them:

```
EmployeeRecord = RECORD
                  Name : string[20];
                  Age, Dependents : integer;
                  Resident : boolean;
```

```
                    CASE EmpCode : char OF
                      'A','B','C' : (DeptCode : char;
                                       HourlyRate : real);
                              'O' : (Salary : real);
                              'S' : (BasePay,
                                       CommissionRate : real;
                                       AutoAllowance : integer);
                      'I','L','U' : ( )
            END;
```

As another example of a variant record, suppose that the following declarations have been made:

```
    TransactionType = ( Deposit, Withdrawal, LoanPayment,
                          Transfer, Void );
    Date = RECORD
              Month, Day, Year : integer
           END;
```

and consider the following definition of a record to store certain items of information related to a banking transaction:

```
    Transaction = RECORD
                     CustomerName : string[20];
                     Number : integer;
                     TransDate : Date;
                     CASE TransType : TransactionType OF
                         Deposit,
                         Withdrawal   : (Amount : real);
                         LoanPayment  : (LoanNumber : integer;
                                          Payment, Interest,
                                          NewBalance : real);
                         Transfer     : (TransferAccount : integer;
                                          AmountOfTransfer : real;
                                          Code : char);
                         Void         : ()
            END;
```

Note that the tag field **TransType** may have any of the five values specified by the enumerated type **TransactionType**. If the value of **TransType** is either **Deposit** or **Withdrawal**, the field in effect is the single real field **Amount**. If the value of **TransType** is **LoanPayment**, then four fields are in effect: one integer field **LoanNumber** and three real fields, **Payment**, **Interest**, and **NewBalance**. For the value **Transfer** of **TransType**, there are three effective fields: **TransferAccount** of integer type, **AmountOfTransfer** of real type, and **Code** of character type (which indicates whether the transfer is to or from **TransferAccount**). Finally, the value of **TransType** may be **Void**, in which case no information is required and thus no field is in effect.

Now suppose that the following variables have been declared:

```
    VAR
       Account : Transaction;
       TransactionCode : char;
```

To read information into the record variable `Account`, one typically first reads values for the fixed field identifiers:

```
WITH Account DO
    BEGIN
        readln( CustomerName );
        readln( Number );
        WITH TransDate DO
            readln( Month, Day, Year )
    END {WITH};
```

Next, a value is read for `TransactionCode` that indicates whether the transaction is a deposit (`D`), withdrawal (`W`), loan payment (`L`), transfer (`T`), or void (`V`). This value can then be used to set the corresponding value of the tag field `TransType`. These codes of type `char`, rather than the actual values of `TransType`, are read, because values of the enumerated type `TransactionType` cannot be read from a text file (including the system file `input`). A `CASE` statement within a `WITH` statement might be used to set the tag field and read the values for items in the corresponding field list:

```
WITH Account DO
    CASE TransactionCode OF
        'D' : BEGIN
                  TransType := Deposit;
                  readln( Amount )
              END;
        'W' : BEGIN
                  TransType := Withdrawal;
                  readln( Amount )
              END;
        'L' : BEGIN
                  TransType := LoanPayment;
                  readln( LoanNumber, Payment )
              END;
        'T' : BEGIN
                  TransType := Transfer;
                  readln( TransferAccount, AmountOfTransfer, Code )
              END;
        'V' : TransType := Void
    END {CASE};
```

As this example illustrates, a record structure may be quite complex, as there may be records nested within records (for example, `TransDate` of record type `Date` nested within `Account` of record type `Transaction`); and although our example does not show it, these nested records may themselves have variant parts.

General Form of Record Declarations

As the following syntax diagrams show, a record may have only a fixed part, like the records in the preceding sections; both a fixed part and a variant part, like those in this section; or only a variant part (see Exercise 12 in this section):

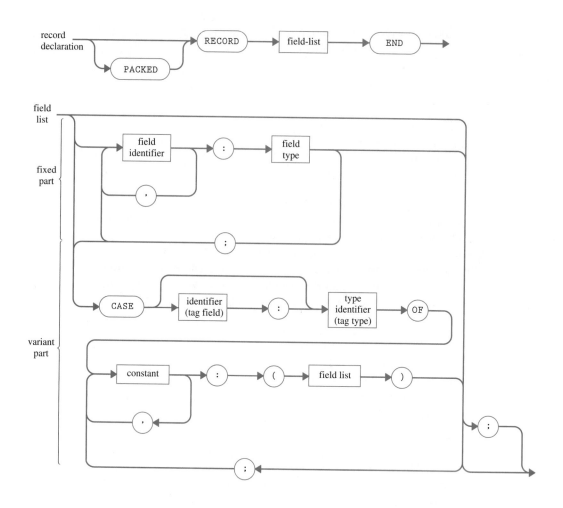

The general form of a record declaration thus is

Record Declaration

Form:

```
RECORD
    fixed-part    (optional)
    variant-part  (optional)
END
```

where:

RECORD and **END** are reserved words;

PACKED may precede the word **RECORD** to declare a packed record;

fixed-part has the form

```
    list-1 : type-1;
    list-2 : type-2;
              .
              .
              .
    list-m : type-m
```
with each **list-i** a single identifier or a list of identifiers,
separated by commas;
variant-part has the form
```
  CASE tag-field : tag-type  OF
      tag-list-1 : (variant-1);
      tag-list-2 : (variant-2);
                 .
                 .
                 .
      tag-list-n : (variant-n)
```
with **tag-field** an identifier and **tag-type** an ordinal type;
each **tag-list-i** is a list of one or more possible values of
tag-field, with no value appearing in more than one list;
each **variant-i** has the same form as a record declaration
except that parentheses are used to delimit it rather than
BEGIN and **END**. (The **tag-field** may be omitted.)

Purpose:
Declares a record that may have a fixed part and/or a variant
part. The fields in the fixed part (if present) are named by the
identifiers in the **list-i**, and **type-i** specifies the type of each
of these fields. For a record containing a variant part, if the
value of **tag-field** is in **tag-list-i**, then the identifiers listed
in **variant-i** have the specified types and are used to store values in this variant.

As noted in the preceding specification, the tag field identifier, but not the type
identifier, in a variant part may be omitted. In this case, access to the items in a
variant field list is still possible, but because no tag field identifier is used, the tag
field itself cannot be accessed. Such records might be used when it is possible to
determine by some other means which variant field list is in effect, for example,
when the first fifty records in an array of one hundred records all use the same
variant field list and the remaining fifty records involve some other variant field
list. Omitting the tag field identifier, however, can easily lead to subtle errors and
should normally be avoided (see Potential Problem 8 at the end of this chapter).

Example: Processing Employee Records

At the beginning of this section we considered processing a file containing information about employees: the employee's name, age, number of dependents, and a

resident-status indicator. In addition, some employees work in the factory and are paid on an hourly basis; others are salaried office employees; and still others are salespersons who receive a fixed base pay plus a certain commission on their sales and an auto allowance. We saw that the following variant record can be used to store this information:

```
RECORD
    Name : string[20];
    Age, Dependents : integer;
    CASE EmpCode : char OF
        'F' : (DeptCode : char;
                HourlyRate : real);
        'O' : (Salary : real);
        'S' : (BasePay, CommissionRate : real;
                AutoAllowance : integer)
END;
```

To illustrate how such variant records are processed, suppose that a payroll program is to be developed that will calculate the biweekly pay for each employee. Factory employees are paid at the hourly rate established for them, with time and a half for overtime pay for employees in departments A and B, but not for those in department C; office employees receive one-twenty-sixth of their salary; and sales personnel receive one-twenty-sixth of their base pay plus a commission on their sales for the past two weeks and a biweekly mileage allowance. From each employee's gross pay, taxes must be withheld, which for simplicity we will assume are determined as follows:

Federal withholding: 20 percent of gross pay less $10.00 for each dependent, or 0 if this figure is negative.

State withholding: 4.5 percent of gross pay.

City withholding: No tax is withheld for those 55 and over. For others, 1 percent of gross pay is withheld for residents, 0.5 percent for nonresidents.

The program in Figure 12.6 calculates the biweekly net pay for these employees. The procedure **ReadARecord** reads the information from the employee file, using a **CASE** statement to store the appropriate information in one of the three variants in the record **Employee**. The function **GrossPay** is then used to calculate the gross pay for an employee; it also uses a **CASE** statement to process the various methods of determining pay. The function **TaxWithheld** calculates the total amount of tax to be withheld, and net pay is obtained by subtracting this amount from gross pay.

FIGURE 12.6   Calculating biweekly pay.

```
PROGRAM Payroll( input, EmployeeFile, output );
{***************************************************************

    Input (file):;    Employee records.
    Input (keyboard): Hours worked for factory employees, dollar sales
                      for salespersons.
    Purpose:          Calculate biweekly pay for employees.  Factory
                      employees are paid on an hourly basis; office
                      personnel receive 1/26-th of their salaries; and
                      salespersons receive 1/26-th of their base pay
                      plus a commission on their sales and a mileage
                      allowance.  Federal, state, and city taxes are
                      withheld.  A variant record is used to store the
                      information read from EmployeeFile.
    Output (screen):  User prompts and biweekly pay for each employee.


***************************************************************}

CONST
    EmpFileName = 'FIL12-6.DAT';   {actual name of employee file}

TYPE
    EmployeeRecord = RECORD
                        Name : string[20];
                        Age, Dependents : integer;
                        Resident : boolean;
                        CASE EmpCode : char OF
                            'F' : (DeptCode : char;
                                   HourlyRate : real);
                            'O' : (Salary : real);
                            'S' : (BasePay, CommissionRate : real;
                                   AutoAllowance : integer)
                        END;

VAR
    Employee : EmployeeRecord;     {an employee record}
    EmployeeFile : text;           {file containing employee information}
    GrPay,                         {employee's gross pay}
    NetPay : real;                 {employee's net pay}

PROCEDURE ReadARecord
          ( VAR EmployeeFile : text;          {file of employee records}
            VAR Employee: EmployeeRecord );    {an employee record}
{-------------------------------------------------------------------------

    Accepts:     File variable EmployeeFile.
    Input (file): An employee record.
    Purpose:     Read an employee record from the text file EmployeeFile.
    Returns:     The variant record Employee.


-------------------------------------------------------------------------}
```

FIGURE 12.6   Calculating biweekly pay. (cont.)

```
    VAR
        ResidentCode : char;      {'Y' if a city resident, else 'N'}

    BEGIN
        WITH Employee DO
            BEGIN
                readln( EmployeeFile, Name );
                readln( EmployeeFile, Age, Dependents );
                read( EmployeeFile, ResidentCode, EmpCode );
                Resident := ResidentCode = 'Y';
                CASE EmpCode OF
                    'F' : {factory worker}
                            readln( EmployeeFile, DeptCode, HourlyRate );

                    'O' : {office employee}
                            readln( EmployeeFile, Salary );

                    'S' : {salesperson}
                            readln( EmployeeFile, BasePay,
                                    CommissionRate, AutoAllowance )
                END {CASE}
            END {WITH}
    END {ReadARecord};

FUNCTION GrossPay( Employee : EmployeeRecord ) : real;
{-----------------------------------------------------------------------

    Accepts:            An Employee record.
    Input (keyboard):   Hours worked for factory employee, dollar sales
                        for salesperson.
    Purpose:            Calculate gross pay for an Employee.
    Returns:            Employee's gross pay.
    Output (screen):    User prompts.

-------------------------------------------------------------------------}

    VAR
        Hours,          {hours worked by a factory worker}
        Sales : real;   {dollar sales by a salesperson}

    BEGIN
        WITH Employee DO
            CASE EmpCode OF
                'F' : BEGIN {factory worker}
                        write ('Hours worked by ', Name, '? ' );
                        readln( Hours );
                        IF ((DeptCode = 'A') OR (DeptCode = 'B')) AND
                            (Hours > 80) THEN
                                GrossPay := 80 * HourlyRate +
                                        1.5 * HourlyRate * (Hours - 80)
                        ELSE
                            GrossPay := HourlyRate * Hours
                    END {factory worker};
```

FIGURE 12.6   Calculating biweekly pay. (cont.)

```
          'O' : {office employee}
                GrossPay := Salary / 26;

          'S' : BEGIN {salesperson}
                    write ( 'Sales for ', Name, '? ' );
                    readln( Sales );
                    GrossPay := BasePay / 26 +
                            CommissionRate * Sales + AutoAllowance
                END {salesperson}
         END {CASE}
  END {GrossPay};


FUNCTION TaxWithheld ( Employee : EmployeeRecord; Pay : real ) : real;
{------------------------------------------------------------------------

   Accepts:  An Employee record and employee's gross Pay.
   Purpose:  Calculate total amount of tax (federal, state, and city)
             to be withheld from the Pay for an Employee.
   Returns:  Amount of tax to be withheld.


-------------------------------------------------------------------------}

   CONST
      DepAllowance = 10.00;    {dependency allowance}
      FedRate = 0.20;          {federal tax withholding rate}
      StateRate = 0.045;       {state tax withholding rate}
      ExemptAge = 55;          {minimum age to be exempt from city tax}
      ResCityRate = 0.01;      {city tax withholding rate for residents}
      NonResCityRate = 0.005;  {city tax withholding rate for nonresidents}

   VAR
      Amount : real;           {amount to be withheld}

   BEGIN
      WITH Employee DO
         BEGIN
            Amount := FedRate * Pay - DepAllowance * Dependents;
            IF Amount < 0 THEN
               Amount := 0;
            Amount := Amount + StateRate * Pay;
            IF Age <= ExemptAge THEN
               IF Resident THEN
                  Amount := Amount + ResCityRate * Pay
               ELSE
                  Amount := Amount + NonResCityRate * Pay
         END {WITH};
      TaxWithheld := Amount
   END {TaxWithheld};
```

FIGURE 12.6   Calculating biweekly pay. (cont.)

```
BEGIN {*************** main program ***************}
   assign( EmployeeFile, EmpFileName );
   reset( EmployeeFile );
   WHILE NOT eof( EmployeeFile ) DO
      BEGIN
         ReadARecord( EmployeeFile, Employee );
         GrPay := GrossPay( Employee );
         NetPay := GrPay - TaxWithheld( Employee, GrPay );
         writeln( 'Pay for ', Employee.Name );
         writeln( 'is $', NetPay:5:2 );
         writeln
      END {WHILE}
END {main program}.
```

Listing of FIL12-6.DAT:

```
Alberts, Alan
35 3
YO 35000
Johnson, James
49 1
NFC 11.75
Jones, Fred
58 4
YFA 13.55
Roberts, Mary
22 0
NO 31150
Smith, Samuel
19 0
NFD 8.35
VanderVan, Peter
29 1
YS 15000 0.15 150
```

Sample run:

```
Pay for Alberts, Alan
is $1032.88

Hours worked by Johnson, James      ? 80
Pay for Johnson, James
is $715.00

Hours worked by Jones, Fred      ? 82
Pay for Jones, Fred
is $889.11
```

FIGURE 12.6   Calculating biweekly pay. (cont.)

```
Pay for Roberts, Mary
is $898.56


Hours worked by Smith, Samuel        ? 75
Pay for Smith, Samuel
is $469.69


Sales for VanderVan, Peter      ? 1000
Pay for VanderVan, Peter
is $663.31
```

Exercises

1. Consider the following declarations:

```
TYPE
    ColorType = ( red, yellow, blue, green, white, black );
    ShirtRecord = RECORD
                    NeckSize : 14..18;
                    SleeveLength : 32..36;
                    Color : ColorType
                  END;
    ShirtArray = ARRAY[1..10] OF ShirtRecord;
    TypeOfFabric = 'A'..'G';
    PriceArray = ARRAY[TypeOfFabric] OF real;
    InventoryRecord = RECORD
                        StockNumber : integer;
                        ShirtInfo : ShirtRecord;
                        Price : PriceArray
                      END;

VAR
    Shirt : ShirtRecord;
    ShirtStock : ShirtArray;
    Item : InventoryRecord;
```

Write statements to

(a) Assign the color red to the appropriate field of **Shirt**.
(b) Read a neck size and store it in the appropriate field of **Shirt**.
(c) Display the sleeve length of **Shirt**.
(d) Read a neck size for **ShirtStock[5]**.
(e) Display the neck size, sleeve length, and color of **ShirtStock[3]**.
(f) Read values for the neck sizes and sleeve lengths of each record in the array **ShirtStock**.
(g) Assign 11782 to the stock number in **Item**.
(h) Read a neck size and a sleeve length for the shirt information stored in **Item**.
(i) Display a message indicating whether the color in the shirt information stored in **Item** is red.

(**j**) Assign a price of $19.95 for fabric type **A** in **Item**.

(**k**) Display all of the prices in **Item** for each type of fabric.

2. Suppose that the following type definition is added to those in Exercise 1:

```
OrderRecord = RECORD
                  Quantity : integer;
                  Item : InventoryRecord
              END;
```

and that **Order** is of type **OrderRecord**. Write statements to

(**a**) Read the stock number of the item in **Order**.

(**b**) Display all of the shirt information in **Order** (in the field **Item**).

(**c**) Assign a price of $18.75 for an item in **Order** of fabric type **G**.

(**d**) Display all of the prices in **Order** for each type of fabric (in the field **Item**).

3. Suppose that **Shipment** is an array that records shipments of 20 different items; its type is **ARRAY[1..20] OF InventoryRecord**, where **InventoryRecord** is the record type defined in Exercise 1. Write statements to

(**a**) Display the stock number of the fifth item shipped.

(**b**) Read a list of stock numbers for all 20 items.

(**c**) Display an appropriate message indicating whether the shirts in the first shipment were blue.

(**d**) Read the stock number, neck size, and sleeve length of the tenth shipment.

(**e**) Assign a price of $17.95 for fabric type **C** in the second shipment.

(**f**) Display a table of prices for the various types of fabric in all of the shipments.

4. For each of the following, develop an appropriate record structure for the given information, and then write type declarations for the records:

(**a**) Cards in a deck of playing cards.

(**b**) Time measured in hours, minutes, and seconds.

(**c**) Length measured in yards, feet, and inches.

(**d**) Listings in a telephone directory.

(**e**) Description of an automobile (make, model, style, color, and the like).

(**f**) Description of a book in a library's card catalogue (author, publisher, and the like).

(**g**) Teams in a baseball league (name, won–lost record, and the like).

(**h**) Position of a checker on a board.

5. The data files **StudentFile**, **InventoryFile**, and **UserIdFile** are described in Appendix E. Write appropriate record declarations to describe the information in these files.

6. For each of the following, develop a record structure using variant records for the given information, and then write type declarations for the records:

(a) Information about a person: name, birthday, age, gender, social security number, height, weight, hair color, eye color, marital status, and, if married, name of spouse.

(b) Statistics about a baseball player: name, age, birthdate, position (pitcher, catcher, infielder, outfielder); for a pitcher: won–lost record, earned-run average, number of strikeouts, number of walks; if a starting pitcher, number of complete games; and if a relief pitcher, number of innings pitched and number of saves; for the other positions: batting average; slugging average; bats right, left, or is a switch hitter; fielding percentage; also, for an infielder, the positions he can play; for a catcher, whether he can catch a knuckleball.

(c) Weather statistics: date; city and state, province, or country; time of day; temperature; barometric pressure; weather conditions (clear skies, partly cloudy, cloudy, stormy); if cloudy conditions prevail, cloud level and type of clouds; for partly cloudy, percentage of cloud cover; for stormy conditions, snow depth if it is snowing; amount of rainfall if it is rainy; size of hail if it is hailing.

7. Like the elements of an array, the fields of a record can be stored in consecutive memory locations, and address translation is required to determine the location of a particular field. To illustrate, suppose that integers are stored in one memory word, real values require two words, and strings of characters are packed two characters per word. The declaration of the record variable **Employee** in Section 12.1 instructs the compiler to reserve a block of fourteen consecutive memory words to store such a record. As for arrays, the address of the first word in this block is called the **base address.** If the base address for **Employee** is b, then the field **Employee.Name** is stored in ten consecutive memory words beginning at b; **Employee.Age** is stored in word $b + 10$; **Employee.Dependents** in word $b + 11$; and **Employee.HourlyRate** in words $b + 12$ and $b + 13$.

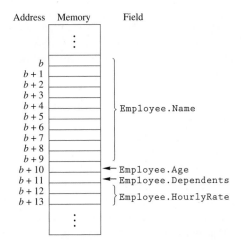

Assuming these storage requirements for integers, reals, and strings, and assuming that values of type **char** require an entire word, give a similar picture showing where each field of the following record types would be stored:

     (a) `Point` in Figure 12.2.
     (b) `StudentRecord` in Figure 12.4.
     (c) `ClassRecord` in Figure 12.3.
     (d) `EmployeeRecord` in Figure 12.6. (See also Potential Problem 10 following this set of exercises.)

8. Extend the program in Figure 12.2 to find

     (a) The midpoint of the line segment joining two points.
     (b) The equation of the perpendicular bisector of this line segment.

9. The **point-slope** equation of a line having slope m and passing through point P with coordinates (x_1, y_1) is

$$y - y_1 = m(x - x_1)$$

     (a) Write a record description for a line, given its slope and a point on the line.
     (b) Write a program that reads the slope of a line and the coordinates of a point on the line and then
       (i) Finds the point-slope equation of the line.
       (ii) Finds the slope-intercept equation of the line.
     (c) Write a program to read the point and slope information for two lines and to determine whether they intersect or are parallel. If they intersect, find the point of intersection and also determine whether they are perpendicular.

10. Write a program that accepts a time of day in military format and finds the corresponding standard representation in hours, minutes, and A.M/P.M. or accepts the time in the usual format and finds the corresponding military representation. For example, the input 0100 should produce 1:00 A.M. as output, and the input 3:45 P.M. should give 1545. Use a record to store the time in the two formats.

11. Write a record declaration for cards in a standard deck having fifty-two cards and two jokers. Then write a program to deal two ten-card hands from such a deck. (See Section 7.4 regarding a random number generator.) Be sure that the same card is not dealt more than once.

12. Write a declaration of a record having only a variant part to store information about four geometric figures: circle, square, rectangle, and triangle. For a circle, the record should store its radius; for a square, the length of a side; for a rectangle, the lengths of two adjacent sides; and for a triangle, the lengths of the three sides. Then write a program that reads one of the letters **C** (circle), **S** (square), **R** (rectangle), **T** (triangle), and the appropriate numeric quantity or quantities for a figure of that type and then calculates its area. For example, the input **R 7.2 3.5** represents a rectangle with length 7.2 and width 3.5; and **T 3 4 6.1** represents a triangle having sides of lengths 3, 4, and 6.1. (For a triangle the area can be found by using **Hero's formula:**

$$\text{area} = \sqrt{s(s - a)(s - b)(s - c)}$$

where a, b, and c are the lengths of the sides and s is one-half of the perimeter.)

13. Write a program to read the records in **InventoryFile** (see Appendix E) and store them in an array of records, read a stock number entered by the user, and then search this array for the item having that stock number. If a match is found, the item name and number currently in stock should be displayed; otherwise, a message indicating that it was not found should be displayed.

14. Write a program to read the records in **StudentFile** (see Appendix E) and store them in an array of records, sort them so that cumulative GPAs are in descending order, and then display the student numbers, names, majors, and GPAs of the records in this sorted array.

15. A **complex number** has the form $a + bi$, where a and b are real numbers and $i^2 = -1$. The four basic arithmetic operations for complex numbers are defined as follows:

addition: $(a + bi) + (c + di) = (a + c) + (b + d)i$

subtraction: $(a + bi) - (c + di) = (a - c) + (b - d)i$

multiplication: $(a + bi) * (c + di) = (ac - bd) + (ad + bc)i$

division: $$\frac{a + bi}{c + di} = \frac{ac + bd}{c^2 + d^2} + \frac{bc - ad}{c^2 + d^2}i$$

provided $c^2 + d^2 \neq 0$.

Write a program to read two complex numbers and a symbol for one of these operations and to perform the indicated operation. Use records to store complex numbers, and use procedures to implement the operations.

16. A rational number is of the form a/b, where a and b are integers with $b \neq 0$. Write a program to do rational number arithmetic, storing each rational number in a record that has a numerator field and a denominator field. The program should read and display all rational numbers in the format a/b, or simply a if the denominator is 1. The following examples illustrate the menu of commands that the user should be allowed to enter:

Input	Output	Comments
3/8 + 1/6	13/24	$a/b + c/d = (ad + bc)/bd$ reduced to lowest terms.
3/8 − 1/6	5/24	$a/b - c/d = (ad - bc)/bd$ reduced to lowest terms.
3/8 * 1/6	1/16	$a/b * c/d = ac/bd$ reduced to lowest terms.
3/8 / 1/6	9/4	$a/b / c/d = ad/bc$ reduced to lowest terms.
3/8 I	8/3	Invert a/b.
8/3 M	2 + 2/3	Write a/b as a mixed fraction.
6/8 R	3/4	Reduce a/b to lowest terms.
6/8 G	2	Greatest common divisor of numerator and denominator.

(continued on p. 644)

Input	Output	Comments
1/6 L 3/8	24	Lowest common denominator of a/b and c/d.
1/6 < 3/8	true	$a/b < c/d$?
1/6 <=3/8	true	$a/b \leq c/d$?
1/6 > 3/8	false	$a/b > c/d$?
1/6 >= 3/8	false	$a/b \geq c/d$?
3/8 = 9/24	true	$a/b = c/d$?
2/3 X + 2 = 4/5	X = −9/5	Solution of linear equation $(a/b)X + c/d = e/f$.

Programming Pointers

Program Design

1. *As with all structured types, record types should be associated with type identifiers in the* **TYPE** *section.*

2. *A record is an appropriate data structure to use for nonhomogeneous data collections, that is, those in which the items of information to be processed are of different types.* For example, in this chapter we considered student information consisting of a student number (**integer**), name (**string[20]**), test scores (**real**), and letter grades (**char**). Using a record to store these data items makes it possible to treat them as a single structure that can be passed to subprograms for processing. This would not be possible if individual simple variables were used to store these items.

Potential Problems

1. *The reserved word* **END** *must be used to mark the end of each record declaration.*

2. *A field in a record is accessed with a field-designated variable, or fielded variable, of the form* **record-name.field-name**. Attempting to use a field name without qualifying it with the name of the record to which it belongs (by attaching the record name to it, perhaps with a **WITH** statement) will result in an **"Unknown identifier"** error message.

3. *The scope of each field identifier is the record in which it appears.* This means that

   ■ *The same identifier may not be used to name two different fields within the same record.*
   ■ *An identifier that names a field within a record may be used for some other purpose outside that record (but see Potential Problem 5).*

4. *Records cannot be read or written as units to or from text files; instead, individual fields must be read or written.* For example, if **InfoRec** is a record of type **InformationRecord** defined by

```
TYPE
   AddressRecord = RECORD
                        StreetAddress : string[20];
                        City, State : string[12];
                        ZipCode : integer
                   END;
   InformationRecord = RECORD
                            Name : string[20];
                            Address : AddressRecord;
                            Age : integer;
                            MaritalStatus : char
                       END;
```

its fields can be displayed as follows:

```
writeln( InfoRec.Name );
writeln( InfoRec.Address.StreetAddress );
writeln( InfoRec.Address.City, ', ', InfoRec.Address.State,
         InfoRec.Address.ZipCode );
writeln( 'Age: ', InfoRec.Age );
writeln( 'Marital Status: ', InfoRec.MaritalStatus );
```

5. *The* **WITH** *statement attaches a given record name(s) to each identifier within the statement that names a field within the specified record(s).* For example, the output statements in Potential Problem 4 could be replaced with

```
WITH InfoRec DO
   BEGIN
      writeln( Name );
      writeln( Address.StreetAddress );
      writeln( Address.City, ', ', Address.State,
               Address.ZipCode );
      writeln( 'Age: ', Age );
      writeln( 'Marital Status: ', MaritalStatus )
   END {WITH};
```

The **WITH** statement attaches a record name to every identifier appearing in the **WITH** statement that names a field within the specified record. Consequently, if one of these identifiers is used for some other purpose outside the record, the **WITH** statement will attach the record name to this identifier so that the field within the record is processed, and not the value of the identifier outside the record.

A **WITH** statement of the form

```
WITH record-name-1, record-name-2 DO
   statement
```

is equivalent to

```
WITH record-name-1 DO
    WITH record-name-2 DO
        statement
```

(and similarly for **WITH** statements with more than two record names). This means that *record-name-2* will first be attached to all identifiers that name fields within it before *record-name-1* is attached. Thus, the preceding **WITH** statement to display the fields in **InfoRec** could also be written as

```
WITH InfoRec, Address DO
    BEGIN
        writeln( Name );
        writeln( StreetAddress );
        writeln( City, ', ', State, ZipCode );
        writeln( 'Age: ', Age );
        writeln( 'Marital Status: ', MaritalStatus )
    END {WITH};
```

One result of this order of attachment is that if an identifier names a field in *record-name-1* and a field in *record-name-2*, then *record-name-2* will be attached to this field identifier.

6. *The value of a record may be copied into another record by using an assignment statement only if the two records have the same type, which means that they must be declared by the same or equivalent type identifiers* (see Section 9.2). Thus, if the type **PersonRecord** is defined by

```
PersonRecord = InformationRecord;
```

where **InformationRecord** is as described in Potential Problem 4, then the record variables **RecA** and **RecB** declared by

```
VAR
    RecA : InformationRecord;
    RecB : PersonRecord;
```

have the same type because **InformationRecord** and **PersonRecord** are equivalent type identifiers.

7. *Records may be used as parameters in functions or procedures, but each actual parameter must have the same type as the corresponding formal parameter. The value of a function may not be a record.*

8. *For variant records, the variant part must be at the end of the record.* It is not permissible, therefore, to have a record declaration of the form

```
RECORD
    fixedfield1 : fixedtype1;
    CASE tag : tagtype OF
        value1 : (varfield1 : vartype1);
        value2 : (varfield2 : vartype2);
    fixedfield2 : fixedtype2
END;
```

Instead, all fixed fields must precede the variant part:

```
RECORD
    fixedfield1 : fixedtype1;
    fixedfield2 : fixedtype2;
    CASE tag : tagtype OF
        value1 : (varfield1 : vartype1);
        value2 : (varfield2 : vartype2)
END;
```

9. *Although the syntax of the variant part of a record declaration resembles that of a* CASE *statement, it is not the same.* In particular, there is no separate END that marks the end of the variant part, only the END at the end of the record declaration.

10. *When variant records are used, sufficient memory is usually allocated to store the variant that requires the most memory, and any other variant of that record is stored using this same portion of memory.* To illustrate, consider declarations of the form

```
TYPE
    EmployeeRecord = RECORD
                        .
                        .    {fixed part of record}
                        .
                        CASE EmpCode : char OF
                            'F' : (DeptCode : char;
                                     HourlyRate : real);
                            'O' : (Salary : real)
                     END;
```

Because the first variant is the larger, sufficient memory is allocated to store it, but the same memory locations are used for the second variant:

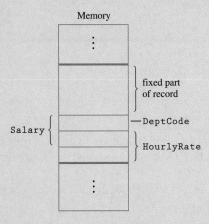

If values such as M and 11.25 are assigned to the fields of the first variant, a subsequent reference to this same record with the second variant is improper.

An error or a "garbage" value for `Salary` may result, because an attempt is made to interpret the internal representation of the character `M` as part of a real value for `Salary`.

11. *The tag field in a variant record must be of ordinal type.*

Program Style

1. *In a record declaration, it is good style to indent and align the field declarations in the record.* In this text we align the reserved words **BEGIN** and **END** that open and close the record declaration and indent the field declarations:

```
RECORD
    field-1 : type-1;
            .
            .
            .
    field-n : type-n
END;
```

2. *In a variant record declaration, it is good style to indent and align the variants within the variant part.* Our style in this text is as follows:

```
RECORD
    fixed-field-1 : fixed-type-1;
                .
                .
                .
    fixed-field-n : fixed-type-n;
    CASE tagfield : tagtype OF
        tag-list-1 : (variant-1);
                .
                .
                .
        tag-list-m : (variant-m)
END;
```

Standard Pascal

As with arrays, there are only a few differences between the way Turbo Pascal and standard Pascal process records. In standard Pascal:

- Records may not be initialized in a constant section.
- In a variant record, each possible value of the tag field must appear in exactly one tag value list.
- The tag field in a variant record may not be passed to a variable formal parameter.

ADTs AND OOP

13

Algorithms + Data Structures = Programs
NIKLAUS WIRTH

CHAPTER CONTENTS

We have learned that solving a problem often involves the manipulation of data and that an important part of the solution is the careful organization of that data. We must identify the relevant data items and the possible relationships between them together with the basic operations to be performed on these items. As we noted in Chapter 10, a collection of data values, together with the basic operations and relations defined on this collection, is called an **abstract data type** (**ADT**) or **data structure.** An **implementation** of an ADT consists of storage structures to store the data items and algorithms for the basic operations and relations. There may be several different implementations, and some may be much better than others. The idea of data abstraction, in which the definition of a data structure is separated from its implementation, is an important concept that is a natural part of a top–down approach to program development. Data abstraction makes it possible to study and use the structure at a logical level without being concerned about the details of its implementation.

The implementation of an ADT generally uses the structured data types provided in the language. For example, in Chapter 10 we saw how arrays are used to implement the string ADT. Several other important data structures are often implemented using arrays and records, and in this chapter we describe two such data structures: stacks and queues. We develop a unit that implements stacks and then use this unit to process expressions written in Reverse Polish Notation (RPN).

The study of ADTs is closely related to the study of **object-oriented programming** (**OOP**), a relatively new method for designing and implementing software systems. The popularity of this new programming paradigm is increasing, and it may become the *modus operandi* in programming and system development. This chapter also includes a brief introduction to OOP, using stacks to illustrate some of its basic concepts and methods.

13.1   Introduction to Stacks

One aspect of the design plan for developing software to solve a problem is choosing data structures to organize the data of the problem. To demonstrate this, we consider four seemingly unrelated problems for which the same data structure may be used to organize the data.

Four Problems

Problem 1.   A program is to be written to simulate a certain card game. One aspect of this simulation is maintaining a discard pile. On any turn, a player may either discard a single card from his hand to the top of this pile or retrieve the top card from this discard pile. What data structure is needed to model this discard pile?

Problem 2.   A program is to be written to model a railroad switching yard. One part of the switching network consists of a main track and a siding onto which cars may be shunted and removed at any time:

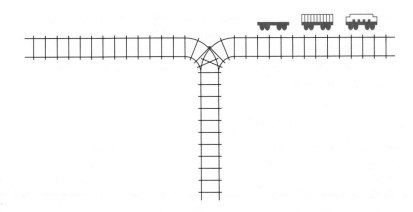

What data structure can be used to model the operation of this siding?

Problem 3. One task that a compiler must perform is scanning an arithmetic expression containing parentheses to determine whether these parentheses balance, that is, whether each left parenthesis has exactly one matching right parenthesis later in the expression. What data structure facilitates this syntax checking?

Problem 4. Data items are stored in computer memory using a binary representation. In particular, positive integers are commonly stored using the base-2 representation described in Section 1.2. This means that the base-10 representation of an integer that appears in a program or in a data file must be converted to a base-2 representation. One algorithm for carrying out this conversion, described in Exercise 13 of Section 1.2, uses repeated division by 2, with the successive remainders giving the binary digits in the base-2 representation from right to left. For example, the base-2 representation of 26 is 11010, as the following computation shows:

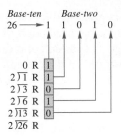

What data structure should be used to keep track of these remainders?

Each of these problems involves a collection of related data items: a deck of cards in Problem 1, a set of railroad cars in Problem 2, a collection of left and right parentheses in Problem 3, and a sequence of remainders in Problem 4. In Problem 1, the basic operations are adding a card to and removing a card from the top of the discard pile. In Problem 2, the basic operations are pushing a car onto the siding or removing the last car previously placed on the siding. To solve Problem 3, we must scan the expression and store each left parenthesis until we encounter a right parenthesis. This right parenthesis matches the last left parenthesis stored, and so this left parenthesis is removed from storage and the scan is continued. From the diagram in Problem 4, we note that the bits comprising the base-2 representation of

26 have been generated in reverse order, from right to left, and that the remainders must therefore be stored in some structure so they can later be displayed in the usual left-to-right order. In each case we need a "last-discarded-first-removed," "last-pushed-onto-first-removed," "last-stored-first-removed," "last-generated-first-displayed" structure.

A LIFO Structure: The Stack

The four preceding problems require a data structure in which items can be stored and retrieved in a **Last-In-First-Out** (**LIFO**) order; that is, the last item stored is the first item to be retrieved. Such a data structure is called a **stack** (or a **push-down stack**) because it functions in the same manner as does a spring-loaded stack of plates or trays used in a cafeteria:

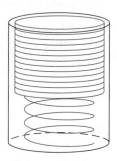

Plates are added to the stack by *pushing* them onto the **top** of the stack. When a plate is removed from the top of the stack, the spring causes the next plate to *pop* up. For this reason, the store and retrieve operations for a stack are commonly called **push** and **pop**, respectively.

To show how a stack can be used in the four preceding problems, we focus on Problem 4. To display the base-2 representation of an integer like 26 in the usual left-to-right sequence, we must "stack up" the remainders generated during the repeated division by 2, as illustrated in the diagram of Problem 4. When the division process terminates, we can retrieve the bits from this stack of remainders in the required "last-in-first-out" order.

Assuming that an ADT for this stack structure is available, we are led to the following algorithm to convert from base 10 to base 2 and display the result:

BASE-CONVERSION ALGORITHM

(* Accepts: Positive integer *Number*.
   Purpose: Convert *Number* from base 10 to base 2.
   Output: The base-2 representation of *Number*. *)

1. Create an empty stack to hold the remainders.
2. While *Number* ≠ 0 do the following:
    a. Calculate the *Remainder* that results when *Number* is divided by 2.
    b. Push *Remainder* onto the stack of remainders.
    c. Replace *Number* by the integer quotient of *Number* divided by 2.

3. While the stack of remainders is not empty do the following:
   a. Remove the *Remainder* from the top of the stack of remainders.
   b. Display *Remainder.*

The following diagram traces this algorithm for the integer 26:

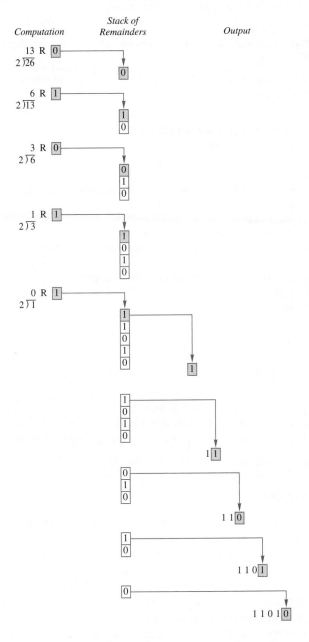

If we assume the availability of procedures **CreateStack**, **Pop**, and **Push** referenced with statements of the form

```
CreateStack( Stack );    {create an empty stack}

Pop( Stack, Item );      {pop Item from Stack, provided
                          the stack is nonempty}

Push( Stack, Item );     {push Item onto Stack }
```

and a boolean function **EmptyStack** referenced by

```
EmptyStack( Stack )      {determine if stack is empty}
```

to implement the basic stack operations, then a program segment to implement the base conversion algorithm is easy to write:

```
CreateStack( StackOfRemainders );
WHILE Number <> 0 DO
   BEGIN
      Remainder := Number MOD 2;
      Push( StackOfRemainders, Remainder );
      Number := Number DIV 2
   END {WHILE};
write( 'Base-two representation:  ' );
WHILE NOT EmptyStack( StackOfRemainders ) DO
   BEGIN
      Pop( StackOfRemainders, Remainder );
      write( Remainder:1 )
   END {WHILE};
writeln;
```

13.2   Implementing Stacks with Arrays and Records

As we noted in Chapter 10, the two steps in implementing an ADT are (1) to select storage structures for the data items and (2) to develop algorithms for the basic operations. We begin therefore by selecting an appropriate storage structure for stacks.

Storage Structure

A stack can be viewed as a special kind of list in which one of the ends is designated as the top of the stack and access to the data items is restricted to this end of the list. Since we have used arrays to process lists, it should also be possible to implement this new data structure using arrays.

In an array, however, each item can be accessed directly, whereas in a stack, only the top item can be accessed. One way to make an array operate as a stack is to designate position 1 in the array as the top of the stack and to adopt the convention that data items will be stored in and retrieved from only this position. For example, in the base-2 conversion problem of the preceding section, if the first three remainders 0, 1, and 0 have already been pushed onto the stack, the stack might be pictured as follows:

```
Stack[1]   0
Stack[2]   1
Stack[3]   0
Stack[4]   ?
            .
            .
            .
Stack[StackLimit]   ?
```

Pushing the next remainder 1 onto the stack, however, requires shifting the elements in array positions 1, 2, and 3 to positions 2, 3, and 4, respectively, so that 1 can be stored in the first position:

```
Stack[1]   0 ~         1
Stack[2]   1 ~    ► 0
Stack[3]   0 ~    ► 1
Stack[4]   ?      ► 0
            .          .
            .          .
            .          .
Stack[StackLimit]   ?       ?
```

Similarly, when an item is popped from the stack, all the array elements must be shifted up by one, so that the top item is in position 1.

This shifting of array elements can easily be avoided. Rather than thinking of a spring-loaded stack of plates, we think of a stack of books on a table. We can add and remove books at the top of this stack without ever moving any of the other books in the stack! For a spring-loaded stack of plates, the top of the stack is fixed, and so the bottom plate (and therefore all of the other plates) move when we add or remove a plate at the top of the stack. For a stack of books, however, only the top moves when we add or remove a book; the bottom of the stack stays fixed (as do all of the other books). To model this view of a stack, we need only "flip the array," fixing position 1 as the bottom of the stack, and let the stack grow toward position **StackLimit**, using a variable **Top** to keep track of the top of the stack, and then push and pop at this location:

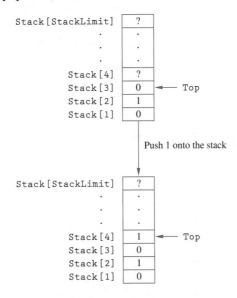

```
Stack[StackLimit]   ?
                     .
                     .
                     .
Stack[4]   ?
Stack[3]   0   ◄— Top
Stack[2]   1
Stack[1]   0
```

Push 1 onto the stack

```
Stack[StackLimit]   ?
                     .
                     .
                     .
Stack[4]   1   ◄— Top
Stack[3]   0
Stack[2]   1
Stack[1]   0
```

A storage structure for a stack in this improved array-based implementation thus has two parts: an array to store the stack elements and a simple variable to store the index of the current top of the stack. It is convenient to combine these two parts into a single structure, namely, a record, and so we are led to declarations of the following form:

```
CONST
    StackLimit = . . .;              {limit on stack size}

TYPE
    StackElementType = . . .;  {type of stack elements}
    StackArray = ARRAY[1..StackLimit] OF StackElementType;
    StackType = RECORD
                    Top : 0..StackLimit;
                    Element : StackArray
                END;
```

Algorithms for the Basic Stack Operations

To complete this implementation of a stack, we must write procedures or functions to perform the basic stack operations:

CreateStack: To create an empty stack.
EmptyStack: To determine whether a stack is empty.
Pop: To retrieve and remove the element at the top of the stack.
Push: To insert a new element at the top of the stack.

The operation of creating an empty stack consists simply of setting **Stack.Top** to 0, and a stack will be empty when the boolean expression **Stack.Top = 0** is true.
An algorithm for the pop operation is

Pop

(∗ Accepts: A *Stack.*
   Purpose: Pop *Item* from the *Stack,* provided the stack is not empty.
   Returns: *Item* and the modified *Stack.*
   Output: ''Stack empty'' message if *Stack* is empty. ∗)

1. Check if the stack is empty.
2. If it is not empty then
    a. Set *Item* equal to the element *Stack.Element*[*Stack.Top*] at the top of the stack.
    b. Decrement *Stack.Top* by 1.
   Otherwise
       Signal that an error (stack empty) has occurred.

And an algorithm for the push operation is

`Push`

(∗ Accepts: A *Stack* and an *Item*.
  Purpose: Push *Item* onto the *Stack,* provided the stack is not full.
  Returns: The modified *Stack.*
  Output: "Stack full" message if *Stack* is full. ∗)

1. Check if the array is full by checking if *Stack.Top* is equal to the array limit.
2. If it is not then
   a. Increment *Stack.Top* by 1.
   b. Set the element *Stack.Element*[*Stack.Top*] equal to *Item.*
   Otherwise
   Signal that an error (stack full) has occurred.

Theoretically, a stack cannot become full; but because an array has a fixed size, a stack-full condition may occur in this implementation. Consequently, it is necessary to determine whether the array is full before performing a push operation.

A Stacks Unit

Since stacks are useful in solving many different problems, it would be convenient to have a stack data type. In some programming languages (such as Modula-2) and in some versions of Pascal, Turbo Pascal in particular, one can, in effect, extend the language to include this ADT by putting the necessary declarations and definitions in a module or unit. As illustrated in Figure 13.1, we can then use this new abstract data type in a program simply by importing these declarations and definitions into the program.

 Unit for the ADT Stack

```
UNIT StackADT;
{************************************************************************

     Purpose:   Define the ADT stack using the array-based implementation
                of stacks.
     Exports:   Constant:    StackLimit
                Types:       StackElementType (supplied by the user),
                             StackArray, StackType
                Function:    EmptyStack
                Procedures:  CreateStack, Pop, Push


 ************************************************************************}
```

Unit for the ADT Stack (cont.)

INTERFACE

```
CONST
   StackLimit  = . . .;  {limit on stack size}

TYPE
   StackElementType  = . . .;   {type of stack elements}
   StackArray  = ARRAY[1..StackLimit] OF StackElementType;
   StackType  = RECORD
                    Top : 0..StackLimit;
                    Element : StackArray
                END;

PROCEDURE CreateStack( VAR Stack : StackType );
{------------------------------------------------------------------------

   Purpose: Create an empty stack.
   Returns: The empty Stack.

------------------------------------------------------------------------}

FUNCTION EmptyStack( Stack : StackType ) : boolean;
{------------------------------------------------------------------------

   Accepts: A Stack.
   Purpose: Check if Stack is empty.
   Returns: True if Stack is empty, false otherwise.

------------------------------------------------------------------------}

PROCEDURE Pop( VAR Stack : StackType; VAR Item : StackElementType );
{------------------------------------------------------------------------

   Accepts:         A Stack.
   Purpose:         Pop Item from the Stack, provided the stack is
                    not empty.
   Returns:         Item and the modified Stack.
   Output (screen): "Stack empty" message if Stack is empty.

------------------------------------------------------------------------}

PROCEDURE Push( VAR Stack : StackType; Item : StackElementType );
{------------------------------------------------------------------------

   Accepts:         A Stack and an Item.
   Purpose:         Push Item onto the Stack, provided the stack is
                    not full.
   Returns:         Item and the modified Stack.
   Output (screen): "Stack full" message if Stack is full.

------------------------------------------------------------------------}
```

Unit for the ADT Stack (cont.)

```
IMPLEMENTATION

   PROCEDURE CreateStack;

      BEGIN
         Stack.Top := 0
      END {CreateStack};

   FUNCTION EmptyStack;

      BEGIN
         EmptyStack := (Stack.Top = 0)
      END {EmptyStack};

   PROCEDURE Pop;

      BEGIN
         IF NOT EmptyStack( Stack ) THEN
            WITH Stack DO
               BEGIN
                  Item := Element[Top];
                  Top := Top - 1
               END {WITH}
         ELSE
            writeln( '*** Attempt to pop from an empty stack ***' )
      END {Pop};

   PROCEDURE Push;

      BEGIN
         IF Stack.Top < StackLimit THEN
            WITH Stack DO
               BEGIN
                  Top := Top + 1;
                  Element[Top] := Item
               END {WITH}
         ELSE
            writeln( '*** Attempt to push onto a full stack ***' )
      END {Push};

END {StackADT}.
```

After this unit has been compiled, the constants, types, procedures, and function defined in its interface part can be imported into and used in any program by simply inserting a **USES** clause at the beginning of the program (immediately after the program heading):

    USES StackADT;

The program in Figure 13.1 illustrates the use of this ADT stack. It solves the base-conversion problem of the preceding section, using the program segment given there and the preceding unit with **StackLimit** set at 50 and **StackElementType** = **integer**.

FIGURE 13.1   Converting from base 10 to base 2—version 1.

```
PROGRAM BaseTenToBaseTwo( input, output );
{***********************************************************

    Input (keyboard): A positive integer in base-ten notation and a
                      user response.
    Purpose:          Calculate the base-two representation of a
                      positive integer.
    Output (screen):  User prompts and base-two representation of
                      input integer.

***********************************************************}

USES StackADT;   {with StackElementType = integer}

VAR
    Number,                          {the number to be converted}
    Remainder : integer;             {remainder when Number is divided by 2}
    StackOfRemainders : StackType;   {stack of remainders}
    Response : char;                 {user response}

BEGIN
    REPEAT
        write( 'Enter positive integer to convert: ' );
        readln( Number );
        CreateStack( StackOfRemainders );
        WHILE Number <> 0 DO
            BEGIN
                Remainder := Number MOD 2;
                Push( StackOfRemainders, Remainder );
                Number := Number DIV 2
            END {WHILE};
        write( 'Base-two representation:  ' );
        WHILE NOT EmptyStack( StackOfRemainders ) DO
            BEGIN
                Pop( StackOfRemainders, Remainder );
                write( Remainder:1 )
            END {WHILE};
        writeln; writeln;
        write( 'More (Y or N)? ' );
        readln( Response )
    UNTIL (Response <> 'Y') AND (Response <> 'y')
END.
```

FIGURE 13.1   Converting from base 10 to base 2—version 1. (cont.)

Sample run:

```
Enter positive integer to convert:   2
Base-two representation:   10

More (Y or N)?   Y
Enter positive integer to convert:   127
Base-two representation:   1111111

More (Y or N)?   Y
Enter positive integer to convert:   128
Base-two representation:   10000000

More (Y or N)?   N
```

Exercises

1. Assume that **S** is of type **StackType** as implemented in this section, **StackElementType** is integer, **StackLimit** is 5, and **I**, **J**, and **K** are integer variables. Give the value of **S.Top** and the contents of **S.Element** after each of the following independent code segments, or indicate why an error occurs:

(a)
```
CreateStack( S );
Push( S, 10 );
Push( S, 22 );
Push( S, 37 );
Pop( S, J );
Pop( S, K );
Push( S, J  + K );
```

(b)
```
CreateStack( S );
Push( S, 10 );
Push( S, 9 );
Push( S, 8 );
WHILE NOT EmptyStack( S ) DO
    Pop( S, K );
```

(c)
```
CreateStack( S );
FOR I := 1 TO 6 DO
    Push( S, 10 * I );
```

(d)
```
Push( S, 1 );
Push( S, 2 );
Pop( S, J );
```

2. Using the ADT stack, write a program that reads a string, one character at a time, and pushes each character onto a stack. Then when the end of the string is reached, pop and display each character on the stack, thus displaying the string in reverse order.

3. Using the ADT stack, write a program that solves Problem 3 of Section 13.1: a program that reads a string, one character at a time, and determines whether the string contains balanced parentheses, that is, whether each left parenthesis (if there are any) has exactly one matching right parenthesis appearing later in the string.

4. Modify the program of Figure 13.1 to convert from base 10 to any of the bases 2, 3, . . . , 16.

5. Proceed as in Exercise 4, but have the program convert from base 10 to base 26; use "digits" 'A' for 1, 'B' for 2, . . . , 'Y' for 25, and 'Z' for 0.

6. Write a procedure **GetTopElement** that returns the top element of its **StackType** parameter but does not delete it from the stack. If **GetTopElement** is called for an empty stack, an error message should be displayed.

   (a) Write **GetTopElement** at the application level. That is, you may use only **Push**, **Pop**, **CreateStack**, and **EmptyStack** to access the top element, if there is one.
   (b) Write **GetTopElement** at the implementation level. That is, you may directly access the storage structure in order to access the top element.

7. Proceed as in Exercise 6, but design a procedure **GetBottomElement** to retrieve the bottom stack element, leaving the stack empty.

8. Proceed as in Exercise 7, but leave the stack contents unchanged.

13.3   PART OF THE PICTURE: Programming Languages

Compilers

The task of a compiler is to generate the machine language instructions required to carry out the instructions of the source program written in a high-level language (see Section 1.2). One part of this task is to generate the machine instructions for evaluating arithmetic expressions like that in the assignment statement

```
X := A * B + C
```

The compiler must generate machine instructions like the following:

1. **LOA A**: Retrieve the value of **A** from the memory location where it is stored, and load it into the accumulator register.
2. **MUL B**: Retrieve the value of **B**, and multiply the value in the accumulator register by it.
3. **ADD C**: Retrieve the value of **C**, and add it to the value in the accumulator register.
4. **STO X**: Store the value in the accumulator register in the memory location associated with **X**.

Arithmetic expressions are ordinarily written using **infix** notation like the preceding, in which the symbol for each binary operation is placed between the operands. In many compilers, the first step in evaluating such infix expressions is to transform them into **postfix** notation in which the operation symbol follows the operands. Machine instructions are then generated to evaluate this postfix expression. Likewise, calculators commonly evaluate arithmetic expressions using postfix notation. The reason for this is that conversion from infix to postfix is straightforward and postfix expressions are generally easier to evaluate mechanically than are infix expressions.

When infix notation is used for arithmetic expressions, parentheses are often needed to indicate the order in which the operations are to be carried out. For example, parentheses are placed in the expression $2 * (3 + 4)$ to indicate that the addition is to be performed before the multiplication. If the parentheses are omitted, giving $2 * 3 + 4$, the standard priority rules dictate that the multiplication is to be performed before the addition.

Reverse Polish Notation

In the early 1950s, the Polish logician Jan Lukasiewicz observed that parentheses are not necessary in postfix notation, also called **Reverse Polish Notation** (**RPN**). For example, the infix expression

$$2 * (3 + 4)$$

can be written in RPN as

$$2\ 3\ 4\ +\ *$$

and

$$(1 + 5) * (8 - (4 - 1))$$

as

$$1\ 5\ +\ 8\ 4\ 1\ -\ -\ *$$

To evaluate such RPN expressions, we scan the expression from left to right until we find an operator. At that point, we combine the last two preceding operands, using this operator. For example, for the RPN expression $1\ 5\ +\ 8\ 4\ 1\ -\ -\ *$, the first operator encountered is +, and its operands are 1 and 5:

$$\underline{1\ 5\ +}\ 8\ 4\ 1\ -\ -\ *$$

Replacing this subexpression with its value 6 yields the reduced RPN expression

$$6\ 8\ 4\ 1\ -\ -\ *$$

Resuming the left-to-right scan, we next encounter the operator - and determine its two operands:

$$6\ 8\ \underline{4\ 1\ -}\ -\ *$$

Applying this operator then yields

6 8 3 - *

The next operator encountered is another -, and its two operands are **8** and **3**:

6 <u>8 3 -</u> *

Evaluating this difference gives

6 5 *

The final operator is *,

<u>6 5 *</u>

and the value 30 is obtained for this expression.

This method of evaluating an RPN expression requires that the operands be stored until an operator is encountered in the left-to-right scan. At this point, the last two operands must be retrieved and combined using this operation. This suggests that a LIFO structure—that is, a stack—should be used to store the operands. Each time an operand is encountered, it is pushed onto the stack. When an operator is encountered, the top two values are popped from the stack, the operator is applied to them, and the result is pushed back onto the stack. The following algorithm summarizes this procedure:

ALGORITHM TO EVALUATE RPN EXPRESSIONS

(* Accepts: An RPN expression.
Purpose: Evaluate the RPN expression.
Returns: A stack whose top element is the value of the RPN expression
(unless an error occurred).
Note: Uses a stack to store operands. *)

1. Initialize an empty stack.
2. Repeat the following until the end of the expression is encountered:
   a. Get the next token (constant, variable, arithmetic operator) in the RPN expression.
   b. If the token is an operand, push it onto the stack. If it is an operator, then do the following:
      (i) Pop the top two values from the stack. (If the stack does not contain two items, an error due to a malformed RPN expression has occurred, and evaluation is terminated.)
      (ii) Apply the operator to these two values.
      (iii) Push the resulting value back onto the stack.
3. When the end of the expression is encountered, its value is on top of the stack (and, in fact, must be the only value in the stack).

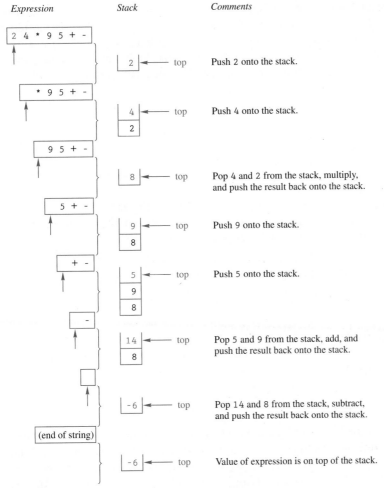

FIGURE 13.2   Evaluation of RPN expression **2 4 * 9 5 + -**.

Figure 13.2 illustrates the application of this algorithm to the RPN expression

$$2 \; 4 \; * \; 9 \; 5 \; + \; -$$

The up arrow (↑) indicates the current token.

A stack is also used in the conversion from infix to RPN. To illustrate, consider the infix expression

$$7 \; + \; 2 \; * \; 3$$

In a left-to-right scan of this expression, **7** is encountered and may be immediately displayed. Next, the operator **+** is encountered, but because its right operand has not yet been displayed, it must be stored and thus is pushed onto a stack of operators:

Output	Stack
7	+

Next, the operand **2** is encountered and displayed. At this point, it must be determined whether **2** is the right operand for the preceding operator **+** or is the left operand for the next operator. We determine this by comparing the operator **+** on the top of the stack with the next operator *****. Since ***** has higher priority than **+**, the preceding operand **2** is the left operand for *****, and so we push ***** onto the stack and search for its right operand:

Output	Stack
7 2	*
	+

The operand **3** is encountered next and displayed. Since the end of the expression has now been reached, the right operand for the operator ***** on the top of the stack has been found, and so ***** can now be popped and displayed:

Output	Stack
7 2 3 *	+

The end of the expression also signals that the right operand for the remaining operator **+** in the stack has been found, and so it too can be popped and displayed, yielding the RPN expression

7 2 3 * +

Parentheses within infix expressions present no real difficulties. A left parenthesis indicates the beginning of a subexpression, and when encountered, it is pushed onto the stack. When a right parenthesis is encountered, operators are popped from the stack until the matching left parenthesis rises to the top. At this point, the subexpression originally enclosed by the parentheses has been converted to RPN, so the parentheses may be discarded and the conversion continues. All of this is contained in the following algorithm:

ALGORITHM TO CONVERT AN INFIX EXPRESSION TO RPN

(* Accepts: An infix expression.
  Purpose: Convert the expression to RPN.
  Output: The RPN expression.
  Note: Uses a stack to store operators. *)

1. Initialize an empty stack of operators.
2. While no error has occurred and the end of the infix expression has not been reached, do the following:

   a. Get the next input *Token* (constant, variable, arithmetic operator, left parenthesis, right parenthesis) in the infix expression.

b. If *Token* is

    (i) A left parenthesis: Push it onto the stack.

    (ii) A right parenthesis: Pop and display stack elements until a left parenthesis is encountered, but do not display it. (It is an error if the stack becomes empty with no left parenthesis found.)

    (iii) An operator: If the stack is empty or *Token* has a higher priority than the top stack element, push *Token* onto the stack.

                          Otherwise, pop and display the top stack element; then repeat the comparison of *Token* with the new top stack item.

                          Note: A left parenthesis in the stack is assumed to have a lower priority than that of operators.

    (iv) An operand: Display it.

3. When the end of the infix expression is reached, pop and display stack items until the stack is empty.

Figure 13.3 illustrates this algorithm for the infix expression

$$7 * 8 - (2 + 3)$$

An up arrow (↑) is used to indicate the current input symbol and the symbol displayed by the algorithm. The program in Example 13.3 of Appendix E implements this algorithm, using the ADT stack described in the preceding section.

Exercises

1. Suppose that A = 7.0, B = 4.0, C = 3.0, and D = −2.0. Evaluate the following RPN expressions:

  (a) A B + C / D *

  (b) A B C + / D *

  (c) A B C D + / *

  (d) A B + C + D +

  (e) A B + C D + +

  (f) A B C + + D +

  (g) A B C D + + +

  (h) A B - C - D -

  (i) A B - C D - -

  (j) A B C - - D -

  (k) A B C D - - -

2. For each of the following RPN expressions trace the algorithm for evaluating RPN expressions by showing the contents of the stack immediately before each of the tokens marked with an arrow is read. Also, give the value of the RPN expression.

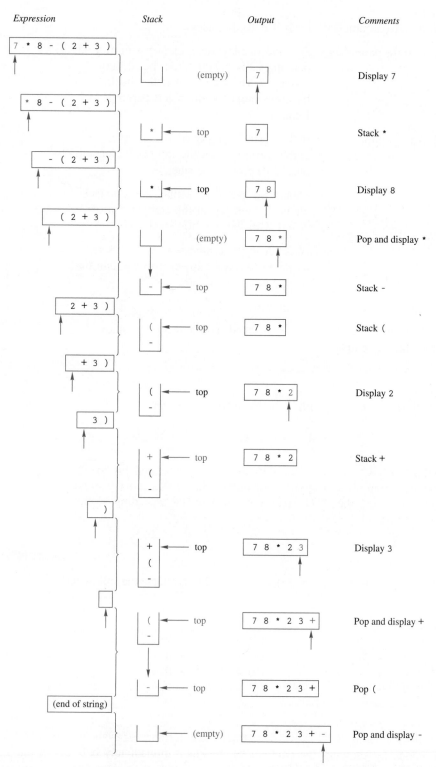

FIGURE 13.3 Converting infix expression **7 * 8 − (2 + 3)** to RPN.

(a) 32 5 3 + / 5 *
          ↑   ↑

(b) 2 17 - 5 / 3 *
            ↑   ↑

(c) 19 7 15 5 - - -
              ↑ ↑ ↑

3. Convert the following infix expressions to RPN:

(a) A * B + C - D
(c) (A + B) / C + D
(e) (A + B) / (C + D)
(g) (((A - B) - C) - D) - E

(b) A + B / C + D
(d) A + B / (C + D)
(f) (A - B) * (C - (D + E))
(h) A - (B - (C - (D - E)))

4. For each of the following infix expressions, trace the algorithm for converting infix to RPN by showing both the stack and the accumulated output immediately before each of the tokens marked with an arrow is read. Also, show the RPN expression.

(a) A + B / C - D
         ↑ ↑ ↑

(b) (A + B) / C - D + E
             ↑   ↑

(c) A + B / (C - D) - E
         ↑   ↑ ↑

(d) A + B / (C - D) * E
          ↑   ↑ ↑

(e) A + B / ((C - D) * E) - F
        ↑   ↑   ↑ ↑

5. Convert the following RPN expressions to infix notation:

(a) A B C + - D *
(c) A B C D + - *
(e) A B / C / D /
(g) A B C / D / /

(b) A B + C D - *
(d) A B + C - D E * /
(f) A B / C D / /
(h) A B C D / / /

6. The symbol - cannot be used for the unary minus operation in postfix notation because ambiguous expressions result. For example, 5 3 - - could be interpreted as either 5 - (-3) = 8 or -(5 - 3) = -2. Suppose instead that ~ is used for unary minus.

(a) Evaluate the following RPN expressions if A = 7, B = 5, and C = 3:

    (i) A ~ B C + -
    (iii) A B C ~ + -
    (v) A B C + - ~

    (ii) A B ~ C + -
    (iv) A B C + ~ -
    (vi) A B C - - ~ ~ ~

(b) Convert the following infix expressions to RPN:

    (i) A * (B + ~C)
    (iii) (~A) * (~B)

    (ii) ~(A + B / (C - D))
    (iv) ~(A - (~B * (C + ~D)))

7. Convert the following boolean expressions to RPN:

(a) A AND B OR C
(b) A AND (B OR NOT C)
(c) NOT(A AND B)

(d) (A OR B) AND (C OR (D AND NOT E))

(e) (A = B) OR (C = D)

(f) ((A < 3) AND (A > 9)) OR NOT(A > 0)

(g) ((B * B - 4 * A * C) >= 0) AND ((A > 0) OR (A < 0))

8. An alternative to postfix notation is **prefix** notation, in which the symbol for each operation precedes the operands. For example, the infix expression 2 * 3 + 4 would be written in prefix notation as + * 2 3 4, and 2 * (3 + 4) would be written as * 2 + 3 4. Convert each of the infix expressions in Exercise 3 to prefix notation.

9. Suppose that A = 7.0, B = 4.0, C = 3.0, and D = −2.0. Evaluate the following prefix expressions (see Exercise 8):

(a) * A / + B C D **(b)** * / + A B C D

(c) - A - B - C D **(d)** - - A B - C D

(e) - A - - B C D **(f)** - - - A B C D

(g) + A B * - C D **(h)** + * A B - C D

10. Convert the following prefix expressions to infix notation (see Exercise 8):

(a) * + A B - C D **(b)** + * A B - C D

(c) - - A B - C D **(d)** - - A - B C D

(e) - - - A B C D **(f)** / + * A B - C D E

(g) / + * A B C - D E **(h)** / + A * B C - D E

(i) + * - A B C D

11. Write a procedure to implement the algorithm for evaluating RPN expressions that involve only one-digit integers and the binary operators +, -, and *.

12. Write a program that reads an RPN expression and determines whether it is well formed, that is, whether each binary operator has two operands and each unary operator ~ has one (see Exercise 6).

13. Write a program that converts an integer expression involving the operators +, -, *, DIV, MOD, and integer constants from infix notation to RPN.

14. For prefix notation as described in Exercise 8, write procedures to

(a) Convert infix expressions into prefix.

(b) Evaluate prefix expressions containing only one-digit integers and the binary operators +, -, and *.

13.4 Queues

Another important data structure is a **queue,** a list in which items may be added only at one end, called the **rear** or **back,** and removed only at the other end, called the **front** or **head.** This **First-In-First-Out** (**FIFO**) structure functions like a waiting line—a line of persons waiting to check out at a supermarket, a line of vehicles at a toll booth, or a queue of planes waiting to take off at an airport. Arriving customers, vehicles, planes, and the like enter the line at the rear and are removed from the line and served when they reach the front of the line.

Examples of Queues in Computer Systems

In addition to lines of people, vehicles, and planes waiting for service, queues are also commonly used to model waiting lines that arise in the operation of computer systems. These queues are formed whenever more than one process requires a particular resource such as a printer or a disk drive or the central processing unit. As processes request a particular resource, they are placed in a queue to wait for service by that resource. For example, several personal computers may be sharing the same printer, and a **spool queue** is used to schedule output requests in a first-come-first-served manner. If a print job is requested and the printer is free, it is immediately assigned to this job. While this output is being printed, other jobs may need the printer, and so they are placed in a spool queue to await their turns. When the output from the current job terminates, the printer is released from that job and is assigned to the first job in the spool queue.

Another important use of queues in computing systems is **input/output buffering.** The transfer of information from an input device or to an output device is relatively slow, and if the processing of a program must be suspended while data is transferred, program execution is slowed dramatically. One common solution to this problem uses sections of main memory known as **buffers** and transfers data between the program and these buffers rather than directly between the program and the input/output device.

In particular, consider a problem in which data being processed by a program is to be read from a disk file. This information is transferred from the disk file to an input buffer in main memory while the central processing unit (CPU) is performing some other task. When data is required by the program, the next value stored in this buffer is retrieved. While this value is being processed, additional data values can be transferred from the disk file to the buffer. Clearly, the buffer must be organized as a first-in-first-out structure, that is, as a queue. A queue-empty condition indicates that the input buffer is empty, and program execution is suspended while the operating system attempts to load more data into the buffer or signals the end of input. Of course, such a buffer has a limited size, and thus a queue-full condition must also be used to signal when the buffer is full and no more data is to be transferred from the disk file to it.

Implementing Queues

Because a queue resembles a stack in many ways, we might imitate the implementation of a stack to construct an implementation of a queue. Thus we might use an array to store the elements of the queue and maintain two variables: **Front** to record the position in the array of the element that can be removed, that is, the first queue element; and **Rear** to record the position in the array at which an element can be added, that is, the position following the last queue element. An element is then removed from the queue by retrieving the array element at position **Front** and then incrementing **Front** by 1. An item is added to the queue by storing it at position **Rear** of the array, provided that **Rear** does not exceed some maximum size **QueueLimit** allowed for the array, and then incrementing **Rear** by 1.

The difficulty with this implementation is that the elements "shift to the right" in the array, so that eventually all the array elements may have to be shifted back to the beginning array positions. For example, consider a queue for which **QueueLimit** = 5 and whose elements are integers. The sequence of operations **AddQ** 70, **AddQ** 80, **AddQ** 50 produces the following configuration:

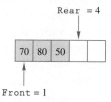

Now suppose that two elements are removed:

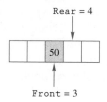

and that 90 and 60 are then added:

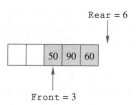

Before another item can be inserted into the queue, the elements in the array must be shifted back to the beginning of the array:

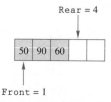

We can avoid this shifting of array elements if we think of the array as **circular,** with the first element following the last. This can be done by indexing the array beginning with 0, and incrementing **Front** and **Rear** using addition modulo **QueueLimit**. For the sequence of operations just considered, this implementation yields the following configurations:

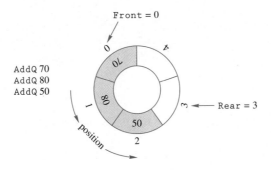

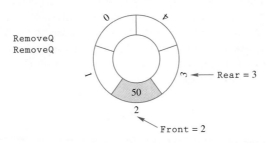

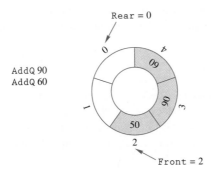

Another insertion is now possible without moving any array elements; we simply store the item in position **Rear** = 0.

Now consider the basic operation **EmptyQ** to determine whether a queue is empty. If the queue contains a single element, it is in position **Front** of the array, and **Rear** is the vacant position following it. If this element is deleted, **Front** is incremented by 1 so that **Front** and **Rear** have the same value. Thus, to determine whether a queue is empty, we need only check the condition **Front** = **Rear**. Initially, **CreateQ** will set both **Front** and **Rear** equal to 0.

Just as the array implementation for a stack introduced the possibility of a stack-full condition, the implementation of a queue raises the possibility of a queue-full condition. To see how this condition can be detected, suppose that the array is almost full, with only one empty location remaining:

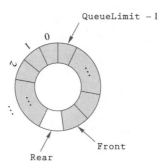

If an item is stored in this location, **Rear** will be incremented by 1 and thus will have the same value as **Front**. However, the condition **Front = Rear** indicates that the queue is empty. Thus, we will not be able to distinguish between an empty queue and a full queue if we use this location to store an element. We can avoid this difficulty if we maintain one empty position in the array; the condition indicating that a queue is full then becomes

> **(Rear + 1) MOD QueueLimit = Front**.

Development of the basic declarations and basic procedures and functions to implement queues using circular arrays as just described is left as an exercise. Declarations for a type **QueueType** are much like those for stacks, and procedures and functions **CreateQ**, **EmptyQ**, **AddQ**, and **RemoveQ** are straightforward.

Exercises

1. Imitating the declarations for stacks given in the text, write constant and type definitions to implement queues using a record having three fields, two of which are integer values providing access to the front and rear of the queue and the third a "circular" array for storing the queue elements.

2. Assuming the declarations in Exercise 1, write

    (a) A procedure **CreateQ** to create an empty queue.
    (b) A function **EmptyQ** to check whether a queue is empty.
    (c) A procedure **AddQ** to add an item at the end of a queue.
    (d) A procedure **RemoveQ** to remove the element at the front of a queue.

3. (a) Complete the following definition of the function **DumpQ** using only the application-level queue operations **CreateQ**, **EmptyQ**, **AddQ**, and **RemoveQ** of Exercise 2.

```
PROCEDURE DumpQ( Q : QueueType );
{  Accepts: A queue Q.
   Purpose: Display the contents of queue Q from
            front to rear, without altering Q.
   Output:  A list of the elements in Q. }
```

(b) Complete the definition of **DumpQ** at the implementation level. That is, you may use information about the storage structure developed in Exercise 1.

4. Write a procedure at **(a)** the application level and **(b)** the implementation level to retrieve the element at the front of a queue, but do not delete it from the queue. (See Exercise 3 for descriptions of application level and implementation level.)

5. Proceed as in Exercise 4, but design procedures to

   (a) Retrieve the element at the rear of a queue, leaving the queue empty.
   (b) Retrieve the element at the rear of a queue, leaving the queue contents unchanged.

6. Write a program that reads a question from a file, displays it, and accepts an answer from the user. If the answer is correct, go on to the next question. If it is not correct, put the question into a queue. When the file of questions is exhausted, the questions that were missed should be displayed again. Keep a count of the correct answers and display the final count. Also, display the correct answer when necessary in the second round of questioning.

7. A **deque** (pronounced "deck") is a double-ended queue, that is, a list into which items may be inserted and from which items may be removed at either end.

   (a) Write a procedure for adding an element to a deque; one of the parameters should specify at which end the item is to be added.
   (b) Write a procedure for removing an element from a deque; one of the parameters should specify from which end the item is to be removed.

13.5   Introduction to OOP (Object-Oriented Programming)

The goals of object-oriented programming (OOP) are to improve programmers' productivity by making it easier to reuse and extend software and to manage its complexity, thereby reducing the cost of developing and maintaining software. As the number and complexity of software systems have continued to increase, it has become clear that development costs can be reduced if portions of existing software can be extended and reused in developing new software systems. This notion of software *extensibility* and *reusability* and the techniques of structured and modular programming are fundamental concepts in object-oriented programming. The popularity of this new programming paradigm is growing, and it is becoming a standard technique in programming and system development.

Three fundamental concepts in object-oriented programming are encapsulation, inheritance, and polymorphism. In object-oriented programming languages, **encapsulation** is provided by **classes.** Each item in a class is called an **object,** and the operations that are defined on it are called **methods,** which play the same role as procedures and functions in non-object-oriented languages. The process of calling one of these methods to modify the data stored in the object is referred to as **sending a message** to the object.

Classes also provide the second important property of object-oriented programming, **inheritance.** A class can be defined to be a **subclass** of another class, and this subclass then inherits the characteristics of the parent class.

Polymorphism (from the Greek, meaning "many forms") is the third important property of object-oriented programming. A **polymorphic method** is one that has the same name for various classes but has different implementations in these classes.

In summary, object-oriented programming focuses on how data types are encapsulated using classes and how these classes can be organized in hierarchies so that their common properties can be reused by subclasses by means of inheritance and shared by means of polymorphism.

Example: Employee Records as Objects

To illustrate the basic aspects of the object-oriented approach, we consider again the example of processing employee information described in Chapter 12. Recall that an employee's name, age, number of dependents, and resident status are stored for all employees and that the function for calculating withholding tax is the same for all employees. Each of the three categories of employees—factory workers, office personnel, and salespersons—is a particular kind of employee, and these three categories may thus be viewed as subclasses of the class **Employee**:

The fields that store an employee's name, age, dependent, and resident status, together with a method **TaxWithheld** for calculating taxes to be withheld are inherited by the subclasses **Factory**, **Office**, and **Sales** from the parent class **Employee**. Each of these subclasses must also contain a method **GrossPay** for calculating an employee's gross pay, but the implementation of this method is different for each subclass, because the way that gross pay is calculated is different for the three kinds of employees. This is therefore an example of polymorphism.

Classes are implemented in Turbo Pascal 5.5 and 6.0 using *object types*. Definitions of object types have a format similar to that of records. For example,

```
Employee = OBJECT
            Name : StringType;
            Age, Dependents : integer;
            Resident : boolean;

            FUNCTION TaxWithheld( GrPay : real );
               {Returns tax to be withheld
                from gross pay GrPay}
        END;
```

is a type definition of the class **Employee**, and

```
Factory = OBJECT (Employee)
            DeptCode : char;
            Hours : real;
            FUNCTION GrossPay;
        END;

Office = OBJECT (Employee)
            Salary : real;
            FUNCTION GrossPay;
        END;

Sales = OBJECT (Employee)
            BasePay,
            CommissionRate,
            AutoAllowance : real;
            FUNCTION GrossPay;
        END;
```

are definitions of the subclasses **Factory**, **Office**, and **Sales**. These type definitions are placed in the interface part of a unit, and the complete definitions of the functions and procedures appear in the implementation part. In the heading of these subprograms, the method name is qualified by the object type name. For example, the definition of method **GrossPay** for subclass **Office** might be

```
FUNCTION Office.GrossPay;

    BEGIN
        GrossPay := Salary / 26
    END {GrossPay};
```

These type definitions can be used in any program to declare a variable to be of one of these object types, for example,

```
VAR
    Emp : Office;
```

The fields and the methods within an object are accessed in much the same manner as for records. For example, to calculate the net pay for **Emp**, we send it a message to calculate its gross pay (using its method **GrossPay**) and then another message to calculate how much tax is to be withheld (using the method **TaxWithheld** inherited from the ancestor class **Employee**):

```
GrPay := Emp.GrossPay;
NetPay := GrPay - Emp.Withholding( GrPay );
```

If we contrast this method of calculating an employee's net pay with that in the Chapter 12, we see a shift from a procedure/function-oriented approach to a data-oriented one: Instead of passing the employee record **Emp** to a procedure or function that performs some operation on it, we send a message to the object (data) **Emp** asking it to perform an operation on itself. Object-oriented programming thus focuses on the data to be processed rather than on the subprograms that do the processing.

Example: Stacks as Objects

As we noted in the introduction to this chapter, the study of abstract data types is tied closely to the study of object-oriented programming. We now illustrate this with an object-oriented approach to the stack ADT. Once again we will see the shift from a procedure/function-oriented approach to a data-oriented one. Instead of passing a stack **S** to a procedure or function that performs some operation on **S**, we send a message to the object (data) **S** asking it to perform an operation on itself. For example, instead of passing **S** to a procedure **Pop** to retrieve the top element of **S**, we send a message to **S** instructing it to pop its top element. Similarly, instead of passing **S** to a procedure **Push** to add a new element to this stack, we send a message to **S** telling it to push an element onto itself.

An object type definition that can be used to implement the class **Stack** is

```
Stack = OBJECT
          Store : StackStorage;     {stores stack elements}
          PROCEDURE Create;
              {Initialize the stack as an empty stack.}
          FUNCTION Empty : boolean;
              {Check if the stack is empty.}
          PROCEDURE Push( Item : StackElementType );
              {Push Item onto the stack.}
          PROCEDURE Pop( VAR Item : StackElementType );
              {Pop Item from the stack.}
        END;
```

Here, **StackStorage** and **StackElementType** are type identifiers (perhaps other object types) that have been previously defined. The field **Store** is the storage structure used to store the stack's elements, and **Create**, **Empty**, **Push**, and **Pop** are the methods that perform the basic stack operations.

As in the preceding example, this object type definition is placed in a type section in the interface part of a unit, and the complete procedures and functions to implement the methods are placed in the implementation part of this unit. For example, the complete definition of procedure **Create** might be

```
PROCEDURE Stack.Create;

   BEGIN
      Store.Top := 0
   END {Create};
```

Complete definitions of the other methods **Empty**, **Push**, and **Pop** are straightforward and are given in the unit **StackClass** that follows.

To complete the definition of the class **Stack**, the type identifiers **StackElementType** and **StackStorage** must be defined and made accessible to **StackStorage**. For simplicity, we have included definitions of **StackLimit**, **StackArray**, and **StackStorage** in this unit. Putting the definition of

StackElementType within StackClass, however, would mean that this unit must be modified each time the type of stack elements is changed. This may not be possible because the user may not have access to the source code for StackClass. Even if the source code is available, it is generally not good practice to modify software that has already been developed and tested. For these reasons, StackClass has been designed so that the user defines StackElementType in a separate unit StackElementInfo, and StackClass imports StackElementType from this unit.

 Unit for the Class Stack.

```
UNIT StackClass;
{*********************************************************************
   Purpose:  Define the class Stack.
   Exports:  The object type Stack whose methods are Create (to
             initialize the stack as an empty stack),  Empty (to check
             if the stack is empty), Push (to push an element onto the
             stack), and Pop (to pop an element from the stack.)


   *****************************************************************}

INTERFACE

   USES StackElementInfo;          {import StackElementType}

   CONST
      StackLimit = . . .;           {limit on stack size}

   TYPE
      StackArray = ARRAY[1..StackLimit] OF StackElementType;
      StackStorage = RECORD
                        Top : 0..StackLimit;
                        Element : StackArray
                     END;
      Stack = OBJECT
                 Store : StackStorage; {stores stack elements}
                 PROCEDURE Create;
                    {Initialize the stack as an empty stack.}
                 FUNCTION Empty : boolean;
                    {Check if the stack is empty.}
                 PROCEDURE Push( Item : StackElementType );
                    {Push Item onto the stack.}
                 PROCEDURE Pop( VAR Item : StackElementType );
                    {Pop Item from the stack.}
              END;

IMPLEMENTATION

   PROCEDURE Stack.Create;

      BEGIN
         Store.Top := 0
      END {Create};
```

Unit for the Class Stack. (cont.)

```
FUNCTION Stack.Empty;

   BEGIN
      Empty := (Store.Top = 0)
   END {Empty};

PROCEDURE Stack.Push;

   BEGIN
      IF Store.Top < StackLimit THEN
         WITH Store DO
            BEGIN
               Top := Top + 1;
               Element[Top] := Item
            END {WITH}
      ELSE
         writeln( '*** Attempt to push onto a full stack ***' )
   END {Push};

PROCEDURE Stack.Pop;

   BEGIN
      IF NOT Stack.Empty THEN
         WITH Store DO
            BEGIN
               Item := Element[Top];
               Top := Top - 1
            END {WITH}
      ELSE
         writeln( '*** Attempt to pop from an empty stack ***' )
   END {Pop};

END {StackClass}.
```

```
UNIT StackElementInfo;

{***************************************************************

   Purpose:  Defines the type StackElementType of stack elements.
   Exports:  Type StackElementType.

***************************************************************}

INTERFACE

   TYPE
      StackElementType = ... ;  {type of stack elements -- set by user}

IMPLEMENTATION

END {ElementInfo}.
```

The program in Figure 13.4 illustrates the declaration and use of objects. It is a modification of the base-conversion program in Figure 13.1. It imports `StackElementType` from the unit `StackElementInfo` in which the user has defined `StackElementType` to be `integer` or `0..1`, for example. It also imports the object type `Stack` from the unit `StackClass` and defines `StackOfRemainders` to be an object of this type. `StackOfRemainders` is initialized by sending it the message

    StackOfRemainders.Create;

As each remainder is generated, it is added to this stack by sending the message

    StackOfRemainders.Push(Remainder);

to `StackOfRemainders` to push this remainder onto its stack. After all of the remainders have been calculated and stored in the stack, the message

    StackOfRemainders.Pop(Remainder)

is sent repeatedly to the object `StackOfRemainders` to pop an element from its stack, which is then displayed, until the message

    StackOfRemainders.Empty

returns a value of true, signaling that the stack is empty.

FIGURE 13.4   Converting from base 10 to base 2—version 2.

```
PROGRAM BaseTenToBaseTwo( input, output );
{*********************************************************************

    Input (keyboard): A positive integer in base-ten notation and a user
                      response.
    Purpose:          Convert the base-ten representation of a positive
                      integer to base two and then display this
                      base-two representation.  It uses an object
                      StackOfRemainders of type Stack to store and
                      process these remainders.
    Output (screen):  Base-two representation of the input integer.
    Imports:          The (user-defined) type StackElementType of stack
                      elements from the unit StackElementInfo and the
                      object type Stack from the unit StackClass.


*********************************************************************}
```

FIGURE 13.4 Converting from base 10 to base 2—version 2. (cont.)

```
USES StackElementInfo, StackClass;

VAR
   Number : LongInt;               {the number to be converted}
   Remainder : StackElementType;   {remainder when Number is divided by 2}
   StackOfRemainders : Stack;      {stack of remainders}
   Response : char;                {user response}

BEGIN
   REPEAT
      write( 'Enter positive integer to convert: ' );
      readln( Number );
      StackOfRemainders.Create;
      WHILE Number <> 0 DO
         BEGIN
            Remainder := Number MOD 2;
            StackOfRemainders.Push( Remainder );
            Number := Number DIV 2
         END {WHILE};
      write( 'Base two representation: ' );
      WHILE NOT StackOfRemainders.Empty DO
         BEGIN
            StackOfRemainders.Pop( Remainder );
            write( Remainder:1 )
         END {WHILE};
      writeln; writeln;
      write( 'More (Y or N)? ' );
      readln( Response )
   UNTIL NOT (Response IN ['Y', 'y'])
END.
```

Sample Run:

```
Enter positive integer to convert:  31
Base two representation:  11111

More (Y or N)?  Y
Enter positive integer to convert:  12345
Base two representation:  11000000111001

More (Y or N)?  N
```

Example: Priority Queues

To demonstrate inheritance, we consider **priority queues** (which also could be called *priority stacks*). These are lists in which the elements are arranged in such a way that those with the highest priority are removed before those of lower priority. We assume that these elements are records, one of whose fields **Priority** stores an integer representing the priority of that element. If we define the class **PriorityQueue** to be a subclass of the class **Stack**, it can inherit the field **Store**

and the methods **Create**, **Empty**, **Push**, and **Pop** from the ancestor class **Stack**.
The method **Push** must be redefined, however, so that an element is inserted below
all those with higher priority. A definition for this subclass is

```
PriorityQueue = OBJECT (Stack)
                    Push( Item : StackElementType )
                        {Add Item to the stack so that it is
                        below all elements of higher
                        priority.}
                END;
```

The following unit **PriorityQueueClass** contains this type definition, together
with the complete procedure **Push**:

 Unit for the Subclass Priority Queue

```
UNIT PriorityQueueClass;
{*********************************************************************

    Imports:  The type StackElementType from the unit StackElementInfo
              and the object type Stack from the unit StackClass.
    Purpose:  Defines the class PriorityQueue as a subclass of the
              class Stack from the unit StackClass.  It inherits the
              fields Store and Error and the methods Create, Empty, and
              Pop; the method Push is overridden.
    Exports:  The object type PriorityQueue.

*********************************************************************}

INTERFACE

    USES StackElementInfo,    {import StackElementType}
         StackClass;          {import ancestor class Stack}

    TYPE
        PriorityQueue = OBJECT (Stack)
                            PROCEDURE Push( Item : StackElementType );
                                {Add Item to the stack so that it is below
                                all elements of equal or higher priority.}
                        END;

IMPLEMENTATION

    PROCEDURE PriorityQueue.Push( Item : StackElementType );

        VAR
            TempStack : Stack;
                        {temporary stack to store higher priority elements}
            TopElement : StackElementType;
                        {top stack element}
            HigherPriority : boolean;
                        {checks priority condition}
```

Unit for the Subclass Priority Queue (cont.)

```
BEGIN
    {Remove elements until one of lower priority is found or
     stack is empty; store these elements in the temporary
     stack TempStack.}
    TempStack.Create;
    HigherPriority := true;
    WHILE NOT Empty AND HigherPriority  DO
        BEGIN
            Pop( TopElement );
            HigherPriority := TopElement.Priority >= Item.Priority;
            IF HigherPriority THEN
                TempStack.Push( TopElement )
            ELSE
                Stack.Push( TopElement );
        END {WHILE};

    {Add the new element to the stack, and then put all
     those from TempStack on top of it.}

    Stack.Push( Item );
    WHILE NOT TempStack.Empty DO
        BEGIN
            TempStack.Pop( TopElement );
            Stack.Push( TopElement )
        END {WHILE}
    END {Push};

END {PriorityQueueClass}.
```

Here again is an example of *polymorphism,* the property of a method's having the same name but different implementations in various classes; both of the classes **Stack** and **PriorityQueue** have a method named **Push**, but its implementations in these classes are different.

In this section we have illustrated the basic elements of object-oriented programming as implemented in Turbo Pascal.[1] It must be emphasized, however, that this has been only a brief introduction to the whole area of OOP and that there is much more that could be said. Nevertheless, the notions of encapsulation, inheritance, and polymorphism introduced in this chapter are fundamental concepts underlying all of object-oriented programming, and this programming paradigm can be used effectively only if these basic ideas are thoroughly understood.

Exercises

1. Name and define the fundamental concepts of object-oriented programming.

---

[1] Turbo Pascal 7.0 has two additional features: a **public** directive and a new reserved word **INHERITED**. See the *Turbo Pascal Language Guide* for a description of these.

2. Another basic operation that is useful for stacks is retrieving the top stack element without removing it from the stack. Describe how to define a subclass **ExtendedStack** of the class **Stack** that adds a new method **Retrieve** to those inherited from **Stack**.

3. Proceed as in Exercise 2 but add a method **Dump** to empty a stack and display its contents.

4. Proceed as in Exercise 3, but add a method **Print** that displays the contents of a stack without emptying it.

5. A *look-ahead stack* differs from a standard stack only in its push method. An element, which is a record, is added to the stack by the push method only if the value in its priority field is greater than the value in the priority field of the top stack element. Describe how to implement the class **LookAheadStack** as a subclass of the class **Stack**.

6. Imitating the object type **Stack** considered in this section, describe how to implement the class **Queue**, which implements a queue ADT.

SETS

No one shall expel us from the paradise which
Cantor has created for us.
DAVID HILBERT

CHAPTER CONTENTS

687

In mathematics and computer science the term **set** denotes an unordered collection of objects called the **elements** or **members** of the set. A set is commonly denoted by listing the elements enclosed in braces, { and }. For example, the set of decimal digits contains the elements 0, 1, 2, 3, 4, 5, 6, 7, 8, and 9 and is denoted {0, 1, 2, 3, 4, 5, 6, 7, 8, 9}. The set of uppercase letters is {A, B, C, . . . , Z}. The set of even prime numbers {2} contains the single element 2; and the set of female U.S. presidents before 1992 is the empty set, denoted ∅ or { }, that is, the set containing no elements.

Sets differ from arrays in that the elements of an array are ordered in a certain sequence, but the elements of a set are unordered. Thus we can speak of the first, second, third, . . . elements of an array, but it does not make sense to refer to the first, second, third, . . . elements of a set. For example, the set whose elements are the even digits 0, 2, 4, 6, and 8 is the same as the set whose elements are 4, 8, 0, 2, and 6 or the set whose elements are 8, 0, 6, 4, and 2. The ordering of array elements makes it possible to access an element directly by specifying its location in the array, but because sets are unordered, no such direct access to the elements of a set is possible.

Sets differ from records in two important ways. Data items stored in a record are directly accessible and may be of different types. In Pascal, however, the elements of a set must be of the same type, and as we have noted, they are not directly accessible.

In this chapter we discuss how sets are implemented in Pascal using the predefined data type **SET** and how they are processed using the operations of set assignment, union, intersection, and difference, the membership relation, and the set relations of subset and equality.

14.1 Set Declarations, Set Values, and Set Assignments

In a problem involving sets, the elements are selected from some given set called the **universal set** for that problem. For example, if the set of vowels or the set whose elements are X, Y, and Z is being considered, the universal set might be the set of all letters. If the universal set is the set of names of months of the year, then one might use the set of summer months: June, July, August; the set of months whose names do not contain the letter r: May, June, July, August; or the set of all months having fewer than 30 days: February.

Set Declarations

In a Pascal program, all of the elements of a set must be of the same type, called the **base type** of the set. This base type must be an ordinal type; thus sets of real numbers, sets of arrays, sets of strings, and sets of records are not allowed. A **set declaration** has the following form:

Set Declaration

Form:

    SET OF *base-type*

where:
    SET and **OF** are reserved words;
    base-type must be an ordinal type.

Purpose:
Specifies that *base-type* is the type of the elements of sets.

For example, if the ordinal types **Digits** and **Months** are defined by

```
TYPE
   Digits = 0..9;
   Months = ( January, February, March, April,
              May, June, July, August,
              September, October, November, December );
```

then

```
SET OF Digits

SET OF Months

SET OF char
```

are valid set declarations.

Turbo Pascal also imposes additional restrictions on sets. The base type must not have more than 256 possible values, and the ordinal numbers of the first and last elements of this base type must be within the range 0 through 255. This limit therefore excludes **integer** as a base type as well as subranges like $[-10..10]$ and $[200..300]$.

To illustrate set declarations, consider the following:

```
TYPE
   Digits = 0..9;
   Months = ( January, February, March, April,
              May, June, July, August,
              September, October, November, December );
   DigitSet = SET OF Digits;
   MonthSet = SET OF Months;
   CapLetterSet = SET OF 'A'..'Z';
   MonthArray = ARRAY[1..4] OF MonthSet;
```

```
VAR
    Dig1, Dig2 : Digits;
    Numbers, Evens, Odds : DigitSet;
    Winter : MonthSet;
    Vowels, Consonants : CapLetterSet;
    Season : MonthArray;
```

The variables **Numbers**, **Evens**, and **Odds** may have as values any sets whose elements are chosen from **0**, **1**, **2**, . . . , **9**; the value of **Winter** may be any set of elements selected from **January**, **February**, . . . , **December**; and the variables **Vowels** and **Consonants** have values that are sets of capital letters. The array **Season** has four components, each of which is a set of months.

Set Values

A **set value** in Pascal has the form

```
[element-list]
```

where *element-list* is a list (possibly empty) of constants, variables, or expressions of the same type, separated by commas, and is enclosed in brackets [and]. Thus, for the base type **Digits**,

```
[0, 2, 4, 6, 8]
```

is a valid set constant that might be the value of **Evens**. This same set constant could also be denoted by

```
[4, 0, 8, 2, 6]
```

or

```
[8, 6, 4, 2, 0]
```

or by using any other arrangement of the elements. If **Dig1** has the value **0** and **Dig2** has the value **4**, then

```
[Dig1, Dig1 + 2, Dig1 + 4, Dig1 + 6, Dig1 + 8]
```

is another representation of this same set value, as is

```
[Dig1, Dig2 DIV 2, Dig2, Dig2 + 2, 2 * Dig2]
```

When some or all of the elements of a set are consecutive values of the base type, it is permissible to use subrange notation to specify them. For example, the set value

```
[0, 1, 2, 3, 4]
```

can also be expressed as

    [0..4]

or

    [Dig1..Dig2]

and the set

    [0, 1, 2, 5, 7, 8, 9]

can be expressed in any of the following ways:

    [0..2, 5, 7..9]

    [0..2, Dig2 + 1, 7..9]

    [Dig1..2, 5, (Dig2 + 3)..(2 * Dig2 + 1)]

Empty Set

The **empty set** is denoted in Pascal by the set constant

    []

and may be assigned to a set variable of any base type. Thus [] could be the value of both **Number** and **Winter**, even though these set variables have different base types.

Set Assignment

To assign a value to a variable of set type, an assignment statement of the form

    set-variable := set

may be used where *set* may be a set value, a set variable, or a set expression (as described in the next section). The base type of *set* must be compatible with the base type of *set-variable*. (Recall that two types are compatible if they are the same type, one is a subrange of the other, or both are subranges of the same type.) Thus, for the base types defined earlier, the statement

    Evens := [0, 2, 4, 6, 8];

is a valid assignment statement and assigns the set constant [0, 2, 4, 6, 8] to the set variable **Evens**. Similarly, the statements

```
Winter := [December, January..March];
Season[1] := [December, January, February];
Consonants := Vowels;
Numbers := [Dig1];
Odds := [];
```

are valid assignment statements. The assignment statement

```
Winter := ['D', 'J', 'F', 'M'];
```

is not valid, however, because the base type of the set constant is not compatible with the base type of **Winter**. Similarly, the assignment statement

```
Season[1] := ['D', 1, February];
```

is not valid because ['D', 1, February] is not a valid set constant (the types of the elements are not the same).

Set Initialization

In Turbo Pascal, a set variable may be initialized as a typed constant by using a declaration of the form

```
CONST
    set-variable : set-type = set-constant;
```

For example,

```
CONST
    Vowels : CapLetterSet = ['A', 'E', 'O', 'I', 'U'];
```

14.2   Set Relations and Operations

The fundamental set relations are the membership (''is an element of'') relation between elements and sets, and the subset, superset and equality relations between sets. The basic set operations are union, intersection, complement, and set difference. In this section we describe how these basic set relations and operations are implemented in Pascal.

The Membership Relation

Because sets are collections of elements, it is important to be able to determine whether a particular element belongs to a given set. This test for set membership is implemented in Pascal by the relational operator **IN**. Boolean expressions used to test set membership have the form

```
element IN set
```

where *set* is a set value, set variable, or set expression, and the type of *element* and the base type of *set* are compatible. For example, if set variables `Vowels`, `Evens`, `Numbers`, and `Bits` are declared by

```
TYPE
   DigitSet = SET OF 0..9;
   BinarySet = SET OF 0..1;
   SetOfCharacters = SET OF char;

VAR
   Evens, Numbers : DigitSet;
   Bits : BinarySet;
   Vowels : SetOfCharacters;
   Num : integer;
```

and have been assigned values by

```
Evens := [0, 2, 4, 6, 8];
Bits := [0, 1];
Numbers := [0..2, 6..9];
Vowels := ['A', 'E', 'I', 'O', 'U'];
```

then

```
2 IN Evens

3 IN Numbers

'I' IN Vowels
```

are valid boolean expressions and have the values **true**, **false**, and **true**, respectively. Similarly, if `Num` has the value 3,

```
Num IN Evens

Num + 3 IN Numbers

'B' IN []
```

are valid boolean expressions that have the values **false**, **true**, and **false**, respectively. The expressions

```
5 IN Vowels

'B' IN Numbers
```

are not valid boolean expressions because of type incompatibility.

The Subset and Superset Relations

The relational operator **IN** is used to determine whether a single element is a member of a given set, but sometimes it is necessary to determine whether all of the elements of some set *set1* are also members of another set *set2*, that is, to determine whether *set1* is a **subset** of *set2*, as pictured in the following **Venn Diagram:**

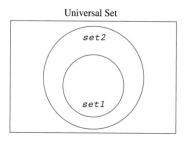

Universal Set

This subset relationship is indicated in Pascal by using the relational operators **<=** and **>=** to construct boolean expressions of the form

$$set1 \text{ <= } set2 \qquad \text{or equivalently} \qquad set2 \text{ >= } set1$$

where *set1* and *set2* are set values, variables, or expressions with compatible base types. These expressions are true if *set1* is a subset of *set2* and are false otherwise. The following table shows some valid boolean expressions and their values, given that the variables have the values previously assigned:

Boolean Expression	Value
[0,1,4] <= [0,1,2,3,4]	true
[2,4] <= Evens	true
Bits >= Evens	false
Vowels <= Vowels	true
Numbers <= Bits	false
['A','B'] >= ['A','C']	false
[] <= Numbers	true

The Equality Relation

Two sets are said to be **equal** if they contain exactly the same elements. Set equality can be checked in Pascal with a boolean expression of the form

    set1 = set2

where *set1* and *set2* must have compatible base types. The relational operator **<>** may be used to check set inequality:

    set1 <> set2

and is equivalent to the boolean expression

    NOT (set1 = set2)

For example,

```
Bits = [0, 1]

Bits <> Evens
```

are valid boolean expressions, and both have the value **true**.

Set Operations

In addition to the relational operators **IN**, **<=**, **>=**, **=**, and **<>**, there are three binary operations that may be used to combine two sets to form another set. These are the union, intersection, and difference operations, which are denoted in Pascal by **+**, *****, and **-**, respectively.

The **union** of two sets *set1* and *set2* is the set of elements that are in *set1* or *set2* or both and is denoted by a set expression of the form

```
set1 + set2
```

This can be pictured by the following Venn Diagram:

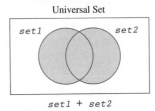

```
set1 + set2
```

The **intersection** of *set1* and *set2* is the set of elements that are in both sets and is denoted by

```
set1 * set2
```

and can be pictured as

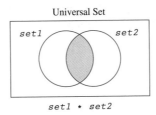

```
set1 * set2
```

The set **difference**

```
set1 - set2
```

is the set of elements that are in *set1* but are not in *set2*, as pictured in the following diagram:

Universal Set

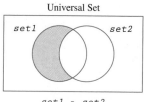

set1 - set2

For each of these set expressions, the base types of *set1* and *set2* must be compatible. The following table illustrates these set operations:

Set Expression	Value
[1,2,3] + [4,5,6]	[1,2,3,4,5,6]
[1,2,3,4] + [2,4,6]	[1,2,3,4,6]
[1,2,3] + []	[1,2,3]
[1,2,3,4] * [2,4,6]	[2,4]
[1,2,3] * [4,5,6]	[]
[1,2,3] * []	[]
[1,2,3,4] - [2,4]	[1,3]
[1,2,3,4] - [2,4,6]	[1,3]
[1,2,3] - [4,5,6]	[1,2,3]
[1,2,3] - [1,2,3,4]	[]
[1,2,3] - []	[1,2,3]

When a set expression contains two or more of these operators, it is evaluated according to the following priorities for the operators:

* $\longleftrightarrow$ high priority

+, - $\longleftrightarrow$ low priority

Thus in the expression

[2, 3, 5] + [2, 4, 7] * [2, 4, 6, 8]

the intersection is performed first, giving the set [2, 4], and

[2, 3, 5] + [2, 4]

is then evaluated, yielding

[2, 3, 4, 5]

Operations having the same priority are evaluated in the order in which they appear in the expression, from left to right. For example,

[1, 2, 3, 4] - [1, 3] + [1, 2, 5] = [2, 4] + [1, 2, 5]
                                  = [1, 2, 4, 5]

Parentheses may be used in the usual way to alter the standard order of evaluation; thus,

```
([2, 3, 5] + [2, 4, 7]) * [2, 4, 6, 8]
                 = [2, 3, 4, 5, 7] * [2, 4, 6, 8]
                 = [2, 4]
```

Compound boolean expressions that are formed using these operators and the boolean operators **NOT**, **AND**, and **OR** are evaluated according to the following priority levels:

Operator	Priority
NOT	(highest)
*, /, DIV, MOD, AND	↑
+, -, OR	↓
<, <=, >, >=, =, <>, IN	(lowest)

The operators +, -, and * may refer to either arithmetic or set operations, and the relational operators <, <=, >, >=, =, and <> may be used with numeric, character, ordinal, string, or set data (except that < and > may not be used with sets). The expression

```
0 IN Evens AND 0 IN Bits
```

is not a valid boolean expression because **AND** has higher priority than **IN**; consequently, the first operation attempted is evaluation of **Evens AND 0**, which results in an error because **AND** is a boolean operator, but **Evens** and **0** are not of **boolean** type. Parentheses must be used to modify the standard order of evaluation:

```
(0 IN Evens) AND (0 IN Bits)
```

Set relations and operations may be used to simplify complex boolean expressions. For example, the boolean expression

```
(ch = 'A') OR (ch = 'L') OR (ch = 'M') OR (ch = 'N')
```

can be expressed more compactly as

```
ch IN ['A', 'L'..'N']
```

The boolean expression

```
((ch >= 'a') AND (ch <= 'z')) OR ((ch >= 'A') AND (ch <= 'Z')) OR
((ch >= '0') AND (ch <= '9'))
```

to determine whenever the value of **ch** is a lowercase or uppercase letter or a digit can be expressed equivalently as

```
ch IN Letters + DigitChars
```

where **Letters** and **DigitChars** are set variables whose values are [`'a'..'z'`, `'A'..'Z'`] and [`'0'..'9'`], respectively.

One application in which such boolean expressions are useful is in programs like that in Section 14.5 for performing lexical analysis. To illustrate, suppose that a program segment must be written to read from a file the longest sequence of characters that constitutes a legal Turbo Pascal identifier, beginning at the present position in the file. Recall that an identifier must begin with a letter and that this letter may be followed by any number of letters, digits, or underscores, The following program segment reads a character **ch** from a text file **SourceFile**, checks if it is a letter, and, if so, continues to read characters from this file as long as they are letters, digits, or underscores:

```
read( SourceFile, ch );
IF ch in Letters THEN
   WHILE ch in (Letters + DigitChars + ['_']) DO
      read( ch );
```

14.3   Processing Sets

In the preceding section we used the assignment statement to assign a value to a set variable. For some sets, however, we need to construct a set by adding elements to it, one at a time. In this section we show how this can be done, how to display the elements of a set, and how to use sets as parameters for subprograms.

To construct a set, we first initialize it to the empty set and then repeatedly add elements to the set, using the union operation. This process is described in the following algorithm:

ALGORITHM TO CONSTRUCT A SET

(* Input: Elements of a set.
   Purpose: Construct a set S by repeatedly adding elements to S.
   Returns: The set S. *)

1. Initialize S to the empty set.
2. While there is more data, do the following:
      a. Get a value for a variable x whose type is the base type of S.
      b. Add x to S.

In Pascal, an element **x** can be added to a set **S** by applying the union operation to **S** and the singleton set **[x]**:[1]

```
S := S + [x]
```

To display the elements of a set, we can use the following algorithm:

ALGORITHM TO DISPLAY A SET

(∗ Accepts: A set *S*.
 Purpose: Display set *S* by repeatedly finding an element *x* of *S*, displaying it, and removing it from *S*.
 Output: Elements of the set *S*.
 Note: The set *S* is destroyed, since it is reduced to the empty set. ∗)

1. Let *x* be a variable whose type is the base type of *S* and initialize *x* to the first element of this base type.
2. While *S* is not empty, do the following:
    a. While *x* is not in *S*, replace *x* with its successor.
    b. Display *x*.
    c. Remove *x* from *S*.

In Pascal, an element **x** can be removed from a set **S**, as required in Step 2c, by applying the difference operation to **S** and the singleton set **[x]**:[2]

```
S := S - [x]
```

Sets may be used as parameters of functions and procedures. Remember, however, that the type of a function must be a simple data type and hence may not be of set type. The program in Figure 14.1 illustrates the use of sets as parameters. It determines which of a set of uppercase letters appear in a given text file. The procedures **ReadSet** and **DisplaySet** implement the preceding algorithms for constructing and displaying a set, respectively. Note that the set parameter **S** in procedure **ReadSet** must be a variable parameter, since the set value must be returned by this procedure. The set parameter **S** in procedure **DisplaySet**, however, is a value parameter, since as we noted, the algorithm for displaying a set reduces the set to an empty set.

---

[1] The **Include** procedure in Turbo Pascal 7.0 can be used to add an element to a set. See Section H.6 of Appendix H.

[2] The **Exclude** procedure in Turbo Pascal 7.0 can be used to remove an element from a set. See Section H.6 of Appendix H.

FIGURE 14.1   Finding letters in text.

```pascal
PROGRAM FindLetters( TextFile, output );
{******************************************************************

    Input (file):     A piece of text.
    Input (keyboard): A set of letters.
    Purpose:          Determine which of a set of upper case letters
                      entered by the user appear in a given text file.
    Output (screen):  User prompts and the set of letters found in
                      the file.


*******************************************************************}

CONST
    TextFileName = 'FIL14-1.DAT';    {actual text file}

TYPE
    ElementType = 'A'..'Z';
    TypeOfSet = SET OF ElementType;

VAR
    TextFile : text;        {text file to be analyzed}
    Symbol : char;          {a character in text file}
    LetterSet,              {set of letters to be found}
    FoundSet : TypeOfSet;   {set of letters found in TextFile}

PROCEDURE ReadSet( VAR S : TypeOfSet );
{-----------------------------------------------------------------

    Input (keyboard): Elements of a set.
    Purpose:          Read the elements of a set S of type TypeOfSet;
                      the base type of the elements of S is ElementType
                      which is char or a subrange of character or
                      integer type.
    Returns:          Set S.

-----------------------------------------------------------------}

    VAR
        x : ElementType;

    BEGIN
        S := [];
        WHILE NOT eoln DO
            BEGIN
                read( x );
                S := S + [x]
            END {WHILE}
    END {ReadSet};
```

FIGURE 14.1   Finding letters in text. (cont.)

```
PROCEDURE SearchFile( VAR TextFile : text;           {a file of text}
                           LetterSet : TypeOfSet; {set of letters}
                           VAR FoundSet : TypeOfSet); {set of found letters}
{----------------------------------------------------------------

   Accepts:       File variable TextFile and set LetterSet.
   Input (file): A piece of text.
   Purpose:       Search TextFile for letters in LetterSet and add
                  them to FoundSet.
   Returns:       FoundSet.


-------------------------------------------------------------------}

   BEGIN
      assign( TextFile, TextFileName );
      reset( TextFile );
      WHILE NOT eof( TextFile ) DO
         BEGIN
            WHILE NOT eoln( TextFile ) DO
               BEGIN
                  read( TextFile, Symbol );
                  IF Symbol IN LetterSet THEN
                     FoundSet := FoundSet + [Symbol]
               END {WHILE NOT eoln};
            readln( TextFile )
         END {WHILE NOT eof};
   END {SearchFile};

PROCEDURE DisplaySet( S : TypeOfSet;
                           {a set}
                        FirstElement : ElementType );
                           {first element of base type ElementType}
{----------------------------------------------------------------

   Accepts:         Set S of type TypeOfSet and the FirstElement of
                    the base type.
   Purpose:         Display the elements of a set S; the base type
                    of the elements of S is ElementType, which is
                    char or a subrange of character or integer type.
                    FirstElement is the first element in this base
                    type.
   Output (screen): Elements of set S.


-------------------------------------------------------------------}

   VAR
      x : ElementType;
```

FIGURE 14.1   Finding letters in text. (cont.)

```
BEGIN
    x := FirstElement;
    WHILE S <> [] DO
        BEGIN
            WHILE NOT (x IN S) DO
                x := succ(x);
            writeln( x );
            S := S - [x]
        END {WHILE}
END {DisplaySet};

BEGIN {*************** main program ***************}
    writeln( 'Enter letters to search for:' );
    ReadSet( LetterSet );
    FoundSet := [];
    SearchFile( TextFile, LetterSet, FoundSet );
    writeln( 'Letters found:' );
    DisplaySet( FoundSet, 'A' )
END {main program}.
```

Listing of FIL14-1.DAT used in sample run:

```
    This program finds which UPPERCASE letters such as A, B, and C
appear in the file TextFile.  It uses the procedure PrintSet to
display these letters after execution of the program is
completed.
```

Sample run:

```
Enter letters to search for:
AEIOUY
Letters found:
A
E
I
U
```

14.4   Example: Checking Major Program Requirements

Students at the University of Dispatch are required to complete a certain set of core courses as part of their major program in computer science. The secretary of the computer science department is responsible for ensuring that each major has satisfied this requirement and would like a program to assist her. A file is maintained that records the computer science courses that each of the current majors takes each semester and that is updated at the end of each semester:

```
John Doe
1 2  5 8
Mary Smith
1 2 5 6 9 10 12
Peter Van
1 2 3 4 5 7 8 9 10 11 13 14 15
        .
        .
        .
```

Each student record in this file consists of two lines: The first contains the student's name, and the second is a list of the computer science courses (encoded as positive integers) that the student has taken.

To solve this problem, we must read these student records and compare the set of courses completed by each student with a set of required core courses. If the set of core courses is contained in the set of completed courses, then the student has satisfied the requirements. Otherwise, the core courses yet to be taken are those which are not in the set of completed courses. This is the approach used in the following algorithm:

ALGORITHM TO CHECK MAJOR PROGRAM REQUIREMENTS

(∗ Input: Records of computer science majors.

Purpose: Read a file of records of computer science majors showing which computer science courses they have taken and determine the required core courses yet to be taken.

Output: Names of students and a list of core courses yet to be taken (if any). ∗)

1. Read first student record.
2. While there are more student records do the following:
    a. If the set of core courses is a subset of the set of completed courses, then
        Display a message that all required courses have been taken.
        Otherwise do the following:
            i. Calculate the set of courses yet to be taken as the set difference

        {core courses} − {completed courses}

            ii. Display this set of courses.
    b. Read the next student record.

The program in Figure 14.2 implements this algorithm. It uses three sets, each of whose base type is an enumerated type: the set **CoreCourses**, which is the set of courses required of each major; the set **Major.Courses**, which are the courses taken by a given major; and **RemainingCourses**, which is the set of courses yet to be taken by that major. The boolean expression **CoreCourses <= Major.Courses** is used to check whether or not the major has taken all of the required core courses, and if not, the set difference `CoreCourses - Major.Courses` is assigned to `RemainingCourses`. The procedures `ReadSet` and `DisplaySet` use the algorithms of the preceding section to read and display sets of courses.

FIGURE 14.2   Checking major program requirements.

```
PROGRAM MajorRequirementChecker( input, MajorsFile, output );
{***************************************************************

    Input (file):   Records of computer science majors.
    Purpose:        Read a file of computer science courses taken by
                    majors in the computer science department and
                    determine which of them have taken all of the
                    required core courses.
    Output (screen): Names of students and a list of core courses yet
                    to be taken (if any).

****************************************************************}

CONST
    MajorsFileName = 'FIL14-2.DAT'; {actual file of course information}

TYPE
    Courses = ( Programming1, Programming2, AssemblyLanguage,
                OperatingSystems, DataStructures, CompilerDesign,
                DataBase, ArtificialIntelligence, Graphics,
                TheoryOfComputation, ProgLanguages, AdvDataStructures,
                ComputerArchitecture, AlgorithmAnalysis, SoftwareDesign );
    CourseSet = SET OF Courses;
    MajorRecord = RECORD
                      Name : string[20];
                      Courses : CourseSet
                  END;

VAR
    MajorsFile : text;                  {file containing majors' records}
    Major : MajorRecord;                {record for one major}
    CoreCourses,                        {set of core courses}
    RemainingCourses : CourseSet;       {set of courses not taken}

PROCEDURE ReadSet( VAR MajorsFile : text;
                                    {file of records of C.S. majors}
                   VAR S : CourseSet );
                                    {set of courses taken by student}
{-------------------------------------------------------------------

    Accepts:     Textfile MajorsFile.
    Input (file): Numbers of courses.
    Purpose:     Read the numbers of courses taken by a student and
                 add the corresponding enumerated constants to the
                 set of courses already taken by the student.
    Returns:     The set S of courses.

-------------------------------------------------------------------}
```

FIGURE 14.2 Checking major program requirements. (cont.)

```
VAR
    Code : integer;  {code of a course}

FUNCTION CourseName( Code {of a course} : integer ) : Courses;
{-------------------------------------------------------------------

    Accepts:  A numeric course Code.
    Purpose:  Find the course name for a course with a given Code.
    Returns:  The course name of enumerated type Courses.


-------------------------------------------------------------------}

    VAR
        i : integer;          {runs through course codes}
        c : Courses;          {runs through Courses}

    BEGIN
        c := Programming1;
        FOR i := 2 TO Code DO
            c := succ(c);
        CourseName := c
    END {CourseName};

BEGIN {ReadSet}
    S := [];
    WHILE NOT eoln( MajorsFile ) DO
        BEGIN
            read( MajorsFile, Code );
            S := S + [CourseName(Code)]
        END {WHILE}
END {ReadSet};

PROCEDURE DisplaySet( S : CourseSet;
                                {set of courses}
                    FirstElement : Courses );
                                {first element of base type Courses}
{-------------------------------------------------------------------

    Accepts:          Set S of courses and the FirstElement of the
                      base type.
    Purpose:          Display the numbers of the courses in set S.
    Output (screen):  Numbers of courses in set S.


-------------------------------------------------------------------}

    VAR
        x : Courses;      {runs through base type}
```

FIGURE 14.2   Checking major program requirements. (cont.)

```
    BEGIN
        x:= FirstElement;
        WHILE S <> [] DO
            BEGIN
                WHILE NOT (x IN S) DO
                    x := succ(x);
                write( 1 + ORD(x):3 );
                S := S - [x]
            END {WHILE}
    END {DisplaySet};

PROCEDURE ReadARecord( VAR MajorsFile : text;
                                    {file of records of C.S. majors}
                        VAR Major : MajorRecord);
                                    {one major's record}
{------------------------------------------------------------------------

    Accepts:      Textfile MajorsFile.
    Input (file): Records of computer science majors.
    Purpose:      Read and return a major's record from the textfile
                  MajorsFile.
    Returns:      The record Major.

------------------------------------------------------------------------}

    BEGIN
        readln( MajorsFile, Major.Name );
        ReadSet( MajorsFile, Major.Courses );
        readln( MajorsFile )
    END{ReadRecord};

BEGIN{*************** main program ***************}
    {Initialize set of required core courses}
    CoreCourses := [Programming1, Programming2, AssemblyLanguage,
                    OperatingSystems, DataStructures,
                    ProgLanguages, ComputerArchitecture];

    assign( MajorsFile, MajorsFileName );
    reset( MajorsFile );
```

FIGURE 14.2   Checking major program requirements. (cont.)

```
    WHILE NOT eof( MajorsFile ) DO
       BEGIN
          ReadARecord( MajorsFile, Major );
          writeln( Major.Name );
          IF CoreCourses <= Major.Courses THEN
             writeln( 'has completed all required core courses.' )
          ELSE
             BEGIN
                RemainingCourses := CoreCourses - Major.Courses;
                write( 'must yet complete courses: ' );
                DisplaySet( RemainingCourses, Programming1 );
                writeln
             END {ELSE};
          writeln
       END {WHILE}
END {main program}.
```

Listing of input file FIL14-2.DAT used in sample run:

```
John Doe
1 2 5 8
Mary Smith
1 2 5 6 9 10 12
Peter Van
1 2 3 4 5 7 8 9 10 11 13 14 15
Fred Johnson
1 2 4 5 7 8 10 11 13 15
Jane Jones
1 2 3 4 5 6 7 8 9 11
Ann Van
1 2 3 4 6 7 8 10 12 13 14 15
Joe Blow
1 2 4 5
Jon Boy
1 2 3 5 6
Alice Girl
1 2 3 4 5 6 7 8 9 10 11 12 13 14 15
Gloria Bee
1 3 5 7 9
Dick Moby
2 4 6 8 10
```

Sample run:

```
John Doe
must yet complete courses:    3   4 11 13

Mary Smith
must yet complete courses:    3   4 11 13
```

FIGURE 14.2   Checking major program requirements. (cont.)

```
Peter Van
has completed all required core courses.

Fred Johnson
must yet complete courses:    3

Jane Jones
must yet complete courses:    13

Ann Van
must yet complete courses:    5 11

Joe Blow
must yet complete courses:    3 11 13

Jon Boy
must yet complete courses:    4 11 13

Alice Girl
has completed all required core courses.

Gloria Bee
must yet complete courses:    2  4 11 13

Dick Moby
must yet complete courses:    1  3  5 11 13
```

14.5   PART OF THE PICTURE: Programming Languages

Compilers

In our discussion of system software in Chapter 1, we mentioned **compilers,** which are programs whose function is to translate a source program written in some high-level language such as Pascal into an object program in machine code. This program is then executed by the computer.

The basic components of the compiler are summarized in the following diagram:

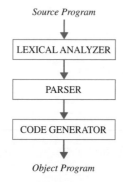

The input to a compiler is a stream of characters that comprise the source program. Before the translation can actually be carried out, this stream of characters must be broken up into meaningful groups, such as identifiers, reserved words, constants, and operators. For example, for a program segment such as

```
BEGIN
    I :=    IFI + 256;
    IF I<500 THEN
        I := I+Num
END
```

or as a "stream" of characters

```
BEGIN●ϸϸϸIϸ:=ϸϸϸϸIFIϸ+ϸ256;●ϸϸϸIFϸI<500ϸTHEN●
ϸϸϸϸϸϸIϸ:=ϸI+Num●END●
```

(where ϸ is a blank and ● is an end-of-line mark) the lexical analyzer must identify the following units:

BEGIN	reserved word
I	identifier
:=	assignment operator
IFI	identifier
+	addition operator
256	integer constant
;	semicolon
IF	reserved word
I	identifier
<	relational operator
500	integer constant
THEN	reserved word
I	identifier
:=	assignment operator
I	identifier
+	arithmetic operator
Num	identifier
END	reserved word

These units are called **tokens,** and the part of the compiler that recognizes these tokens is called the **lexical analyzer.**

It is then the task of the **parser** to group these tokens together to form the basic **syntactic structures** of the language as determined by the syntax rules. For example, it must recognize that the three consecutive tokens

$$\textit{identifier} \quad \textit{relational-operator} \quad \textit{integer-constant}$$
$$\downarrow \qquad\qquad \downarrow \qquad\qquad\qquad \downarrow$$
$$\texttt{I} \qquad\qquad \texttt{<} \qquad\qquad\qquad \texttt{500}$$

can be grouped together to form a valid boolean expression, that the three consecutive tokens

form a valid arithmetic expression, that

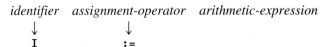

constitutes an assignment statement, and then that

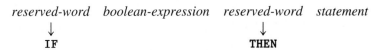

forms a valid **IF** statement. The complete **parse tree** constructed during the compilation of this **IF** statement is

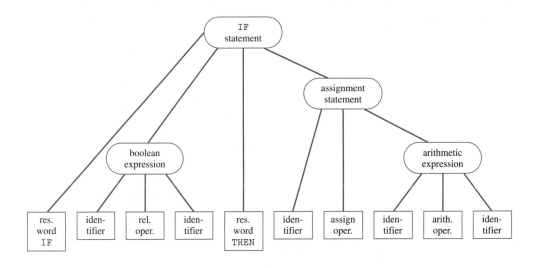

Later phases of the compiling process then generate the machine code for this **IF** statement.

Finite State Automata and Lexical Analysis

When designing a lexical analyzer to recognize various tokens, one can begin by designing a **finite state automaton,** also called a **finite state machine,** to recognize each token. A finite state automaton consists of a finite number of states together with a function that defines transitions from one state to another, depending on the current machine state and the current input character. One state is designated as the *start state* and is the state of the automaton when it begins processing an input string of characters. If the machine is in one of the special states called *accept states* after an input string is processed, then that string is said to be *recognized* or *accepted* by the automaton. For example, a finite automaton to recognize bit strings that contain 01 is

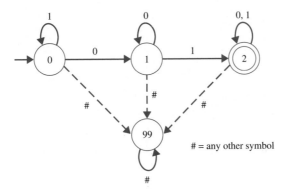

Here, the arrow pointing to state 0 indicates that this is the start state. The automaton begins processing input symbols in state 0 and makes transitions from one state to another state or remains in the current state, as specified by the labels on the arrows.

To illustrate, consider the input string 0011. The finite state automaton begins in state 0, and because the first input symbol is 0, it transfers to state 1. Since the next input symbol is a 0, it remains in state 1. However, the third symbol is a 1, which causes a transition to state 2. The final symbol is a 1 and does not cause a state change. The end of the input string has now been reached, and because the automaton is in an accept state, as indicated by the double circle, we say that it accepts the string 0011. It is easy to see that any bit string containing 01 will be processed in a similar manner and lead to the accept state and that only such strings will cause the automaton to terminate in state 2. For example, the string 11000 is not accepted, since the automaton will be in state 1 after processing this string and state 1 is not an accept state. The bit string 100201 also is not accepted, since the "illegal" symbol 2 causes a transition from state 1 to state 99, which is not an accept state.

State 99 is a "reject" or "dead" state; once it is entered, it is never exited. The transitions to this state are shown as dashed lines, since the existence of such a state is usually assumed and transitions are not drawn in the diagram. For any state and any input symbol for which no transition is specified, it is assumed that the transition is to such a reject state. Thus, the finite state automaton is usually drawn as

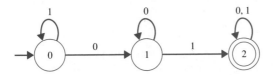

Another example of a finite state automaton is the following automaton that recognizes bit strings ending in 00 or 11:

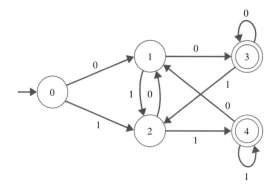

A finite state automaton to recognize Turbo Pascal identifiers is

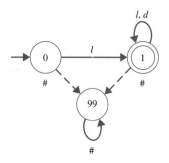

where l denotes a letter and d denotes a digit.

To show how a finite state automaton can aid the design of lexical analyzers, we consider the problem of recognizing Pascal integer constants. A finite state automaton that does this is

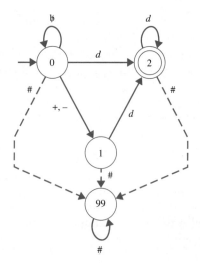

where d denotes one of the digits 0, 1, . . . , 9, ♭ denotes a blank, and state 2 is the only accepting state. The machine begins in state 0, and if the first input symbol is a blank, it stays in state 0, "gobbling up" leading blanks; if it is + or −, it goes to state 1; if it is a digit, it goes to state 2; otherwise, the input character is not valid, and thus the string does not represent a valid integer.

Writing program statements that simulate such a finite state automaton is straightforward. The program in Figure 14.3 illustrates this. It reads a string of characters and determines whether it represents a valid Pascal integer. The part of the program highlighted in color implements the preceding finite state automaton.

 FIGURE 14.3 Lexical analysis.

```pascal
PROGRAM LexicalAnalyzer( input, output );
{**********************************************************************

   Input (keyboard):  A sequence of characters.
   Purpose:           Determines if the sequence of characters
                      represents a valid Pascal integer.
   Output (screen):   User prompts and messages indicating whether
                      inputs represent valid integers.
   Note:              This program simulates a finite state automaton
                      for recognizing integer constants.


***********************************************************************}

CONST
   MaxState = 99;          {largest state number}
   DeadState = MaxState;   {dead (reject) state}

TYPE
   CharacterSet = SET OF char;
   StateSet = SET OF 0..MaxState;

VAR
   Digits : CharacterSet;    {set of digits}
   AcceptStates : StateSet;  {set of accept states}
   State : 0..MaxState;      {current state}
   EndOfToken : boolean;     {signals end of token being checked}
   Symbol,                   {current input symbol}
   Response : char;          {user response}

BEGIN
   Digits := ['0'..'9'];
   AcceptStates := [2];
   REPEAT
      {begin in initial state}
      State := 0;
      write( 'Enter the string to be checked: ' );
```

FIGURE 14.3   Lexical analysis. (cont.)

```
    WHILE NOT eoln DO
        BEGIN
            read( Symbol );
            CASE State OF
                     0 : IF Symbol = ' ' THEN
                             State := 0
                         ELSE IF Symbol IN ['+', '-'] THEN
                             State := 1
                         ELSE IF Symbol IN Digits THEN
                             State := 2
                         ELSE
                             State:= DeadState;
                   1,2 : IF Symbol IN Digits THEN
                             State := 2
                         ELSE
                             State:= DeadState;
               DeadState : {stay in dead state}
            END {CASE}
        END {WHILE};
    IF State IN AcceptStates THEN
        writeln( 'Valid integer' )
    ELSE
        writeln( 'Not a valid integer' );
    readln;
    writeln;
    write( 'More data (Y or N)? ' );
    readln( Response )
  UNTIL NOT( Response IN ['y', 'Y'] )
END.
```

Sample run:

```
Enter the string to be checked: 1234
Valid integer

More data (Y or N)? Y
Enter the string to be checked: -1
Valid integer

More data (Y or N)? Y
Enter the string to be checked: +9999
Valid integer

More data (Y or N)? Y
Enter the string to be checked: 123+4
Not a valid integer

More data (Y or N)? Y
Enter the string to be checked: abccdef
Not a valid integer

More data (Y or N)? N
```

1. Given that A, B, C, and D are set variables assigned values as follows:

   ```
   A := [3, 5..9, 11];
   B := [1..5, 11, 12];
   C := {2, 4, 6, 8];
   D := [6..10];
   ```

   calculate the following:

(a) A * B	**(b)** A + B	**(c)** A - B
(d) B - A	**(e)** A + D	**(f)** A - D
(g) A * D	**(h)** D - A	**(i)** C + C
(j) C * C	**(k)** C - C	**(l)** C - []
(m) A + B + C + D	**(n)** (A - B) - C	**(o)** A - (B - C)
(p) A * B * C * D	**(q)** A + B * C	**(r)** A * B + C
(s) A * B - C * D	**(t)** (A - (B + C)) * D	**(u)** A * B - (A + B)
(v) A - B - C - D	**(w)** B - B - C	**(x)** B - (B - C)

2. Write appropriate declarations for the following set type identifiers:

   (a) SmallIntegers: set of integers from 1 through 99.
   (b) FirstLetters: set of letters in the first half of the alphabet.
   (c) Days: the set of names of days of the week.
   (d) Suit: set of 13 cards in a suit.

3. Write appropriate variable declarations for the following set variables, and write statements to assign to each the specified value:

   (a) Evens: the set of all even integers from 1 through 99; and Odd: the set of all odd integers in the range from 1 through 99.
   (b) OneModThree: the set of all numbers of the form $3k + 1$ in the range from 1 through 99, with k an integer.
   (c) Null: the empty set.
   (d) LargeFactors: the set of all numbers in the range 1 through 99 that are not divisible by 2, 3, 5, or 7.
   (e) Divisors: the set of all divisors of a given integer Number.
   (f) Vowels: the set of all vowels; and Consonants: the set of all consonants.
   (g) WeekDays: the set of all weekdays.
   (h) FaceCards: the set of all face cards in a suit; and NumberCards: the set of all number cards in a suit.

4. Write a procedure to print any set of characters or integers using the usual mathematical notation in which the elements are enclosed in braces { and } and are separated by commas. For example, the set of numbers 2, 5, and 7 should be displayed as {2, 5, 7}, the set whose element is 4 as {4}, and the empty set as { }.

5. Write

   (a) a nonrecursive function
   (b) a recursive function

   to calculate the cardinal number of a set, that is, the number of elements in the set.

6. Sets are commonly stored in computer memory as bit strings. The length of these bit strings is the number of elements in the universal set, each bit corresponding to exactly one element of the universal set. Thus sets of base type 0..9 are represented by bit strings of length 10, the first bit corresponding to 0, the second to 1, and so on. A given set S is then represented by a bit string in which the bits corresponding to the elements of S are 1 and all other bits are 0. For example, the set S = [1, 3, 7..9] would be represented by the bit string

$$
\begin{array}{lcccccccccc}
\text{S:} & 0 & 1 & 0 & 1 & 0 & 0 & 0 & 1 & 1 & 1 \\
 & | & | & | & | & | & | & | & | & | & | \\
\text{base type:} & 0 & 1 & 2 & 3 & 4 & 5 & 6 & 7 & 8 & 9
\end{array}
$$

   (a) Assuming this same universal set, give the bit string representations of the following sets:
      (i) The set of odd digits.
      (ii) The set of prime digits.
      (iii) The set of digits divisible by 1.
      (iv) The set of digits not divisible by 1.
   (b) For the base type 'A'..'Z', describe the bit strings for the following sets:
      (i) The set of vowels.
      (ii) ['A'..'E', 'X', 'Y', 'Z']

7. Write a program to find the set of vowels and the set of consonants that appear in a given line of text.

8. Write a program to read two lines of text, and find all characters that appear in both lines.

9. Write a program to find all letters that are not present in a given line of text, and display them in alphabetical order.

10. Write a program to read several lines of text, and find all words having three or more distinct vowels.

11. Write a program to deal two ten-card hands from a standard deck of fifty-two cards. Use a random number generator (see Section 7.4), and use sets to ensure that the same card is not dealt twice.

12. The Greek mathematician Eratosthenes developed an algorithm for finding all prime numbers less than or equal to a given number n, that is, all primes in the range 2 through n. This algorithm was described in Exercise 15 of Section 9.3 and can be rephrased using sets as follows:

ALGORITHM FOR THE SIEVE METHOD

1. Initialize the set *Sieve* to contain the integers from 2 through n.
2. Select the smallest element *Prime* in *Sieve*.

3. While *Prime*^{2} ≤ *n*, do the following:
   a. Remove from *Sieve* all elements of the form *Prime* ∗ *k* for *k* > 1.
   b. Replace *Prime* with the smallest element in *Sieve* that is greater than *Prime*.

The elements remaining in *Sieve* when this algorithm terminates are the primes in the range 2 through *n*. Write a program to implement this algorithm.

13. Because some versions of Pascal allow only rather small sets, the Sieve Method of Eratosthenes for finding prime numbers described in Exercise 12 cannot be used to find large primes. Write a program that can. (*Hint:* Use an array `Sieve` of sets `Sieve[0]`, `Sieve[1]`, `Sieve[2]`, . . . whose elements are integers in the range 0 through 99. Each element of `Sieve[1]` must be interpreted as 100 plus its value, each element of `Sieve[2]` as 200 plus its value, and so on.)

14. Write a program similar to that in Figure 14.2 for a computer dating service. It should allow the user to enter a set of characteristics that he or she desires and should then search a file of names and characteristics to find all the persons in the file who have these traits.

15. Proceed as in Exercise 14, but search the file to find the best match(es) in case there are no persons who have all of the desired traits.

16. Write a program similar to that in Figure 14.2 for a real estate firm. It should allow the user to enter a set of features that he or she is looking for in a home and should then search a file of features of homes on the market to find all the homes in the file that have these features.

17. Proceed as in Exercise 16, but search the file to find the best match(es) in case there are no homes that have all of the desired features.

18. Design a finite state automaton to recognize bit strings

   (a) Containing 00 or 11.
   (b) Containing an even number of 1's.
   (c) Containing an even number of 0's and an even number of 1's.
   (d) In which *n* MOD 3 = 1 where *n* is the number of 1's.

19. A real number in Pascal has one of the forms `m.n`, `+m.n`, or `-m.n`, where *m* and *n* are nonnegative integers; or it may be expressed in exponential form `xEk`, `xek`, `xE+k`, `xe+k`, `xE-k`, `xe-k`, where *x* is an integer or a real number not in exponential form and *k* is a nonnegative integer. Write a program that accepts a string of characters and then checks to see whether it represents a valid real constant.

20. Write a program for a lexical analyzer to process assignment statements of the form *identifier* := *string-constant*. Have it recognize the following tokens: identifier, assignment operator (:=), and string constant.

21. Write a program for a lexical analyzer that processes assignment statements of the form *set-variable* := *set-value*. Have it recognize the following tokens: identifier, set constant, set operation (+, *, -), and assignment operator (:=).

Programming Pointers

Program Design

1. *A set may be an appropriate structure to use for storing data values that are all of the same (ordinal) type and the order in which they are stored is not important.* For example, in a program like that in Figure 14.2 in which it is necessary to determine whether each item in a certain collection of data values also belongs to some other collection of like values, a set is an appropriate storage structure, since the order of the data items is irrelevant and one need only determine whether the first collection is a subset of the second.

2. *The IN relation for set membership can be used to simplify complex boolean expressions and to determine whether the value of the selector in a CASE statement is one of the case labels.* The examples at the end of Section 14.2 illustrate.

Potential Problems

1. *All of the elements of a set must be of the same type, called the base type for that set. This base type must be an ordinal type.* Consequently, collections of real numbers, collections of strings, collections of records, and so on cannot be stored using the set data type.

2. *Turbo Pascal limits to 256, the number of elements that a set may contain and requires that the ordinal numbers of the first and last elements of the base type be in the range 0 through 255.* In particular, the declaration

        SET OF integer

is not allowed, but

        SET OF char

is allowed. To use sets whose elements are integers, a subrange must be specified for these elements, for example,

        SET OF 1..100

3. *The only set operations are + (union), * (intersection), and - (difference).*

4. *The only relational operators that may be used to compare sets are* <= *(subset),* >= *(superset),* = *(equal), and* <> *(not equal).*

5. *A set value cannot be read by including the name of the set in the input list of a* read *or* readln *statement.* Instead, each element of the set must be read and added to the set. See the algorithm in Section 14.3 for constructing a set.

6. *A set value cannot be displayed by including the name of the set in the output list of a* write *or* writeln *statement.* Instead, each element must be displayed individually. The algorithm in Section 14.3 for displaying a set indicates how this can be done.

Standard Pascal

There are few variations between the way Turbo Pascal and standard Pascal process sets. Standard Pascal:

- Does not impose a limit on the size of sets (although most implementations do).
- Does not allow initialization of sets as typed constants.

FILES

CHAPTER CONTENTS

The programs that we have written up to this point have involved relatively small amounts of input/output data. In most of our examples, we have assumed that the input data was read from the standard system file **input** and output has been directed to the standard system file **output**. However, many applications involve large data sets—motor vehicle registrations, telephone listings, and so on—and these can be processed more conveniently if stored on magnetic tape or a magnetic disk or some other **secondary (auxiliary) memory.** Once data has been stored on such media, it may be used as often as desired without being reentered from the keyboard. Also, several different data sets can be processed by a program, and the output produced by one program can be stored and used as input to another program.

A collection of related data items stored on some external medium is called a **file,** and the individual items are often called **components** or **records.** Usually the programmer is not concerned with the details of the actual external medium on which the data is stored because these details are handled by the operating system. Instead, the programmer deals with the logical structure of the file, that is, with the relationships among the items stored in the file and with the algorithms needed to process these items.

There are two basic types of files: **sequential** and **direct** (or **random**) **access.** In a sequential file, the data items must be accessed in the order in which they are stored; that is, to access any particular item, one must start at the beginning of the file and pass through all the items that precede it. In contrast, each item in a direct access file can be accessed directly by specifying its location, usually by means of a component number. Direct access files can, however, be processed sequentially when necessary, by simply accessing the components in order by component number. Standard Pascal supports only sequential files, but Turbo Pascal supports both kinds.

Another distinction between files is based on the way in which information is represented in the file. Files in which information is stored in external character form are called **text files,** and those in which the information is stored using internal binary representation are called **binary** or **nontext** files. Pascal supports both kinds, and they are processed in Pascal programs by using the structured data types **text** and **file.** In this chapter we describe the file-processing capabilities of Turbo Pascal, beginning with a review of text files considered in Chapter 6.

15.1   Review of Text Files

As a data structure, a **file** is an ordered collection of related data items, usually stored in external memory, for input to or output by a program; that is, information can be read from the file and/or written to the file. The files we have used in Pascal programs up to this point are **text files,** whose components are characters and these characters are organized into lines. The file type **text** is a predefined type identifier used to declare text files. The system files **input** and **output** associated with the standard input (keyboard) and output (screen) devices are examples of text files, and in Chapter 6, we described user-defined text files. The procedures **readln**, **writeln**, and **eoln** may be used only with text files.

As we noted in the introduction, Pascal also supports nontext files, whose components may be of any type, simple or structured, except that they may not be of file type. Although we restrict our attention in this section to text files, much of the discussion also applies to the other types of files considered in subsequent sections.

The principal rules governing the use of text files in Turbo Pascal programs as discussed in Chapter 6 may be summarized as follows:

1. *Program heading:* Although not required in Turbo Pascal, it is good practice to include the names of all files used in a program (including the standard text files **input** and **output**) in the file list of the program heading.

2. *Declaration:* Each user-defined file must be declared as a file variable in the declaration part of the program. For text files, the predefined type identifier **text** can be used to specify the types of file variables.

3. *Associating file variables with actual files:* In Turbo Pascal, before a file can be used for input or output in a program, it must be associated with a disk file by calling the predefined procedure **assign** in a statement of the form

```
assign( file-variable, file-name )
```

4. *Opening files for input:* Each file from which data is to be read must be opened for input by using the predefined procedure **reset** in a statement of the form

```
reset( file-variable )
```

Each such procedure call resets the data pointer to the beginning of the specified file. (The standard system file **input** need not be opened for input.)

5. *Opening files for output:* Each file to which data is to be written must be opened for output. For text files, this can be done by using the predefined procedure **rewrite**, in a statement of the form

```
rewrite( file-variable )
```

In Turbo Pascal the predefined procedure **append** may also be used. It is called with a statement of the form

```
append( file-variable )
```

Each call to the procedure **rewrite** empties the specified file, so that any previous contents of the file are destroyed. A call to **append** positions the data pointer at the end of the file so that output values will be appended to the file. (The standard system file **output** need not be opened for output.)

6. *File input:* Information can be read from a text file by using the predefined procedures **read** and **readln** in the forms

```
read( file-variable, input-list )

readln( file-variable, input-list )
```

If *file-variable* is omitted, values are read from the system file **input**.

7. *File output:* Output can be directed to a text file by using the predefined procedures **write** and **writeln** in the forms

```
write( file-variable, output-list )

writeln( file-variable, output-list )
```

If *file-variable* is omitted, output is directed to the system file **output**.

8. *Closing files:* In Turbo Pascal, after output to a file is completed, it should be closed by calling the predefined procedure `close` with a statement of the form

```
close( file-variable )
```

Failure to do so may result in the loss of data values because they are not transferred from the output buffer to the file.

9. *Copying files:* The contents of one file cannot be copied to another by using an assignment statement of the form *file-variable-1 := file-variable-2*. Rather, the components must be copied one at a time.

10. *Files as parameters:* Formal parameters that represent files must be variable parameters. This is a consequence of Rule 9, since value parameters require copying the values of the corresponding actual parameters.

In addition to the predefined procedures and functions described here, Turbo Pascal also provides procedures `ChDir`, `Erase`, `GetDir`, `MkDir`, `Rename`, and `RmDir` and the function `IOResult` for processing files in general, and procedures `flush` and `SetTextBuff` and functions `SeekEof` and `SeekEoln` for processing text files. Descriptions of these can be found in the Turbo Pascal reference manuals.

15.2   Binary Files

The files reviewed in the preceding section are text files, that is, files whose components are of type `char` and these characters are organized into lines. As we noted, however, the components of a file may be of any predefined or user-defined data type except file type. In this section we consider such nontext files.

File Declarations

A general file declaration has the following form:

File Declaration

Form:

    FILE OF *component-type*

where:
    FILE and **OF** are reserved words;
    component-type may be any type except another file type.

Purpose:
Specifies that *component-type* is the type of the components in a file.

The following illustrate some file declarations:

```
TYPE
    DaysOfWeek = ( Sunday, Monday, Tuesday, Wednesday,
                   Thursday, Friday, Saturday );
    List = ARRAY[1..100] OF integer;
    EmployeeRecord = RECORD
                        Name : string[20];
                        Number, Dependents : integer;
                        HourlyRate : real
                     END;
    FileOfNumbers = FILE OF integer;
    FileOfDays = FILE OF DaysOfWeek;
    LongStringsFile = FILE OF string[80];
    FileOfLists = FILE OF List;
    EmployeeFile = FILE OF EmployeeRecord;

VAR
    CharacterSetFile : text;
    NumberFile : FileOfNumbers;
    DayFile : FileOfDays;
    AddressFile : LongStringsFile;
    ListFile : FileOfLists;
    EmpFile : EmployeeFile;
```

Data Representation in Binary Files

Binary files such as **NumberFile**, **DayFile**, **AddressFile**, **ListFile**, and **EmpFile** can usually be created only by a program, and access to the components of such files is possible only within a program. Attempting to list the file contents by using a system command or trying to access them by using a system text editor usually results in "garbage" output or some other error message.

The characters that make up a text file are stored using a coding scheme (ASCII in Turbo Pascal), as described in Section 1.2, and when a text file is listed, these codes are automatically converted to the corresponding characters by the terminal, printer, or other output device and become legible to the user. On the other hand, the information in a binary file is illegible because it is stored using the internal binary representation scheme for the particular computer being used— hence the name, *binary files*—and this representation usually cannot be correctly displayed in character form by the output device.

To illustrate, consider the integer 27195. If the usual binary representation described in Section 1.2 were used, this integer would be stored internally in a 16-bit word as the bit string

$$0110101000111011$$

and this would also be its representation in a file of type **integer** such as **NumFile**:

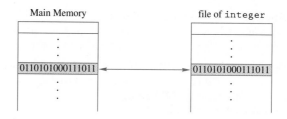

In a text file, however, it would be stored as a sequence of codes for the five characters '2', '7', '1', '9', '5':

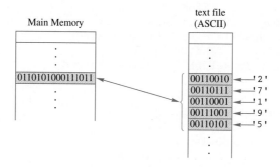

As these diagrams suggest, information in binary files can be transferred more rapidly between main memory and secondary memory, as it is already in a form that requires no decoding or encoding. Also, a data item is usually stored more compactly if it is stored using its internal representation rather than its external representation in one of the standard coding schemes.

In Turbo Pascal, each file used in a program must be associated with a disk file by using the procedure **assign** before any of its components can be accessed. A call to **assign** has the same form for all file:

    assign(*file-variable*, *file-name*)

This statement associates the disk file ***file-name*** with the name ***file-variable*** used to refer to the file within the program so that any subsequent reference to ***file-variable*** will in fact be carried out using the disk file ***file-name***. The file must then be opened by calling the procedures **reset** or **rewrite** with one of the statements

    reset(*file-variable*)

or

    rewrite(*file-variable*)

The procedure **append** may not be used for nontext files.

Reset is used to open an existing file, and it positions the data pointer at the beginning of the file. It is an error if the disk file associated with ***file-variable*** by the **assign** procedure does not exist. If the file is a text file, then it is opened only for input, but there is no such restriction for binary files.

The procedure **rewrite** creates a new empty disk file with the name associated with *file-variable* by the **assign** procedure. If such a file already exists, it is deleted and a new empty file with the same name is created in its place. If the file is a text file, **rewrite** opens it for output only.

Writing to a Binary File

Because a binary file must be created by a Pascal program, we first consider the **write** procedure that is used for this purpose. Values can be written to a file by using an output statement of the form

```
write( file-variable, output-list )
```

where *output-list* is an expression (constant, variable, or formula) or a list of expressions separated by commas, each of which must be compatible with the type of the components of *file-variable*. Note that the procedure **writeln** may *not* be used for binary files. Also, as noted in the preceding section, after output to a file is complete, it should be closed with a statement of the form

```
close( file-variable )
```

to ensure that all the data has in fact been transferred to the file.

Example: Creating a File of Computer Usage Records

As a simple illustration of file output, suppose that a file of computer-usage records is needed and that we wish to create a data file containing such records, one for each user. Each record is to contain the user's id number, the computer system (A, B, C, or D) to be used, the limit on resources for this user, and the amount of resources used to date.

The type definitions and variable declarations needed to declare a file **UsersFile** with components of type **UserRecord** are

```
TYPE
    UserRecord = RECORD
                    IdNumber : integer;
                    CompSystem : char;
                    ResourceLimit,
                    UsedToDate : integer
                 END;
    FileOfUserRecords = FILE OF UserRecord;

VAR
    UsersFile : FileOfUserRecords;
```

The program in Figure 15.1 creates the desired file. The **assign** procedure is called first to associate the disk file whose name is **UsersFileName** with the file variable **UsersFile**, and then the **rewrite** procedure opens this file for output.

The program then repeatedly reads values for the fields of a user record **UserRec** and writes each record to **UsersFile** with the statement

```
write( UsersFile, UserRec );
```

After the user signals the end of input, the **close** procedure is called to close **UsersFile**.

FIGURE 15.1   Creating a binary file.

```
PROGRAM CreateUsersFile1( input, output, UsersFile );
{******************************************************************

    Input (keyboard): Values for the fields of a record of type
                      UserRecord.
    Purpose:          Create the binary file UsersFile whose
                      components are records of type UserRecord.
                      The fields of a record UserRec are entered by
                      the user during execution, and the procedure
                      write is used to write UserRec to UsersFile.
    Output (file):    The binary file UsersFile.
    Output (screen):  User prompts and a message signaling that file
                      creation is complete.

******************************************************************}

CONST
    UsersFileName = 'FIL15-1.DAT';   {name of actual disk file}

TYPE
    UserRecord = RECORD
                     IdNumber : integer;
                     CompSystem : char;
                     ResourceLimit,
                     UsedToDate : integer
                 END;
    FileOfUserRecords = FILE OF UserRecord;

VAR
    UserRec : UserRecord;              {record entered by user}
    UsersFile : FileOfUserRecords;   {binary file created}
```

FIGURE 15.1   Creating a binary file. (cont.)

```
BEGIN
    assign( UsersFile, UsersFileName );
    rewrite( UsersFile );
    WITH UserRec DO
        BEGIN
            write( 'User''s id number (0 to stop)? ' );
            readln( IdNumber );
            WHILE IdNumber > 0 DO
                BEGIN
                    write( 'System (A,B,C,D), resource limit, ' );
                    write( 'resources used to date? ' );
                    readln( CompSystem, ResourceLimit, UsedToDate );
                    write( UsersFile, UserRec );
                    write( 'User''s id number (0 to stop)? ' );
                    readln( IdNumber )
                END {WHILE}
        END {WITH};
    writeln;
    writeln ('*** Creation of UsersFile completed ***');
    close( UsersFile )
END.
```

Sample run:

```
User's id number (0 to stop)? 12300
System (A,B,C,D), resource limit, resources used to date? B 200 159
User's id number (0 to stop)? 12310
System (A,B,C,D), resource limit, resources used to date? B 200 110
User's id number (0 to stop)? 13320
System (A,B,C,D), resource limit, resources used to date? C 300 228
User's id number (0 to stop)? 13400
System (A,B,C,D), resource limit, resources used to date? A 100  28
User's id number (0 to stop)? 13450
System (A,B,C,D), resource limit, resources used to date? B 200 105
User's id number (0 to stop)? 13490
System (A,B,C,D), resource limit, resources used to date? C 300 128
User's id number (0 to stop)? 14000
System (A,B,C,D), resource limit, resources used to date? D 400 255
User's id number (0 to stop)? 14010
System (A,B,C,D), resource limit, resources used to date? A 100  84
User's id number (0 to stop)? 14040
System (A,B,C,D), resource limit, resources used to date? A 100  17
User's id number (0 to stop)? 14100
System (A,B,C,D), resource limit, resources used to date? C 300 185
User's id number (0 to stop)? 0
*** Creation of UsersFile completed ***
```

Reading from a Binary File

The components of a file that has been opened for input can be read using the procedure **read** in a reference of the form

```
read( file-variable, input-list )
```

where *input-list* is a single variable or a list of variables separated by commas. The type of each variable in the input list and the type of the file components must be compatible. Note that the procedure **readln** may *not* be used for binary files because they have no line structure.

Example: Reading Records from `UsersFile`

As an illustration of input from files, suppose that we wish to examine the contents of the file **UsersFile** created by the program in Figure 15.1. This file must first be associated with the corresponding disk file by calling the **assign** procedure

```
assign( UsersFile, UsersFileName );
```

and then opened for input by using the statement

```
reset( UsersFile );
```

Each component of the file can then be read and assigned to the variable **UserRec** of record type **UserRecord** by using the procedure **read**:

```
read( UsersFile, UserRec );
```

and the values of the four fields of **UserRec** can then be displayed:

```
WITH UserRec DO
    writeln( IdNumber:7, CompSystem:8,
             ResourceLimit:11, UsedToDate:11 )
```

In the program in Figure 15.2, these two statements are repeated until the end-of-file mark in **UsersFile** is encountered. This end-of-file mark is automatically placed at the end of each file created by a Pascal program.

 FIGURE 15.2   Reading from a binary file.

```
PROGRAM ReadUsersFile1( UsersFile, output );
{*******************************************************************

    Input (file):     The binary file UsersFile whose components are
                      records of type UserRecord.
    Purpose:          Read and display the contents of the binary file
                      UsersFile created by the program of Figure 15.1.
    Output (screen):  The fields of the records in UsersFile.

********************************************************************}
```

FIGURE 15.2   Reading from a binary file. (cont.)

```
CONST
   UsersFileName = 'FIL15-2.DAT';     {name of disk file}

TYPE
   UserRecord = RECORD
                     IdNumber : integer;
                     CompSystem : char;
                     ResourceLimit,
                     UsedToDate : integer
                END;
   FileOfUserRecords = FILE OF UserRecord;

VAR
   UserRec : UserRecord;              {a record from UsersFile}
   UsersFile : FileOfUserRecords;     {binary file being read}

BEGIN
   assign( UsersFile, UsersFileName );
   rewrite( UsersFile );
   writeln( '******** Contents of UsersFile ********' );
   writeln( 'Id Number  System  Res. Limit  Res. Used' );
   writeln( '=========  ======  ==========  =========' );
   WHILE NOT eof( UsersFile ) DO
      BEGIN
         read( UsersFile, UserRec );
         WITH UserRec DO
            writeln( IdNumber:7, CompSystem:8,
                     ResourceLimit:11, UsedToDate:11 )
      END {WHILE}
END.
```

Sample run:

```
******** Contents of UsersFile ********

Id Number  System  Res. Limit  Res. Used
=========  ======  ==========  =========
   12300      B       200         159
   12310      B       200         110
   13320      C       300         228
   13400      A       100          28
   13450      B       200         105
   13490      C       300         128
   14000      D       400         255
   14010      A       100          84
   14040      A       100          17
   14100      C       300         185
```

Example: Creating and Verifying a Binary File of Computer Usage Records

In the preceding examples, we used one program to create **UsersFile** and a separate program to read the file. The program in Figure 15.3 does both, and thus combines the functions of the programs in Figures 15.1 and 15.2 into a single program.

 FIGURE 15.3   Creating and verifying a binary file.

```
PROGRAM CreateAndVerifyUsersFile( input, output, UsersFile );
{**************************************************************************

    Input (keyboard): Values for the fields of a record of type
                      UserRecord.
    Input (file):     The binary file UsersFile whose components are
                      records of type UserRecord.
    Purpose:          Create the binary file UsersFile having components
                      of type UserRecord. User records are input
                      directly into the file buffer variable by the user
                      during execution.  The contents of the file are
                      then verified by opening it for input, reading the
                      contents, and displaying each user record.
    Output (file):    The binary file UsersFile.
    Output (screen):  User prompts, a label, and the fields of the
                      records in UsersFile.

**************************************************************************}

CONST
    UsersFileName = 'FIL15-2.DAT';    {name of disk file}

TYPE
    UserRecord = RECORD
                    IdNumber : integer;
                    CompSystem : char;
                    ResourceLimit,
                    UsedToDate : integer
                 END;
    FileOfUserRecords = FILE OF UserRecord;

VAR
    UserRec : UserRecord;             {a record from UsersFile}
    UsersFile : FileOfUserRecords;    {binary file being created and read}
```

FIGURE 15.3   Creating and verifying a binary file. (cont.)

```
BEGIN
   {Create UsersFile}
   assign( UsersFile, UsersFileName );
   rewrite( UsersFile );
   WITH UserRec DO
      BEGIN
         write( 'User''s id number (0 to stop)? ' );
         readln( IdNumber );
         WHILE IdNumber > 0 DO
            BEGIN
               write( 'System (A,B,C,D), resource limit, ' );
               write( 'resources used to date? ' );
               readln( CompSystem, ResourceLimit, UsedToDate );
               write( UsersFile, UserRec );
               write( 'User''s id number (0 to stop)? ' );
               readln( IdNumber )
            END {WHILE}
      END {WITH};

   {Verify the contents of UsersFile}
   reset( UsersFile );
   writeln;
   writeln( '********* Contents of UsersFile ********' );
   writeln( 'Id Number  System  Res. Limit  Res. Used' );
   writeln( '=========  ======  ==========  =========' );
   WHILE NOT eof( UsersFile ) DO
      BEGIN
         read( UsersFile, UserRec );
         WITH UserRec DO
            writeln( IdNumber:7, CompSystem:8,
                     ResourceLimit:11, UsedToDate:11 )
      END {WHILE}
   close( UsersFile );
END.
```

Sample run:

```
User's id number (0 to stop)? 12300
System (A,B,C,D), resource limit, resources used to date? B 200 159
User's id number (0 to stop)? 12310
System (A,B,C,D), resource limit, resources used to date? B 200 110
User's id number (0 to stop)? 13320
System (A,B,C,D), resource limit, resources used to date? C 300 228
User's id number (0 to stop)? 13400
System (A,B,C,D), resource limit, resources used to date? A 100  28
User's id number (0 to stop)? 13450
System (A,B,C,D), resource limit, resources used to date? B 200 105
User's id number (0 to stop)? 13490
System (A,B,C,D), resource limit, resources used to date? C 300 128
```

FIGURE 15.3 Creating and verifying a binary file. (cont.)

```
User's id number (0 to stop)? 14000
System (A,B,C,D), resource limit, resources used to date? D 400 255
User's id number (0 to stop)? 14010
System (A,B,C,D), resource limit, resources used to date? A 100  84
User's id number (0 to stop)? 14040
System (A,B,C,D), resource limit, resources used to date? A 100  17
User's id number (0 to stop)? 14100
System (A,B,C,D), resource limit, resources used to date? C 300 185
User's id number (0 to stop)? 0
```

```
******** Contents of UsersFile ********
```

Id Number	System	Res. Limit	Res. Used
12300	B	200	159
12310	B	200	110
13320	C	300	228
13400	A	100	28
13450	B	200	105
13490	C	300	128
14000	D	400	255
14010	A	100	84
14040	A	100	17
14100	C	300	185

The eof Function

As the preceding examples illustrate, the procedure **read** (and **readln** for text files) reads the next file component unless the end of the file has been reached. In this case, the value of

```
eof( file-variable )
```

becomes true (it is false otherwise). Any subsequent calls to the procedure **read** results in an error, because an attempt is made to access information beyond the end of the file.

Files as Parameters

As an illustration of the use of files as parameters, consider the following procedure, which copies the contents of one file into another:

```
PROCEDURE CopyFile( VAR FromFile, ToFile : FileType );
{-----------------------------------------------------------------

    Input (file):   FromFile.
    Purpose:        Copies the contents of FromFile to ToFile.
    Output (file):  ToFile.


-----------------------------------------------------------------}
```

```
VAR
   Component : ComponentType;

BEGIN
   WHILE NOT eof( FromFile ) DO
      BEGIN
         read( FromFile, Component );
         write( ToFile, Component )
      END {WHILE}
END {Copyfile};
```

This procedure copies one component at a time from **FromFile** to **ToFile**. This is necessary because the contents of a file can be accessed only one component at a time; it is not possible to copy one file into another file by using an assignment statement of the form *file-1* := *file-2*.

One consequence is that files used as parameters, as in procedure **CopyFile**, must be variable parameters. Value parameters cannot be used, because this would require copying an entire actual file into the corresponding formal file parameter. Corresponding actual file parameters and formal file parameters must have the same type, and as for the other predefined data structures in Pascal, this requirement means that they must be declared by the same or equivalent type identifiers (see Section 9.2).

Example: Appending Data to a File

As an illustration of how procedure **CopyFile** can be used, consider the problem of appending data to an existing binary file. Because the procedure **append** cannot be used for nontext files, it is not possible to add the data by simply opening the file with **append** and then writing to it. Instead, we first must copy the permanent file to a temporary work file, then add the additional data to this file, and finally copy the resulting work file back to the permanent file. The program in Figure 15.4 uses the file **WorkFile** to append data entered by the user to the file **UsersFile** created earlier.

FIGURE 15.4   Appending data to a file.

```
PROGRAM AppendToUsersFile( input, output, UsersFile );
{****************************************************************

    Input (keyboard): Values for the fields of a record of type
                      UserRecord.
    Purpose:          Read user records entered during execution and
                      add these records to the end of the previously
                      created UsersFile.  The contents of UsersFile
                      are first copied into the temporary file
                      WorkFile, the new records are appended to
                      WorkFile, and the contents of WorkFile are
                      then copied back to UsersFile.  The contents
                      of UsersFile are then verified by reading and
                      displaying each record in it.
    Output (file):    The binary file UsersFile.
    Output (screen):  User prompts and the fields of the records
                      in UsersFile.


 ****************************************************************}

CONST
    UsersFileName = 'FIL15-4.DAT'; {disk file -- copy of FIL15-3.DAT}
    WorkFileName = 'TEMPFILE.DAT'; {name of disk file used as a work file}

TYPE
    UserRecord = RECORD
                     IdNumber : integer;
                     CompSystem : char;
                     ResourceLimit,
                     UsedToDate : integer
                 END;
    FileOfUserRecords = FILE OF UserRecord;
    FileType = FileOfUserRecords;
    ComponentType = UserRecord;

VAR
    UserRec : UserRecord;              {a record from UsersFile}
    WorkFile,                          {temporary file of GPA records}
    UsersFile : FileOfUserRecords;     {file of GPA records created}

PROCEDURE CopyFile( VAR FromFile, ToFile : FileType );
{----------------------------------------------------------------

    Accepts:       File variables FromFile and ToFile.
    Input (file):  FromFile.
    Purpose:       Copy the contents of FromFile to ToFile.
    Output (file): ToFile.


 ----------------------------------------------------------------}
```

FIGURE 15.4   Appending data to a file. (cont.)

```
    VAR
        Component : ComponentType;     {a file component}

    BEGIN
        WHILE NOT eof( FromFile ) DO
            BEGIN
                read( FromFile, Component );
                write( ToFile, Component );
            END {WHILE}
    END {Copyfile};

BEGIN {*************** main program ***************}
    assign( UsersFile, UsersFileName );
    assign( WorkFile, WorkFileName );

    {Copy contents of UsersFile to WorkFile}
    reset( UsersFile );
    rewrite( WorkFile );
    CopyFile( UsersFile, WorkFile );

    {Append new records to the end of WorkFile}

    WITH UserRec DO
        BEGIN
            write( 'User''s id number (0 to stop)? ' );
            readln( IdNumber );
            WHILE ( IdNumber > 0 ) DO
                BEGIN
                    write( 'System (A,B,C,D), resource limit, ' );
                    write( 'resources used to date? ' );
                    readln( CompSystem, ResourceLimit, UsedToDate );
                    write( WorkFile, UserRec );
                    write( 'User''s id number (0 to stop)? ' );
                    readln( IdNumber )
                END {WHILE}
        END {WITH};

    {Now copy the contents of WorkFile to UsersFile}

    reset( WorkFile );
    rewrite( UsersFile );
    CopyFile ( WorkFile, UsersFile );
```

FIGURE 15.4   Appending data to a file. (cont.)

```
{Finally, verify the contents of UsersFile}

reset( UsersFile );
writeln;
writeln( '********* Contents of UsersFile ********' );
writeln( 'Id Number  System  Res. Limit  Res. Used' );
writeln( '=========  ======  ==========  =========' );
WHILE NOT eof( UsersFile ) DO
   BEGIN
      read( UsersFile, UserRec );
      WITH UserRec DO
         writeln( IdNumber:7, CompSystem:8,
                  ResourceLimit:11, UsedToDate:11 );
   END {WHILE}
close( UsersFile );
close( WorkFile )
END {main program}.
```

Sample run:

```
User's id number (0 to stop)? 15000
System (A,B,C,D), resource limit, resources used to date? A 100 0
User's id number (0 to stop)? 15100
System (A,B,C,D), resource limit, resources used to date? B 200 0
User's id number (0 to stop)? 15200
System (A,B,C,D), resource limit, resources used to date? C 300 0
User's id number (0 to stop)? 15300
System (A,B,C,D), resource limit, resources used to date? D 400 0
User's id number (0 to stop)? 0

********* Contents of UsersFile ********
Id Number  System  Res. Limit  Res. Used
=========  ======  ==========  =========
  12300      B        200         159
  12310      B        200         110
  13320      C        300         228
  13400      A        100          28
  13450      B        200         105
  13490      C        300         128
  14000      D        400         255
  14010      A        100          84
  14040      A        100          17
  14100      C        300         185
  15000      A        100           0
  15100      B        200           0
  15200      C        300           0
  15300      D        400           0
```

Exercises

In these exercises, the files **StudentFile** and **UserIdFile** should be processed as files of records. For descriptions of these files, see Appendix E.

1. Each of the following program segments is intended to read a text file **Infile**, each line of which contains an integer, and to count the integers in the file. Explain why each fails to do so.

   (a)
   ```
   Count := 0;
   WHILE NOT eof( InFile ) DO
      BEGIN
         read( InFile, Number );
         Count := Count + 1
      END {WHILE};
   ```

   (b)
   ```
   Count := 0;
   readln( InFile, Number );
   WHILE NOT eof( InFile ) DO
      BEGIN
         Count := Count + 1;
         readln( InFile, Number )
      END {WHILE};
   ```

2. Write a procedure to concatenate two files of identical type.

3. Modify Exercise 6 of Section 10.4 to print "personalized" junk-mail letters in which certain blanks in a form letter are filled in with personal information obtained from a file containing that information.

4. Write a program to read **UserIdFile** to find and display the password for a specified user's identification number.

5. Write a program to read **StudentFile** and produce a report for all freshmen with GPAs below 2.0. This report should include the student's first name, middle initial, last name, major, and cumulative GPA, with appropriate headings.

6. At the end of each month, a report is produced that shows the status of the account of each user in **UserIdFile**. Write a program to read the current date and produce a report having the following form:

   ```
                    USER ACCOUNTS--12/31/92

                                     RESOURCE        RESOURCES
   USER NAME            USER-ID        LIMIT           USED
   ------------------------------------------------------------
   Joseph Miltgen       10101         $750            $381
   Isaac Small          10102         $650            $599***
         .                 .            .               .
         .                 .            .               .
         .                 .            .               .
   ```

in which the three asterisks (∗∗∗) indicate that the user has already used 90 percent or more of the resources available to him or her.

7. Write a simple **text-formatting** program that reads a text file and produces another text file in which no lines are longer than some given length. Put as many words as possible on the same line. You will have to break some lines of the given file, but do not break any words or put punctuation marks at the beginning of a new line.

8. Extend the text-formatting program of Exercise 7 to right-justify each line in the new text file by adding evenly distributed blanks in lines where necessary. Also, preserve all indentation of lines in the given text file that begin a new paragraph.

9. (Project) Most system text formatters also allow command lines to be placed within the unformatted text. These command lines might have forms like the following:

.P *m n*	Insert *m* blank lines before each paragraph, and indent each paragraph *n* spaces.
.W *n*	Width of page (line length) is *n*.
.L *n*	Page length (number of lines per page) is *n*.
.I *n*	Indent all lines following this command line *n* spaces.
.U	Undent all following lines and reset to previous left margin.

Extend the program of Exercises 7 and 8 to implement command lines.

10. (Project) A **pretty printer** is a special kind of text formatter that reads a text file containing a program and then prints it in a ''pretty'' format. For example, a pretty printer for Pascal programs might insert blank lines between procedures and indent and align statements within other statements, such as **IF** statements, compound statements, type declarations, and variable declarations, to produce a format similar to that used in the sample programs of this text. Write a pretty-print program for Pascal programs to indent and align statements in a pleasing format.

15.3   PART OF THE PICTURE: Databases

A database is a collection of files, and one important part of managing a database is updating the files in the database so that the information they contain is current, correct, and consistent. In this section we consider this problem of file updating, looking first at the problem of updating a sequential file using the information from a transaction file. Since most update algorithms require that the records in the files be sorted so that some key fields are in order, we consider next the problem of sorting a file. Finally, we describe how individual records in direct access files can be updated and illustrate these techniques using direct access files as implemented in Turbo Pascal.

Updating a Sequential File

One important file-update problem is updating a master file with the contents of a transaction file. For example, the master file may be an inventory file that is to be updated with a transaction file containing the day's sales, or the master file may be a file of students' records and the transaction file a file containing the students' grades for the semester just concluded.

Here we consider the problem of updating a master file containing information regarding the users of a university's computing system. Suppose that components of the master file **UsersFile** are records containing the identification number, computer system used, limit on resources, and resources used to date for each system user. A daily log of the system's activity is also maintained. Among other items of information, this log contains a list of user identification numbers and resources used for each job entered into the system. This list is maintained in the transaction file **UpdateFile**. At the end of each day, the master file **UsersFile** must be updated with the contents of **UpdateFile** to incorporate the activities of that day.

This type of updating of sequential files can be done most easily and efficiently if both files have been previously sorted so that the values in some common key field appear in ascending (or descending) order. An algorithm for performing such file updating is as follows:

ALGORITHM FOR UPDATING A MASTER FILE USING A TRANSACTION FILE

(* Input: Two files, *MasterFile* and *TransFile*. It is assumed that the records in these fields are ordered so that values in some common key field are in ascending order and that all values in *TransFile* are valid.

Purpose: Update records in *MasterFile* with information from *TransFile* to produce *NewMasterFile*.

Output: The file *NewMasterFile*. *)

1. Read the first record from *MasterFile* and assign it to *MasterRec*.
2. Read the first record from *TransFile* and assign it to *TransRec*.
3. Initialize a boolean variable *EndOfUpdate* to false.
4. While not *EndOfUpdate* do the following updating:

   Compare the key fields of *MasterRec* and *TransRec*. If they match, do the following:
       a. Update *MasterRec* using the information in *TransRec*.
       b. If the end of *TransFile* has been reached, set *EndOfUpdate* to true; otherwise read the next value for *TransRec* from *TransFile*.

   If the key fields do not match, do the following:
       a. Write *MasterRec* to *NewMasterFile*.
       b. Read a new value for *MasterRec* from *MasterFile*.

5. Because the last updated master record has not been written, write *MasterRec* to *NewMasterFile*.
6. Copy any remaining records in *MasterFile* into *NewMasterFile*.

The program in Figure 15.5 implements this algorithm to update the contents of **UsersFile** with the entries in **UpdateFile**; these files have been previously sorted so that the identification numbers are in ascending order. Also shown are the contents of two small files used in a test run and the output file produced. These listings were obtained by executing a program that reads each record from a binary file and then displays each field of the record by using a program segment of the form

```
assign( BinaryFile, BinFileName );
reset( BinaryFile );
WHILE NOT eof( BinaryFile ) DO
   BEGIN
      read( BinFile, Component );
      WITH Component DO
         writeln( field-1, field-2, ... )
   END {WHILE}
```

FIGURE 15.5   Updating a file.

```
PROGRAM UserFileUpdate( UsersFile, UpdateFile, NewUsersFile) ;
{***********************************************************************

   Input (file):   UsersFile and UpdateFile.
   Purpose:        Update the entries in the master file UsersFile with
                   the entries in the transactions file UpdateFile.
                   The records in UsersFile contain the id-number,
                   computer system used, resource limit, and resources
                   used to date for each system user;  UpdateFile
                   represents the log of a day's activities; each record
                   contains a user's id-number and resources used for a
                   job entered into the system.  Both files are sorted
                   so that id-numbers are in ascending order, and all
                   id-numbers in UsersFile are assumed to be valid.
                   The updated records are written to the output file
                   NewUsersFile.
   Output (file): NewUsersFile.


***********************************************************************}

CONST
   UsersFileName = 'FIL15-5A.DAT';    {disk file -- master file}
   UpdateFileName = 'FIL15-5B.DAT';   {disk file -- transactions file}
   NewUsersFileName = 'FIL15-5C.DAT'; {disk file -- new master file}
```

FIGURE 15.5   Updating a file. (cont.)

```
TYPE
   UserRecord = RECORD
                     IdNumber : integer;
                     CompSystem : char;
                     ResourceLimit,
                     UsedToDate : integer
                END;
   UserUpdateRecord = RECORD
                          UpdateNumber,
                          ResourcesUsed : integer
                      END;
   MasterFile = FILE OF UserRecord;
   TransactionFile = FILE OF UserUpdateRecord;

VAR
   UserRec : UserRecord;                {record from UsersFile}
   UpdateRec : UserUpdateRecord;        {record from UpdateFile}
   UsersFile,                           {file containing user information}
   NewUsersFile : MasterFile;           {updated user file}
   UpdateFile : TransactionFile;        {file to update UsersFile}
   EndOfUpdate : boolean;               {signals end of UpdateFile}

BEGIN
   assign( UsersFile, UsersFileName );
   assign( UpdateFile, UpdateFileName );
   assign( NewUsersFile, NewUsersFileName );
   reset( UsersFile );
   reset( UpdateFile );
   rewrite( NewUsersFile );

   {Read first record from each file}

   read( UsersFile, UserRec );
   read( UpdateFile, UpdateRec );

   {Update records of UsersFile with records of UpdateFile}

   EndOfUpdate := false;
   WHILE NOT EndOfUpdate DO
      BEGIN
         WITH UserRec, UpdateRec DO
            IF IdNumber = UpdateNumber THEN      {id-numbers match}
               BEGIN
                  UsedToDate := UsedToDate + ResourcesUsed;
                  IF eof( UpdateFile ) THEN
                     EndOfUpdate := true
                  ELSE
                     read( UpdateFile, UpdateRec )
               END {IF}
            ELSE                                        {no match}
               BEGIN
                  write( NewUsersFile, UserRec );
                  read( UsersFile, UserRec )
               END {ELSE}
      END {WHILE};
```

FIGURE 15.5   Updating a file. (cont.)

```
   {Write UserRec to NewUsersFile; then copy any
      remaining records from UsersFile}

   write( NewUsersFile, UserRec );
   WHILE NOT eof( UsersFile ) DO
      BEGIN
         read( UsersFile, UserRec );
         write( NewUsersFile, UserRec )
      END {WHILE};
   close( NewUsersFile )
END.
```

Contents of FIL15-5A.DAT (master file):

```
12300 B 200 159
12310 B 200 110
13320 C 300 228
13400 A 100  28
13450 B 200 105
13490 C 300 128
14000 D 400 255
14010 A 100  84
14040 A 100  17
14100 C 300 185
15000 A 100   0
15100 B 200   0
15200 C 300   0
15300 D 400   0
```

Contents of FIL15-5B.DAT (transactions file):

```
12300 10
12300 24
12310 17
12310  3
12310  5
14000 22
14000  5
14000 12
14000  7
15000  3
15000  7
```

FIGURE 15.5   Updating a file. (cont.)

Contents of FIL15-5C.DAT (new master file):

```
12300 B 200 193
12310 B 200 135
13320 C 300 228
13400 A 100  28
13450 B 200 105
13490 C 300 128
14000 D 400 301
14010 A 100  84
14040 A 100  17
14100 C 300 185
15000 A 100  10
15100 B 200   0
15200 C 300   0
15300 D 400   0
```

Mergesort

The preceding file-update algorithm requires that the files be sorted. However, all of the sorting algorithms we considered in Chapter 9 are **internal** sorting schemes; that is, the entire collection of items to be sorted must be stored in main memory. But large files contain too much data to store in main memory, and so an **external** sorting algorithm is needed. One popular and efficient external sorting method is the **mergesort** technique, a variation of which, called **natural mergesort,** we examine next.

As the name mergesort suggests, the basic operation in this sorting scheme is merging data files. The merge operation combines two files that have previously been sorted so that the resulting file is also sorted. As a simple illustration, suppose that *File1* contains eight integers in increasing order:

$$File1: \quad 15 \quad 20 \quad 25 \quad 35 \quad 45 \quad 60 \quad 65 \quad 70$$

and *File2* contains five integers in increasing order:

$$File2: \quad 10 \quad 30 \quad 40 \quad 50 \quad 55$$

In practice, of course, files contain many more items, and each item is usually a record containing several different types of information, and as we have commented before, sorting is then based on some key field within these records.

To merge files *File1* and *File2* to produce sorted *File3,* we read one element from each file, say, *X* from *File1* and *Y* from *File2:*

$$File1: \quad \boxed{15} \quad 20 \quad 25 \quad 35 \quad 45 \quad 60 \quad 65 \quad 70$$
$$\uparrow$$
$$X$$
$$File2: \quad \boxed{10} \quad 30 \quad 40 \quad 50 \quad 55$$
$$\uparrow$$
$$Y$$

We compare these items and write the smaller, in this case Y, to *File3:*

File3 :   10

and then read another value for Y from *File2:*

```
File1:  [15]  20  25   35  45  60  65  70
         ↑
         X
File2:  10  [30]  40  50  55
             ↑
             Y
```

Now X is smaller than Y, so it is written to *File3*, and a new value for X is read from *File1:*

```
File1:  15  [20]  25  35  45  60  65  70
             ↑
             X
File2:  10  [30]  40  50  55
             ↑
             Y
File3:  10   15
```

Again, X is less than Y, so it is written to *File3*, and a new value for X is read from *File1:*

```
File1:  15  20  [25]  35  45  60  65  70
                 ↑
                 X
File2:  10  [30]  40  50  55
             ↑
             Y
File3:  10   15   20
```

Continuing in this manner, we eventually read the value 60 for X and the last value of *File2*, 55, for Y:

```
File1:  15  20  25  35  45  [60]  65  70
                             ↑
                             X
File2:  10  30  40  50  [55]
                         ↑
                         Y
File3:  15  20  25  30  35  40  45  50
```

Because $Y < X$, we write Y to *File3:*

File3:   15   20   25   30   35   40   45   50   55

Because the end of *File2* has been reached, we simply copy the remaining items in *File1* to *File3* to complete the merging:

File3: 15 20 25 30 35 40 45 50 55 60 65 70

The general algorithm for merging two sorted files is

MERGE

(* Input: Sorted files *File1* and *File2*.
   Purpose: Merge sorted files *File1* and *File2*, giving *File3*.
   Output: *File3*. *)

1. Open *File1* and *File2* for input, *File3* for output.
2. Read the first element *X* from *File1* and the first element *Y* from *File2*.
3. Repeat the following until the end of either *File1* or *File2* is reached:
   If $X < Y$, then
      a. Write *X* to *File3*.
      b. Read a new *X* value from *File1*.
   Otherwise:
      a. Write *Y* to *File3*.
      b. Read a new *Y* value from *File2*.
4. If the end of *File1* was encountered, copy any remaining elements from
   File2 into *File3*. If the end of *File2* was encountered, copy the rest of *File1*
   into *File3*.

In this algorithm, we have assumed that the file components are simple components. If the files contain records that are sorted on the basis of some key field, the key field of *X* is compared with the key field of *Y* in Step 3.

To see how the merge operation can be used in sorting a file, consider the following file *F* containing sixteen integers:

F: 75 55 15 20 85 30 35 10 60 40 50 25 45 80 70 65

Notice that several segments of *F* consist of elements that are already in order:

F: 75 | 55 | 15 20 85 | 30 35 | 10 60 | 40 50 | 25 45 80 | 70 | 65

These segments are called **subfiles** or **runs** in *F*, and they subdivide *F* in a natural way.

We begin by reading these subfiles of *F* and alternately writing them to two other files, *F1* and *F2:*

F1: 75 | 15 20 85 | 10 60 | 25 45 80 | 65

F2: 55 | 30 35 | 40 50 | 70

and then identifying the sorted subfiles in *F1* and *F2*.

F1: 75 | 15 20 85 | 10 60 | 25 45 80 | 65

F2: 55 | 30 35 40 50 70

Notice that although the subfiles of *F1* are the same as those copied from *F*, the last three subfiles written to *F2* have combined to form a larger subfile.

Next we merge the first subfile of *F1* with the first one in *F2* to produce a sorted subfile in *F:*

F: | 55   75 |

and then merge the second subfiles:

F: | 55   75 | | 15   20   30   35   40   50   70   85 |

Corresponding subfiles are merged until the end of either or both of the files *F1* and *F2* is reached. If either file still contains subfiles, they are simply copied into *F*. Thus in our example, because the end of *F2* has been reached, the remaining subfiles of *F1* are copied back into *F*.

F: | 55   75 | | 15   20   30   35   40   50   70   85 | | 10   60 | | 25   45   80 | | 65 |

Now file *F* is again split into files *F1* and *F2*, by copying its subfiles alternately into *F1* and *F2*.

F1: | 55   75 | | 10   60 | | 65 |

F2: | 15   20   30   35   40   50   70   85 | | 25   45   80 |

This time we see that two subfiles of *F1* combine to form a larger subfile:

F1: | 55   75 | | 10   60   65 |

F2: | 15   20   30   35   40   50   70   85 | | 25   45   80 |

Once again we merge corresponding subfiles of *F1* and *F2* back into *F*.

F: | 15   20   30   35   40   50   55   70   75   85 | | 10   25   45   60   65   80 |

When we now split *F* into *F1* and *F2*, each of the files *F1* and *F2* contains a single sorted subfile, and therefore each is completely sorted.

F1: | 15   20   30   35   40   50   55   70   75   85 |

F2: | 10   25   45   60   65   80 |

Thus when we merge *F1* and *F2* back into *F*, *F* will also contain only one sorted subfile and hence will be sorted.

F: | 10   15   20   25   30   35   40   45   50   55   60   65   70   75   80   85 |

From this example we see that the mergesort method has two steps: (1) splitting file *F* into two other files, *F1* and *F2,* and (2) merging corresponding subfiles in these two files. These steps are repeated until each of the smaller files contains a single sorted subfile, and when these are merged, the resulting file is completely sorted.

The splitting operation is carried out by the following algorithm:

SPLIT ALGORITHM FOR NATURAL MERGESORT

(* Input: File *F*.
    Purpose: Split file *F* into files *F1* and *F2* by copying natural sorted
                 subfiles of *F* alternately to *F1* and *F2*.
    Output: Files *F1* and *F2*. *)

1. Open the file *F* for input and the files *F1* and *F2* for output.
2. While the end of *F* has not been reached, do the following:
    a. Copy a sorted subfile of *F* into *F1* as follows: Repeatedly read an
       element of *F* and write it into *F1* until the next element in *F* is
       smaller than this copied item or the end of *F* is reached.
    b. If the end of *F* has not been reached, copy the next sorted subfile of
       F into *F2* in a similar manner.

And the following algorithm implements the merge operation illustrated in the example:

MERGE ALGORITHM FOR NATURAL MERGESORT

(* Input: Files *F1* and *F2*.
    Purpose: Merge corresponding sorted subfiles in *F1* and *F2* back into file
                 F. NumSubFiles is the number of sorted subfiles produced in *F*.
    Output: File *F.* *)

1. Open files *F1* and *F2* for input, *F* for output.
2. Initialize *NumSubFiles* to 0.
3. While neither the end of *F1* nor the end of *F2* has been reached, do the
   following:
    a. While no end of a subfile in *F1* or in *F2* has been reached, do the
       following:
          If the next element in *F1* is less than the next element in *F2,* then
          copy the next element from *F1* into *F*; otherwise, copy the next
          element from *F2* into *F*.
    b. If the end of a subfile in *F1* has been reached, then copy the rest of
       the corresponding subfile in *F2* to *F;* otherwise, copy the rest of the
       corresponding subfile in *F1* to *F*.
    c. Increment *NumSubFiles* by 1.
4. Copy any subfiles remaining in *F1* or *F2* to *F,* incrementing *NumSubFiles*
   by 1 for each.

The program in Example 15.3A of Appendix E uses mergesort to sort a file. It repeatedly calls the split and merge algorithms until the file is sorted, using the "look-ahead" property provided by the file window to locate the end of a sorted subfile.

The worst case for mergesort occurs when the items are in reverse order. In this case the subfiles have sizes 1, 2, 4, 8, and so on. It follows that to sort a file or list of n items, $\log_2 n$ split and merge operations are required, and each of the n items must be examined in each of them. Hence, in the worst case, and as can be shown for the average case as well, the computing time for mergesort is $O(n \cdot \log_2 n)$.

Updating Direct Access Files

Direct access or **random access files** are files in which each component can be accessed directly by specifying its location in the file, thus making it possible to read or write components anywhere in the file. As we have noted, standard Pascal does not support direct access files, but Turbo Pascal does.

A particular component in a direct access file can be accessed by using the predefined procedure **seek**. It is called with a statement of the form

```
seek ( file-variable, component-number )
```

where **component-number** is an integer expression specifying the number of the component to be located in the file; the numbering of the components begins with 0. Seeking a component whose number is one more than the number of the last component is permitted, and this positions the data pointer at the end of the file so that a new component can be added there. Using a component number that is larger than this or that is negative is an error.

Once a component has been located with **seek**, the procedure **read** can be used to read this component. For example, to read the user record that is the **RecNum**th component in **UsersFile**, we can use the statements

```
seek( UsersFile, RecNum );
read( UsersFile, UserRec );
```

The procedure **write** can be used to replace the component at which the data pointer is currently positioned. For example, to modify some of the fields such as the resource limit in the user record that is the **RecNum**th component of **UsersFile**, we can use

```
seek( UsersFile, RecNum );
read( UsersFile, UserRec );
WITH UserRec DO
   BEGIN
      writeln( 'User id ', IdNumber );
      write( 'Enter new resource limit:  ' );
      readln( ResourceLimit )
   END {WITH};
seek( UserFile, RecNum );
write( UserFile, UserRec );
```

The program in Example 15.3B of Appendix E shows how direct access files are implemented in Turbo Pascal. It updates a direct access file in which component numbers correspond to user ids in a file of user records.

Indexed Files

To access a particular component in a direct access file, it is necessary to know its component number. In the computer-user update example, this is easy because the *n*th record in the file of user records is the record of the user whose id number is *n*. Usually this is not the case, however; for example, if social security numbers were used for id numbers, the record for user 567-34-9999 would be stored in the 567,349,999th record in the file, but most of the file components numbered 0 through 567,349,998 would probably not be used.

One common approach is to use an **index** to establish a correspondence between key values and component numbers. This index is a list of key values stored in main memory—in an array, for example—arranged in the same order as they appear in the file. Thus the location of a given key value in this list is the same as the number of the corresponding record in the file. We search this index for a particular key value using some internal search method such as binary search, and its position in this index is the number of the desired record in the file:

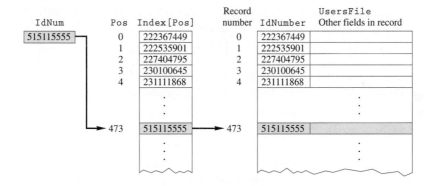

Exercises

In these exercises, the files **InventoryFile**, **InventoryUpdate**, **StudentFile**, **StudentUpdate**, and **UserIdFile** should be processed as files of records. For descriptions of these files, see Appendix E.

1. The file update algorithm in this section assumes that all identification numbers in **TransFile** are valid. Modify this algorithm and the program in Figure 15.5 so that they will work correctly even if some records in **TransFile** have invalid identification numbers.

2. Write a program to update **InventoryFile** with **InventoryUpdate** to produce a new inventory file. Each record in **InventoryFile** for which there is no

record in **InventoryUpdate** with a matching item number should remain unchanged. Each record with one or more corresponding records in **InventoryUpdate** should be updated with the entries in the update file. For transaction code **R**, the number of items returned should be added to the number in stock. For transaction code **S**, the number of items sold should be subtracted from the number currently in stock; if more items are sold than are in stock, display a message showing the order number, stock number, item name, and how many should be back ordered (that is, the difference between the number ordered and the number in stock), and set the number currently in stock to zero.

3. Write a program to read the files **StudentFile** and **StudentUpdate** and pro-duce an updated grade report. This grade report should show

(a) The current date.

(b) The student's name and student number.

(c) A list of the names, grade, and credits for each of the current courses under the headings **COURSE**, **GRADE**, and **CREDITS**.

(d) Current GPA (multiply credits by numeric grade—A = 4.0, A− = −3.7, B+ = 3.3, B = 3.0, . . . , D− = 0.7, F = 0.0—for each course to find honor points earned for that course, sum these to find total new honor points, and then divide total new honor points by total new credits to give the current GPA, rounded to two decimal places).

(e) Total credits taken (old credits from **StudentFile** plus total new credits).

(f) New cumulative GPA (first calculate old honor points = old credits times old cumulative GPA and then new cumulative GPA = sum of old honor points and new honor points divided by updated total credits).

4. (Project) Write a menu-driven program that uses **StudentFile** and **StudentUpdate** and allows (some of) the following options. For each option, write a separate procedure so that options and corresponding procedures can be easily added or removed.

1. Locate a student's permanent record when given his or her student number and print it in a nicer format than that in which it is stored.
2. Same as Option 1, but locate the record when given his or her name.
3. Print a list of all student names and numbers in a given class (1, 2, 3, 4, 5).
4. Same as Option 3, but for a given major.
5. Same as Option 3, but for a given range of cumulative GPAs.
6. Find the average cumulative GPAs for all
   (a) females   (b) males   (c) students with a specified major
   (d) all students. (These are suboptions of Menu Option 6.)
7. Produce updated grade reports having the following format:

```
          GRADE REPORT--SEMESTER #1
                 12/31/92
            DISPATCH UNIVERSITY
     10103       James L. Johnson
                            GRADE      CREDITS
     ==========================================
     ENGL 176                  C          4
     EDUC 268                  B          4
     EDUC 330                  B+         3
     P E 281                   C          3
     ENGR 317                  D          4
     Cumulative Credits:      33
     Current GPA:            2.22
     Cumulative GPA:         2.64
```

(See Exercise 3 for descriptions of these last items.)

8. Same as Option 7, but instead of producing grade reports, produce a new permanent file containing the updated total credits and new cumulative GPAs.

9. Produce an updated file when a student (a) drops or (b) adds a course.

10. Produce an updated file when a student (a) transfers to or (b) withdraws from the university.

5. Following the example of the text, show the various splitting–merging stages of mergesort for the following lists of numbers:

   (a) 1, 5, 3, 8, 7, 2, 6, 4
   (b) 1, 8, 2, 7, 3, 6, 5, 4
   (c) 1, 2, 3, 4, 5, 6, 7, 8
   (d) 8, 7, 6, 5, 4, 3, 2, 1

6. Write a program to read records from **UserIdFile** and sort them so that the resources used to date are in increasing order.

7. Write a program that uses mergesort, appropriately modified, to sort a list stored in an array.

8. Information about computer terminals in a computer network is maintained in a direct access file. The terminals are numbered 1 through 100, and information about the nth terminal is stored in the nth record of the file. This information consists of a terminal type (string), the building in which it is located (string), its transmission rate (integer), an access code (character), and the date of last service (month, day, year). Write a program to read a terminal number, retrieve and display the information about that terminal, and modify the date of last service for that terminal.

9. Write a program to process **InventoryFile**, considered as a direct access file of records described in Appendix E. The program should first construct an index that contains item numbers as key values. (For this, you might first write a "preprocessor" program that reads through **InventoryFile**, regarded as a

sequential file, and constructs an index containing the item numbers. Note that the records in `InventoryFile` are arranged so that the item numbers are in ascending order.) The program should then allow the user to enter item numbers, and it should retrieve the information in the file for that item. This search should be carried out using a binary search of the index.

Programming Pointers

In this chapter we reviewed text files and introduced files of other types. Many of the programming pointers at the end of Chapter 6 regarding text files apply to files in general. These are summarized here; for additional details, see the Programming Pointers for Chapter 6.

1. *In text files:*

   ■ *After values have been read for each variable in the input list,* `readln` *advances the data pointer past the next end-of-line mark, but* `read` *positions it immediately after the last character read.*

   ■ *Leading blanks, leading tabs, and leading end-of-line marks are ignored when reading numeric values but not when reading values for character or string variables. If an end-of-file mark is encountered while skipping these leading characters for a numeric variable, 0 is assigned to the variable.*

   ■ *Every numeric value must be followed by a blank, a tab, an end-of-line mark, or an end-of-file mark.*

   ■ *Characters are read for a string variable up to the next end-of-line or end-of-file mark. If the data pointer is already positioned at an end-of-line mark or at an end-of-file mark, an empty string is assigned to the variable.*

   ■ *The data pointer always points to the next character to be read.*

2. *All file variables should appear in the file list of the program heading and must be declared in a variable section of the program.*

3. *Before a user-defined file can be used for input or output, it must be associated with an actual file name by using the procedure* `assign` *and then opened using one of the procedures* `reset`, `rewrite`, *or* append. *Remember the following, however:*

   ■ Each call to `reset` positions the data pointer at the beginning of the file.

   ■ Each call to `rewrite` creates an empty file, and any previous contents that the file may have had are destroyed.

   ■ Each call to `append` positions the data pointer at the end of the output file so that data can be appended to the file; `append` may be used only with text files.

   ■ A text file must be opened with `reset` if it is to be used for input, with `rewrite` if it is to be used for output.

4. *Every file to which values have been written should be closed using procedure* `close` *after output to it has been completed.* Failure to do so may cause some values to be left in the output buffer and not transferred to the file.

5. *Binary files have no line structure, and thus the procedures* `readln` *and* `writeln` *and the function* `eoln` *cannot be used with them.*

6. *Assignment statements of the form* `file-variable-1 := file-variable-2` *are not allowed. The components of one file must be copied to another file individually.*

7. *File variables used as formal parameters in functions and procedures must be variable parameters.*

Standard Pascal

Text files were introduced in Chapter 6, and the differences in the file-processing features of Turbo Pascal and standard Pascal described in the Standard Pascal section at the end of that chapter should be reviewed at this point. In addition to the differences noted there, in standard Pascal:

- Procedures `reset` must be used to open all input files and procedure `rewrite` to open all output files.
- Declaring a file variable creates a *file buffer* and an associated file buffer variable whose name has the form *file-variable*↑, which can be used to access this buffer. The type of this file buffer variable is the same as the type of the components of the associated file, and its value is always the next component in the file. A call to procedure `reset` loads this file buffer with the first component of the file.
- Procedures `get` and `put` are provided. `Get( file-variable )` loads the next component of the file into the buffer, so that it becomes the value of *file-variable*↑. `Put( file-variable )` transfers the contents of the buffer to the file, leaving *file-variable*↑ undefined. The statement

  ```
  read( file-variable, component );
  ```

  is equivalent, therefore, to the pair of statements

  ```
  component := file-variable↑;
  get( file-variable );
  ```

  and the statement

  ```
  write( file-variable, component );
  ```

  is equivalent to

  ```
  file-variable↑ := component;
  put( file-variable );
  ```

- Direct access files are not supported.

POINTERS AND LINKED STRUCTURES

16

[Pointers] are like jumps, leaping wildly from one part of a data structure to another. Their introduction into high-level languages has been a step backward from which we may never recover.
C. A. R. HOARE

I've got a little list, I've got a little list.
GILBERT AND SULLIVAN, *The Mikado*

I think that I shall never see,
A poem lovely as a tree.
JOYCE KILMER

CHAPTER CONTENTS

The data structures we have considered in earlier chapters—arrays, records, and sets—all are **static data structures** whose maximum sizes and associated memory locations are fixed at compile time. It is also possible to design **dynamic data structures** that expand or contract as required during execution, and whose associated memory locations change. Such dynamic structures are especially useful for storing and processing data sets whose sizes change during program execution, for example, the collection of jobs that have been entered into a computer system and are awaiting execution or the collection of passenger names and seat assignments on a given airplane flight. A dynamic data structure is a collection of elements called **nodes** of the structure which are linked together.

This linking is established by associating with each node a pointer that points to the next node in the structure. One of the simplest linked structures is a *linked list,* which might be pictured as follows:

In this chapter we consider dynamic data structures and how they can be implemented in Pascal using pointers and the procedures **new** and **dispose**.

16.1 Introduction to Linked Lists

In Chapter 9, we described how arrays can be used to store and process lists. Although this array-based implementation of lists works well for static lists, that is, lists whose sizes remain quite constant, it is not an efficient way of processing dynamic lists that grow and shrink as elements are inserted and deleted. The reason is that each time a new element is inserted into the list, array elements may have to be shifted to make room for it. For example, suppose we wish to insert the new value 56 after the element 48 in the list of integers

$$23, 25, 34, 48, 61, 79, 82, 89, 91, 99$$

to produce the new list

$$23, 25, 34, 48, 56, 61, 79, 82, 89, 91, 99$$

If the list elements are stored in an array, the array elements in positions 5 through 10 must first be shifted into positions 6 through 11 before the new element can be inserted at position 5:

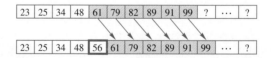

Removing a list element also requires shifting array elements. For example, to delete the second item in the list

$$23, 25, 34, 48, 56, 61, 79, 82, 89, 91, 99$$

we must shift the array elements in positions 3 through 11 into locations 2 through 10 to ''close the gap'' in the array:

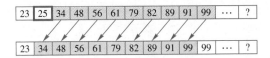

A linked list is an alternative structure for storing the elements of a list, and as we will see, it provides a better implementation of dynamic lists. A **linked list** consists of a collection of elements called **nodes,** each of which stores two items of information: (1) an element of the list and (2) a **link** or **pointer** that indicates the location of the node containing the successor of this list element. Access to the node storing the first list element must also be maintained. For example, a linked list storing the list of names **Brown, Jones**, and **Smith** might be pictured as follows:

In this diagram, arrows represent links, and **List** points to the first node in the list. The *Data* part of each node stores one of the names in the list, and the *Next* part stores the pointer to the next node. The dot in the *Next* part of the last node having no arrow emanating from it represents a **nil pointer** and indicates that this list element has no successor.

Inserting New Elements into a Linked List

One of the strengths of a linked list is that no list elements need be moved when a new element is inserted into the list or when an element is removed. We demonstrate this first for the insertion operation.

To insert a new data value into a linked list, we must first obtain a new node and store the value in its data part. We assume that there is a storage pool of available nodes and some mechanism for obtaining nodes from it as needed. The second step is to connect this new node to the existing list, and for this, there are two cases to consider: (1) insertion at the beginning of the list and (2) insertion after some element in the list.

To illustrate the first case, suppose we wish to insert the name **Adams** at the beginning of the preceding linked list. We first obtain a new node and store the name **Adams** in its data part:

Get a node pointed to by **TempPtr**.
Store **'Adams'** in the *Data* part of this node.

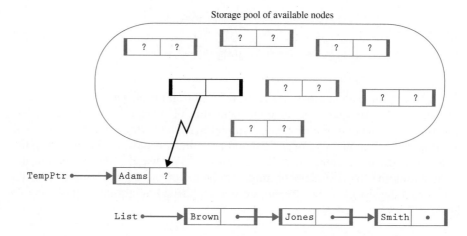

We then insert this node into the list by setting its link part to point to the first node in the list:

Set the *Next* part of the node pointed to by **TempPtr** equal to **List**.

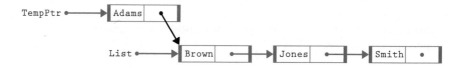

and then setting **List** to point to this new first node:

Set **List** equal to **TempPtr**.

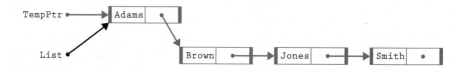

As an illustration of the second case, suppose that we wish to insert the name **Lewis** after the node containing **Jones** and that **PredPtr** is a pointer to this predecessor.

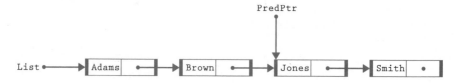

We begin as before by obtaining a new node in which to store the name **Lewis**:

Get a node pointed to by **TempPtr**.
Store **'Lewis'** in the *Data* part of this node.

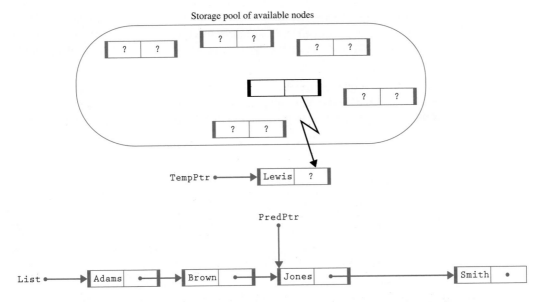

We insert this node into the list by first setting its link part equal to the pointer in the *Next* part of the node pointed to by **PredPtr** so that it points to its successor:

> Set the *Next* part of the node pointed to by **TempPtr** equal to the *Next* part of the node pointed to by **PredPtr**.

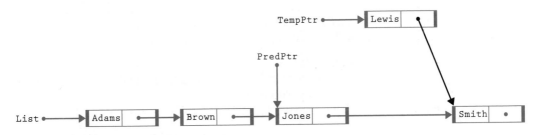

and then resetting the link part of the predecessor node to point to this new node:

> Set the *Next* part of the node pointed to by **PredPtr** equal to **TempPtr**.

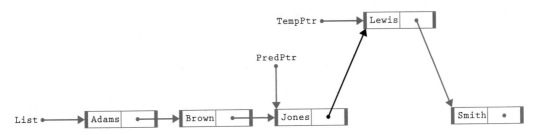

Deleting Items from a Linked List

Like insertion, there are two cases to consider for deletion: (1) deleting the first element in the list and (2) deleting an element that has a predecessor. To demonstrate the first case, suppose we wish to delete the name **Adams** from the preceding list. This case is easy and consists of simply resetting **List** to point to the second node in the list and then returning the first node to the storage pool of available nodes:

> Set **TempPtr** equal to **List**.
> Set **List** equal to the *Next* part of the node pointed to by **List**.
> Return the node pointed to by **TempPtr** to the storage pool of available nodes.

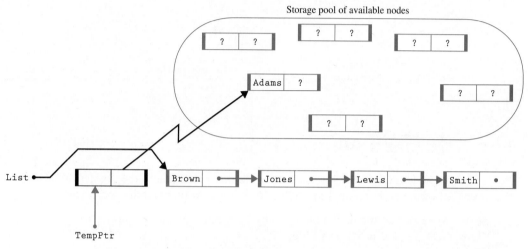

The second case is almost as easy as the first. For example, to delete the node containing **Lewis** from the preceding list, we need only set the link of its predecessor to point to the node containing its successor (if there is one):

> Set **TempPtr** equal to the *Next* part of the node pointed to by **PredPtr**.
> Set the *Next* part of the node pointed to by **PredPtr** equal to the *Next* part of the node pointed to by **TempPtr**.
> Return the node pointed to by **TempPtr** to the storage pool of available nodes.

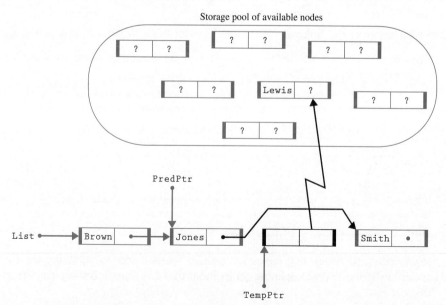

Summary

As the preceding examples demonstrate, it is possible to insert and delete data items in a linked list without shifting list elements, as required in the array-based implementation of a list. At this stage, however, we have described linked lists only abstractly, at a logical level, and have not considered an implementation for them. To implement linked lists, we need at least the following capabilities:

1. Some means of dividing memory into nodes, each having a *Data* part and a *Next* part, and some implementation of pointers.
2. Operations and/or functions to access the values stored in the *Data* and *Next* parts of a node.
3. Some means of keeping track of the nodes in use and the available free nodes and of transferring nodes between those in use and the pool of free nodes.

Unfortunately, there are only a few programming languages (such as LISP, an acronym for LISt Processing) that provide lists as predefined data structures. In other languages it is necessary to implement linked lists using other predefined data types. In the next section we show how they can be implemented using records and the pointer data type in Pascal.

Exercises

1. Write an algorithm to count the nodes in a linked list with first node pointed to by *List*.

2. Write an algorithm to determine the average of a linked list of real numbers with first node pointed to by *List*.

3. Write an algorithm to append a node at the end of a linked list with first node pointed to by *List*.

4. Write an algorithm to determine whether the data items in a linked list with first node pointed to by *List* are in ascending order.

5. Write an algorithm to search a linked list with first node pointed to by *List* for a given item, and if found, return a pointer to the predecessor of the node containing that item.

6. Write an algorithm to insert a new node into a linked list with first node pointed to by *List* after the *n*th node in this list for a given integer *n*.

7. Write an algorithm to delete the *n*th node in a linked list with first node pointed to by *List*, where *n* is a given integer.

8. Suppose the items stored in two linked lists are in ascending order. Write an algorithm to merge these two lists to yield a list with the items in ascending order.

9. Write an algorithm to reverse a linked list with first node pointed to by *List*. Do not copy the list elements; rather, reset links and pointers so that *List* points to the last node and all links between nodes are reversed.

16.2   Pointers; the Procedures `new` and `dispose`

Variables are symbolic addresses of memory locations. This relationship between a variable and the memory location it names is a static one that is established when the program is compiled and remains fixed throughout the execution of the program. Although the contents of a memory location associated with a variable may change during execution—that is, the value of the variable may change—the variables themselves can be neither created nor destroyed during execution. Consequently, these variables are called **static variables.**

As we have seen, however, the number of memory locations needed for a dynamic structure varies during program execution as the structure grows and shrinks. Consequently, because the memory requirements are not known in advance, static variables are not adequate for processing dynamic structures. What is required is a method for acquiring additional memory locations as needed during execution and for releasing them when they are no longer needed. Pascal provides for such dynamic memory allocation and deallocation by using **pointers** and the predefined procedures `new` and `dispose`.

Pointer Variables

A **pointer variable,** or simply a **pointer,** is a variable whose value is the address of some memory location. A type declaration for a pointer has the following form:

Pointer Type Declaration

Form:

    ↑*type-identifier*   or   ^*type-identifier*

Purpose:
Used to declare the type of a pointer variable whose value is to be an address of a memory location where a data value of type *type-identifier* can be stored. The variable is said to be **bound** to this type, because it may only be used to reference memory locations storing data of this type.

For example, if the data values are strings, then a pointer to a memory location that may be used to store a string may be declared by

```
TYPE
    .
    .
    .
    StringType = string[8];
    PointerToString = ↑StringType;

VAR
    StringPtr : PointerToString;
```

This pointer variable **StringPtr** is bound to the type **StringType** and may be used only to reference memory locations in which values of this type can be stored.

The Procedure new

The predefined Pascal procedure **new** is used to acquire memory locations and assign their addresses to pointer variables during program execution. This procedure is called with a statement of the following form:

The Procedure new

Form:

new(*pointer*)

Purpose:
Assigns the address of a memory location to
pointer. Its effect, therefore, is as though the
statement *pointer* := *memory-address* were executed.

Thus the statement

    new(StringPtr)

assigns to **StringPtr** a memory address, say 1005, so that the value of **StringPtr** is this memory address:

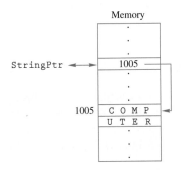

This is the address of a memory location where a string such as **COMPUTER** can be stored. (In this particular case, it would, in fact, be the address of the first word in a block of consecutive memory locations in which the characters of the string are stored.) We say that **StringPtr** "points" to this memory location and picture this with a diagram like the following:

StringPtr ●──────▶ | COMPUTER |

Because this area of memory can be used to store values of type **StringType**, it is a variable, but it has no name! Such variables are thus sometimes referred to as **anonymous variables,** and pointers are said to point to anonymous variables. Since these variables come into existence during program execution and may later cease to exist, we shall instead refer to them as **dynamic variables.** At one point during execution, there may be a particular memory location associated with a dynamic variable, and at a later time, no memory location or a different one may be associated with it.

Each call of the procedure **new** acquires a new memory location and assigns its address to the specified pointer. Thus, if **TempPtr** is also a pointer of type **PointerToString**, the statement

    new(TempPtr)

acquires a new memory location pointed to by **TempPtr**:

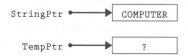

Nil Pointers

Pascal provides the special pointer constant **NIL** for those situations in which it is necessary to assign a value to a pointer variable that indicates that it does not point to any memory location. This value may be assigned to a pointer of any type in an assignment statement of the form

    pointer := NIL

We picture a nil pointer as simply a dot with no arrow emanating from it:

pointer ●

Operations on Pointers

Because the values of pointers are addresses of memory locations, the operations that may be performed on them are limited: Only assignment and comparison using the relational operators = and <> are allowed. If *pointer1* and *pointer2* are bound to the same type, an assignment statement of the form

    pointer1 := *pointer2*

copies the value of *pointer2* to *pointer1* so that both have the same memory address as their value (or both are nil); that is, both point to the same memory location. The previous location (if any) pointed to by *pointer1* can no longer be accessed unless it is pointed to by some other pointer. The following diagrams illustrate:

Before assignment:

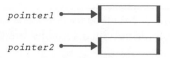

After assignment *pointer1* := *pointer2:*

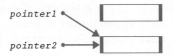

Before assignment:

After assignment *pointer1* := *pointer2:*

As an illustration, suppose that both **StringPtr** and **TempPtr** are pointer variables of type **PointerToString** = ↑**StringType** and point to memory locations containing the strings **COMPUTER** and **SOFTWARE**, respectively:

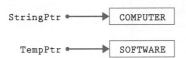

The assignment statement

```
TempPtr := StringPtr
```

assigns the memory address that is the value of **StringPtr** to **TempPtr**, so that **TempPtr** points to the same memory location as does **StringPtr**:

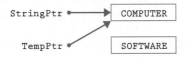

The string **SOFTWARE** stored in the first location can no longer be accessed (unless it is pointed to by some other pointer of type **PointerToString**).

The relational operators = and <> can be used to compare two pointers *bound to the same type* to determine if they both point to the same memory locations or both are nil. Thus the boolean expression

```
TempPtr = StringPtr
```

is valid and is true if and only if **TempPtr** and **StringPtr** point to the same memory location or both are nil. Similarly,

```
TempPtr <> NIL
```

is a valid boolean expression and is true if and only if **TempPtr** has a nonnil value.[1]

Pointers may also be used as parameters in functions and procedures. These parameters may be either value or variable parameters, but corresponding pointer parameters must be bound to the same type. The value of a function may also be a pointer.

Dereferencing Pointers

The value of a nonnil pointer is the *address* of the memory location to which it points, *not* the data item stored in this location. This data item can be accessed by appending the **dereferencing operator** ↑ or ^ to the pointer:

$$pointer\uparrow \quad \text{or} \quad pointer^\wedge$$

If the pointer is nil or undefined, however, then there is no memory location associated with this variable, and so an attempt to dereference it is an error. Otherwise, *pointer*↑ is a variable whose type is that to which *pointer* is bound. It is a dynamic variable, however, because at one point during program execution, there may be a particular memory location associated with it, and at a later time, no memory location or a different one may be associated with it. This differs from ordinary variables for which memory locations are allocated at compile time, and this association remains fixed throughout the execution of the program.

To illustrate, suppose that pointer variable **StringPtr** has a nonnil value. Then **StringPtr**↑ is a variable of type **StringType** and may be used in the same manner as any other variable of this type. For example, a value can be assigned to it by an assignment statement

```
StringPtr↑ := 'COMPUTER';
```

and its individual characters accessed as in

```
IF StringPtr↑[1] = 'A' THEN
   writeln( StringPtr↑ )
END {IF};
```

If, however, **StringPtr** is nil or undefined so that no memory location is associated with the dynamic variable **StringPtr**↑, an attempt to execute either of these statements is an error.

If both **TempPtr** and **StringPtr** have nonnil values, the statement

```
TempPtr↑ := StringPtr↑;
```

is a valid assignment statement because both of the dynamic variables **TempPtr**↑ and **StringPtr**↑ exist and they have the same type **StringType**, since both **TempPtr** and **StringPtr** are bound to this type. This statement copies the contents of the memory location(s) pointed to by **StringPtr** into the location(s) pointed to by **TempPtr**:

---

[1] Turbo Pascal 7.0 provides an **Assigned** procedure to determine whether a pointer is nil. See Section H.7 of Appendix H.

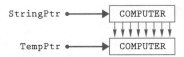

Note that this result is quite different from that produced by the assignment statement

```
TempPtr := StringPtr;
```

considered earlier, which causes `TempPtr` to point to the same memory location pointed to by `StringPtr`:

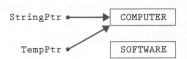

To illustrate further the difference between a pointer and a dereferenced pointer, consider the relational operators = and <>. As we have noted, these operators can be used to determine whether two pointers bound to the same type point to the same memory location. Thus, the boolean expression

```
TempPtr = StringPtr
```

is true only if `TempPtr` and `StringPtr` point to the same memory location or both are nil. This is not equivalent to the boolean expression

```
TempPtr↑ = StringPtr↑
```

however, since this compares the string pointed to by `TempPtr` with the string pointed to by `StringPtr`. Obviously if `TempPtr = StringPtr` is true and both pointer variables have nonnil values, then `TempPtr↑ = StringPtr↑` also is true; the string values of these two variables are identical, since `TempPtr` and `StringPtr` point to the same memory location and thus to the same string. The converse is not true, however. The values of `TempPtr↑` and `StringPtr↑` may be equal but may be stored in different locations; that is, `TempPtr` and `StringPtr` point to different memory locations. Also note that if one of the pointers `TempPtr` or `StringPtr` is nil, then the boolean expression `TempPtr = StringPtr` is valid, but `TempPtr↑ = StringPtr↑` is not.

The Procedure dispose

If the memory location pointed to by a pointer is no longer needed, it may be released and made available for later allocation by calling the procedure `dispose`:

The Procedure dispose

Form:

dispose(*pointer*)

Purpose:
Frees the memory location pointed to by *pointer*
and leaves *pointer* undefined.

For example, the statement

```
dispose( StringPtr )
```

releases the memory location pointed to **StringPtr**, making it available for allocation later. The pointer variable **StringPtr** is now undefined, and so any attempt to use its value as in a reference **StringPtr**↑ is an error.

16.3 Implementing Linked Lists

Pointer variables, which we introduced in the preceding section, are not very useful by themselves. Rather, their importance lies in the fact that they make it possible to implement dynamic data structures such as linked lists. As we have noted, dynamic structures are more suitable than are static structures for modeling a data set whose size changes during processing. In this and the next section we show how linked lists can be implemented using records and Pascal pointers.

Linked List Declarations

The nodes in a linked list are represented in Pascal as records having two kinds of fields, data fields and link fields. The data fields are of a type that is appropriate for storing a list element, and the types of the link fields are pointer types. Declarations for a linked list might thus have the form

```
TYPE
    ListElementType = . . .;   {type of list elements}
    ListPointer = ↑ListNode;   {type of pointers to list nodes}
    ListNode = RECORD
                   Data : ListElementType;
                   Next : ListPointer
               END;
    LinkedListType = ListPointer;
```

The type **ListElementType** of the first field **Data** is the type of the values being stored. For a linked list of names,

`ListElementType` would be a string type:

```
ListElementType = string[5];
```

For a linked list of employee records

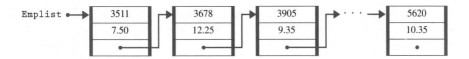

`ListElementType` might be defined by

```
EmployeeRecord = RECORD
                    Number : integer;
                    HourlyRate : real
                 END;
ListElementType = EmployeeRecord;
```

The value of a variable `List` declared by

```
VAR
    List : LinkedListType;
```

will be a pointer to the first node in the linked list.

Note that in the preceding type declarations, the definition of the pointer type `ListPointer`

```
ListPointer = ↑ListNode;
```

precedes the definition of the record type `ListNode`. This is the only situation in which it is permissible to use an identifier (`ListNode`) before it is defined.

Creating an Empty Linked List

To construct a linked list, we first must be able to create an empty list. The variable `List` is a pointer to the first node of the linked list, but since there is no such node for an empty list, we simply initialize `List` to be a nil pointer, thus indicating that it points to no node:

`List ●`

A procedure for creating an empty list thus is

```
PROCEDURE CreateList( VAR List : LinkedListType );
{-----------------------------------------------------------------

    Purpose:   Create an empty linked List.
    Returns:   Empty linked List (a nil pointer).

--------------------------------------------------------------}
```

```
BEGIN
   List := NIL
END {CreateList};
```

Checking If a Linked List Is Empty

Since an empty linked list is represented by a nil pointer, it is easy to determine whether a linked list is empty. The following boolean-valued function does this and returns the value true if the list is empty and the value false otherwise:

```
FUNCTION EmptyList( List : LinkedListType ) : boolean;
{---------------------------------------------------------------

   Accepts:   A linked List.
   Purpose:   Check if a linked List is empty.
   Returns:   True if the list is empty and false otherwise.


-------------------------------------------------------------}

BEGIN
   EmptyList := (List = NIL)
END {EmptyList};
```

Adding Elements at the Front of a Linked List

One method of constructing a linked list is to repeatedly add new nodes at the front of the list, beginning with an empty list. To illustrate, consider again the linked list of names:

To add **Adams** at the front of this list, we saw that we must first acquire a new node in which to store this new name. The procedure **new** can be used for this:

```
new( TempPtr );
```

The statement

```
TempPtr↑.Data := 'Adams';
```

can then be used to store the name **Adams** in the data part of this node:

This node is then added at the front of the list by setting its link field so that it points to the first node:

```
TempPtr↑.Next := List;
```

and then by setting **List** to point to this new first node:

```
List := TempPtr;
```

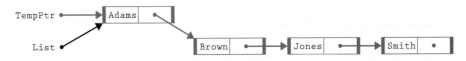

The following procedure implements this approach:

```
PROCEDURE AddToFrontOfList( VAR List : LinkedListType;
                                Item : ListElementType );

{--------------------------------------------------------------

    Accepts:    A linked List and an Item.
    Purpose:    Add Item at the front of a linked list with
                first node pointed to by List.
    Returns:    Modified linked List.

---------------------------------------------------------------}

    VAR
       TempPtr : ListPointer;    {pointer to new node}

    BEGIN
       new( TempPtr );
       TempPtr↑.Data := Item;
       TempPtr↑.Next := List;
       List := TempPtr
    END {AddToFrontOfList};
```

Traversing a Linked List

Once a linked list has been constructed, we may want to **traverse** it from beginning to end and process (for example, display) each element in it. To traverse a list stored in an array, we move through the list from one element to the next by varying an array index in some repetition structure. The analog for a linked list is to move through the list by varying a pointer variable in a repetition structure, moving from one node to the next by following the link fields.

To illustrate, suppose we wish to display the names stored in the linked list

We begin by initializing some auxiliary pointer **CurrPtr** to point to the first node and display the list element **Brown** stored in this node:

CurrPtr := List;

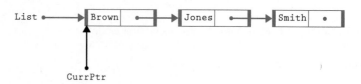

writeln(CurrPtr↑.Data);

To move to the next node, we follow the link from the current node, setting **CurrPtr** equal to **CurrPtr↑.Next**—analogous to incrementing an index in an array by 1—and display the name **Jones** stored there:

CurrPtr := CurrPtr↑.Next;

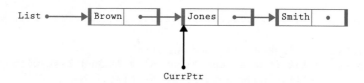

writeln(CurrPtr↑.Data);

After displaying the name in this node, we move to the next node and display the list element **Smith** stored there:

CurrPtr := CurrPtr↑.Next;

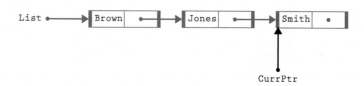

writeln(CurrPtr↑.Data);

When we attempt to move to the next node, **CurrPtr** becomes nil, signaling the end of the list:

CurrPtr := CurrPtr↑.Next;

CurrPtr

In summary, a linked list can be traversed as follows:

ALGORITHM TO TRAVERSE A LINKED LIST

(* Accepts: A linked list with first node pointed to by *List*.
   Purpose: Traverse this linked list, processing each list element
                   exactly once.
   Returns/Output: Depends on the kind of processing. *)

1. Initialize *CurrPtr* to *List*.
2. While *CurrPtr* is not nil, do the following:
    a. Process *CurrPtr↑.Data*, the data part of the node pointed to by
       CurrPtr.
    b. Move to the next node by setting *CurrPtr* equal to *CurrPtr↑.Next*,
       the link in the next field of the current node.

Note that this algorithm is correct even for an empty list, since in this case *List* is a nil pointer and the while loop is bypassed.

Example: Reversing a String

The program in Figure 16.1 uses these techniques for constructing and traversing a linked list to reverse the characters in a string. It first calls procedure **CreateList** to create an empty list and then reads the characters, using procedure **AddToFrontOfList** to add each character to the beginning of the list. When the special symbol **$** is read, signaling the end of the string, the list is traversed, using the procedure **LinkedTraverse**, which implements the preceding list-traversal algorithm. Since the last characters read are at the beginning of the list, the characters in the string are displayed in reverse order. (This Last-In-First-Out processing suggests an alternative to the array-based implementation of stacks described in Chapter 13. Linked stacks and queues are considered in the exercises.)

   FIGURE 16.1   Reversing a string.

```
PROGRAM Reverse( input, output );
{****************************************************************************

    Input (keyboard): A string of characters.
    Purpose:          Reverse a string of characters.  As each character
                      is read, it is stored at the beginning of a linked
                      list.  This list is then traversed and the
                      characters displayed.
    Output (screen):  User prompts and reversed strings of characters.

    ****************************************************************************}

CONST
    EndMark = '$';     {signals end of string}
```

FIGURE 16.1 Reversing a string. (cont.)

```
TYPE
   ListElementType = char;
   ListPointer = ^ListNode;
   ListNode = RECORD
                  Data : ListElementType;
                  Next : ListPointer
              END;
   LinkedListType = ListPointer;

VAR
   List : LinkedListType;   {pointer to first node in linked list}
   Ch : char;                {current character being processed}

PROCEDURE CreateList( VAR List : LinkedListType );
{-----------------------------------------------------------------------

   Purpose: Create an empty linked List.
   Returns: Empty linked List (a nil pointer).

-----------------------------------------------------------------------}

   BEGIN
      List := NIL
   END {CreateList};

PROCEDURE AddToFrontOfList( VAR List : LinkedListType;
                                Item : ListElementType );
{-----------------------------------------------------------------------

   Accepts:  A linked List and an Item.
   Purpose:  Add Item at the front of a linked list with first
             node pointed to by List.
   Returns:  Modified linked List.

-----------------------------------------------------------------------}

   VAR
      TempPtr : ListPointer;   {pointer to new node}

   BEGIN
      new( TempPtr );
      TempPtr^.Data := Item;
      TempPtr^.Next := List;
      List := TempPtr
   END {AddToFrontOfList};
```

FIGURE 16.1   Reversing a string. (cont.)

```
PROCEDURE LinkedTraverse( List : LinkedListType );
{-----------------------------------------------------------------

   Accepts:          A linked list with first node pointed to by List.
   Purpose:          Traverse a linked list, processing each data
                     item exactly once.
   Output (screen): Data items stored in the list.

   -----------------------------------------------------------------}

   VAR
      CurrPtr : ListPointer;   {pointer to current node being processed}

   BEGIN
      CurrPtr:= List;
      WHILE CurrPtr <> NIL DO
         BEGIN
            write( CurrPtr^.Data );
            CurrPtr:= CurrPtr^.Next
         END {WHILE};
      writeln
   END {LinkedTraverse};

BEGIN {*************** main program ***************}
   CreateList( List );
   writeln( 'Enter the string, using ', EndMark,
           ' to signal its end:' );
   read( Ch );
   WHILE Ch <> EndMark DO
      BEGIN
         AddToFrontOfList( List, Ch );
         read( Ch )
      END {WHILE};
   readln;
   writeln( 'Reversed string is:' );
   LinkedTraverse( List );
END {main program}.
```

Sample runs:

```
Enter the string, using $ to signal its end:
SHE SELLS SEASHELLS BY THE SEASHORE$
Reversed string is:
EROHSAES EHT YB SLLEHSAES SLLES EHS
```

FIGURE 16.1   Reversing a string. (cont.)

```
Enter the string, using $ to signal its end:
abcdefghijklmnopqrstuvwxyz$
Reversed string is:
zyxwvutsrqponmlkjihgfedcba

Enter the string, using $ to signal its end:
ABLE WAS I ERE I SAW ELBA$
Reversed string is:
ABLE WAS I ERE I SAW ELBA
```

Exercises

1. Assume the following declarations:

   ```
   VAR
       X: integer;
       P1, P2 : ↑integer;
       Q1, Q2 : ↑real;
   ```

   What (if anything) is wrong with each of the following statements?

   (a) `writeln( P1 );`   **(b)** `readln( P1↑ );`

   (c) `P1 := Q1;`   **(d)** `new( X );`

   (e) `IF P1↑ = NIL THEN`   **(f)** `BEGIN`
   `        Q1 := Q2;`   `            P1↑ := 17;`
   `                          `   `            new( P1 )`
   `                          `   `        END;`

2. Write type declarations needed for a linked list of records from the files

   (a) `InventoryFile`   **(b)** `StudentFile`   **(c)** `UsersFile`

   (See Appendix E for descriptions of these files.)

3. Assume the following declarations:

   ```
   TYPE
       NumberPointer = ↑NumberNode;
       NumberNode = RECORD
                        Data : integer;
                        Next : NumberPointer
                    END;

   VAR
       P1, P2 : NumberPointer;
       P3 : ↑integer;
   ```

and also assume that the following three statements have already been executed:

```
new( P1 );
new( P2 );
new( P3 );
```

Tell what will now be displayed by each of the following program segments, or explain why an error occurs:

(a)
```
P1↑.Data := 123;
P2↑.Data := 456;
P1↑.Next := P2;
writeln( P1↑.Data );
writeln( P1↑.Next↑.Data );
```

(b)
```
P1↑.Data := 12;
P2↑.Data := 34;
P1 := P2;
writeln( P1↑.Data );
writeln( P2↑.Data );
```

(c)
```
P1↑.Data := 123;
P2↑.Data := 456;
P1↑.Next := P2;
writeln( P2↑.Data );
writeln( P2↑.Next↑.Data );
```

(d)
```
P1↑.Data := 12;
P2↑.Data := 34;
P3↑.Data := 34;
P1↑.Next := P2;
P2↑.Next := P3;
writeln( P1↑.Data );
writeln( P2↑.Data );
writeln( P3↑.Data );
```

(e)
```
P1↑.Data := 111;
P2↑.Data := 222;
P1↑.Next := P2;
P2↑.Next := P1;
writeln( P1↑.Data, P2↑.Data );
writeln( P1↑.Next↑.Data );
writeln( P1↑.Next↑.Next↑.Data );
```

(f)
```
P1↑.Data := 12;
P2↑.Data := 34;
P1 := P2;
P2↑.Next := P1;
writeln( P1↑.Data );
writeln( P2↑.Data );
writeln( P1↑.Next↑.Data );
writeln( P2↑.Next↑.Data );
```

4. Given the following linked list and pointers **P1**, **P2**, **P3**, and **P4**:

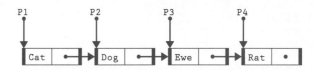

draw a similar diagram for each of the following, to show how this configuration changes when the given program segment is executed, or explain why an error occurs:

(a) `P1 := P2↑.Next;`

(b) `P4 := P1;`

(c) `P4↑.Data := P1↑.Data;`

(d) `P4↑.Next↑.Data := P1↑.Data;`

(e) `P2↑.Next := P3↑.Next;`

(f) `P4↑.Next := P1;`

(g) `P1↑.Next := P3↑.Next;`
    `P1 := P3;`

(h) `P1 := P3;`
    `P1↑.Next := P3↑.Next;`

(i) `P4↑.Next := P3↑.Next;`
    `P3↑.Next := P2↑.Next;`
    `P2↑.Next := P1↑.Next;`

(j) `P4↑.Next := P3;`
    `P4↑.Next↑.Next := P2;`
    `P4↑.Next↑.Next↑.Next := P1;`
    `P1 := NIL;`

5. Write a

(a) nonrecursive function
(b) recursive function

to count the nodes in a linked list.

6. Write a

(a) nonrecursive boolean-valued function
(b) recursive boolean-valued function

that determines whether the data items in a linked list are arranged in ascending order.

7. Write a

(a) nonrecursive function
(b) recursive function

that returns a pointer to the last node in a linked list.

8. Write a procedure to reverse a linked list; that is, the last node becomes the first node, and all links between nodes are reversed.

9. Type definitions like those for linked lists can be used to define a **linked stack:**

```
TYPE
   StackElementType = ...;   {type of stack elements}
   StackPointer = ↑StackNode;
   StackNode = RECORD
                  Data : StackElementType;
                  Next : StackPointer
               END;
   StackType = StackPointer;

VAR
   Stack : StackType;
```

The value of **Stack** will be a pointer to the top of the stack. For example, a linked stack of integers might be pictured as

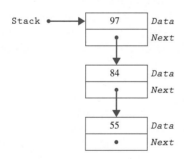

(a) Describe how an element would be popped from this linked stack. Include a picture of the modified stack.
(b) Assuming that this linked stack has been modified as in part (a), describe how the integer 77 would be pushed onto the linked stack. Include a picture of the modified stack.
(c) Modify the procedures **CreateStack**, **Push**, and **Pop** and the function **EmptyStack** given in Section 13.2 for this implementation.
(d) Use your procedures in a program like that in Figure 13.1 to convert integers from base-10 to base-2 notation.

10. Like stacks, queues also can be implemented as linked lists. For **linked queues,** we might use two pointers, **FrontPtr**, which points to the node at the front of the queue, and **RearPtr**, which points to the node at the rear. For example, a linked queue containing the integers 573, −29, and 616 in this order, might be pictured as

(a) Describe how an element would be removed from this linked queue. Include a picture of the modified queue.

(b) Assuming that this linked queue has been modified as in part (a), describe how the integer 127 would be added to the linked queue. Include a picture of the modified queue.

(c) Write appropriate declarations for a linked queue.

(d) Write procedures/functions for the basic queue operations: **CreateQ**, **EmptyQ**, **AddQ**, **RemoveQ** (see Section 13.4).

16.4   Other Operations on Linked Lists

In the preceding section we implemented the basic operations on linked lists of creating an empty linked list, checking if a list is empty, and traversing a linked list, but we considered only a special case of the insert operation, namely, adding an item at the beginning of the list. In this section we implement the general insert operation together with the delete and search operations.

Inserting Items into a Linked List

In Section 16.1, we described how to insert a new node into a linked list after a node pointed to by a pointer **PredPtr**. To show how this is done in our implementation of linked lists, consider again the problem of inserting the name **Lewis** after the node containing **Jones** in the following linked list:

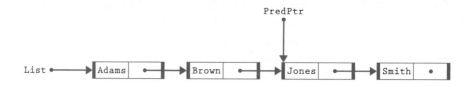

We first obtain a new node and store the name **Lewis** in its data part:

```
new( TempPtr );
TempPtr↑.Data := 'Lewis';
```

TempPtr ●———▶ | Lewis | ● |

We insert it into the list by first setting its link part equal to **PredPtr↑.Next** so that it points to its successor:

TempPtr↑.Next := PredPtr↑.Next;

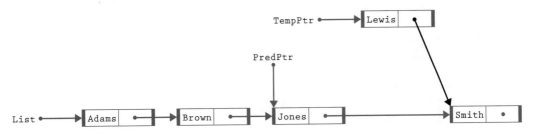

and then resetting the link part of the predecessor node to point to this new node:

PredPtr↑.Next := TempPtr;

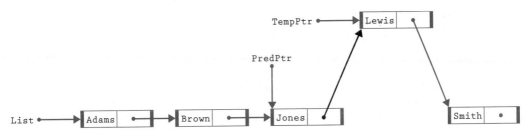

The following algorithm handles insertion at any point in a linked list:

ALGORITHM FOR INSERTION INTO A LINKED LIST

(* Accepts: A linked list with first node pointed to by *List*, a data *Item*, and a pointer *PredPtr*.

Purpose: Insert a node containing *Item* into the linked list following the node pointed to by *PredPtr*, or at the front of the list if *PredPtr* is nil.

Returns: Modified linked list with first node pointed to by *List*. *)

1. Get a node pointed to by *TempPtr*.
2. Set *TempPtr↑.Data* equal to *Item*.
3. If *PredPtr* = nil then do the following:
   (* Insert *Item* at beginning of list *)
   a. Set *TempPtr↑.Next* equal to *List*.
   b. Set *List* equal to *TempPtr*.

   Else do the following:
   (* There is a predecessor *)
   a. Set *TempPtr↑.Next* equal to *PredPtr↑.Next*.
   b. Set *PredPtr↑.Next* equal to *TempPtr*.

Deleting Items from a Linked List

As we saw in Section 16.1, there are two cases to consider for deletion: (1) deleting the first element in the list and (2) deleting an element that has a predecessor. For the first case we simply change the pointer **List** to the first node so that it points to the second node:

```
TempPtr := List;
List  := List↑.Next;
```

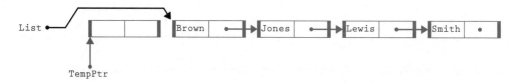

and then use the procedure **dispose** to return the first node to the storage pool of available nodes:

```
dispose( TempPtr );
```

The second case is almost as easy as the first. For example, to delete the node containing **Lewis** from the preceding list, we need only set the link of its predecessor to point to the node containing its successor (if there is one):

```
TempPtr := PredPtr↑.Next;
PredPtr↑.Next:= TempPtr↑.Next;
dispose( TempPtr );
```

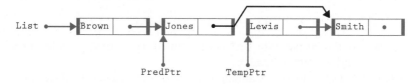

The following algorithm handles all cases of deletion from a linked list:

ALGORITHM FOR DELETION FROM A LINKED LIST

(∗ Accepts: A linked list with first node pointed to by *List* and a pointer
                 PredPtr.
   Purpose: Delete the node from the linked list whose predecessor is pointed
                 to by *PredPtr* or delete the first node if *PredPtr* is nil, unless
                 the list is empty.
   Returns: The modified linked list with first node pointed to by *List*.
   Output: A list-empty message if the list is empty. ∗)

If the list is empty then
     Display a list-empty message.

Else do the following:
    1. If **PredPtr** = nil then   (∗ deleting the first node ∗)
        a. Set **TempPtr** equal to **List**.
        b. Set **List** equal to **List**↑**.Next**.
    Else do the following: (∗ node has a predecessor ∗)
        a. Set **TempPtr** equal to **PredPtr**↑**.Next**.
        b. Set **PredPtr**↑**.Next** equal to **TempPtr**↑**.Next**.
    2. Return the node pointed to by **TempPtr** to the storage pool of available free nodes.

Searching a Linked List

The algorithms for insertion and deletion use a pointer to the predecessor of the item to be inserted or deleted (nil if there is no predecessor). If the elements in the list are not arranged in any particular order, so that it makes no difference where new items are inserted in the list, then we may as well insert them at the beginning of the list. For such unordered lists, the third step of the insertion algorithm simplifies to

    3. Set **TempPtr**↑**.Next** equal to **List**.
    4. Set **List** equal to **TempPtr**.

Procedure **AddToFrontOfList** in the program of Figure 16.1 implemented this simplified insertion algorithm. (Note that the insertion operation for such lists is precisely the push operation for stacks.)

    Before an item can be deleted from a linked list, however, a pointer **PredPtr** must be positioned so that it points to the predecessor of the node to be deleted, given only the value to be deleted. The following algorithm, which performs a linear search of a linked list, can be used to position **PredPtr**. It assumes that the data part of a node is a record, one of whose fields is designated as the **key field** and which contains the items being sought.

ALGORITHM TO SEARCH A LINKED LIST

(∗ Accepts: A data value **KeyValue** and a linked list with first node pointed to by **List**.

  Purpose: Carry out a linear search of the linked list for a node containing a specified **KeyValue** in its key field.

  Returns: If the search is successful, **Found** is true, **CurrPtr** points to the node containing **KeyValue**, and **PredPtr** points to its predecessor or is nil if there is none. **Found** is false for an unsuccessful search. ∗)

    1. Initialize **CurrPtr** to **List**, **PredPtr** to nil, and **Found** to false.
    2. While not **Found** and **CurrPtr** ≠ nil do the following:
        If **CurrPtr**↑**.Data.Key** = **KeyValue** then
           Set **Found** to true.

Else do the following:
 a. Set *PredPtr* equal to *CurrPtr*.
 b. Move to the next node by setting *CurrPtr* equal to *CurrPtr↑.Next*.

In an **ordered** or **sorted list,** the nodes are linked together in such a way that the items stored in the nodes are visited in ascending (or descending) order as the list is traversed. If the data part of a node is a record, the ordering is based on the values that appear in a key field. When a new item is inserted, it must be inserted in such a way that this ordering is maintained. Both the insertion algorithm and the deletion algorithm require a pointer *PredPtr* to the predecessor of the item being inserted or deleted (if there is one), and because the list is sorted, the following modified search algorithm can be used to position this pointer:

ALGORITHM TO SEARCH AN ORDERED LINKED LIST

(* Accepts: A data value *KeyValue* and an ordered linked list in which the items in the key fields are in ascending order, with first node pointed to by *List*.

  Purpose: Carry out a linear search of the ordered linked list for the first node containing *KeyValue* in its key field or for a position to insert a new node.

  Returns: *CurrPtr* points to the first node having a key ≥ *KeyValue* or is nil if *KeyValue* is greater than the keys of all nodes in the list. *PredPtr* points to its predecessor or is nil if *KeyValue* is smaller than the keys of all nodes in the list. *Found* is returned as true if a node containing *KeyValue* is already in the list; otherwise, *Found* is false. *)

1. Initialize *CurrPtr* to *List*, *PredPtr* to nil, *Found* to false, and *DoneSearching* to false.
2. While not *DoneSearching* and *CurrPtr* ≠ nil do the following:
   If *CurrPtr↑.Data.Key* ≥ *KeyValue* then
    a. Set *DoneSearching* to true.
    b. Set *Found* to true if *CurrPtr↑.Data.Key* = *KeyValue*.
   Else do the following:
    a. Set *PredPtr* equal to *CurrPtr*.
    b. Set *CurrPtr* equal to *CurrPtr↑.Next*.

The search technique we have used here is a **linear search** and is the only feasible searching strategy for linked lists. The more efficient binary search described in Section 9.4 for ordered lists implemented as arrays is not a real option for linked lists, since it requires repeatedly accessing the middle element of the part of the list being searched, and this can be done efficiently only when each list element can be accessed directly. For a linked list, however, we have direct access only to the first node; to access any other node, we must traverse the first part of the list, following the links, until we reach that node. (In Section 16.7 we describe a **multiply linked structure,** called a **binary search tree,** in which a binarylike search is possible.)

16.5   A Unit for the ADT Linked List

We have looked at several examples of linked lists and have given declarations for them in Pascal and algorithms for the basic operations of this abstract data type: creation of an empty list, checking if a list is empty, insertion, deletion, and searching. In this section we collect together these declarations and subprograms for the algorithms into a unit that may be used in any program in which linked lists are needed.

 Unit for the ADT Linked List

```
UNIT LinkedListADT;
{*******************************************************************

    Imports:    ListElementType from unit ListElementInfo.
    Purpose:    Process linked lists whose nodes store items of type
                ListElementType, which is defined by the user in a unit
                ListElementInfo.  For generality, we assume that the
                list elements are records, one of whose fields has been
                designated as a Key field of type KeyType.
    Exports:    Types:      ListElementType
                                (imported from ListElementInfo),
                            ListPointer, LinkedListType
                Function:   EmptyList
                Procedures: CreateList, LinkedTraverse,
                            LinearSearch, OrderedLinearSearch,
                            LinkedInsert, LinkedDelete


    *******************************************************************}

INTERFACE

    USES ListElementInfo;      {import ListElementType}

    TYPE
        ListPointer = ^ListNode;
        ListNode = RECORD
                        Data : ListElementType;
                        Next : ListPointer
                   END;
        LinkedListType = ListPointer;
```

Unit for the ADT Linked List (cont.)

```
PROCEDURE CreateList( VAR List : LinkedListType );
{-----------------------------------------------------------------------

    Purpose:   Create an empty linked List.
    Returns:   Empty linked List (a nil pointer).


-----------------------------------------------------------------------}

FUNCTION EmptyList( List : LinkedListType ) : boolean;
{-----------------------------------------------------------------------

    Accepts:   A linked List.
    Purpose:   Check if a linked List is empty.
    Returns:   True if the list is empty and false otherwise.


-----------------------------------------------------------------------}

PROCEDURE LinkedTraverse( List : LinkedListType );
{-----------------------------------------------------------------------

    Accepts:        A linked list with first node pointed to by List.
    Purpose:        Traverse the linked list, processing each data item
                    exactly once.
    Returns/Output: Depends on the kind of processing.


-----------------------------------------------------------------------}

PROCEDURE LinearSearch(     List : LinkedListType;
                            KeyValue : KeyType;
                        VAR Found : boolean;
                        VAR PredPtr, CurrPtr : ListPointer );
{-----------------------------------------------------------------------

    Accepts:   A data value KeyValue and a linked list with first node
               pointed to by List.
    Purpose:   Carry out a linear search of the (unordered) linked list
               for a node containing KeyValue in its key field.
    Returns:   If the search is successful, Found is true, CurrPtr points
               to the node containing KeyValue and PredPtr points to its
               predecessor or is nil if there is none.  Found is false
               for an unsuccessful search.


-----------------------------------------------------------------------}
```

Unit for the ADT Linked List (cont.)

```
PROCEDURE OrderedLinearSearch(       List : LinkedListType;
                                     KeyValue : KeyType;
                                VAR Found : boolean;
                                VAR PredPtr, CurrPtr : ListPointer );
  {-------------------------------------------------------------------

     Accepts:  A data value KeyValue and an ordered linked list
               in which the items in the key fields are in ascENDing
               order with first node pointed to by List.
     Purpose:  Carry out a linear search of the ordered linked list
               for the first node containing KeyValue in its key field
               or for a position to insert a new node.
     Returns:  CurrPtr points to the first node having a key >= KeyValue
               or is nil if KeyValue is greater than the keys of all
               nodes in the list.  PredPtr points to its predecessor
               or is nil if KeyValue is smaller than the keys of all
               nodes in the list.  Found is returned as true if a node
               containing KeyValue is already in the list; otherwise,
               Found is false.

  -------------------------------------------------------------------}


PROCEDURE LinkedInsert( VAR List : LinkedListType;
                            Item : ListElementType;
                            PredPtr : ListPointer );
  {-------------------------------------------------------------------

     Accepts:  A linked list with first node pointed to by List, a new
               list Item, and a pointer PredPtr.
     Purpose:  Insert a node containing Item into the linked list
               following the node pointed to by PredPtr, or at the
               front of the list if PredPtr is nil.
     Returns:  Modified linked list with first node pointed to by List.

  -------------------------------------------------------------------}


PROCEDURE LinkedDelete( VAR List : LinkedListType;
                            PredPtr : ListPointer );
  {-------------------------------------------------------------------

     Accepts:  A linked list with first node pointed to by List and a
               pointer PredPtr.
     Purpose:  Delete the node from the linked list whose predecessor is
               pointed to by PredPtr, or delete the first node if
               PredPtr is nil, unless the list is empty.
     Returns:  Modified linked list with first node pointed to
               by List.
     Output:   A list-empty message if the list was empty.

  -------------------------------------------------------------------}
```

Unit for the ADT Linked List (cont.)

```
IMPLEMENTATION

PROCEDURE CreateList;

   BEGIN
      List := NIL
   END {CreateList};

FUNCTION EmptyList;

   BEGIN
      EmptyList := List = NIL
   END {EmptyList};

PROCEDURE LinkedTraverse;

   VAR
      CurrPtr : ListPointer;   {pointer to current node being processed}

   BEGIN
      CurrPtr := List;
      WHILE CurrPtr <> NIL DO
         BEGIN
            {Appropriate statements to process CurrPtr^.Data are
             inserted here}
            CurrPtr := CurrPtr^.Next
         END {WHILE}
   END {LinkedTraverse};

PROCEDURE LinearSearch;

   VAR
      CurrPtr : ListPointer;    {pointer to current node}

   BEGIN
      CurrPtr := List;
      PredPtr := NIL;
      Found := false;
      WHILE NOT Found and (CurrPtr <> NIL) DO
         IF CurrPtr^.Data.Key = KeyValue THEN
            Found := true
         ELSE
            BEGIN
               PredPtr := CurrPtr;
               CurrPtr := CurrPtr^.Next
            END {ELSE}
   END {LinearSearch};
```

Unit for the ADT Linked List (cont.)

```
PROCEDURE OrderedLinearSearch;

    VAR
        CurrPtr : ListPointer;    {pointer to current node}
        DoneSearching : boolean; {signals when search is complete}

    BEGIN
        CurrPtr := List;
        PredPtr := NIL;
        Found := false;
        DoneSearching := false;
        WHILE NOT DoneSearching and (CurrPtr <> NIL) DO
            IF CurrPtr^.Data.Key >= KeyValue THEN
                BEGIN
                    DoneSearching := true;
                    Found := (CurrPtr^.Data.Key = KeyValue)
                END {IF}
            ELSE
                BEGIN
                    PredPtr := CurrPtr;
                    CurrPtr := CurrPtr^.Next
                END {ELSE}
    END {OrderedLinearSearch};

PROCEDURE LinkedInsert;

    VAR
        TempPtr : ListPointer;   {points to new node to be inserted}

    BEGIN
        new( TempPtr );
        TempPtr^.Data := Item;
        IF PredPtr = NIL THEN    {insert at beginning of list}
            BEGIN
                TempPtr^.Next := List;
                List := TempPtr
            END {IF}
        ELSE                        {node has a predecessor}
            BEGIN
                TempPtr^.Next := PredPtr^.Next;
                PredPtr^.Next := TempPtr
            END {ELSE};
    END { LinkedInsert};

PROCEDURE LinkedDelete;

    VAR
        TempPtr : ListPointer;       {points to node to be deleted}
```

Unit for the ADT Linked List (cont.)

```
    BEGIN
        IF EmptyList( List ) THEN
            BEGIN
                writeln( '***Attempt to delete from an empty list ***' );
            END {IF}
        ELSE
            BEGIN
                IF PredPtr = NIL THEN   {first node being deleted}
                    BEGIN
                        TempPtr := List;
                        List := TempPtr^.Next
                    END {IF}
                ELSE                         {node has a predecessor}
                    BEGIN
                        TempPtr := PredPtr^.Next;
                        PredPtr^.Next := TempPtr^.Next
                    END {ELSE};
                dispose( TempPtr )
            END {ELSE}
    END {LinkedDelete};

END {LinkedListADT}.
```

```
UNIT ListElementInfo;
{*************************************************************************

    Purpose:   Defines the type ListElementType of list elements,
               which is a record, one of whose fields has been
               designated as a Key field of type KeyType.
    Exports:   Type ListElementType.

*************************************************************************}

INTERFACE

TYPE
    KeyType = . . .;                  {type of key field -- defined by user}
    ListElementType = RECORD          {type of data part of nodes}
                           .          {defined by the user}
                           .
                           .
                        KEY : KeyType;
                           .
                           .
                           .
                        END;

IMPLEMENTATION

END {ListElementInfo}.
```

16.6   Example: Maintaining a Linked List of Employee Records

As an example of processing linked lists, suppose we wish to create and maintain an ordered linked list of employee records, each of which contains an employee's number, age, number of dependents, and hourly pay rate. These records are in a file, so the first task is to create the initial ordered linked list by reading these records and inserting them into the list, beginning with an empty list. The second task is to update this list by adding new records to the list, deleting records, and modifying existing records. Finally, after all of the updating is complete, the list must be copied back to the file. A first-level algorithm for solving this problem is as follows:

ALGORITHM TO MAINTAIN A LINKED LIST OF EMPLOYEE RECORDS

1. Create the initial ordered linked list by reading records from a file and inserting them into the list, beginning with an empty list.
2. Repeat the following until *Option* = 0:
   a. Read an *Option*.
   b. If *Option* is
      1: Read a new employee record and insert it into the list.
      2: Read an employee number and delete the record for that employee.
      3: Modify an existing record.
      0: Copy the list to a file and terminate processing.

The program in Figure 16.2 implements this algorithm. It obtains the type **LinkedListType**, the function **EmptyList**, and procedures **CreateList**, **OrderedLinearSearch**, **LinkedInsert**, and **LinkedDelete** from the unit for the ADT linked list described in the preceding section; procedure **CopyListToFile** is a modification of **LinkedTraverse**. **ListElementType** is defined in the unit **ListElementInfo** to be the record type **EmployeeRecord** in which the **Key** field stores an employee's number and is of type **KeyType = integer**. The program begins by constructing the linked list of employee records, calling the procedure **CreateList** to create an empty list and then repeatedly calling **AddRecord**, which uses **LinkedInsert** to add records from a file to the list. The user then selects from a menu of options for inserting, deleting, or modifying an employee record or for terminating processing. The insert and delete options are implemented using procedures **AddRecord** and **DeleteRecord**, which call **LinkedInsert** and **LinkedDelete**, respectively. A record is modified by calling procedure **ModifyRecord**, which uses **OrderedLinearSearch** to locate the desired record and then allows the user to enter new values for the fields in this record. When the quit option is selected, the updated list is copied back into a file, using the list-traversal techniques described in the preceding section. The structure of this program is displayed in the following structure diagram. (Recall that a shaded corner in a box indicates a procedure that is shared by two or more program units.)

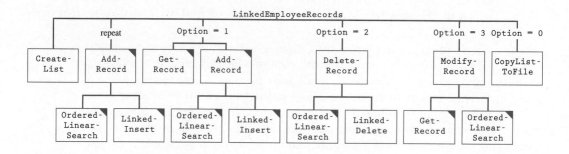

FIGURE 16.2   Maintaining a linked list of employee records.

```
UNIT ListElementInfo;
{*****************************************************************

    Purpose:   Defines the type ListElementType of list elements,
               which is an employee record with the employee number
               as the key field.
    Exports:   Types KeyType, EmployeeRecord, and ListElementType.


******************************************************************}

INTERFACE

TYPE
    KeyType = integer;               {type of key field -- defined by user}
    EmployeeRecord = RECORD
                        Key,      {key field -- employee number}
                        Age, Dependents : integer;
                        HourlyRate : real
                     END;
    ListElementType = EmployeeRecord;

IMPLEMENTATION

END {ListElementInfo}.
```

FIGURE 16.2   Maintaining a linked list of employee records. (cont.)

```pascal
PROGRAM LinkedEmployeeRecords( input, EmpFile, output );
{*****************************************************************

    Input (file):      Employee records.
    Input (keyboard):  Menu options and employee records.
    Purpose:           Process employee records.  Options are displayed
                       by procedure PrintMenu.  The records are stored
                       in an ordered linked list, with employee numbers
                       in ascending order.
    Output (file):     Updated employee records.
    Output (screen):   User prompts and messages.
    Imports:           Types KeyType, EmployeeRecord, and ListElementType
                       from ListElementInfo and procedures CreateList,
                       OrderedLinearSearch, LinkedInsert, and
                       LinkedDelete from LinkedListADT.


    *****************************************************************}

USES ListElementInfo, LinkedListADT;

CONST
    EmpFileName = 'FIL16-2.DAT'; {disk file of employee records}
    NumberOfOptions = 3;          {number of options in menu}

TYPE
    EmployeeFile = FILE of EmployeeRecord;

VAR
    EmpList : LinkedListType;       {linked list of employee records}
    Option : integer;              {option selected by user}
    EmpRecord : EmployeeRecord;    {record for an employee}
    EmpFile : EmployeeFile;        {permanent file of employee records}
    EmpNumber : integer;           {number of an employee}
    Response : char;               {user response}

PROCEDURE AddRecord( VAR EmpList : LinkedListType;
                     EmpRecord : EmployeeRecord );
{-----------------------------------------------------------------

    Accepts:         Linked list EmpList of employee records and
                     employee record EmpRecord.
    Purpose:         Insert the record of an employee into a linked
                     list ordered by employee number.
    Returns:         The modified linked list EmpList.
    Output (screen): Message if a record for this employee has
                     already been added to the list.


    -----------------------------------------------------------------}
```

FIGURE 16.2   Maintaining a linked list of employee records. (cont.)

```
    VAR
        PredPtr,                   {pointers to predecessor}
        SuccPtr : ListPointer; {and successor of record being inserted}
        Found : boolean;           {indicates if record was found}

    BEGIN
        OrderedLinearSearch( EmpList, EmpRecord.Key,
                              Found, PredPtr, SuccPtr );
        IF NOT Found THEN
            LinkedInsert( EmpList, EmpRecord, PredPtr )
        ELSE
            BEGIN
                write( 'Record for ', EmpRecord.Key, ' already exists -- ' );
                writeln( 'ignoring this record.' )
            END {ELSE}
    END {AddRecord};

PROCEDURE DeleteRecord( VAR EmpList : LinkedListType;
                             EmpNumber : integer );
{---------------------------------------------------------------------

    Accepts:        Linked list EmpList of employee records and
                    employee number EmpNumber.
    Purpose:        Delete the record of an employee.
    Returns:        The modified linked list EmpList.
    Output (screen): Message if record not found.


---------------------------------------------------------------------}

    VAR
        EmpRecPtr,                     {pointer to old record}
        PredPtr : ListPointer;         {and its predecessor}
        Found : boolean;               {indicates if record was found}

    BEGIN
        OrderedLinearSearch( EmpList, EmpNumber, Found, PredPtr, EmpRecPtr );
        IF Found THEN
            LinkedDelete( EmpList, PredPtr )
        ELSE
            writeln( '** Record for employee ', EmpNumber:1,
                    ' not found **' )
    END {DeleteRecord};

PROCEDURE GetRecord( VAR EmpRecord : EmployeeRecord );
{---------------------------------------------------------------------

    Input (keyboard): An employee record.
    Purpose:          Get an employee record from the user.
    Returns:          The record EmpRecord.
    Output (screen):  User prompt.


---------------------------------------------------------------------}
```

FIGURE 16.2   Maintaining a linked list of employee records. (cont.)

```
BEGIN
    writeln( 'Enter employee''s number, age, dependents, ',
             'and hourly rate:' );
    WITH EmpRecord DO
        readln( Key, Age, Dependents, HourlyRate )
END {GetRecord};

PROCEDURE ModifyRecord( EmpList : LinkedListType );
{----------------------------------------------------------------------

    Accepts:         Linked list EmpList of employee records.
    Purpose:         Modify the record of an employee.
    Returns:         The modified linked list EmpList.
    Output (screen): User prompts, labels, and contents of an
                     employee record.

-----------------------------------------------------------------------}

    VAR
        EmpNumber : integer;        {employee's number}
        EmpRecPtr,                  {pointers to old record}
        PredPtr : ListPointer;      {and its predecessor}
        Found : boolean;            {indicates if record was found}

    BEGIN
        write ('Employee''s number?  ');
        readln( EmpNumber );
        OrderedLinearSearch( EmpList, EmpNumber, Found, PredPtr, EmpRecPtr );
        IF Found THEN
            WITH EmpRecPtr^.Data DO
                BEGIN
                    writeln( 'Age: ', Age:1, '   Dependents: ', Dependents:1,
                             '   Hourly Rate:  $', HourlyRate:4:2 );
                    write( 'Enter new age, dependents, and hourly rate:  ' );
                    readln( Age, Dependents, HourlyRate )
                END {WITH}
        ELSE
            writeln( '** Record for employee ', EmpNumber:1, ' not found **' )
    END {ModifyRecord};

PROCEDURE CopyListToFile(    EmpList: LinkedListType;
                         VAR EmpFile : EmployeeFile );
{----------------------------------------------------------------------

    Accepts:       Linked list EmpList of employee records.
    Purpose:       Write the linked list to the file EmpFile.
    Output (file): List of employee records.

-----------------------------------------------------------------------}

    VAR
        CurrPtr: ListPointer;    {pointer to current node}
```

FIGURE 16.2   Maintaining a linked list of employee records. (cont.)

```
    BEGIN
        rewrite( EmpFile );
        CurrPtr := EmpList;
        WHILE CurrPtr <> NIL DO
            BEGIN
                write( EmpFile,CurrPtr^.Data );
                CurrPtr := CurrPtr^.Next
            END {WHILE}
    END {CopyListToFile};


BEGIN {*************** main program ***************}
    {First create the linked list of employee records}
    assign( EmpFile, EmpFileName );
    reset( EmpFile );
    CreateList( EmpList );
    WHILE NOT eof( EmpFile ) DO
        BEGIN
            read( EmpFile, EmpRecord );
            AddRecord( EmpList, EmpRecord );
        END {WHILE};

    {Now process this linked list}
    REPEAT
        writeln( 'To add, delete, or modify an employee''s record, enter' );
        write  ( '    1      2      or    3      (0 to quit):  ' );
        readln( Option );
        IF Option IN [0..NumberOfOptions] THEN
            CASE Option OF
                1 : BEGIN
                        GetRecord( EmpRecord );
                        AddRecord( EmpList, EmpRecord )
                    END {case 1};
                2 : BEGIN
                        write( 'Number of employee to be deleted:  ' );
                        readln( EmpNumber );
                        write( 'Sure (Y or N)?  ' );
                        readln( Response );
                        IF Response IN ['Y', 'y'] THEN
                            DeleteRecord( EmpList, EmpNumber )
                    END {case 2};
                3 : ModifyRecord( EmpList );
                0 : BEGIN
                        CopyListToFile( EmpList, EmpFile );
                        close( EmpFile )
                    END {case 0}
            END {CASE}
        ELSE
            writeln( '*** Illegal Option ***' );
        writeln
    UNTIL Option = 0
END {main program}.
```

FIGURE 16.2   Maintaining a linked list of employee records. (cont.)

Listing of `FIL16-2.DAT` used in sample run:

```
2100 17 0  9.60
3889 19 1 10.25
2222 65 3 16.05
1801 39 4 14.15
4144 31 2 12.85
1111 39 3 13.50
1357 25 2 12.50
2534 40 5 14.95
3011 21 0 12.75
2888 29 1 13.95
3414 22 2 12.80
```

Sample run:

```
To add, delete, or modify an employee's record, enter
     1     2     or   3      (0 to quit):
To add, delete, or modify an employee's record, enter
     1     2     or   3      (0 to quit):  3
Employee's number?  1112
Employee 1112 not found

To add, delete, or modify an employee's record, enter
     1     2     or   3      (0 to quit)::  3
Employee's number?  1111
Age: 39   Dependents: 3   Hourly Rate:  $10.50
Enter new age, dependents, and hourly rate:  39 2 10.75

To add, delete, or modify an employee's record, enter
     1     2     or   3      (0 to quit):  2
Enter employee's number, age, dependents, and hourly rate:
3137 44 2 11.25

To add, delete, or modify an employee's record, enter
     1     2     or   3      (0 to quit):  1
Number of employee to be deleted?  2222
Sure (Y or N)?   Y

To add, delete, or modify an employee's record, enter
     1     2     or   3      (0 to quit):  4
*** Illegal Option ***

To add, delete, or modify an employee's record, enter
     1     2     or   3      (0 to quit):  0
```

Exercises

1. Modify the unit for the ADT linked list by adding a procedure **LinkedErase** that erases a linked list, leaving it empty. It should traverse the linked list, removing each node and returning it to the storage pool of available nodes.

2. The procedures **LinkedInsert** and **LinkedDelete** in the linked-list unit require checking whether the item to be inserted or deleted has a predecessor in the list. These procedures can be shortened if we require every linked list to have a dummy node, called a **head node,** at the beginning of the list so that the first node that stores the actual data has the head node as a predecessor. Modify the procedures **LinkedInsert** and **LinkedDelete** for linked lists having head nodes.

3. Suppose that jobs entering a computer system are assigned a job number and a priority from 0 through 9. The numbers of jobs awaiting execution by the system are kept in a **priority queue.** A job entered into this queue is placed ahead of all jobs of lower priority but after all those of equal or higher priority. Write a program to read one of the letters **R** (remove), **A** (add), or **L** (list). For **R**, remove the first item in the queue; for **A**, read a job number and priority and then add it to the priority queue in the manner just described; and for **L**, list all the job numbers in the queue. Maintain the priority queue as a linked list.

4. A limited number of tickets for the Frisian Folk Singers concert go on sale tomorrow, and ticket orders are to be filled in the order in which they are received. Write a program that reads the names and addresses of the persons ordering tickets together with the number of tickets requested, and stores these in a linked list. The program should then produce a list of names, addresses, and number of tickets for orders that can be filled.

5. Modify the program in Exercise 4 so that multiple requests from the same person are not allowed.

6. Write a program to read the records from **StudentFile** (see Appendix E), and construct five linked lists of records containing a student's name, number, and cumulative GPA, one list for each class. Each list is to be an ordered linked list in which the names are in alphabetical order. After the lists have been constructed, print each of them with appropriate headings.

7. Write a menu-driven program that allows at least the following options:

   GET: Read the records from **StudentFile** (see Appendix E) and store them in five linked lists, one for each class, with each list ordered so that the student numbers are in ascending order.

   INS: Insert the record for a new student, keeping the list sorted.

   RET: Retrieve and display the record for a specified student.

   UPD: Update the information in the record for a specified student.

   DEL: Delete the record for some student.

   LIS: List the records (or perhaps selected items in the records) in order.

This option should allow the following suboptions:

ALL: List for all students.
CLA: List for only a specified class.
GPA: List for students with GPAs above/below a specified value.
MAJ: List for a given major.
GEN: List for a given gender.
SAV: Save the updated list of records by writing them to
`NewStudentFile`.

8. A **polynomial of degree** n has the form

$$a_0 + a_1 x + a_2 x^2 + \cdots + a_n x^n$$

where $a_0, a_1, \ldots, a_n$ are numeric constants called the **coefficients** of the polynomial and $a_n \neq 0$. For example,

$$1 + 3x - 7x^3 + 5x^4$$

is a polynomial of degree 4 with integer coefficients 1, 3, 0, -7, and 5.

(a) Develop an ordered linked list that can represent any such polynomial. Let each node store a nonzero coefficient and the corresponding exponent.

(b) Write a program to read the nonzero coefficients and exponents of a polynomial, construct its linked representation, and print the polynomial using the usual mathematical format with x^n written as $x \uparrow n$ or $x \wedge n$. The program should then read values for x and evaluate the polynomial for each of them.

9. Write a program that reads the nonzero coefficients and exponents of two polynomials, possibly of different degrees, stores them in linked lists (as described in Exercise 8), and then calculates and displays their sum and product.

10. The Cawker City Candy Company maintains two warehouses, one in Chicago and one in Detroit, each of which stocks a large number of different items. Write a program that first reads the product numbers of items stored in the Chicago warehouse and stores them in a linked list `Chicago`, and then repeats this for the items stored in the Detroit warehouse, storing these product numbers in a linked list `Detroit`. The program should then find and display the **intersection** of these two lists of numbers, that is, the collection of product numbers common to both lists. Do not assume that the lists have the same number of elements.

11. Repeat Exercise 10, but find and display the **union** of the two lists, that is, the collection of product numbers that are elements of at least one of the lists.

12. The number of elements in an ordered list may grow so large that searching the list, always beginning with the first node, is not efficient. One way to improve efficiency is to maintain several smaller linked lists with an array of pointers to the first nodes of these lists. Write a program to read several lines of uppercase text and to produce a **text concordance**, which is a list of all distinct words in the text. Store distinct words beginning with **A** alphabetically ordered in one linked list, those beginning with **B** in another, and so on. Use an array with indices of type `'A'..'Z'`, with each array element being a pointer to the first node in the list of words that begin with the corresponding index. After all the text lines have been read, print a list of all these words in alphabetical order.

13. Modify the program of Exercise 12 so that the concordance also includes the frequency with which each word occurs in the text.

14. In addition to the words in a section of text, a concordance usually stores the numbers of selected pages on which there is a significant use of the word. Modify the program of Exercise 12 so that the line numbers of the first ten or fewer references to a word are stored along with the word itself. The program should display each word together with its references in ascending order.

15. Proceed as in Exercise 14, but modify the data structure used for the text concordance so that the numbers of *all* lines in which a word appears are stored.

16. **Directed graphs** and their representations using adjacency matrices were described in Exercise 6 of Section 11.4.

   (a) Imitating the construction in Exercise 12, develop a representation of a directed graph by using an array of pointers (one for each vertex) to linked lists containing the vertices that can be reached directly (following a single directed arc) from the vertex corresponding to the index.

   (b) Draw a diagram showing the linked representation for the following directed graph:

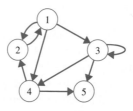

   (c) Write a program to read the numbers (or names) of the vertices of a directed graph and ordered pairs of vertices representing the directed arcs, construct the linked representation for the digraph, and then use it to display the adjacency matrix.

17. In Chapter 11 we represented matrices by two-dimensional arrays. But for a **sparse matrix,** that is, one with only a few nonzero entries, this is not an efficient representation.

   (a) Imitating the construction in Exercise 12, develop a representation for a sparse matrix by using one ordered linked list for each row and an array of pointers to the first nodes in these lists. Do not store zero entries of the matrix. (*Hint:* Store a matrix entry and the number of the column in which it appears.)

(b) Write a program to read the nonzero entries of a sparse matrix and their locations in the matrix, and construct its linked representation. Then print the matrix in the usual table format with all entries (including 0's) displayed.

18. Extend the program of Exercise 17 to read two sparse matrices and calculate their sum and product (see Section 11.4).

16.7 Multiply Linked Structures: Trees

In Section 16.4 we observed that a linear search can be carried out with a linked list, but a binary search is not feasible, because it requires direct access to each item in the list. It is possible, however, to store the elements of an ordered list in a linked structure that can be searched in a binarylike manner. To illustrate, consider the following ordered list of integers:

$$13, 28, 35, 49, 62, 66, 80$$

The first step in a binary search requires examining the middle element in the list. Direct access to this element is possible if we maintain a pointer to the node storing it:

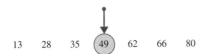

For the next step, one of the two sublists, the left half or the right half, must be searched and both must therefore be accessible from this node. This is possible if we maintain two pointers, one to each of these sublists. Since these sublists are searched in the same manner, these pointers should point to nodes containing the middle elements in these sublists:

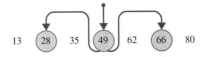

By the same reasoning, pointers from each of these "second-level" nodes are needed to access the middle elements in the sublists at the next stage:

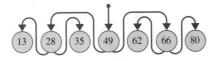

The resulting structure is usually drawn so that it has a treelike shape:

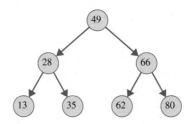

It is called a *binary search tree* and is a special kind of *binary tree,* which is a special instance of a more general structure called a *tree.*

Trees

A **tree** consists of a finite set of elements called **nodes** or **vertices,** and a finite set of **directed arcs** that connect pairs of nodes. If the tree is nonempty, then one of the nodes, called the **root,** has no incoming arcs, but every other node in the tree can be reached from the root by following a unique sequence of consecutive arcs.

Trees derive their names from the treelike diagrams that are used to picture them. For example,

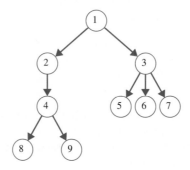

shows a tree having nine vertices in which vertex 1 is the root. As this diagram indicates, trees are usually drawn upside down, with the root at the top and the **leaves**—that is, vertices with no outgoing arc—at the bottom. Nodes that are directly accessible from a given node (by using only one directed arc) are called the **children** of that node, and a node is said to be the **parent** of its children. For example, in the preceding tree, vertex 3 is the parent of vertices 5, 6, and 7, and these vertices are the children of vertex 3 and are called **siblings.**

Applications of trees are many and varied. For example, a **genealogical tree** such as the following is a convenient way to picture a person's descendants:

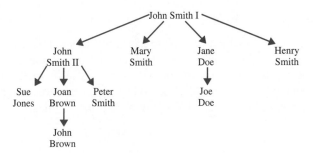

Game trees like the following, which shows the various configurations possible in
the Towers of Hanoi problem with two disks (see Section 7.7), are used to analyze
games and puzzles.

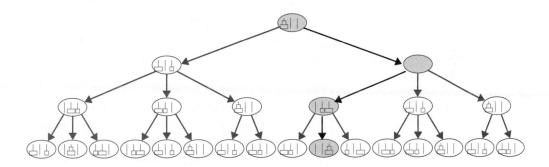

Parse trees constructed during the compilation of a program are used to check the
program's syntax. For example, the following is a parse tree for the expression
$2 * (3 + 4)$,

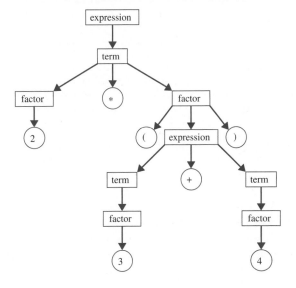

Binary Trees

Binary trees are trees in which each node has at most two children. Such trees are especially useful in modeling processes in which some experiment or test with two possible outcomes (for example, off or on, 0 or 1, false or true, down or up) is performed repeatedly. For example, the following binary tree might be used to represent the possible outcomes of flipping a coin three times:

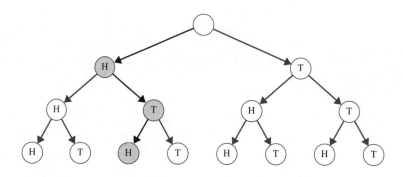

Each path from the root to one of the leaf nodes corresponds to a particular outcome, such as HTH (a head followed by a tail followed by another head), as highlighted in the diagram.

Similarly, a binary tree can be used in coding problems such as in encoding and decoding messages transmitted in Morse code, a scheme in which characters are represented as sequences of dots and dashes, as shown in the following table (see Exercise 8 of Section 10.5):

A ·—	M ——	Y —·——
B —···	N —·	Z ——··
C —·—·	O ———	1 ·————
D —··	P ·——·	2 ··———
E ·	Q ——·—	3 ···——
F ··—·	R ·—·	4 ····—
G ——·	S ···	5 ·····
H ····	T —	6 —····
I ··	U ··—	7 ——···
J ·———	V ···—	8 ———··
K —·—	W ·——	9 ————·
L ·—··	X —··—	0 —————

In this case, the nodes in a binary tree are used to represent the characters, and each arc from a node to its children is labeled with a dot or a dash, according to whether it leads to a left child or to a right child, respectively. Thus, part of the tree for Morse code is

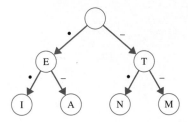

The sequence of dots and dashes labeling a path from the root to a particular node corresponds to the Morse code for that character; for example, ·· is the code for I, and −· is the code for N.

Here we confine our attention to binary trees. This is not a serious limitation, however, because any tree can be represented by a binary tree, using a technique described in the exercises.

Binary trees can be represented as multiply linked structures in which each node has two link fields, one a pointer to the left child of that node and the other a pointer to the right child. Such nodes can be represented in Pascal by records whose declarations have the form

```
TYPE
    BinTreeElementType = ...;    {type of data items
                                  stored in the nodes}
    BinTreePointer = ↑TreeNode;
    TreeNode = RECORD
                   Data : BinTreeElementType;
                   LChild, RChild : BinTreePointer
               END;
    BinaryTreeType = BinTreePointer;
```

The two link fields **LChild** and **RChild** are pointers to nodes representing the left and right child, respectively,

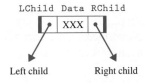

or are nil if the node does not have a left or right child. A leaf node is thus characterized by having nil values for both **LChild** and **RChild**:

The binary tree

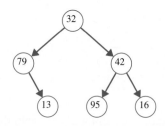

can thus be represented as the following linked tree of records:

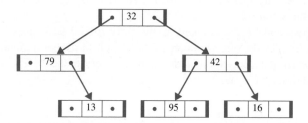

The root node of this binary tree contains the integer 32 and has pointers to the nodes containing 79 and 42, each of which is itself the root of a binary **subtree:**

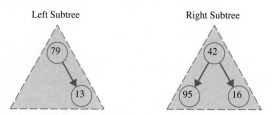

Now consider the left subtree. Its root node contains the integer 79 and has a right child but no left child. Nevertheless, we can still regard this node as having pointers to two binary subtrees, a left subtree and a right subtree, provided that we allow empty binary trees:

Both the left and right subtrees of the one-node tree containing 13 are empty binary trees.

This leads to the following recursive definition of a binary tree:

RECURSIVE DEFINITION OF A BINARY TREE

A binary tree either

    a. is empty ←————————————————— Anchor

or

    b. consists of a node called the root,
       which has pointers to two disjoint ←———— Inductive step
       binary subtrees called the **left**
       subtree and the **right subtree.**

Because of the recursive nature of binary trees, many of the basic operations on them can be carried out most simply and elegantly using recursive algorithms. These algorithms are typically anchored by the special case of an empty binary tree, and the inductive step specifies how a binary tree is to be processed in terms of its root and either or both of its subtrees.

The first operation for binary trees that we consider is **traversing** the tree, that is, "visiting" each node in the binary tree exactly once. Suppose for now that the order in which the nodes are visited is not relevant. What is important is that we visit each node, not missing any, and that the information in each node is processed exactly once.

One simple recursive scheme is to traverse the binary tree as follows:

1. Visit the root and process its contents.
2. Traverse the left subtree.
3. Traverse the right subtree.

Thus, in our example, if we simply display a node's contents when we visit it, we begin by displaying the value 32 in the root of the binary tree. Next we must traverse the left subtree, and after this traversal is finished, we must traverse the right subtree. When this traversal is completed, we will have traversed the entire binary tree.

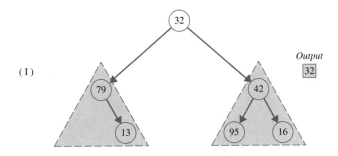

(I)

Thus the problem has been reduced to the traversal of two smaller binary trees. We consider the left subtree and visit its root. Next we must traverse its left subtree and then its right subtree.

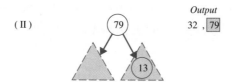

(II)

Output

32 , 79

The left subtree is empty, and so we have reached the anchor case of the recursive definition of a binary tree, and to complete the traversal algorithm, we must specify how an empty binary tree is to be traversed. But this is easy. We do nothing.

Because traversal of the empty left subtree is thus finished trivially, we turn to traversing the right subtree. We visit its root and then must traverse its left subtree followed by its right subtree:

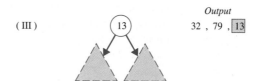

(III)

Output

32 , 79 , 13

As both subtrees are empty, no action is required to traverse them. Consequently, traversal of the binary tree in diagram III is complete, and since this was the right subtree of the tree in diagram II, traversal of this tree is also complete.

This means that we have finished traversing the left subtree of the root in the original binary tree in diagram I and are ready to begin traversing the right subtree. This traversal proceeds in a similar manner. We first visit its root, displaying the value 42 stored in it, then traverse its left subtree, and finally its right subtree:

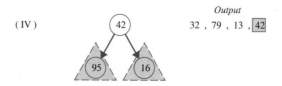

(IV)

Output

32 , 79 , 13 , 42

The left subtree consists of a single node with empty left and right subtrees and is traversed as described earlier for a one-node binary tree:

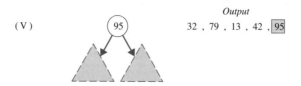

(V)

Output

32 , 79 , 13 , 42 , 95

The right subtree is traversed in the same way:

(VI)

Output

32 , 79 , 13 , 42 , 95 , 16

This completes the traversal of the binary tree in diagram IV and thus completes the traversal of the original tree in diagram I.

As this example demonstrates, traversing a binary tree recursively requires three basic steps, which we shall denote N, L, and R:

N: Visit a node.
L: Traverse the left subtree of a node.
R: Traverse the right subtree of a node.

We performed these steps in the order listed here, but in fact, there are six different orders in which they can be carried out:

LNR
NLR
LRN
NRL
RNL
RLN

For example, the ordering LNR corresponds to the following traversal algorithm:

If the binary tree is empty then   (* anchor *)
    Do nothing.
Else do the following: (* inductive step *)
    L: Traverse the left subtree.
    N: Visit the root.
    R: Traverse the right subtree.

For the preceding binary tree, this LNR traversal visits the nodes in the order 79, 13, 32, 95, 42, 16.

The first three orders, in which the left subtree is traversed before the right, are the most important of the six traversals and are commonly called by other names:

LNR ↔ Inorder
NLR ↔ Preorder
LRN ↔ Postorder

To see why these names are appropriate, consider the following **expression tree,** a binary tree used to represent the arithmetic expression

$$A - B * C + D$$

by representing each operand as a child of a parent node representing the corresponding operator:

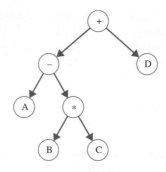

An **inorder** traversal of this expression tree produces the **infix** expression

$$A - B * C + D$$

A **preorder** traversal gives the **prefix** expression (see Exercise 8 in Section 13.3):

$$+ - A * B C D$$

And a **postorder** traversal yields the **postfix** (RPN) expression (see Section 13.3):

$$A B C * - D +$$

A recursive procedure to implement any of these traversal algorithms is easy. For example, a procedure for an inorder traversal is the following:

```
PROCEDURE InOrder( Root : BinaryTreeType );
{-----------------------------------------------------------------------

   Accepts:       A binary tree with root node pointed to by Root.
   Purpose:       Perform an inorder traversal of the binary tree,
                  processing each node exactly once.
   Returns/Output: Depends on the type of processing.

-------------------------------------------------------------------}
   BEGIN
      IF Root <> NIL THEN                 {tree is not empty}
         BEGIN
            InOrder( Root↑.LChild );      {L operation}
            Visit( Root );                {N operation}
            InOrder( Root↑.RChild )       {R operation}
         END {IF}
      {ELSE
         do nothing}
   END {InOrder};
```

The following table traces the action of **InOrder** as it traverses the binary tree:

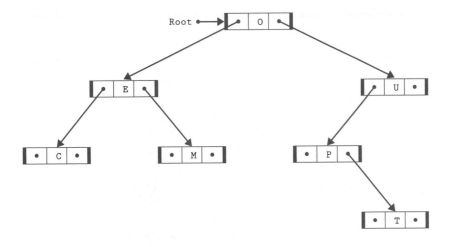

Contents of Current Node	Level in the Tree	Action	Output
O	1	Call **InOrder** with pointer to root (**E**) of left subtree.	
E	2	Call **InOrder** with pointer to root (**C**) of left subtree.	
C	3	Call **InOrder** with pointer (nil) to root of left subtree.	
none	4	None; return to parent node.	
C	3	Display contents of node.	C
C	3	Call **InOrder** with pointer (nil) to root of right subtree.	
none	4	None; return to parent node.	
C	3	Return to parent node.	
E	2	Display contents of node.	E
E	2	Call **InOrder** with pointer to root (**M**) of right subtree.	
M	3	Call **InOrder** with pointer (nil) to root of left subtree.	
none	4	None; return to parent node.	
M	3	Display contents of node.	M
M	3	Call **InOrder** with pointer (nil) to root of right subtree.	
none	4	None; return to parent node.	
M	3	Return to parent node.	
E	2	Return to parent node.	
O	1	Display contents of node.	O

(continues)

Contents of Current Node	Level in the Tree	Action	Output
O	1	Call **InOrder** with pointer to root (**U**) of right subtree.	
U	2	Call **InOrder** with pointer to root (**P**) of left subtree.	
P	3	Call **InOrder** with pointer (nil) to root of left subtree.	
none	4	None; return to parent node.	
P	3	Display contents of node.	P
P	3	Call **InOrder** with pointer to root (**T**) of right subtree.	
T	4	Call **InOrder** with pointer (nil) to root of left subtree.	
none	5	None; return to parent node.	
T	4	Display contents of node.	T
T	4	Call **InOrder** with pointer (nil) to root of right subtree.	
none	5	None; return to parent node.	
T	4	Return to parent node.	
P	3	Return to parent node.	
U	2	Display contents of node.	U
U	2	Call **InOrder** with pointer (nil) to root of right subtree.	
none	3	None; return to parent node.	
U	2	Return to parent node.	
O	1	Terminate procedure; traversal complete.	

Procedures for any of the other traversals are obtained by simply changing the order of the statements representing the L, N, and R operations. For the preceding binary tree, the output produced by preorder and postorder traversals would be

Preorder: O E C M U P T
Postorder: C M E T P U O

Binary Search Trees

In the preceding example, the output produced by **InOrder** was

```
C E M O P T U
```

Note that the letters are in alphabetical order. This is because this binary tree has the special property that the items in the left subtree of each node are less than the item in that node, which in turn is less than all items in the right subtree. A binary tree having this property is called a **binary search tree (BST)** because, as we noted in the introduction to this section, it can be searched using an algorithm, much like the binary search algorithm for arrays.

To illustrate, consider again the binary tree given earlier:

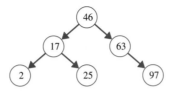

Suppose we wish to search this BST for 25. We begin at the root, and since 25 is less than the value 46 in this root, we know that the desired value is located to the left of the root; that is, it must be in the left subtree, whose root is 17:

Now we continue the search by comparing 25 with the value in the root of this subtree. Since $25 > 17$, we know that the right subtree should be searched:

Examining the value in the root of this one-node subtree locates the value 25.

Similarly, to search for the value 55, after comparing 55 with the value in the root, we are led to search its right subtree:

Now, because $55 < 63$, if the desired value is in the tree, it will be in the left subtree. However, since this left subtree is empty, we conclude that the value 55 is not in the tree.

The following procedure **BSTSearch** for searching a binary search tree incorporates these techniques. The pointer **LocPtr** begins at the root of the BST and then is repeatedly replaced by its left or right link, according to whether the item for which we are searching is less than or greater than the value stored in this node. This process continues until either the desired item is found or **LocPtr** becomes nil, indicating an empty subtree, in which case the item is not in the tree. The procedure is designed to handle trees in which the data parts of the nodes are records; **Item** is compared with some key field in these nodes, and the outcome of this comparison is used to determine whether to descend to the left subtree or to the right subtree or to terminate the search because the item has been found.

```
PROCEDURE BSTSearch(     Root : BinaryTreeType; KeyValue : KeyType;
                    VAR Found : boolean;
                    VAR LocPtr : BinTreePointer );
{-----------------------------------------------------------------

    Accepts:  BST with root pointed to by Root and a KeyValue.
    Purpose:  Search a BST for a node containing a specified
              KeyValue in its keyfield.
    Returns:  Found is true and LocPtr points to a node containing
              KeyValue if the search is successful; otherwise,
              Found is false.


-----------------------------------------------------------------}

    BEGIN
       LocPtr := Root;                         {begin at the root}
       Found := false;
       WHILE NOT Found AND (LocPtr <> NIL) DO
          IF KeyValue < LocPtr↑.Data.Key THEN
             LocPtr := LocPtr↑.LChild          {search left subtree}
          ELSE IF KeyValue > LocPtr↑.Data.Key THEN
             LocPtr := LocPtr↑.RChild          {search right subtree}
          ELSE
             Found := true                     {KeyValue found}
       END {BSTSearch};
```

Because each time we move down to a subtree, we search it in the same manner as the preceding (sub)tree, we could have written this procedure recursively (as the exercises ask you to do). This recursive procedure, however, is no shorter or easier to understand than the nonrecursive one given here.

A binary search tree can be constructed by repeatedly calling the following procedure to insert elements into a BST that is initially empty (**Root = NIL**). The method used to determine where an element is to be inserted is similar to that used in **BSTSearch**. We move down to a left or right subtree of a node, beginning at the root, depending on whether the element is less than or greater than the value in that node. (For elements that are records, a key field in these records is the basis for comparison.) If the element is not already in the tree, we will eventually reach an empty subtree in which the item is to be inserted. As in the case of the search procedure, an insert procedure can be written either recursively or nonrecursively; in this case, the recursive formulation is somewhat easier.

```
PROCEDURE RecBSTInsert( VAR Root : BinaryTreeType;
                        Item : BinTreeElementType );
{-----------------------------------------------------------------

    Accepts:  BST with root pointed to by Root and a data Item.
    Purpose:  Recursively insert Item into the BST.
    Returns:  Modified BST with root pointed to by Root.


-----------------------------------------------------------------}
```

```
BEGIN
   IF Root = NIL THEN                         {insert into empty tree}
      BEGIN
         new( Root );
         Root↑.Data := Item;
         Root↑.LChild := NIL;
         Root↑.RChild := NIL
      END (* IF *)
   ELSE
      IF Item.Key < Root↑.Data.Key THEN          {insert into:  }
         RecBSTInsert( Root↑.LChild, Item )      {left subtree}
      ELSE IF Item.Key > Root↑.Data.Key THEN
         RecBSTInsert( Root↑.RChild, Item )      {right subtree}
      ELSE                                  {Item already in tree}
         writeln( 'Item already in the tree' )
END {RecBSTInsert};
```

The order in which items are inserted into a BST determines the shape of the tree. For example, inserting the letters O, E, T, C, U, M, P into a BST of characters in this order gives the nicely *balanced* tree

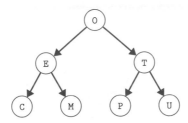

but inserting them in the order C, O, M, P, U, T, E yields the unbalanced tree

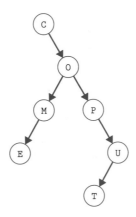

and inserting them in alphabetical order, C, E, M, O, P, T, U, causes the tree to degenerate into a linked list:

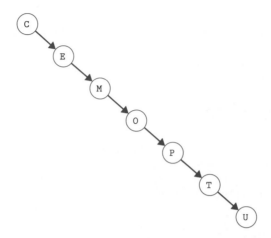

For such unbalanced BSTs, search times increase, since the search procedure degenerates into a linear search. Insertion algorithms that avoid constructing such unbalanced trees are known but are beyond the level of this introductory text.[1]

Deleting a leaf node in a binary search tree is easy to do, but deleting an interior node (one having at least one child) is more complicated. The exercises explore the deletion operation in more detail.

Treesort

If we combine this method of constructing a binary search tree with that for performing an inorder traversal, we obtain a new scheme for sorting a list of elements. We simply insert the list items into a BST that is initially empty and then use an inorder traversal to copy them back into the list. The following algorithm uses this technique to sort a list stored in an array:

TREESORT ALGORITHM

(* Accepts: A list of *n* items stored in an array **X**.
   Purpose: Use a BST to sort the list into ascending order.
   Returns: The sorted list. *)

1. Initialize an empty BST.
2. For *i* ranging from 1 to *n*:
       Insert **X[i]** into the BST.
3. Initialize an index *i* to 0.
4. Perform an inorder traversal of the BST, in which visiting a node consists of the following two steps:
       a. Increment *i* by 1.
       b. Set **X[i]** equal to the data item in the current node.

---

[1] See, for example, Larry Nyhoff and Sanford Leestma, *Data Structures and Program Design in Pascal,* 2nd ed. (New York: Macmillan, 1991).

1. For each of the following lists of letters,

    (a) Draw the binary search tree that is constructed when the letters are inserted in the order given.

    (b) Perform inorder, preorder, and postorder traversals of the tree, and show the sequence of letters that results in each case.

        (i) M, I, T, E, R   **(ii)** T, I, M, E, R

        (iii) R, E, M, I, T   **(iv)** C, O, R, N, F, L, A, K, E, S

2. For the trees in Exercise 1, traverse each tree, using the following orders:

    (a) NRL   **(b)** RNL   **(c)** RLN

3. For each of the following arithmetic expressions, draw a binary tree that represents the expression, and then use tree traversals to find the equivalent prefix and postfix (RPN) expressions:

    (a) A + B + C / D

    (b) (A + B) / C - D

    (c) (A + B) * ((C + D) / (E + F))

    (d) A - (B - (C - (D - E)))

4. Write procedures for preorder and postorder traversals of a binary tree.

5. (a) Preorder traversal of a certain binary tree produced

        A D F G H K L P Q R W Z

    and inorder traversal produced

        G F H K D L A W R Q P Z

    Draw the binary tree.

    (b) Postorder traversal of a certain binary tree produced

        F G H D A L P Q R Z W K

    and inorder traversal gave the same result as in part (a). Draw the binary tree.

    (c) Show by example that knowing the results of a preorder traversal and a postorder traversal does not uniquely determine the binary tree. That is, give an example of two different binary trees for which a preorder traversal of each gives the same result, and so does a postorder traversal.

6. As noted in the text, every tree can be represented by a binary tree. This can be done by letting node **x** be a left child of node **y** in the binary tree if **x** is the leftmost child of **y** in the given tree, and by letting **x** be the right child of **y** if **x** and **y** are siblings (have the same parent) in the original tree. For example, the tree

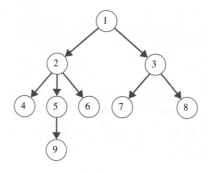

can be represented by the binary tree

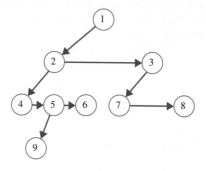

or, if it is drawn in the more customary manner,

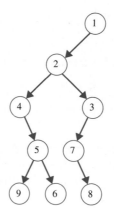

Represent each of the following by binary trees:

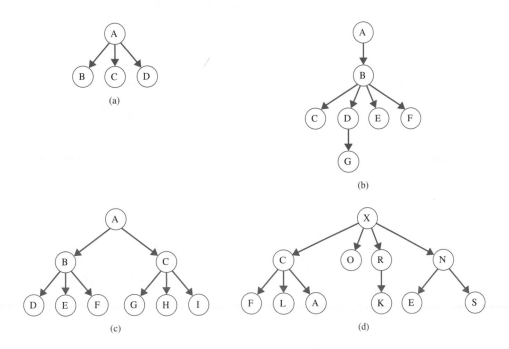

7. Write a recursive version of the procedure **BSTSearch**.

8. Write a recursive function to count the leaves in a binary tree. (*Hint:* How is the number of leaves in the entire tree related to the number of leaves in the left and right subtrees of the root?)

9. Write a recursive function to find the depth of a binary tree. The depth of an empty tree is 0, and for a nonempty tree it is one more than the larger of the depths of the left and right subtrees of the root.

10. Write a recursive function to find the level in a BST at which a given item is located. The root is at level 0, and its children are at level 1.

11. Repeat Exercise 10, but do not assume that the binary tree is a BST.

12. Write a program to process a BST whose nodes contain characters. Allow the user to select from the following menu of options:

> **I** followed by a character: To insert that character into the BST
> **S** followed by a character: To search for that character in the BST
> **TI**: For inorder traversal of the BST
> **TP**: For preorder traversal of the BST
> **TR**: For postorder traversal of the BST
> **QU**: To quit

13. Write a procedure `TreeSort` that implements the treesort algorithm for sorting a list of items stored in (a) an array and (b) a linked list. You may assume that the procedures `InOrder` and `BSTInsert` are available.

14. Write a program that reads a collection of records consisting of student numbers and names and then uses the procedure `TreeSort` of Exercise 13 to sort them so that the student numbers are in ascending order.

15. Complete the binary tree begun in this section for decoding messages in Morse code.

16. Write a program that uses a binary tree as described in Exercise 15 to decode messages in Morse code.

17. To delete a node **x** from a BST, three cases must be considered: (1) **x** is a leaf; (2) **x** has only one subtree; and (3) **x** has two subtrees. Case 1 is handled easily. For Case 2, simply replace **x** with the root of its subtree by linking the parent of **x** to this root. For Case 3, **x** must be replaced with its inorder successor (or predecessor). The following diagram illustrates this case:

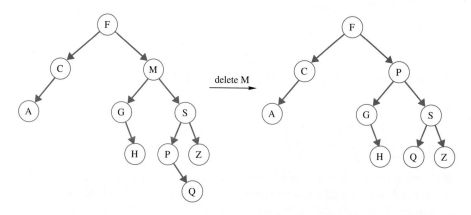

Write a procedure to delete an item from a BST. A procedure like `BSTSearch` can be used to locate the item and its parent in the tree.

18. (Project) For a certain company, the method by which the pay for each employee is computed depends on whether that employee is classified as an Office employee, a Factory worker, or a Salesperson. Suppose that a file of employee records is maintained in which each record is a variant record containing the following information for each employee:

Name (20 characters).
Social security number (integer).
Age (integer).
Number of dependents (integer).
Employee code (character O, F, S representing Office, Factory, and Salesperson, respectively).
Hourly rate if the employee is a Factory worker.

Annual salary if the employee is an Office employee.

A base pay (real) and a commission percentage (real) if the employee is a Salesperson.

Write a menu-driven program that allows at least the following options to be selected by the user of the program:

GET: Get the records from the employee file and store them in a binary search tree, sorted so that the names are in alphabetical order.

INS: Insert a new employee's record into the BST.

UPD: Update the record of an employee already in the tree.

RET: Retrieve and display the record for a specified employee.

LIS: List the records (or perhaps selected items in the records) in order. This option should allow the following suboptions.

  ALL—to list for all employees.

  OFF—to list for only Office employees.

  FAC—to list for only Factory workers.

  SAL—to list for only Salespersons.

SAV: Copy the records from the BST into a permanent file.

DEL: Delete an employee's record from the BST.

19. An alternative storage structure for a BST is an array. We simply number each of the possible positions in the BST from top to bottom, numbering from left to right on each level

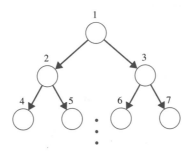

and then store an item in the ith position of the BST in the ith location of an array **B**.

(a) Show what each element of array **B** would be for the BSTs in Exercise 1.

(b) In general, why is this an inefficient way to store BSTs? For what kinds of BSTs is this a good storage structure to use?

20. Assume that array **B** is used to store a BST containing positive integers, as described in Exercise 19. Write a procedure to perform **BSTSearch** for this implementation.

21. In a **doubly** or **symmetrically linked list,** each node has two link fields, one containing a pointer to the predecessor of that node and the other containing a pointer to its successor. It might be pictured as follows:

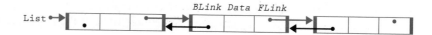

and is especially useful when it is necessary to traverse a linked list or a part of it in either direction.

(a) Write the necessary type declarations for such a doubly linked list.
(b) Write a procedure for traversing the list from left to right.
(c) Write a procedure for traversing the list from right to left.
(d) Write a procedure for inserting an item (1) after or (2) before some other given element in a doubly linked list.
(e) Write a procedure to delete an item from a doubly linked list.

22. A **doubly linked ring** or **doubly linked circular list** is a doubly linked list in which the nil right pointer in the last node is replaced with a pointer to the first node, and the nil left pointer in the first node is replaced with a pointer to the last node.

Assuming that **List** points to the first node, write procedures to

(a) Traverse the list from left to right.
(b) Traverse the list from right to left.
(c) Insert an item (1) after or (2) before a given element in the list.
(d) Delete an item from the list.

23. Another application of multiply linked lists is to maintain a list sorted in two or more different ways. For example, consider the following multiply linked list having two links per node:

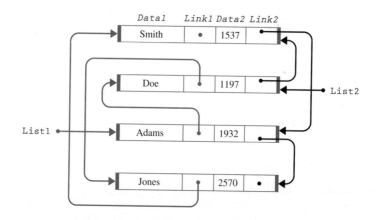

If this list is traversed and the data fields are displayed by using `List1` to point to the first node and following the pointers in the field `Link1`, the names will be in alphabetical order:

Adams   1932
Doe   1197
Jones   2570
Smith   1537

A traversal using `List2` to point to the first node and following pointers in the field `Link2` gives the identification numbers in ascending order:

Doe   1197
Smith   1537
Adams   1932
Jones   2570

This list is logically ordered, therefore, in two different ways. Write a program to read the first ten records from `UserIdFile` (see Appendix E) and store them in a multiply linked list that is logically sorted so that the user identification numbers are in ascending order and the resources used to date are in descending order. Traverse the list and display the records so that the identification numbers are in ascending order. Then traverse the list and display the records so that the resources used to date are in descending order.

24. In Exercise 8 of Section 16.6, a linked list representation for a polynomial in x

$$P(x) = a_0 + a_1x + a_2x^2 + \cdots + a_nx^n$$

was described. A **polynomial in two variables** x and y can be viewed as a polynomial in one variable y, with coefficients that are polynomials in x; that is, it has the form

$$P(x,y) = A_0(x) + A_1(x)y + \cdots + A_{m-1}(x)y^{m-1} + A_m(x)y^m$$

where each $A_i(x)$ is a polynomial in x. For example,

$$6 + 8x^4 + y^2 - 3xy^2 + 4x^5y^2 + 5x^2y^3 + 7x^5y^3$$

can be rewritten as

$$(6 + 8x^4) + (1 - 3x + 4x^5)y^2 + (5x^2 + 7x^5)y^3$$

A multiply linked representation for such polynomials is obtained by representing each term of the form $A_k(x)y^k$ by a node that stores the exponent of y and two links, one containing a pointer to a linked list representing the polynomial $A_k(x)$ and the other a pointer to the next term. For example, the first term in the preceding example can be represented as

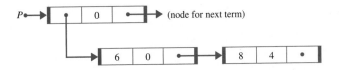

(a) Draw a multiply linked representation for

$$P(x, y) = 1 + 4x + x^2 + 9y + 2xy + xy^4 + 6x^2y^4 - 7xy^5 + 5x^7y^5 + 3x^9y^5$$

(b) Write a program to read triples of the form

(coefficient, x-exponent, y-exponent)

for a polynomial in x and y and construct its linked representation. Then read values for x and y and evaluate the polynomial.

(c) Modify the program in part (b) so that the exponents of x and the exponents of y need not be read in increasing order.

Programming Pointers

The variables that we have considered in previous chapters have as values specific data items such as integers, real numbers, characters, strings, sets, and records. Pointer variables, however, have memory addresses as values. Consequently, the manner in which pointer variables are used is quite different from that in which other kinds of variables are processed; thus, pointers can cause special difficulties for both beginning and experienced programmers. Pointers are used to create dynamic data structures, such as linked lists, which are processed in a way quite different from that in which static data structures, such as arrays, records, and sets, are processed. The following are some of the main features to remember when using pointer variables and dynamic structures in Pascal programs:

1. *Each pointer variable is bound to a fixed type; a pointer is the address of a memory location in which only a value of that type can be stored.* For example, if **P** and **Q** are pointer variables declared by

   ```
   VAR
       P : ↑integer;
       Q : ↑string[20];
   ```

   then **P** is bound to the type **integer** and **Q** to the type **string[20]**. Memory locations pointed to by **P** can store only integers, whereas those to which **Q** points can store only strings of length 20.

2. *Only limited operations can be performed on pointers because they have memory addresses as values.* In particular:

   ■ *A pointer **P** can be assigned a value in only the following ways:*

   (a) `new(P)`
   (b) `P := NIL`
   (c) `P := Q {where Q is bound to the same type as P}`

   ■ *No arithmetic operations can be performed on pointers.* For example, the values (memory addresses) of two pointer variables cannot be added, nor can a numeric value be added to the value of a pointer variable.

- *Only = and <> can be used to compare pointers.* The two pointers must be bound to the same type, or one or both may be nil. The relational operators <, <=, >, and >= may not be used to compare pointers.
- *Pointer values cannot be read or displayed.*
- *Pointers may be used as parameters in functions and procedures, but corresponding actual and formal parameters cannot be bound to different types.* Also, if pointer variable P of type ↑integer is used as a formal parameter of a function or procedure, it cannot be declared in the subprogram heading using

      ...P : ↑integer;...

because the types of formal parameters must be specified using type identifiers. A type identifier must be associated with the pointer type ↑integer

      TYPE
          IntegerPointer = ↑integer;

and this type identifier used to specify the type of P:

      ...P : IntegerPointer;...

Similarly, the value of a function may be a pointer, but it must also be specified by a type identifier.

3. *Don't confuse memory locations with the contents of memory locations.* If P is a pointer, its value is the address of a memory location; P↑ refers to the contents of that location. P := P + 1 is not valid, but P↑ := P↑ + 1 may be (if P is bound to a numeric type); similarly, you cannot display the value of P, but you may be able to display the value of P↑.

4. *Nil ≠ undefined.* A pointer becomes defined when it is assigned the address of a memory location or the value NIL. Assigning a pointer the value NIL is analogous to "blanking out" a character (or string) variable or "zeroing out" a numeric variable.

5. *If P is a pointer that is undefined or nil, then an attempt to use P↑ is an error, but these errors are not detected in Turbo Pascal; rather, unpredictable results occur.*

6. *Memory locations that were once associated with a pointer variable and that are no longer needed should be returned to the "storage pool" of available locations by using the procedure* dispose. Special care is required so that inaccessible memory locations are avoided. For example, if P and Q are pointer variables bound to the same type, the assignment statement

      P := Q

causes P to point to the same memory location as that pointed to by Q. Any memory location previously pointed to by P becomes inaccessible and cannot be disposed of properly unless it is pointed to by some other pointer. Temporary pointers should be used to maintain access, as the following statements demonstrate:

```
TempPtr := P;
P := Q;
dispose( TempPtr )
```

7. *Pay attention to special cases in processing linked lists, and be careful not to lose access to nodes.* In particular, remember the following "programming proverbs":

■ *Don't take a long walk off a short linked list.* It is an error to attempt to process elements beyond the end of the list. As an example, consider the following incorrect attempts to search a linked list with first node pointed to by `List` for some `ItemSought`:

Attempt 1:

```
CurrPtr:= List;
WHILE Curr↑.Data <> ItemSought DO
   CurrPtr := CurrPtr↑.Next;
```

If the item is not present in any node of the linked list, `CurrPtr` will eventually reach the last node in the list. `CurrPtr` then becomes nil, and an attempt is made to examine the `Data` field of a nonexistent node, resulting in an error. However, as we noted in Programming Pointer 5, this error is undetected in Turbo Pascal and the results are unpredictable. In particular, an infinite loop may result!

Attempt 2:

```
{ This time I'll make sure I don't fall off the end of
  the list by stopping if I find ItemSought or reach
  a node whose link field is nil. }

Found := false;
CurrPtr := List;
WHILE NOT Found AND (CurrPtr↑.Next <> nil) do
   IF CurrPtr↑.Data = ItemSought THEN
      Found := true
   ELSE
      CurrPtr := CurrPtr↑.Next;
```

Although this avoids the problem of moving beyond the end of the list, it will fail to locate the desired item (that is, set `Found` to `true`) if this item is the last one in the list. When `CurrPtr` reaches the last node, the value of `CurrPtr↑.Next` is nil, and repetition is terminated without examining the `Data` field of this last node. Another problem is that if the item is found in the list, the remaining nodes (except the last) will also be examined.

Attempt 3:

```
{ Another attempt to avoid running past
  the end of the list. }
```

```
CurrPtr := List;
WHILE (Curr↑.Data <> ItemSought) AND (CurrPtr <> NIL) DO
   CurrPtr := CurrPtr↑.Next;
```

This solution is almost correct, but like the first attempted solution, it results in an error if the item is not in the list. The reason is that as we noted in Chapter 4, boolean expressions in Turbo Pascal are evaluated from left to right (unless the **Complete boolean eval** compiler option is turned on to change from the default short-circuit evaluation of boolean expressions to complete evaluation). Thus, when the end of the list is reached and **CurrPtr** becomes nil, the first part of the boolean expression controlling repetition is evaluated, and the result of dereferencing a nil pointer is unpredictable, as we noted earlier.

Attempt 4:

```
{Okay, so I'll just reverse the two parts
 of the boolean expression.}

CurrPtr := List;
WHILE (CurrPtr <> NIL) AND (Curr↑.Data <> ItemSought) DO
   CurrPtr := CurrPtr↑.Next;
```

This is a correct solution provided that the **Complete boolean eval** compiler option has not been activated (or equivalently, the program contains the compiler directive {$B-}). However, because this solution depends on setting a compiler switch, it is preferable to use a boolean variable together with an end-of-list check to control repetition, as in the following solution:

Attempt 5:

```
{ This solution does work! }

Found := false;
CurrPtr := List;
WHILE (CurrPtr <> NIL) AND (NOT Found) DO
   IF CurrPtr↑.Data = ItemSought THEN
      Found := true
   ELSE
      CurrPtr := CurrPtr↑.Next;
```

If the item is found in the list, then **Found** will be set to **true** and repetition will be terminated. If it is not in the list, **CurrPtr** will eventually become nil and repetition will terminate.

■ *You can't get water from an empty well.* Don't try to access elements in an empty list; this case usually requires special consideration. For example, if **List** is nil, then initializing **CurrPtr** to **List** and attempting to access **CurrPtr↑.Data** or **CurrPtr↑.Next** is an error. However, as we noted earlier, this error is not detected in Turbo Pascal and unpredictable results occur, including the possibility of an infinite loop.

■ *Don't burn bridges before you cross them.* Be careful that you change links in the correct order, or you may lose access to a node or to many nodes! For example, in the following attempt to insert a new node at the beginning of a linked list,

```
  List := NewNodePtr;
  NewNodePtr↑.Next := List;
```

the statements are not in correct order. As soon as the first statement is executed, List points to the new node, and access to the remaining nodes in the list (those formerly pointed to by List) is lost. The second statement then simply sets the link field of the new node to point to itself:

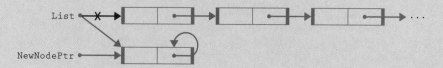

The correct sequence is first to connect the new node to the list and then to reset List:

```
  NewNodePtr↑.Next := List;
  List := NewNodePtr;
```

Standard Pascal

There are a number of differences between Turbo Pascal and standard Pascal in how pointers are used. In standard Pascal:

- Alternative forms of reference to procedures **new** and **dispose** may be used for variant records, which allow the system to allocate memory locations more efficiently:

```
new( pointer, tag-value-1, tag-value-2, . . . , tag-value-n )
dispose( pointer, tag-value-1, tag-value-2, . . . , tag-value-n )
```

Here, *tag-value-1*, *tag-value-2*, . . . , *tag-value-n* represents values of tag fields in increasingly nested variant parts of the record.
- If **f** is a pointer-valued function, a function reference of the form **f(***actual-parameter***)**↑ is not permitted. The value of the function must
- be assigned to a pointer variable, and this variable used to access the contents of the memory location to which it points.
- Attempting to dereference an undefined or nil pointer is an error.

ASCII AND EBCDIC

ASCII and EBCDIC codes of printable characters

Decimal	Binary	Octal	Hexadecimal	ASCII	EBCDIC
32	00100000	040	20	SP (Space)	
33	00100001	041	21	!	
34	00100010	042	22	"	
35	00100011	043	23	#	
36	00100100	044	24	$	
37	00100101	045	25	%	
38	00100110	046	26	&	
39	00100111	047	27	' (Single quote)	
40	00101000	050	28	(	
41	00101001	051	29	)	
42	00101010	052	2A	*	
43	00101011	053	2B	+	
44	00101100	054	2C	, (Comma)	
45	00101101	055	2D	– (Hyphen)	
46	00101110	056	2E	. (Period)	
47	00101111	057	2F	/	
48	00110000	060	30	0	
49	00110001	061	31	1	
50	00110010	062	32	2	
51	00110011	063	33	3	
52	00110100	064	34	4	
53	00110101	065	35	5	
54	00110110	066	36	6	
55	00110111	067	37	7	
56	00111000	070	38	8	
57	00111001	071	39	9	
58	00111010	072	3A	:	
59	00111011	073	3B	;	
60	00111100	074	3C	<	
61	00111101	075	3D	=	
62	00111110	076	3E	>	
63	00111111	077	3F	?	
64	01000000	100	40	@	SP (Space)
65	01000001	101	41	A	
66	01000010	102	42	B	

ASCII and EBCDIC codes of printable characters (cont.)

Decimal	Binary	Octal	Hexadecimal	ASCII	EBCDIC
67	01000011	103	43	C	
68	01000100	104	44	D	
69	01000101	105	45	E	
70	01000110	106	46	F	
71	01000111	107	47	G	
72	01001000	110	48	H	
73	01001001	111	49	I	
74	01001010	112	4A	J	¢
75	01001011	113	4B	K	. (Period)
76	01001100	114	4C	L	<
77	01001101	115	4D	M	(
78	01001110	116	4E	N	+
79	01001111	117	4F	O	|
80	01010000	120	50	P	&
81	01010001	121	51	Q	
82	01010010	122	52	R	
83	01010011	123	53	S	
84	01010100	124	54	T	
85	01010101	125	55	U	
86	01010110	126	56	V	
87	01010111	127	57	W	
88	01011000	130	58	X	
89	01011001	131	59	Y	
90	01011010	132	5A	Z	!
91	01011011	133	5B	[	$
92	01011100	134	5C	\	*
93	01011101	135	5D	]	)
94	01011110	136	5E	^	;
95	01011111	137	5F	(Underscore)	¬ (Negation)
96	01100000	140	60	`—	- (Hyphen)
97	01100001	141	61	a	/
98	01100010	142	62	b	
99	01100011	143	63	c	
100	01100100	144	64	d	
101	01100101	145	65	e	
102	01100110	146	66	f	
103	01100111	147	67	g	
104	01101000	150	68	h	
105	01101001	151	69	i	
106	01101010	152	6A	j	^
107	01101011	153	6B	k	, (Comma)
108	01101100	154	6C	l	%
109	01101101	155	6D	m	(Underscore)
110	01101110	156	6E	n	>
111	01101111	157	6F	o	?
112	01110000	160	70	p	
113	01110001	161	71	q	
114	01110010	162	72	r	
115	01110011	163	73	s	
116	01110100	164	74	t	
117	01110101	165	75	u	
118	01110110	166	76	v	
119	01110111	167	77	w	
120	01111000	170	78	x	

ASCII and EBCDIC codes of printable characters (cont.)

Decimal	Binary	Octal	Hexadecimal	ASCII	EBCDIC
121	01111001	171	79	y	
122	01111010	172	7A	z	:
123	01111011	173	7B	{	#
124	01111100	174	7C	|	@
125	01111101	175	7D	}	' (Single quote)
126	01111110	176	7E	~	=
127	01111111	177	7F		"
128	10000000	200	80		
129	10000001	201	81		a
130	10000010	202	82		b
131	10000011	203	83		c
132	10000100	204	84		d
133	10000101	205	85		e
134	10000110	206	86		f
135	10000111	207	87		g
136	10001000	210	88		h
137	10001001	211	89		i
.	.	.	.		.
.			.		.
.	.	.	.		.
145	10010001	221	91		j
146	10010010	222	92		k
147	10010011	223	93		l
148	10010100	224	94		m
149	10010101	225	95		n
150	10010110	226	96		o
151	10010111	227	97		p
152	10011000	230	98		q
153	10011001	231	99		r
.	.	.	.		.
.			.		
.	.	.	.		.
162	10100010	242	A2		s
163	10100011	243	A3		t
164	10100100	244	A4		u
165	10100101	245	A5		v
166	10100110	246	A6		w
167	10100111	247	A7		x
168	10101000	250	A8		y
169	10101001	251	A9		z
.	.	.	.		.
.			.		
.	.	.	.		
192	11000000	300	C0		}
193	11000001	301	C1		A
194	11000010	302	C2		B
195	11000011	303	C3		C
196	11000100	304	C4		D
197	11000101	305	C5		E
198	11000110	306	C6		F
199	11000111	307	C7		G
200	11001000	310	C8		H
201	11001001	311	C9		I

ASCII and EBCDIC codes of printable characters (cont.)

Decimal	Binary	Octal	Hexadecimal	ASCII	EBCDIC
.	.	.	.		.
.	.	.	.		.
.	.	.	.		.
208	11010000	320	D0		}
209	11010001	321	D1		J
210	11010010	322	D2		K
211	11010011	323	D3		L
212	11010100	324	D4		M
213	11010101	325	D5		N
214	11010110	326	D6		O
215	11010111	327	D7		P
216	11011000	330	D8		Q
217	11011001	331	D9		R
.	.	.	.		.
.	.	.	.		.
.	.	.	.		.
224	11100000	340	E0		\
225	11100001	341	E1		
226	11100010	342	E2		S
227	11100011	343	E3		T
228	11100100	344	E4		U
229	11100101	345	E5		V
230	11100110	346	E6		W
231	11100111	347	E7		X
232	11101000	350	E8		Y
233	11101001	351	E9		Z
.	.	.	.		.
.	.	.	.		.
.	.	.	.		.
240	11110000	360	F0		0
241	11110001	361	F1		1
242	11110010	362	F2		2
243	11110011	363	F3		3
244	11110100	364	F4		4
245	11110101	365	F5		5
246	11110110	366	F6		6
247	11110111	367	F7		7
248	11111000	370	F8		8
249	11111001	371	F9		9
.	.	.	.		.
.	.	.	.		.
.	.	.	.		.
255	11111111	377	FF		

ASCII codes of control characters

Decimal	Binary	Octal	Hexadecimal	Character
0	00000000	000	00	NUL (Null)
1	00000001	001	01	SOH (Start of heading)
2	00000010	002	02	STX (End of heading and start of text)
3	00000011	003	03	ETX (End of text)
4	00000100	004	04	EOT (End of transmission)
5	00000101	005	05	ENQ (Enquiry—to request identification)
6	00000110	006	06	ACK (Acknowledge)
7	00000111	007	07	BEL (Ring bell)
8	00001000	010	08	BS (Backspace)
9	00001001	011	09	HT (Horizontal tab)
10	00001010	012	0A	LF (Line feed)
11	00001011	013	0B	VT (Vertical tab)
12	00001100	014	0C	FF (Form feed)
13	00001101	015	0D	CR (Carriage return)
14	00001110	016	0E	SO (Shift out—begin non-ASCII bit string)
15	00001111	017	0F	SI (Shift in—end non-ASCII bit string)
16	00010000	020	10	DLE (Data link escape—controls data transmission)
17	00010001	021	11	DC1 (Device control 1)
18	00010010	022	12	DC2 (Device control 2)
19	00010011	023	13	DC3 (Device control 3)
20	00010100	024	14	DC4 (Device control 4)
21	00010001	025	15	NAK (Negative acknowledge)
22	00010110	026	16	SYN (Synchronous idle)
23	00010111	027	17	ETB (End of transmission block)
24	00011000	030	18	CAN (Cancel—ignore previous transmission)
25	00011001	031	19	EM (End of medium)
26	00011010	032	1A	SUB (Substitute a character for another)
27	00011011	033	1B	ESC (Escape)
28	00011100	034	1C	FS (File separator)
29	00011101	035	1D	GS (Group separator)
30	00011110	036	1E	RS (Record separator)
31	00011111	037	1F	US (Unit separator)

EBCDIC codes of control characters

Decimal	Binary	Octal	Hexadecimal	Character
0	00000000	000	00	NUL (Null)
1	00000001	001	01	SOH (Start of heading)
2	00000010	010	02	STX (End of heading and start of text)
3	00000011	011	03	ETX (End of text)
4	00000100	002	04	PF (Punch off)
5	00000101	003	05	HT (Horizontal tab)
6	00000110	006	06	LC (Lower case)
7	00000111	007	07	DEL (Delete)
10	00001010	012	0A	SMM (Repeat)
11	00001011	013	0B	VT (Vertical tab)
12	00001100	014	0C	FF (Form feed)
13	00001101	015	0D	CR (Carriage return)
14	00001110	016	0E	SO (Shift out—begin non-ASCII bit string)
15	00001111	017	0F	SI (Shift in—end non-ASCII bit string)
16	00010000	020	10	DLE (Data link escape—controls data transmission)
17	00010001	021	11	DC1 (Device control 1)
18	00010010	022	12	DC2 (Device control 2)
19	00010011	023	13	DC3 (Device control 3)
20	00010100	024	14	RES (Restore)
21	00010101	025	15	NL (Newline)
22	00010110	026	16	BS (Backspace)
23	00010111	027	17	IL (Idle)
24	00011000	030	18	CAN (Cancel—ignore previous transmission)
25	00011001	031	19	EM (End of medium)
26	00011010	032	1A	CC (Unit backspace)
28	00011100	034	1C	IFS (Interchange file separator)
29	00011101	035	1D	IGS (Interchange group separator)
30	00011110	036	1E	IRS (Interchange record separator)
31	00011111	037	1F	IUS (Interchange unit separator)
32	00100000	040	20	DS (Digit select)
33	00100001	041	21	SOS (Start of significance)
34	00100010	042	22	FS (File separator)
36	00100100	044	24	BYP (Bypass)
37	00100101	045	25	LF (Line feed)
38	00100110	046	26	ETB (End of transmission block)
39	00100111	047	27	ESC (Escape)
42	00101010	052	2A	SM (Start message)
45	00101101	055	2D	ENQ (Enquiry—to request identification)
46	00101110	056	2E	ACK (Acknowledge)
47	00101111	057	2F	BEL (Ring bell)
50	00110010	062	32	SYN (Synchronous idle)
52	00110100	064	34	PN (Punch on)
53	00110101	065	35	RS (Record separator)
54	00110110	066	36	UC (Upper case)
55	00110111	067	37	EOT (End of transmission)
60	00111100	074	3C	DC4 (Device control 4)
61	00111101	075	3D	NAK (Negative acknowledge)
63	00111111	077	3F	SUB (Substitute a character for another)

PASCAL RESERVED WORDS, STANDARD IDENTIFIERS, AND OPERATORS

Reserved Words

AND	END	NIL	SHR
ARRAY	FILE	NOT	STRING
ASM	FOR	OBJECT	THEN
BEGIN	FUNCTION	OF	TO
CASE	GOTO	OR	TYPE
CONST	IF	PACKED	UNIT
CONSTRUCTOR	IMPLEMENTATION	PROCEDURE	UNTIL
DESTRUCTOR	IN	PROGRAM	USES
DIV	INLINE	RECORD	VAR
DO	INTERFACE	REPEAT	WHILE
DOWNTO	LABEL	SET	WITH
ELSE	MOD	SHL	XOR

Standard Identifiers

Predefined Constants

false	maxint	maxlongint	true

Predefined Directives

ABSOLUTE	FAR	INTERRUPT	PRIVATE
ASSEMBLER	FORWARD	NEAR	VIRTUAL
EXTERNAL			

Predefined Types

boolean	double	longint	single
byte	extended	real	text
char	integer	shortint	word
comp			

Predefined Files

```
input     output
```

Predefined Functions[1]

```
abs       exp         ln        round
arctan    filepos     odd       sin
chr       filesize    ord       sqr
concat    frac        pi        sqrt
cos       int         pos       succ
copy      ioresult    pred      trunc
eof       length      random    upcase
eoln
```

Predefined Procedures[1]

```
append    erase       randomize   seek
assign    exit        read        str
close     halt        readln      val
dec       inc         rename      write
delete    insert      reset       writeln
dispose   new         rewrite
```

Units[1]

```
crt       graph       printer
dos       overlay     system
```

Operators

Unary Arithmetic Operators

Operator	Operation	Type of Operands	Type of Result
+	unary plus	integer	integer
		real	real
-	unary minus	integer	integer
		real	real

---

[1] Additional standard functions, procedures, and units are described in the Turbo Pascal reference manuals.

Binary Arithmetic Operators

Operator	Operation	Type of Operands	Type of Result
+	addition	**integer** or **real**	**integer** if both operands are **integer**, otherwise **real**
-	subtraction	**integer** or **real**	**integer** if both operands are **integer**, otherwise **real**
*	multiplication	**integer** or **real**	**integer** if both operands are **integer**, otherwise **real**
/	division	**integer** or **real**	**real**
DIV	integer division	**integer**	**integer**
MOD	modulo	**integer**	**integer**

Relational Operators

Operator	Operation	Type of Operands	Type of Result
=	equality	simple, string, set, or pointer	**boolean**
<>	inequality	simple, string, set, or pointer	**boolean**
<	less than	simple or string	**boolean**
>	greater than	simple or string	**boolean**
<=	less than or equal to, or subset	simple, string, or set	**boolean**
>=	greater than or equal to, or superset	simple, string, or set	**boolean**
IN	set membership	first operand: ordinal type second operand: set type	**boolean**

Boolean Operators

Operator	Operation	Type of Operands	Type of Result
AND	conjunction	**boolean**	**boolean**
NOT	negation	**boolean**	**boolean**
OR	disjunction	**boolean**	**boolean**
XOR	exclusive or	**boolean**	**boolean**

Set Operators

Operator	Operation	Type of Operands	Type of Result
+	set union	set type	same as operands
-	set difference	set type	same as operands
*	set intersection	set type	same as operands

Assignment Operator

Operator	Operation	Type of Operands
:=	assignment	any type except file types

Logical Operators

Operator	Operation	Type of Operands	Type of Result
AND	bitwise and	integer	integer
NOT	bitwise negation	integer	integer
OR	bitwise or	integer	integer
shl	shift left	integer	integer
shr	shift right	integer	integer
XOR	bitwise exclusive or	integer	integer

String Operator

Operator	Operation	Type of Operands	Type of Result
+	concatenation	string	string

Address Operator

Operator	Operation	Type of Operands	Type of Result
@	address	variable or procedure or function identifier	pointer

SYNTAX DIAGRAMS

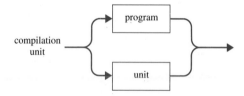

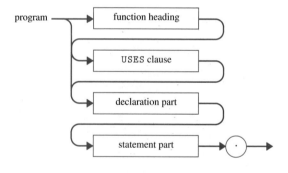

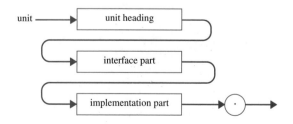

program
heading

unit heading
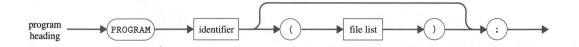

identifier
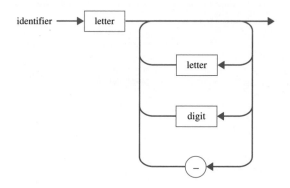

file list
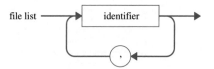

USES
clause
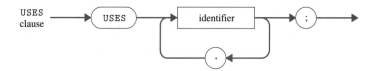

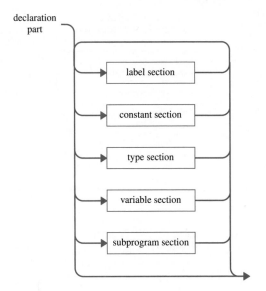

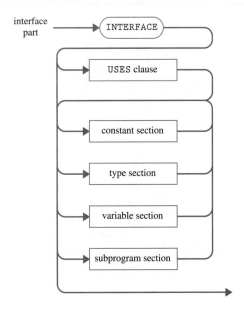

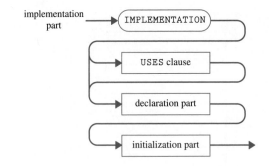

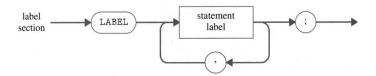

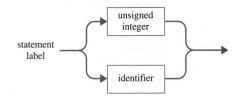

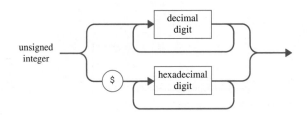

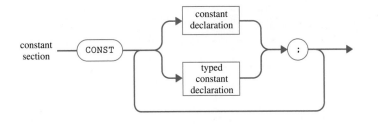

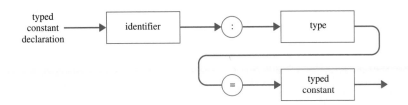

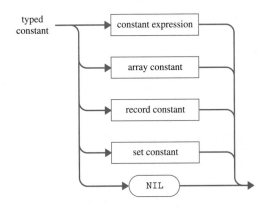

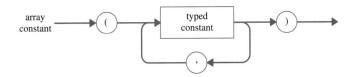

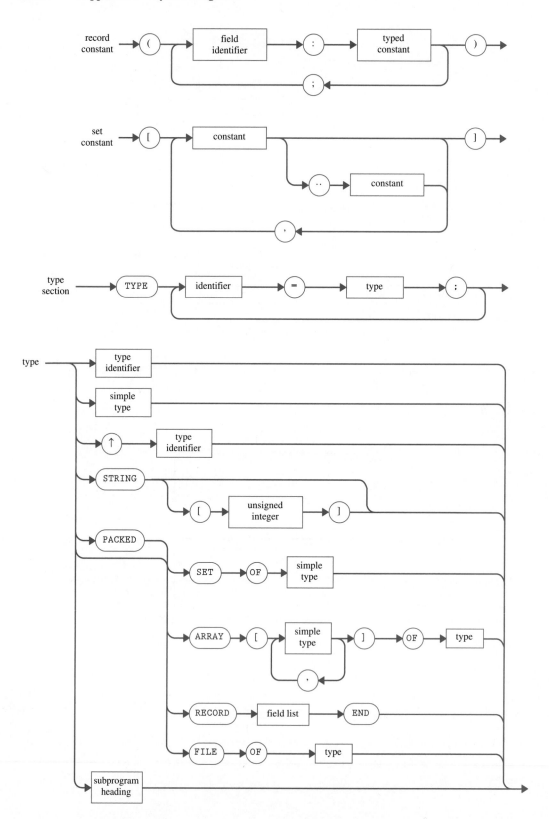

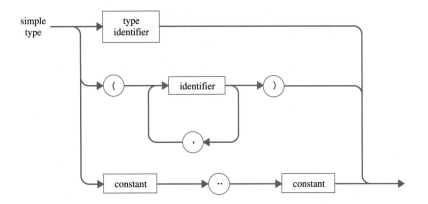

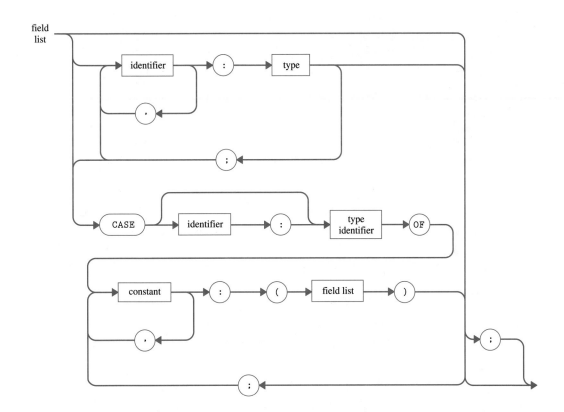

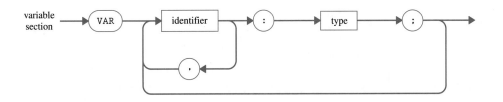

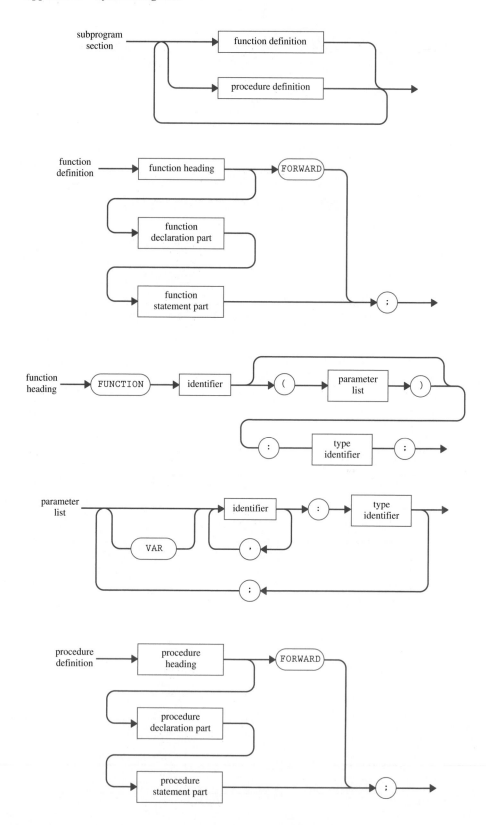

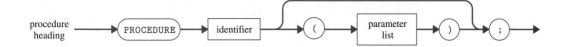

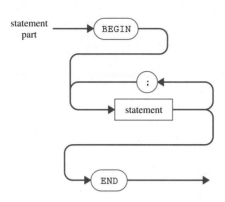

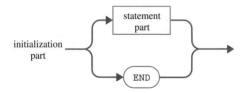

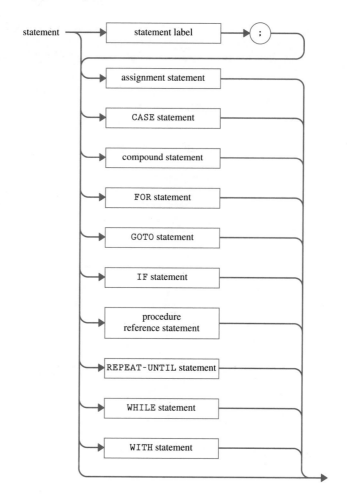

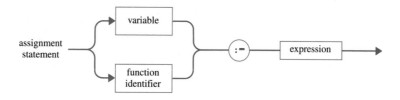

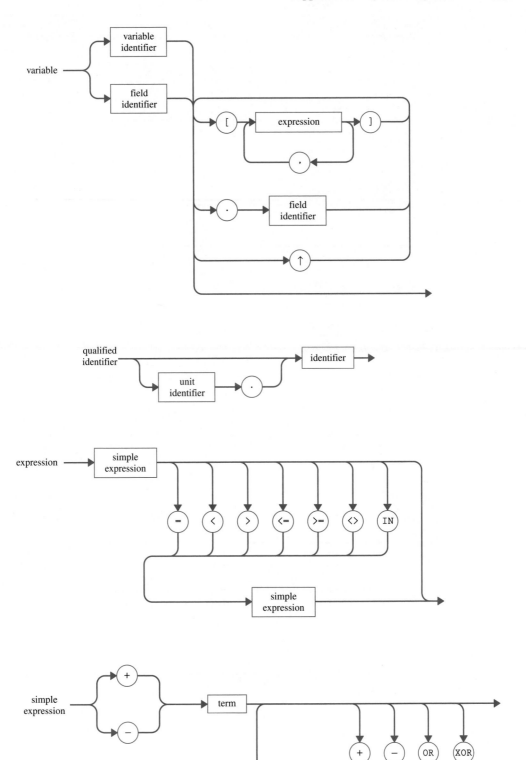

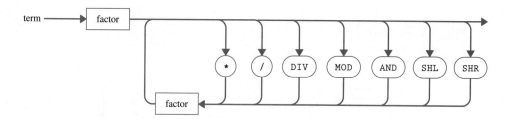

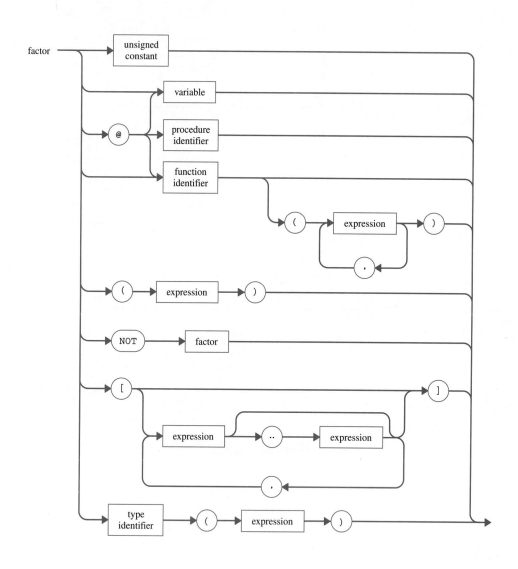

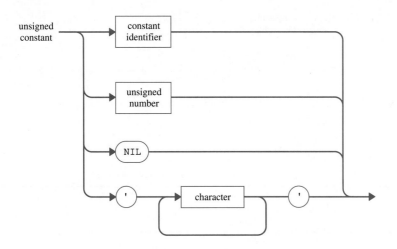

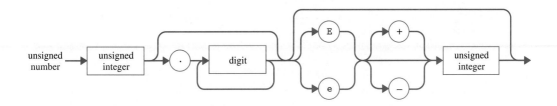

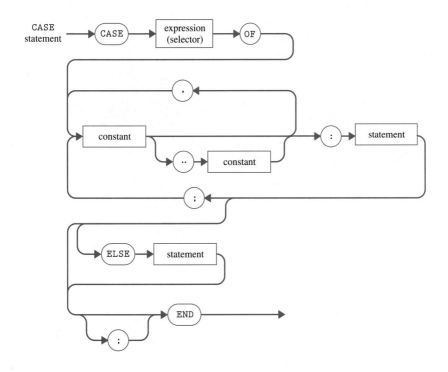

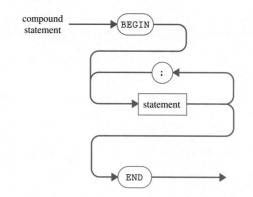

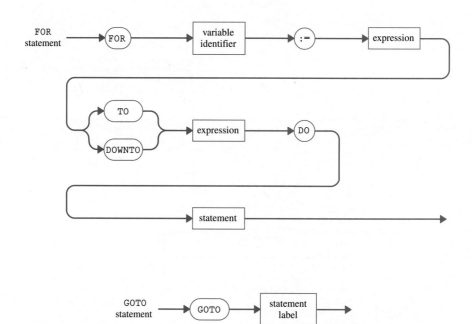

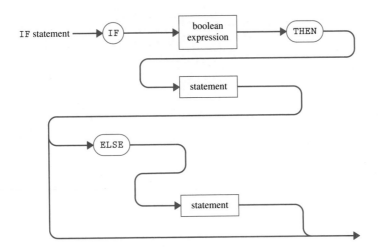

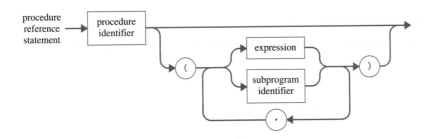

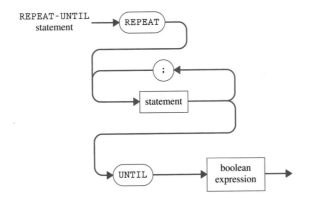

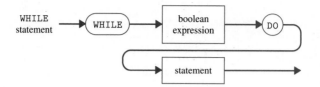

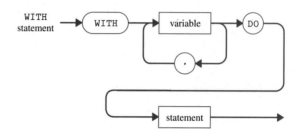

PASCAL PREDEFINED FUNCTIONS AND PROCEDURES

Predefined Functions[1]

Function	Description	Type of Argument	Type of Value
`abs(x)`	absolute value of **x**	`integer` or `real`	same as argument
`arctan(x)`	inverse tangent of **x** (value in radians)	`integer` or `real`	`real`
`chr(n)`	character whose ordinal number is **n**	`integer`	`char`
`concat(s₁,..., sₙ)`	concatenation of $s_1, \ldots, s_n$	string	string
`copy(s, m, n)`	substring of **s** consisting of **n** characters beginning at position **m**	**s**: string **m, n**: `integer`	string
`cos(x)`	cosine of **x** (in radians)	`integer` or `real`	`real`
`eof(F)`	end-of-file function	file	`boolean`
`eoln(F)`	end-of-line function	`text`	`boolean`
`exp(x)`	exponential function e^x	`integer` or `real`	`real`
`filepos(F)`	current position in file **F**	file	`integer`
`filesize(F)`	number of components in **F**	file	`integer`
`frac(x)`	fractional part of **x**	`real`	`real`
`int(x)`	integer part of **x**	`real`	`integer`
`ioresult`	error number for last i/o operation; 0 if no error		`integer`
`length(s)`	length of **s**	string	`integer`
`ln(x)`	natural logarithm of **x**	`integer` or `real`	`real`
`odd(x)`	true if **x** is odd, false otherwise	`integer`	`boolean`
`ord(t)`	ordinal number of **t**	ordinal	`integer`
`pi`	value of π		`real`
`pos(s₁, s₂)`	index of s_1 in s_2	string	`integer`
`pred(t)`	predecessor of **t**	ordinal	ordinal
`random`	random real number in the interval [0, 1]		`real`
`random(n)`	random integer in the range 0 to **n**	`integer`	`integer`
`round(x)`	**x** rounded to nearest integer	`real`	`integer`
`sin(x)`	sine of **x** (in radians)	`integer` or `real`	`real`
`sqr(x)`	x^2	`integer` or `real`	same as argument
`sqrt(x)`	square root of **x**	`integer` or `real`	`real`
`succ(x)`	successor of **x**	ordinal	ordinal
`trunc(x)`	**x** truncated to its integer part	`real`	`integer`
`upcase(c)`	uppercase equivalent of **c** or **c** if there is none	`char`	`char`

[1] Turbo Pascal 7.0 also has `Low` and `High`. See Section H.3 of Appendix H.

Predefined Procedures[2]

Procedure	Description
append(F)	Opens text file F for output and positions the data pointer in F at the end of the file.
assign(F, *file-name*)	Associates the external file *file-name* with the file variable F.
close(F)	Closes file F.
dec(v), dec(v, n)	Decrements the ordinal variable v by 1 in the first form, n in the second.
delete(s, m, n)	Deletes from string s the n characters beginning at position m.
dispose(P)	Releases the memory location pointed to by pointer variable P, leaving P undefined.
erase(F)	Erases the external file associated with file variable F.
exit	Halts execution of the current subprogram (program) and returns control to the calling program unit (operating system).
halt	Halts execution of the current program and returns control to the operating system.
inc(v), inc(v, n)	Increments the ordinal variable v by 1 in the first form, n in the second.
insert(s_1, s_2, m)	Inserts string s_1 into string s_2 at position m in s_2.
new(P)	Acquires a memory location and assigns its address to pointer variable P.
randomize	Initializes the random number generator.
read(F, *input-list*)	Reads values from the file F and assigns these to the variables in the input list. If F is not specified, the standard file **input** is assumed.
readln(F, *input-list*)	Reads values from the text file F, assigns these to the variables in the input list, and then advances the data pointer in F past the next end-of-line mark. If F is not specified, the standard file **input** is assumed.
rename(F, *file-name*)	Renames as *file-name* the external file associated with the file variable F.
reset(F)	Opens the file F for input, positions the data pointer in F at the first file component.
rewrite(F)	Creates the empty file F and opens it for output. Any previous contents of F are destroyed.
seek(F, n)	Positions the data pointer in file F at the nth component. The number of the first component is 0.
str(x, s)	Converts the numeric value x to a string and assigns it to the string variable s.
val(s, x, n)	Converts the string s to an integer or real value if possible and assigns it to x, n is set to 0 if conversion is successful; otherwise, it is the index of the first invalid character in s.
write(F, *output-list*)	Writes the values of the items in the output list to file F. If F is not specified, the standard file **output** is assumed.
writeln(F, *output-list*)	Writes the value of the items in the output list to text file F followed by an end-of-line mark. If F is not specified, the standard file **output** is assumed.

[2] Turbo Pascal 7.0 also has **Assigned, Break, Continue, Exclude,** and **Include.** See Sections H.2, H.6, and H.7 of Appendix H.

SAMPLE DATA FILES AND PROGRAMS

Several exercises in the text use the files **InventoryFile**, **InventoryUpdate**, **LeastSquaresFile**, **StudentFile**, **StudentUpdate**, and **UserIdFile**. Descriptions of these files and sample listings follow.

InventoryFile

Item number: an integer
Number currently in stock: an integer in the range 0 through 999
Unit price: a real value
Minimum inventory level: an integer in the range 0 through 999
Item name: a 25-character string

File is sorted so that item numbers are in increasing order.

Sample `InventoryFile`

```
1011  20   54.95   15 TELEPHOTO POCKET CAMERA
1012  12   24.95   15 MINI POCKET CAMERA
1021  20   49.95   10 POL. ONE-STEP CAMERA
1022  13  189.95   12 SONAR 1-STEP CAMERA
1023  15   74.95    5 PRONTO CAMERA
1031   9  279.99   10 8MM ZOOM MOVIE CAMERA
1032  15  310.55   10 SOUND/ZOOM 8MM CAMERA
1041  10  389.00   12 35MM SLR XG-7 MINO. CAM.
1042  11  349.95   12 35MM SLR AE-1 PENT. CAM.
1043  20  319.90   12 35MM SLR ME CAN. CAM.
1044  13  119.95   12 35MM HI-MATIC CAMERA
1045  20   89.99   12 35MM COMPACT CAMERA
1511   7  129.95    5 ZOOM MOVIE PROJECTOR
1512   9  239.99    5 ZOOM-SOUND PROJECTOR
1521  10  219.99    5 AUTO CAROUSEL PROJECTOR
1522   4  114.95    5 CAR. SLIDE PROJECTOR
2011   4   14.95    5 POCKET STROBE
2012  12   48.55   10 STROBE SX-10
2013  10   28.99   15 ELEC.FLASH SX-10
3011  13   32.99   15 TELE CONVERTER
3012  14   97.99   15 28MM WIDE-ANGLE LENS
3013  13   87.95   15 135MM TELEPHOTO LENS
3014   8  267.95    5 35-105 MM ZOOM LENS
3015   7  257.95    5 80-200 MM ZOOM LENS
3111   4   67.50    5 HEAVY-DUTY TRIPOD
3112  10   19.95    5 LIGHTWEIGHT TRIPOD
3511  10  159.99    5 35MM ENLARGER KIT
4011   4   35.98    5 40X40 DELUXE SCREEN
4012  10   44.98    5 50X50 DELUXE SCREEN
5011  17    4.29   25 120-SLIDE TRAY
5012  33    2.95   25 100-SLIDE TRAY
5021  12    6.25   15 SLIDE VIEWER
5031  12   55.95   10 MOVIE EDITOR
6011  10   59.95    5 CONDENSER MICROPHONE
6111  80    0.89  100 AA ALKALINE BATTERY
7011  19   19.79   20 GADGET BAG
8011  45    1.49   50 135-24 COLOR FILM
8021  60    0.99   50 110-12 COLOR FILM
8022  42    1.45   50 110-24 COLOR FILM
8023  37    0.59   25 110-12 B/W FILM
8024  43    0.95   25 110-24 B/W FILM
8031  44    0.89   50 126-12 COLOR FILM
8032  27    0.59   25 126-12 B/W FILM
8041  39    6.89   50 8MM FILM CASSETTE
8042  25   11.89   20 16MM FILM CASSETTE
9111  10  959.99   12 COMBINATION CAMERA KIT
```

InventoryUpdate

Order number: three letters followed by four digits
Item number: an integer (same as those in **InventoryFile**)
Transaction code: a character (**S** = sold, **R** = returned)
Number of items sold or returned: an integer in the range 0 through 999

The file is sorted so that item numbers are in increasing order. (Some items in **InventoryFile** may not have update records; others may have more than one.)

 Sample **InventoryUpdate**

CCI7543	TAV3604	VDZ2970
1012 S 2	1512 S 2	4012 S 6
LTB3429	DCW9363	BOJ9069
1012 S 7	1522 S 1	5011 S 6
DJS6762	EXN3964	MNL7029
1021 S 9	1522 R 1	5011 S 9
NQT1850	OIN5524	MRG8703
1022 S 1	1522 S 1	5021 S 10
WYP6425	EOJ8218	DEM9289
1023 S 4	1522 S 1	5021 S 1
YOK2210	YFK0683	BXL1651
1023 R 2	2011 S 2	5031 S 2
QGM3144	PPX4743	VAF8733
1023 S 1	2012 S 4	6111 S 65
NPQ8685	DBR1709	UYI0368
1031 S 5	2013 S 4	7011 S 2
MAP8102	JOM5408	VIZ6879
1031 S 13	2013 S 3	8011 S 16
JRJ6335	PKN0671	GXX9093
1031 S 1	2013 S 1	8011 S 19
UWR9386	LBD8391	HHO5605
1032 S 3	3011 S 9	8021 S 41
TJY1913	DNL6326	BOL2324
1032 S 11	3012 S 9	8021 S 49
YHA9464	BTP5396	PAG9289
1041 S 5	3013 S 1	8023 S 15
SYT7493	GFL4913	MDF5557
1041 S 3	3013 S 8	8023 S 17
FHJ1657	EHQ7510	IQK3388
1042 S 7	3013 S 7	8024 S 12
OJQ2215	QQL6472	OTB1341
1043 S 8	3013 S 5	8024 S 28
UOX7714	SVC6511	SVF5674
1043 S 2	3014 S 4	8031 S 24
ERZ2147	XJQ9391	ZDP9484
1043 S 7	3014 S 4	8031 S 15
MYW2540	ONO5251	OSY8177
1044 S 1	3111 S 3	8032 S 15
UKS3587	CXC7780	GJQ0185
1045 S 2	3111 S 1	8032 S 8

Sample **InventoryUpdate** (cont.)

AAN3759			VGT8169			VHW0189		
1045	S	2	3112	S	8	8041	S	20
WZT4171			IMK5861			WEU9225		
1045	S	12	3511	S	2	8041	S	6
TYR9475			QHR1944			YJO3755		
1511	S	1	3511	S	1	8041	S	8
FRQ4184			ZPK6211					
1511	S	1	4011	S	2			

LeastSquaresFile

This is a text file in which each line contains a pair of real numbers representing the x coordinate and the y coordinate of a point.

 Sample **LeastSquaresFile**

2.18	1.06		5.63	8.58
7.46	12.04		8.94	15.27
5.75	8.68		7.34	11.48
3.62	4.18		6.55	9.92
3.59	3.87		4.89	7.07
7.5	12.32		9.59	15.82
7.49	11.74		1.81	0.45
7.62	12.07		0.99	-0.71
7.39	12.17		4.82	6.91
1.88	0.58		9.68	16.24
6.31	10.09		1.21	-0.22
2.53	2.04		4.54	5.64
5.44	8.25		1.48	0.3
1.21	-0.76		6.58	9.8
9.07	15.5		3.05	3.56
3.95	5.0		6.19	9.62
9.63	17.01		6.47	9.83
9.75	16.91		8.13	10.75
9.99	16.67		7.31	11.73
3.61	4.69		0.33	-1.93
9.06	15.0		5.12	7.41
5.03	6.62		5.23	7.73
4.45	6.12		7.14	11.02
4.54	5.89		1.27	-0.21
0.92	-1.02		2.51	1.59
0.82	-1.5		5.26	7.86
2.62	2.1		4.74	6.19
5.66	8.53		2.1	2.12
8.05	13.05		5.27	7.73
8.99	14.85		2.85	2.63
5.12	7.03		1.99	1.09
3.85	4.43		8.91	15.03

Sample **LeastSquaresFile** (cont.)

6.08	9.21	2.19	1.21
1.42	0	1.6	-0.05
2.58	2.38	8.93	15.12
5.99	9.42	3.19	3.56
0.63	-1.63	3.37	3.64
9.98	17.25		

StudentFile

Student number: an integer
Student's name: a string of the form last-name, first-name, middle-initial
Hometown: a string
Phone number: a 7-character string
Gender: a character (**M** or **F**)
Class level: a 1-digit integer (**1**, **2**, **3**, **4**, or **5** for special)
Total credits earned to date: an integer
Cumulative GPA: a real value
Major: a 4-character string

The file is arranged so that student numbers are in increasing order.

 Sample **StudentFile**

```
10103 JOHNSON, JAMES L
WAUPUN, WISCONSIN
7345229
M 1 15 3.15
ENGR
10104 ANDREWS, PETER J
GRAND RAPIDS, MICHIGAN
9493301
M 2 42 2.78
CPSC
10110 PETERS, ANDREW J
LYNDEN, WASHINGTON
3239550
M 5 63 2.05
ART
10113 VANDENVANDER, VANESSA V
FREMONT, MICHIGAN
5509237
F 4 110 3.74
HIST
10126 ARISTOTLE, ALICE A
CHINO, CALIFORNIA
3330861
F 3 78 3.10
PHIL
```

```
10144 LUCKY, LUCY L
GRANDVILLE, MICHIGAN
7745424
F 5 66 2.29
HIST
10179 EULER, LENNIE L
THREE RIVERS, MICHIGAN
6290017
M 1 15 3.83
MATH
10191 NAKAMURA, TOKY O
CHICAGO, ILLINOIS
4249665
F 1 12 1.95
SOCI
10226 FREUD, FRED E
LYNDEN, WASHINGTON
8340115
M 1 15 1.85
PSYC
10272 SPEARSHAKE, WILLIAM W
GRAND RAPIDS, MICHIGAN
2410744
M 5 102 2.95
ENGL
```

Sample **StudentFile** (cont.)

10274 TCHAIKOVSKY, WOLFGANG A
BYRON CENTER, MICHIGAN
8845115
M 3 79 2.75
MUSC
10284 ORANGE, DUTCH V
GRAAFSCHAAP, MICHIGAN
3141660
M 2 42 2.98
ENGR
10297 CAESAR, JULIE S
DENVER, COLORADO
4470338
F 4 117 3.25
HIST
10298 PSYCHO, PRUNELLA E
DE MOTTE, INDIANA
5384609
F 4 120 2.99
PSYC
10301 BULL, SITTING U
GALLUP, NEW MEXICO
6632997
M 1 14 2.95
EDUC
10302 CUSTER, GENERAL G
BADLANDS, SOUTH DAKOTA
5552995
M 3 40 1.95
HIST
10303 FAHRENHEIT, FELICIA O
SHEBOYGAN, WISCONSIN
5154997
F 2 40 3.85
CHEM
10304 DEUTSCH, SPRECHEN Z
SPARTA, MICHIGAN
8861201
F 5 14 3.05
GERM
10307 MENDELSSOHN, MOZART W
PEORIA, ILLINOIS
2410747
M 3 76 2.87
MUSC
10310 AUGUSTA, ADA B
LAKEWOOD, CALIFORNIA
7172339
F 2 46 3.83
CPSC

10319 GAUSS, CARL F
YORKTOWN, PENNSYLVANIA
3385494
M 2 41 4.00
MATH
10323 KRONECKER, LEO P
TRAVERSE CITY, MICHIGAN
6763991
M 3 77 2.75
MATH
10330 ISSACSON, JACOB A
SILVER SPRINGS, MD
4847932
M 5 25 2.99
RELI
10331 ISSACSON, ESAU B
SILVER SPRINGS, MD
4847932
M 5 25 2.98
RELI
10339 DEWEY, JOHANNA A
SALT LAKE CITY, UTAH
6841129
F 2 41 3.83
EDUC
10348 VIRUS, VERA W
SAGINAW, MICHIGAN
6634401
F 4 115 3.25
CPSC
10355 ZYLSTRA, ZELDA A
DOWNS, KANSAS
7514008
F 1 16 1.95
ENGL
10377 PORGY, BESS N
COLUMBUS, OHIO
4841771
F 2 44 2.78
MUSI
10389 NEWMANN, ALFRED E
CHEYENNE, WYOMING
7712399
M 4 115 0.99
EDUC
10395 MEDES, ARCHIE L
WHITINSVILLE, MA
9294401
M 3 80 3.10
ENGR

Sample **StudentFile** (cont.)

10406 MACDONALD, RONALD B
SEATTLE, WASHINGTON
5582911
M 1 15 2.99
CPSC
10415 AARDVARK, ANTHONY A
GRANDVILLE, MICHIGAN
5325912
M 2 43 2.79
ENGR
10422 GESTALT, GLORIA G
WHEATON, ILLINOIS
6631212
F 2 42 2.48
PSYC
10431 GOTODIJKSTRA, EDGAR G
CAWKER CITY, KANSAS
6349971
M 1 15 4.00
CPSC
10448 REMBRANDT, ROBERTA E
SIOUX CENTER, IOWA
2408113
F 1 77 2.20
ART
10458 SHOEMAKER, IMELDA M
HONOLULU, HAWAII
9193001
F 1 15 3.15
POLS
10467 MARX, KARL Z
HAWTHORNE, NEW JERSEY
5513915
M 3 78 2.75
ECON
10470 SCROOGE, EBENEZER T
TROY, MICHIGAN
8134001
M 4 118 3.25
SOCI
10482 NIGHTINGALE, FLORENCE K
ROCHESTER, NEW YORK
7175118
F 1 15 3.15
NURS
10490 GAZELLE, GWENDOLYN D
CHINO, CALIFORNIA
3132446
F 2 43 2.78
PE

10501 PASTEUR, LOUISE A
WINDOW ROCK, ARIZONA
4245170
F 1 16 3.10
BIOL
10519 ELBA, ABLE M
BOZEMAN, MONTANA
8183226
M 3 77 3.40
SPEE
10511 LEWIS, CLARK N
NEW ERA, MICHIGAN
6461125
M 4 114 3.37
GEOG
10515 MOUSE, MICHAEL E
BOISE, IDAHO
5132771
M 5 87 1.99
EDUC
10523 PAVLOV, TIFFANY T
FARMINGTON, MICHIGAN
9421753
F 1 13 1.77
BIOL
10530 CHICITA, JUANITA A
OKLAHOMA CITY, OK
3714377
F 5 95 2.66
ENGL
10538 BUSCH, ARCH E
ST LOUIS, MISSOURI
8354112
M 3 74 2.75
ENGR
10547 FAULT, PAIGE D
PETOSKEY, MICHIGAN
4543116
F 5 55 2.95
CPSC
10553 SANTAMARIA, NINA P
PLYMOUTH, MASSACHUSETTS
2351181
F 1 15 1.77
HIST
10560 SHYSTER, SAMUEL D
EVERGLADES, FLORIDA
4421885
M 1 13 1.95
SOCI

Sample **StudentFile** (cont.)

10582 YEWLISS, CAL C
RUDYARD, MICHIGAN
3451220
M 376 2.99
MATH
10590 ATANASOFF, ENIAC C
SPRINGFIELD, ILLINOIS
6142449
F 1 14 1.88
CPSC
10597 ROCKNE, ROCKY K
NEWY YORK, NEW YORK
4631744
M 4 116 1.98
PE
10610 ROOSEVELT, ROSE Y
SPRING LAKE, MICHIGAN
9491221
F 5 135 2.95
POLS
10623 XERXES, ART I
CINCINATI, OHIO
3701228
M 4 119 3.25
GREE
10629 LEIBNIZ, GOTTFRIED W
BOULDER, COLORADO
5140228
M 1 13 1.95
MATH
10633 VESPUCCI, VERA D
RIPON, CALIFORNIA
4341883
F 5 89 2.29
GEOG
10648 PRINCIPAL, PAMELA P
ALBANY, NEW YORK
7145513
F 1 14 1.75
EDUC

10652 CICERO, MARSHA
RAPID CITY, SD
3335910
F 3 77 2.87
LATI
10657 WEERD, DEWEY L
DETROIT, MICHIGAN
4841962
M 4 115 2.99
PHIL
10663 HOCHSCHULE, HORTENSE C
LINCOLN, NEBRASKA
7120111
F 5 100 2.70
EDUC
10668 EINSTEIN, ALFRED M
NEWARK, NEW JERSEY
3710225
M 2 41 2.78
ENGR
10675 FIBONACCI, LEONARD O
NASHVILLE, TENNESSEE
4921107
M 4 115 3.25
MATH
10682 ANGELO, MIKE L
AUSTIN, TEXAS
5132201
M 4 117 3.74
ART
10688 PASCAL, BLAZE R
BROOKLYN, NEW YORK
7412993
M 1 15 1.98
CPSC

StudentUpdate

Student number: an integer (same as those used in **StudentFile**)
For each of five courses:

Course name: a seven-character string (e.g., **CPSC131**)
Letter grade: a two-character string (e.g., **A-**, **B+**, **C♭**)
Course credit: an integer

The file is sorted so that student numbers are in increasing order. There is one update record for each student in `StudentFile`.

 Sample `StudentUpdate`

```
10103 ENGL176 C   4 EDUC268 B   4 EDUC330 B+  3 PE281   C   3 ENGR317 D   4
10104 CPSC271 D+  4 ESCI208 D-  3 PHIL340 B+  2 CPSC146 D+  4 ENGL432 D+  4
10110 ART 520 D   3 ESCI259 F   1 ENGL151 D+  4 MUSC257 B   4 PSYC486 C   4
10113 HIST498 F   3 PE  317 C+  4 MUSC139 B-  3 PHIL165 D   3 GEOG222 C   3
10126 PHIL367 C-  4 EDUC420 C-  3 EDUC473 C   3 EDUC224 D-  3 GERM257 F   4
10144 HIST559 C+  3 MATH357 D   3 CPSC323 C-  2 PE246   D-  4 MUSC379 D+  4
10179 MATH169 C-  4 CHEM163 C+  4 MUSC436 A-  3 MATH366 D-  2 BIOL213 A-  4
10191 SOCI177 F   4 POLS106 A   4 EDUC495 A-  3 ENGR418 B+  2 ENGR355 A   4
10226 PSYC116 B   3 GERM323 B-  4 ART350  A   4 HIST269 B+  4 EDUC214 C+  3
10272 ENGL558 A-  4 EDUC169 D+  3 PSYC483 B+  4 ENGR335 B+  2 BIOL228 B   4
10274 MUSC351 B   4 PSYC209 C-  4 ENGR400 F   1 ESCI392 A   4 SOCI394 B-  3
10284 ENGR292 D   4 PSYC172 C   4 EDUC140 B   4 MATH274 F   4 MUSC101 D+  4
10297 HIST464 F   1 HIST205 F   1 ENGR444 F   1 MATH269 F   1 EDUC163 F   1
10298 PSYC452 B   3 MATH170 C+  4 EDUC344 C-  2 GREE138 C-  2 SPEE303 A-  3
10301 EDUC197 A   4 PE372   B   3 ENGR218 D   4 MATH309 C   4 ESCI405 C-  4
10302 CHEM283 F   1 PE440   A   2 MATH399 A-  3 HIST455 C-  4 MATH387 C-  3
10303 HIST111 D-  3 ART151  C+  3 ENGL100 C-  3 PSYC151 D+  3 PE104   A-  1
10304 GERM526 C-  2 CHEM243 C   4 POLS331 B-  4 EDUC398 A   3 ENGR479 D+  4
10307 MUSC323 B+  3 MATH485 C   4 HIST232 B+  4 EDUC180 A   3 ENGL130 B+  4
10310 CPSC264 B   2 POLS227 D+  3 ENGR467 D-  3 MATH494 D-  4 ART420  C+  4
10319 MATH276 B   2 ESCI434 A   3 HIST197 B-  4 GERM489 B-  2 ART137  C-  3
10323 MATH377 D-  4 EDUC210 D   4 MATH385 D-  4 ENGR433 C   2 HIST338 A-  4
10330 HIST546 C+  3 ESCI440 B+  3 GREE472 C+  3 BIOL186 B   4 GEOG434 C+  2
10331 HIST546 C   3 ESCI440 B+  3 GREE472 C   3 BIOL186 B+  4 GEOG434 C+  2
10339 EDUC283 B   3 CPSC150 B   3 ENGR120 D   4 CPSC122 F   4 ART216  B   4
10348 CPSC411 C-  3 HIST480 C+  4 PSYC459 B   4 BIOL299 B+  4 ECON276 B+  3
10355 ENGL130 C-  3 CPSC282 C+  4 CPSC181 A-  4 CPSC146 C-  4 SOCI113 F   1
10377 SOCI213 D+  3 PSYC158 D   4 MUSC188 C   3 PSYC281 D-  4 ENGR339 B+  4
10389 EDUC414 D+  4 PSYC115 C-  2 PSYC152 D-  4 ART366  D-  3 ENGR366 F   4
10395 ENGR396 B   4 HIST102F   3 ENGL111 A   4 PSYC210 D-  2 GREE128 A   4
10406 CPSC160 C+  4 CPSC233 C   1 LATI494 C+  3 ENGL115 C-  3 MATH181 A   3
10415 ENGR287 C   4 EDUC166 B-  4 EDUC106 A-  3 PE190   F   3 MATH171 B-  3
10422 PSYC275 A-  4 MATH497 A   4 EDUC340 F   1 GERM403 C-  4 MATH245 D+  4
10431 CPSC187 D-  4 CPSC426 F   4 ENGR476 B-  4 BIOL148 B+  3 CPSC220 F   3
10448 ART171  D+  3 CPSC239 C-  3 SOCI499 B-  4 HIST113 D+  3 PSYC116 C   4
10458 POLS171 F   1 CPSC187 C+  4 CHEM150 B   2 PHIL438 D-  4 PHIL254 D   4
10467 ECON335 D-  3 ESCI471 B+  4 MATH457 C+  3 MATH207 C   2 BIOL429 D   4
10470 MUSC415 C+  3 POLS177 C   3 CPSC480 A   4 PSYC437 B   3 SOCI276 D   4
10482 ENGL158 D-  4 EDUC475 B   3 HIST172 B-  2 PE316   F   4 ENGR294 A-  3
10490 PE239   F   4 ENGL348 F   3 LATI246 F   4 CPSC350 F   4 MATH114 F   1
10501 BIOL125 F   4 CPSC412 F   3 ESCI279 F   4 ENGR153 F   2 ART293  F   1
10519 SPEE386 B+  4 HIST479 C   4 PSYC249 B-  2 GREE204 B-  4 PE421   A   1
10511 ESCI416 B   3 MATH316 D-  4 MATH287 C   2 MATH499 A-  4 ESCI288 D   3
10515 EDUC563 D+  3 PHIL373 D-  3 ART318  B   4 HIST451 F   1 ART476  C+  3
10523 BIOL183 D-  2 HIST296 D+  4 HIST380 B+  4 ENGR216 C   4 MATH412 B-  2
10530 ENGL559 F   1 EDUC457 D+  4 CPSC306 A   3 ENGR171 B+  1 CPSC380 A   4
```

Sample **StudentUpdate** (cont.)

```
10538 ENGR328 A- 4 ENGR336 C  3 EDUC418 D+ 3 PHIL437 B+ 4 CPSC475 D  4
10547 CPSC537 A- 4 ART386  D  4 HIST292 D- 4 ENGR467 A- 4 PE464   B+ 4
10553 HIST170 A- 4 SOCI496 D- 3 PHIL136 B+ 4 CPSC371 D- 4 CPSC160 A- 1
10560 SOCI153 D+ 3 MATH438 D+ 4 CPSC378 C  4 BIOL266 F  3 EDUC278 D+ 3
10582 MATH388 A- 3 PE311   B  3 ECON143 D  4 MATH304 C+ 3 PE428   C+ 4
10590 CPSC134 B- 3 ESCI114 B+ 3 CPSC492 C  4 ENGL121 C  4 ENGR403 A- 4
10597 PE423   A- 3 BIOL189 D+ 3 PHIL122 D- 4 ENGL194 C- 4 SOCI113 D+ 3
10610 ESCI594 C- 3 PHIL344 F  4 CPSC189 B+ 2 ENGR411 D- 3 MATH241 A  4
10623 GREE412 B- 4 ENGL415 D- 3 ENGL234 D- 4 MATH275 F  1 SOCI124 B+ 3
10629 MATH137 D  2 MATH481 F  3 ESCI445 F  1 MATH339 D  4 ART219  B+ 4
10633 GEOG573 B  4 ENGL149 C+ 4 EDUC113 B+ 4 ENGR458 C- 2 HIST446 D+ 4
10648 EDUC132 D+ 4 MUSC103 D- 4 ENGL263 C  4 ENGL134 B+ 4 ESCI392 A  3
10652 LATI363 F  3 BIOL425 F  1 CPSC267 C  4 EDUC127 C+ 3 MATH338 B  4
10657 PHIL429 F  1 ART412  D- 4 MUSC473 B- 4 SOCI447 C- 4 MATH237 D+ 2
10663 EDUC580 B- 4 ENGR351 B+ 4 SOCI283 D  4 ART340  C  4 PSYC133 D+ 3
10668 ENGR274 B+ 4 SOCI438 C  1 PE327   C  4 BIOL158 A  4 EDUC457 A- 4
10675 MATH457 A  4 ENGR114 C  4 CPSC218 C  3 ESCI433 C- 3 PSYC243 C+ 1
10682 ART483  D+ 3 GERM432 C  3 ENGL103 B+ 4 MUSC169 C- 3 SOCI381 C- 2
10688 CPSC182 F  1 HIST371 C+ 4 PSYC408 F  1 MUSC214 B+ 4 MATH151 C  3
```

UserIdFile

Identification number: an integer
User's name: A string in the form last-name, first-name
Password: a string with at most five characters
Resource limit (in dollars): an integer with up to four digits
Resources used to date: a real value

The file is arranged so that identification numbers are in increasing order.

  Sample **UserIdFile**

```
10101 MILTGEN,JOSEPH          10106 PIZZULA,NORMA
MOE                          PIZZA
750 380.81                   350 223.95
10102 SMALL,ISAAC            10107 VANDERVAN,HENRY
LARGE                        VAN
650 598.84                   750 168.59
10103 SNYDER,SAMUEL          10108 FREELOADER,FREDDIE
R2-D2                        RED
250 193.74                   450 76.61
10104 EDMUNDSEN,EDMUND       10109 ALEXANDER,ALVIN
ABCDE                        GREAT
250 177.93                   650 405.04
10105 BRAUNSCHWEIGER,CHRISTOPHER  10110 MOUSE,MICHAEL
BROWN                        EARS
850 191.91                   50 42.57
```

Sample **UserIdFile** (cont.)

10111 LUKASEWICZ,ZZYZK
RPN
350 73.50
10112 CHRISTMAS,MARY
NOEL
850 33.28
10113 SINKEY,CJ
TRAIN
750 327.53
10114 NIJHOFF,LARAN
KKID
550 382.03
10115 LIESTMA,STAN
SAAB
650 38.36
10116 ZWIER,APOLLOS
PJ
350 249.48
10117 JAEGER,TIM
BIKE
250 246.73
10118 VANZWALBERG,JORGE
EGYPT
850 466.95
10119 JESTER,COURTNEY
JOKER
450 281.16
10120 MCDONALD,RONALD
FRIES
250 35.00
10121 NEDERLANDER,BENAUT
DUTCH
550 28.82
10122 HAYBAILER,HOMER
FARM
850 37.32
10123 SPEAR,WILLIAM
SHAKE
450 337.01
10124 ROMEO,JULIET
XOXOX
150 100.19
10125 GREEK,JIMMY
WAGER
250 0.03
10126 VIRUS,VERA
WORM
750 67.35
10127 BEECH,ROCKY
BOAT
950 256.18

10128 ENGEL,ANGEL
WINGS
150 16.39
10129 ABNER,LIL
DAISY
950 89.57
10130 TRACY,DICK
CRIME
550 392.00
10131 MCGEE,FIBBER
MOLLY
750 332.12
10132 BELL,ALEXANDER
PHONE
850 337.43
20101 COBB,TYRUS
TIGER
50 32.81
20102 GEORGE,RUTH
BABE
350 269.93
20103 DESCARTES,RONALD
HORSE
250 109.34
0104 EUCLID,IAN
GREEK
350 63.63
20105 DANIELS,EZEKIEL
LIONS
350 128.69
20106 TARZAN,JANE
APES
150 100.31
20107 HABBAKUK,JONAH
WHALE
950 183.93
20108 COLUMBUS,CHRIS
PINTA
850 202.24
20109 BYRD,RICHARD
NORTH
550 168.49
20110 BUNYAN,PAUL
BABE
550 333.47
20111 CHAUCER,JEFF
POEM
950 37.02
20112 STOTLE,ARI
LOGIC
750 337.74

Sample `UserIdFile` (cont.)

```
20113 HARRISON,BEN          20119 SAWYER,TOM
PRES                        HUCK
550 262.97                  950 460.30
20114 JAMES,JESSE           20120 NEWMANN,ALFRED
GUNS                        MAD
250 58.81                   450 116.00
20115 SCOTT,FRANCINE        20121 SIMPLE,SIMON
FLAG                        SAYS
350 168.11                  550 486.05
20116 PHILLIPS,PHYLLIS      20122 SCHMIDT,MESSER
GAS66                       PLANE
650 322.22                  250 35.31
20117 DOLL,BARBARA          20124 LUTHER,CALVIN
KEN                         REF
350 26.34                   777 666.66
20118 FINN,HUCK             20125 YALE,HARVARD
TOM                         IVY
350 22.86                   150 127.70
```

Algorithms and Programs

Several of the PART OF THE PICTURE sections in the text refer to programs and, in some cases, algorithms for problems described in these sections. These algorithms and/or program listings follow.

Example 9.4 Quicksort

Section 9.4, PART OF THE PICTURE: Sorting and Searching, described two sorting methods—simple selection sort and quicksort—and several other methods were described in the exercises. The following program is similar to that in Figure 9.6 for sorting a list of numbers, but it uses quicksort rather than selection sort.

 Quicksort

```pascal
PROGRAM SortWithQuicksort( input, output );
{*****************************************************************

   Input (keyboard): List of items and user response.
   Purpose:          Read and count a list of items Item[1], Item[2],
                     ..., Item[n], sort them in ascending order,
                     and then display the sorted list.
   Output (screen):  User prompts and a sorted list of items

*****************************************************************}

CONST
   ListLimit = 100;   {maximum # of items in the list}
```

Quicksort (cont.)

```
TYPE
   ListElementType = integer;
   ListType = ARRAY[1..ListLimit] OF ListElementType;

VAR
   NumItems,          {number of items}
   i: integer;        {index}
   Item : ListType;   {list of items to be sorted}

PROCEDURE ReadList( VAR Item : ListType;    {list of items to be read}
                    VAR Count : integer );  {number of items}

{-----------------------------------------------------------------

   Input (keyboard): List elements.
   Purpose:          Read list elements into array Item and Count
                     the elements read.
   Returns:          Array Item and Count.
   Output (screen):  User prompts.

-----------------------------------------------------------------------}

   VAR
      Response : char;   {user response}

   BEGIN
      writeln( 'Enter the list of items, as many per line as desired.' );
      writeln( 'Note:  At most ', ListLimit:1, ' items can be read.' );
      writeln;
      Count := 0;
      REPEAT
         write( 'Items:  ' );
         WHILE NOT eoln DO
            BEGIN
               Count := Count + 1;
               read( Item[Count] )
            END {WHILE};
         readln;
         write( 'More (Y or N)?  ' );
         readln( Response )
      UNTIL Response <> 'Y'
   END {ReadList};

PROCEDURE Split( VAR X : ListType; Low, High : integer;
                 VAR Mid : integer );
{-----------------------------------------------------------------

   Accepts:  A list of items stored in locations Low..High of the
             array X.
   Purpose:  Rearrange X[Low], ..., X[High] so that one item is
             properly positioned.
   Returns:  The rearranged list and the final position Mid of that
             item.

-----------------------------------------------------------------------}
```

Quicksort (cont.)

```
VAR
    Left,                           {index for searching from the left}
    Right : integer;                {index for searching from the right}
    TempItem : ListElementType;   {temporary item used for interchanging}

BEGIN
    {Initialize indices for left and right searches}
    Left := Low;
    Right := High;

    {Carry out the searches}
    WHILE Left < Right DO        {While searches haven't met}
        BEGIN
            {Search from the right}
            WHILE X[Right] > X[Low] DO
                Right := Right - 1;

            {Search from the left}
            WHILE (Left < Right) AND (X[Left] <= X[Low]) DO
                Left := Left + 1;

            {Interchange items if searches have not met}
            IF Left < Right THEN
                BEGIN
                    TempItem := X[Left];
                    X[Left] := X[Right];
                    X[Right] := TempItem
                END {IF}
        END {WHILE};

    {End of searches; place selected item in proper position}
    Mid := Right;
    TempItem := X[Mid];
    X[Mid] := X[Low];
    X[Low] := TempItem
END {Split};

PROCEDURE QuickSort( VAR X : ListType; Low, High : integer );
{-----------------------------------------------------------------------

    Accepts:   A list of items stored in locations Low..High of the
               array X.
    Purpose:   Sort X[Low], ..., X[High] into ascending order using
               quicksort.
    Returns:   The sorted list.

------------------------------------------------------------------------}

VAR
    Mid : integer;            {final position of selected item}
```

Quicksort (cont.)

```
    BEGIN
       IF Low < High THEN     {list has more than one item}
          BEGIN
             Split (X, Low, High, Mid);     {split into two sublists}
             QuickSort (X, Low, Mid -1);    {sort first sublist}
             QuickSort (X, Mid + 1, High)   {sort second sublist}
          END {IF}
    END {QuickSort};

PROCEDURE PrintList( VAR Item : ListType;        {list of items}
                         NumItems : integer ); {number of items}
{-----------------------------------------------------------------

   Accepts:         List of NumItems items stored in array Item.
   Purpose:         Display the list of items.
   Output (screen): Items in list.

------------------------------------------------------------------}

   VAR
      i : integer;        {index}

   BEGIN
      writeln;
      writeln( 'Sorted list of ', Numitems:1, ' items:' );
      writeln;
      FOR i := 1 TO NumItems DO
         writeln( Item[i] )
   END {PrintList};

BEGIN {************** main program **************}
   ReadList( Item, NumItems );
   QuickSort( Item, 1, NumItems );
   PrintList( Item, NumItems )
END {main}.
```

Sample run:

```
Enter the list of items, as many per line as desired.
Note:  At most 100 items can be read.

Items:  55 88 34 84 21
More (Y or N)?  Y
Items:  99 5 83 71
More (Y or N)?  N
```

Quicksort (cont.)

Sorted list of 9 items:

        5
       21
       34
       55
       71
       83
       84
       88
       99

Example 11.4 Gaussian Elimination

Section 11.4, PART OF THE PICTURE: Numerical Methods, illustrated the method of Gaussian Elimination for solving a system of linear equations. The following algorithm summarizes this method. To minimize the effect of roundoff error in the computations, it rearranges the rows to obtain as a pivot that element which is largest in absolute value. Note that if it is not possible to find a nonzero pivot element at some stage, then the linear system is said to be a singular system and does not have a unique solution.

GAUSSIAN ELIMINATION ALGORITHM

(* Accepts: An $n \times n$ coefficient matrix A and an $n \times 1$ constant vector b.
   Purpose: Solve the linear system $Ax = b$, using Gaussian elimination, where x is the $n \times 1$ vector of unknowns.
   Returns: The solution vector x, if one can be found.
   Output: A message if the matrix is found to be singular. *)

1. Form the $n \times (n + 1)$ augmented matrix Aug by adjoining b to A:

$$Aug = [A \mid b]$$

2. For i ranging from 1 to n, do the following:
   a. Find the entry $Aug[k, i]$, $k = i, i + 1, \ldots, n$ that has the largest absolute value.
   b. Interchange row i and row k.
   c. If $Aug[i, i] = 0$, display a message that the matrix A is singular and stop processing.
   d. For j ranging from $i + 1$ to n, do the following:

   Add $\dfrac{-Aug[j, i]}{Aug[i, i]}$ times the ith row of Aug to the ith row of Aug

   to eliminate $x[i]$ from the jth equation.

3. Set $x[n]$ equal to $\dfrac{Aug[n, n + 1]}{Aug[n, n]}$.

4. For j ranging from $n - 1$ to 1 in steps of 1, do the following:
   Substitute the values of $x[j + 1], \ldots, x[n]$ in the jth equation and
   solve for $x[j]$.

The following program implements this algorithm for Gaussian elimination.
Because real numbers cannot be stored exactly, the statement implementing step 2c
checks if `abs(Aug[i, i])` is less than some small positive number `Epsil` rather
than if `Aug[i, i]` is exactly 0.

 Gaussian Elimination

```
PROGRAM GaussianElimination( input, output );
{**********************************************************************

    Input (keyboard): The coefficient matrix A and the constant vector b
                      of a linear system Ax = b.
    Purpose:          Solve the linear system using Gaussian elimination.
    Output (screen):  User prompts and the solution vector.


**********************************************************************}

CONST
    MaxEquations = 10;                    {maximum number of equations}
    AugColumns = MaxEquations + 1;  {and columns in augmented matrix}

TYPE
    AugmentedMatrix = ARRAY[1..MaxEquations, 1..AugColumns] OF real;
    SolutionVector = ARRAY[1..MaxEquations] OF real;

VAR
    Aug : AugmentedMatrix;     {augmented matrix}
    X : SolutionVector;        {solution vector}
    n : integer;               {number of equations and unknown}
    Singular : boolean;        {indicates if matrix is (nearly) singular}

PROCEDURE ReadEquations( VAR Aug : AugmentedMatrix; {augmented matrix}
                         VAR n : integer );         {number of equations}
{-------------------------------------------------------------------

    Input (keyboard): Coefficient matrix and constant vector.
    Purpose:          Read the number of equations, the coefficient
                      matrix, and the constant vector and initialize
                      the augmented matrix.
    Output (screen):  Prompts to the user.
    Returns:          The augmented matrix Aug and the number n of
                      equations.


-------------------------------------------------------------------}
```

Gaussian Elimination (cont.)

```
VAR
    i, j : integer;    {indices}

BEGIN
    write( 'Enter the number of equations in the system: ' );
    readln( n );
    writeln( 'Enter the coefficient matrix rowwise: ' );
    FOR i := 1 TO n DO
        BEGIN
            FOR j := 1 TO n DO
                read( Aug[i,j] );
            readln
        END {FOR i};
    writeln( 'Enter the constant vector: ' );
    FOR i := 1 TO n DO
        read( Aug[i, n + 1] );
    readln
END {ReadEquations};

PROCEDURE Reduce( VAR Aug : AugmentedMatrix;    {augmented matrix}
                      n : integer;              {number of equations}
                  VAR Singular : boolean );     {signals if matrix singular}
{-----------------------------------------------------------------------

    Accepts:      Augmented matrix Aug and number n of equations.
    Purpose:      Use Gaussian elimination to reduce the augmented
                  matrix of a linear system, provided the matrix
                  of coefficients is nonsingular.
    Returns:      The reduced augmented matrix and boolean value
                  Singular, which is true if the coefficient matrix
                  is (nearly) singular and is false otherwise.

-----------------------------------------------------------------------}

CONST
    Epsilon = 1E-6;       {a small positive real value ("almost zero")}

VAR
    i, j, k,              {indices}
    PivotRow : integer;   {row containing pivot element}
    Mult,                 {multiplier used to eliminate an unknown}
    AbsPivot,             {absolute value of pivot element}
    Temp : real;          {used to interchange rows of matrix}
```

Gaussian Elimination (cont.)

```
     BEGIN
        Singular := false;
        i := 1;
        WHILE (NOT Singular) AND (i <= n) DO
           BEGIN
              {Locate pivot element}
              AbsPivot := abs(Aug[i,i]);
              PivotRow := i;
              FOR k := i + 1 TO n DO
                 IF Abs(Aug[k,i]) > AbsPivot THEN
                    BEGIN
                       AbsPivot := abs(Aug[k,i]);
                       PivotRow := k
                    END {IF};
              {Check if matrix is (nearly) singular}
              Singular := AbsPivot < Epsilon;
              IF NOT Singular THEN
                 BEGIN
                    {Interchange rows PivotRow and i if necessary}
                    IF i <> PivotRow THEN
                       FOR j := 1 TO n + 1 DO
                          BEGIN
                             Temp := Aug[i,j];
                             Aug[i,j] := Aug[PivotRow, j];
                             Aug[PivotRow, j] := Temp
                          END {FOR j};

                    {Eliminate i-th unknown from equations i + 1, . . .  n}
                    FOR j := i + 1 TO n DO
                       BEGIN
                          Mult := -Aug[j,i] / Aug[i,i];
                          FOR k := i TO n + 1 DO
                             Aug[j,k] := Aug[j,k] + Mult * Aug[i,k]
                       END {FOR j}
                 END{IF};
              i := i + 1
           END {WHILE};
     END {Reduce};


PROCEDURE Solve( VAR Aug : AugmentedMatrix;   {reduced augmented matrix}
                 n : integer;                 {number of equations}
                 VAR X : SolutionVector);     {solution vector}
{-------------------------------------------------------------------

   Accepts:    Augmented matrix Aug and number n of equations.
   Purpose:    Find the solution of a linear system of n equations with
               a given reduced augmented matrix by back substitution.
   Returns:    The solution vector X.


----------------------------------------------------------------------}
```

Gaussian Elimination (cont.)

```
    VAR
       i, j : integer;   {indices}

    BEGIN
       X[n] := Aug[n, n + 1] / Aug[n,n];
       FOR  i := n - 1 DOWNTO 1 DO
          BEGIN
             X[i] := Aug[i, n + 1];
             FOR j := i + 1 TO n DO
                X[i] := X[i] - Aug[i,j] * X[j];
             X[i] := X[i] / Aug[i,i]
          END {FOR i}
    END {Solve};

PROCEDURE PrintSolution( VAR X : SolutionVector;   {the solution vector}
                             n : integer );         {number of unknowns}
{-------------------------------------------------------------------------

   Accepts:         Solution vector X and number n of unknowns.
   Purpose:         Display the n components of the solution vector.
   Output (screen): The solution vector X.

-------------------------------------------------------------------------}

   VAR i : integer;   {index}

   BEGIN
      writeln;
      writeln( 'The solution is: ' );
      FOR i := 1 TO n DO
         writeln( 'X[', i:1, '] = ', X[i]:5:3 );
   END {PrintSolution};

BEGIN {*************** main program ****************}
   ReadEquations( Aug, n );
   Reduce( Aug, n, Singular );
   IF NOT Singular THEN
      BEGIN
         Solve( Aug, n, X );
         PrintSolution(X, n)
      END{IF}
   ELSE
      writeln( 'Coefficient matrix is (nearly) singular')
END {main program}.
```

Sample run:

```
Enter the number of equations in the system: 3
Enter the coefficient matrix rowwise:
 5 -1 -2
-1  5 -2
-2 -2  7
```

Gaussian Elimination (cont.)

```
Enter the constant vector:
11
0
0

The solution is:
X[1] = 2.842
X[2] = 1.008
X[3] = 1.100
```

Sample run:

```
Enter the number of equations in the system: 4
Enter the coefficient matrix rowwise:
 4  4 -5  2
 3  3  5 -1
 2  1 -1  1
-1  1 -1  1
Enter the constant vector:
7
9
4
1

The solution is:
X[1] = 1.000
X[2] = 1.000
X[3] = 1.000
X[4] = 2.000
```

Sample run:

```
Enter the number of equations in the system: 3
Enter the coefficient matrix rowwise:
1 1 1
2 3 4
3 4 5
Enter the constant vector:
1
2
3
Coefficient matrix is (nearly) singular
```

Example 11.5A Graph Plotting

Section 11.5, PART OF THE PICTURE: Computer Graphics, described how a two-dimensional character array can be used to model a graphics window. The procedure **Plot** in the following program uses this approach to plot the graph of a function defined by a function **f**. It uses a **NumRows** × **NumColumns** character array **Window**, each element of which is a single character corresponding to a point in a graphics window. The user enters values for **xMin** and **xMax**, the minimum and maximum **x** values, and for **yMin** and **yMax**, the minimum and maximum **y** values. The rows of the two-dimensional array **Window** correspond to **x** values ranging from **xMin** to **xMax** in increments of **Deltax** = (xMax - xMin) / NumColumns, and the columns correspond to **Y** values ranging from **YMin** to **YMax** in steps of **Deltay** = (yMax - yMin) / NumRows. For each **x** value, the **y** value nearest the actual function value **y** = **f(x)** is determined, and the point **Window[x,y]** is set to some plotting character such as '*****' (''on''); all other elements of **Window** are blank (''off'').

 Graph plotting

```pascal
PROGRAM Plotter( input, output, GraphFile );
{***********************************************************************

    Input (keyboard): Minimum and maximum x values and minimum and
                      maximum y values.
    Purpose:          Plot the graph of a function y = f(x).
    Output (screen):  User prompts.
    Output (file):    Graph of f.


***********************************************************************}

CONST
    GraphFileName = 'EX11-5A.DAT';

VAR
    xMin, xMax,          {min. & max. x values}
    yMin, yMax : real;   {min. & max. y values}
    GraphFile : text;    {file containing graph of y = f(x)}

FUNCTION f( x : real ) : real;
{-----------------------------------------------------------------------

    Accepts:  Real number x.
    Purpose:  Define the function whose graph is to be plotted.
    Returns:  Value of f at x.

-----------------------------------------------------------------------}

    BEGIN
       f := x * cos(x)
    END{f};
```

Graph plotting (cont.)

```
PROCEDURE Plot(      xMin, xMax, yMin, yMax : real;
              VAR GraphFile : text );
{-----------------------------------------------------------------------

    Accepts:        Real numbers xMin, xMax, yMin, yMax; text file
                    GraphFile.
    Function:       Plot the graph of a function y = f(x) for x ranging
                    from xMin to xMax; y is allowed to range from yMin
                    to yMax.  Graph is drawn in the file GraphFile.
    Output (file): Graph of f.


------------------------------------------------------------------------}

    CONST
        NumRows = 20;     {number of rows and}
        NumColumns = 70; {columns in the plotting Window}
        Symbol = '*';     {character used to represent a point on the graph}

    TYPE
        PlottingWindow = PACKED ARRAY[0..NumRows, 0..NumColumns] OF char;

    VAR
        Window : PlottingWindow;   {the plotting window}
        Deltax,                    {x increment}
        Deltay,                    {y increment}
        x, y : real;               {a point on the graph}
        xLoc, yLoc,                {location of a point in the window}
        Count : integer;           {counts units on y axis for labeling}

BEGIN
    Deltax := (xMax - xMin) / NumColumns;
    Deltay := (yMax - yMin) / NumRows;

    {Clear the plotting window}
    FOR yLoc := 0 TO NumRows DO
       FOR xLoc := 0 TO NumColumns DO
          Window[yLoc, xLoc] := ' ';

    {Turn on points in WINDOW corresponding to points on graph}
    x := xMin;
    FOR xLoc := 0 TO NumColumns DO
       BEGIN
           y := f(x);
           IF (y >= yMin) AND (y <= yMax) THEN
              BEGIN
                  yLoc := round( (y - yMin) / Deltay );
                  Window[yLoc, xLoc] := Symbol
              END{IF};
           x := x + Deltax
       END{FOR};
```

Graph plotting (cont.)

```
        {Draw the WINDOW in the file together with labeled Y axis}
        y := yMax;
        Count := 5 * (NumRows DIV 5);
        FOR yLoc := NumRows DOWNTO 0 DO
            BEGIN
                IF Count MOD 5 = 0 THEN
                    write( GraphFile, y:8:2, ':' )
                ELSE
                    write( GraphFile,':' : 9 );
                FOR xLoc := 0 TO NumColumns DO
                    write( GraphFile, Window[yLoc, xLoc] );
                writeln( GraphFile );
                Count := Count - 1;
                y := y - Deltay
            END{FOR};

        {Draw a labeled X axis in the file}
        write(GraphFile,' ' : 9 );
        FOR xLoc := 0 TO NumColumns DO
            write( GraphFile,' ');
        writeln( GraphFile );
        write( GraphFile, '    ' );
        xLoc := 0;
        WHILE xLoc <= NumColumns DO
            BEGIN
                write( GraphFile, xMin + xLoc * DeltaX :10:3 );
                xLoc := xLoc + 10
            END{WHILE};
        writeln( GraphFile )

    END{Plot};

BEGIN {*************** main program ***************}
    write( 'Enter minimum and maximum x values: ' );
    readln( xMin, xMax );
    write( 'Enter minimum and maximum y values: ' );
    readln( yMin, yMax );
    assign( GraphFile, GraphFileName );
    rewrite( GraphFile );
    Plot( xMin, xMax, yMin, yMax, GraphFile )
END{main program}.
```

Example 11.5B Density Plots

Section 11.5, PART OF THE PICTURE: Computer Graphics, also described how a two-dimensional character array can be used to generate density plots. The procedure `GenerateDensityPlot` in the following program produces such a density plot. An example of the output produced is given in Section 11.5.

Density Plots

```
PROGRAM DensityPlot( input, output, DensityFile );
{**********************************************************************

    Input (keyboard): Minimum and maximum x values and minimum and
                      maximum y values.
    Purpose:          Produce a density plot of a function z = f(x,y).
    Output (screen):  User prompts.
    Output (file):    The density plot.

 **********************************************************************}

CONST
    GraphFileName = 'EX11-5B.DAT';

VAR
    xMin, xMax,            {min. & max. x values}
    yMin, yMax,            {min. & max. y values}
    zMin, zMax : real;     {min. & max. z values}
    DensityFile : text;    {file containing the density plot for z = f(x,y)}

FUNCTION f( x, y : real ) : real;
{-----------------------------------------------------------------------

    Accepts:  Real numbers x and y.
    Purpose:  Define the function for which density plot is generated.
    Returns:  Value of f at (x, y).

 -----------------------------------------------------------------------}

    BEGIN
        f := exp( -(x*x + y*y) )
    END{f};

PROCEDURE GenerateDensityPlot(     xMin, xMax, yMin, yMax,
                                   zMin, zMax : real;
                               VAR DensityFile : text );
{-----------------------------------------------------------------------

    Accepts:        Real numbers xMin, xMax, yMin, yMax, zMin, zMax;
                    text file DensityFile.
    Purpose:        Generate a density plot of a function z = f(x, y) for
                    x ranging from xMin to xMax and y ranging from yMin to
                    yMax; z is allowed to range from zMin to zMax.  Graph
                    is drawn in the file DensityFile.
    Output (file):  Density plot of f.

 -----------------------------------------------------------------------}

    CONST
        NumRows = 45;      {number of rows and}
        NumColumns = 75;   {columns in the plotting Window}
        MaxGray = 9;       {largest index in array Gray}
```

Density Plots (cont.)

```
TYPE
    PlottingWindow = PACKED ARRAY[0..NumRows, 0..NumColumns] OF char;
    GrayShades = ARRAY[0..MaxGray] of char;

VAR
    Window : PlottingWindow;     {the plotting window}
    Gray : GrayShades;           {symbols representing shades of gray}
    Deltax,                      {x increment}
    Deltay,                      {y increment}
    Deltaz,                      {z increment}
    x, y,                        {a point}
    z : real;                    {z = f(x,y)}
    xLoc, YLoc,                  {location of a point in the window}
    zShade : integer;            {shade of gray used to represent height z}

BEGIN
    {Initialize array of characters to indicate "densities of gray"
     that in turn represent heights of function f}
    Gray[0] := '0'; Gray[1] := '1'; Gray[2] := '2'; Gray[3] := '3';
    Gray[4] := '4'; Gray[5] := '5'; Gray[6] := '6'; Gray[7] := '7';
    Gray[8] := '8'; Gray[9] := '9';

    {Calculate increments}
    Deltax := (xMax - xMin) / NumColumns;
    Deltay := (yMax - yMin) / NumRows;
    Deltaz := (zMax - zMin) / MaxGray;

    {"Shade" each element of Window with appropriate gray}
    y := yMin;
    FOR yLoc := 0 TO NumRows DO
        BEGIN
            x := xMin;
            FOR xLoc := 0 TO NumColumns DO
                BEGIN
                    z := f(x, y);

                    {Find gray shade corresponding to z value}
                    IF z >= zMax THEN
                        zShade := MaxGray
                    ELSE
                        zShade := round( (z - zMin) / Deltaz );
                    Window[yLoc, xLoc] := Gray[zShade];
                    x := x + DeltaX
                END{FOR xLoc};
            y := y + Deltay
        END{FOR yLoc};

    {Draw the Window in the file}
    FOR yLoc := NumRows DOWNTO 0 DO
        BEGIN
            FOR xLoc := 0 TO NumColumns DO
                write( DensityFile, Window[yLoc, xLoc] );
            writeln( DensityFile )
        END{FOR yLOC}
END{GenerateDensityPlot};
```

Density Plots (cont.)

```
BEGIN{************** main program **************}
   writeln( 'Enter minimum and maximum x values, then y values:' );
   readln( xMin, xMax, yMin, yMax );
   writeln( 'Enter minimum and maximum values of the function:' );
   readln( zMin, zMax );
   assign( GraphFile, GraphFileName );
   rewrite( DensityFile, 'FIL11-14.DAT' );
   GenerateDensityPlot( xMin, xMax, yMin, yMax, zMin, zMax, DensityFile )
END{main program}.
```

Example 13.3 Converting Infix Expressions to RPN

Section 13.3, PART OF THE PICTURE: Programming Languages, described Reverse Polish Notation (RPN) and gave an algorithm for converting an infix expression to RPN that used a stack to store the various operators. The following program implements this algorithm. It uses the compiler directive **#include** to insert into the program the contents of the stack package described in Section 13.2.

 Converting infix to RPN

```
PROGRAM InfixToRPN (input, output);
{*******************************************************************

    Input (keyboard): An infix expression and user responses.
    Purpose:          Converts the infix expression to Reverse Polish
                      Notation.
    Output (screen):  The RPN expression.

*******************************************************************}

USES StackADT;   {with StackElementType = char};

CONST
   MaxExpression = 80;            {limit on expression length}

TYPE
   Expression = string[MaxExpression];

VAR
   Exp : Expression;              {infix expression}
   Response : char;               {user response}

PROCEDURE ConvertToRPN( Exp : Expression ); {infix expression}
{------------------------------------------------------------

    Accepts:          Infix expression Exp.
    Purpose:          Convert Exp to RPN.
    Output (screen):  RPN Expression and/or error messages.

------------------------------------------------------------}
```

Converting infix to RPN (cont.)

```pascal
VAR
   OpStack : StackType;    {stack of operators}
   i,                      {index}
   ExpLen : integer;       {length of expression}
   Token : char;           {a character in the expression}
   Error : boolean;        {signals error in expression}

FUNCTION Priority (Operator : char) : integer;
{-------------------------------------------------------------------

   Accepts: The character Operator.
   Purpose: Find the priority of Operator, an arithmetic operator
            or (.
   Returns: Returns priority (0 - 2) of Operator.


--------------------------------------------------------------------}

BEGIN
   CASE Operator OF
      '('      : Priority := 0;
      '+', '-' : Priority := 1;
      '*', '/' : Priority := 2
   END {CASE}
END {Priority};

PROCEDURE ProcessRightParen
                  ( VAR OpStack : StackType;   {stack of operators}
                    VAR Error : boolean );      {signals error}
{-------------------------------------------------------------------

   Accepts:          The stack OpStack.
   Purpose:          Pop and display operators from OpStack until
                     a left parenthesis is on top of the stack;
                     it too is popped, but not displayed.
   Returns:          Modified stack OpStack, and Error, which is
                     true if the stack becomes empty with no left
                     parenthesis being found.
   Output (screen): Arithmetic operators popped from OpStack.


--------------------------------------------------------------------}

VAR
    TopToken : char;       {token at top of stack}

BEGIN
   REPEAT
      Error := EmptyStack(OpStack);
      IF NOT Error THEN
         BEGIN
            Pop( OpStack, TopToken );
            IF TopToken <> '(' THEN
               write( TopToken:2 )
         END {IF}
   UNTIL (TopToken = '(') OR Error
END {ProcessRightParen};
```

Converting infix to RPN (cont.)

```
PROCEDURE ProcessOperator
        (     Operator : char;         {an operator symbol}
            VAR OpStack : StackType );  {stack of operators}


{-----------------------------------------------------------------

    Accepts:        A character denoting an arithmetic Operator,
                    and a stack OpStack of operators.
    Purpose:        Process an arithmetic operator.  Operators are
                    popped from OpStack until the stack becomes
                    empty or an operator appears on the top of the
                    stack whose priority is less than or equal to
                    that of the Operator.  Operator is then pushed
                    onto the stack.
    Returns:        Modified stack OpStack.
    Output (screen): Arithmetic operators popped from OpStack.

-----------------------------------------------------------------}

    VAR
        TopOperator : char;        {operator on top of stack}
        DonePopping : boolean;     {signals when stack-popping is
                                      completed}

    BEGIN
        DonePopping := false;
        REPEAT
            IF EmptyStack( OpStack ) THEN
                DonePopping := true
            ELSE
                BEGIN
                    Pop( OpStack, TopOperator );
                    IF (Priority(Operator) <= Priority(TopOperator)) THEN
                        write( TopOperator : 2 )
                    ELSE
                        BEGIN
                            Push( OpStack, TopOperator );
                            DonePopping := true
                        END {ELSE}
                END {ELSE}
        UNTIL DonePopping;
        Push( OpStack, Operator )
    END {ProcessOperator};
```

Converting infix to RPN (cont.)

```
    BEGIN {ConvertToRPN}

        {Initialize an empty stack}
        CreateStack( OpStack );
        Error := false;

        {Begin the conversion to RPN}
        ExpLen := length( Exp );
        i := 1;
        REPEAT
            IF Token <> ' ' THEN                            {skip blanks}
                IF Token = '(' THEN                         {left paren}
                    Push( OpStack, Token )
                ELSE IF Token = ')' THEN                    {right paren}
                    ProcessRightParen( OpStack, Error )
                ELSE IF (Token = '+') OR (Token = '-') OR
                        (Token = '*') OR (Token = '/') THEN {operator}
                    ProcessOperator( Token, OpStack )
                ELSE                                        {operand}
                    write( Token:2 );
                i := i + 1
        UNTIL (i > ExpLen) OR Error;

        {If no error detected, pop and display any operands on the stack}
        WHILE NOT EmptyStack( OpStack ) AND NOT Error DO
            BEGIN
                Pop( OpStack, Token );
                IF Token <> '(' THEN
                    write( Token:2 )
                ELSE
                    Error := true
            END {WHILE};
        IF Error THEN
            writeln( '<<< Error in infix expression >>>' )
        ELSE
            writeln
    END {ConvertToRPN};

BEGIN {*************** main program ***************}
    REPEAT
        write( 'Infix Expression?  ' );
        readln( Exp );
        write( 'RPN Expression is ' );
        ConvertToRPN( Exp );
        writeln;
        write( 'More(Y or N)?  ' );
        readln( Response )
    UNTIL (Response <> 'Y') AND (Response <> 'y')
END {main program}.
```

Converting infix to RPN (cont.)

Sample run:

```
Infix Expression?  A + B
RPN Expression is  A B +

More (Y or N)?   Y
Infix Expression?  A - B - C
RPN Expression is  A B - C -

More (Y or N)?   Y
Infix Expression?  A - (B - C)
RPN Expression is  A B C - -

More (Y or N)?   Y
Infix Expression?  ((A + 5)/B - 2)*C
RPN Expression is  A 5 + B / 2 - C *

More (Y or N)?   Y
Infix Expression?  (A + B))
RPN Expression is  A B + <<< Error in infix expression >>>

More (Y or N)?   Y
Infix Expression?  ((A + B)
RPN Expression is  A B + <<< Error in infix expression >>>

More (Y or N)?   N
```

Example 15.3A Mergesort

Section 15.3, PART OF THE PICTURE: Databases, gave algorithms for the split and merge operations used in the natural mergesort scheme. The following program uses natural mergesort to sort the file **UsersFile** of computer usage records as described in Chapter 15, using the key field **IdNumber** so that the records are arranged in such a way that the user id numbers are in ascending order. Procedures **SplitFile** and **Merge** implement the split and merge algorithms. Both use the procedures **CopyRecord** and **CopySubFile** to copy one item or a sorted subfile, respectively, from one file to another.

Mergesort

```pascal
PROGRAM SortWithMergesort( UsersFile, output );
{*****************************************************************

    Input (file):    The binary file UsersFile whose components are
                     records of type UserRecord.
    Purpose:         Sort UsersFile using the natural mergesort
                     algorithm.
    Output (file):   The sorted file UsersFile.
    Output (screen): Message indicating that sorting is complete.


*****************************************************************}
CONST
    UsersFileName = 'EX15-3A.DAT';
    NameF = 'TEMPFILF.DAT';
    NameF1 = 'TEMPFIL1.DAT';
    NameF2 = 'TEMPFIL2.DAT';

TYPE
    RecordType = RECORD
                     IdNumber : integer;
                     CompSystem : char;
                     ResourceLimit,
                     UsedToDate : integer
                 END;
    FileType = FILE OF RecordType;

VAR
    UsersFile,          {file of computer usage records}
    F : FileType;       {copy of UsersFile that is sorted}
    Rec : RecordType;   {a record from UsersFile}

PROCEDURE Mergesort( VAR F : FileType );
{----------------------------------------------------------------

    Input (file):  Records from F.
    Purpose:       Mergesort file F.
    Output (file): Records to F.


----------------------------------------------------------------}

    VAR
        F1, F2 : FileType;      {auxiliary files used in mergesort}
        NumSubfiles : integer;  {number of subfiles in F}
```

Mergesort (cont.)

```
PROCEDURE CopyRecord( VAR FileA, FileB : FileType;
                      VAR BufferA, BufferB : RecordType;
                      VAR EndSubfile, EndFileA : boolean );
{-------------------------------------------------------------

   Accepts:         File variables FileA and FileB with
                    file buffers BufferA and BufferB.
   Input (file):    A record from FileA.
   Purpose:         Copy one record from FileA to FileB and
                    check if the field IdNumber in the next record
                    in FileA is smaller than that in the record
                    just copied or the end of FileA has been
                    reached (both of which indicate the end of
                    a subfile in FileA).
   Output (file):   A record to FileB.
   Returns:         Boolean value EndSubFile, which is true if
                    the end of a subfile in FileA has been
                    reached and is false otherwise; EndFileA,
                    which is true if the end of FileA has been
                    reached; updated file buffers BufferA and
                    BufferB.

-----------------------------------------------------------------}

BEGIN
   BufferB := BufferA;
   write( FileB, BufferB );
   IF eof(FileA) THEN
      BEGIN
         EndFileA := true;
         EndSubfile := true
      END (* IF *)
   ELSE
      BEGIN
         EndFileA := false;
         read( FileA, BufferA );
         EndSubfile := (BufferA.IdNumber < BufferB.IdNumber)
      END (* ELSE *)
END {CopyRecord};

PROCEDURE CopySubFile( VAR FileA, FileB : FileType;
                       VAR BufferA, BufferB : RecordType;
                       VAR EndSubFile, EndFileA : boolean );
{-------------------------------------------------------------

   Input (file):  Records from FileA.
   Purpose:       Copy a sorted subfile from FileA to FileB.
   Output (file): Records to FileB.

-----------------------------------------------------------------}
```

Mergesort (cont.)

```
BEGIN
   REPEAT
      CopyRecord( FileA, FileB, BufferA, BufferB,
                     EndSubfile, EndFileA )
   UNTIL EndSubfile
END {CopySubFile};

PROCEDURE SplitFile( VAR F, F1, F2 : FileType );
{-----------------------------------------------------------------

     Input (file):   Records from F.
     Purpose:        Split file F into files F1 and F2 by
                     copying natural sorted subfiles of F
                     alternately to F1 and F2.
     Output (file):  Records to F1 and F2.


----------------------------------------------------------------}

VAR
   FileNum : 1..2;          {# of file being written to}
   EndSubfile,              {indicates end of subfile}
   EndFileF : boolean;      {indicates end of file F}
   BufferF, BufferF1,
   BufferF2 : RecordType;   {file buffers}

BEGIN

   {Open the files}

   reset( F );
   rewrite( F1 );
   rewrite( F2 );

   {Split the file}

   IF NOT eof(F) THEN
      BEGIN
         EndFileF := false;
         read( F, BufferF )
      END {IF}
   ELSE
      EndFileF := true;
   FileNum := 1;
```

Mergesort (cont.)

```
        WHILE NOT EndFileF DO
           BEGIN
              CASE FileNum OF
                     1 : CopySubFile( F, F1, BufferF, BufferF1,
                                       EndSubfile, EndFileF );
                     2 : CopySubFile( F, F2, BufferF, BufferF2,
                                       EndSubfile, EndFileF );
              END {CASE};

              {Switch to other file}

              FileNum := 3 - FileNum
           END {WHILE}
     END {SplitFile};

PROCEDURE Merge( VAR F, F1, F2 : FileType; VAR NumSubfiles : integer );

   {*************************************************************

      Input (file):  Records from F1 and F2.
      Purpose:       Merge corresponding sorted subfiles in F1
                     and F2 back into file F.  NumSubFiles is the
                     number of sorted subfiles produced in F.
      Output (file): Records to F.

      *************************************************************}

   VAR
      FileNum :    1..2;          {# of file being used}
      EndFile1, EndFile2,         {indicates end of F1, F2}
      EndSubfile1,                {indicates end of subfile in F1}
      EndSubfile2 : boolean;      {    "      "    "    "    " F2}
      BufferF, BufferF1,
      BufferF2 : RecordType;      {file buffers}

   BEGIN
      {Open the files}

      reset (F1 );
      reset( F2 );
      rewrite( F );

      {Now merge subfiles of F1 & F2 into F}

      IF NOT eof(F1) THEN
         BEGIN
            EndFile1 := false;
            read( F1, BufferF1 )
         END {IF}
      ELSE
         EndFile1 := true;
```

Mergesort (cont.)

```
      IF NOT eof(F2) THEN
         BEGIN
            EndFile2 := false;
            read( F2, BufferF2 )
         END {IF}
      ELSE
         EndFile2 := true;
      NumSubFiles := 0;
      WHILE NOT (EndFile1 OR EndFile2) DO
         BEGIN

            {set end-of-subfile indicators}

            EndSubFile1 := false;
            EndSubFile2 := false;

            {merge two subfiles}

            WHILE NOT (EndFile1 OR EndFile2 OR
                       EndSubFile1 OR EndSubFile2) DO
               IF BufferF1.IdNumber < BufferF2.IdNumber THEN
                  CopyRecord( F1, F, BufferF1, BufferF,
                              EndSubFile1, EndFile1 )
               ELSE
                  CopyRecord( F2, F, BufferF2, BufferF,
                              EndSubFile2, EndFile2 );

            {copy rest of other subfile}

            IF EndSubFile1 THEN
               CopySubFile( F2, F, BufferF2, BufferF,
                            EndSubFile2, EndFile2 )
            ELSE
               CopySubFile( F1, F, BufferF1, BufferF,
                            EndSubFile1, EndFile1 );
            NumSubFiles := NumSubFiles + 1
         END {WHILE};

      {Now copy any remaining subfiles in F1 or F2 to F}

      WHILE NOT EndFile1 DO
         BEGIN
            CopySubFile( F1, F, BufferF1, BufferF,
                         EndSubFile1, EndFile1 );
            NumSubFiles := NumSubFiles + 1
         END {WHILE};
      WHILE NOT EndFile2 DO
         BEGIN
            CopySubFile( F2, F, BufferF2, BufferF,
                         EndSubFile2, EndFile2 );
            NumSubFiles := NumSubFiles + 1
         END {WHILE};
   END {Merge};
```

Mergesort (cont.)

```pascal
BEGIN {Mergesort}
    assign (F1, NameF1);
    assign (F2, NameF2);
    NumSubfiles := 0;
    REPEAT
        SplitFile( F, F1, F2 );
        Merge( F, F1, F2, NumSubfiles )
    UNTIL NumSubfiles = 1
END {Mergesort};

BEGIN {*************** main program ***************}
    assign (UsersFile , UsersFileName);
    assign (F, NameF );
    { Copy records from UsersFile into file F}
    reset( UsersFile );
    rewrite( F );
    WHILE NOT eof( UsersFile ) DO
        BEGIN
            read( UsersFile, Rec );
            write( F, Rec )
        END {WHILE };
    close(F);

    {Now sort F}
    Mergesort( F );
    writeln( 'Sorting completed'  );
    close( UsersFile )
END {main program}.
```

Example 15.3B Updating Direct Access Files

Section 15.3 also described direct access files. The following program shows how
a direct access file of computer usage records can be updated in Turbo Pascal.

 Updating a direct access file

```pascal
PROGRAM UserFileUpdate( input, output, UsersFile );
{****************************************************************

    Input (file):      Records from UsersFile.
    Input (keyboard):  User id numbers and new resource limits.
    Purpose:           Update a direct access file UsersFile in which
                       the numbers of records in the file are inter-
                       preted as id numbers.  An id number is entered
                       by the user, the corresponding record is
                       retrieved and displayed, modifications are made,
                       and the updated record then rewritten to the
                       file.
    Output (file):     Updated records to UsersFile.
    Output (screen):   User prompts.

    ****************************************************************}
```

Updating a direct access file (cont.)

```pascal
CONST
   MaxNumRecords = 100;              {upper limit on record numbers}

TYPE
   UserRecord = RECORD
                    IdNumber : integer;
                    CompSystem : char;
                    ResourceLimit,
                    UsedToDate : integer
                END;
   FileOfUserRecords = FILE OF UserRecord;

VAR
   UsersFile : FileOfUserRecords;  {file to be updated}
   FileName : string[20];          {actual name of file}
   UserRec : UserRecord;           {a record from PartsFile}
   IdNum : integer;                {user id}

BEGIN
   {Open UsersFile}
   write( 'Name of file to be updated?  ' );
   readln( FileName );
   assign( UsersFile, FileName );
   reset( UsersFile );

   {Update the file}
   writeln ('Enter negative id number to stop.' );
   writeln;
   write( 'Id #?  ' );
   readln( IdNum );
   WHILE IdNum >= 0 DO
      BEGIN
         IF IdNum <= MaxNumRecords THEN
            BEGIN
               seek( UsersFile, IdNum );
               read( UsersFile, UserRec );
               WITH UserRec DO
                  BEGIN
                     writeln( 'User id ', IdNumber );
                     write( 'Enter new resource limit:  ' );
                     readln( ResourceLimit )
                  END {WITH};
               seek( UsersFile, IdNum );
               write( UsersFile, UserRec );
            END {IF}
         ELSE
            writeln( 'ID # > ', MaxNumRecords:1, ' -- out of range' );
         writeln;
         write( 'Id #?  ' );
         readln( IdNum )
      END {WHILE};
   writeln;
   writeln( 'File updating completed' );
   close( UsersFile )
END.
```

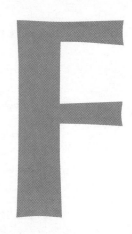

MISCELLANY

In the main part of this text we mentioned some special features of Pascal that were not described in detail. For completeness they are briefly described in this appendix.

Indirect Recursion

The examples of recursion given in the main part of the text have illustrated **direct recursion,** in which the fuctions and procedures reference themselves directly. **Indirect recursion** occurs when a subprogram references other subprograms, and some chain of subprogram references eventually results in a reference to the first subprogram again. For example, function **A** may reference function **B**, which references procedure **C**, which references **A** again. Since Pascal requires that a subprogram be defined before it is referenced, **B** would have to be defined before **A**, since **A** references **B**, and **C** must be defined before **B**, since **B** references **C**. However, since **C** references **A**, **A** would have to be defined before **C**. Thus it would seem that indirect recursion is not possible in Pascal programs.

To allow indirect recursion without violating Scope Rule 4 in Section 5.6, Pascal allows **dummy definitions** of functions and procedures in addition to actual definitions. A dummy definition consists only of the subprogram heading followed by the reserved word **FORWARD**, which is a directive to the compiler that the actual definition appears later in the subprogram section of the program. It thus has the form

```
FUNCTION name( formal-parameter-list ) : result-type; FORWARD;
```

or

```
    PROCEDURE name( formal-parameter-list ); FORWARD;
```

In the heading of the corresponding actual definition of the subprogram, the formal parameter list and the result type for a function are omitted so that it has the form

```
    FUNCTION name;
```

or

```
PROCEDURE name;
```

Now consider again the situation of function **A** referencing function **B** referencing procedure **C**, which references **A** again. The following arrangement of dummy and actual subprogram definitions makes this indirect recursion possible without violating Scope Rule 4:

```
FUNCTION A( formal-parameter-list ) : result-type; FORWARD;
   {Dummy definition of A}

PROCEDURE C( formal-parameter-list ); FORWARD;
   .
   .
   .

   {Actual definition of C}
   .
   .
   .

FUNCTION B( formal-parameter-list ) : result-type;
   .
   .
   .

   {Actual definition of B}
   .
   .
   .

FUNCTION A;
   .
   .
   .

   {Actual definition of A}
   .
   .
   .
```

A can reference **B** (in its actual definition), since **B** has already been defined. Similarly, **B** can reference **C**, since **C** has been defined earlier. And **C** can reference **A**, since **A** is defined before **C** (albeit in a dummy fashion).

Turbo Pascal also provides the directives **INLINE** and **EXTERNAL**, which are used to incorporate subprograms written in assembly language into a Pascal program. These directives are described in the Turbo Pascal reference manuals.

Statement Labels and the GOTO Statement

Pascal provides two statements for implementing repetition structures: the **WHILE** statement for constructing pretest loops in which the termination test is at the top of the loop, and the **REPEAT-UNTIL** statement for constructing posttest loops in which the termination test is made at the bottom of the loop. More general repetition structures can also be implemented in Pascal. In these structures there may be several termination tests and they may be placed anywhere within the body of the loop, or there may be no termination test at all in which case the loop is an **infinite loop.**

A **repeat-forever** loop is an example of an infinite loop. It can be constructed in Pascal as a while loop,

```
WHILE true DO
    body of the loop
```

or as a repeat loop:

```
REPEAT
    body of the loop
UNTIL false
```

When these statements are executed, the body of the loop is executed repeatedly. Since the termination test is never false in the first case and is never true in the second, these loops will never terminate. Such infinite loops may be useful in some special applications. For example, control programs in an operating system are meant to run forever. Similarly, a program might use a nonterminating loop to continually collect data from a device monitoring some process such as the operation of a nuclear reactor.

Most programs, however, are not intended to execute forever; consequently, most loops must contain some mechanism for terminating repetition. To illustrate, consider a program for which the input data may contain errors and provision must be made to detect these errors. When an error is found, control might be passed to some other part of the program for error handling and/or execution of the program terminated. These abnormal situations can be handled easily by using statement labels and the **GOTO** statement. For example, if all the data values processed by a program are to be no greater than 100, the following while loop might be used:

```
WHILE true DO
    BEGIN
        read( Data );
        IF Data > 100 THEN GOTO 50;
        { else process Data }
            .
            .
            .
    END {WHILE};
50: writeln( '*** Bad data value ***', Data );
        .
        .
        .
```

In this example, **50** is a **statement label.** Such labels must be declared in the label section in the declaration part of the program. This section has the form

```
LABEL
    label-1, label-2, . . . , label-n;
```

and must be the first section in the declaration part. Each *label-i* must be a positive integer or identifier and can be used to label only one statement. Control can then be transferred to that statement by using a **GOTO** statement of the form

```
GOTO label-i
```

In the preceding example, if a data value greater than 100 is read, control is transferred to the statement with label 50. A label section such as the following must therefore be used to define this statement label:

```
LABEL 50;
```

The statement label **50** followed by a colon (**:**) can then be attached as a prefix to any statement in the program unit in which this label section appears. In our example, it is attached to an output statement that displays an error message.

A statement of the form

```
IF boolean-expression THEN GOTO statement-label
```

can be placed anywhere within a loop to cause an exit from it.[1] For example,

```
WHILE true DO
   BEGIN
      statement-sequence-1;
      IF boolean-expression THEN GOTO ##;
      statement-sequence-2
   END {WHILE};
##: next-statement
```

If *statement-sequence-1* is omitted, this loop is a pretest loop; if *statement-sequence-2* is omitted, it is a posttest loop; if both *statement-sequence-1* and *statement-sequence-2* are present, it is a **test-in-the-middle loop.** The loop might also contain multiple exits

---

[1] A better alternative in Turbo Pascal 7.0 is to use the **Break** procedure described in Section H.1 of Appendix H.

```
WHILE true DO
   BEGIN
      statement-sequence-1;
      IF boolean-expression-1 THEN GOTO ##;
      statement-sequence-2;
      IF boolean-expression-2 THEN GOTO ##;
                         .
                         .
                         .
      statement-sequence-k;
      IF boolean-expression-k THEN GOTO ##;
      statement-sequence-k + 1
   END {WHILE};
##: next-statement
```

In most applications, however, while and repeat-until loops are preferred because the logical flow in such single-exit loops is easier to follow than it is in loops that allow multiple exits. Moreover, loops having the termination test at the top or at the bottom of the loop are easier to read and understand than are those that allow exits in the middle.

The familiar scope rules for identifiers in Pascal programs also apply to statement labels. Thus the **fundamental scope principle for labels** is

> The scope of a statement label is the program unit in which it is declared.

More specifically, the three basic **scope rules for labels** are

1. A statement label declared in a program unit is not accessible outside that unit.
2. A global statement label is accessible in any subprogram in which that label is not declared locally.
3. Statement labels declared in a subprogram can be accessed by any subprogram defined within it, provided that the label is not declared locally in the internal subprogram.

USING
TURBO
PASCAL

CONTENTS

G.1   The Turbo Pascal Integrated Environment

To enter the Turbo Pascal environment on most hard-disk systems it is necessary first to change the active directory to the subdirectory **TP**. For a floppy-disk system one must usually insert a disk containing the Turbo system in a disk drive and make directory **TP** on this disk the current directory. In either case, one usually then needs only to type the command **TURBO**.[1]

The first thing one sees upon entering the Turbo Pascal integrated environment is the main menu screen, similar to that shown in Figure G.1 for Version 7.0 of Turbo Pascal.[2] The *main menu bar* at the top of the screen shows the various operations available to the user; at its left end is a *close box,* which if clicked with a mouse closes the window. Below the main menu bar is the *title bar,* which contains the name (**NONAME00.PAS**) of the window, the number assigned to this window, and a *zoom box,* which if clicked with a mouse will zoom the window to fill the screen or will restore it to its original size. The *status line* at the bottom of the screen shows shortcuts for some of the commonly used commands. The area between these is the *desktop* or *editing window* in which programs are entered and modified. The *scroll bars* can be used with a mouse to scroll the contents of the

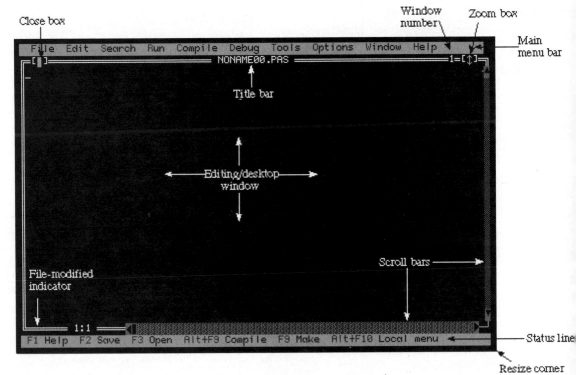

FIGURE G.1   The main menu screen in Turbo 7.0.

---

[1] A protected-mode integrated environment is also provided in Turbo Pascal 7.0. It is activated with the command **TPX**.

[2] Here we assume that Version 7.0 of Turbo Pascal is being used; see Section G.6 for a description of the main differences in Versions 6.0 and 5.5.

window up and down or from side to side, and the *size box* at the lower right corner can be dragged with a mouse to change the size of the window. The *file-modified indicator* at the lower left corner will be an asterisk (*) if the file has been modified since it was last opened or since it was last saved.

Using the Editor

When the integrated environment is entered, an Edit window is open. (To open other windows, use the **File|Open** [or **F3**] command.) A program or other file is then created simply by typing its contents, ending each line with the **Enter** key. If a typing error is made, the **Backspace** key can be used to backspace the cursor to the error, erasing characters along the way. The arrow keys can be used to move the cursor to the error without erasing characters. The cursor's current position is displayed at the bottom of the window. For example, if we have just begun entering a Pascal program by typing

```
PROGRAM Savings_
```

(where _ represents the cursor), the coordinates **1:16** will be displayed, indicating that the cursor is in line 1 and column 16.

If a color monitor is being used, different parts of the program will appear in different colors. The default *syntax coloring* is white for reserved words and yellow for all other parts of the program. These coloring conventions can be changed using the **Options|Environment|Color** command described in the next section.

The **Edit** menu (see section G.2) contains commands for various editing operations, such as cutting, copying, and pasting, and the **Search** menu (also described later) has commands for the familiar search and replace operations. One especially useful command added in Version 7.0 is the **Undo** (or **Alt+Backspace**) command, which undoes the last editing operation. It can be used repeatedly to undo several operations. In addition, several editor commands are provided for cursor movement, inserting and deleting text, locating text, and so on. These special commands are summarized in Section G.3.

Hot Keys

The status line at the bottom of the screen indicates the *hot keys* and shortcuts that are currently active; for example:

F1-Help	Opens a help window and displays information about the selected item (as indicated by the highlight bar). If no item is highlighted, information about edit commands is provided.
F2-Save	Saves the contents of the active window on disk, using the name in the title bar.
F3-Open	Activates a dialog box in which the user can select or type the name of a file to be opened.

To use any of these, simply click on it with the mouse or press the specified key or combination of keys. Note that the status line changes to show other tasks that can be performed while in this window.

Hot keys

Key(s)	Menu/Mouse (🖱️)Equivalents	Description
General		
F1	Help	Activates help utility.
F1 F1	Help|Help on Help	Displays information about how to use the help utility.
Shift+F1	Help|Index	Activates the help index.
Alt+F1	Help|Previous Topic	Recalls last help screen.
Ctrl+F1	Help|Topic Search	Gives language-specific help.
F2	File|Save	Saves current file.
F3	File|Open	Opens a file.
F6	Window|Next	Activates the next open window.
F10		Activates the main menu.
Menu Activators		
Alt+C	Compile	Pulls down the **Compile** menu.
Alt+D	Debug	Pulls down the **Debug** menu.
Alt+E	Edit	Pulls down the **Edit** menu.
Alt+F	File	Pulls down the **File** menu.
Alt+H	Help	Pulls down the **Help** menu.
Alt+O	Options	Pulls down the **Options** menu.
Alt+R	Run	Pulls down the **Run** menu.
Alt+S	Search	Pulls down the **Search** menu.
Alt+T	Tools	Pulls down the **Tools** menu.
Alt+W	Window	Pulls down the **Window** menu.
Alt+X	File|Exit	Quits Turbo Pascal and returns to DOS.
Alt+F10	🖱️Click right button	Pulls down a local menu.
Compiling/Running/Debugging		
F9	Compile|Make	Invokes the Make utility to compile and link program.
Alt+F9	Compile|Compile	Compiles the last file that was edited.
Ctrl+F9	Run|Run	Executes the current program.
Ctrl+F2	Run|Program Reset	Stops debugging; resets running program.
F4	Run|Go to cursor	Executes program to line where cursor is located
F7	Run|Trace Into	Traces into procedures and functions.

Some hot keys are combinations of the **Alt** key or **Ctrl** key with other keys. For example, pressing **Alt+F9** (the function key **F9** while holding down the **Alt** key) causes the current Pascal program to be compiled. The table above shows most of the hot keys available in the Turbo Pascal environment.

The Main Menu

When the Turbo Pascal integrated environment is entered (or whenever F10 is pressed), the main menu bar at the top of the screen is active:

File Edit Search Run Compile Debug Tools Options Window Help

One of the options in this menu can be selected in any of the following ways:

1. Click on it with the mouse.
2. Activate the main menu (**F10**) and either:
   a. Use the arrow keys (← and →) to move the highlight bar to the desired item and then press the **Enter** key.
   b. Press the first letter of the desired command.

Hot keys (cont.)

Key(s)	Menu/Mouse (🖱⤶)Equivalents	Description
F8	**Run|Step Over**	Steps over a procedure or function reference.
Ctrl+F4	**Debug|Evaluate/Modify**	Evaluates an expression in debugging session.
Ctrl+F7	**Debug|Add Watch**	Adds an expression to be watched.
Ctrl+F8	**Toggle Breakpoint** on Local Edit Menu	Sets or clears a breakpoint.
Windowing		
F5	**Window|Zoom** 🖱⤶ Click zoom box or double click on title bar	Zooms current window to fill up screen.
F6	**Window|Next**	Activates the next open window.
Shift+F6	**Window|Previous**	Makes previous open window active.
Alt+F3	**Window|Close** 🖱⤶ Click close box	Closes the active window.
Alt+F5	**Window|User Screen**	Switches to the User screen.
Alt+0	**Window|List**	Displays a list of all open windows.
Alt+*n*	🖱⤶ Click anywhere in the window.	Activates window whose number is *n*.
Ctrl+F5	**Window|Size/Move** 🖱⤶ Drag resize corner 🖱⤶ Drag title bar.	Changes size or position of the current window.
Editing		
F2	**File|Save**	Saves current file.
F3	**File|Open**	Opens a file.
Alt+BackSpace	**Edit|Undo**	Undoes the previous editing operation. Can be used repeatedly.
Shift+Del	**Edit|Cut**	Deletes selected text and saves it on the clipboard.
Shift+Ins	**Edit|Paste**	Pastes text from the clipboard into the current window.
Ctrl+Del	**Edit|Clear**	Clears selected text without saving it on the clipboard.
Ctrl+Ins	**Edit|Copy**	Copies selected text to the clipboard.
Ctrl+L	**Search|Search Again**	Repeats last **Find** or **Replace** command.

3. Press the **Alt** key with the first letter of the desired option.

Each of these options has a *pull-down menu* showing several suboptions, some of which have their own submenus or information windows. For example, selecting the **Files** option produces the following pull-down menu:

```
File
┌─────────────────────────┐
│ New                     │
│ Open...        F3       │
│ Save           F2       │
│ Save as...              │
│ Save all                │
├─────────────────────────┤
│ Change dir...           │
│ Print                   │
│ Printer setup...        │
│ DOS shell               │
│ Exit           Alt+X    │
└─────────────────────────┘
```

An item in a pull-down menu can be selected in any of the following ways:

1. Click on it with the mouse.
2. Use the arrow keys (↑ and ↓) to move the highlight bar to the desired item and then press the **Enter** key.
3. Press the first letter of the item.
4. Press the hot keys shown for that item.

To exit from a menu, simply press the **Esc** key.

G.2   The Main Menu Options

The **File** Menu (**Alt+F**)

```
File
┌─────────────────────┐
│ New                 │
│ Open...        F3   │
│ Save           F2   │
│ Save as...          │
│ Save all            │
├─────────────────────┤
│ Change dir...       │
│ Print               │
│ Printer setup...    │
│ DOS shell           │
│ Exit        Alt+X   │
└─────────────────────┘
```

Command (hot key)	Description of Command
New	Opens a new empty Edit window with the name **NONAME##.PAS**, where **##** is a number in the range from 00 through 99.

Open **(F3)**	Opens an Edit window containing a file previously saved on disk. When selected, this command opens a dialog box containing the following items:
	
	    An input box
	    A file list
	    Open, **Replace**, **Cancel**, and **Help** buttons
	    An information window
	
	The **Tab** key can be pressed to move the cursor from the input box to the file list; then to the **Open** button, the **Replace** button, the **Cancel** button, the **Help** button, and then back to the input box; or a mouse can be used to select any one of these items.
	    Specifying the file to be opened can be done in any of several ways:
	
	1. Type its name in the input window and press **Enter**. If a file with this name cannot be found, a new window having this name will be opened.
	2. Double-click on its name in the file list.
	3. Select its name in the file list (either with the mouse or using the arrow keys) and then press **Enter**.

Command (hot key)	Description of Command
	If a directory name appears in the file list, it can be opened using either method 2 or 3 and a file selected from it. Also, entering a file name containing the standard DOS wildcards ***** or **?** in the input box will filter the names in the file list so that only those having the specified form appear.
Save **(F2)**	Saves the file in the current Edit window to disk. If this file is a modification of the file originally loaded into the Edit window, the original file will be renamed with the extension **.BAK** before the current file is saved. If the current file has a name of the form **NONAME##.PAS**, the user will be prompted to rename it. If no extension is specified for the file name, the default extension **.PAS** is used.

Save as...	Saves the file in the current Edit window to disk under a different name. When selected, this command opens a dialog box containing the following items:
	
	    An input box
	    A file list
	    OK, **Cancel**, and **Help** buttons
	    An information window
	
	The **Tab** key can be pressed to move the cursor from the input box to the file list; then to the **OK** button, the **Cancel** button, the **Help** button, and then back to the input box; or a mouse can be used to select any one of these items.
	    The new name (which may be a path name) is typed in the input box and either the **Enter** key is pressed or the **OK** button is clicked or selected. The file is then saved on disk under this name (replacing any disk file that already has this name) and all windows containing this file are updated with the new name.

Save all	Like the **Save** command except that all modified files are saved.

Change Dir	Allows the user to change the current directory (which is the one in which all files are saved/retrieved). When selected, this command opens a dialog box containing the following items:
	
	    An input box
	    A directory tree
	    OK, **Chdir**, **Revert**, and **Help** buttons
	    An information window
	
	The **Tab** key can be pressed to move the cursor from the input box to the file list; then to the **OK** button, the **Chdir** button, the **Revert** button, the **Help** button, and then back to the input box; or a mouse can be used to select any one of these items.
	    There are two ways in which the directory can be changed:
	
	1. Type the path of the new directory in the input box and either press the **Enter** key or click or select the **OK** button.
	2. Use the mouse or arrow keys to select the desired directory in the directory tree and press the **Enter** key or click or select the **OK** button. If the directory name is double-clicked or if the **Chdir** button is selected, the directory tree changes; pressing **Enter** or using the **OK** button then effects the change; the **Revert** button is used to revert to the previous directory tree.

Print	Prints the contents of the current Edit window. Use **Ctrl-K P** to print selected text only.
Printer setup...	Used to choose a printer filter; for example, **PRNFLTR** for printing text so that syntax elements are highlighted.
Dos Shell	Allows the user to temporarily leave the Turbo Pascal integrated environment and execute DOS commands. Typing **EXIT** causes a return to the Turbo Pascal environment.
Exit **(Alt+X)**	Quits the Turbo Pascal environment and returns to DOS. The user is first prompted to save the current file if it hasn't already been saved.

The Edit Menu (Alt+E)

Edit

Undo	Alt+BkSp
Redo	
Cut	Shift+Del
Copy	Ctrl+Ins
Paste	Shift+Ins
Clear	Ctrl+Del
Show Clipboard	

Most of these editing commands require first selecting (highlighting) the piece of text to be edited. This can be done in several ways:

1. *With the mouse:*
   a. Drag the mouse pointer over the piece of text.
   b. Double-click anywhere in a line to select the entire line.
   c. Hold down the **Shift** key while clicking and dragging to extend or reduce a selection.
2. *From the keyboard:*
   a. Hold down the **Shift** key while pressing an arrow key.
   b. To select a word, move the cursor to the word and then press **Ctrl-K T**.
   c. To select an entire line, move the cursor to the line and then press **Ctrl-K L**.
   d. To select a block of text, press **Ctrl-K B** at the beginning of the block of text to be selected, move the cursor to the end of the block, and then press **Ctrl-K K**.

Once a piece of text has been selected, the edit commands become available.

Command (hot key)	Description of Command
Undo **(Alt+Bksp)**	Undoes the last editing operation.
Redo	Restores the last editing operation that was undone.
Cut **(Shift+Del)**	Removes the selected text and places it on the Clipboard.
Copy **(Ctrl+Ins)**	Copies the selected text to the Clipboard but does not remove it.
Paste **(Shift+Ins)**	Inserts text from the Clipboard into the current window at the current position of the cursor.
Clear **(Ctrl+Del)**	Removes the selected text but does not save in on the Clipboard.
Show Clipboard	Opens the Clipboard window, which can be edited like other Edit windows.

The Search Menu (Alt+S)

Search

```
Find
Replace...
Search Again

Go to line number...
Show last compiler error
Find error...
Find procedure...
```

Command (hot key)	Description of Command
Find... (Ctrl+Q F)	When selected, this command opens a dialog box containing the following items:

- An input box labeled **Text to find**
- Four check boxes labeled **Options**, **Direction**, **Scope**, and **Origin**.
- **OK**, **Cancel**, and **Help** buttons

The **Tab** key can be used to move the cursor from one box or button to the next in the order listed; or a mouse can be used to select any one of these items.

A string to be searched for can be specified in any of the following ways:

1. Type it in the input box.
2. Press ↑ to produce a list of strings searched for previously, and select a string from this history list.
3. Position the cursor on the word or select the words to be searched for before invoking the Search menu.

Pressing the **Enter** key or pressing the **OK** button begins a search of the file in the current Edit window to find the first occurrence of the specified string. If the string is not located, a **"Search string not found"** message is displayed.

The four check boxes that can be used to effect different kinds of searches are:

- **Options:**
  [ ] **Case sensitive**
  To distinguish between uppercase and lowercase.

  [ ] **Whole words only**
  To search for complete words only and not parts of words.

  [ ] **Regular expression**
  To recognize search strings with the following wildcards:

^	At the start of the string, ^ matches the start of a line.
$	At the end of the string, $ matches the end of a line.
.	Matches any character.
*	An expression of the form $x*$ matches any number of occurrences (including zero) of the character x.
+	An expression of the form $x+$ matches any number of occurrences (but not zero) of the character x.

Command (hot key)	Description of Command
	[] [*str*] matches any one character that appears in the string *str*.
	[^] [^*str*] matches any one character that does *not* appear in the string *str*.
	[-] [*x-y*] matches any character in the range *x* through *y*.
	\ *w*, where *w* is a wildcard character, is the character *w* treated literally, not as a wildcard.

■ **Direction:**

(●) Forward

   To search forward.

( ) Backward

   To search backward.

■ **Scope:**

(●) Global

   To search the entire file.

( ) Selected text

   To search only a selected part of text.

■ **Origin:**

( ) From Cursor

   To begin the search at the current position of the cursor.

(●) Entire Scope

   To start the search at the beginning or end of the file, depending on whether the selected direction is forward or backward.

Command (hot key)	Description of Command
Replace... (Ctrl-Q A)	When selected, this command opens a dialog box that is identical to that produced by the **Find** option except that there are two input windows labeled

   Text to find

and

   New text

There is one additional item in the **Options** check box:

   [X] Prompt on replace: To prompt for each change.

And there is one additional button labeled **Change all** that can be selected to find and replace all occurrences found.

Command (hot key)	Description of Command
Search Again	To repeat the last **Find** or **Replace** command.
Go to Line Number...	To move the cursor to a specified line number.
Find Error	To find the location of a run-time error.
Find Procedure	This command is available only during debugging. When selected, it searches for the definition of a specified procedure or function.

The Run Menu (Alt+R)

Run

```
┌──────────────────────────────┐
│ Run            Ctrl+F9        │
│ Step over           F8        │
│ Trace into          F7        │
│ Go to cursor        F4        │
│ Program reset  Ctrl+F2        │
│ Parameters                    │
└──────────────────────────────┘
```

Command (hot key)	Description of Command
Run (Ctrl+F9)	Executes the current program, recompiling it first if it has been modified since the last time it was compiled.
Step over (F8)	Like **Trace Into** except that when the statement contains a procedure or function call, the entire subprogram is executed.
Trace into (F7)	Executes the next statement of the current program. If this statement contains a procedure or function refererence, the first statement in the procedure or function is executed.
Go to cursor (F4)	Executes the current program from the current execution position (initially, the first line) to the line containing the cursor.
Program reset (Ctrl+F2)	Cancels the current debugging session and reinitializes the debugger. (For more information see the discussion of the integrated debugger.)
Parameters	Used to give command-line arguments to a running program.

The Compile Menu (Alt+C)

```
Compile

Compile        Alt+F9
Make              F9
Build

Destination   Memory
Primary file:
Clear primary file

Information...
```

Command (hot key)	Description of Command
Compile (Alt+F9)	Compiles the current program. During compilation, a status box displays various items of information about the compilation process, including an indication of whether compilation was successful. If it was, pressing any key removes the compilation window and returns to the Edit window. If an error is detected during compilation, an error message is displayed at the top of the Edit window and the cursor is positioned at the error.
Make (F9)	Compiles the current program (or the file designated as the primary file in the **Primary File** command) and all files upon which it depends and which have been modified since their last compilation.
Build	Like **Make**, but recompiles all files upon which the current (or primary) file depends, regardless of whether they are out of date.

Command (hot key)	Description of Command
`Destination Disk/Memory`	The first form specifies that the executable version of the current program is to be saved on disk (as an **.EXE** file). The second form specifies that no such **.EXE** file is to be created, and this executable version is thus lost when the Turbo Pascal environment is exited. The **Enter** key toggles between **Destination Disk** and **Destination Memory**.
`Primary File`	Used to specify the file to be compiled when the **Make** or **Build** options are used.
`Clear primary file`	Clear the previous file set as the primary file.
`Information...`	Displays information about the last program compiled, current memory usage, and the environment.

The Debug Menu (Alt+D)

```
Debug
┌─────────────────────────────────┐
│ Breakpoints                     │
│ Call stack          Ctrl+F3     │
│ Register                        │
│ Watch                           │
│ Output                          │
│ User screen         Alt+F5      │
├─────────────────────────────────┤
│ Evaluate/modify...  Ctrl+F4     │
│ Add watch           Ctrl+F7     │
│ Add breakpoint                  │
└─────────────────────────────────┘
```

The items in the **Debug** menu are used in connection with Turbo Pascal's integrated debugger, which is described in more detail in Section G.4.

The Tools Menu (Alt+T)

```
Tools
┌──────────────────────────────┐
│ Messages                     │
│ Go to next        Alt+F8     │
│ Go to previous    Alt+F7     │
├──────────────────────────────┤
│ Grep...           Shift+F2   │
└──────────────────────────────┘
```

The **Tools** menu makes it possible to run other programs and utilities such as GREP without leaving the integrated environment. The bottom of the **Tools** menu shows which programs and utilities can be used. Others can be added using the **Options|Tools** command.

Command (hot Key)	Description of Command
Messages	Opens a window where messages can be viewed.
Go to next (Alt+F8)	Move to the next message in the Message window.
Go to previous (Alt+F7)	Move to the previous message in the Message window.
Grep... (Shift+F2)	The GREP programming tool, which is automatically installed in the Tools window.

The Options Menu (Alt+O)

The items in the **Options** menu allow the user to specify various options for the components of the Turbo Pascal integrated environment. Of these, some of the **Compiler** options are of special interest to the beginning programmer. These options are described in Section G.3. Another option that may prove useful is:

Environment

Suboption **Preferences** can be used to change the number of lines displayed from 25 to 43/50 lines.
Suboption **Editor** has the following check boxes:

    [X] Create backup files
    [X] Insert mode (unchecked means overwrite mode)
    [X] Autoindent mode
    [ ] Use tab character (unchecked replaces tabs with spaces)
    [ ] Optimal fill
    [ ] Backspace unindents
    [ ] Cursor through tabs
    [X] Group Undo (checked allows undoes of same-type objects)
    [X] Persistent blocks
    [ ] Overwrite blocks
    [X] Syntax highlight (enables/disables syntax highlighting)
    [ ] Block insert cursor (block or underbar cursor)
    [X] Find text at cursor

a box labeled **Tab size** that can be used to set the number of spaces caused by a tab, and a box labeled **Highlight extensions** that allows you to specify which files are to be displayed with syntax highlighting.

Information about these and other items in the **Options** menu can be obtained by using the **Help** utility (select the item about which information is desired and press **F1**) or by consulting the *Turbo Pascal User's Guide*.

The Window Menu (Alt-W)

Window

```
Tile
Cascade
Close all
Refresh display

Size/Move    Ctrl+F5
Zoom
Next              F6
Previous    Shift+F6
Close         Alt+F3

List...       Alt+0
```

Command (hot key)	Description of Command
Tile	Tiles the open Edit windows so that all can be viewed.
Cascade	Stacks the open Edit windows with the active window in front.
Close all	Close all windows on the desktop.
Refresh display	Redraw the screen.
Size/Move (Ctrl+F5)	Use to change the size or position of the active window. After selecting this command, the arrow keys can be used to move the window and **Enter** when done. Hold down the **Shift** key while using the arrow keys to change the size of the window.
Zoom (F5)	Resizes the active window to its maximum size or restores it to its previous size.
Next (F6)	Makes the next window active.
Previous (Shift+F6)	Makes the previous window active.
Close (Alt+F3)	Closes the active window.
Watch	Opens the Watch window used during debugging to display expressions and changing values.

Command (hot key)	Description of Command
`Register`	Opens the Register window, which displays CPU registers.
`Output`	Opens the Output window, which displays the output produced by a program.
`Call stack` (Ctrl+F3)	Opens a window that displays the names or procedures and values of parameters in the sequence of procedure calls needed to reach the procedure currently being executed.
`User Screen` (Alt+F3)	Used for full-screen display of a program's output.
`List` (Alt+0)	Produces a list of all windows that have been opened.

The Help Menu (Alt+H)

```
Help

┌────────────────────────────┐
│ Contents                   │
│ Index          Shift+F1    │
│ Topic search   Ctrl+F1     │
│ Previous topic  Alt+F1     │
│ Using help                 │
│ Files...                   │
├────────────────────────────┤
│ Compiler directives        │
│ Reserved words             │
│ Standard units             │
│ Turbo Pascal Language      │
│ Error messages             │
├────────────────────────────┤
│ About...                   │
└────────────────────────────┘
```

Command (hot key)	Description of Command
`Contents`	Opens the Help window and displays the main table of contents. Press **F1** while the Help window is open to get help on Help.
`Index` (Shift+F1)	Displays a full list of help keywords.
`Topic search` (Ctrl+F1)	Displays help about an item selected in the Edit window.
`Previous topic` (Alt+F1)	Opens the Help window and displays the previous help text.
`Using help`	Explains how to use the help system.
`Files...`	Used to add or remove additional help files.

Command (hot key)	Description of Command
Compiler directives	Displays a list of compiler directives.
Reserved words	Displays a list of reserved words.
Standard units	Displays a list of the standard Turbo Pascal units.
Turbo Pascal Language	Displays a list of Turbo Pascal language elements.
Error messages	Displays a list of error messages.
About...	Displays version and copyright information.

G.3   Editing Commands

The **Edit** menu (described earlier) contains commands for various editing operations, such as cutting, copying, and pasting, and the **Search** menu (also described earlier) has commands for the familiar search and replace operations. For many of these commands there is an associated hot-key shortcut; in addition, several other commands are available for cursor movement, inserting and deleting text, locating text, and so on. The following tables summarize these useful hot keys.

Edit mode toggles

Command	Keystroke
Autoindent mode on/off	**Ctrl+O I**
Unindent mode on/off	**Ctrl+O U**
Cursor through tabs	**Ctrl+O C**
Insert mode on/off	**Ins**
Fill mode on/off	**Ctrl+O F**
Tab mode on/off	**Ctrl+O T**

Cursor movement

To move the cursor	Keystroke
To any position	▬➥ Click the mouse at that position
One character left	← or **Ctrl+S**
One character right	→ or **Ctrl+D**
One line up	↑ or **Ctrl+E**
One line down	↓ or **Ctrl+X**
One word left	**Ctrl+←** or **Ctrl+A**
One word right	**Ctrl+→** or **Ctrl+F**
One screen up (scroll up)	**Ctrl+W**
One screen down (scroll down)	**Ctrl+Z**
One page up	**PgUp** or **Ctrl+R**
One page down	**PgDn** or **Ctrl+C**
To beginning of line	**Home** or **Ctrl+Q S**
To end of line	**End** or **Ctrl+Q D**
To top of window	**Ctrl+Home** or **Ctrl+Q E**
To bottom of window	**Ctrl+End** or **Ctrl+Q X**
Beginning of file	**Ctrl+PgUp** or **Ctrl+Q R**
End of file	**Ctrl+PgDn** or **Ctrl+Q C**
Beginning of block	**Ctrl+Q B**
End of block	**Ctrl+Q K**
Last cursor position	**Ctrl+Q P**
Position of last error	**Ctrl+Q W**

Insert/delete commands

Command	Keystroke
Insert a new line	**Ctrl+N**
Insert default compiler directives	**Ctrl+O O**
Delete to end of line	**Ctrl+Q Y**
Delete entire line	**Ctrl+Y**
Restore line	**Ctrl+Q L**
Delete character to left of cursor	**Backspace** or **Ctrl+H** or **Shift+Tab**
Delete character under cursor	**Del** or **Ctrl+G**
Delete word to right of cursor	**Ctrl+T**

Find/replace commands

Command	Keystroke
Find Equivalent to the **Search|Find** command.	**Ctrl+Q F**
Find and replace Equivalent to the **Search|Replace** command.	**Ctrl+Q A**
Repeat last **Search|Find** or **Search|Replace** command	**Ctrl+L**
Set a place marker $(0 \leq n \leq 9)$	**Ctrl+K** n
Find place marker n	**Ctrl+Q** n

Block commands

Command	Keystroke
Set beginning of block	**Ctrl+K B**
Set end of block	**Ctrl+K K**
Mark (highlight) a block	☞ Click and drag mouse over the block
	Hold down **Shift** key and use ←, →, ↑, or ↓.
Mark single word as a block	☞ Double-click mouse **Ctrl+K T**
Copy a marked block to the Clipboard	**Ctrl+Ins**
Cut a marked block to the Clipboard	**Shift+Del**
Paste a marked block from the Clipboard	**Shift+Ins**
Delete a marked block	**Ctrl+Del**
Indent a marked block	**Ctrl+K I**
Unindent a marked block	**Ctrl+K U**
Hide/display block marks	**Ctrl+K H**
Move a marked block to current position	**Ctrl+K M**
Print a selected block	**Ctrl+K P**
Write a marked block to disk	**Ctrl+K W**
Read a block from disk	**Ctrl+K R**

Miscellaneous commands

Command	Keystroke
Prefix for a control character	**Ctrl+P**
Activate main menu	**F10**
Obtain language help with current item (constant, variable, etc.)	**Ctrl+F1**
Open a file	**F3**
Pair matching Move cursor to a {, [, (*, ", ', <, >, *),], <, >, *),], or } that matches the current character	**Ctrl+Q [** for forward search **Ctrl+Q]** for backward search
Save current file	**F2** or **Ctrl+K S**
Tab	**Tab** or **Ctrl+I**

G.4   Compiler Options and Directives

Selecting the **Compiler** option on the **Options** menu displays a dialog box containing five check boxes labeled **Code generation**, **Runtime errors**, **Syntax** options, Numeric processing, and Debugging, an input box labeled Conditional defines, and OK, Cancel, and Help buttons.

The check boxes and the input box can be used to set various compiler options. These options can also be set by using a *compiler directive* within the source program. Most (but not all) of these directives have the form

$xy

where *x* is the first letter of the option name and *y* is its value (usually + or - corresponding to on [checking a box] or off [not checking a box], respectively). In a program, each directive or a list of directives, separated by commas (but no spaces), is enclosed within braces:

{$xy,uv, . . . ,wz}

The following list describes the various compiler options. The checked boxes denote the default values. The corresponding compiler directives are also given. The $Include directive is one compiler option that does not appear in any of the check boxes. Additional information about these and other directives can be found in the Turbo Pascal reference manuals.

Runtime errors
[ ] Range checking {$R+}, {$R-}
    Enables or disables range checking. When this option is on, code is generated to check if values of expressions of ordinal type are in range; if they are not, program execution is terminated.
[X] Stack checking {$S+}, {$S-}
    Enables or disables stack checking. When this option is on, code is generated to check that stack space is available for procedure and function calls; if it is not, program execution is terminated.
[X] I/O checking {$I+}, {$I-}
    Enables or disables i/o checking. When this option is on, code is generated to check for i/o errors with each i/o operation. Program execution is terminated if an i/o-error occurs.
[X] Overflow checking {$O+}, {$O-}
    Enables or disables generation of code for overflow checking of the integer operations +, -, *, Abs, sqr, succ, and pred. If an overflow occurs, program execution terminates.

Syntax options
[X] Strict var-strings {$V+}, {$V-}
    Used to switch between strict (+) and relaxed (-) checking of string variable parameters. In strict mode, the actual parameter and the corresponding variable formal parameter must have identical string types. In relaxed mode, any string type variable may be used as an actual parameter.
[ ] Complete boolean eval {$S+}, {$S-}
    Used to switch between short circuit (-) and complete (+) evaluation of boolean expressions. In short-circuit mode, evaluation stops as soon as the value of the expression can be determined. For example, in the bool-

ean expression **P AND Q**, if **P** is found to be false, **Q** is not evaluated. In complete mode, boolean expressions are evaluated in their entirety.

[ ] **Extended syntax {$X+}, {$X-}**

When this option is on, user-defined function calls may be statements, as if they were procedures.

—[ ] **Typed @ operator {$T+}, {$T-}**

Used to enable (+) or disable (–) type-checking or pointer values returned when the @ operator is applied to a variable.

[ ] **Open parameter {$P+}, {$P-}**

Used to enable (+) or disable (–) open string and array parameters.

Code generation

[ ] **Force far calls {$F+}, {$F-}**

Used to set compiler's call mode selection (near or far). If it is off (–), the appropriate mode is selected automatically; turning it on (+) forces far calls.

[X] **Word align data {$W+}, {$W-}**

Used to switch between word (+) and byte (–) alignment of variables and typed constants.

[ ] **Overlays allowed {$O+}, {$O-}**

Enables or disables overlay code generation.

[ ] **286 instructions {$G+}, {$G-}**

Enables or disables code generation for the 80286 instruction set.

Numeric processing

[ ] **8087/80287 {$N+}, {$N-}**

Used to switch between software (–) and 8087/80287 (+) modes for floating-point operations. In the 8087/80287 mode, code is generated to use the 8087 numeric coprocessor for all real-type operations; in particular, the **single**, **double**, **extended**, and **comp** data types may be used. In software mode all such calculations are done in software by calling special library subprograms; only the **real** data type may be used unless the **Emulation** option is on.

[X] **Emulation {$E+}, {$E-}**

Enables or disables a special set of library subprograms that emulate the 8087 numeric coprocessor, thus making it possible to use the **single**, **double**, **extended**, and **comp** data types even when the machine does not have the coprocessor.

Debugging

[X] **Debug information {$D+}, {$D-}**

Enables or disables the generation of special debugging information. This information is needed by the debugger and by the **Search|Find Error** command.

[X] **Local symbols {$L+}, {$L-}**

Enables or disables the generation of special local symbol information. This information is needed by the debugger when local variables are to be examined and/or modified.

`{$include filename}`

Instructs the compiler to insert the contents of *filename* at the point in the program where this directive appears. This directive may not appear in the statement part of the program or any subprogram. The default extension for *filename* is `.PAS`.

`Conditional defines` box `{$DEFINE name}` `{$UNDEF name}`

Used to define or undefine special symbols to be used in conditional compilation. Each symbol has the same syntax as a Turbo Pascal identifier, and two or more symbols must be separated by semicolons. These conditional symbols are used in conditional compilation constructs of the form

```
{$IFDEF name}
statement-sequence-1
{$ELSE}
statement-sequence-2
{$ENDIF}
```

where the `{$ELSE}` part is optional. When the compiler encounters such a construct, it generates code for *statement-sequence-1*, if *name* has been defined to be a conditional symbol. If *name* is undefined, *statement-sequence-1* is ignored; and if the `{$ELSE}` clause is included, code for *statement-sequence-2* is generated. For example, suppose `Debug` has been entered in the `Conditional defines` box, or equivalently, the program contains the compiler directive

```
{$DEFINE Debug}
```

If the compiler encounters the conditional compilation sequence

```
{$IFDEF Debug}
    writeln( 'Sum = ', Sum );
{$ENDIF}
```

code for the `writeln` statement will be generated and thus this statement will be executed when the program is run. The conditional directive

```
{$IFOPT xy}
```

may also be used in such constructs to compile code for the associated statement-sequence if the compiler (switch) option x has value y (+ or -).

G.5   The Integrated Debugger

The debugger in the Turbo Pascal integrated environment can be of great help in locating logical errors in a program. Using it, one can interact with the program while it is executing, watch the values of certain variables and expressions, and stop execution at specified points so that certain variables can be examined and perhaps assigned new values. Debugging commands are found on several of the menus and submenus. The following table summarizes these commands; additional information can be found in the Turbo Pascal reference manuals.

Debugging commands

Menu|Command	Hot key Equivalent	Description
Run|Run	Ctrl+F9	Run program to a break point.
Run|Step over	F8	Execute current line, but do not trace into procedures or functions.
Run|Trace into	F7	Execute current statement, and if it contains a procedure or function reference, trace into it and execute its statements one at a time.
Run|Go to cursor	F4	Execute program from current location (highlighted bar) to the line containing the cursor.
Run|Program reset	Ctrl+F2	End debugging session and return to the Edit window.
Debug|Breakpoints...		Opens a dialog box that shows all breakpoints, line numbers, and conditions and **Ok**, **Edit**, **Delete**, **View**, **Clear all**, and **Help** buttons.
Debug|Call stack	Ctrl+F3	Displays the current contents of the stack used to save local variables in procedure and function references.
Debug|Register		Activate the Register window, which displays the contents of the cpu registers.
Debug|Watch		Activate the Watch window, which displays expressions and their changing values.
Debug|Output		Activate the Output window, which displays the output produced by the program.
Debug|User screen	Alt+F5	Switch to the User screen.
Debug|Evaluate/Modify	Ctrl+F4	Opens a dialog box in which one may evaluate variables and expressions and/or modify variables.
Debug|Add watch	Ctrl+F7	Add a variable or expression to the Watch window.
Debug|Add breakpoint	Ctrl+F8	Opens a dialog box for adding breakpoints.
Local Edit Menu	Alt+F10	
Toggle breakpoint	Ctrl+F8	Set/clear a breakpoint at the current line.
Go to cursor	F4	Same as **Run|Go to cursor**.
Evaluate/Modify	Ctrl+F4	Same as **Debug|Evaluate/Modify**.
Add watch	Ctrl+F7	Same as **Debug|Add watch**.
Local Watch Menu	Alt+F10	
Add	Ins or Ctrl+N	Same as **Debug|Add watch**.
Modify	Enter	Edit the selected variable or expression.
Remove	Del or Ctrl+Y	Delete the selected variable or expression.
Clear all		Remove all variables and expressions from the Watch window.
Enable		Enable the selected variable or expression.
Disable		Disable the selected variable or expression.

Debugging commands

Menu|Command	Hot key Equivalent	Description
Search|Find procedure		Find and display the first line in a subprogram declaration
Options|Compiler [X]Debug Information		Makes debugging possible by generating debugging information. Default value is on.
[X]Local Symbols		Enables evaluation of local symbols. Default value is on.
Options|Debug [X]Integrated		Must be on to enable the debugger. Default value is on.
[]Standalone		Enables debugging with the Turbo Debugger that is outside the integrated environment. Default value is off.

Starting/Restarting/Stopping the Debugger

Before the debugger can be used, certain debugging information for the program must be generated by the compiler. To accomplish this, the **Debug Information** and **Local Symbols** compiler options must be set to on (their default values), or equivalently, the compiler directives {$D+,L+} must be included in the program (and/or units) to be debugged.

The simplest way to initiate the debugger is to press **F7**, or select the **Trace Into** option on the **Run** menu. The program will be compiled and a highlight bar called the *execution bar* will be positioned at the beginning of the statement part of the program.

The **Program Reset** command on the **Run** menu (hot key equivalent **Ctrl+F2**) can be used to terminate the debugger at any time and return to the Edit window. It can then be restarted by pressing **F7** or selecting the **Trace Into** option on the **Run** menu. The debugger can also be restarted if any part of the program is modified during debugging and a command is given to continue execution. The user will be asked to respond to the query **Source modified, rebuild? (Y/N)**. A response of 'Y' causes the program to be recompiled and the debugger reinitialized; 'N' continues the current debugging session.

Tracing Program Execution

The program can be executed one statement at a time by using the **Trace Into** and **Step Over** options on the **Run** menu, or more simply, by pressing their hot-key equivalents **F7** and **F8**.[2] The difference between these two debugging commands is that the first will trace into each subprogram that is called and execute it one statement at a time. The **Step Over** command treats a subprogram reference as a single statement and moves on to the next statement.

---

[2] Lines containing multiple statements will be executed in their entirety.

The `Go to Cursor` option (hot key `F4`) can be used to execute several statements. Simply position the cursor on the line where execution is to pause and press `F4` (or select `Run|Go to Cursor`) to execute the statements from the current location to that point.

Another alternative is to set *breakpoints* at those lines where execution is to stop. This is done by moving the cursor to the desired line, and select `Toggle Breakpoint` on the `Local Edit` Menu (`Alt+F10`) or press `Ctrl-F8`. This command sets a breakpoint at that line if none is there and removes a breakpoint if one has previously been set. The `Clear all` button in the dialog box displayed by the `Debug|Breakpoints...` command can be used to remove all breakpoints in the program.

Selecting `Run` on the `Run` menu (or pressing `Ctrl+F9`) executes statements from the current location to the next breakpoint. If this statement is within a loop, execution will stop each time the breakpoint is reached. Execution can be continued by using any of the `Run` (`Ctrl+F9`), `Go to Cursor` (`F4`), `Trace Into` (`F7`), or `Step Over` (`F8`) options on the `Run` menu.

Execution can be terminated at any time by pressing `Ctrl+Break`. This causes a return to the Edit window and the execution bar is positioned at the next statement of the program and the debugger prompts the user to press the `Esc` key to terminate the debugging session.

Watching Values

The values of variables and expressions can be monitored while a program's execution is being traced by placing them in the Watch window. As each line of the program is executed, the values of these *watches* are displayed in this window. Watches may be removed and new ones added whenever execution has been interrupted.

To watch the value of certain variables, simply move the cursor to each one and press `Ctrl+F7` or use the `Add Watch` command on the `Debug` menu, or the Local Edit Menu (press `Alt+F10` when the Edit window is active), or the `Add` command (`Ins`) on the Local Watch Menu (press `Alt+F10` when the Watch window is active). This copies the variable's name into the `Add Watch` box, and pressing `Enter` adds it to the Watch window, where it and its current value will be displayed. An expression can be added to the Watch window by copying the first operand of the expression to the `Add Watch` box as just described, using the right-arrow key ($\rightarrow$) to copy the rest of the expression and then pressing `Enter`. A variable or expression can also be added by simply typing it in the `Add Watch` box. The `Esc` key can be used to cancel the current `Add Watch` command without adding anything to the Watch window.

Enumerated type values are displayed as strings of uppercase characters; pointers are displayed as addresses in (*segment:offset*) format; arrays and records are displayed as lists of elements enclosed within parentheses, separated by commas; nested lists are used for multidimensional arrays and nested records; the elements of sets are displayed within brackets, separated by commas, with subrange notation used where possible; a file variable is displayed as (*status*, *filename*), where *status* is one of `CLOSED`, `OPEN`, `INPUT`, or `OUTPUT`, and *filename* is the name of the disk file associated with the file variable. Values that are too large to fit on a line can be examined by using the left- and right-arrow keys to move through the line.

The Watch window can be edited so that items can be added, removed, or modified. To do this, first select the Watch window by pressing **F6** and/or **Shift+F6** if necessary to switch from the Output window to the Watch window. The arrow keys ↓ and ↑ can be used to move through the variables and expressions in the window; the highlight bar shows which one can be edited in the following ways:

- **Add** (**Ins** or **Ctrl+N**): Opens the **Add Watch** box so that a new variable or expression can be added just above the highlighted item.
- **Modify** (**Enter**): Opens an **Edit Watch** box containing the selected item, which can be edited by retyping and by using the →, ←, **Home**, and **End** keys. After editing is completed, pressing **Enter** replaces the selected item; pressing **Esc** retains the original item.
- **Remove** (**Del** or **Ctrl+Y**): Deletes the selected item.
- **Clear All**: Removes all watches.
- **Enable, Disable**: Enables or disables a watched variable or expression.

Evaluation

If the value of a variable or expression needs to be checked only a few times, there is an alternative to adding it to the Watch window and then removing it. Also, one might wish to change its value for debugging purposes. The debugger provides the Evaluate window for this purpose.

Positioning the cursor on a variable name and then choosing the **Evaluate/modify** command on the **Debug** menu (or pressing **Ctrl+F4**) opens an **Evaluate and Modify** window that contains an **Expression** box that contains the variable name, a **Result** box, and a **New value** box. The **Tab** key can be used to move between these boxes. The **Expression** box can be edited in the same manner as the **Add Watch** box described earlier. Pressing the **Enter** key causes the value of the variable or expression in the **Expression** box to appear in the **Result** box. Typing a new name or expression in the **Expression** box replaces the old one, and pressing **Expression** causes it to be evaluated.

The **New value** box can be used to assign a new value to the variable whose name appears in the **Expression** box. A constant, a variable name, or an expression can be entered in the **New value** box. Structured variables such as arrays and records can not be modified in this manner, but an array element or a field of a record can.

Navigation Aids

The debugger provides two features to help with determining where one is in a complicated program that may have many subprograms and use several units. These are the **Debug|Call Stack** and **Search|Find Procedure** commands.

The **Debug|Call Stack** command (with equivalent hot key **Ctrl+F3**) produces a window that shows a stack of the most recent active subprogram calls. For example, if the main program named **Payroll** has just executed the procedure reference statement `CalcWages(Hours, 40)`, and if within this procedure, the function reference `Taxes(Brackets, Wages)`, where `Brackets` is an array, has just been executed, the Call Stack window would appear as

```
                     Call Stack
          TAXES((...), WAGES)
          CALCWAGES(HOURS, 40)
          PAYROLL
```

The up- and down-arrow keys can be used to move through the stack. Pressing the space bar or `Enter` when at a particular reference in the stack will show the place in that subprogram where the reference above it on the stack occurred. Execution tracing does not continue in this subprogam, however, but continues where it left off.

The **Find Procedure** command on the **Search** menu is used to locate a particular procedure or function. Selecting it opens a small window in which the user is asked to enter the name of the subprogram to be located. This subprogram is then placed in the Edit window, where it may be examined. As with the **Call Stack** option, this does not change the point in the program at which execution is being traced.

G.6   The Integrated Environment in Other Versions

Version 6.0

There are several features of the integrated environment of Version 7.0 that are not provided in Version 6.0:

- Syntax highlighting.
- **Undo** and **Redo** options on the **Edit** menu.
- **Tools** menu.
- Local menus.
- Messages window.
- ObjectBrowser, for browsing through objects and units, examining source code, obtaining cross references, and so on. See the *Turbo Pascal User's Guide* for a description of ObjectBrowser.
- Symbol information saved across sessions and across compilations (see the *Turbo Pascal User's Guide*).

Most of the hot keys described in the earlier sections for Version 7.0 may also be used in Version 6.0. The same is true for the main menu commands, except that some of the options are not provided in 6.0 (e.g., **Tools** options) and others are located in different menus and submenus. The following table summarizes these differences.

Command	Description/Equivalent Command in 7.0
≡ (System) Menu (**Alt+Spacebar**)	
About...	Same as **Help|About...**
Refresh Display	Same as **Window|Refresh Display**
Clear Desktop	Same as **Window|Close all**
File menu (**Alt+F**)	
Open...	Same as **File|Open**
New	Same as **File|New**
Save	Same as **File|Save**
Save as...	Same as **File|Save as**
Save all	Like **Save** except that all modified files are saved.
Change dir...	Same as **File|Change dir...**
Print	Same as **File|Print**
Get info...	Same as **Compile|Information...**
DOS Shell	Same as **File|DOS shell**
Exit (**Alt+X**)	Same as **File|Exit**
Edit menu (**Alt+E**)	
Restore line	Undoes last editing command performed on a line.
Cut (**Shift+Del**)	Same as **Edit|Cut**
Copy (**Ctrl+Ins**)	Same as **Edit|Copy**
Paste (**Shift+Ins**)	Same as **Edit|Paste**
Copy Example	Copies the preselected example text in the current Help window to the Clipboard
Show Clipboard	Same as **Edit|Show Clipboard**
Clear (**Ctrl+Del**)	Same as **Edit|Clear**
Search menu (**Alt+S**)	
Find...	Same as **Search|Find...**
Replace...	Same as **Search|Replace...**
Search Again	Same as **Search|Search Again**
Go to line number...	Same as **Search|Go to line number...**
Find procedure	Same as **Search|Find procedure**
Find Error	Find the location of a run-time error.
Run menu (**Alt+R**)	
Run (**Ctrl+F9**)	Same as **Run|Run**
Program reset (**Ctrl+F2**)	Same as **Run|Program reset**
Go to cursor (**F4**)	Same as **Run|Go to cursor**
Trace into (**F7**)	Same as **Run|Trace into**
Step over (**F8**)	Same as **Run|Step over**
Parameters	Same as **Run|Parameters**
Compile menu (**Alt+C**)	
Compile (**Alt+F9**)	Same as **Compile|Compile**
Make (**F9**)	Same as **Compile|Make**
Build	Same as **Compile|Build**
Destination	Same as **Compile|Destination**
Primary file:	Same as **Compile|Primary file:**
Debug menu (**Alt+D**)	
Evaluate/modify (**Ctrl+F4**)	Same as **Debug|Evaluate/modify**
Watches	Activates a watch menu containing commands like those on the Local Watch Menu.
Toggle breakpoint	Same as **Toggle breakpoint** on the Local Edit Menu.
Breakpoints	Same as **Debug|Breakpoints**

Command	Description/Equivalent Command in 7.0
`Options` menu (`Alt+O`)	
`Compiler...`	Essentially the same as `Options|Compiler...`
`Memory sizes...`	Same as `Options|Memory sizes...`
`Linker...`	Same as `Options|Linker...`
`Debugger...`	Same as `Options|Debugger...`
`Directories...`	Same as `Options|Directories...`
`Environment`	Same as `Options|Environment`
`Save options...`	Opens a dialog box used to save various settings.
`Retrieve options...`	Opens a dialog box used to retrieve settings.
`Window` menu (`Alt+W`)	
`Size/Move (Ctrl+F5)`	Same as `Window|Size/Move`
`Zoom (F5)`	Same as `Window|Zoom`
`Tile`	Same as `Window|Tile`
`Cascade`	Same as `Window|Cascade`
`Next (F6)`	Same as `Window|Next`
`Previous (Shift+F6)`	Same as `Window|Previous`
`Close (Alt+F3)`	Same as `Window|Close`
`Watch`	Same as `Debug|Watch`
`Register`	Same as `Debug|Register`
`Output`	Same as `Debug|Output`
`Call stack (Ctrl+F3)`	Same as `Debug|Call stack`
`User screen (Alt+F5)`	Same as `Debug|User screen`
`List...`	Same as `Window|List...`
`Help` menu (`Alt+H`)	
`Contents`	Same as `Help|Contents`
`Index (Shift+F1)`	Same as `Help|Index`
`Topic search (Ctrl+F1`	Same as `Help|Topic search`
`Previous topic (Alt+F1)`	Same as `Help|Previous topic`
`Help on Help`	Same as `Help|Using help`

The compiler options and directives described in Section G.4 for Version 7.0, except those for open string and array parameters (`{$P}`), type-checked pointers (`{$T}`), and overflow checking (`{$C}`), can also be used in Version 6.0. The integrated debugger is used in Version 6.0 in the same way as described in Section G.5, except that some debugger commands and options are located on different menus and submenus as described in the preceding table.

Version 5.5

One of the main differences between Versions 5.5 and later versions is that the integrated environment is a one-window environment (not multiwindow) and all commands must be selected from the keyboard (not using a mouse). The main menu screen is also a bit different from those in Versions 6.0 and 7.0. There are fewer options in the main menu bar:

```
File  Edit  Run  Compile  Options  Debug  Break/watch
```

The window is split into an Edit window and a small Watch window at the bottom of the screen. The first line of the Edit window displays the current position, the edit modes (**Insert**, **Indent**, **Unindent**) that are currently active, and the name of the file:

```
Line 1  Col 1    Insert  Indent     Undent    C:NONAME.PAS
```

Before characters can be typed in the **Edit** window, it must be activated by selecting the Edit option on the main menu.

Most of the hot keys described in the earlier sections for Version 7.0 can also be used in Version 5.5. The same is true for the main menu commands, except that some of the options are not provided in 5.5 (e.g., **Tools** and **Window** options) and others are located in different menus and submenus. The following table summarizes these differences.

Command	Description/Equivalent Command in 6.0
File menu (**Alt+F**)	
Load (**F3**)	Same as **File|Open**
Pick (**Alt+F3**)	Used to select a file from a list of the eight most recent files loaded into the Edit window.
New	Same as **File|New**
Save	Same as **File|Save**
Write to	Same as **File|Save as**
Directory	Used to display a list of all files in a specified directory
Change dir	Same as **File|Change dir**
OS Shell	Same as **File|DOS shell**
Exit (**Alt+X**)	Same as **File|Exit**
Run menu (**Alt+R**)	
Run (**Ctrl+F9**)	Same as **Run|Run**
Program reset (**Ctrl+F2**)	Same as **Run|Program reset**
Go to cursor (**F4**)	Same as **Run|Go to cursor**
Trace into (**F7**)	Same as **Run|Trace into**
Step over (**F8**)	Same as **Run|Step over**
User screen (**Alt+F5**)	Displays the program outout (User) screen; similar to **Debug|User screen**
Compile menu (**Alt+C**)	
Compile (**Alt+F9**)	Same as **Compile|Compile**
Make (**F9**)	Same as **Compile|Make**
Build	Same as **Compile|Make**
Destination	Same as **Compile|Destination**
Primary file:	Same as **Compile|Primary file:**
Get info	Same as **Compile|File|Get info**
Options menu (**Alt+O**)	
Compile (**Alt+F9**)	Essentially the same as **Options|Compiler...**

Other options:
     Linker, **Environment**,
     Directories, **Parameters**,
     Save options,
     Retrieve options
	See the Turbo Pascal 5.5 reference manuals.

Command	Description/Equivalent Command in 6.0
Debug menu (Alt+D)	
Evaluate (Ctrl+F4)	Same as Debug|Evaluate/modify
Call stack (Ctrl+F3)	Same as Debug|Call stack
Find procedure	Same as Search|Find procedure
Integrated debugging	Same as Options|Debug|Integrated
Stand-alone debugging	Same as Options|Debug|Standalone
Display swapping	Used to set display-swapping settings; same as Options|Debug|Display swapping
Refresh display	Same as Window|Refresh Display
Break/watch menu (Alt+B)	
Add watch (Ctrl+F7)	Same as Debug|Add watch
Delete watch	Same as Delete option on Local Watches Menu
Edit watch	Same as Edit option on Local Watches Menu
Remove all watches	Same as Clear all option on Local Watches Menu
Toggle breakpoint (Ctrl+F8)	Same as Toggle breakpoint on Local Edit Menu
Clear all breakpoints	Same as selecting Clear all button in Debug|Breakpoints dialog box
View next breakpoint	Same as selecting View button in Debug|Breakpoints dialog box

The compiler options and directives described in Section G.4 for Version 7.0 except those noted earlier for Version 6.0 can also be used in Version 5.5. The integrated debugger is used in Version 5.5 in the same way as that described in Section G.5, except that some debugger commands and options are located on different menus and submenus as described in the preceding table.

NEW FEATURES OF TURBO PASCAL 7.0

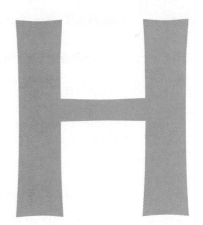

CONTENTS

H.1   Procedures `Break` and `Continue`

Version 7.0 of Turbo Pascal has added several new procedures to the **System** unit (which is imported automatically into every program). Two of these are the **Break** and **Continue** procedures that can be used to alter the manner in which a while, for, or repeat-until loop is executed.

The Break Procedure

The **Break** procedure has no parameters and is thus called with the statement

```
Break
```

This causes termination of the innermost while, for, or repeat-until loop containing this procedure call.

The effect of **Break** within a loop is the same as that described in Appendix F of using a **GOTO** statement to jump to a labeled statement following the end of a loop. This is, in fact, the preferred method of constructing **test-in-the-middle loops** such as

```
WHILE true DO
   BEGIN
      statement-sequence-1;
      IF boolean-expression THEN Break;
      statement-sequence-2
   END {WHILE};
```

As noted in Chapter 4, this provides a nice alternative to the type of **sentinel-controlled loop** described there that does not require two input statements (one ahead of the while loop and one at the bottom of the loop):

While **true** do the following
    a. Read a data value.
    b. If the data value is the data sentinel,
        Break;
    c. (*Else*)
        Process the data value.

For example, the sentinel-controlled loop in the program in Figure 4.8 could be modified as follows:

```
WHILE true DO
   BEGIN
      write( 'Fail Time (negative to stop):  ' );
      readln( FailTime );
      IF FailTime < 0 THEN Break;
      INC( NumTimes );
      Sum := Sum + FailTime
   END {WHILE};
```

Break can also be used to construct loops with multiple exits equivalent to those described in Appendix F. Simply replace each statement of the form

```
IF boolean-expression-i THEN GO TO ##;
```

used there with

```
IF boolean-expression-i THEN Break;
```

The Continue Procedure

The **Continue** procedure has no parameters and is thus called with the statement

```
Continue
```

This causes the innermost while, for, or repeat-until loop containing this procedure call to proceed immediately with the next iteration.

To illustrate, consider a for loop of the form

```
FOR control-var := first TO last DO
    BEGIN
        statement-sequence-1;
        IF boolean-expression THEN
            BEGIN
                statement-sequence-2
            END {IF}
    END {FOR};
```

where each time the **boolean-expression** is true, **statement-sequence-2** is executed; but each time **boolean-expression** is false, **statement-sequence-2** is bypassed and the next iteration of the loop begins. Such loops could be written more compactly using **Continue** as follows:

```
FOR control-var := first TO last DO
    BEGIN
        statement-sequence-1;
        IF NOT boolean-expression THEN Continue;
        statement-sequence-2
    END {FOR};
```

H.2   Constant Parameters

In standard Pascal and in earlier versions of Turbo Pascal, formal parameters may be either *value* or *variable* parameters. Version 7.0 of Turbo Pascal also allows **constant parameters.** Formal parameters are declared to be constant parameters by preceding their names by the reserved word **CONST** in the subprogram heading:

```
CONST param-list : type;
```

Like a value parameter, a constant parameter gets its value from the corresponding actual parameter when the procedure or function is called. However, unlike value parameters, the value of a constant parameter may not be changed during execution of that subprogram, nor may its value be "threatened" by passing it to another subprogram for which the corresponding formal parameter is a variable parameter. Constant parameters thus make it possible to protect a formal parameter from being changed. In some cases (especially for structured and string types) they also allow the compiler to generate more efficient code.

H.3   Functions Low and High

The functions **Low** and **High** are provided in the **System** unit of Turbo Pascal 7.0 (and are thus imported automatically into every program). These functions are called with references of the form

```
Low(X)      and      High(X)
```

where X is either a type identifier or a variable. The type denoted by X must be an ordinal type, an array type, or a string type. For an ordinal type, these functions return the lowest and highest values of that type. Thus, for example, `Low(integer) = -32768`, `High(integer) = maxint = 32767`, `Low(boolean) = false`, `High(boolean) = true`, `Low(char) = char(0)` and `High(chr) = chr(255)`. For an array type, they return the lowest and highest index for that array. For a string type X, `Low(X)` returns 0 and `High(X)` returns the declared length of strings of that type.

H.4   Open-Array Parameters

In Section 9.2 we illustrated the use of arrays as parameters using a function to calculate the mean of a list of numbers stored in an array. The heading and specification for this function were as follows:

```
FUNCTION Mean( VAR Item : ListType;      {a list of items}
               NumItems : integer )   {number of items}
               : real;
{--------------------------------------------------------------------

   Accepts: A list of NumItems numbers stored in an array item.
   Returns: The mean of the numbers

---------------------------------------------------------------------}
```

If the type identifier **ListType** is defined in the main program by

```
TYPE
   ListType = ARRAY[1..100] OF integer;
```

then this function can be used only for arrays whose component type is integer and whose index type is the subrange `1..100`. If there are other arrays with a different index type declared in the program, such as

```
VAR
    Score : ListType:
    InStock : ARRAY[100..999] OF integer;
    DigitCount : ARRAY[0..9] OF integer;
    CharCount : ARRAY['A'..'Z'] OF integer;
```

then **Mean** could not be used to calculate the mean of the numbers stored in the arrays **InStock**, **DigitCount**, and **CharCount**.

In Turbo Pascal 7.0, this function can be modified so that it can process each of these arrays by declaring the formal parameter **Item** to be an **open-array parameter.** An open-array declaration has the form

```
ARRAY OF element-type
```

where **element-type** is a type identifier that specifies the type of array elements. For example,

```
ARRAY OF integer
```

is an open-array declaration and can be used to specify the type of formal array parameter **Item** in the function **Mean**. The heading for this modified function thus is

```
FUNCTION Mean( VAR Item : ARRAY OF integer; {a list of integers}
               NumItems : integer )      {number of integers}
               : real;
```

Before open-array parameters can be used, the **Open parameters** compiler option must be enabled. This is done either by checking the **Open parameters** box on the **Compiler** submenu of the **Options** menu or by including the compiler directive {P+} in the program.

Open-array parameters may be value, variable, or constant parameters and can be used in the same manner as ordinary array parameters except that they must be processed elementwise. They may not be used in array assignment statements and may not be passed to other subprograms unless the corresponding formal parameter is an open-array parameter.

For an open-array parameter declared by

```
open-array-param : ARRAY OF element-type
```

the corresponding actual parameter must be a variable of type **element-type** or an array whose elements are of type **element-type**. (If the open-array parameter has elements of type **char**, the actual parameter may be a string constant.) In the case that the actual parameter is an array, any index type is allowed. Consequently, any of the arrays **Score**, **Instock**, **DigitCount**, and **CharCount** can be used as actual parameters corresponding to the formal parameter **Item** in the modified function **Mean**.

Within the function or procedure that has an open-array parameter, the index type is always a subrange of type integer with the first value 0, regardless of the index type of an actual array parameter. The effect is as though the index type was declared to be **0..# - 1**, where # is the number of elements in the actual array parameter; if the actual parameter is a variable, the open array is treated as an array with one element.

This means that the for loop in the modified function **Mean** must be rewritten so that the indices of the open array **Item** are varied from **0** to **NumItems - 1** rather than from **1** to **NumItems**:

```
FUNCTION Mean( VAR Item : ARRAY OF integer; {a list of integers}
               NumItems : integer )      {number of integers}
               : real;
{-------------------------------------------------------------------

   Accepts: A list of NumItems integers stored in an array item.
   Returns: The mean of the integers.

   ------------------------------------------------------------------}

VAR
   i : integer; {index}
   Sum : real;  {sum of the numbers}

BEGIN
   IF NumItems = 0 THEN
      BEGIN
         writeln( 'No elements -- returning mean of 0' );
         Mean := 0
      END {IF}
   ELSE
      BEGIN
         Sum := 0;
         FOR i := 0 TO NumItems - 1 DO
            Sum := Sum + Item[i];
         Mean := Sum / NumItems
      END {ELSE}
END {Mean};
```

As we described in the preceding section, the function **High** can be used to find the highest index of an array. In particular, if **A** is an open array, its highest index is **High(A)**, and its index type is therefore **0..High(A)**. This can be used to design rather generic subprograms that process all the elements of an array. To illustrate, consider a procedure that is to read and count a list of integers and store them in an array, and suppose we use an open-array parameter for this array. An appropriate heading for this procedure thus is as follows:

```
PROCEDURE ReadIntList(
              VAR IntArray : ARRAY OF integer; {list of integers}
              VAR Count : integer )            {number of integers}
{------------------------------------------------------------------

   Input:    A list of integers.
   Purpose:  Read and Count a list of integers, storing them in
             the (open) array IntArray.
   Returns:  The array IntArray and Count.

------------------------------------------------------------------}

   CONST
      Sentinel = -maxint;

   VAR
      NextNum,        {next number read}
      i : integer; {index}

BEGIN
   writeln( 'Enter the list of integers.  Note:  At most' );
   writeln( High( IntArray ) + 1 : 1, ' integers can be read.' );
   writeln( 'Enter ', Sentinel:1, ' to stop.' );
   Count := 0;
   WHILE true DO
      BEGIN
         read( NextNum );
         IF NextNum = Sentinel THEN
            Break;
         IF Count = High( IntArray ) THEN
            BEGIN
               writeln( '*** Array is full ***' );
               Break
            END {IF};
         IntArray[Count] := NextNum;
         INC( Count );
      END {WHILE};
   readln
END {ReadIntList};
```

This modified procedure can be used to read and store values in any array whose elements are integers. For example, if the actual parameter in a reference to **ReadIntList** is of type

```
TYPE
   ListOfInts = ARRAY[1..10] OF integer;
```

then the formal open array **IntArray** in procedure **ReadIntList** is a 10-element array whose indices range from 0 through 9. If the actual array parameter is of type

```
ARRAY[5..20] OF integer
```

then `IntArray` is a 16-element array whose indices range from 0 through 15. If the type of the actual parameter is

    ARRAY['A'..'Z'] OF integer

and the encoding scheme is ASCII, `IntArray` is a 26-element array whose indices range from 0 through 25.

H.5   Open-String Parameters

In addition to open-array parameters, Turbo Pascal 7.0 provides open-string parameters to facilitate string processing. An open-string parameter is a variable parameter whose type is specified using the

    Openstring

identifier, or if the **Open parameters** compiler option is enabled (by checking the **Open parameters** box on the **Compiler** submenu of the **Options** menu or by including the compiler directive {P+} in the program), the reserved word

    STRING

may be used. Open-string parameters behave like variable parameters of a string type, except that they may not be passed as regular variable parameters, only as open-string parameters, to other subprograms.

The actual parameter corresponding to an open-string parameter may be a variable of any string type. Within the subprogram, the length of the corresponding formal open-string parameter will be the same as that of the corresponding actual parameter. For example, consider the following procedure to convert a string to uppercase:

```
PROCEDURE UpcaseString( VAR S : OpenString );
{-----------------------------------------------------------------------

    Accepts:  String S.
    Returns:  Modified string S with all uppercase characters.

    -------------------------------------------------------------------}

VAR
    i : integer;      {index}

BEGIN
    FOR i := 1 TO SizeOf(S) DO
        S[i] := upcase(S[i]);
END {UpcaseString};
```

In a reference to **UpcaseString** with an actual parameter of type **string[30]**, within the procedure the maximum length of **S** will be 30, while for a reference with an actual parameter of type **STRING**, the maximum length of **S** will be 255.

An open-string parameter must be a variable parameter. If it is not but rather is a value or a constant parameter, then it is treated as though it was declared to be a string type with maximum length 255.

H.6   Procedures `Include` and `Exclude`

Version 7.0 of Turbo Pascal has added two new set-processing procedures to the `System` unit (imported automatically into every program): `Include` and `Exclude`. The `Include` procedure is called with a statement of the form

```
Include( S, x )
```

where *S* is a set variable and *x* is a set expression whose type is compatible with the base type of *S*. This statement adds *x* to *S* (unless it is already a member of *S*) and is thus equivalent to the statement

```
S := S + [x]
```

The `Exclude` procedure is called with a statement of the form

```
Exclude( S, x )
```

where *S* is a set variable and *x* is a set expression whose type is compatible with the base type of *S*. This statement removes the element *x* from *S* (unless it is not a member of *S*) and is thus equivalent to the statement

```
S := S - [x]
```

H.7   The Assigned Procedure

Another procedure provided in Turbo Pascal 7.0 (in the `System` unit) is the procedure `Assigned`. It is a boolean-valued function that is called with a reference of the form

```
Assigned( ptr )
```

where *ptr* is a pointer variable (or a procedural variable). This function reference returns true if the *ptr* is not nil and false otherwise. It thus corresponds to the boolean expression

```
ptr <> NIL
```

(`@P <> NIL` for a procedure variable).

ANSWERS TO SELECTED EXERCISES

Section 1.2 (p. 25)

1. (a) Combined the concepts of mechanized calculation and automatic control in the design of his "Analytical Engine."

(c) Credited with the development of the stored program concept.

(e) Inventor of a loom that was controlled by a "program" stored on punched cards.

(g) Developed the first fully electronic computer.

(i) A pioneer in the development of transistors and a cofounder of the Intel Corporation.

(k) Designed the programming languages Pascal and Modula-2.

2. (a) The most well-known of the first fully electronic computers.

(c) Early use of a "program" to control a mechanical device.

(e) An early electromechanical computer, built in the U. S. in 1944.

4. (a) The concept of storing a program in the memory of the computer rather than on some external media such as punched cards.

(c) A structured programming language used for teaching programming.

(e) That part of the central processing unit that performs basic arithmetic and logical operations.

(g) A digit, 0 or 1, in the binary number system.

(i) A basic storage unit consisting of a machine-dependent number of bits (commonly 16 or 32).

(k) A popular operating system developed by Microsoft Corporation for use on personal computers.

(m) A machine-language program produced by a compiler.

(o) A language used directly by the computer in all its calculations and processing.

5. (a) Allocate storage for programs and data, perform supervisory functions, and act as an interface between the user and the machine.
   (c) Translate assembly language programs into machine language.

6. (a) 9   (c) 64   (e) 1.5

7. (a) 83   (c) 4096   (e) 7.25

8. (a) 18   (c) 2748   (e) 8.75

9. (a) 1010011   (c) 1000000000000   (e) 111.01

10. (a) 10010   (c) 101010111100   (e) 1000.11

11. (a) 11   (c) 100   (e) 1.4

12. (a) 9   (c) 40   (e) 1.8

13. (a) (i) 11011_2 (ii) 33_8 (iii) $1B_{16}$
    (c) (i) 100111010_2 (ii) 472_8 (iii) $13A_{16}$

14. (a) (i) 0.1_2 (ii) 0.4_8 (iii) 0.8_{16}
    (c) (i) 0.101_2 (ii) 0.5_8 (iii) $0.A_{16}$

15. (a) (i) $0.0\overline{1001}_2$ (ii) $0.2\overline{3146}_8$ (iii) $0.4\overline{C}_{16}$
    (c) (i) $0.0000\overline{11}_2$ (ii) $0.03\overline{146}_8$ (iii) $0.0\overline{C}_{16}$

16. (a) 64   (c) −65   (e) −256

17. (a) 0000000011111111
    (c) 1111111100000001
    (e) 1100011010001001

19. (a) (i) 0110000000011111   (ii) Same as (i)
    (c) (i) 0100000000011100   (ii) Same as (i)
    (e) (i) 0110011001111101   (ii) Same as (i)

20. (a) (i)

0	1	0	1	0	1	0	0	0	1	0	0	1	1	1	1
T								O							

(ii)

1	1	1	0	0	0	1	1	1	1	0	1	0	1	1	0
T								O							

(d) (i)

0	1	0	0	0	1	0	1	0	1	0	1	0	1	0	0	0	1	0	0	0	1	0	0	0	0	1	0	1	1	1	0
E								T								C								•							

(ii)

1	1	0	0	0	1	0	1	1	1	1	0	0	0	1	1	1	1	0	0	0	0	1	1	0	1	0	0	1	0	1	1
E								T								C								•							

21. (a) 1. LOAD A   **(b)** 00010000 00001111
　　 2. ADD B　　　　 00100011 00010000
　　 3. MULT C　　　　 00100100 00010001
　　 4. STORE X　　　 00010001 00010111

Section 2.6 (p. 59)

1.

Statement	A	B	X	Y	Z
1	?	?	0	5	25
2	?	?	0	5	25
2-a	1	?	1	20	25
2-b	1	?	1	20	25
2	1	?	1	20	25
2-a	2	?	2	5	25
2-b	4	15	2	5	20
2	4	15	2	5	20
2-a	3	15	3	15	20
2-b	9	0	3	15	15
2	9	0	3	15	15
2-a	4	0	4	0	15
2-b	16	10	4	0	10
2	16	10	4	0	10
2-a	5	10	5	10	10
2-b	25	−5	5	10	5
3	25	−5	5	10	5

?=undefined

5. Input—A temperature on the Celsius temperature scale.
Ouput—The corresponding temperature on the Fahrenheit temperature scale.

We first must find the specific linear relationship between the two scales. In general, $C°$ Celsius corresponds to $F°$ Fahrenheit, where $F = aC + b$ for some constants a and b. Because $0°$ Celsius corresponds to $32°$ Fahrenheit, we must have

$$32 = a \cdot 0 + b$$

so that $b = 32$. This means, then, that

$$F = aC + 32$$

Because $100°$ Celsius corresponds to $212°$ Fahrenheit, we must have

$$212 = a \cdot 100 + 32$$

which gives $a = 9/5$, so that our equation becomes

$$F = \frac{9}{5}C + 32$$

The algorithm for solving the problem is now straightforward:

(∗ Input: A temperature (*Celsius*) in degrees Celsius
　 Purpose: Convert a temperature of *Celsius* degrees on the Celsius scale to the corresponding degrees (*Fahren*) on the Fahrenheit scale.
　 Ouput: *Fahren.* ∗)

1. Enter *Celsius.*
2. Calculate

$$Fahren = \frac{9}{5}Celsius + 32$$

3. Display *Fahren.*

9. Input—Pollution index: *Index*
Ouput—Air quality description: Pleasant, unpleasant, or hazardous

ALGORITHM

(∗ Input: A pollution *Index.*
　 Purpose: Determine the air quality based on the pollution *Index.* A negative value of *Index* is used to signal the end of data.
　 Ouput: An indicator of air quality—pleasant, unpleasant, or hazardous. ∗)

1. Enter first value of *Index.*
2. While *Index* ≥ 0 do the following:
   a. If *Index* < 35 then display "Pleasant"
      else if *Index* ≤ 60 display "Unpleasant"
      else display "Hazardous",
   b. Enter next value of *Index.*

17.
```
PROGRAM ConvertTemps( input, output );
{**************************************************

    Input:   Temperature in degrees Celsius.
    Purpose: Convert a temperature of Celsius degrees
             to the corresponding temperature Fahren
             on the Fahrenheit scale.
    Output:  The value of Fahren.


***************************************************}

VAR
    Celsius,        {temperature on Celsius scale}
    Fahren : real; {temperature on Fahrenheit scale}
```

```
BEGIN
    writeln( 'Enter temperature in degrees Celsius:' );
    readln( Celsius );
    Fahren := (9/5) * Celsius + 32.0;
    writeln( 'Fahrenheit temperature is :', Fahren:7:2 )
END.
```

Section 3.2 (p. 74)

2. (a) Integer.

   (c) Real

   (e) Neither

3. (a) Legal.

   (c) Not legal (missing first quote).

   (e) Legal.

4. (a) CONST
```
        Rate = 1.25;
```

   (c) CONST
```
        Year = 1776;
        Female = 'F';
        Blank = ' ';
```

5. (a) VAR
```
        Item, Number, Job : real;
```

   (c) VAR
```
        Mileage : real;
        Cost, Distance : integer;
```

6. (a) CONST
```
        FirstMonth : string = 'January';
```

Section 3.3 (p. 79)

1. (a) 1.

   (d) Not a valid expression. **9 / 2** is a real value, and **DIV** requires integer operands.

   (g) 2

   (j) 2

   (m) 0

   (p) 18.0

   (s) 3.25

   (v) 4.0

2. (a) 8.0   **(c)** 2.$\overline{6}$ **(e)** 5.1   **(g)** 6.25

3. (a) `10 + 5 * B - 4 * A * C`

(c) `sqrt( a + 3 * sqr(b) )`

(e) `abs( A / (m + n) )`

Section 3.4 (p. 86)

1. (a) Valid

(d) Valid

(g) Not valid; variable must be to the left of an assignment operator.

(j) Valid

(m) Not valid; string constant may not be assigned to a boolean variable.

2. (a) 15.0

(d) 6

(g) Not valid; an integer value may not be assigned to a character variable.

(j) Not valid; a real value may not be assigned to a character variable.

(m) Not valid; a character value may not be assigned to a real variable.

(p) 2

3. (a)   (i) `Number := Number + 77;`
           (ii) `Inc( Number, 77 )`

(d)   (i) `Number := Number + Number MOD 10;`
         (ii) `INC( Number, Number MOD 10 )`

4. (a) `Distance := Rate * Time;`

(d) `Area := (b * h) / 2;`

5. (a) For a = 2, b = 3, c = 4, a * (b DIV c) = 0, a * b DIV c = 1.

Section 3.5 (p. 101)

1. (d) ƀƀ436ƀƀ872   **(e)** ƀƀ-567.4ƀƀ436
         ƀƀƀ0.00040   Tolerance:ƀ0.00040

(*Note:* ƀ denotes a blank.)

2. (a) ƀƀNewƀbalanceƀ=ƀ2559.50
         ƀƀƀƀCƀƀƀƀ8.02

3. (a) `writeln( R1:9:4, C:4, N1:5 );`
         `writeln( N2:5, 'PDQ', R2:8:5 );`

4. (a) A ← 1, B ← 2, C ← 3, X ← 4.0, Y ← 5.5, Z ← 6.6

   (e) Same as (a).

Section 3.8 (p. 111)

1. (a) Valid   **(d)** Not valid

8.
```
PROGRAM Triangle( input, output );
{*********************************************************

      Input (keyboard): The lengths of two legs of a
                        right triangle.
      Purpose:          Compute the area of the triangle and
                        the length of the hypotenuse.
      Output (screen):  The area of the triangle and the
                        length of the hypotenuse.

      *****************************************************}

VAR
   a, b,         {the legs of the triangle}
   Hypotenuse,   {its hypotenuse}
   Area : real;  {and its area}

BEGIN
   writeln( 'Enter the lengths of the two legs of the ',
            'right triangle.' );
   readln( a, b );
   Area := a * b / 2;
   Hypotenuse := sqrt( sqr(a) + sqr(b) );
   writeln( 'Area = ', Area:5:2 );
   writeln( 'Hypotenuse = ', Hypotenuse:5:2 )
END.
```

Section 4.3 (p. 133)

1. (a)

a	b	a OR NOT b
true	true	true
true	false	true
false	true	false
false	false	true

   (d)

a	a AND true OR (1 + 2 = 4)
true	true
false	false

2. (a) x > 3

   (d) (Alpha > 0) and (Beta > 0)

   (g) (a < 6) OR (a > 10)

3. (a) a AND b AND NOT c

6. (a) (i) Sum1 := (A OR B) AND NOT (A AND B);
```
        Carry1 := A AND B;
```

   (ii) Sum := (Sum1 OR CIn) AND NOT (Sum1 AND CIn);
```
        Carry := Carry1 OR (Sum1 AND CIn);
```

Section 4.4 (p. 148)

1. (a) IF TaxCode = 'T' THEN
```
        Price := Price + TaxRate * Price;
```

   (c) IF (0 < A) and (A < 5) THEN
```
        B := 1 / sqr(A)
    ELSE
        B := sqr(A);
```

   (e) IF (Distance >= 0) AND (Distance <= 100) THEN
```
        Cost := 5.00
    ELSE IF Distance <= 500 THEN
        Cost := 8.00
    ELSE IF Distance <= 1000 THEN
        Cost := 10.00
    ELSE
        Cost := 12.00;
```

Section 4.6 (p. 163)

1. (a) 4
   5
   6

2. (a) WHILE x > 0 DO
```
        BEGIN
            writeln( 'x = ', x);
            x := x - 0.3
        END {WHILE};
```

   (c) Number := 1;
```
    WHILE Number <= 100 DO
        BEGIN
            writeln( sqr(Number) );
            Number := Number + 1
        END {WHILE};
```

   (e) Number := 1;
```
    WHILE Number < 50 DO
        BEGIN
            writeln( sqrt(Number) );
            Number := Number + 2
        END {WHILE};
```

Section 5.1 (p. 181)

2. Here is procedure `PrintZero`:

```
PROCEDURE PrintZero;
{------------------------------------------------------

   Purpose:            Create and display a stick number
                       for zero.
   Output (screen): The stick figure for 0 (zero).

------------------------------------------------------}

   BEGIN
      writeln( ' --- ' );
      writeln( '|     |' );
      writeln( '|     |' );
      writeln( '|     |' );
      writeln( ' --- ' )
   END {PrintZero};
```

4. (a)

```
PROCEDURE ProcessCircle;
{------------------------------------------------------

   Input (keyboard): Radius of a circle.
   Purpose:            Calculate and display the
                       circumference and area of a circle
                       with a given radius.
   Output (screen): User prompt, circumference and
                       area of circle.

------------------------------------------------------}

   CONST
      Pi = 3.14159;

   VAR
      Radius : real;          {radius of circle}

   BEGIN
      write( 'Enter the radius of the circle: ' );
      readln( Radius );
      writeln( 'Circumference = ', 2 * Pi * Radius :4:2 );
      writeln( 'Area = ', Pi * sqr(Radius) : 4:2 )
   END {ProcessCircle};
```

Section 5.4 (p. 214)

2. (a) Can be used.

(d) Cannot be used; character string `'16'` cannot be associated with real formal parameter `a`; real constant `pi` cannot be associated with integer formal parameter `m`; constant `13` cannot be associated with variable formal parameter `k`.

(g) Can be used; however, because the variable **u** is associated with a value parameter, its value will never be changed so that either the loop will not be entered (u ≤ 0) or an infinite loop will result (u > 0).

(j) Cannot be used; the expression **p** + **q** cannot be associated with the variable formal parameter **k**.

6.
```
PROCEDURE Switch( VAR First, Second : integer );
    {------------------------------------------------------------

        Accepts:  Integers First and Second.
        Purpose:  Interchange the values of First and Second.
        Returns:  Modified First and Second.


    ------------------------------------------------------------}

    VAR
        Temp : integer;       {holds one of the two values}

    BEGIN
        Temp := First;
        First := Second;
        Second := Temp
    END {Switch};
```

Section 5.5 (p. 225)

1. (a) Can be used.

(d) Cannot be used; illegal function reference (**f** is a function, not a procedure).

(g) Can be used.

(j) Cannot be used; invalid boolean expression since there is no value associated with a procedure.

(m) Can be used.

5.
```
FUNCTION IsADigit( Ch : char ) : boolean;
    {------------------------------------------------------------

        Accepts:  Character Ch.
        Purpose:  Determine if Ch is a digit.
        Returns:  True if Ch is a digit, false otherwise.


    ------------------------------------------------------------}

    BEGIN
        IsADigit := ('0' <= Ch) AND (Ch <= '9')
    END {IsADigit};
```

8. FUNCTION NumberOfBacteria(N, k, t : real) : real;
   {--

       Accepts: Real values N, k, and t.
       Purpose: Calculate the number of bacteria present
                  at time t for initial population N and
                  rate constant k.
       Returns: N * e∧(k * t).

   ---}

   BEGIN
       NumberOfBacteria := N * exp(-k * t)
   END {NumberOfBacteria};

Section 5.6 (p. 237)

1. **(a)** true   **(d)** true   **(g)** true   **(j)** false

2. ҍҍҍҍ6ҍҍҍ13
   ҍҍҍ41ҍҍҍ51

Section 6.1 (p. 294)

1. **(a)** Num1 ← 1, Num2 ← -2, Num3 ← 3, Num4 ← 4

   (d) Num1 ← 1, Num2 ← -2, Num3 ← 4, Num4 ← -5

2. **(a)** N1 ← 123   **(d)** C1 ← 'X'
       R1 ← 45.6   N1 ← 78
       C1 ← 'X'   R1 ← -909.8
       N2 ← 78   R2 ← 7.0
       R2 ← -909.8   N2 ← -65
       C2 ← '-'   C2 ← ' ' (blank)
       N3 ← 65   C3 ← '$'
       C3 ← ' ' (blank)   R3 ← 432.10
       C4 ← '$'
       R3 ← 432.10
       S1 ← 'CAT DOG'
       S2 ← 'HORSE'

   (g) 123 is read and assigned to N1; 45.6 is read and assigned to R1; the end-of-line mark is read and a blank assigned to C1; then an error occurs because the next character X is nonnumeric and thus cannot be read for N2.

3. **(a)** N1 ← 54 | 5 4 | 3 2 E 1 |←|↓| - 6 . 7 8 | $ 9 0 |←|↓|←|↓| 1 |←|↓|
       R1 ← 32E1
       R2 ← -6.78
       S1 ← ' $90'
       N2 ← 1

(d) N1 ← 54

     `| 5 4 | 3 2 E 1 ←↓ - 6 . 7 8 | $ 9 0 ←↓←↓ 1 ←↓`

     C1 ← ' ' (blank)

     C2 ← '3'

     C3 ← '2'

     C4 ← 'E'

     R1 ← 1.0

     R2 ← -6.78

     S1 ← ' $90'

     R3 ← 1.0

(g) R1 ← 54.0

     `| 5 4 | 3 2 E 1 ←↓ - 6 . 7 8 | $ 9 0 ←↓←↓ 1 ←↓`

     R2 ← 32E1

     C1 ← '-'

     C2 ← '6'

An error now occurs, since a real constant cannot begin with a period.

Section 6.3 (p. 315)

1. (a) I think that I shall never see
     A poem lovely as a tree.
                 -JOYCE KILMER (1914)

Section 7.1 (p. 332)

1. (a)
```
CASE TransCode OF
     'D' : Balance := Balance + Amount;
     'W' : Balance := Balance - Amount;
     'P' : writeln( Balance )
     ELSE
          writeln( 'VOID' )
END {CASE};
```

Section 7.4 (p. 360)

1. (a)
```
-2 squared = 4
-1 squared = 1
 0 squared = 0
 1 squared = 1
 2 squared = 4
 3 squared = 9
```

(d)
```
11 1
12 1
12 2
13 1
13 2
13 3
21 1
22 1
22 2
```

```
23 1
23 2
23 3
31 1
32 1
32 2
33 1
33 2
33 3
```

(g)   0   0   0   2   4   4   8   6 12

Section 7.6 (p. 397)

1. (a) (i) (blank line)
        123

  (b) (i) (blank line)
        876543

  (c) (i) 321

  (d) (i) 321
        123

3. (a) Q(14,2) produces as output:

  (blank line)
  13
  14
  15

  and Q(14,3) produces as output:

  (blank line)
  12
  13
  14
  14
  14
  15
  16

4. (a) Calculates 3 * n!.

  (d) Calculates the sum of the digits of **n**.

5. (a) `FUNCTION F( n : integer ) : integer;`

```
        VAR
            i, Prod : integer;
```

```
BEGIN
   Prod := 3;
   FOR i := n DOWNTO 1 DO
      Prod := Prod * i;
   F := Prod
END {F};
```

(d) FUNCTION F(n : integer) : integer;

```
VAR
   Sum : integer;

BEGIN
   Sum := 0;
   WHILE n > 0 DO
      BEGIN
         Sum := Sum + n MOD 10;
         n := n DIV 10
      END {WHILE};
   F := Sum
END {F};
```

Section 8.4 (p. 436)

1. (a) TYPE

```
MonthAbbrev = ( Jan, Feb, Mar, Apr, May, Jun,
                Jul, Aug, Sep, Oct, Nov, Dec );
MonthNumber = 1..12;
```

2. (b) FUNCTION NumberToNumeral(Num : Numeral) : Number;

```
BEGIN
   NumberToNumeral := ord(Num) - ord('0')
END {NumberToNumeral};
```

3. (a) true   **(d)** Mar   **(g)** Mar   **(j)** 8

Section 9.3 (p. 469)

1. (a) Number[1] ← 0   **(d)** Number[1] ← 1
Number[2] ← 1   Number[2] ← 2
Number[3] ← 1   Number[3] ← 4
Number[4] ← 2   Number[4] ← 8
Number[5] ← 2   Number[5] ← 16
Number[6] ← 3   Number[6] ← 32
Number[7] ← 3   Number[7] ← 64
Number[8] ← 4   Number[8] ← 128
Number[9] ← 4   Number[9] ← 256
Number[10] ← 5   Number[10] : no value assigned

(g) `Price[red]` ← 19.95
`Price[yellow]` ← 12.75
`Price[blue]` ← 19.95
`Price[green]` ← 14.50
`Price[white]` : no value assigned
`Price[black]` ← 14.50

2. (a) TYPE
```
    SmallIntArray = ARRAY[0..5] OF 0..5;
```

VAR
```
    Number : SmallIntArray;
    i : 0..5;
```

Statement:

```
  FOR i := 0 TO 5 DO
    Number[i] := i;
```

(d) TYPE
```
    BooleanArray = ARRAY[1..20] OF boolean;
```

VAR
```
    TFQuestion : BooleanArray;
    Num : 1..20;
```

Statement:

```
  FOR Num := 0 TO 20 DO
    TFQuestion[Num] := NOT odd(Num);
```

(g) TYPE
```
    LetterArray = ARRAY['a'..'z'] OF boolean;
```

VAR
```
    Vowel : LetterArray;
    ch : 'a'..'z';
```

Statement:

```
    FOR ch := 'b' TO 'z' DO
      Vowel[ch] := false;
  Vowel['a'] := true;
  Vowel['e'] := true;
  Vowel['i'] := true;
  Vowel['o'] := true;
  Vowel['u'] := true;
```

3. (b)

A[i] is stored in two consecutive words beginning at $b + 2(i - 1)$.

4.
```
FUNCTION Max( VAR Number : NumberArray;
                  NumElements : integer ) : integer;
{-------------------------------------------------------------

    Accepts:  An array Number of integers and NumElements.
    Purpose:  Find the largest integer among the first
              NumElements elements of the integer array
              Number.
    Returns:  The largest integer found.

-----------------------------------------------------------}

    VAR
       i,                    {index}
       Largest : integer;    {largest integer found so far}

    BEGIN
       IF NumElements = 0 THEN
          writeln( 'No array elements' )
       ELSE
          BEGIN
             Largest := Number[1];
             FOR i := 2 TO NumElements DO
                IF Number[i] > Largest THEN
                   Largest := Number[i];
             Max := Largest
          END {ELSE}
    END {Max};
```

Section 9.4 (p. 491)

1. (a)

i	1	2	3	4	5	6	7	8	
X[i]	10	50	80	30	60	20	70	40	← After pass
X[i]	10	20	80	30	60	50	70	40	← After pass
X[i]	10	20	30	80	60	50	70	40	← After pass
X[i]	10	20	30	40	60	50	70	80	← After pass

2. (a)

i	1	2	3	4	5	6	7	8	
X[i]	10	50	40	30	60	20	70	80	← After pass 1
X[i]	10	20	40	30	60	50	70	80	← After pass 2
X[i]	10	20	30	40	50	60	70	80	← After pass 3
X[i]	10	20	30	40	50	60	70	80	← After pass 4

5. (a)

(Sub)List Being Sorted	Low	High	Mid	Action
5, 1, 6, 4, 3, 2	1	6		Call **Quicksort** with original list.
3, 1, 2, 4, 5 , 6			5	Split positions 5 in location 5.
3, 1, 2, 4, 5 , 6	1	4		Call **Quicksort** with left sublist.
2, 1, 3 , 4, 5 , 6			3	**Split** positions 3 in location 3.
2, 1, 3 , 4, 5 , 6	1	2		Call **Quicksort** with left sublist.
1, 2 , 3 , 4, 5 , 6			1	**Split** positions 2 in location 2.
1, 2 , 3 , 4, 5 , 6	1	1		Call **Quicksort** with left (one-element) sublist. **Low ≮ High**, so sublist is already sorted. Return to previous reference to **Quicksort**.
1 , 2 , 3 , 4, 5 , 6	1	2		Left sublist is now sorted.
1 , 2 , _ 3 , 4, 5 , 6	3	2		Call **Quicksort** with right (empty) sublist. **Low ≮ High**, so sublist is already sorted. Return to previous reference to **Quicksort**.
1 , 2 , 3 , 4, 5 , 6	1	4		Right sublist has been sorted, so return to previous reference to **Quicksort**.
1, 2 , 3 , 4, 5 , 6	1	4	3	Left sublist is now sorted.
1, 2 , 3 , 4, 5 , 6	4	4		Call **Quicksort** with right (one-element) sublist. **Low ≮ High**, so sublist is already sorted. Return to previous reference to **Quicksort**.
1, 2 , 3 , 4 , 5 , 6	1	6		Right sublist has been sorted, so return to previous reference to **Quicksort**.
1, 2, 3, 4 , 5 , 6	1	6	5	Left sublist is now sorted.

(Sub)List Being Sorted	Low	High	Mid	Action
1, 2, 3, 4 , 5 , 6̲	6	6		Call **Quicksort** with right (one-element) sublist. **Low ≮ High**, so sublist is already sorted. Return to previous reference to **Quicksort**.
1, 2, 3, 4 , 5 , 6	1	6	5	Right sublist is sorted, so return to previous reference to **Quicksort**.
1, 2, 3, 4, 5, 6	1	6		Original reference to **Quicksort** is complete, so entire list has been sorted.

Section 9.5 (p. 500)

1. (a) $O(n^3)$ **(c)** $O(n)$

3. (a) $O(n)$ **(c)** $O(n^2)$ **(e)** $O(n^2)$

Section 10.4 (p. 538)

2. (a) SXEOLF   **(c)** HXWSOE   **(e)** 0554 1486 2112

Section 11.3 (p. 555)

1. (a) 5000   **(d)** 4   **(g)** 792

2. (a) $\begin{bmatrix} 2 & 3 & 4 \\ 3 & 4 & 5 \\ 4 & 5 & 6 \end{bmatrix}$

3. (a) ABCDEF   **(d)** AG
GHIJKL   BH
                CI
                DJ
                EK
                FL

5. (a)

Address   Memory   Array Element

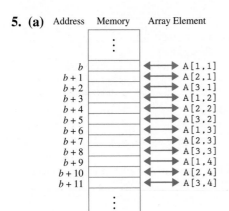

A[i, j] is stored in two consecutive words beginning at
$b + 3(j − 1) + (i − 1)$.

Section 12.6 (p. 639)

1. (a) Shirt.Color := red;

(d) readln(ShirtStock[5].NeckSize);

(g) Item.StockNumber := 11782;

(j) Item.Price['A'] := 19.95;

2. (a) readln(Order.Item.StockNumber);

(c) Order.Item.Price['G'] := 18.75;

3. (a) writeln('Stock number: ', Shipment[5].StockNumber:1);

(d) WITH Shipment[10], ShirtInfo DO
        readln(StockNumber, NeckSize, SleeveLength);

4. (a) TYPE
        CardSuit = (Hearts, Diamonds, Spades, Clubs);
        PlayingCard = RECORD
                        Suit : CardSuit;
                        Value : 1..13
                    END;

(d) TYPE
        Listing = RECORD
                    Name, Address : string[20];
                    PhoneNumber : string[7]
                END;

6. (a) TYPE
```
        Color = ( blue, brown, green, other );
        MaritalStatus = ( Married, Single );
        Date = RECORD
                    Month : 1..12;
                    Day : 1..31;
                    Year : 1900..2000
               END;
        PersonalInfo =
               RECORD
                    Name : string[20];
                    BirthDay : Date;
                    Age : integer;
                    Gender : char;
                    SocSecNumber : string[11];
                    Height, Weight : integer;
                    EyeColor : Color;
                    CASE MarStat : MaritalStatus OF
                       Married : (NumChildren : integer);
                       Single : ()
               END;
```

7. (a)   Address   Memory   Record Field

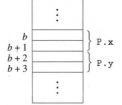

Here **P** is a record of type **Point**.

Section 13.2 (p. 661)

1. (a) S.Top = 2
```
    S.Element[5] = ?        (? = undefined)
    S.Element[4] = ?
    S.Element[3] = 37
    S.Element[2] = 59
    S.Element[1] = 10
```

(c) S.Top = 5
```
    S.Element[5] = 50       (? = undefined)
    S.Element[4] = 40
    S.Element[3] = 30
    S.Element[2] = 20
    S.Element[1] = 10
```

Output: *** Attempt to push onto a full stack ***

6. (a)
```
PROCEDURE GetTopElement
                  (      S : StackType;
                   VAR TopElement : StackElementType );
    BEGIN
      IF NOT EmptyStack( S ) THEN
          BEGIN
             Pop( S, TopElement );
             Push( S, TopElement )
          END {IF}
      ELSE
          writeln( 'Empty stack' )
    END {GetTopElement};
```

(b)
```
PROCEDURE GetTopElement
                  (      S : StackType;
                   VAR TopElement : StackElementType );
    BEGIN
      IF S.Top <> 0 THEN
          TopElement := S.Element[S.Top]
      ELSE
          writeln( 'Empty stack' )
    END {GetTopElement};
```

Section 13.3 (p. 667)

1. (a) -7.$\overline{3}$ **(d)** 12.0   **(g)** 12.0   **(j)** 8.0

2. (a) Before + is read: Before * is read:

```
| 3  |           
| 5  |        | 5 |
| 32 |        | 4 |
```

Value of RPN expression is 20

3. (a) A B * C + D -   **(d)** A B C D + /+

(g) A B - C - D - E -

4. (a) Before C is read: Before - is read:

Stack is
```
| / |
| + |
```
               Stack is `| + |`

Accumulated output: A B   Accumulated output: A B C /

Before D is read:

Stack is `| - |`

Accumulated output: A B C / +

Final RPN expression: A B C / + D-

5. (a) (A - (B + C)) * D   (d) ((A + B) - C) / (D * E)

    (g) A / ((B / C) / D)

6. (a) (i) -15   (iv) 15

    (b) (i) A B C ~ + *   (iii) A ~ B ~ *

7. (a) A B AND C OR   (e) A B = C D = OR

8. (a) - + * A B C D   (d) + A / B + C D

    (g) - - - - A B C D E

9. (a) -24.5   (d) -2.0

    (g) 55.0

10. (a) (A + B) * (C - D)   (d) A - (B - C) - D

    (g) (A * B + C) / (D - E)

Section 14.5 (p. 715)

1. (a) [3, 5, 11]   (d) [1, 2, 4, 12]   (g) [6..9]

    (j) [2, 4, 6, 8]   (m) [1..12]   (p) [ ]

    (s) [3, 5, 11]   (v) [ ]

2. (a) TYPE
       SmallIntegers = SET OF 1..99;

    (c) TYPE
           DaysOfWeek = (Sunday, Monday, Tuesday, Wednesday,
                          Thursday, Friday, Saturday);
           Days = SET OF DaysOfWeek;

3. (a) Declarations:

       TYPE
           SetOfNumbers = SET OF 1..99;

       VAR
           Even, Odd : SetOfNumbers;
           Number : integer;

    Statements:

       Even := [ ];
       FOR Number := 1 TO 49 DO
           Even := Even + [2 * Number];
       Odd := [1..99] - Even;

(c) Declarations:

```
TYPE
   SetOfNumbers = SET OF 1..99;

VAR
   Null : SetOfNumbers;
```

Statements:

```
Null := [ ];
```

(e) Declarations:

```
TYPE
   SetOfNumbers = SET OF 1..99;

VAR
   Divisors : SetOfNumbers;
   D, Number : integer;
```

Statements:

```
Divisors := [1, Number];
FOR D := 2 TO Number DIV 2 DO
   IF Number MOD D = 0 THEN
      Divisors := Divisors + [D];
```

(g) Declarations:

```
TYPE
   DaysOfWeek = ( Sunday, Monday, Tuesday, Wednesday,
                  Thursday, Friday, Saturday );
   SetOfDays = SET OF DaysOfWeek;

VAR
   WeekDays : SetOfDays;
```

Statements:

```
WeekDays := [Monday..Friday];
```

6. (a) (i) 0101010101
              | | | | | | | | | |
              0123456789 ← base type

(b) (i) 100010001000001000001000000
            | | | | | | | | | | | | | | | | | | | | | | | | | |
            ABCDEFGHIJKLMNOPQRSTUVWXYZ ← base type

18. (b)

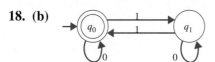

Section 15.2 (p. 739)

1. (a) Attempts to read beyond the end of the file when the data pointer is positioned at the last end-of-line mark.

2. (a) Fails for all text files whose first character is not a blank.

Section 15.3 (p. 751)

5. (a)
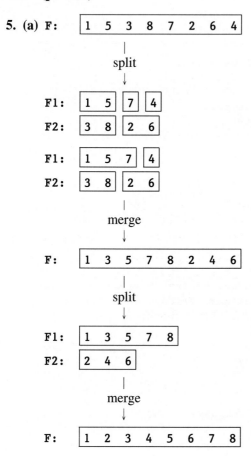

Section 16.3 (p. 778)

1. (a) Values of pointer variables cannot be displayed.

(d) The procedure **new** is used only to assign a value to a pointer variable.

2. For InventoryFile:

```
TYPE
    ListElementType = RECORD
                          Number : integer;
                          InStock : 0..999;
                          Price : real
                          InvLevel : 0..999;
                          Name : string[25]
                      END;
    ListPointer = ↑ListNode;
    ListNode = RECORD
                  Data : ListElementType;
                  Next : ListPointer
               END;
    LinkedListType = ListPointer;
```

3. (a) 123
456

(d) Error occurs—P3↑ is not a record with a field **Data**.

4. (a)

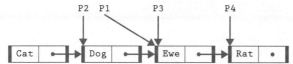

(d) Error occurs—**P4↑.Next↑.Data** is undefined because **P4↑.Next** is nil.

5. (a) FUNCTION Length(List : LinkedList) : integer;

```
    VAR
      Count : integer;
      Ptr : ListPointer;

    BEGIN
      Count := 0;
      Ptr := List;
      WHILE Ptr <> NIL DO
        BEGIN
          Ptr := Ptr↑.Next;
          Count := Count + 1
        END {WHILE};
      Length := Count
    END {Length};
```

(b) FUNCTION Length(List : LinkedList) : integer;

```
    BEGIN
      IF List = NIL THEN
        Length := 0
      ELSE
        Length := 1 + Length(List↑.Next)
    END {Length};
```

9. (a) 1. Retrieve the top stack element:

```
Item := Stack↑.Data;
```

2. Delete this node from the linked list:

```
TempPtr := Stack;
Stack := StackPtr↑.Next;
dispose( TempPtr );
```

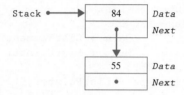

10. (a) 1. Retrieve the front queue element:

```
Item := FrontPtr↑.Data;
```

2. Delete this node from the linked list:

```
TempPtr := FrontPtr;
FrontPtr:= FrontPtr↑.Next;
dispose( TempPtr );
```

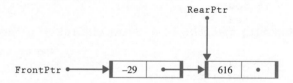

Section 16.7 (p. 819)

1. (a) (i)

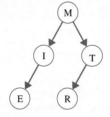

(b) (i) Inorder: EIMRT
Preorder: MIETR
PostOrder: EIRTM

2. (a) (i) M T R I E

(b) (i) T R M I E

(c) (i) R T E I M

3. (a)

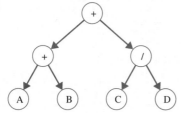

Prefix: **+ + A B / C D**
Postfix: **A B + C D / +**

6. (a)

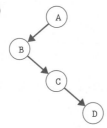

8. FUNCTION LeafCount(Root : BinaryTreeType) : integer;
```
{-------------------------------------------------------
    Accepts:  Binary tree with a pointer to Root.
    Purpose:  Count the leaves in the binary tree.
    Returns:  Number of leaves.
-------------------------------------------------------}

    BEGIN
        IF Root = NIL THEN
            LeafCount := 0
        ELSE IF (Root↑.LChild = NIL) AND
                (Root↑.RChild = NIL) THEN
            LeafCount := 1
        ELSE
            LeafCount := LeafCount(Root↑.LChild)
                        + LeafCount(Root↑.RChild)
```

19. (a) (i) B[1] ← 'M'
```
            B[2] ← 'I'
            B[3] ← 'T'
            B[4] ← 'E'
            B[5] ← ?
            B[6] ← 'R'
            B[7] ← ?
```
(All other array elements are undefined; also, ? = undefined.)

GLOSSARY

abstract data type (ADT)   See *data structure.*

ACM (Association for Computing Machinery)   A professional society for computer scientists.

actual parameter   A parameter that appears in a procedure/function reference and is associated with the corresponding formal parameter in the procedure/function heading.

address   A label associated with a memory location. Each word (or byte for byte-addressable machines) in memory has a unique address that makes it possible to access its contents.

address translation   A computation that must be performed to determine the address of the location in memory where a particular item in a structured data type is stored.

ADT   Abstract data type.

algorithm   A sequence of clearly stated simple steps for solving a problem in a finite amount of time.

ALU   See *arithmetic logic unit.*

anchor   A part of a recursive definition in which values of a function or actions of a procedure are specified for one or more values of the parameters.

anonymous variable   A variable that has no name. It is usually created by a call to **new** and is referenced through a pointer variable. (See also *dynamic variable.*)

arithmetic-logic unit (ALU)   That part of the central processing unit that performs basic arithmetic and logical operations.

array   A data structure consisting of a fixed number of data items, all of the same type, organized in a sequence, each of which can be accessed directly by specifying its location in this sequence.

ASCII   American Standard Code for Information Interchange. One of the standard coding schemes for characters.

assembler   System software that translates programs written in assembly language into machine language.

assembly language   A language that is closely related to machine language but that uses instruction mnemonics (names) in place of numeric opcodes and symbolic addresses (variables) in place of numeric addresses.

assignment operator   An operator denoted in Pascal by := that assigns a value to a variable or to a function identifier.

assignment statement   A Pascal statement that uses an assignment operator to assign a value to a variable or to a function identifier.

auxiliary memory   See *secondary memory.*

Backus-Naur Form   A notation used in specifying the syntax rules of a particular statement or construct in a language.

base address   The address of the first memory word in a block of consecutive words used to store the elements of an array or record.

base of a number system   In a positional number system, the digits in a numeral are coefficients of powers of the base of that number system. For example, in the decimal or base-10 number system, each digit in a numeral is a coefficient of a power of 10; thus $234 = 2 \times 10^2 + 3 \times 10^1 + 4 \times 10^0$.

base type   An ordinal type used in defining subrange and set types. For a subrange type it specifies the larger collection of values containing the subrange. For a set type it specifies the type of elements in the universal set.

batch processing   A mode of processing in which a file containing a program, data, and certain command lines is submitted to the system, and execution proceeds without any user interaction.

big Oh notation   See *order of magnitude.*

binary digit   A digit, 0 or 1, in the binary number system.

binary number system   A number system, using only the binary digits 0 and 1, that is commonly used for internal computer representation.

binary search   A scheme for searching an ordered list by repeatedly examining the middle item in the (sub)list to determine which half of the (sub)list contains the desired item, and then continuing the search with that sublist.

binary search tree   A binary tree in which the data item stored in each node is greater than the data item in its left child but less than the data item in its right child.

binary tree   A tree in which each node has at most two children.

bit   See *binary digit.*

BNF   See *Backus-Naur Form.*

boolean   A predefined Pascal data type in which the only possible values are **true** and **false**.

buffer   Portion of main memory used for temporary storage of data values being transferred between main memory and secondary memory. Buffers are used to reduce the effects of differences in operating speeds of various devices.

bug   A program error.

byte   A group of bits, usually eight.

CASE statement   A Pascal statement implementing a multialternative selection structure in which the selection is based on the value of a selector variable or expression. Cases specifying the alternative courses of action are labeled with lists of possible values of this selector.

central processing unit (CPU)   Controls the operation of the entire computer system, performs arithmetic/logic operations, stores and retrieves instructions and data.

char   A predefined Pascal data type in which the values are single characters.

character   Any symbol in the Pascal character set including letters, both upper case and lower case, digits, and various special symbols.

character constant   A constant of type `char`. In Pascal, this character must be enclosed within single quotes (apostrophes).

children of a node   Nodes in a tree pointed to by a given node called their *parent*.

class   A collection of related objects that share common attributes; sometimes used as a synonym for *abstract data type* in object-oriented languages.

coding   Writing a program or subprogram in a high-level language.

collating sequence   A sequence used in a particular computer to establish an ordering of the character set.

comments   Used to provide documentation within a Pascal program and enclosed between the comment delimiters { `and` } or (* `and` *).

compatible types   Two simple data types are said to be compatible if they are the same type, one is a subrange of the other, or both are subranges of the same type.

compile-time error   See *syntax error.*

compiler   System software used to translate source programs written in a high-level language into object programs in machine or assembly language.

component   An element of a data structure such as an array or file.

compound statement   A Pascal statement formed by combining several statements into a block by enclosing them between the reserved words **BEGIN** and **END** and separating them by semicolons.

concatenation   A string operation that appends one string to another.

constant   A quantity that does not change during program execution.

constant section   That section of the declaration part of a Pascal program in which named constants are defined.

control structure   Structures that control the logical flow in an algorithm or program. Structured algorithms and programs use only the control structures: *sequence, repetition,* and *selection.*

control unit   That part of the central processing unit that fetches instructions from memory, decodes them, and directs the system to execute the operations indicated by the instructions.

control variable   A variable used to control repetition in a for loop.

CPU   See *central processing unit.*

data structure   A collection of related data items together with basic operations defined on this collection. They may be *predefined* data structures such as arrays and records, or they may be *user-defined* structures such as linked lists and trees.

debug   To locate and correct errors (bugs) in a program.

declaration part   That part of a Pascal program in which variables are declared and constants, types, functions, procedures, and labels are defined.

deque   Double-ended queue.

dereferencing operator (↑)   Provides access to the memory location pointed to by a pointer variable.

design plan   A plan for developing a program or a system of programs that meets a problem's specification. Two important aspects of this design plan are the selection and design of data structures to store the data items and the development of algorithms to process them.

digraph   See *directed graph.*

direct access   (Also called *random access.*) Accessing a given component in a data structure by specifying its position in the structure without examining other components as in sequential access.

direct access file   A file in which each component can be accessed directly.

direct recursion   Recursion in which a function or procedure references itself directly.

directed graph   A structure consisting of a finite set of vertices (nodes) together with a finite set of directed arcs that connect pairs of vertices.

disk   See *magnetic disk.*

divide-and-conquer   An algorithm design strategy in which problems are repeatedly divided into simpler subproblems until a solution to each subproblem is straightforward.

documentation   Information that explains what a program does, how it works, what variables it uses, any special algorithms it implements, and so on.

dummy definition   A definition of a function or procedure that consists of only a heading together with the **FORWARD** directive that indicates that the actual definition of the subrogram appears later.

dynamic data structure   A data structure whose size changes during processing.

dynamic variables   Variables that are created and disposed of during program execution. Dynamic variables are accessed by means of a pointer rather than by a variable name; they are created by using the procedure **new** and are disposed of with the procedure **dispose**.

EBCDIC   Extended Binary Coded Decimal Interchange Code. One of the standard coding schemes for characters.

editor   System software used to create and modify files.

empty statement   A Pascal statement used to indicate that no action is required.

encapsulation   One of the fundamental concepts of OOP; the other two are *inheritance* and *polymorphism.* A collection of data values and the basic operations on them are encapsulated into classes in OOP languages.

end-of-data flag (or **sentinel**)   An artificial data value used to mark the end of a collection of input data.

end-of-file-mark   A special control character used to indicate the end of a file.

end-of-line-mark   A special control character used to indicate the end of a line of text.

enumerated type   A user-defined ordinal data type. The definition consists of listing the values of this data type, which must be identifiers, separated by commas, and enclosed within parentheses.

equivalent type identifiers   Type identifiers whose definitions can be traced back to a common type identifier.

external file   See *permanent file.*

external memory   See *secondary memory.*

external sorting   A sorting scheme appropriate for sorting large files stored in secondary memory.

field (of a record)   An element of a record.

field-designated variable   A variable used to access the value stored in a field within a record. It has the form `record-name.field name`.

fielded variable   See *field-designated variable.*

FIFO structure   See *queue.*

file   A collection of data items, usually stored in secondary memory, that are input to, or output by, a program.

fixed part (of a record)   Those fields in a variant record that occur in all variants.

flag See *sentinel.*

floating point number Synonym for *real number.*

floating point representation See *scientific representation.*

FOR statement A Pascal statement implementing a repetition structure in which the body of the loop is repeated once for each value of a control variable in some specified range of values.

formal parameter A parameter used in a subprogram heading to transfer information to or from the subprogram.

format descriptor An expression used in an output statement to specify the format in which values are to be displayed.

FORWARD directive See *dummy definition.*

function A subprogram that (ordinarily) returns a single value via the function name.

function heading A function definition begins with a function heading of the form: **FUNCTION** *function-name* **(** *formal-parameter-list* **) :** *result-type***;**

function parameter A parameter that is a function.

Fundamental Scope Principle *The scope of an entity is the program or subprogram in which it is declared.*

global entity Any item declared in the declaration part of the main program or listed in the program heading is said to be *global,* because it is accessible throughout the entire program, except within subprograms in which a local entity has the same name as the global entity.

GOTO statement A seldom-used Pascal statement that transfers control to a statement with a specified label.

hardware The actual physical components of a computer system such as disk drives, printers, central processing unit, memory, and so on.

heading See *function heading, procedure heading,* and *program heading.*

hexadecimal number system A base-16 number system.

hierarchical records See *nested.*

high-level language A language such as Pascal that is similar to natural language and that is intended to facilitate program development. Programs written in such languages must be converted into machine language using a compiler (or interpreter) before they can be executed.

identifier Names given to programs, constants, variables, functions, procedures, and other entities in a program.

IEEE (Institute of Electrical and Electronics Engineers) A professional society for computer engineers and other computer professionals.

IF statement A Pascal statement that implements a selection structure in which selection is controlled by a boolean expression.

IF-ELSE IF construct A compound form of an **IF** statement that implements a multialternative selection structure.

implementation of a data structure Selection of storage structures to store the data items and the design of algorithms to carry out the basic operations.

in parameter See *value parameter.*

in-out parameter See *variable parameter.*

index An expression that indicates the position in an array of a particular component.

indexed variable A variable of the form *array-name*[*index*] used to access a particular component of an array.

indirect recursion Recursion in which a subprogram references other subprograms and in which some chain of subprogram references eventually results in a reference to the first subprogram again.

inductive step Part of a recursive definition of a function (or procedure) that specifies the value of a function (or parameters) in terms of previously defined values.

infinite loop A loop that does not terminate.

infix notation Notation for arithmetic expressions in which the symbol for each binary operation is placed between its operands.

inheritance The concept in object-oriented programming of a subclass inheriting the attributes of the parent class.

inorder traversal Traversal of a binary tree in which the left subtree of a node is visited, then the node itself, and then the right subtree of that node.

input Data obtained by a program from an external source during execution.

input file A standard default input file in Pascal. It is a text file and usually refers to an external input device, the keyboard in Turbo Pascal.

integer A predefined Pascal data value in which the values are all of the integers in the range **-maxint** through **maxint** where the value of **maxint** is 32767 in Turbo Pascal.

interactive processing A mode of processing in which the user communicates with a program during execution.

interpreter System software that translates each statement in a source program into one or more machine language instructions. These instructions are executed before the next statement is translated.

internal memory See *memory unit*.

internal sorting A sorting scheme appropriate for lists stored in the main memory.

key field A field in a record on which sorting or searching is based.

label section That section of the declaration part of a program or subprogram in which statement labels are declared.

leaf node A tree node that has no children.

lexical analyzer The part of a compiler that groups characters in a source program into logical units such as identifiers, reserved words, operators, and so on.

LIFO structure See *stack*.

linear search A strategy for searching a list by examining the items sequentially, beginning with the first item.

link A field in a node of a linked structure that points to another node.

linked list A data structure consisting of nodes linked together by pointers, together with a pointer to the first node in the list. Each node contains two kinds of information: the actual data item being stored and a link (pointer) to the next node in the list.

local variable A variable whose scope is a subprogram.

logical error An error in the logical structure of a program (or algorithm). These errors usually do not prevent the program from executing, but incorrect results are produced.

loop See *repetition structure*.

machine language The language used directly by a particular computer for all calculations and processing.

magnetic disk A secondary mass storage medium that stores information on rotating disks coated with a substance that can be magnetized.

magnetic tape A secondary mass storage medium that stores information on plastic tape coated with a substance that can be magnetized.

main memory See *memory unit.*

`maxint` A predefined identifier representing a machine-dependent integer constant that is the largest integer value that can be stored in a particular computer's memory (32767 in Turbo Pascal).

memory unit That part of the computer hardware in which the instructions and data of the currently executing program are stored.

mergesort A sorting scheme, usually external, based on the operations of creating and merging sorted subfiles.

modular programming A programming strategy in which major tasks to be performed are identified and individual procedures/functions (called modules) for these tasks are designed and tested.

multialternative selection structure A control structure in which one of several (usually more than two) actions is selected for execution.

multidimensional array An array with two or more dimensions.

multiply indexed variable A variable used to access a component of a multidimensional array. It is formed by attaching the appropriate number of indices enclosed within brackets to the array's name.

multiply linked structure A linked structure in which each node has two or more link fields.

n-dimensional array An array having n dimensions.

named constant A constant that has been named in the constant section of a Pascal program.

nested A term describing the placement of one structure with another, e.g., nested **IF** statements and nested records.

`NIL` A predefined pointer constant. Assigning this value to a pointer variable indicates that it does not point to any memory location.

nil pointer A pointer to which the value `NIL` has been assigned.

node A component of a linked structure.

object-oriented programming A relatively new method of designing and implementing software systems whose goals are to increase programmer productivity by reusing and extending software. It's fundamental concepts are *encapsulation, inheritance,* and *polymorphism.*

octal number system A base-8 number system.

one-dimensional array Often used as a synonym for *array.*

OOP See *object-oriented programming.*

opcode A numeric code for a machine language instruction.

operating system System software that controls the overall operation of the computer system and serves as an interface between the user and the machine.

order of magnitude An approximate measure of the computing time of an algorithm. $T(n)$ is said to have order of magnitude $g(n)$, denoted $T(n) = O(g(n))$, if there exists a constant C such that $T(n) \leq C \cdot g(n)$ for all sufficiently large values of n.

ordinal number The number of the position of a value of ordinal type in the ordering for that type.

ordinal type A simple data type in which the values of that type are ordered so that each one except the first has an immediate predecessor and each one except the last has an immediate successor.

output Information produced by a program.

output file A standard default output file in Pascal. It is a text file and usually refers to an external device, the screen in Turbo Pascal.

overflow A condition that results when a value is generated that is too large to be stored in the computer being used.

packed array An array in which more than one array component is stored in a single memory word.

parameter A variable used to pass information between program units.

parent of a node See *children of a node*.

parser The part of a compiler that groups tokens together according to the syntax rules of the language.

peripheral devices Hardware devices such as terminals, printers, disk drives, and tape drives that are not part of the central processing unit.

permanent file A file usually stored in secondary memory that exists not only during execution of a program but also before and/or after execution.

pointer, pointer variable A variable whose value is a memory address.

polymorphism The concept in object-oriented programming of a method that has the same name in two different classes but different implementations in these classes.

pop The deletion operation for a *stack*.

postfix notation Notation for arithmetic expressions in which the symbol for each binary operation is placed after its operands.

postorder traversal Traversal of a binary tree in which the left subtree of a node is visited, then the right subtree, and then the node itself.

precedence (or **priority**) **rules** Rules that specify the order in which the operators in an expression are to be performed.

prefix notation Notation for arithmetic expressions in which the symbol for each binary operation is placed before its operands.

preorder traversal Traversal of a binary tree in which a node is visited, then its left subtree, and then its right subtree.

primary memory See *memory unit*.

priority See *precedence rules*.

procedure A subprogram that performs a particular task. Information is passed between a procedure and other program units by means of parameters.

procedure heading A procedure definition begins with a procedure heading of the form: **PROCEDURE** *procedure-name(formal-parameter-list)*;

procedure parameter A parameter that is a procedure.

procedure reference statement A Pascal statement of the form *procedure-name(actual-parameter-list)* that is used to call a procedure.

procedure stub Incomplete subprograms used temporarily in designing a program in a top-down manner.

program heading Pascal programs begin with a program heading of the form: **PROGRAM** *program-name(file-list)*;

pseudocode A loosely defined language that resembles a programming language and is used to describe algorithms.

pseudorandom numbers A sequence of numbers that are generated by an algorithm but that appear to be random, i.e., they appear to be uniformly distributed over some range.

push The insertion operation for a stack.

queue A list in which items may be added only at one end, called the *back* or *rear*, and removed only at the other end, called the *front* or *head*. A queue is a *First-In-First-Out (FIFO)* structure.

quicksort A recursive sorting scheme based on correctly positioning one element of a (sub)list so that all list items that precede it are less than this item and all those that follow it are greater than this item. The two sublists that result are then sorted independently in the same way.

random access file See *direct access file*.

random number generator An algorithm or subprogram that generates pseudorandom numbers.

real A predefined Pascal data type used for values that are real numbers. They may be represented either in decimal form or in scientific notation.

record A data structure in which a collection of related data items of possibly different types may be stored. The positions in which these data items are stored are called the *fields* of the record.

recursion, recursive A process of a function or procedure referencing itself.

relational operators The operators $=$, $<$, $>$, $<>$, $<=$, $>=$, and **IN**. They are used to form simple boolean expressions.

repeat-until loop A posttest loop, i.e., a repetition structure in which the boolean expression that controls repetition is tested after the body of the loop is executed.

REPEAT-UNTIL statement A Pascal statement that implements a repeat-until loop.

repetition structure A control structure in which one or more statements are repeatedly executed. Repetition must be controlled so that these statements are executed only a finite number of times.

reserved words Keywords such as **BEGIN**, **END**, and **VAR** that have a special meaning in Pascal and may be used only in the special ways required by the syntax of the language.

Reverse Polish Notation (RPN) See *postfix notation*.

root node See *tree*.

roundoff error The error that results in storing a real number because of the limited number of bits used to store its fractional part.

run-time error An error such as division by zero that occurs during execution of a program.

same type Two types are the *same* if they are declared by the same type identifier or by equivalent type identifiers.

scientific representation Representation of a real number (also called *floating point representation*) that consists of an integer or a real constant in decimal form followed by the letter **E** (or **e**) followed by an integer constant that is interpreted as an exponent on the base 10.

scope That part of a program or subprogram in which an entity is accessible.

secondary memory Storage devices such as magnetic disks and magnetic tapes that provide relatively inexpensive long-term storage for large collections of information.

selection sort   A simple sorting scheme in which the smallest (or largest) element in a sublist of the given list is located and positioned at the beginning (or end) of the sublist.

selection structure   A control structure in which one of a number of alternative actions is selected.

semantics   The interpretation or meaning of the statements in a language.

sentinel   An artificial data value used to mark the end of a collection of input data.

sequential access   A method of access in which an item can be accessed only by examining all those items that precede it.

sequential file   A file in which the components must be accessed sequentially.

sequential structure   A control structure in which the statements comprising the structure are executed in the order in which they appear.

SET   A predefined structured data type used to process unordered collections of items that are all of the same type.

simple data type   A data type in which each datum is atomic, i.e., it consists of a single entity that cannot be subdivided.

simulation   Modeling a dynamic process and using this model to study the behavior of the process.

software   Computer programs.

sorting   Arranging a list of items so that they are in either ascending or descending order.

source program   A program written in a high-level language such as Pascal.

stack (push-down stack)   A list in which elements may be inserted (*pushed*) and deleted (*popped*) at only one end, called the *top* of the stack. A stack is a *Last-In-First-Out* (*LIFO*) structure.

statement part   The part of a Pascal program that contains the statements that actually carry out the steps of an algorithm.

static data structure   A data structure whose size remains fixed during program execution.

static variable   A variable to which memory locations are allocated at compile time. This association does not change during program execution. (See also *dynamic variable.*)

string   A finite sequence of characters; also, in Turbo Pascal, a predefined structured data type for values that are strings.

string constant   In Pascal, a string enclosed within single quotes (apostrophes).

structure diagram   A diagram that displays the structure of an algorithm by displaying the major tasks that must be performed and the relationship between them.

structured algorithm (program)   An algorithm (program) that is designed using only the three basic control structures: sequential, selection, and repetition.

structured data type   A data type in which a datum consists of a collection of items.

subprogram   A function or procedure.

subprogram section   That section of the declaration part of a Pascal program or subprogram in which functions and procedures are defined.

subrange type   An ordinal type that is defined by specifying the first and last elements in the range of values for a datum of this type.

subscript, subscripted variable   See *index* and *indexed variable.*

successive refinement See *divide-and-conquer.*

syntax The grammar of a language, i.e., the set of rules for forming words and statements in that language.

syntax diagram A diagram used to display a syntax rule for a particular statement or construct in a language.

syntax error A violation of the syntax of the language that is detected during compilation of the program.

system software A collection of programs such as editors, compilers, interpreters, debuggers, etc. supplied as part of the computer system.

tag field A field within a variant record whose value determines which variant is in effect.

tape See *magnetic tape.*

temporary file A file that exists only during execution of a program.

text file A file of characters that is organized into lines.

top-down design See *divide-and-conquer.*

trace table A table of values of all or certain key variables in a program segment obtained by tracing the execution of that program segment step by step.

tree A directed graph with a root node that has no incoming arcs but from which each node in the tree can be reached by exactly one path, i.e., by following a unique sequence of consecutive arcs.

type A formal specification of the set of values that a variable may have.

type section That section of the declaration part of a Pascal program in which data types are defined.

typed constant A variable in a Turbo Pascal program that is initialized in a special constant section.

unit A file containing constant definitions, type definitions, and subprogram definitions that can be compiled and whose items can be imported into a program or another unit by using a **USES** clause.

USES clause A declaration of the form **USES *unit-name*** that can be placed in a program or unit ahead of the declaration part and that makes available to the program/unit the items defined in the specified unit.

validation Checking that algorithms, programs, and subprograms meet a problem's specfication.

value parameter A formal parameter of a subprogram that is used to pass information to the subprogram but not to return information from it.

variable An identifier associated with a particular memory location. The value stored in this location is the value of the variable, and this value may be changed during program execution.

variable parameter A formal parameter of a subprogram that is used both to pass information to, and to return information from, the subprogram. In Pascal, variable parameters must be indicated as such by preceding them with the reserved word **VAR**.

variable section That section of the declaration part of a program or subprogram in which variables are declared.

variant part The last part of a variant record.

variant record A record that may contain a variant part in addition to the usual fixed part. The number and types of the fields in the fixed part do not change during program execution, but those in the variant part may change in number and/or type.

verification   Checking that algorithms, programs, and subprograms are correct and complete.

while loop   A pretest loop, i.e., a repetition structure in which the boolean expression that controls repetition is tested before the body of the loop is executed.

WHILE statement   A Pascal statement that implements a while loop.

window   See *file window*.

WITH statement   A Pascal statement used to attach a record name to identifiers of fields within that record to form fielded variables.

word   A basic storage unit consisting of a machine-dependent number of bits (commonly 16 or 32).

INDEX OF EXAMPLES AND PROGRAMMING EXERCISES

Exercises

INDEX

989

Statements	Example
Assignment (81–88, 111, 455, 512, 557, 605, 691, 735, 766)	``` Count := 0; Wages := RoundCents(Hours * Rate); DeptCode := 'A'; OverTime := (Hours > 40); ProductName := 'Ford-Carburetor'; Letters := ['A'..'F', 'P', 'S']; EmpRec.Number := 12345; TempPtr := NIL; FirstPtr↑.Data := ProductName; ```

Sequential (122–124)
 Compound (123)
	``
	BEGIN
	  Wages := RoundCents(Hours * Rate);
	  OverTime := false
	END;
	``

Selection (135–150)
 IF (135–150)
	``
	IF Hours <= 40 THEN
	  Wages := RoundCents(Hours * Rate)
	ELSE
	  BEGIN
	    OverTime := true;
	    Wages := RoundCents(HoursLimit * Rate +
	        OTMult * Rate * (Hours - HoursLimit))
	  END {ELSE};
	``

CASE (328–335)	```
	CASE DeptCode of
	  'o', 'O' : Dept := Office;
	  'f', 'F' : Dept := Factory;
	  's', 'S' : Dept := Sales
	  ELSE
	          writeln('Illegal code')
	END {CASE};
	``